T0374559

Ilex Foundation Series 6

The *History* of Beyhaqi

Also in the Ilex Foundation Series

Poet and Hero in the Persian Book of Kings
by Olga M. Davidson
third edition

Comparative Literature and Classical Persian Poetics
by Olga M. Davidson
second edition

Ferdowsi's Shāhnāma: *Millennial Perspectives*
edited by Olga M. Davidson and Marianna Shreve Simpson

Global Medieval: Mirrors for Princes Reconsidered
edited by Regula Forster and Neguin Yavari

Erin and Iran: Cultural Encounters between the Irish and the Iranians
edited by H.E. Chehabi and Grace Neville

Dreaming across Boundaries:
The Interpretation of Dreams in Islamic Lands
edited by Louise Marlow

The Rhetoric of Biography: Narrating Lives in Persianate Societies
edited by L. Marlow

Ruse and Wit: The Humorous in Arabic, Turkish, and Persian Narrative
edited by Dominic Parvis Brookshaw

Persian Literature and Judeo-Persian Culture:
Collected Writings of Sorour S. Soroudi
edited by H.E. Chehabi

On the Wonders of Land and Sea: Persianate Travel Writing
edited by Roberta Micallef and Sunil Sharma

Methodists and Muslims: My Life as an Orientalist
by Richard W. Bulliet

Naqqali Trilogy
by Bahram Beyzaie
translated by Richard Saul Chason and Nikta Sabouri

Cyrus the Great: Life and Lore
edited by Rahim Shayegan

more at *www.ilexfoundation.org*

The *History* of Beyhaqi

(The History of Sultan Masʿud of Ghazna, 1030–1041)

by

Abu'l-Fażl Beyhaqi

Translated with a historical, geographical, linguistic and cultural commentary and notes by

C. E. Bosworth

Fully revised and with further commentary by

Mohsen Ashtiany

VOLUME I

Introduction and Translation of Years 421–423 A.H. = 1030–1032 A.D.

Ilex Foundation
Boston, Massachusetts

Distributed by Harvard University Press
Cambridge, Massachusetts and London, England

The *History* of Beyhaqi (The History of Sultan Masʿud of Ghazna, 1030–1041) by Abu'l-Fażl Beyhaqi
Translated with a historical, geographical, linguistic and cultural commentary and notes by C. E. Bosworth; and fully revised and with further commentary by Mohsen Ashtiany

The *History* of Beyhaqi project was sponsored by the Center for Iranian Studies, Columbia University.

Copyright © 2011 Ilex Foundation
All Rights Reserved

Published by the Ilex Foundation, Boston, MA
Third printing, April 2023

Distributed by Harvard University Press, Cambridge, MA and London, England

Cover design: Joni Godlove
Printed in the United States of America

The image on the cover is of a silver plate in the collection of The State Hermitage Museum, St. Petersburg. Photograph © The State Hermitage Museum / photo by Vladimir Terebenin, Leonard Kheifets, Yuri Molodkovets

Library of Congress Cataloging-in-Publication Data

Bayhaqi, Abu al-Fazl Muhammad ibn Husayn, ca. 996-1077.
[Tarikh-i Bayhaqi. English]
The history of Beyhaqi : (the history of Sultan Mas'ud of Ghazna, 1030-1041) / by Abu'l-Fazl Beyhaqi ; translated with a historical, geographical, linguistic and cultural commentary and notes by C.E. Bosworth ; fully revised and with further commentary by Mohsen Ashtiany.
v. <1-3> ; cm.
Translated from Persian.
Includes bibliographical references and index.
ISBN 978-0-674-06233-7 (alk. paper) -- ISBN 978-0-674-06234-4 (alk. paper) -- ISBN 978-0-674-06235-1 (alk. paper) -- ISBN 978-0-674-06236-8 (alk. paper) -- ISBN 978-0-674-06238-2 (alk. paper) -- ISBN 978-0-674-06239-9 (alk. paper)
1. Ghaznevids. 2. Iran--History--640-1256. 3. Afghanistan--History. I. Bosworth, Clifford Edmund. II. Ashtiany, Mohsen, 1943- III. Title.
DS288.7.B313 2011
955'.022--dc23

2011028511

To the memory of
Vladimir Fedorovich Minorsky
(1877–1966)

Contents

Translation of the *Tārikh-e Masʿudi*

About the Translator

C. Edmund Bosworth graduated in Modern History from Oxford University and in Arabic, Persian and Turkish from Edinburgh University, and was until his retirement Professor of Arabic Studies in the University of Manchester; he is at present Visiting Professor at the Institute of Arabic and Islamic Studies in the University of Exeter. He is a Fellow of the British Academy and an Honorary Member of the Hungarian Academy of Sciences. He was for almost thirty years British Editor of the *Encyclopaedia of Islam*, new edition, was Co-Editor of the *Journal of Semitic Studies* and edited two volumes of the UNESCO *History of the Civilizations of Central Asia*. He is Co-Editor of *Iran, Journal of the British Institute of Persian Studies*, and consultant on medieval Islamic history and historical geography for the *Encyclopaedia Iranica*. The subjects of his many books range over Arabic literature, Arabic social history, Islamic chronology and dynastic history, Iranian and Turkish history, and seventeenth-century British travellers to the Middle East. He has contributed extensively to the *Encyclopaedia of Islam* and the *Encyclopaedia Iranica*, and several of his very numerous articles have been collected together in three Variorum Collected Studies volumes.

About the Reviser

Mohsen Ashtiany, Associate Editor of the *Encyclopaedia Iranica*, has studied at the Universities of St. Andrews and Oxford and has held research fellowships at the Universities of Harvard and Princeton. He has also taught Persian literature and history at the Universities of Oxford, Manchester, and California at Los Angeles. He is the author of a number of articles in the field of Persian studies and is well known for his extensive knowledge of Persian history and culture as well as for his bibliographical scholarship and his elegant English style. He is currently working on a book on the twelfth-century Persian poet Nezami of Ganjeh. The Center for Iranian Studies would like to thank the Ilex Foundation for their generous grant which enabled him to carry out a major part of the revision during his year's Fellowship at Princeton in 2002–3.

Foreword by Ehsan Yarshater

Beyhaqi's *History*, arguably the best known and most liked of all Persian histories, stands out among other Persian chronicles for its objectivity, its analytical approach to reporting events, its attention to detail, the skill displayed in weaving the rich texture of its narrative with its often ironic implications—all contributing to the highly dramatic quality which is its hallmark. No other Persian history, with the possible exception of Rashid al-Din's thirteenth-century universal history, *Jāmeʿ-al-tavārikh,* has been the subject of more scholarly studies in either Western languages or Persian.

The author, Abu'l Fażl Beyhaqi (995–1077), a court secretary of a number of Ghaznavid rulers in eastern Persia and Afghanistan, was born in Beyhaq (modern Sabzevār) in Khorasan. He studied in Nishapur, at the time an important cultural centre. As a young man he joined the Secretariat of the Ghaznavid Sultan Maḥmud (998–1030), where for almost two decades he worked under the chief secretary Abu Naṣr Moshkān. He continued working under Maḥmud's successors, observing at close quarters the reigns of eight successive kings in the course of some fifty-five years, and was involved in the preparation of important documents and diplomatic correspondence with neighbouring sovereigns. He was promoted under Sultan ʿAbd-al-Rashid (1049–52), became the head of the Secretariat and then he retired from court service and settled down in Ghazna, the capital of the early Ghaznavids, to write his *History.* His proximity to the centre of power at the court gives his chronicle a sense of immediacy, reinforced by frequent accounts of his own direct observations during his years in office.

Throughout his long career, Beyhaqi had made copious notes, which he later used in compiling his *History*. The result was a voluminous opus, comprising some thirty "books," covering the dynastic history of the Ghaznavids and the life and times of its major players. Only five "books" (books 5–10) have survived, the rest having disappeared as a result of political upheavals in which most of his manuscript and notes were pillaged and destroyed. However, the extant volumes in themselves amount to a substantial corpus, with the printed text running into almost a thousand pages in the critical edition by ʿA.-A. Fayyāż (Tehran, 1971; repr. 2004).

The *History* has been translated into Arabic by Yaḥyā al-Khashshāb and Ṣādeq Nash'at (Cairo, 1956), and into Russian with notes as *Istoriya Masʿūda* by A.K. Arends (Tashkent, 1962; 2nd ed. Moscow, 1969).

A collection of essays entitled, *Yād-nāme-ye Abu'l Fażl Beyhaqi* (*Abu'l Fażl Beyhaqi's Memorial Volume,* Mashhad, 1971), contains a number of important studies in Persian and English on various aspects of Beyhaqi's *History,* including for example, Nazir Ahmad's "A Critical Examination of Baihaqi's Narration of the Indian Expeditions during the Reign of Masʿud of Ghazna," pp. 34–83 (also in *Afghanistan* 24/4, 1972, pp. 68–92), Kenneth Allin Luther's "Bayhaqi and the Later Seljuq Historians: Some Comparative Remarks" (pp. 14–33), and Roger M. Savory's "Abo'l Faẓl Bayhaqi as an Historiographer," pp. 84–128.

Several monographs have been devoted to a discussion of Beyhaqi's *magnum opus*; R. Gelpke, *Sulṭān Masʿūd I. von Ġazna, Die drei ersten Jahre seiner Herrschaft (421/1030–424/1033)* (Munich, 1957); Marilyn Waldman, *Toward a Theory of Historical Narrative: A Case Study in Perso-Islamicate Historiography* (Columbus, Ohio, 1980); Filippo Bertotti, *L'Opera dello storico persiano Bayhaqī* (Istituto Italiano Orientale, Naples, 1991).

The *History* is also discussed at length as an essential document in recent works on historiography. Stephen Humphreys examines Beyhaqi's *History* as the most representative specimen of Persian historiography in a chapter entitled "Bayhaqī and Ibn Taghrībirdī: The Art of Narrative in Islamic Historical Writing during the Middle Periods" in his perceptive work: *Islamic History: A Framework for Inquiry* (Princeton, 1991, pp. 128–47). Julie Scott Meisami's "Bayhaqī's History of Masʿūd of Ghazna" in her *Persian Historiography to the End of the Twelfth Century,* (Edinburgh, 1999, pp. 79–108) re-examines the implications of Beyhaqi's narrative methods in their historical context.

Among numerous other essays and articles on Beyhaqi, one may mention the authoritative overview of Beyhaqi's life and work and various editions of his *History* by Gholām-Ḥoseyn Yusofi in the *Encyclopædia Iranica* (under "Bayhaqī, Abu'l Fażl," Vol. III, pp. 889–94, 1988); Mujtaba Minovi, "The Persian Historian Bayhaqī," in B. Lewis and P.M. Holt, eds., *Historians of the Middle East* (London 1962, pp. 138–40); C.E. Bosworth's "Early sources for the First Four Ghaznavid Sultans (977–1041)," in *Islamic Quarterly* (7/1–2, 1963, pp. 10–14, reprinted in idem, *The Medieval History of Iran, Afghanistan and Central Asia,* London, 1977); idem, "The Poetical Citations in Baihaqī's *Ta'rīkh-i Masʿūdī,*" in *XX. Deutscher Orientalistentag … 1977 in Erlangen, Vorträge (ZDMG,* Suppl. IV, Wiesbaden, 1980, pp. 41–56); and Gilbert Lazard, "Un mémorialiste persan, Beyhaqi," in *Mélanges Labande* (Poitiers, 1974, pp. 471–78); and Houra Yavari, "Some thoughts on the Narrative Structure of Bayhaqi's *History* and the Role of Added Narratives" (in Persian), in *Irān-shenāsi,* XIII/1, Spring 2001, pp. 117–38.

Essentially, the *History* is devoted to the narration of the events and the description of the personalities of the reign of Masʿud (1030–41) and his brother Moḥammad, whom he defeated as successor to the throne, and, by extension, those of his father, Maḥmud, the most powerful of all the Ghaznavid sultans. However, as a backdrop to Masʿud's reign, Beyhaqi frequently introduces accounts of past events and relates in flashbacks the important occurrences, not only of Sultan Maḥmud's reign, but also of Sebüktegin, the founder of the Ghaznavid dynasty. There are also accounts of earlier dynasties, notably the Samanids (819–1005), which preceded the Ghaznavids in Central Asia and Eastern Iran, and the Buyids (932–1062) in central and western Persia, as well as a number of events related to the ʿAbbasid and Fatimid caliphs. He also provides a valuable history of Chorasmia, a Central Asian kingdom, occasioned by Sultan Maḥmud's conquest of it.

What distinguishes Beyhaqi's *History* from other medieval Persian histories is his concept of history and his avowed notion of his task as a historian, encapsulated in frequent asides in his narrative. Thus in an often quoted passage as a critique of other chronicles (see e.g. Stephen Humphreys, *op.cit*, p. 128) Beyhaqi writes,

> One usually reads that a certain king sent a certain general to such and such a war, and that on such and such a day they made war or peace, and that this one defeated that one or that one this one, and then proceeded somewhere else. But I write what is worthy to be recorded.

What is to Beyhaqi worthy of recording is not merely the narration of events but also the elucidation of their circumstances and their underlying context and the motives of the protagonists involved in them, which he attempts to unravel and explain. Furthermore, to him "events" do not consist of only political occurrences, conflicts and wars, peace agreements and treaties; he has a much broader view of history. His panoramic view embraces and integrates political and diplomatic events, social phenomena, court customs and ceremonial, and administrative structure and processes. His invocation of the general decline of a reign, as refracted in the abeyance of ceremonies and neglect of decorum, is an obvious example.

Beyhaqi's evocation of scenes and his enlivening the interest of his readers with subtle ironical innuendoes, are buttressed by a strong sense of morality and a firm belief in justice and ethical conduct. Without being explicitly judgmental, his *History* can also be seen as a vehicle for the moral education of the reader; it shows the virtues of justice and simple piety and the banality and the ultimate futility of spiteful intrigues and blind ambitions at the court. Frequently he uses an indirect way to impart his criticism of royal conduct or the greed, vengefulness, and thoughtlessness of the officials in charge by citing parallel events from other times and other regimes. A case in point is his dramatic description of the downfall, arrest and impaling of Ḥasanak, a capable vizier of Sultan Maḥmud. He describes a number of events to serve as a moral pointer for the injustice done to Ḥasanak and the complicity and culpability of Sultan Masʿud in his execution.

As already suggested above, it is neither possible nor desirable to separate the "matter" of this masterpiece from its "manner." Nevertheless, setting aside the considerable literary and stylistic merits of the work, it must be pointed out that no other historical work in Persian contains so much information about the administrative divisions of a government (the *Divāns*), diplomatic negotiations and correspondence, the place of the military in the dynastic rule, the siege of cities and imposition of tolls and tributes, collection of taxes, management of royal domains, the working of tribunals, relations of local dynasts with the ʿAbbasid court in Baghdad, the rivalries in the bipolar Islamic world of the time between the Fatimid caliphs in Egypt and North Africa and the ʿAbbasid caliphs in the eastern lands of Islam, the position of slaves and their training as soldiers or servants or companions, the daily life at court (important in an autocratic royal system of government), the relation between the king and his courtiers, court ceremonies, celebrations and mournings; the patronage of poets and authors by the royal court and the notables, secretarial lore, and the machinations and intrigues among the court dignitaries and officials. Here indeed is God's plenty.

It should be noted that the administrative apparatus of the Ghaznavids, as one of the most powerful dynasties of the ʿAbbasid realm, was inherited from their predecessors, the Samanids, which had been modelled on that of the ʿAbbasids, itself influenced to a certain extent by the practices of the Sasanians (224–651). The system thus established was continued in its basic features in Persia and Central Asia until the Mongol invasion in the thirteenth century and even beyond up to pre-modern times. No other source furnishes such detailed information about this administrative system as does Beyhaqi. His *History* is indispensable for the knowledge of the *Divān* system (administrative divisions) in Iran and Central Asia.

About the Present Annotated Translation

More than forty years ago when I started the Persian Heritage Series, which consisted of the translation of Persian classics into major Western languages and Japanese, more particularly into English, one of my strong desires was to have Beyhaqi's *History* translated into English. Some thirty-five years ago, I approached Professor C.E. Bosworth, the well-known historian and the outstanding expert on the Ghaznavid dynasty, to see whether he could spare necessary time for such a translation. But at the time and for many years afterwards, he was busy not only with teaching but also with carrying the major burden of editing the second edition of the *Encyclopaedia of Islam,* apart from writing frequent entries for it and for the *Encyclopaedia Iranica* as well as for a variety of learned journals. Therefore, his reluctance to commit himself to a very time consuming task was understandable.

In the years that followed, I could not find a satisfactory translator for this gem of Persian historiography until 1997, when Professor Bosworth was nearing retirement and the second edition of *Encyclopaedia of Islam* was approaching its completion, I thought I had a better chance of persuading him to undertake the task. Much to my delight, he agreed, but as befits the integrity of his scholarly character he said that he would need the cooperation of a scholar of Persian literature to check his translation and help him with some of the obscure or difficult passages, especially some of the poems that Beyhaqi cites.

To respond to his request, first I approached Professor Heshmat Moayyad of Chicago University for the purpose and he cooperated with the project by checking the first fifty pages of the translation. In the meantime, I sent a request to the National Endowment for the Humanities for financial support of the project—a request that was approved in due course.

The arrangement with Professor Moayyad, however, did not work out. As a result, I persuaded my colleague Mr. Mohsen Ashtiany, a scholar with a vast knowledge of Persian literature and history and with an exceptional mastery of the English language and style to collaborate with Prof. Bosworth in his task and serve as a reviser of Prof. Bosworth's translation. In practice, Prof. Bosworth would regularly send batches of his translation and annotation to me, or to Mr. Ashtiany who would go over them and check them against the original and return them to Prof. Bosworth with his comments and corrections. As a rule, Prof. Bosworth in his translation paid meticulous attention to the wording and turn of phrases of the original, and Mr. Ashtiany tried to make the translation read more smoothly and fluently, while registering at the same time his comments on the translation of difficult passages and notes. I often benefited by the scholarship of the erudite translator and reviser while keeping the process uninterrupted and steady.

The translation proceeded with considerable speed. Prof. Bosworth had decided early that a translation of Beyhaqi without historical, geographical, and philological explanatory notes could not be thoroughly understood or appreciated by those readers who might not be familiar with the context of the events and their venues. Therefore, he embarked on not only full explanation of all the proper names and philological points, but also on commenting on the events and their historical contexts with reference to parallel passages in other sources when necessary. He also placed at the head of his translation a full Introduction in which he discussed the history of the Ghaznavid domains in Iran, Central Asia, and Northwestern India as well as delineating the method of Beyhaqi's historiography and the characteristics of his style as a historian.

As the notes grew copious, amounting to about half the translation, I suggested that a separate volume be devoted to the publication of the Notes, of use mostly to researchers and scholars, with a Glossary of Terms to be placed after the Introduction. This was agreed upon and this is how the annotated translation of this classic of Persian historiography and literature is presented to its readers.

It is a distinct pleasure to see one of my old wishes realized. This is the only translation of Beyhaqi's *History* that exists in Western languages except Russian. It is hoped that it will prove of assistance to all the students of Islamic history and the history of Iranian lands during the tenth to the twelfth centuries in a broad sense.

Acknowledgements

It is my pleasant duty to thank first of all, Professor Bosworth and Mr. Ashtiany for their several years of arduous and dedicated work on Beyhaqi's translation, as well as Professor Moayyad for his initial cooperation. I should like to express also a profound gratitude to the National Endowment for the Humanity for their encouragement and support, and The Persian Heritage Foundation for its providing the needed matching funds. I am particularly grateful to Dr. Helen Agüera, the Senior Officer at the National Endowment's Division of

Preservation and Access and Mr. George Farr, the former head of the Division, for their support and their facilitating the progress of the project. I am also grateful to the Alavi Foundation for their support of the project through Columbia University. I am thankful to Ms. Dina Amin and Dr. Mahnaz Moazami of The Center for Iranian Studies and of The Persian Heritage Foundation, respectively, who have been of great help with the administrative aspects of the Project. My thanks are due also to Mr. Claudius Naumann of the Freie Universität Berlin who was responsible for the careful layout and the choice of the fonts with admirable taste, and to Mr. Alex Popovkin for his meticulous preparation of the Index.

Preface and Acknowledgements

The present translation, having been begun in 1999, represents the work of several years. Its genesis lies in an invitation from Professor Ehsan Yarshater to produce an English version of Beyhaqi's *History* for his Persian Heritage Series, and I am very grateful to him for his encouragement and support during the protracted period of this book's gestation. It is over four decades ago that the late Professor V.F. Minorsky suggested to me, while I was visiting him in his welcoming house in Bateman Street, Cambridge, and near the end of his long and richly-fulfilled life, that I should undertake this work. At that stage of my academic life I felt that I lacked both the considerable amount of time and concentration required and also the maturity of experience and knowledge necessary for embarking on such a massive work. But Professor Yarshater's invitation, coming as it did over thirty years later, in the later nineteen-nineties, was timely in that, having retired from full-time University life, I was then able to devote much of my time to what was obviously going to be a complex and lengthy undertaking.

Such an English translation represents the first rendering of this masterpiece of early Persian historiography, the *Tārikh-e Masʿudi*, into a Western European language (for details of existing texts and other translations, see below, Introduction, section 3). It appeared to me, however, that a bare translation of the Persian text would be of very limited value when dealing with a work of such significance for the history of the Islamic lands to the east of the Arab heartland. Beyhaqi's *History* is not only valuable for the light that it throws on the dynastic, diplomatic and military history of the Eastern Islamic world in the later tenth and early eleventh centuries AD, with the Iranian principalities there faced with incoming waves of Turkish military adventurers and tribesmen from the Inner Asian steppes who were to transform that world, but valuable also for its uniquely illuminating picture of the working of a medieval Islamic chancery and its personnel. It has, moreover, long been recognized as a key text—not least because of its great length—in the development of early New Persian prose style during what the historian of Persian prose writing, Malek al-Shoʿarāʾ Bahār, has described as its second period. It displays significant pointers to the linguistic usages of the time when it was written (*ca.* AD 1060), despite the regrettable normalisations of the text by later copyists that probably took place over subsequent centuries (see below, Introduction, section 5).

For all these reasons, I felt that the work would bear a detailed commentary, predominantly historical and geographical, but with some note of literary and linguistic questions, and that it would not, indeed, be properly intelligible without it. This commentary I have accordingly endeavoured to supply, and it forms Volume III of the present work. The reader of the translation can accordingly consult this commentary for detailed, specific information on historical, literary and linguistic points, but the translation will be intelligible to him as it stands provided he or she first reads section 1 of the Introduction, which delineates the historical background of Beyhaqi's work, and utilizes the *Select glossary of names of significant persons, places, dynasties and peoples occurring in the History* and the *Glossary of technical terms* given below.

It is a bold modern Westerner who tries to understand the personality of a Persian bureaucrat working in what is now eastern Afghanistan almost a millennium ago. Much of the mindset of such a person as this, nurtured as he was in an alien religious and cultural world, must be inevitably closed for us and be incapable of full recovery after such an long expanse of time; we can only observe from outside the culture and over a great temporal distance and then hope in part to comprehend. And if the Persian language has changed less in a thousand years than say English, in its transition during a comparable period from the Early English of late Anglo-Saxon times to Modern English, it nevertheless has inevitably developed, so that Beyhaqi's style and linguistic usages are not always easy for modern Persians fully to grasp.

Hence I have been fortunate in having Mr Mohsen Ashtiany, with his profound knowledge of all periods of New Persian language and literature, and his sense of English literary style, to review and correct my translation and to make many valuable contribution to the notes and commentary, these last being marked thus [M.A.]. He has corrected erroneous translations; has made sense of many difficult passages, ones which may well have been corruptly transmitted by copyists; and has made many modifications to my original translation in the direction of lightening its style. For there is always a tension between the aim of providing a literal translation, one which is as faithful as possible to the original and which displays the fact that the translator has understood, as far as is possible with the lapse of centuries, the original, and the aim of producing a version which is smooth-reading and has a modicum at least of literary attractiveness. Moreover, the necessity for having a scholar of ethnically Persian origin like Mr Ashtiany undertake such a work of review is especially pressing with regard to the Persian poetry which Beyhaqi quotes frequently and at length. Citations from Samanid period authors like Daqiqi and Rudaki are relatively straightforward—insofar as any Persian poetry is straightforward to the outsider—but the historian gives the texts of four substantial odes by a contemporary of his in Ghazna during the middle decades of the eleventh century, one Abu Ḥanifa Eskāfi (see below, Introduction, sections 1, 4). The style of these poems is far from easy and, since Beyhaqi is the sole author to preserve their texts, we have no check on whether they have been correctly transmitted over the centuries. Various other Persian scholars whom I have consulted here have offered differing translations and interpretations for many of the verses, so that the translations given here are tentative and cannot be regarded as definitive; Mr Ashtiany has in fact come to the conclusion that the received text is so corrupt in certain places that no intelligible translation of it there can in fact be given. Clearly, more work needs to be done on the poems by experts in classical Persian poetry.

An enterprise on the scale of the present work has required input and help from specialists on a wide range of subjects. In addition to Mr Ashtiany's wide-ranging contribution, acknowledged above, I am grateful to Professor Heshmat Moayyad (University of Chicago) for checking my translation of the first forty or fifty pages of Beyhaqi's text. Dr Ebrāhim Nurā'i (University of Isfahan), Dr

Leonard Lewisohn (University of Exeter) and Mr Moḥammad Reza Jowzi (Institute of Ismaili Studies, London) made valuable comments on translating the Persian poetry. Professor Geert Jan Van Gelder (University of Oxford) gave advice on aspects of the rendering of the Arabic poetry. Professor Rudolf Sellheim (University of Frankfurt) gave especially copious and detailed information on the many Arabic proverbial sayings and adages, identifying these in the classical collections wherever possible. Professors Christopher Shackle (School of Oriental and African Studies, University of London) and Irfan Habib (Aligarh Muslim University) answered queries about Indian names and terms used by Beyhaqi and about points of Indo-Muslim history. Professor Michael Fedorov (Karlsruhe, Germany) shared with me his specialist knowledge of medieval Islamic Central Asian numismatics. Dr Benedek Péri (University of Budapest) and Professor Peter B. Golden (Rutgers University, N.J.) were sources of enlightenment on points of Turkish onomastics and philology. For linguistic information on the older Iranian languages, the late and lamented Professor D.N. MacKenzie (University of Göttingen) showed his customary helpfulness. For certain architectural terms used by Beyhaqi but of obscure significance today, I derived help from the encyclopaedic knowledge of Persian art and architecture of Professor Robert Hillenbrand (University of Edinburgh). Other scholars who have been helpful in supplying information and help with bibliographical materials include Professor Iraj Afshār (University of Tehran); Dr Mohammed Ben Madani (London); Professor A.D.H. Bivar (SOAS, University of London); Professor Claude Gilliot (University of Aix-en-Provence); and Professor Edmund Herzig (University of Oxford) and Professor G.R. Smith (University of Manchester).

C. Edmund Bosworth

Castle Cary, Somerset
April 2008

I would like to thank Dr. Adel Adamova and Ms. Olga Novoseltseva of The State Hermitage Museum for their kind assistance in providing the illustration for the cover. I am also indebted to my friends at the Ilex Foundation, Niloo Fotouhi and Chris Dadian, for overseeing the final stages of the publication of these volumes.

Mohsen Ashtiany

Note on Presentation, Transliteration, Bibliography and Dating

As a chancery secretary, with the training of an *adib* or connoisseur steeped in Islamic literature, the basis of an Islamic humanistic education at that time, Beyhaqi may well have been equally at home in Arabic as in his native Persian. He certainly quotes much Arabic poetry (see below, Introduction, section 4), and he gives the lengthy Arabic texts of documents such as the letter that arrived in Ghazna from Baghdad announcing the accession in 1031 of the new ʿAbbasid caliph al-Qāʾem and the response, the pledge of allegiance *(beyʿat)* to the caliph, by Sultan Masʿud. As well as the poetry and these texts of documents, Beyhaqi frequently cites Arabic proverbial sayings and adages, and his Persian style is often interspersed with Arabic phrases and idioms, many of which must have been felt by educated Persian speakers of the time as being as much a part of their language as when we today speak of habeas corpus or a blitzkrieg or a coup d'état. I have adopted the practice in my translation of giving these Arabic passages and quotations in italics, with the exception, however, of pious formulae uttered after certain categories of names on certain occasions, like the *taṣliya*, the *tarḥim*, the *tarżiya*, etc., which, again, must have been effortlessly integrated into the speech patterns of Persian speakers of the time and not felt as foreign. Unless they seem to have some special significance, they have largely been omitted in the present translation except when they occur within the texts of formal diplomatic and similar documents.

The edition which has been used as the main basis for the translation is that of ʿAli Akbar Fayyāż (Mashhad, 1350/1971), and the pagination of this is denoted within the translation by the siglum F, but the pagination of the preceding edition of Qāsem Ghani and Fayyāż (Tehran, 1324/1945), which is cited in many historical works of the mid-twentieth century utilising Beyhaqi's *History*, has also been indicated and is denoted by the siglum Gh.

The Qor'ānic translations are my own, made after consultation with various existing translations such as those of A.J. Arberry and Marmaduke Pickthall and the commentaries of Richard Bell and Rudi Paret.

In citing the titles of Arabic books and other works, the system of the standard bibliographies of Arabic literature, those of Carl Brockelmann and Fuat Sezgin, is followed: i.e. for purposes of the capitalisation of the first word of a title, words like *Ketāb* "book," *Resāla* "epistle" and *Ta'rikh* "history" are disregarded, as in e.g. *Ketāb al-Tāj, Resālat al-Qovvād, Ta'rikh al-Rosol va 'l-moluk*.

For transliteration, the system basically adopted is that used increasingly now for the rendering of Modern Persian and recently adopted by the *Encyclopaedia Iranica*; it has the advantage of expressing in a simple fashion the vowel system of Persian. As noted above, there are in Beyhaqi's text many Arabic quotations and expressions, and for the sake of uniformity, these also have been rendered in the Persian system just mentioned. The results may look rather strange to Arabists used to the standard schemes for Classical and Modern Arabic but the reconstitution of the Arabic originals should present no problem. The main aberrancy, among the consonants, between this Persian system and the Arabic schemes is in regard to the transliteration of the quintessentially Arabic consonant, probably in origin a voiced lateralised velarised interdental fricative, *ḍād* /ḍ/, rendered here as /ż/ and pronounced in fact in New Persian as the voiced alveolar fricative /z/. However, for the many Turkish names and terms occurring in the *History*, an exact rendering of the vowel system of Turkish, one much richer than those of Arabic and Persian, has necessarily been adopted.

The Bibliography gives full details of most works consulted for the translation and commentary, with the exception of certain works mentioned only once or concerned with topics very peripheral to the book's main thrust. However, when these last are cited in the notes, full bibliographical details are given at that place.

Regarding dating, it should be noted that pre-modern Islamic historians and writers usually followed in their works the Muslim, so-called Hijri system of dating (for Beyhaqi's dating usages, see below, Introduction, section 5) which began in AD 622, the year of the Prophet Moḥammad's *hejra* or migration from Mecca to Medina. Such dates are often expressed in Western writings as AH (*anno hegirae* "in the year of the Hijra"). However, although there is very roughly a disparity of six centuries between Christian era and Hijra, the correspondence is only approximate, given that the Christian era is a solar one and the Muslim one a lunar one so that the years in each system have differing lengths; for calculating exact correspondences, recourse can most conveniently be made to printed tables or a special computer programme. Within the present book, it is felt that the extended Introduction to the translation is of a wider, general scope than one just for Islamic historians and that exact Hijri dates are not necessary and possibly distracting. Within the translation itself, Beyhaqi normally gives dates in the Hijri form, and for these the Christian era equivalent is shown. Likewise, for the commentary on the translation, where historical parallels or the wider historical background to events are often given, exactness is required; hence both Hijri and Christian era dates are given there.

Abbreviations of the Names of Journals and Books Frequently Cited

AEMAe	*Archivum Eurasiae Medii Aevi* (Wiesbaden)
ArO	*Archiv Orientální* (Prague)
BGA	*Bibliotheca geographicorum arabicorum* (Leiden)
Bi.Or.	*Bibliotheca Orientalis* (Leiden)
BSO[A]S	*Bulletin of the School of Oriental [and African] Studies* (London)
CAJ	*Central Asiatic Journal* (The Hague, Wiesbaden)
CHAL	*The Cambridge History of Arabic Literature* (Cambridge)
CHIr	*The Cambridge History of Iran* (Cambridge)
EAL	*Encyclopedia of Arabic Literature* (London, New York)
EI[1]	*Encyclopaedia of Islam*, first edition (Leiden)
EI[2]	*Encyclopaedia of Islam*, second edition (Leiden)
EIr	*Encyclopaedia Iranica* (New York)
EQ	*Encyclopaedia of the Qur'ān* (Leiden, Boston)
EW	*East and West* (Rome)
F	Beyhaqi, *Tārikh*, ed. Fayyāż
GAL	C. Brockelmann, *Geschichte der arabischen Literatur* (Leiden)
GAS	Fuad Sezgin, *Geschichte des arabischen Schrifttums* (Leiden)
Gh	Beyhaqi, *Tārikh*, ed. Ghani and Fayyāż
GIE	*The Great Islamic Encyclopaedia*, ed. Kazem Musavi Bojnurdi, Tehran, 1984–
GMS	E. J. W. Gibb Memorial Series (Leiden, London)
HdO	Handbuch der Orientalistik (Leiden)
IC	*Islamic Culture* (Hyderabad, Deccan)
IQ	*Islamic Quarterly* (London)

Iran JBIPS	*Iran, Journal of the British Institute of Persian Studies* (London)
Ir. St.	*Iranian Studies* (London, New York)
Isl.	*Der Islam* (Strassburg/Berlin and Leipzig/Berlin)
ISMEO	Istituto Italiano per il Medio ed Estremo Oriente (Rome)
JA	*Journal Asiatique* (Paris)
JAOS	*Journal of the American Oriental Society* (New Haven)
JESHO	*Journal of the Economic and Social History of the Orient* (Leiden)
JNES	*Journal of Near Eastern Studies* (Chicago)
JRAS	*Journal of the Royal Asiatic Society* (London)
M	Beyhaqi, *Tārikh*, ed. Morley
MDAT	*Majalla-ye Dāneshkada-ye Adabiyāt (va ʿolum-e ensāni)* (Tehran University)
N	Beyhaqi, *Tārikh*, ed. Nafisi
R	Beyhaqi, *Tārikh*, ed. Khaṭib-Rahbar
REI	*Revue des Études Islamiques* (Paris)
RO	*Rocznik Orientalistycny* (Warsaw)
RSO	*Revista degli Studi Orientali* (Rome)
SBÖAW	*Sitzungsberichte der Österreichischen Akademie der Wissenschaften* (Vienna)
SBWAW	*Sitzungsberichte der Kaiserlichen Akademie der Wissenschaften zu Wien* (Vienna)
St. Ir.	*Studia Iranica* (Paris)
UAJB	*Ural-altaische Jahrbücher* (Wiesbaden)
WKAS	*Wörterbuch der klassischen arabischen Sprache* (Wiesbaden)
WI	*Die Welt des Islams* (Wiesbaden)
ZDMG	*Zeitschrift der Deutschen Morgenländischen Gesellschaft* (Leipzig, Berlin, Wiesbaden)

Glossaries

1. Select Glossary of Names of Significant Persons, Places, Dynasties and Peoples Occurring in the *History*

Brief information only is given here. For fuller information and explanatory references, see these names as they appear in their appropriate places within the *History* and its Commentary.

A

ʿAbd al-Jabbār b. Aḥmad b. ʿAbd al-Ṣamad, son of Sultan Masʿud of Ghazna's vizier Aḥmad b. ʿAbd al-Ṣamad (*q.v.*). He was sent to Khwarazm as the Sultan's representative when Altuntāsh's son Hārun (*q.v.*) was showing signs of rebelliousness, but was killed there in 425/1034 by Hārun's partisans.

ʿAbd al-Malek (II) b. Nuḥ (II), penultimate ruler of the Samanid dynasty (*q.v.*), r. 389–90/999–1000, before its extinction and the partition of the Samanid lands between the Ghaznavids and Qarakhanids (*q.v.*).

ʿAbd al-Rashid b. Maḥmud, son of Sultan Maḥmud of Ghazna and uncle of Masʿud. He is little mentioned by Beyhaqi as playing a role in Masʿud's reign, but eventually himself became sultan in Ghazna, r. ?440–43/?1049–52.

ʿAbd al-Razzāq b. Aḥmad b. Ḥasan, son of the vizier to Sultans Maḥmud and Masʿud, Aḥmad b. Ḥasan Meymandi (*q.v.*). He served in Masʿud's administration and became vizier to Sultan Mowdud b. Masʿud (*q.v.*) and died after 450/1058.

ʿAbdus, secretary in the Ghaznavid bureaucracy who was close to Sultan Masʿud and was employed by him for confidential tasks and negotiations.

Abivard or Bāvard, a town in northern Khorasan, now just within the Turkmen Republic. It was one of the frontier posts ceded by Masʿud to the incoming Seljuq marauders in a vain hope of satisfying their aspirations.

Abu ʿAli Moḥammad Simjuri, son of Abu'l-Ḥasan Moḥammad Simjuri (*q.v.*), military commander from the Turkish family of the Simjurids (*q.v.*) and twice governor of Khorasan for the Samanids.

Abu'l-ʿAskar Ḥoseyn Maʿdān, member of the Maʿdānid family of lords of Makrān (*q.v.*), placed on the throne there by his suzerain Sultan Masʿud in 421/1030.

Abu Dolaf Qāsem ʿEjli, Arab commander for the ʿAbbasid caliphs and lord of a small western Persian principality centred on Karaj [Abi Dolaf], d. 225/840. Beyhaqi records an anecdote involving him and the Afshin Ḥeydar (*q.v.*).

Abu'l-Ḥasan Moḥammad Simjuri, father of Abu ʿAli Moḥammad (*q.v.*) of this family and twice governor of Khorasan for the Samanids, d. 378/989.

Abu (or **Bā**) **Kālijār**, prince of the Ziyarid dynasty, of Deylamite origin, r. 420–?441/1029–?1049 in the Caspian coastal provinces of Gorgān and Ṭabarestān (*qq.v.*) as a reluctant vassal and tributary of Sultan Masʿud.

Abu'l-Moẓaffar ʿAbd al-Jabbār Jomaḥi, official from Beyhaq who was Sultan Masʿud's *ṣāḥeb-barid* or postal and intelligence officer in Nishapur during the first occupation of that town by the Seljuqs 429–31/1038–39. He was also a good poet in both Arabic and Persian.

Abu Naṣr Moshkān, outstanding head of the Chancery or department of state responsible for all correspondence, domestic and diplomatic, until his death in 431/1039, and Beyhaqi's superior there. He may have been the author, and was certainly the subject of, a work on his official activities, the *Maqāmāt-e Abu Naṣr-e Moshkān*, which Beyhaqi clearly used in his *History*.

Abu Sahl Zowzani, official who was head of the Army Department and then head of the Chancery during Masʿud's reign. Beyhaqi regards his influence over the Sultan as making him something like the latter's evil genius.

Afghān-shāl, a place just outside Ghazna often mentioned in the *History* as the venue for the sultans' *al fresco* celebrations and wine-drinking parties.

Afshin Ḥeydar or **Kheydhar b. Kāvus**, Iranian local ruler of the region of Oshrusana in Transoxania, now in the Uzbek Republic. He served as a commander in the army of the ʿAbbasid caliphs and was killed in 226/841. Beyhaqi records an anecdote involving him and Abu Dolaf Qāsem ʿEjli (*q.v.*).

Aḥmad b. ʿAbd al-Ṣamad Shirāzi, vizier to Sultan Masʿud in succession to Aḥmad b. Ḥasan Meymandi (*q.v.*), hence appointed in 424/1033, having previously been *kadkhodā* or administrative assistant and counsellor to the Khwarazm Shah Altuntāsh (*q.v.*). For two years he served Masʿud's son Mowdud as his first vizier, but fell from favour and died shortly after this.

Aḥmad b. Ḥasan Meymandi, famed vizier to Sultan Maḥmud till his fall in 416/1025, and then re-appointed to the same office by the new sultan, Masʿud, in 422/1031. He assumed the post ostensibly with reluctance but clearly enjoyed the exercise of power again; he died in office two years later.

Aḥmad b. Ināltegin, Turkish military commander of Sultans Maḥmud and Masʿud. In 422/1031 Masʿud appointed him commander-in-chief of the army in India, based on Lahore, where however he rebelled in 424/1033; his outbreak was suppressed and he was killed a year later.

ʿAlāʾ al-Dowla Moḥammad, Ebn Kāku, founder of a line of Deylamite princes in western Persia, the Kakuyids (*q.v.*), with his capital at Isfahan, r. before 398–433/before 1008–1041. After 429/1030 he was nominally a vassal of the Ghaznavids, but in practice, because of the great distance of his lands from the sultans' centre of power, he was virtually independent, and especially so after the Ghaznavids were compelled to relinquish Ray.

Alexander of Macedon, called **the Great**, appearing in Islamic lore as Eskandar, Greek emperor who led his army across Western Asia as far as India, r. BC 336–323. His fame later gave rise to a series of epic romances, versions of which are to be found in almost all the languages of the Middle East and Caucasus region, in Persian as the *Eskandar-nāma*. Beyhaqi has an anecdote about his campaign against the Indian king Porus.

ʿAli b. ʿAbdallāh Mikāli, member of the illustrious Nishapur family of Mikāʾilis (*q.v.*), high in the sultans' favour, as *raʾis* or mayor of Ghazna for Maḥmud and then in 422/1031 as leader of the Pilgrimage for Masʿud.

ʿAli Dāya, Turkish commander of Sultans Maḥmud and Masʿud. He was one of the old guard or Maḥmudiyān (*q.v.*) during Masʿud's reign who nevertheless managed to retain his master's favour until in 431/1040 he was made a scapegoat for the disaster of the battle of Dandānqān (*q.v.*).

ʿAli Qarib or **Khᵛishāvand**, Turkish commander of Sultan Maḥmud, who played a leading role in placing the latter's son Moḥammad (*q.v.*) on the throne at Ghazna in 421/1030, exercising *de facto* supreme power during his brief reign. He then deserted Moḥammad in favour of his brother Masʿud, but this did not save him from the new Sultan's suspiciousness and mistrust, and he was speedily arrested and died in captivity.

ʿAlitegin, ʿAli b. Hārun or **b. Ḥasan Bughrā Khān**, brother of Yusof Qadïr Khān (*q.v.*), wily and capable prince of the Turkish Qarakhanid dynasty (*q.v.*), who carved out for himself a principality in Transoxania based on Samarqand and Bokhara (*qq.v.*). Regarded as basically hostile by the Ghaznavid Sultans, he nevertheless warded off their attacks, dying in 425/1034.

Alptegin, Turkish slave commander of the Samanids who was in 350/961 unsuccessfully involved in a succession putsch within the ruling family and decided to withdraw to the eastern periphery of the Samanid lands, establishing in Ghazna what was virtually an autonomous principality of his own. He died in 352/963, and one of his successors there was his Turkish slave soldier Sebüktegin (*q.v.*), founder of the Ghaznavid dynasty.

Altuntāsh Khwarazm Shah, trusty Turkish slave commander of Sebüktegin and Maḥmud, who was entrusted with the governorship of Khwarazm after the latter conquered it in 408/1017, assuming the ancient title of Khwarazm Shah. Despite Masʿud's suspicious attitude towards him, he faithfully governed the province for the Ghaznavids till his death in battle against ʿAlitegin (*q.v.*) in 423/1032.

Āmol of Ṭabarestān, a town of the Caspian coastal region, now in the Persian province of Māzandarān. It was savagely sacked by the Ghaznavid army in 426/1035 when Sultan Masʿud marched there to collect arrears of tribute owed by the Ziyarid Abu Kālijār Anushirvān (*q.v.*).

Āmol-e Shaṭṭ, i.e. the town situated on the left bank of the Oxus river at a strategic crossing place where the highroad across Khorasan led onwards to Bokhara and Transoxania. It is now the town of Charzhou in the Turkmen Republic.

ʿAmr b. Leyth, the second amir of the Saffarid dynasty in Sistan (*q.v.*), r. 265–87/879–900. He inherited from his brother Yaʿqub (*q.v.*) a vast military empire, but most of this was lost when he unwisely challenged the Samanids in war in 287/900. The *History* has an anecdote about his fortitude on the loss of his son.

Amu Darya, the classical Oxus, a river of Central Asia which rises in the Pamirs and debouches into the Aral Sea through the region of Khwarazm (*q.v.*)

Andkhud or **Andkhuy**, a town of northeastern Khorasan on the road from Merv to Balkh, now in the Faryab province of modern Afghanistan and adjacent to the border with the Turkmen Republic.

Anushirvān, Khosrow I, see **Khosrow I Anushirvān**.

Arslān Jādheb, Turkish slave commander of Maḥmud, who towards the end of the Sultan's reign was sent against the Turkmens harrying the northern fringes of Khorasan; he died before the end of Maḥmud's reign.

Arslān Khān Soleymān, Qarakhanid ruler in the eastern parts of the Khanate 423–48/1032–56 and the son of Sultan Maḥmud's ally Yusof Qadïr Khān (*q.v.*). The previous friendly relations of his father with the Ghaznavids were continued in Masʿud's reign, and marriage links were established between him and his family and that of the Sultan.

Astarābād, a town of the province of Gorgān at the southeastern corner of the Caspian sea, now the modern town of Gorgān.

Ayāz b. Uymaq, celebrated Turkish slave and catamite of Sultan Maḥmud, a relationship much celebrated in subsequent Persian poetry and romance. He retained Sultan Masʿud's favour but with a reduced role in events, and apparently died in 449/1057.

ʿAżod al-Dowla Fanā-Khosrow, the most forceful and successful ruler of the Buyid dynasty (*q.v.*), r. 338–72/949–83 from his capital Shiraz; Beyhaqi has an anecdote about his vengeance against the vizier of his cousin ʿEzz al-Dowla Bakhtiyār, Ebn Baqiyya.

B

Bā Kālijār, see Abu Kālijār.

Bādghis, a region of Khorasan, now in northwestern Afghanistan, on the middle Heri Rud river with its centre at Herat.

Baghlān, a town of northern Afghanistan situated to the north of the Hindu Kush, and on the route connecting Balkh (*q.v.*) with Ghazna.

Balkh, an ancient city of northern Afghanistan to the south of the middle Oxus river in the region known in medieval Islamic times as Tokhārestān (*q.v.*). It was a key point in Ghaznavid strategy against incoming marauders such as the Qarakhanids and the Oghuz Turkmens (*qq.v.*).

Balkhān Kuh, a mountainous region to the east of the Caspian sea, now in the Turkmen Republic, to which the Oghuz invaders of

Khorasan were on various occasions hurled back by the generals of Sultans Maḥmud and Masʿud.

Barghashi, Abu'l-Moẓaffar Moḥammad, vizier to two of the last Samanid amirs, Nuḥ (II) b. Manṣur (I) and his son Manṣur II. According to an anecdote in the *History*, he foresaw the collapse of the Samanid dynasty and sought his demission from office by a ruse.

Barmakids, celebrated Iranian family of officials and viziers for the early ʿAbbasid caliphs. Their downfall at the hands of Hārun al-Rashid (*q.v.*) in 187/803 became for later historians and littérateurs a much-cited graphic tale and moral example; members of the family such as Yaḥyā b. Khāled b. Barmak and his sons Fażl and Jaʿfar are the subjects of various favourable anecdotes and mentions in the *History*.

Bāvard, see Abivard.

Begtegin, Turkish slave commander of Sultans Maḥmud and Masʿud, active in promoting the succession of Masʿud to the sultanate in 429/1030.

Begtughdï, Turkish slave commander of Sultan Masʿud and Commander of his élite force of the Palace Gholāms. He was employed in the attempts to stem Turkmen incursions into Khorasan, although by that time elderly and infirm; he was arrested as a scapegoat for the Dandānqān disaster of 431/1040.

Beyhaq, a town of Khorasan, on the highroad connecting northern Persia with Nishapur and beyond, which produced many ulema, secretaries and literary men, notably Abu'l-Fażl Beyhaqi himself.

Bilgetegin, Turkish slave commander of Sultan Masʿud and his *Ḥājeb-e Bozorg* or Great Chamberlain, the senior military commander, d. 426/1035.

Bokhara, an ancient city of Sogdia in Transoxania, the seat of the Samanid amirate and then in early Ghaznavid times a centre of the principality of the Qarakhanid ʿAlitegin (*q.v.*), now in the Uzbek Republic.

Böritegin Ebrāhim, Tamghach Khān, Qarakhanid of the Western branch of the confederation, who ruled in Transoxania *ca.* 444–60/*ca.* 1052–68, in later Islamic literature achieving a reputation as a wise and exemplary ruler. He appears in the *History* as a wily and tenacious enemy of Sultan Masʿud, harrying the upper Oxus territories of the Ghaznavid empire.

Bost, a town of southeastern Afghanistan situated at the confluence of the Helmand and Arghandab rivers whose site today is known as Qalʿa-ye Bist. It was an early conquest of Sebüktegin (*q.v.*), and an extensive palace and military complex was built nearby at Lashkari Bāzār and is apparently mentioned by Beyhaqi.

Bozorjmehr, said to have been the chief minister of the Sasanid Emperor Khosrow I Anushirvān (*q.v.*), who may, however, have been a semi-legendary figure, famed in later Islamic literature for his wisdom. In a story given in the *History*, he is martyred by his master for his uncompromising monotheism and thus made into something like a proto-Muslim.

Bughrā Khān Hārun or **Ḥasan b. Soleymān,** Qarakhanid (*q.v.*) leader whose invasion in 382/992 of the Samanid lands and temporary occupation of the capital Bokhara (*q.v.*) heralded the disintegration of the Samanid empire within the following few years; d. 382/992.

Buyids or **Boveyhids**, a family of what were originally Delamite soldiers of fortune from northwestern Persia, on occasion referred to by Beyhaqi as the Shāhanshāhis from the ancient title "King of Kings" adopted by some members of the family. In the course of the fourth/tenth century, the Buyids established a series of amirates in Persian and Iraq forming something like a family confederation (320–454/932–1062). Just before his death, Sultan Maḥmud conquered from them the northern Buyid amirate based on Ray, but Masʿud was unsuccessful in his attempt to annex the Buyid province of Kerman.

C

Chaghāniyān, a principality on the right or northern bank of the upper Oxus river, now falling mainly in the Uzbek Republic; its Iranian princes were in Masʿud's time vassals of the Ghaznavids.

Chaghrï Beg Dāvud, brother of Ṭoghrïl Beg (*q.v.*), one of the three leaders of the Seljuq family from the Oghuz (*q.v.*) or Ghuzz tribe of the Turks who during the later part of Sultan Masʿud's reign overran Khorasan and wrested it from the Ghaznavids after the battle of Dandānqān (*q.v.*).

D

Dabusiyya, a small town of Sogdia in Transoxania, whose site is now in the Uzbek Republic. It was here that there was fought in 432/1033 an indecisive battle between the Qarakhanid ʿAlitegin (*q.v.*) and his Seljuq allies, and the Ghaznavid forces, in which the commander of the latter, Altuntāsh (*q.v.*), was however killed.

Dandānqān, a small town of northern Khorasan in the desert between Merv and Sarakhs, whose site is now in the Turkmen Republic. In spring 431/1040 was fought there one of the decisive battles of Eastern Islamic history, when the Seljuqs and their Turkmen followers defeated Sultan Masʿud's army, thus opening the way for the Turkmens to overrun Khorasan and lay the foundation of the Great Seljuq empire.

Daqiqi, Abu Manṣur Aḥmad, important early poet in New Persian who flourished in the later Samanid period, probably d. *ca.* 366/*ca.* 976. Beyhaqi cites his lyric poetry, but his greatest achievement was his embarking on a poetical version of the Iranian national epic, the *Shāh-nāma* or "Book of Kings," a work taken up and completed by his younger contemporary Ferdowsi.

Dehestān, a region lying to the east of the Caspian Sea, now in the Turkmen Republic, with a famed *rebāṭ* or frontier post which was a bastion against Oghuz Turkmen marauders coming from the Central Asian steppes.

E

[Ebn] ʿAbd al-ʿAziz ʿOmari, Abu ʿAbd al-Raḥmān, d. 184/800, ascetic of Mecca, and **Ebn al-Sammāk, Abu'l-ʿAbbās Moḥammad,** d. 183/799, ascetic of Kufa. Beyhaqi gives an anecdote on the caliph Hārun al-Rashid's visit to them and their rebukes to him for his worldliness.

Ebrāhim b. Masʿud, Ghaznavid sultan, r. 451–92/1059–99, who restored the now truncated sultanate to something like its former glory; it was in the early years of his reign that Beyhaqi completed his *History*.

Ebrāhim Ināl, see **Yināliyān**.

Ertegin, Turkish slave commander of Masʿud. He served as *Ḥājeb-e Sarāy* or Major-Domo of the Palace; towards the end of the reign he was appointed Commander of the Palace Gholāms in place of Begtughdï (*q.v.*).

Eryāruq, Turkish slave commander of Masʿud. He had taken Masʿud's side during the succession struggle with Moḥammad, but was nevertheless brought under the new Sultan's suspicion through the intrigues of the Maḥmudiyān (*q.v.*) so that the downfalls of Eryāruq and his fellow-general Ghāzi (*q.v.*) were procured, and he was arrested in 422/1031 and killed.

Esfarāyen, a town of northern Khorasan on the route from Nishapur and Ṭus to the Caspian provinces of Gorgān and Ṭabarestān (*qq.v.*).

Esfezār, a town of what is now the Farah province of western Afghanistan, in Ghaznavid times a stage on the southerly route from Ghazna to Herat via Bost and Sistan (*qq.v.*).

Eskāfi, Abu Ḥanifa, poet who was a contemporary and friend of Beyhaqi, and still alive when the latter was composing his *History*. Beyhaqi gives the texts of four long odes by him and is a main source for what little is known about this poet and his work.

Esmāʿil Khandān, son of the Khwarazm Shah Altuntāsh (*q.v.*), who after the murder of his brother Hārun (*q.v.*) was in 426/1035 hailed as Shah in Khwarazm. He held power there till 432/1041 when Masʿud's ally, Shāh Malek of Jand (*q.v.*), expelled him from Khwarazm and he had to take refuge with the Seljuqs.

F

Fāʾeq Khāṣṣa ("Close Retainer, Intimate"), Turkish slave eunuch commander of the later Samanids, much involved in the fighting in Khorasan over the partition of the Samanid lands, d. 389/999.

Farāmorz b. 'Alā' al-Dowla Moḥammad, son and successor of his father (see **'Alā' al-Dowla Moḥammad, Ebn Kāku**) in the Kakuyid amirate of Isfahan, d. after 455/1063. He was with the Seljuq forces at the battle of Dandānqān (*q.v.*) in 431/1040, and eventually had to submit to Seljuq overlordship.

Farāva, town on the northern rim of the mountains of northern Khorasan, facing the Qara Qum desert, hence harried by the Oghuz Turkmens during Sultan Mas'ud's reign. Its site is now marked by the place Qizil Arvat in the Turkmen Republic.

Farrokh-zād b. Mas'ud, Ghaznavid sultan, r. 443–51/1052–59. It was during his reign that Beyhaqi was putting together his *History.*

Farrokhi Sistāni, poet and eulogist of the early Ghaznavids, and especially of Maḥmud and Mas'ud, though his verse is not actually quoted by Beyhaqi in the extant part of his *History*; d. during Mas'ud's reign.

Fażl b. Rabi', chief minister to the 'Abbasid Caliphs Hārun al-Rashid (*q.v.*) and his son Amin, d. 207 or 208/822–24. He figures in anecdotes about a visit of his with Hārun to Mecca and about the commander 'Abdallāh b. Ṭāher's intercession on his behalf with the next caliph, Ma'mun.

Fażl b. Sahl, Persian of Zoroastrian antecedents who acted as vizier and military commander for the Caliph Ma'mun, d. 202/818. He appears as a sensible adviser to Ma'mun in anecdotes given by Beyhaqi about his master.

Fażl b. Yaḥyā Barmaki, commander and governor for Hārun al-Rashid, see **Barmakids**.

G

Gardiz, a town of eastern Afghanistan, in the modern Pakhtia province, early conquered by the Turkish amirs succeeding Alptegin (*q.v.*) in Ghazna.

Gharchestān, a region of Afghanistan to the north of the Heri Rud which had had its own prince with the title of Shir until conquered by Sultan Maḥmud in 403/1012

Ghāzi, Turkish slave commander of Maḥmud and Masʿud, and after the death of Arslān Jādheb (*q.v.*), commander-in-chief of the Ghaznavid army in Khorasan. But, as with his fellow-commander Eryāruq (*q.v.*), Masʿud's mind was poisoned against him by the clique of Maḥmudiyān (*q.v.*), and he was arrested in 422/1031, dying in captivity in 425/1034.

Ghazna, Ghaznin, a town of eastern Afghanistan, in the modern Ghazni province, the seat of the Ghaznavid dynasty until it was pushed out by the rising Ghurids (*q.v.*) in the mid-sixth/twelfth century so that the last Ghaznavid sultans ruled only in northwestern India.

Ghur, the mountainous and inaccessible region of central Afghanistan, the modern province of Ghorat. Sultan Maḥmud and his son Prince Masʿud led raids into it so that its chiefs subsequently recognized Ghaznavid overlordship. Masʿud took refuge with friendly chiefs in Ghur when fleeing from the Dandānqān (*q.v.*) battlefield in 431/1040.

Ghurids, a line of chieftains from Ghur (*q.v.*), r. early fifth century–612/early eleventh century–1215, who rose to power in the course of the early sixth/twelfth century until they were able to sack Ghazna in 545/1150 and eventually drive the last Ghaznavids into India.

Giri, a Ghaznavid fortress in northwestern India, possibly in the region of Peshawar, mentioned in contemporary sources as a place of imprisonment.

Gorgān and **Ṭabarestān**, two adjacent regions of the Caspian coastlands at the Sea's southeastern end, in early Ghaznavid times under the rule of the Ziyarids (*q.v.*). In 426/1035 Masʿud led an expedition into the area in order to recover arrears of tribute from the Ziyarid princes there.

Guzgān(ān), a region of northern Afghanistan, roughly corresponding to the modern provinces of Faryab and Jowzjan. Maḥmud brought its line of native Iranian princes, the Farighunids, under his control, and in the latter part of the Sultan's reign it was governed by his son, Prince Moḥammad.

H

Ḥamdavi or **Ḥamduni, Abu Sahl Aḥmad**, official and secretary who functioned as Moḥammad's vizier during his short sultanate. He nevertheless managed to retain the new ruler Masʿud's favour: he served as interim vizier for him until Aḥmad b. Ḥasan Meymandi (*q.v.*) could be brought back from India, and subsequently was appointed in 424/1033 civil governor in Ray.

Hānsi, a fortress and town of northern India, now in the Hariyana province of the Indian Union, against which Sultan Masʿud led an expedition; it subsequently became a forward base for further Muslim attacks into the Gangetic plain.

Hārun al-Rashid, ʿAbbasid caliph famed in later story and myth as ruler in the supposedly palmiest days of the dynasty, r. 170–93/786–809, cited in various anecdotes of the *History*.

Hārun b. Altuntāsh, son of the Khwarazm Shah Altuntāsh (*q.v.*). who after his father's death in 423/1032 became lieutenant in Khwarazm for the nominal Khwarazm Shah, Sultan Masʿud's son Saʿid. He soon threw off the control of Ghazna and probably assumed the title of Shah for himself, but Masʿud was able to procure his murder in 425/1034.

Hārun or **Ḥasan b. Soleymān**, see **Bughrā Khān Hārun** or **Ḥasan b. Soleymān.**

Ḥasanak, Abu ʿAli Ḥasan, member of the important Nishapur family of Mikālis (*q.v.*) who became vizier to Sultan Maḥmud in 416/1025 after the fall of Aḥmad b. Ḥasan Meymandi (*q.v.*). However, after the accession of his old enemy the new Sultan Masʿud, a charge of collusion with the Ismaʿili Fatimids of Egypt and Syria was brought against him and he was killed in 422/1031; the account of his trial and judicial murder is one the most graphic episodes in the *History*.

Herat, Harāt, an ancient city of western Afghanistan, situated on the Heri Rud river and centre of the region of Bādghis (*q.v.*); in the later part of Sultan Maḥmud's reign it was governed by Prince Masʿud.

Ḥorra-ye Khottali, aunt of Sultan Masʿud, strong proponent of his succession as Sultan on his father's death and consoler of Masʿud in his depressed and defeated state at the end of his reign.

I

ʿIsā b. Maʿdān, of the family of rulers of Makrān, who succeeded his father in 416/1025–26 but was in 421/1030 displaced and killed by a Ghaznavid expedition under the Amir Yusof b. Sebüktegin (*q.v.*) and his brother Abu'l-ʿAskar (*q.v.*) placed on the throne as a Ghaznavid tributary.

Isfahan, a city of western Persia that, together with Hamadan, marked the farthest limit westwards of Sultan Maḥmud's campaign across Persia of 420/1029 and the capital of the principality of the Kakuyids (*q.v.* and see **ʿAlāʾ al-Dowla Moḥammad, Ebn Kāku**).

J

Jaʿfar b. Yaḥyā Barmaki, vizier to Hārun al-Rashid, see **Barmakids**.

Jebāl or **ʿErāq-e ʿAjam** ("Iraq of the Persians"), the western part of the Iranian plateau, annexed by Sultan Maḥmud at the end of his reign but only held by the Ghaznavids for a few years of Masʿud's reign.

K

Kabul, Kābol, an ancient town of eastern Afghanistan, It was conquered by Sebüktegin (*q.v.*) from its local rulers, the Kabul Shahs, and used as a springboard for Ghaznavid raids into India.

Kakuyids, a dynasty of Deylamite origin founded by ʿAlāʾ al-Dowla Moḥammad, Ebn Kākuya (q.v.), which ruled in Jebāl, with centres at Isfahan and Hamadan, before 398/before 1008 to the Seljuq conquest in 443/1051, and thereafter in the two towns of central Persia of Yazd and Abarquh, till ?536/?1141.

Kerman, a province of southeastern Persia which Sultan Masʿud endeavoured to conquer from the Buyids (*q.v.*) but was only able to hold for two or so years.

Khalaj, a Turkish people who had apparently migrated to eastern Afghanistan, against whom the Sultans had at times to lead punitive expeditions but whom they also recruited as auxiliary troops in their armies.

Khorasan, Khurasan, now the northeastern province of Persia but in medieval Islamic times a term of much wider application, largely comprising all lands lying between the region of Ray as far as eastern Afghanistan and the frontiers of India.

Khosrow I Anushirvān, outstanding emperor of the pre-Islamic Persian dynasty of the Sasanids, r. 531–79. In Islamic Arabic and Persian wisdom literature and the "Mirrors for Princes" genre, he often figures as the model of a wise, benevolent and just ruler, but an anecdote given in the *History* consigns him to Hell for his persecution and killing of his minister Bozorjmehr (*q.v.*).

Khottal(ān), a district to the north of the upper Oxus, now in the Uzbek Republic, that was held by the early Ghaznavids as a buffer zone against the Qarakhanids (q.v.).

Khwarazm, the classical Chorasmia, a province of Central Asia, situated on the lower Oxus river and under an independent line of rulers (see **Ma'munids**) until the Ghaznavid conquest of 408/1017. It now comes within the Karakalpak region of the Uzbek Republic.

Komijis, a people of uncertain origin, often mentioned together with the Kanjina Turks, and located in the upper Oxus region of what is now the Tadjik Republic, mentioned as harrying the Ghaznavid frontiers of northeastern Afghanistan.

L

Lahore, Lāhawr, the main centre of Ghaznavid military power, a resort of *ghāzi*s or fighters for the faith in northwestern India, now a city of the Panjab province of Pakistan. From Lahore, raids were launched against the Indian princes, and in the last decades of the Ghaznavid empire, it was the capital of the realm.

M

Maḥmudiyān, a somewhat shadowy group of persons at Mas'ud's court who went back to the former reign of Sultan Maḥmud, also called by Beyhaqi the Pedariyān "Men from the Father's Reign." They are contrasted with the Mas'udiyān "Men of Mas'ud's Reign," also called "New Men, Upstarts."

Majdud b. Mas'ud, a favoured son of the Sultan, who was, towards the end of his father's reign, sent to India with an army. When Mas'ud was killed, he attempted to assert his own claims to the succession against his brother Mowdud (*q.v.*), but died in mysterious circumstances.

Makrān, the region of what is now the southern part of Pakistani and Iranian Baluchistan, in early Ghaznavid time ruled by its own line of chiefs, the Ma'dānids.

Ma'mun b. Hārun al-Rashid, governor in the Eastern caliphate and then 'Abbasid caliph, r. 189–218/813–33, cited by Beyhaqi in various anecdotes.

Ma'munids, the last independent line of Iranian Khwarazm Shahs, ruling from 385/995 in Gorgānj, before Sultan Maḥmud's conquest of 408/1017.

Mandish, one of the principal fortresses in Ghur (*q.v.*), mentioned in the accounts of the early Ghaznavid raids into that region.

Manṣur II b. Nūḥ II, ephemeral, and in effect the last Samanid amir, r. 389–90/997–99. His deposition gave Sebüktegin (*q.v.*) an opportunity to pose as his avenger, leading to the disintegration of the Samanid rule, a process described in anecdotal flashbacks of the *History*.

Manuchehr b. Qābus, Falak al-Ma'āli, amir of the Ziyarid dynasty in Gorgān and Ṭabarestān (*q.v.*), r. 402–20/1012–29, whom Sultan Maḥmud regarded as his tributary.

Manuchehri Dāmghāni, court poet of the Ghaznavids whose birth and death dates are unknown. He eulogized Sultan Mas'ud and his servants extensively but his verses are, somewhat surprisingly, not cited by Beyhaqi in the extant part of the *History*.

Masʿud b. Maḥmud, Ghaznavid sultan, r. 421–32/1030–40, whose reign takes up the greater part of the surviving section of Beyhaqi's *History*, the *Mojalladāt*. He was deposed by his army en route for India and then killed in 432/1041.

Masʿudiyān, see **Maḥmudiyān**.

Mengütirek, Turkish commander of the Ghaznavids and brother of ʿAli Qarib (*q.v.*), whose fate he shared in 421/1030 at the hands of the vengeful new Sultan Masʿud.

Merv, Marv, an ancient oasis and town of northern Khorasan, the bastion of Arab power in Khorasan at the time of the Arab conquests, now in the Turkmen Republic. It was used as base for the Ghaznavid forces endeavouring to stem the influx of Oghuz Turkmens into Khorasan.

Mikālis, Mikā'ilis, an influential, aristocratic family of ulema, literary men and landowners in Nishapur during the Samanid and Ghaznavid periods. Various of them served the sultans such as ʿAli b. ʿAbdallāh Mikāli (*q.v.*) and Maḥmud's vizier Ḥasanak (*q.v.*).

Moḥammad b. Maḥmud, Ghaznavid sultan with an ephemeral first reign in 421/1039 and an even shorter second one, after his brother Masʿud's deposition, in 432/1040–41. Beyhaqi has much detail on the events surrounding the collapse of his first sultanate and Masʿud's accession.

Monjuq, Turkish commander of the Küjet Turkish tribal auxiliary troops of the Ghaznavid forces in Khwarazm. Masʿud endeavoured to incite him against the Khwarazm Shah Altuntāsh but he was killed by the latter before he could make the attempt.

Mosaferids or **Sal(l)arids**, a Deylamite dynasty of the western Alborz mountains, with their centres at Ṭārom and Samirān, and in Azerbaijan and Arrān (before 304-*c.* 483/before 916-*c.* 1090); their territories in Deylam were briefly occupied by Ghaznavid forces under Prince Masʿud in 420/1029.

Moʿtaṣem b. Hārun al-Rashid, ʿAbbasid caliph, r. 218–27/833–42, mentioned in various anecdotes given in the *History*.

Movaffaq, Abu Moḥammad Hebatallāh, Imam or leader of the Shafiʿite scholars in Nishapur. He gave his support to the Seljuq leaders during their first occupation of Nishapur, left with them when they withdrew temporarily and later became administrator of Nishapur for the Seljuqs after they had overrun Khorasan.

Mowdud b. Masʿud, Ghaznavid sultan, r. 432-?440/1041-?1048. As his father's avenger, he suppressed Moḥammad's second brief period of rule and succeeded then as sultan.

Multan, a city of northern Sind in western India which had its own line of local Muslim rulers until it was brought under Ghaznavid control by such sultans as first Maḥmud and then Mowdud.

Musā Yabghu or **Bïghu,** one of the Seljuq family leaders and close kinsman of Ṭoghrïl Beg and Chaghrï Beg (*qq.v.*). He was involved in the Seljuqs' overrunning of Khorasan and allotted Sistan and adjoining regions in the subsequent share-out of territories.

N

Nasā, a town on the northern fringes of Khorasan, on the edge of the Qara Qum desert and now in the Turkmen Republic. With Abivard and Farāva (*qq.v.*), it was one of the towns ceded to the incoming Oghuz Turkmens by Sultan Masʿud in a vain attempt to contain them.

Naṣr (II) b. Aḥmad (II), Samanid amir, r. 301–31/914–43, the subject of an anecdote given in the *History*.

Naṣr b. ʿAli, Qarakhanid prince holding the princely title of **Ilig Khān** ("Territorial Khān"), d. 403/1012–13. He disputed militarily with Sultan Maḥmud control of northern Khorasan, invading the province in 396/1006.

Naṣr b. Sebüktegin, brother of Sultan Maḥmud who was commander-in-chief of the army in Khorasan and governor of Sistan till his death in 412/1021.

Nishapur, ancient city of Khorasan, the seat of the Samanid and Ghaznavid administrations of the province and headquarters of the army of Khorasan.

Nushtegin, the name of three Turkish commanders and courtiers of Sultan Masʿud, distinguished as N. Khāṣṣa, N. Nowbati and N. Valvāleji.

O

Oghuz or **Ghuzz**, a tribe of the Turks known from the time of the early Turkish empire in Mongolia and Inner Asia, out of which sprang the Seljuq family, who from the later fourth/tenth century were involved with the Samanids and Qarakhanids (*qq.v.*). In the decade of the 1030s they gradually increased their power till they were able to overrun Khorasan, having defeated Sultan Masʿud at the battle of Dandānqān (*q.v.*), and establish the Great Seljuq sultanate in Persia and Iraq.

ʿOnṣori, one of the leading poets at Sultan Maḥmud's court, cited by Beyhaqi, d. 441/1049–50.

Ostovā, a town of the mountain region of northern Khorasan, in the corridor leading to the Caspian coastlands.

Özkend or **Uzgand**, a town in the Ferghana valley of Central Asia, now in the Kyrgyz Republic, the seat of the early Qarakhanid khans who harried and eventually overthrew the last Samanids.

P

Panjhir, a valley of the southern slopes of the Hindu Kush, famed in early Islamic times for its silver mines and a corridor connecting the Kabul river valley with northern Afghanistan.

Parvān, a town of eastern Afghanistan in the lower part of the Panjhir valley (*q.v.*) and a stage on the route from Ghazna and Kabul to Balkh and the upper Oxus lands.

Peshawar, Peshāvur, fortress and town in the valley of the Kabul river adjacent to the entrance to the Khyber Pass, now in the Northwest Frontier region of Pakistan.

Pushang, Pushanj, a town to the west of Herat (*q.v.*) and on the route from that city to Nishapur and the West.

Q

Qāder, ʿAbbasid caliph, r. 381–422/991–1031, with whom Sultan Maḥmud was careful to cultivate a reputation for Sunni orthodoxy and hostility to radical Shi'ism in the form of the Fatimids of Egypt and their movement.

Qā'em, ʿAbbasid caliph, r. 422–67/1031–75, who hailed Masʿud as sultan, awarding him honorific titles and confirming him in his territories.

Qadïr Khān Yusof, see **Yusof Qadïr Khān.**

Qarakhanids, a Turkish confederation, possibly of Qarluq tribal origin, r. 382–609/992–1212, which established itself in Transoxania, Ferghana and Eastern Turkestan at the end of the fourth/tenth century.

Qāżi Shirāzi, Bu'l-Ḥasan b. ʿAli, judge and official from Shiraz whom Sultan Masʿud appointed to head the civil administration in India at the same time as he made Aḥmad Ināltegin (*q.v.*) commander-in-chief of the army there.

Qobādhiyān, a district to the north of the upper Oxus substantially in what is now the Tadjik Republic.

Qoṣdār, a district of what is now northeastern Pakistani Baluchistan, whose line of local princes was subject to the early Ghaznavids.

R

Ray, Rayy, a historic city of northern Persia on the highroad connecting Iraq with Khorasan, whose site is now engulfed by the urban sprawl of modern Tehran. It was the capital of the northern amirate of the Buyids (*q.v.*), conquered by Maḥmud in 420/1029 but only held by Masʿud for a few years in the face of Oghuz Turkmen pressure further east; see also **Jebāl.**

Rebāṭ-e Karvān, a place on the upper Heri Rud, to the south of Guzgān (*q.v.*) and on the direct route from Ghazna to Herat, the modern Rabat-Kerman, where the Sultans had pasture grounds for their riding beasts.

Rudaki, early poet in New Persian who enjoyed the patronage of the Samanids (*q.v.*), d. towards the middle of the fourth/tenth century; several of his verses are cited in the *History*.

S

Ṣāʿed, Qāżi Abu'l-ʿAlā', d. 431/1040, member of a leading family of Hanafite ulema and jurists in Nishapur, the Ṣāʿedis, in high favour with both Sultans Maḥmud and Masʿud.

Saffarids, a dynasty centred on Sistan (*q.v.*), founded by Yaʿqub b. Leyth (*q.v.*) (247–393/861–1003). Its last ruler, Khalaf b. Aḥmad, was deposed by Sultan Maḥmud and his principality annexed to the Ghaznavid empire.

Ṣāḥeb [Esmāʿil] Ebn ʿAbbād, famed vizier of the Buyids (*q.v.*) in Isfahan and Ray, in the latter place for the Amir Fakhr al-Dowla; patron of scholars and littérateurs, and himself an important stylist and scholar in Arabic, d. 385/995.

Saʿid, favourite son of Sultan Masʿud, for a while his designated heir (*vali ʿahd*), d. 430/1038 after which Mowdud (*q.v.*) was once more the heir.

Sakāvand, a place with a fortress which probably lay in southern Tokhārestān (*q.v.*).

Samangān, a town of Tokhārestān (*q.v.*), now the chef-lieu of the modern Afghan province of that name.

Samanids, a dynasty of Iranian origin, *dehqān*s or landowners in Transoxania and the upper Oxus region, who were at first governors for the Tahirids and then a largely autonomous line of amirs ruling over Transoxania and Khorasan 204–395/819–1005.

Samarqand, an ancient city of Transoxania, one of the main centres of Samanid rule and, subsequently, of the western branch of the Qarakhanids (*q.v.*), now within the Uzbek republic.

Sarakhs, a town in the steppeland of the northern fringes of Khorasan, on the road from Nishapur and Ṭus to Merv, now in the Khorasan province of Iran. It was the base from which Sultan Masʿud set off in 431/1040 for his ill-fated campaign against the Oghuz Turkmens which ended at Dandānqān (*q.v.*) in his defeat.

Sāri, a town of Ṭabarestān (see **Gorgān and Ṭabarestān**) in the Caspian coastlands.

Sebüktegin, in origin a Turkish slave in the Samanid army, he succeeded to power, after Alptegin (*q.v.*) and some other Turkish commanders, in 366/977 at Ghazna, and used this as the springboard for constituting an amirate in eastern Afghanistan that became after his death the Ghaznavid sultanate.

Seljuqs, a family of the Oghuz tribe of Turkmens; see **Oghuz or Ghuzz.**

Shābahār, Shāhbahār, a plain outside Ghazna, mentioned in the *History* as a favoured review ground of the Ghaznavid troops.

Shādyākh, a suburb of the city of Nishapur (*q.v.*) favoured as the seat of the governors of Khorasan from Tahirid times onwards.

Shāh Malek, an Oghuz chief based at Jand on the lower Syr Darya river who held the ancient Turkish noble title of Yabghu and was the rival and enemy of the Seljuq family. He conquered Khwarazm (*q.v.*) in the name of Sultan Masʿud, but soon lost it to the expanding Seljuqs and was killed *ca.* 435/1044.

Shoburqān, a town of Guzgān (*q.v.*) on the road from Herat to Balkh, the modern Shebargān, chef-lieu of the modern Afghan province of Juzjān.

Simjurids, a line of commanders of the Samanids (*q.v.*), originally of Turkish slave origin, who played a leading role in events of the Eastern Iranian lands in the fourth/tenth century, often as governors of Khorasan for the Amirs.

Sistan or **Nimruz**, a historic region of eastern Iranian lands, now divided between Iran and Afghanistan. In the early years of the fifth/eleventh century it was brought under Ghaznavid rule by Sultan Maḥmud.

Somnāth, a great Hindu shrine in the Kathiawar peninsula of western India, the goal of Sultan Maḥmud's famed plunder raid of 416/1025–26.

Sübashï, Turkish commander of Sultans Maḥmud and Masʿud, who achieved some successes against the Oghuz in Khorasan but was in 431/1040 arrested by Masʿud as one of the scapegoats for the Dandānqān (*q.v.*) disaster.

Suri, Abu'l-Fażl, *ʿamid* or civil governor of Khorasan for Sultan Masʿud, notorious for his exactions there which must have made the local population predisposed in favour of the incoming Seljuqs. He later became Sultan Mowdud's head of the civil administration but fell from favour and died in captivity.

Syr Darya, the classical Jaxartes, a river of Central Asia which rises in the Tien Shan mountains on the borders of the Kirghiz Republic and the Chinese province of Sinkiang and debouches into the Aral Sea.

T

Ṭabarestān, see **Gorgān and Ṭabarestān**.

Tabbānis, a family of Hanafite jurists and scholars of Nishapur, high in the favour of Sultans Maḥmud and Masʿud. The latter employed one of them, the Qazi Abu Ṭāher Tabbāni, on a diplomatic mission to the Qarakhanid Yusof Qadïr Khān (*q.v.*).

Tahirids, a line of governors of Khorasan for the ʿAbbasid caliphs, 205–59/821–73.

Ṭālaqān, the name of several places in the eastern Islamic world, the significant ones in Ghaznavid times being the one in Guzgān (*q.v.*), whose modern site is uncertain, and the one in Tokhārestān (*q.v.*) on the road from Balkh to Badakhshān, now the chef-lieu of the modern Afghan province of Takhar.

Tāsh Farrāsh, Turkish commander who was left as commander of the Ghaznavid forces in Isfahan after Sultan Maḥmud's conquest of 420/1029 and whom Sultan Masʿud in 424/1033 appointed as commander of the garrison at Ray.

Teginābād, a place and fortress in the medieval Islamic region of Rokhkhaj in southeastern Afghanistan, where the deposed Sultan

Moḥammad was at first imprisoned. Its exact site is unknown but must have been near the modern Kandahar.

Termedh, a town on the right bank of the Oxus river (see **Amu Darya**), of great strategic importance as the crossing-place on the route from Balkh to the upper Oxus right-bank provinces (see **Chaghāniyān; Khottal(ān); Kobādhiyān; Vakhsh**), now the town of Termez in the Uzbek republic.

Tilak, Indian who served as a translator and secretary for Indian affairs in the Ghaznavid administration, and was then in 425/1034 sent by Sultan Masʿud to India to suppress the revolt there of Aḥmad b. Ināltegin (*q.v.*).

Ṭoghrïl Beg Moḥammad, senior member of the Seljuq family who led the Oghuz against the Ghaznavid forces in Khorasan and subsequently became the founder of the Great Seljuq sultanate in western Persia and Iraq, r. 431–55/1040–63.

Tokhārestān, the region to the south of the middle and upper Oxus, now in northern Afghanistan, which had Balkh (*q.v.*) as its centre. It was a lordship of the first Samanids, and then part of the Ghaznavid sultanate, but in the later 1040s passed under Seljuq control.

Ṭus, a district of Khorasan on the Nishapur-Sarakhs road, famed as being the site of the shrine of the Eighth Imam of the Shiʿa. The modern city of Mashhad has in recent times grown up in its vicinity.

V

Valvālej, a town of the district of Tokhārestān (*q.v.*) in northern Afghanistan, whose site was probably that of the modern Qonduz.

Vakhsh, a district on the right bank of the Oxus, adjacent to Khottal(ān) (*q.v.*) and now in the Tadjik Republic.

Y

Yaḥyā b. Khāled Barmaki, see **Barmakids**.

Yaʿqub b. Leyth, founder of the Saffarid military empire in the third/ninth century (see **Saffarids**).

Yāruq-tughmush, Turkish slave commander of the Sultans, who under Masʿud was Keeper of the Royal Wardrobe.

Yināliyān, Ināliyān, a group within the Oghuz Turkmens (*q.v.*) associated with the Seljuqs during their incursions into Khorasan, and a family rather than a tribal grouping, one under the leadership of the Seljuqs' kinsman Ebrāhim Ināl.

Yusof Qadïr Khān b. Hārun or **b. Ḥasan Bughrā Khān,** brother of ʿAlitegin (*q.v.*), Qarakhanid ruler of the eastern lands of the confederation, with his capital at Kāshghar in Eastern Turkestan, d. 423/1032. Through a common hostility to ʿAlitegin, he and the Ghaznavids were allies, with marriage links between his family and that of Sultans Maḥmud and Masʿud.

Yusof b. Sebüktegin, younger brother of Sultan Maḥmud and uncle of Masʿud, commander-in-chief of the army when Masʿud secured the throne. But like others associated with the former régime, he incurred the chronic suspiciousness of Masʿud, who in 422/1031 procured his downfall and subsequent captivity, in which he died.

Z

Zābolestān, a region of eastern Afghanistan in which lay Ghazna; it had been, anciently, a principality apparently within the Indian cultural and religious world, conquered in the third/ninth century by the Saffarids (*q.v.*).

Zamindāvar, a region of southeastern Afghanistan which corresponds with the modern region around Kandahar.

Zeynabi or **Zinati ʿAlavi,** court poet of Sultan Masʿud, whose munificent gifts to him are mentioned in the *History*.

Ziyarids, a dynasty of Deylamite origin who reigned in Gorgān and Ṭabarestān (*q.v.*) (319–*ca.* 483/931–*ca.* 1090). In the time of Sultans Maḥmud and Masʿud, the Ziyarid amirs Manuchehr b. Qābus and Abu Kālijār (*qq.v.*) were considered by the Ghaznavids as their vassals.

2. Select Glossary of Technical Terms

ākhur-sālār, the Master of the Royal Stables, an office held in the Ghaznavid and succeeding dynasties by a high Turkish military commander. See Year 422 n. 428.

ʿamid, lit. "mainstay," i.e. of the bureaucracy, hence the formal title often given to the Chief Secretary and other high civilian officials. See Year 421 n. 557.

ʿāreż, lit. "one who inspects, examines something," but with the technical military and administrative sense of the official responsible for reviewing the army and ensuring that the troops and their mounts were ready for service. He was also in charge of the Department of the Army (see ***divān-e ʿarż***) within the Ghaznavid bureaucracy, a post normally held by Persian secretaries, since administrative rather than military expertise was required. See Year 421 n. 11.

aʿyān, lit. "persons in the public eye, prominent persons," hence the notables and leading figures e.g. at court or in a local, urban society context. See Year 421 n. 32.

ʿayyār, a term used in the Persian world with varied connotations, at one place in Beyhaqi, with a distinctly negative one, "urban ruffian, rural bandit and desperado" (see Year 430 n. 26), but in another place (Year 431, Gh 643, F 869) with the sense of "irregular troops."

barāt, in the Ghaznavid context, an assignment of salary on a specific source, to be collected by the payee, often linked with the similar term *tasbib*. See Year 422 n. 480.

barid, the postal and intelligence service of the ʿAbbasid caliphate and its successor-states. In Beyhaqi, the *ṣāḥeb-barid* functions as a postmaster conveying official messages to and from the provinces by means of a network of post-horses, but is also an intelligence-gatherer, sending back reports on local events to the central administration. See Year 421 n. 340.

beg, a Turkish term originally denoting a tribal chief or leader, but below the supreme ruler, the qaghan or khān, in Beyhaqi often the leader of a tribal contingent within the army. See Year 421 n. 26.

biruniyān, lit. "those outside," in Beyhaqi used for the members of the outside palace service, as opposed to those of the inside service, the sultan's intimates and boon-companions, and the eunuchs in charge of the harem, etc. See Year 421 n. 525.

bistagāni, a term found in the official terminology of eastern Islamic states, such as the Samanids, Ghaznavids and Seljuqs, at this time denoting the quarterly payment of salaries to the troops and other officials. See Year 421 n. 237.

bondār, in the fiscal terminology of the period, a tax-farmer who bought up assignments of taxation in kind, hence usually a rich and powerful person. See Year 422 n. 107.

chākar, in Ghaznavid times a general term for "servant, retainer," but in earlier Eastern Iranian usage particularly applied to the personal guard corps of a potentate or ruler. See Year 421 n. 156.

chatr, the ceremonial parasol of a ruler, in battle a rallying-point for the troops. The holder of the parasol in the sultan's entourage was the *chatr-dār*, a high dignitary. See Year 422 n. 74.

dāneshmand, lit. "learned scholar," the Persian equivalent of Arabic *ʿālem*, a person learned in the Islamic sciences of theology, law, Arabic language, etc. See Year 421 n. 63.

davāt-dār, davit-dār, lit. "keeper of the inkstand," the official of the bureaucracy in charge of this, but apparently functioning also as a keeper of archives and records; however, a further storeplace for important documents, the *khezāna-ye ḥojjat*, separate from the *davit-khāna*, is also mentioned. See Year 422 n. 29, Year 429 n. 56.

divān-e ʿarż, the department of the bureaucracy concerned with the recruitment, mustering, supplying and payment of the army, and headed by the *ʿāreż* (q.v.). See Year 421 n. 11.

divān-e eshrāf[-e mamlakat], the department concerned with inspectorial duties within the palace complex and also with the organising of espionage and intelligence-gathering, in particular, monitoring the behaviour of provincial officials. Its agents were known as *moshrefs* (*q.v.*).

divān-e resālat/rasā'el, the chancery, responsible for issuing documents, investiture diplomas, etc., and for undertaking diplomatic correspondence, the whole body of literary composition involved here being known as *enshā'*. It was headed by the Chief Secretary.

divān-e vazir, the department of the sultan's vizier, the ruler's right-hand man, something like a chief executive in the state. It was essentially a finance department, responsible for the collection of taxes and other revenue sources, and for the disbursement of money for official salaries, payments to the army, etc.

dorrā'a, the characteristic robe worn by the secretarial and official classes. See Year 422 n. 141.

'eqābeyn ('oqābeyn), a framework constructed with two poles and used as a flogging-frame. See Year 422 n. 81.

eshrāf, see ***divān-e eshrāf*** and ***moshref***.

esteqbāl, lit. "presenting oneself before someone, entering someone's presence," specifically, going out to meet an important person or messenger on his arrival and then escorting him back in a prestigious fashion. See Year 421 n. 161.

faqih, a scholar learned in *feqh*, jurisprudence, i.e. in the *Shari'a* and other aspects of Islamic law.

ghāshiya, lit. "covering," a ceremonial cloth used by a ruler or great man as a protection from pollution, and regarded as one of the emblems of sovereignty. See Year 423 n. 231.

ghāzi, lit. "fighter for the faith," one who indulges in *ghazv*, combat with unbelievers. In Beyhaqi's milieu, it was especially used for religious enthusiasts who combated the pagan Turks on the frontiers with Inner Asia or the infidel Hindus in India. see Year 421 n. 113.

gholām, lit. "lad, youth, famulus," but especially used in the military context for slave soldiers, usually recruited from lands beyond the borders of the Islamic world such as South Russia, Inner Asia and the Indian subcontinent. In the Ghaznavid empire, these slave soldiers would be largely Turks.

gholāmān-e sarāy, lit. "palace gholāms," the élite force within the general body of slave soldiers within the Ghaznavid army who formed the sultan's bodyguard. See Year 421 n. 13.

ḥājeb, lit. "one who veils something," in early Islamic palace organisation, the official charged with protecting the ruler from intruders, hence a chamberlain. In the eastern Iranian lands of Beyhaqi's time, this court office came to be held by a high-ranking soldier, generally a Turk, hence the title became used in a military context for "senior commander," something like a general officer in modern armies. The supreme commander of an army was often designated "the Great Ḥājeb," *Ḥājeb-e Bozorg, al-Ḥājeb al-Kabir* or *Ḥājeb al-Ḥojjāb*. See Year 421 nn. 6, 28, 152.

ḥashar, lit. "assemblage, collection of people." In an administrative-military context, this term can denote a group of auxiliary troops, often recruited locally for a campaign, to augment the regular, professional army, but in a more general one, a body of people, usually peasants, brought together for labouring purposes, such as construction work or beating for a hunt, hence a corvée. See Year 421 n. 471, Year 422 n. 567, Year 427 n. 38.

jāma-dār, lit. "one who keeps the clothing," the official of the sultan's household responsible for the Royal Wardrobe. See Year 421 n. 293.

jān-dār, lit. "one who guards someone's person," hence a bodyguard, in Beyhaqi, the personal guard of the sultan. See Year 421 n. 491.

kadkhodā, lit. "head of a household, family," in Beyhaqi's general usage a landowner, headman or similar local dignitary, and in later times the standard term for the headman of a community, tribe, craft guild, etc. However, Beyhaqi frequently uses it for a specific military-administrative post, that of the person attached to a governor or military commander as his administrative officer and counsellor, hence combining the functions of adjutant to a commander and of quartermaster in a modern army. See Year 421 n. 64.

khādem, basically "servant, slave." It is a general term for the sultan's servants; it can also mean, specifically, in the context of the royal household, a eunuch who e.g. guards the women's quarters, though this is not an invariable meaning of the term. See Year 421 n. 146, Year 422 n. 458.

khᵛāja, lit. "master," in Beyhaqi's time a title of honour for eminent scholars and officials. See Year 421 n. 97.

khāṣṣa, lit. "what is special," is used by Beyhaqi in various senses: as a general term for "the upper ranks of society, those specially close to the sultan, his special guard" for the ruler's share of captured plunder; and for the crown estates, the ruler's personal properties. See Year 421, 462, Year 428 n. 91.

khaṭib, lit. "orator," in early Arabic the spokesman for the tribe, in Islamic usage the preacher, usually state-salaried, who delivered a standardised oration at the Friday congregational worship (the *khoṭba*, *q.v.*) and offered up the formal intercessory prayer for the ruler. See Year 421 n. 31.

khażrā, an architectural term whose exact meaning is unclear. In Beyhaqi, it is clearly a building which was part of palaces and pavilions, in some contexts apparently an elevated structure, possibly open to the sky and having an outward view over e.g. a parade or polo ground. See Year 421 n. 299.

khelʿat, the robe of honour presented by a ruler or great man to e.g. a visiting envoy as a manifestation of favour or to one of his servants as a reward for service. See Year 421 n. 209.

kheyltāsh, a group within the army, apparently mounted (*kheyl* "horses, cavalrymen") and noted for their swift, dashing qualities, hence often used for conveying important dispatches as quickly as possible. See Year 421 n. 28.

kheyma, a general term for "tent," but more specifically, it seems, a guyed tent. As one would expect in a context where the court was often peripatetic and armies were frequently out campaigning, there is an extensive vocabulary in Beyhaqi for various kinds of tents. See Year 421, n. 34, Year 422, n. 450.

khoṭba, primarily, the stylised oration or sermon delivered by the *khaṭib* (*q.v.*) or official preacher. However, it is also used by Beyhaqi in the sense of an exordium, a discourse introducing an episode or story within his *History*. See Year 421 nn. 30, 380.

kutvāl, a term, originally Indian, denoting the castellan or keeper of a fortress. See Year 421 n. 40.

laqab or ***naʿt***, an honorific title conferred on a rule by the caliph or on subordinate officials by the ruler himself. See Year 421 n. 397, Year 422 n. 236.

māl-e beyʿat, lit. "allegiance money," money and gifts which had to be distributed at the accession of a new sovereign, one uncertain of his strength and forcefulness, to the troops and officials in order to secure their allegiance. See Year 422 n. 479.

manshur, lit. "what is spread out, laid open to view," an investiture diploma, letters patent.

maqāma, lit. "standing-place," a well-known literary genre of several Islamic languages, but in Beyhaqi it is used in the special sense of a self-contained episode of the *History*. See Year 421 nn. 435, 436.

martaba-dār, lit. "one holding a rank or function," apparently one of a body of officials at the Ghaznavid court who marshalled people into their places at court according to their official rank and social status, i.e. acted as masters of ceremonies and in charge of protocol. See Year 421 n. 114.

maẓālem, lit. "acts of tyranny," but coming to denote the sessions where the sovereign, in his role of supreme justiciar in the land, or his representative, heard complaints by his subjects of oppression and corruption. See Year 421 n. 175.

methqāl, a weight used especially for weighing out gold or registering the weight of (gold) dinars. See Year 421 n. 121.

mokhāṭaba, lit. "the act or form of addressing someone," denotes specifically an official form of address granted by the ruler as a sign of his favour and trust and regarded as a sign of closeness to the sovereign. See Year 421 n. 52.

molaṭṭafa, lit. "something slender," in Beyhaqi a slim message which could be kept easily concealed in a narrow place. See Year 421 n. 24.

moqaddam, lit. "one who is sent forward, placed in the van," hence "leader, chief," a military rank denoting a senior officer. See Year 421 n. 28.

moṣādara, lit. "squeezing," the routine confiscation and mulcting of a high official when he left office, often by the use of violence, whence a general term for forced confiscation. See Year 421 n. 372.

moṣallā, lit. "place of prayer, instrument or appliance used in prayer," is a large open space where the whole Muslim community of a town or district could worship en bloc at the two festivals of the Ending of the Fast and of the Sacrifice. The equivalent of this Arabic term in the Persian cultural world is *namāz-gāh* or *ʿid-gāh*. See Year 421 n. 185, Year 427 n. 71. *Moṣallā* can also denote a prayer rug, used for performing the *ṣalāt* (*q.v.*).

moshāfaha, lit. "the act of delivering lip-to-lip," hence instructions given to diplomatic envoys which are to be delivered orally. See Year 422 n. 217.

moshref, lit. "one who looks out, who inspects or oversees something," in Beyhaqi applied first, to a group of officials with inspectorial duties within the palace; and second, to officials sent out to the provinces of the empire with police and intelligence-gathering duties or else secretly attached to governors, commanders, etc. as spies to report on their behaviour. The central administration contained a *divān-e eshrāf* (*q.v.*) from which such operations were organised. See Year 421 n. 259, Year 422 n. 59.

mostakhrej or ***mostaḥeththh***, lit. "one who extracts," a collector of taxation, usually one designated to get this together by force if need be. See Year 422 n. 47.

mostowfi, the chief accountant in the central administration, attached to the *divān-e vazir* (*q.v.*) for supervisory and auditing purposes in a separate, ancillary office, the *divān-e estifāʾ*. See Year 421 n. 369.

moṭṭavveʿ, ***motaṭavveʿ***, lit. "one who does something beyond the call of duty," a volunteer fighter for the faith, the equivalent of a *ghāzi* (*q.v.*).

movāżaʿat, lit. "what is laid down mutually," a contract of service, in Beyhaqi a formal agreement between the sultan and his servants, such as by a vizier on coming into office, which defines duties and spheres of competence. See Year 421 n. 514, Year 422 n. 27.

mowlā, lit. "someone who is close to a person." In early Islamic usage this term has a wide range of meanings, including a "manumitted slave or client" but also "lord, master." In more than one place, Beyhaqi uses the phrase *mowlā-zāda* "a person born of a *mowlā*" in what seems to be the sense of "a low-born person." See Year 422 n. 186, Year 426 n. 58, Year 431 n. 158.

naqib is used, first, in a military context, for an army rank, the holder of which seems to have been in charge of ethnic and other component groups of the forces; it is often rendered in the present translation as "troop commander." Second, in a social-religious context it is used for the marshal or head of the body of ʿAlids within a town or other administrative units. See Year 421 nn. 28, 55, 112, year 429 n. 88.

nethār, lit. "what is scattered," specifically, showerings of coins distributed on ceremonial and festive occasions, but often used by Beyhaqi to mean "presents, offerings" in general. See Year 421 nn. 33, 452.

nim-tark, a somewhat mysterious architectural term, apparently denoting a domed tent or similar building. See Year 421 n. 118.

nowbatiyān, lit. "those who take turns," the courtiers or palace guards who had specified turns of duty in the sultan's service. A *ḥājeb-e nowbat*, the duty court chamberlain, is also mentioned. See Year 421 nn. 151, 498.

owliyāʾ va ḥasham, lit. "those close [to the ruler] and the group [of attendant courtiers]," a phrase much used by Beyhaqi for the group of courtier and retainers in close attendance on the sultan, hence notables and leading figures at court. See Year 421 n. 49.

qāʾed, lit. "leader," a high military rank, equivalent to that of general in modern military parlance. In Beyhaqi it is sometimes used specifically for the commander of a tribal, auxiliary contingent in the army. See Year 421 nn. 28, 354.

qavvāl, lit. "someone who recites, intones, sings," hence especially connected in later times with the singing of Sufi hymns and chants. See Year 421 n. 35.

qāżi, the general term for "judge," but Beyhaqi also mentions a "judge of the army," *ḥākem-e lashkar*. See Year 422 n. 153.

qeṣṣa, lit. "story, narration," but also used in administrative terminology with the specific sense of "petition, request" made to a higher authority. See Year 421 n. 503.

ra'is, lit. "headman, chief," the leading figure amongst the notables of a town and their spokesman *vis-à-vis* the central administration. It thus approximates to the European office of a mayor. See Year 421 n. 97.

rasul-dār, lit. "one who conducts, looks after a messenger," the court official charged with the reception, lodging and presentation to the ruler of official envoys and diplomatic agents. A special lodging for such envoys, the *rasul-khāna*, is also mentioned by Beyhaqi. See Year 421 n. 193.

rebāṭ, lit. "a place where horses are tethered," but with the particular meaning of "a frontier post where ghāzis (*q.v.*) come together for launching raids and jihad against the infidels." It then comes to mean a place where devotees can gather together for contemplation, pious exercises, etc., something like a hospice, as a term for which *zāviya*, lit. "angle, corner," is also found. See Year 421 n. 451, Year 422 n. 70.

revāq, an architectural term denoting a chamber with columns open to the air.

ṣāḥeb-barid, see ***barid***.

sālār, with *ḥājeb*, the most senior rank in the army, hence something like a general, but also the term often applied to the head of a band of *ghāzis* (*q.v.*). See Year 422 n. 536.

ṣalāt, the set pattern of uttered formulae and prayers and bodily movements making up the Muslim sequence of worship, whose performance five times a day is incumbent upon the believer.

sarāy-parda, lit. "palace-curtain," a protective screen round the quarters of the sultan or an army commander separating him from the courtiers or troops at large, hence the camp-enclosure, with its component parts. See Year 421 n. 25.

sardāb, a basement or underground chamber in houses used in summer to escape the heat. See 421 n. 523.

sarhang, a military rank denoting an officer of considerable seniority but below a *ḥājeb*, *qā'ed* or *sālār*, hence perhaps something like the holder of field rank in modern military terminology, so that in the present translation it is often rendered as "field officer." See Year 421 n. 39.

sepahsālār, lit. "commander of the army," hence "commander-in-chief."

sheḥna, lit. "materials of war, armaments," by Beyhaqi's time applied to a person who had these military resources at his disposal, hence "commander of a garrison or city", "police commander in a city," such a person being the sultan's personal representative in a town or province. see Year 421 n. 62.

siyāh-dār, lit. "someone wearing black," in Beyhaqi applied to the court attendants, ushers, door-keepers, etc., who seem to have worn black as a kind of uniform. See Year 421 n. 117, Year 422 n. 347.

takkor, an Indian word used by Beyhaqi for the Rajput Indian princes who were amongst the Ghaznavids' most strenuous opponents in India. See Year 424 n. 203.

taqbil al-arż, lit. "kissing the ground," a form of obeisance, known from Ancient Near Eastern times onwards, performed before the sultan or in the presence of a letter or command from him. See Year 421 n. 53.

ṭāram, ṭārom, an architectural term meaning, it appears, an open portico or loggia which served as an anteroom to the *divān-e resālat* or chancery. See Year 421 n. 537, Year 427 n. 11.

ṭasht-dār or ***āb-dār***, lit. "bearer of the ewer, water jug," a high official of the sultan's household, at the Ghaznavid court normally a Turkish soldier. See Year 421 n. 303.

tégin, in earliest Turkish the exalted rank of "prince", but by Beyhaqi's time one which had sunk in social status and was then frequently part of the onomastics of Turkish slave soldiers. See Year 421 n. 1.

ṭerāz, the embroidered bands on robes of honour, luxury garments, etc., woven in special state workshops. See Year 421 n. 339.

ṭeylasān, a hood-like garment worn over a robe and regarded as the characteristic garb of the learned and religious classes. See Year 422 n. 121.

towqiʿ, the authentification of an official document by the affixing of the ruler's personal device (*ʿalāma*) or signature.

vakil-e dar, the official in charge of the running of the sultan's palace.

vāli, lit. "someone in a close relationship with someone else," but in military-administrative usage, someone entrusted (in Sunni constitutional theory, as an act of delegation by the caliph) with power as a deputy, hence a vassal ruler, governor, etc. See Year 422 n. 641.

vali ʿahd, lit. "successor by virtue of a covenant," the specific designation by the ruler, in a legally-attested document, of his intended heir and successor. See Year 421 n. 23.

vothāq, apparently with a basic sense of "tent, room in a building," but in Beyhaqi used specifically for the parts of the palace where the palace gholāms were accommodated, hence "barracks," with *vothāqiyān* being "those quartered in barracks." See Year 421 n. 231.

yak-sovār, lit. "one-horse trooper," a military term apparently denoting a lightly-laden cavalryman, as opposed to a *do-sovār* "two-horse trooper" with a spare horse and heavier equipment. See Year 421 n. 148.

Maps

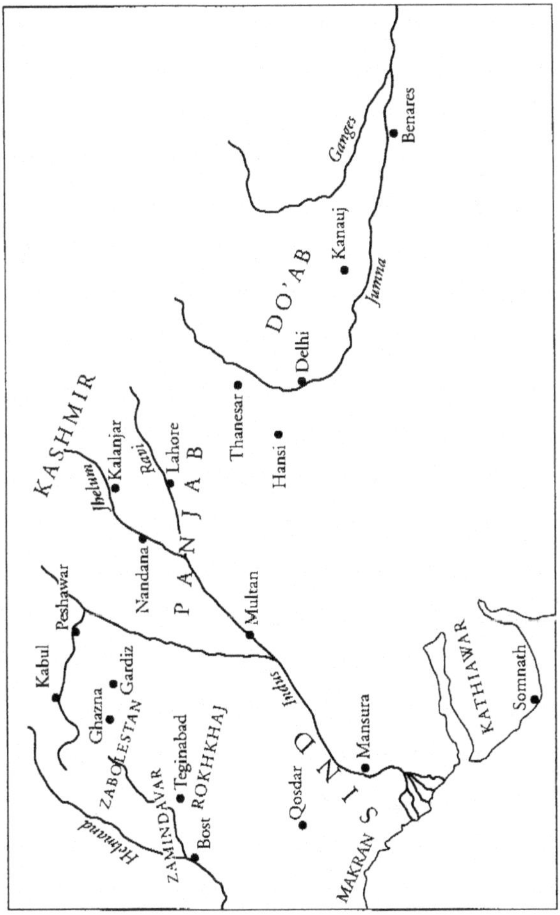

Map 1: Eastern Afghanistan and Northwestern India

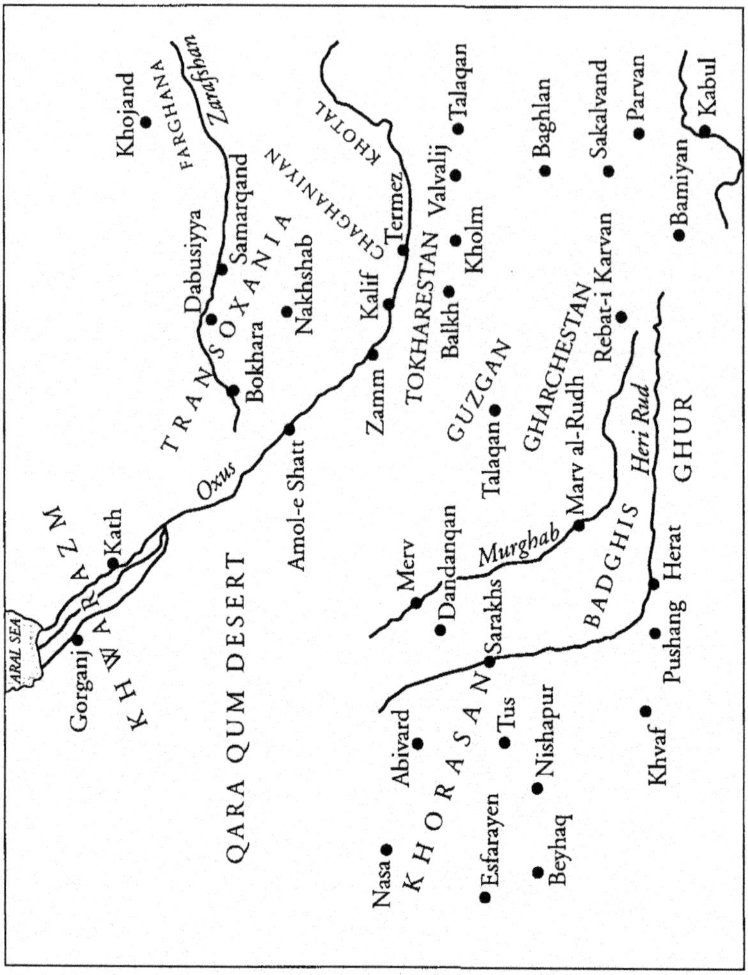

Map 2: Khorasan and the lands along the Oxus

Genealogical Tables

Table 1: The early Ghaznavid Amirs as they figure in Beyhaqi's *History*[1]

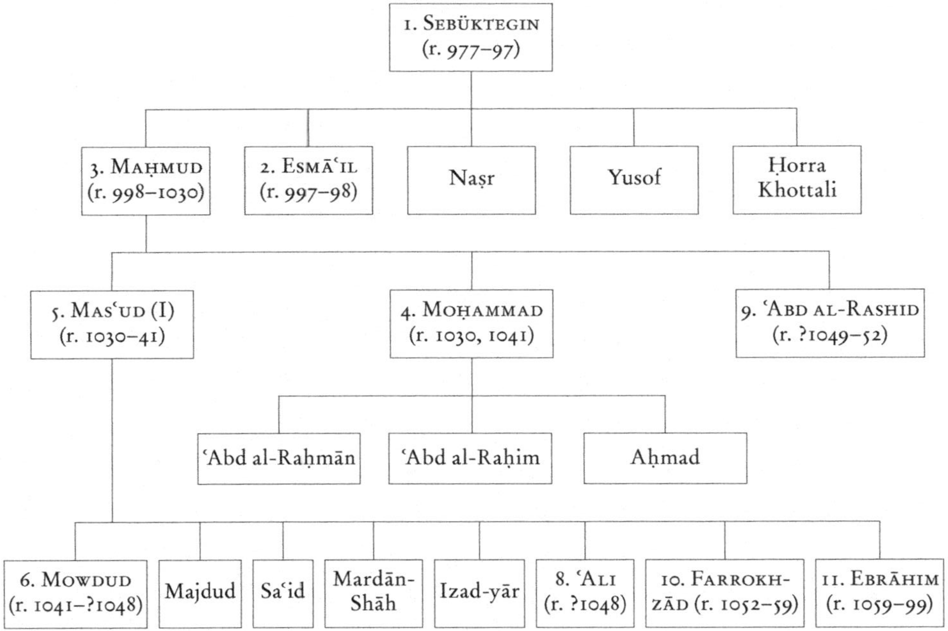

1. For a complete table of the dynasty, see Genealogical Table 1 in C.E. Bosworth, *The Ghaznavids, their empire in Afghanistan and eastern Iran 994–1040*, at the end; for the chronology of the dynasty, see *idem*, *The New Islamic dynasties. A chronological and genealogical manual*, 296–97 no. 158.

Table 2: The Ma'munid Khwarazm Shahs

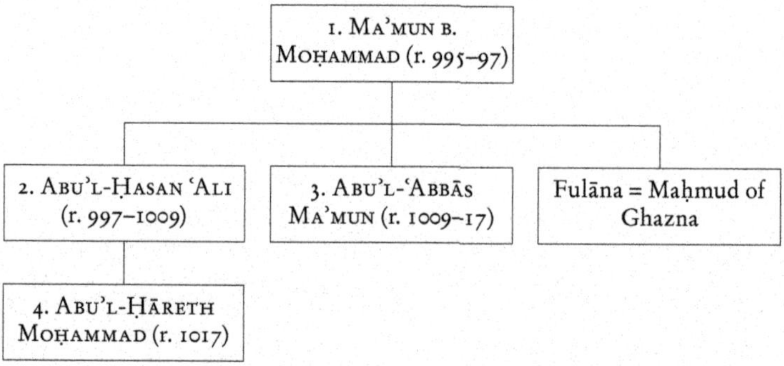

Table 3: The Khwarazm Shahs of Altuntāsh's line

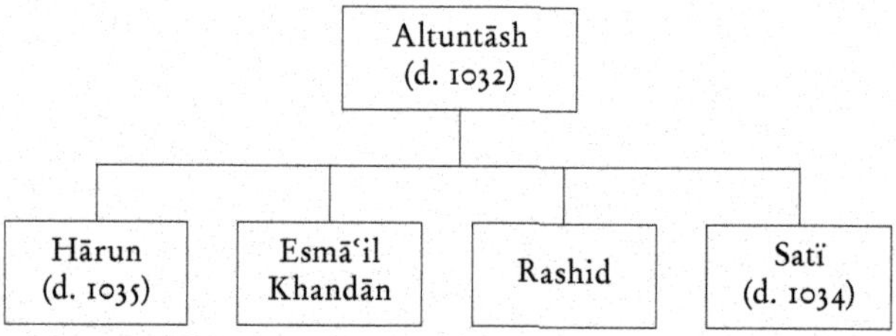

Introduction

1. The eastern Islamic world in early Islamic times and the formation of the Ghaznavid amirate

The Ghaznavid amirate, later sultanate, arose as one of the powers that emerged as the earlier idea of a universal Islamic caliphate disintegrated, at least, at its political, practical level. Since the later ninth century AD, ambitious provincial governors and military commanders had started carving out their own principalities in the more distant parts from Iraq of the caliphate. Some of them merely claimed autonomy and continued to acknowledge the suzerainty of the ʿAbbasid caliphs in Baghdad through the traditional means of the *khoṭba*, mention of the supreme overlord's name in the bidding prayer at the Friday congregational worship,[1] and in the *sekka*, the right of coinage, with the primacy of the caliph's name on gold and silver coinage minted by governors and commanders within their territories. This was the case with the Tulunids in Egypt and Syria towards the end of the ninth century and the opening of the next century, and with the Tahirids in Khorasan and the East in the middle decades of the ninth century. It was also nominally the case with the Samanids of Transoxania and then of Khorasan in the later ninth and the tenth centuries, although the great distance of their territories from Baghdad meant that, in practice, the Samanid amirs behaved as independent sovereigns, continuing to acknowledge the ʿAbbasids in the *khoṭba* and *sekka* and at

[1] See on the significance of this, below, Year 421 n. 30.

times sending gifts, but not forwarding to Baghdad the annual tribute regarded as another token of dependence.[2]

Other newly-emergent provincial powers were less deferential to ʿAbbasid theoretical suzerains and even at times hostile. Such was the case of the Saffarid brothers Yaʿqub and ʿAmr b. Leyth who, in the later ninth century, built up a powerful if transient military empire in southern Persia, in what is now Afghanistan, and then in Khorasan from their base in Sistan. Of plebeian origin and proud of it (*ṣaffār* = "coppersmith"), they were unimpressed by the *sharaf*, the hereditary noble descent of the ʿAbbasids and of the landowning classes such as, in Persia, the *dehqāns*, having achieved their own dominant position by force of arms alone.

Yet other powers were ideologically opposed to the idea of the ʿAbbasid caliphate as the embodiment of Sunni orthodoxy, as this concept had evolved since the time of the Prophet and the Patriarchal Caliphs. The Deylamite Buyids were originally from the fastnesses of the Alborz chain in northern Persia and the adjacent Caspian coastlands, where they had been exposed to the preaching of Zeydite Shiʿism by missionaries from Yemen. Hence they carried their personal Shiʿite beliefs into the lands of western and southern Persia and of Iraq which they overran during the middle years of the tenth century. The practicalities of the resultant situation—a minority Deylamite warrior caste ruling over a majority Sunni population—led the Buyid amirs, as moderate rather than extremist Shiʿites, to come to an accommodation with the ʿAbbasid Caliphs. They took over the ʿAbbasids' sole remaining territories in central Iraq, circumscribing their political and financial freedom of action, but left them with the moral authority of religious headship of orthodox, Sunni Islam. The ambiguities arising from the resultant situation were to provide useful pretexts for the early Ghaznavid sultans to expand westwards from their province of Khorasan inherited from the Samanids (see below) into northern and northwestern Persia at the expense of the northern Buyid amirate and other local Deylamite and Kurdish petty rulers. The express aim in 1029 of Maḥmud of Ghazna, in his persona as an ultra-zealous Sunni ruler, was to free the ʿAbbasids from their tutelage under the Buyids,

---

[2] R.N. Frye, "The Sāmānids," in *CHIr. IV. From the Arab invasion to the Saljuqs*, ed. Frye, Cambridge 1975, 140.

once the outstandingly powerful figures of the Buyid family, ʿAżod al-Dowla (949–83) and his son Bahāʾ al-Dowla (989–1012) were out of the way.[3]

More threatening, however, to the ʿAbbasids on both the moral and religious plane and then on the political and military one were the Fatimid Caliphs who, from 358/969 onwards built up their power in Egypt and Syria into the most powerful state of its age in the Islamic heartlands. As exponents of Ismaʿilism, a radical form of Shiʿism, they regarded the descendants of the Prophet's uncle ʿAbbās as having usurped the Imamate, the divinely-inspired headship of the Muslim community, that should properly be exercised by the house of Moḥammad's nephew and son-in-law ʿAli and his wife the Prophet's daughter Fāṭema. Egypt and Syria were geographically remote from the empire which Sebüktegin and Maḥmud were to build up in the Islamic East, and it was not till the middle years of the eleventh century, when the Ghaznavids themselves had been pushed to the far eastern fringes of the *Dār al-Eslām* "Abode of Islam" by the incoming Seljuq Turks, that partisans of the Fatimids actually threatened militarily the ʿAbbasid Caliphs in central Iraq. But there was a potential flashpoint arising from the Fatimids' control of the Pilgrimage route through Palestine and Syria to the Holy Cities of western Arabia, and the rivalries between Ghaznavids and Fatimids engendered here were to form the backdrop for one of the most dramatic episodes of Beyhaqi's *History*, the disgracing and execution of Maḥmud's former vizier Ḥasanak, now accused in the early part of the new reign of Masʿud of collusion with the Fatimids when he had come home from the Pilgrimage through Fatimid-controlled territory and of sympathy with their doctrines.[4]

Furthermore, propagandists for the Ismaʿili Shiʿism eventually espoused by the Fatimids had from the early part of the tenth century

[3] See for overviews of these processes, D. Sourdel, "The ʿAbbasid caliphate," in P.M. Holt, A.K.S. Lambton and B. Lewis (eds.), *The Cambridge history of Islam. I. The central Islamic lands*, Cambridge 1970, 104–39; B. Spuler, "The disintegration of the caliphate in the east. The period of the Buyids, Samanids and Ghaznavids," in *ibid.*, 143–74; J.-Cl. Garcin, "Les pouvoirs princières en Orient," in *idem et alii*, *États, sociétés et cultures du monde musulman médiéval Xe–XVe siècle. I. L'évolution politique et sociale*, Paris 1995, 13–48.

[4] See below, Gh 178ff., F 221ff.

been working in selected areas of the Islamic East, such as in Sistan, at the court of the Samanids in Bokhara and, with more enduring success, in the northwest Indian province of Sind, where there was an anciently-established Arab colony; the existence there of these sectaries, called in the Ghaznavid sources—without regard for historical accuracy—Qarāmeṭa or Carmathians, was to provide a pretext for Maḥmud to undertake operations during the early part of his reign against Multan in Upper Sind.[5] It seems, indeed, that the material successes of the Fatimids in North Africa and the Near East, and the brilliance of their culture, far eclipsing that of the penurious and restricted ʿAbbasids in Baghdad, engendered amongst many Sunnis feelings that they were being threatened by the activities of Ismaʿili *doʿāt* or propagandists that were part of a vast plot to subvert orthodox Islam; Maḥmud and Masʿud were able, on occasion, to play on these fears and use them as a shield for their own expansionist policies.[6]

As well as being a delayed consequence of the break-up of caliphal unity in the Islamic world, the constituting of the Ghaznavid empire was also a consequence of another great trend in the history of the caliphate during the ninth century, namely, the increased militarisation of the caliphate, which had effects not only in the sphere of political and social life but also in such economic ones as taxation and landholding. Predominant in this trend was the role of Turkish mercenary slave soldiers (*ghelmān*, sing. *gholām*, and *mamālek*, sing. *mamluk*). Such troops speedily became a prominent, if not dominant, element in almost all armies of the central and eastern Islamic lands. These Turkish elements were praised by contemporary observers, from the time of the Arab littérateur Jāḥeẓ in the mid-ninth century onwards, as embodying some of the virtues of the noble savage. With their harsh and frugal Inner Asian steppe background, they were regarded as hardy and intrepid warriors, and praised for their loyalty to their masters, since they had been cut off from all ties of birth and home-

[5] See Muḥammad Nāẓim, *The life and times of Sulṭān Maḥmūd of Ghazna*, Cambridge 1931. 96–99.

[6] See for the significance of the Fatimids as shield bearers for Ismaʿili Shiʿism, H. Halm, *The Fatimids and their traditions of learning*, London 1977, and for Ghaznavid attitudes here, C.E. Bosworth, "The imperial policy of the early Ghaznawids," *Islamic Studies, Journal of the Central Institute of Islamic Research*, Karachi, I/2 (1962), 60ff.

land (although the course of events within many states was to show up this loyalty as a delusion). Turkish slave soldiers had been recruited by the ʿAbbasid caliphs from as far back as the reign of Hārun al-Rashid (786–809) in the hope of reducing reliance on the older Arab and Iranian military classes. With a decline in the caliphs' personal qualities, evident as the ninth century went on, the Turkish soldiery in Sāmarrā and Baghdad (recruited from the South Russian steppes controlled by the Khazars and from the Central Asian steppes beyond the amirates of the Tahirids and then of the Samanids in Khorasan and Transoxania) became increasingly the real masters of the political situation in Iraq, making and unmaking caliphs.[7]

The military value of Turkish cavalrymen, with their weapons of the compound bow and the lance, meant that, in the tenth century, the Buyids recruited substantial numbers of Turks to supplement their own Deylamite tribal following, essentially one of mountaineer infantrymen. Likewise, Turkish slave soldiers became the nucleus of the army of the Samanids in Transoxania and Khorasan, and an influential factor in court life and politics there from the opening years of this same century. As time went on, the Amirs in Bokhara became increasingly unable to hold their territories together, and power tended to pass to their Turkish generals; it was out of the ambitions and rivalries of these commanders in Khorasan that the Ghaznavids were to emerge. Similarly, Turkish soldiers apparently came to play a role in the adjacent Central Asian state of Khwarazm, although details are lacking. They are mentioned as prominent in the events leading to the downfall of the line of Ma'munid Shahs of Gorgānj and in the ensuing invasion of Khwarazm by Maḥmud of Ghazna in 1017; certainly, the names of the commanders of the Khwarazmian forces opposing the Ghaznavids are all Turkish.[8] The Samanids and Khwarazm Shahs were, of course, especially well placed to draw directly on Inner Asian resources of Turkish manpower, whether as free, tribal auxiliaries or as slaves imported to the markets within their lands;

[7] Bosworth, "Barbarian incursions: the coming of the Turks into the Islamic world," in D.S. Richards (ed.), *Islamic civilisation 950–1150*, Oxford 1973, 1–16; Patricia Crone, *Slaves on horses. The evolution of the Islamic polity*, Cambridge 1980, 74ff.; D. Pipes, *Slave soldiers and Islam. The genesis of a military system*, New Haven and London 1981.

[8] See below, Gh 675, 678, F 919, 924.

the Samanids systematically organised the import of slaves from the Turkish steppes to frontier markets at places like Shāsh/Tashkent and Esfijāb and levied transit dues as these slaves were transported to the lands further west.[9]

It was directly from the slave guard of the Samanids in their capital Bokhara that the founder of the Ghaznavid line, Sebüktegin, sprang. He had been born, naturally a pagan, at Barskhān on the shores of the Issik Kol in Semirechye or Yeti Su "the land of the seven rivers," in what is now the northeastern part of the Kyrgyz Republic.[10] His master Alptegin had been Commander-in-Chief of the Samanid army in Khorasan and was deeply embroiled in the court politics of the time. In alliance with the Vizier Abu ʿAli Moḥammad Balʿami, he had endeavoured to place his own candidate on the throne in Bokhara when the Amir ʿAbd al-Malek (I) b. Nuḥ (I) died in 961. The two conspirators' putsch failed, and Alptegin had to withdraw to the southeastern periphery of the Samanid empire, the region of Zābolestān, in which lay the town of Ghazna, till then having figured very little in recorded history. The local rulers of the town were dispossessed, and various commanders from Alptegin's following succeeded after his death in 963 briefly as amir in Ghazna, until the Turkish troops there raised Sebüktegin to power as their leader, so that he thereby began a rule of twenty years (977–97).

Although Alptegin's stance had latterly been that of a quasi-rebel, the new Samanid Amir Manṣur (I) b. Nuḥ (I) had been content to leave him neutralised on the far frontier of his dominions, and he recognized Alptegin as official governor there. Sebüktegin continued in this status of theoretical subordination to the Amirs in Bokhara, as attest the legends on his coins and the inscription on his tomb at Ghazna describing him, not as an independent ruler, but as *al-Ḥājeb al-Ajall* "Most Exalted Commander." Once firmly installed at Ghazna, Sebüktegin showed his newly-acquired strength by moving southwards into the region of Bost and to Qoṣdār in what was later to become northern Baluchistan, and by leading raids down the Kabul river valley to the Indus basin against the Hindushahi Rajahs of Wayhind.

---

[9] Bosworth, *The Ghaznavids, their empire in Afghanistan and eastern Iran 994–1040*, Edinburgh 1963, 208–09.

[10] See below, Year 421 n. 381.

Some of the lines for future expansion had thus been already sketched out for Sebüktegin's son Maḥmud when he eventually succeeded his father in 998. Under his leadership, the Turkish commanders who had been rival contenders with him and his father for dominion in Khorasan were finally vanquished in 999. Henceforth, Maḥmud was no longer theoretically a governor owing allegiance to an overlord in Bokhara but in practice an independent sovereign. Soon afterwards, the lands of the now defunct Samanid amirate were partitioned, with Maḥmud taking the lands south of the Oxus, i.e. Khorasan and Tokhārestān, while the lands north of the river, that is, Transoxania, were taken over by the Qarakhanids, incoming Turks from Inner Asia (on the dynasty constituted by these tribesmen, who were probably from the Qarluq group—by Islamic standards a long-enduring dynasty, lasting as it did till the Anushteginid Khwarazm Shahs and the Mongols appeared in Transoxania at the opening of the thirteenth century—see below, Year 421 n. 273).

In the early part of his thirty years' reign, Maḥmud consolidated his position by annexing petty principalities in northern Afghanistan and the upper Oxus region and by ending the rule in Sistan of the last Saffarid; and towards the end of his reign he expanded southwards towards the Arabian Sea shores by making the rulers of Makrān, in what is now coastal Baluchistan, his tributaries. But Maḥmud had an uneasy relationship with the Qarakhanids, a line which he would have liked to treat as his vassals but which in practice he had to treat as equals. Although in the partition of the Samanid dominions, the Oxus had been made the boundary between the two powers (see above), the Qarakhanid chief, the Ilig Naṣr b. ʿAli, was ill-disposed to accept this river as a permanent frontier, and in 1007–08 Maḥmud had to repel an invasion of the Cisoxanian, Balkh, region by the Ilig's army which was aided by a contingent from his cousin Yusof Qadïr Khān of Kāshghar and Khotan. The Sultans' acquisition ten years later of the lower Oxus province of Khwarazm, graphically described by Beyhaqi in the special section of his *History* devoted to the affairs of Khwarazm (below, section 3, p. 42), was intended to turn the flank of the branch of the Qarakhanids now established in Sogdia and to exert pressure upon it. In practice, diplomatic contacts, involving marriage alliances between the two houses, were now used to achieve a *modus vivendi*, with peace lasting until the early part of Masʿud's reign when his general, the Khwarazm Shah Altuntāsh, led an abortive invasion into Sogdia against the Khāns centred on Samarqand and Bokhara. It was only in the latter part of the Sultan's reign that Qarakhanid incursions led by another member of the family, Ebrāhim b. Naṣr, the later Tamghach Khān, Beyhaqi's Böritegin, into the Ghaznavid territories on the upper Oxus began seriously to hamper Mas'ud's attempts to deal with the menace in Khorasan of the Turkmens and their Seljuq chiefs.

The great contemporary reputation that Maḥmud achieved, buttressed by assiduous cultivation of links with the 'Abbasid caliphs as moral heads of the Sunni world and the astute publication abroad of his victories, was above all that of hammer of the infidel Hindus and despoiler of their temple treasures, out of which the Sultan could forward to Baghdad impressive presents and adorn splendid new public buildings in his capital Ghazna. This public relations exercise was so effective that the Ghāzi Sultan acquired an immediate fame as *bot-shekan* "idol breaker,"[11] and this has redounded through the ages in the Indo-Muslim world. Winter expeditions through the Indus and Ganges-Jumna valleys enabled Ghaznavid armies to penetrate as far as Gwalior, Kanauj and Kālanjar, i.e. almost to Benares (this last famed city of rich temples not, however, to be actually reached and despoiled by the Muslims till the next reign, that of Mas'ud, see below, p. 21), and an especially glorious victory was gained in 1025–26 when a Muslim force penetrated across the Kathiawar peninsula of western India and captured the great shrine of Somnath. In reality, the motive force behind Maḥmud's raids here was *Realpolitik*, greed and the acquisition of plunder—gold, elephants and slaves—rather than religious zeal and the permanent occupation of territory in India. The Sultan cheerfully incorporated pagan Indian troops into his army, and there were no attempts, either by Maḥmud or by his successors, at a mass conversion of the Hindus, an impractical proposition anyway; it was not till the thirteenth century, under the Ghurids and their epigoni, the Slave Kings of Delhi, that territory began to be permanently taken

[11] See, e.g., Gertrud Spiess, *Maḥmūd von Ġazna bei Farīdu'd-dīn 'Aṭṭār*, Basel 1959, 26ff.; H. Ritter, *The Ocean of the Soul. Man, the World and God in the Stories of Farīd al-Dīn 'Aṭṭār*, tr. J. O'Kane and B. Radtke, Leiden 2003, 128–32.

over and an appreciable number of conversions to Islam took place in northwestern India.[12]

Towards the end of his reign, Maḥmud abandoned his policy of studied non-interference in the affairs of his western neighbours, the Buyids. Taking advantage of a period of weak rule in the northern Buyid amirate based on Ray, in 1029 he marched westwards. He deposed the young Amir Majd al-Dowla, on the plea that the latter had been unable to keep order amongst the unruly Deylamite troops once the strong hand of his mother, the regent Sayyeda, had been removed by her death the previous year. He took over the Buyid territories of Ray and Jebāl, which now provided a base for further operations in northwestern Persia, the region that Beyhaqi and later historians call ʿErāq[-e ʿAjam] "Persian Iraq." His son Masʿud was appointed governor in Ray, with instructions to campaign in western Persia against the petty Deylamite and Kurdish princes there such as the Kakuyids of Isfahan and Hamadan and the Mosāferids of Ṭārom.[13]

When Maḥmud died in 1030, worn out by a lifetime of furious campaigning and with his judgement and political sense showing signs of impairment (see below), Masʿud, his eventual successor in 1031 (on the events of the intervening period, see below), inherited a vast assemblage of lands stretching from the fringes of Azerbayjan in the west to Lahore and the Panjab in the east, from Khwarazm in Central Asia in the north to the shores of the Indian Ocean in the south. Masʿud was not the man his father was, but subsequent events were to show that the boundaries of the Ghaznavid empire were seriously overstretched and could probably not have been held together permanently even by a sultan of Maḥmud's calibre.

The succession to Maḥmud turned out to be a troubled one. Perhaps as a result of the general ascendancy of military-directed dynasties in the central and eastern Islamic lands, the failure to develop

---

[12] Cf. the pioneer reappraisal in the modern Indo-Muslim world of Maḥmud's work and achievement here, that of the Aligarh historian Moḥammad Habib, *Sultan Mahmud of Ghaznin*, 2nd ed. Delhi, Jullundur and Lucknow 1952, 75ff., who notes in his Preface to the 2nd ed., Delhi 1967, p. iv, that the first edition of his book had been "hailed by a storm of criticism in the Urdu press ... vindictive, bitter, hostile ... based on a complete ignorance of the originals."

[13] Nāẓim, *Sulṭān Maḥmūd of Ghazna*, 80–85; Bosworth, "The imperial policy of the early Ghaznawids," 68–72.

enduring political structures, and endemic faction and intrigue at the courts involved, the Ghaznavids failed to enunciate laws, or even informal guidelines, for inheritance and succession to power on the death of a ruler. Whether there was any lingering inheritance here from the Inner Asian Turkish tribal tradition, in which the most capable male member of the chiefly family, and not necessarily a son of the dead ruler, usually assumed leadership of the tribe, is doubtful.[14] (Such an influence is, however, clearly discernible among the various Seljuq family lines, for the Seljuqs came into the Islamic environment directly from the steppes, and older traditions remained strong even when the Great Seljuq sultans became enveloped by their Perso-Islamic cultural and ethical environment.)[15] Although the old Turkish aspects of the Ghaznavid sultans' behaviour, their psychology and their cultural baggage, including language, cannot have been negligible,[16] these things are poorly documented by the Arabic and Persian historians, who were totally ill-equipped to detect or understand them anyway. As it happened, the Ghaznavid sultans speedily slotted themselves into their new, Perso-Islamic environment and enthusiastically modelled themselves on the traditions characteristic of that milieu, including that of the despotic ruler, for whom *force majeure* rather than consensus was the prime impulse in exercising power.

When Sebüktegin had died, there had ensued a struggle between two of his sons, Maḥmud and Esmāʿil. Sebüktegin does not seem to have designated a specific, covenanted heir (*vali ʿahd*, lit. "successor by virtue of a covenant"), though Maḥmud had fought at Sebüktegin's side in Khorasan and elsewhere. Esmāʿil, on the other hand, does not seem to have had any military experience and was a younger son; the sole factor in his favour was that his mother had been a daughter of Sebüktegin's old master Alptegin. Yet at the end of his life, apparently following the

[14] The view put forward by the present author in his article "A Turco-Mongol practice amongst the early Ghaznavids?", *CAJ*, VII (1962), 237–40, remains possible but unproven.

[15] The form adopted here, Seljuq, is really a hybrid one. The vowel harmony of Turkic languages demands either Seljük/Selchük or Saljuq/Salchuq. The tradition of Arabic (and later, Syriac) rendering of the name, *s.l.j.w.q*, implies the latter form, i.e. with back vowels, but Maḥmud Kāshghari says that "Seljük/Selchük (*s.l.j.k*) [is] the name of the grandfather of the present sultans." See P. B. Golden, *An introduction to the history of the Turkic peoples*, Wiesbaden 1992, 217.

[16] See Bosworth, *The Ghaznavids*, 130. 133–34, and below, Year 421 n. 100.

older Turkish tradition and not envisaging the setting-up of a principality completely independent of the Samanids, Sebüktegin shared out his power as military commands and governorships among his brother and his sons, with Esmāʿil to have the heartland, Ghazna and Balkh: an act that perplexed later Muslim historians, affected as they must have been by Maḥmud's dazzling successes as ruler and commander. In fact, a battle in 998 between Maḥmud and Esmāʿil left the former victorious, so that he was hailed as amir and began a reign of over thirty years.[17]

Yet, as if no lessons had been learnt, a similar situation arose towards the end of Maḥmud's life. The sequence of events spanning the last days of Maḥmud's life, the brief sultanate of Moḥammad and the speedy triumph of Masʿud, is clear enough, but the motives and the thought-processes of Maḥmud during the closing months of his life remain somewhat opaque.

According to the Ghurid historian Juzjāni, Maḥmud had seven sons, and the existence of at least three daughters is known. Juzjāni names the sons, but not, it appears, in any particular order of age.[18] Apart from Masʿud and Moḥammad, none of the other sons was of significance for the general history of the Ghaznavids (except for ʿAbd al-Rashid, who makes a brief appearance in Beyhaqi's pages as having been present at the battle of Dandānqān against the Seljuqs and who in the end became sultan *ca.* 1049) and virtually nothing is known about them. Masʿud and Moḥammad seem to have been almost the same age, and projecting back from 1010–11 when Beyhaqi says that the two princes were fourteen years old, their birth date must have been around 997–98.[19] Moḥammad seems to have been only slightly younger, pointing to the fact that they were either born of different mothers or were twins of one mother.[20]

---

[17] Nāẓim, *op. cit.*, 38–41, 179; Bosworth, "A Turco-Mongol practice amongst the early Ghaznavids?", 238–39.

[18] Menhāj al-Din b. Serāj al-Din Juzjāni, *Ṭabaqāt-e nāṣeri*, ed. ʿAbd al-Ḥayy Ḥabibi, 2nd ed. Tehran 1342–43/1963–64, I, 232, Eng. tr. H.G. Raverty, *Ṭabaḳát-i Náṣirí, a general history of the Muhammadan dynasties of Asia, including Hindustan*, London 1881–99, I, 91.

[19] Gh 111, F 132; cf. R. Gelpke, *Sulṭān Masʿūd I. von Ġazna. Die drei ersten Jahre seiner Herrschaft (421/1030–424/1033),* Munich 1957, 22.

[20] Gelpke, *op. cit.*, 16, 22; a late source like the Indo-Muslim historian Fereshta states that they were indeed twins but that Masʿud had been born slightly ahead of Moḥammad.

As a young man of seventeen or eighteen years old, Masʿud participated with such bravery and distinction in the campaign of 1015 against Khᵛābin in southwestern Ghur, in the mountainous heartland of Afghanistan, that, one year afterwards, Maḥmud formally appointed Masʿud heir-designate to the throne.[21] Even before this, Masʿud had been accorded precedence as the eldest son and heir presumptive. As the story of the three princes, Masʿud, Moḥammad and Yusof b. Sebüktegin (uncle of the two preceding, but in fact only three years older than them) and their stay in Zamindāvar in 1010–11 shows, their tutor-guardian Reyḥān Khādem always accorded Masʿud and then Moḥammad precedence on formal occasions and at polo and other outdoor activities, Masʿud was served by the other two.[22] Moḥammad, on the other hand, had little administrative experience beyond having governed for a while the province of Guzgān in northern Afghanistan and had no known military capability, although events at the time he was raised to power showed that he was popular at court and was a man of considerable culture and aesthetic sensibility.

The course of Maḥmud's relations with his covenanted heir Masʿud had not run smoothly during the remainder of the Sultan's life. Although he had, as stated above, appointed him as heir in 1015–16, he placed spies over him in his governorate of Herat, including ones planted within Masʿud's closest circle of boon-companions, domestic attendants, musicians, etc.[23] At one point Masʿud fell from grace enough to be temporarily exiled to Multan in India and held there, as he later related, "like a captive, although it was not actually called that," before being restored to his governorship in Herat.[24] According to Juzjāni, at some time unspecified, Maḥmud sent a request to the ʿAbbasid court at Baghdad asking that Moḥammad should have precedence over Masʿud, with his names and honorific titles placed after those of Moḥammad in formal usage (*mokhāṭaba*) (presumably in the headings of official documents, in the *khoṭba*, etc.).[25] This must be the occasion noted by Beyhaqi, when Masʿud complains that, on the oc-

---

[21] Gh 216, F 275; cf. Gelpke, *op. cit.*, 23.
[22] Gh 112, F 133; cf. Gelpke, *op. cit.*, 22.
[23] Gh 121–22, F 145–46; cf. Gelpke, *op. cit.*, 24.
[24] Gh 217, F 276; cf. Gelpke, *op. cit.*, 16.
[25] *Ṭabaqāt-e nāṣeri*, I, 232, tr. I, 91. On the *mokhāṭaba*, see below, Year 421 n. 52.

casion of Maḥmud's writing to the Caliph al-Qāder for an additional grant of honorifics for himself, the two sons and Yusof b. Sebüktegin, the Sultan instructed the Chancery secretaries to put Moḥammad's name first in the letter. The occasion for the Sultan's request to Baghdad may have been after his Somnath campaign, when the sacking of the celebrated Hindu shrine there resounded round the orthodox Sunni world, after which the Caliph sent honorifics for Maḥmud and the princes with, according to Gardizi, a rider attached that he would approve and recognize whichever person Maḥmud chose to nominate as his heir.[26]

Towards the end of his life, Maḥmud's battle-weariness was exacerbated by increasing illness which he strove to surmount but which inevitably had a debilitating effect for his body. His mental faculties and judgement also deteriorated, as Beyhaqi noted; he became resentful of healthy people and would fly into rages at the slightest provocation.[27] When the Sultan actually died at Ghazna on 30 April 1030, Masʿud was at Isfahan, on the far western confines of the empire. Just before this, when the latter had been in the newly-conquered city of Ray preparing for operations in western Persia, Maḥmud had, without informing him, made the apparently capricious decision to transfer the succession from the battle-hardened Masʿud to the less obviously capable Moḥammad. The reasoning behind Maḥmud's action here puzzled contemporaries as much as it has continued to puzzle later generations. Amongst reasons adduced by the historians were the ones that Maḥmud envied brave people or that the Sultan wished the patently less capable Moḥammad to have some share of power and honour. Masʿud himself later asserted that his father had deliberately left him at Ray with a weak military force so that he would not be able to achieve any spectacular successes in western Persia and would consequently appear incompetent and unsuccessful. The historians inevitably noted the parallel with what had happened at Sebüktegin's death

---

[26] Gh 218, F 277; Abu Saʿid ʿAbd al-Ḥayy b. Żahhāk Gardizi, *Ketāb Zeyn al-akhbār*, ed. Muhammad Nazim, Berlin-Steglitz 1928, 87–88, ed. ʿAbd al-Ḥayy Ḥabibi, Tehran 1347/1968, 191. Cf. Gelpke, *op. cit.*, 16; Bosworth, "The titulature of the early Ghaznavids," *Oriens*, XV (1962), 219.

[27] Gh 80, 217–18, F 91, 277; Moḥammad b. ʿAli Shabānkāra'i, *Majmaʿ al-ansāb fi 'l-tavārikh*, ed. Mir Hāshem Moḥaddeth, Tehran 1363/1984, 64. On Maḥmud's last illness and death, see Nāẓim, *Sulṭān Maḥmūd of Ghazna*, 123–24.

when the latter had bequeathed power in Ghazna and Balkh to the less experienced son Esmāʿil rather than to Maḥmud, bringing about a short period of civil warfare before Maḥmud made firm his own claims (see above).[28] That Maḥmud deliberately planned the division of an empire which had become too unwieldy for one man to control, as asserted by Nāẓim, seems, as correctly observed by Gelpke, very improbable; he would hardly have given the less capable son the lion's share.[29]

With hindsight, it does seem strange that Maḥmud did not realize that Moḥammad would be unlikely to maintain his power in Ghazna, in face of his brother's superior military experience and popularity with the army as someone who would obviously be a successful war leader and maintain the inflow of plunder for the state and its servants. The adverse effects of the Sultan's declining health, as mentioned above, were probably also strengthened (although we do not know the details in the absence of the earlier part of Beyhaqi's *Mojalladāt*, see below, section 3, p. 42) by the efforts of Moḥammad's supporters at court in Ghazna, who denigrated Masʿud during his absence from the centre of power at Ghazna, first in his governorship of Herat and then in the newly-conquered western Persian lands, and promoted Moḥammad's claims. The outstanding role during Moḥammad's brief sultanate in Ghazna of the Great Chamberlain ʿAli Qarib or Khᵛishāvand b. Il Arslān suggests that magnates like him hoped to enjoy the real substance of power in a state where Moḥammad would be nominal ruler only. This is, indeed, the analysis of motives put forward by the later historian Shabānkāraʾi: that Moḥammad was well aware of his inferiority to his brother in wisdom, experience and popularity with the army, and was reluctant to accept the throne when his father died. The topic was discussed for a week, and Moḥammad was propelled into acceptance by his ambitious counsellors who hoped to

---

[28] Marilyn R. Waldman has remarked that Maḥmud's change of mind and his fresh succession arrangements form a remarkable parallel to the arrangements made by Hārun al-Rashid for his sons in the so-called "Meccan Letters" of 802, so productive of internecine strife and prolonged instability within the caliphate once Hārun had died. See her *Toward a theory of historical narrative. A case study in Perso-Islamicate historiography*, Columbus, Ohio 1980, 31.

[29] Nāẓim, *op. cit.*, 169–70; Gelpke, *op. cit.*, 18.

share extensively in the fruits of royal power.[30] But against this idea of an inadequate man pushed unwillingly into rule is the undoubted fact that, when offered by Masʿud a division of power which would have left Moḥammad in control of the heartlands of Afghanistan and Khorasan and of the position in India, leaving Masʿud with a free hand to carve out further conquests in the west, provided that he acknowledge Masʿud's precedence in the *khoṭba*, i.e. recognize him as supreme monarch, Moḥammad refused this very favourable offer.[31]

Moḥammad was proclaimed Sultan in Ghazna shortly after his father's death, but was to reign only for six or seven months, while his resentful brother marched inexorably eastwards from the region of Isfahan, gathering support en route at Ray and such great centres of Khorasan as Nishapur and Herat. According to Gardizi, Moḥammad's succession in Ghazna was at the outset received there very favourably, probably in reaction to the preceding harsh régime of Maḥmud and the arbitrariness of his last days. Complaints of tyranny and wrongdoing (*maẓālem*) were immediately heard; the tax registers were examined and those taxes on lands which had become infertile or deserted were removed; prices were fixed at a low level; merchants flocked to the capital as confidence in a future of just rule and prosperity grew; and the treasuries were thrown open to reward the troops of the army and high civilian officials and to secure their allegiance.[32] The need for donatives like these (*māl-e beyʿati va ṣelat-hā* "accession money and presents," as Beyhaqi calls them) showed a weakness in Moḥammad's position; it does not seem that such handouts were made by Maḥmud when he overcame his brother Esmāʿil.[33] Abu Sahl Aḥmad b. Ḥasan Ḥamdavi became Moḥammad's vizier and Yusof b. Sebüktegin Commander-in-Chief of the army, but it was the Great Chamberlain ʿAli Qarib who dominated the civilian administrators like the vizier, the deputy officials (*novvāb*) and secretaries, himself becoming the *nā'eb-e koll* "person responsible for everything."[34]

30 *Majmaʿ al-ansāb*, 71–72.

31 Gh 80–81, F 91–92; Shabānkāra'i, 73–74. Cf. Gelpke, *op. cit.*, 18, 35–36.

32 Gardizi, ed. Nazim, 93, ed. Ḥabibi, 194.

33 Masʿud, when firmly on the throne, was to make an ill-advised, and, in the event, only partially successful, attempt to recover this money and these presents for the royal treasury. See Gh 257–60, F 336–40.

34 Gardizi, *loc. cit.*

According to the historians, Moḥammad was in fact content to occupy himself in Ghazna with merry-making and wine-drinking, allowing Mas'ud to march back through Khorasan without impediment, so that, despite the burgeoning prosperity for the civilian population, a feeling grew amongst the great men of state that it would be Mas'ud who would provide the vigorous leadership necessary to preserve the integrity of Maḥmud's legacy of power and ensure the continued exploitation of India, with its resultant bounty of rich plunder.[35] Hence leading military figures in Ghazna, the Great Chamberlain 'Ali, Yusof b. Sebüktegin and 'Ali Dāya, plus Maḥmud's old favourite Ayāz, withdrew their support from Moḥammad and headed for Nishapur to make their peace with Mas'ud. During his stay in Nishapur, the latter had in mid-August 1030 received an envoy sent from Baghdad by the Caliph al-Qāder bringing congratulations on the Ghaznavids' conquests in northern and northwestern Persia and their humbling of the Buyids of Ray and other sectaries, together with a splendid array of honorific titles (*alqāb*, sing. *laqab*, or *no'ut*, sing. *na't*).[36] Such emphatic approval from the moral head of Sunni Islam was a powerful psychological weapon for Mas'ud in the impending struggle with his brother, and he assiduously publicised these tokens of caliphal favour amongst the populations of the towns lying ahead en route in his march eastwards. Mas'ud approached Herat and Moḥammad's support started to melt away. Ayāz suborned the Turkish palace gholāms and these left the capital for Bost. Moḥammad, at last stirred into action, sent after them elements of the army that were still loyal to him, including the Indian troops under their commander Suvendharāy. A fierce battle took place, with many casualties on both sides, Suvendharāy being amongst the dead, and the heads of the slain rebels were sent back to the Sultan in Ghazna.[37] Moḥammad set out with his troops for Bost,

[35] An ode addressed by the court poet Farrokhi of Sistān to Moḥammad at this time, actually at the *'Īd al-Feṭr*, the Festival of the Ending of the Fast of this year, AH 421/AD 1030 (*Divān*, ed. Moḥammad Dabir-Siyāqi, Tehran 1335/1956, 104–07), hence only a few days before Moḥammad's deposition, seems to express, in a guarded fashion, the poet's premonition of that event and his feeling that Moḥammad was inadequate for the supreme power; see Julie S. Meisami, "Ghaznavid panegyrics: some political implications," *Iran JBIPS*, XXVIII (1990), 36–39.

[36] See Gelpke, *op. cit.*, 42–43; Bosworth, "The imperial policy of the early Ghaznawids," 63–64; *idem*, "The titulature of the early Ghaznavids," 224–25.

[37] Gardizi, ed. Nazim, 94, ed. Ḥabibi, 194–95. Cf. Gelpke, *op. cit.*, 34–35.

presumably with the intention of marching by the southern route via the Helmand valley, Sistan, Farāh and Esfezār to confront Masʿud at Herat, but at Teginābād in Arachosia or Rokhkhaj, his leading commanders mutinied, declaring that he had no hope of withstanding Masʿud. They imprisoned Moḥammad in a fortress which both mss. of Gardizi's history call *v.l.ḥ*, which ʿAbd al-Ḥayy Ḥabibi restored as *Rokhkhaj, i.e. "the fortress of Rokhkhaj," but which we know from Beyhaqi was actually called Kuhtiz, and then they went to join Masʿud, by now at Herat.[38]

The new Sultan Masʿud was hailed as such in Herat, but then went on to Balkh, apparently anxious to show his new royal authority and his military might to the Qarakhanids beyond the Oxus, whose potential hostility he feared, and he only reached the capital Ghazna in April 1031. Much of the narrative in Beyhaqi's *History* of the months of autumn 1030 is taken up with a recounting of these events, with an implicit justification of Masʿud's action in disregarding and controverting his father's express appointment of his brother as the covenanted heir, whatever the state of Maḥmud's mind might have been at the time. A similar, more explicit justification of Masʿud's seizure of power forms the theme of a long *qaṣida* or ode composed by a poet of Ghazna personally known to Beyhaqi, the *faqih* or religious lawyer Abu Ḥanifa Eskāfi and addressed to the new Sultan that Beyhaqi cites in its entirety in the events of 1031;[39] there were doubtless many other such *pièces justificatives* uttered by other of the Ghaznavid family's panegyrists (see further, below, section 4, p. 59).[40]

Instability in the succession and resultant discord were to dog the Ghaznavids at various points in the dynasty's subsequent history.[41] There was a "time of troubles" after the death of Mowdud b. Masʿud (I) in *ca.* 1048, that included an usurpation of the throne from ʿAbd al-Rashid b. Maḥmud by one of the dynasty's slave commanders, a

[38] Gardizi, *loc. cit.*; Juzjāni, I, 231–32, tr. I, 89–90; Ebn al-Athir, *al-Kāmel fi 'l-ta'rikh*, Beirut 1385–87/1965–67, IX, 298–300; Shabānkāra'i, 71–75. Cf. Gelpke, *op. cit.*, 37–38; Bosworth, *The Ghaznavids*, 227–29.

[39] Gh 275–80, F 361–71.

[40] A poet like Farrokhi, who had praised extensively Moḥammad and Yusof b. Sebüktegin, was able without any difficulty—so far as we know—now to transfer his encomia to the new Sultan, Masʿud; see Meisami, *op. cit.*, 38ff.

[41] Gelpke, *op. cit.*, 16, speaks of discords between brothers as a *Leitmotiv* of Ghaznavid history.

certain Ṭoghrïl, followed by a long period of internal stability under two sons of Masʿud, Farrokh-zād and Ebrāhim and the latter's son Masʿud (III).[42] But after this last sultan's death in 1115, three of his sons disputed his inheritance, with Bahrām Shāh emerging in 1117 as the victor, but only with military aid from the Seljuq ruler of the East, Sanjar, so that for the next three or so decades, the Ghaznavid dominions were tributary to the Great Seljuqs. This subordinate status, not onerous because distant from the suzerains in Iraq and Western Persia, was ended by what was a much worse disaster for the Ghaznavids, the onslaught of the Ghurids; in the end Bahrām Shāh's son Khosrow Shāh had to abandon Ghazna for northwestern India and Lahore until the final extinguishing of the dynasty took place towards the end of the twelfth century.[43] Thus the Ghaznavids had been no more successful than other medieval Islamic lines in solving the problem of smooth transmission of rulership, in the absence of any institutions strong enough to assure continuity in the state when its head died or had his authority successfully challenged.

Once Masʿud's position as sultan in Ghazna was secure, he set about consolidating his authority internally, and the first two or three years of his reign, covered by Beyhaqi in immense detail,[44] were largely taken up with the resultant struggles for power, some overt and some covert, amongst his courtiers, officials and army commanders. It was natural enough that a new ruler should wish to surround himself with his own partisans, his circle of advisers and executives, servants whom he could hopefully mould to his own intentions and use to carry out his plans. In an age when loyalties were essentially to persons rather than to ideas, it was not inevitable that the loyalties of state servants should automatically be transferred from a former to a new ruler, although we can, in fact, discern from Beyhaqi's pages that there was a nucleus of servants faithful to the idea in itself of a Ghaznavid *dowla* or state, irrespective of who was ruling at any one

[42] Bosworth, *The later Ghaznavids, splendour and decay. The dynasty in Afghanistan and northern India 1040–1186*, Edinburgh 1977, 37ff.

[43] *Ibid.*, 89ff.

[44] The events of the years 421, 422 and 423 take up almost half of the whole extant part of the *Tārikh-e Masʿudi.*

time, a notable figure here being Beyhaqi's master in the Chancery and his mentor, the Chief Secretary Abu Naṣr b. Moshkān.[45]

However, Masʿud's suspicious nature—perhaps fuelled by the climate of fear and suspicion engendered by the internal system of espionage and the atmosphere of delation that had developed within the empire under Maḥmud (and in which Masʿud himself had participated when governor in Herat for his father, see below), and by cynicism arising out of the abrupt changes of loyalty during the succession struggle with his brother—led him to disregard or to downplay the wise counsel and disinterested advice of old and faithful servants, men who had devoted their whole lives and careers to the dynasty's well-being.[46] Instead, Masʿud cultivated and promoted the careers of his own followers, those whom Beyhaqi calls *masʿudiyān* "partisans of Masʿud" or *now-khāstagān* or *bar-kashidagān* "parvenus, upstarts," and at the same time endeavoured to get rid of the *maḥmudiyān* or *pedariyān* "men of his father's time," the old guard associated with the previous reign. This last group included persons who had slighted him in the past and who, as he thought, had persuaded Maḥmud to divert the succession to Moḥammad, and persons who had supported his brother during his brief reign, even though they might have later made opportunist switches of allegiance to the rising star of Masʿud.

In narratives which are amongst the most compelling and dramatic of the *History*, Beyhaqi accordingly describes the execution of Maḥmud's former vizier Ḥasanak and the removal and imprisonment of military commanders like ʿAli Qarib, Eryāruq, Asïghtegin Ghāzi and even the Amir's own uncle, Yusof b. Sebüktegin. Masʿud thereby deprived himself of a fund of experience and military skill, the lack of which was to show itself in the Ghaznavid army's inability to contain or repel the Turkmen incursions into Khorasan (see below) and created a vast fund of resentment and fear; in the final cataclysm for

[45] That Moshkān was Abu Naṣr's father's name and not his own *esm* is clear from his formal designation at Gh 373, F 475 as "Abi Naṣr b. Moshkān" instead of the usual form with the Persian *eżāfa* "Bu Naṣr-e Moshkān."

[46] Concerning Masʿud's character, the verdict of W. Barthold was that he "inherited only his father's faults," see his *Turkestan down to the Mongol invasion*, 3rd ed. London, 1968, 293, and also the picture of Masʿud as he emerges from Beyhaqi's pages delineated by Jalāl Matini, "Simā-ye Masʿud Ghaznavi dar Tārikh-e Beyhaqi," in *Yād-nāma-ye Abu'l-Fażl-e Beyhaqi*, Mashhad 1350/1971, Persian section, 520–607.

Masʿud at Dandānqān (see below) were former gholāms of the four commanders mentioned above who had deserted to the side of the Seljuqs and fought against Masʿud. The Sultan was even so ill-advised as to plot the overthrow and death of one of the oldest and most faithful of his father's commanders, the Khwarazm Shah Altuntāsh, who had been appointed to govern Khwarazm after its conquest from the Ma'munids (see above, pp. 7–8) and who had a great store of knowledge and experience of the affairs and personalities of Central Asia, a sensitive region for the Ghaznavids given their uneasy relations with the Qarakhanids ruling there. Masʿud's agents attempted to procure Altuntāsh's assassination but failed to achieve this. Although Altuntāsh was subsequently in 1032 to die in battle against the Qarakhanid ruler in Sogdia, ʿAli b. Ḥasan or Hārun Bughrā Khān, called in the sources ʿAlitegin, and although he was to remain faithful to the end in his allegiance to his old masters Sebüktegin and Maḥmud, he was never rash enough to visit Masʿud's court again.

This vendetta against certain members of the Maḥmudiyān has many obscure aspects. The division between the men of the old régime and the new men seems not always to have been clearcut, and several remaining Maḥmudiyān were apparently a powerful and influential body still. It was they who, from motives that are unclear, hounded the general Ghāzi, provoking him into an act of rebellion through trickery, and who were able to muster on their own initiative troops to pursue him in his flight, even though, according to Beyhaqi, the Sultan still had a favourable opinion of Ghāzi. Certain persons did somehow manage to make successful and enduring changes of allegiance, such as the former vizier of Moḥammad in Ghazna, Abu Sahl Ḥamdavi, who nevertheless achieved high regard from the new sultan and was eventually sent out as civil governor of Ray and Jebāl.

In external policy, Masʿud tried to follow the expansionist path of his father. An invasion of Transoxania was launched in 1032 against the above-mentioned ʿAlitegin; it proved militarily inconclusive but displayed the strength of the Ghaznavids. An army was sent to annex the Buyid province of Kerman, but Ghaznavid rule there proved so harsh and unpopular that the Buyids of Fārs had little difficulty in recovering it in 1034. The Ziyarid ruler of the Caspian provinces of Gorgān and Ṭabarestān had fallen behind in payment of tribute to Ghazna, hence in the winter of 1034–35 Masʿud led a punitive expedition thither.[47] In India, Masʿud's commander Aḥmad b. Ināltegin led a raid as far as Benares (apparently the first Muslim commander to penetrate this far down the Ganges valley) but used the spoils collected there to rebel against the Sultan, and his outbreak had to be suppressed by an Indian general sent out from Ghazna with an army; then, later in his reign, Masʿud personally led a successful campaign against the stronghold of Hānsi in the eastern Panjab (winter of 1037–38), so that for some six years Hānsi remained in Ghaznavid hands as a bastion of their power there.[48]

But all these efforts by Masʿud, some successful, some unsuccessful, were more and more overshadowed by his failure to deal with the Oghuz Turkmen hordes whose chiefs included the Seljuq family. The Turkmens had been first admitted in the later tenth century from the steppes to the north of Transoxania into Samanid Sogdia, as auxiliaries of the Amirs in Bokhara, but towards the end of his reign, Sultan Maḥmud had admitted several thousand families of these Turkmens into the northern fringes of Khorasan, where they terrorised the local population by their violence and by the ravages of their flocks. Maḥmud's generals were compelled to push many of them back across the Qara Qum desert to the Balkhān Kuh mountains to the east of the Caspian Sea and to divert others of them westwards into the Buyid lands.[49]

During Masʿud's reign, Turkmens who had been expelled from Transoxania were utilized as allies by Hārun, son of the former Khwarazm Shah Altuntāsh, who from 1032 onwards began to display a hostile attitude towards Masʿud. Turkmen raids into Khorasan from Balkhān Kuh had been resumed early in Masʿud's reign, until in 1035 the Seljuq chiefs Ṭoghrïl Beg, Chaghrï Beg Dāvud and Musā Yabghu sought from the Ghaznavid governor of Khorasan permission to settle with their herds of horses and flocks of sheep on the northern edge of Khorasan and in Dehestan, at the southeastern end of the Caspian Sea, undertaking in return to repel any further Turkmen incursions

[47] Barthold, *op. cit.*, 295–96; Bosworth, *The Ghaznavids*, 90–91.

[48] See for these incursions into India the detailed study of Nazir Ahmad, "A critical examination of Baihaqi's narration of the Indian expeditions during the reign of Masʿud of Ghazna," in *Yād-nāma-ye Abu'l-Fażl-e Beyhaqi*, English section, 34–83.

[49] See Nāẓim, *Sulṭān Maḥmūd of Ghazna*, 62–66; Cl. Cahen, "Le Malik-Nameh et l'histoire des origines seljukides," *Oriens*, II (1949), 44ff., 51–56.

from Inner Asia. Inevitably, the Seljuqs' promises proved hollow ones, and the inhabitants of Khorasan suffered increasingly from the Turkmens' beasts overrunning the oases and agricultural lands and from the tribesmen's depredations, disrupting caravan traffic and the economic life of the province.[50]

Accordingly, much of Beyhaqi's narrative of Masʿud's later years is taken up with the saga of armies sent against the Turkmens led by various of the Sultan's generals, who were on occasion successful but more often the reverse: they were operating with insufficient troops and encumbered by extensive baggage trains, in terrain where water was scanty or non-existent and which favoured the highly-mobile, lightly-burdened Turkmen raiders. Masʿud, meanwhile, refused to take the Turkmen menace seriously enough or to give it his full personal attention; against all the advice of his civilian and military counsellors, he was diverted, on the plea of fulfilling a vow, into personally leading an expedition against the fortress of Hānsi in India in the winter of 1037–38.[51] Further, in the winter of 1038–39, climatically a totally inappropriate time, he led a disastrous expedition across the Oxus into the right-bank principality of Chaghāniyān against the Qarakhanid Böritegin, who had been harrying the upper Oxus lands.[52] In Khorasan, the Ghaznavid forces were gradually worn down, and the Turkmens were able temporarily to occupy some of the Khorasanian towns, including, in the spring of 1038, Nishapur for several months. At last persuaded to conduct counter-operations in Khorasan in person, the Sultan nevertheless once more went against the unanimous advice of his officials and commanders that the army was ill-prepared for a campaign into the desert in the scorching heat of late spring 1040 and that the army should rest and recover its fighting efficiency at Herat. Masʿud insisted on marching out with an ill-equipped and ill-supplied army across the waterless desert from Sarakhs to Merv. In a pitched battle at Dandānqān, one of the decisive ones of Eastern Islamic history and one which is graphically described in detail by Beyhaqi, who was present on the field, the Ghaznavid troops were all but annihilated. Nishapur once more, Merv and the whole of western Khorasan passed into Seljuq hands; the Ghaznavid position in Ray

[50] *Ibid.*, 55–60.
[51] Ahmad, *op. cit.*, 56–65.
[52] Barthold, *op. cit.*, 301–02.

and Jebāl had already become untenable and the region now reverted to the local, indigenous rulers there until the Seljuqs later arrived.[53]

The psychological effects on Masʿud of the defeat were serious, and his nerve seems now to have gone. He took his revenge on the unfortunate commanders of his army at Dandānqān, although they had only been carrying out his disastrous orders with reluctance and against their own better judgement. Despite assurances by his advisers that the Seljuqs were unlikely to move eastwards into the highly mountainous terrain of Afghanistan when they could sweep westwards through more open country, Masʿud fell into something like despair, and he made plans to abandon Ghazna and Balkh and retire to India. However, a section of his troops mutinied at the Indus crossing. The mutineers raised Moḥammad once more briefly to the sultanate as a puppet ruler and the deposed Masʿud was killed.[54] That Masʿud's advisers had been right and that the position in eastern Afghanistan was far from untenable was shown by the Seljuq chiefs' decision, whether made consciously or not, against pushing eastwards into Afghanistan towards India but rather to follow the lure of rich pickings in the West and to overrun Persia and the lands beyond, thus inaugurating the Great Seljuq sultanate. Masʿud's son and successor, Mowdud (1041-?1048) still had hopes of recovering lost territory, but after an interval his other son Ebrāhim (1059–99) eventually gave up irredentist dreams and established a permanent frontier with the Seljuqs, one which ran roughly north-south, bisecting what is the modern state of Afghanistan and leaving Kabul and Ghazna in the possession of the Ghaznavids for a further century or so. Hence Ghaznavid power survived there and in northern India as an empire truncated territorially but still one with important contributions to make in the cultural sphere, above all in that of Persian literature.[55] Its end was not to come from the Seljuqs or any other Turkish group from the Inner Asian steppes but from a dynamic family of chiefs from the inaccessible and only recently Islamised mountainous core of Afghanistan, the region of Ghur, still known today as the Ghorāt province. It was the Ghurid Amir ʿAlāʾ al-Din Ḥoseyn b. Ḥoseyn, unenviably called *Jahān-suz* "the World Incendiary," who sacked Ghazna in 1150 and dealt that

[53] Cahen, op. cit., 61ff.; Bosworth, *The Ghaznavids*, 246–52.

[54] Bosworth, *The later Ghaznavids*, 15–20.

[55] *Ibid.*, 25ff., 50ff., 74–77.

town a blow from which it never recovered; and in 1186 another Ghurid chief, Moʿezz al-Din Moḥammad b. Sām, ended for ever the rule of the last Ghaznavid in Lahore, Khosrow Malek.[56]

The distinctive quality of the Ghaznavid empire as built up by Sebüktegin and Maḥmud and taken over by their successors was the culmination of a process which, as has been noted above in regard to the militarisation of government and society in the central and eastern Islamic lands, had been going on for a century and a half under the direction of Arab and Persian rulers, but with the difference that the advent of the Ghaznavids and Qarakhanids brought the greater part of the eastern Islamic world under the direction of Turkish leaders. The rules of previous Turkish governors like the Ṭulunids and Ikhshidids in Egypt and Syria had been on the whole short-lived and had involved autonomy from the caliphate rather than complete independence and freedom of action, or else rule had been local and circumscribed, like that of the Simjurid family within Samanid Khorasan. The Ghaznavids, however, were Turks who made it to the top and stayed there for several generations. Their own Turkish ethnicity was doubtless buttressed by the continuous arrival into their military following of Turkish manpower freshly recruited or purchased from the steppes, though what this feeling of Turkishness amounted to is difficult to estimate, since it was never as such the concern of the Arabic or Persian chroniclers and can only be inferred from passing references. Nevertheless, such rulers as Maḥmud and Masʿud, and a *fortiori* their successors had from the start to function within as monarchs within a Persian administrative system staffed by Persian officials, and were linguistically as much at home in Persian as in Turkish;[57] we know from Beyhaqi that Maḥmud ensured that his own son Masʿud and his younger brother Yusof had a thorough Islamic education, one which seems to have given Masʿud at least a good competence in Arabic language and culture.[58]

[56] Bosworth, "The political and dynastic history of the Iranian world (A.D. 1000–1217)," in *CHIr. V. The Saljuq and Mongol periods*, ed. J.A. Boyle, Cambridge 1968, 157–61; *idem*, *The later Ghaznavids*, 111–31.

[57] Their immersion in Persian culture is stressed by Maḥmud Omidsālār in his article "Shāhnāma-ye Ferdowsi va huviyyat-e farhangi-ye Maḥmud Ghaznavi" *Irān-shenāsi*, XI/3 (1999), 619–20.

[58] See below, Gh 111–12, F 133. That Maḥmud himself was an authority on Islamic law and, according to what the Ottoman Turkish bibliographer Ḥājji

Thus it was the case that the Ghaznavid Amirs, on attaining supreme control of the state, took over the full apparatus of monarchical authority as it had evolved in the Perso-Islamic tradition whose roots stretched back into the pre-Islamic Iranian past; and they buttressed this inheritance with an assiduous cultivation of all the moral and religious authority of their role as theoretical delegates of the ʿAbbasid caliphs, though this delegated status meant virtually nothing in practice.[59] Theorists of this Perso-Islamic tradition, such as the authors of the "Mirrors for Princes" literature, or a theologian exercised by the moral aspects of political power like Ghazāli, asserted the pattern of an autocratic ruler whose authority, being backed by divine approval, had to be accepted; in any case, all scholars and divines who mused upon the problems of power held firmly to the belief that autocracy, however capriciously exercised, was preferable to mob-rule and anarchy. Thus when, towards the end of the eleventh century, the great statesman and vizier Neẓām al-Molk composed his work on political theory and practice, the *Siyāsat-nāma* or "Treatise on statecraft," for his Seljuq masters—whom he considered as too relaxed in their attitude towards such a serious topic as royal power—he looked back nostalgically at the first Ghaznavids and the power structures that they erected, and made Maḥmud, together with his equally forceful Buyid predecessor ʿAżod al-Dowla, the hero of several anecdotes illustrating firm monarchical rule tempered by justice towards subjects and regard for the rights of God.[60]

This "power state" of the Ghaznavids under Maḥmud and Masʿud, as we know it from the contemporary authors ʿOtbi, Gardizi and Beyhaqi, rested on various presuppositions. One was the cliché that the ruler was the shadow of God upon earth and was therefore answerable only to the deity. There followed from this that the subjects (*raʿiyya*, pl. *raʿāyā*) had an unqualified duty of obedience and no right of resistance;

Khalifa mentions, composed a work on it, hence was necessarily literate in Arabic (see Nāẓim, *Sulṭān Maḥmūd of G͟hazna*, 156–57), is unbelievable.

[59] It is notable that Neẓām al-Molk in his *Siyāsat-nāma* (see on this below and next note), makes no mention of the caliph or the caliphate of his time, nor of the conditions for legitimising royal power expressed in the writings on constitutional law, as was observed by Ritter, *op. cit.*, 107–08.

[60] See his *Siyāsat-nāma*, ed. H. Darke, Tehran 1340/1962, tr. *idem*, *The book of government or rules for kings*, London 1978, indices s.vv.

the lively debates in medieval Christian Europe on whether monarchical divine right was to be tempered by a right of resistance found little echo in the corresponding period of Islam. Neẓām al-Molk, again, expressed the view that the relationship between ruler and ruled was always in tension. Any latitude or indulgence shown to the subjects diminished the majesty and awesomeness of the ruler, and any slackening of the reins of power inevitably provokes disobedience and rebelliousness. There was in the nature of things a great gulf fixed between the persons making up the ruling institution, military or civilian, what the Ottomans were later to call collectively the *ʿaskeri*s, on one side and the *raʿāyā*, merchants, shopkeepers, artisans or peasants, on the other. In the light of this, what might anachronistically be called the "trade union of rulers" was set up over and against the mass of the subject population, even though the various territorial and political units—empires, principalities, city states, etc.—might in practice be sharply divided from each other. Rulers in general had more in common with each other than had a particular ruler with his subjects.

Such an attitude was well seen in Maḥmud's reprimand to the populace of Balkh, as described by Beyhaqi, when in 1006 they were faced with an incoming Qarakhanid army under the Ilig Naṣr's general Sübashïtegin. The townspeople of Balkh had resisted vigorously, and in the course of this resistance a market belonging to the Sultan, that brought in much revenue, had been damaged. The Balkhis got no thanks for their efforts against the invader but, instead, reproaches from the Sultan: they should not have allowed royal property to be harmed but should have resigned themselves to whichever ruler proved the stronger. Subjects had no right to defend themselves against the enemy; fighting was the business of the Sultan and his troops.[61]

Under a forceful ruler like Maḥmud, there was a good chance that the royal army would rescue a town or rural district that had been compelled by circumstances to yield to an enemy, as Ghaznavid troops had recovered Balkh on the above-mentioned occasion. But this became less certainly the case under Masʿud, when the Sultan proved increasingly unable to defend the towns and agricultural oases of Khorasan against the Turkmens, yet was filled with wrath and indignation when the local people attempted to salvage something of the

[61] Gh 551, F 729. Cf. Barthold, *Turkestan*, 291; Bosworth, *The Ghaznavids*, 253.

situation for themselves by coming to an agreement with the Seljuqs. In the summer of 1039, Masʿud's troops ravaged the regions of Herat, Bādghis and Ganj Rostāq in northern Afghanistan on the pretext that the locals had colluded with the Seljuqs when the latter had entered the area, and persons who had collaborated with the Seljuqs in Herat were executed. Those town notables who had co-operated with the three Seljuq chiefs during their first occupation of the town during 1038–39 did not wait for vengeance to descend upon them when the Sultan temporarily recovered Nishapur in 1040, but decamped to the Seljuq side with the Turkmens when they left.[62]

Only at the very end, after the overwhelming defeat at Dandānqān, when Masʿud despairingly concluded that his position within the Iranian lands of his empire was untenable (see above, p. 23), did he abandon these attempts at terrorising his subjects into a show of loyalty which had now no practical basis, and before departing to India gave his officials in Ghazna permission to make terms as best they could with what he thought was an imminent Seljuq occupation: the ultimate acknowledgment of his failure.[63]

For a state to be truly totalitarian, total supervision of its constituent elements is necessary, and this implies an internal spy system whose tentacles reach down to the humblest citizen, as was the case with the Stasi and its multitude of informers in pre-1991 East Germany. Medieval Islam had its fair share of autocracies and despotisms, indeed, these were the norms within settled society there, and the Ghaznavid sultanate may fairly be included amongst them. Yet these régimes of medieval Islam were not totalitarian, with the ruling power claiming a right to control every sector of its subjects' lives. Medieval Islamic polities were made up of carefully delimited spheres: within the public sphere, the ruler might exercise close military and political control, but there was left a wide private sphere, embracing the life of the spirit (provided that this did not involve overt heterodoxy) and economic and commercial activities, and within this sphere, the subjects were left to pursue their own avocations.

Hence the system of internal espionage and social control, which was a prominent feature of the early Ghaznavid state apparatus, aimed

---

62 Gh 588–89, 607, F 782–83, 810. Cf. Bosworth, *The Ghaznavids*, 262–66.

63 Gh 664, F 899. Cf. Bosworth, *The later Ghaznavids*, 16.

mainly at curbing the propensities of governors and commanders outside the heartland for revolt, and at preventing financial officials and tax collectors from pocketing a greater share of the state revenues than convention allowed them. For it was regarded as axiomatic that provincial governors, often hundreds of miles distant from the court and the capital, would act in an insubordinate fashion if unchecked; they might recruit gholāms for their private armies and appropriate local revenues. Likewise, tax collectors, who were in any case usually pressed and harassed by the powers above them, would act tyrannically and oppress the populace. In this last connection, apart from the loss of revenue for the central government that defalcation caused, the ruler might be mindful of the fact that his sovereign power under God brought with it the responsibilities of dealing out justice to God's creation and of redressing wrongs, duties stressed in the "Mirrors for Princes" literature and illustrated by a wealth of anecdotes in the *adab* or polite literature going back to the Sasanid emperors and the early Islamic Patriarchal Caliphs.

We can discern clearly from Beyhaqi that the network of local intelligence agents, that of the *aṣḥāb-e barid*, with a system of *manāzel* or *marāḥel*, relay stations along the important routes of the empire, was a vital instrument for keeping control of distant provinces and knowing what was going on there, and such examples as the Ghaznavid system must have influenced Neẓām al-Molk, with his Khorasanian background, in devoting no fewer than four chapters of his *Siyāsat-nāma* to the topics of internal and external security and the use of spies and informers. It was through such agents of the postal and intelligence service, so Beyhaqi tells us, that Sultan Masʿud was kept informed of what was happening in remote Khwarazm when the late Khwarazm Shah's son and *de facto* successor, Hārun, in 1033–34 broke away from his allegiance to Ghazna, and similarly, it was from the *ṣāḥeb-barid* of Nishapur, at that time in concealment but able to communicate secretly with the outside world, that Masʿud knew about events in the town when Ṭoghrïl Beg and his Turkmen followers first occupied it in 1038.[64]

At the side of these postal and intelligence officials there was a host of lesser spies and informers, *moshrefs*, whose activities were control-

[64] Bosworth, *The Ghaznavids*, 238, 252.

led by a special department of the central bureaucracy, the *divān-e shoghl-e eshrāf*. Under Maḥmud and Masʿud, these spies were everywhere, from the entourages of the royal princes downwards. It was normal practice that members of the ruling family should set spies over each other, as did Sultan Maḥmud over Prince Masʿud when the latter was governor of Herat, while reciprocally, Masʿud received confidential reports about happenings at the Sultan's court from sympathisers and from an aunt, Ḥorra Khottali. Military commanders sent forth on expeditions to the provinces or on raids into Central Asia or India had *moshref*s secretly attached to them as a matter of course, even when, in one instance, an expedition to Qoṣdār in what is now northern Baluchistan, the commander was Masʿud's own uncle, Yusof b. Sebüktegin. The resultant climate of fear and suspicion, combined with the personal divisions and rivalries amongst the Sultan's officials at court, did much during Masʿud's reign to inhibit the proffering of disinterested, sincere advice and to paralyse sound decision-making.[65]

2. Beyhaqi's life and career

We are indeed fortunate to possess the small part of Beyhaqi's *History* which has, apparently fortuitously, survived, but given its comparative exiguousness it is hardly surprising that few data on his life and career are available. Some scattered details on his early life, together with some rather more numerous, but still far from lavish, comments on what befell him in the course of his secretarial career during the decades after Sultan Masʿud's death, can be gleaned from the *Tārikh-e Masʿudi* "History of Sultan Masʿud" itself; but all these are disparate and disconnected. It would have been good if Beyhaqi had figured in the literary-biographical work of his older contemporary, Abu Manṣur ʿAbd al-Malek Moḥammad b. Esmāʿil Thaʿālebi, the *Yatimat al-dahr fi maḥāsen ahl al-ʿaṣr* "The unique pearl concerning the praiseworthy aspects of the people of the age", and its sequel, the *Tatemmat al-yatima* "The completion of the Unique pearl", or in the continuation of Thaʿālebi's two works, the *Domyat al-qaṣr*

[65] *Ibid.*, 63–64, 93–97.

va-ʿoṣrat ahl al-ʿaṣr "The handsome idol of the palace and the refuge of the people of the age," of Abu'l-Ḥasan (or Abu'l-Qāsem) ʿAli b. al-Ḥasan Bākharzi, in the same way that certain of his colleagues in the Ghaznavid administration figure, such as the Head of the Army Department (*ʿārez̤*) Abu Sahl Zowzani and the postal and intelligence officer, *ṣāḥeb-barid*, of Nishapur Abu'l-Moẓaffar Jomaḥi. Thaʿālebi certainly knew Beyhaqi from their common Khorasanian, Nishapuri, background, and he did not die until 1038 when Beyhaqi was still in mid-career, while Bākharzi, likewise a Khorasanian, was Beyhaqi's almost exact contemporary.[66]

However, Thaʿālebi was concerned above all with the Arabic scholarship of the poets and writers of ornate, chancery prose, *enshā'*, and it does not seem that Beyhaqi by the time of the older man's death had achieved any special reputation as a poet and stylist in Arabic. It goes without saying that, like any literate person of his time and especially a person with a secretarial training, Beyhaqi would have almost certainly been able to turn his hand to Arabic and Persian verse. His daily round in the Ghaznavid Chancery must have entailed inditing letters to outside powers such as the ʿAbbasid caliphs and the Buyids (at whose courts in western and northern Persia there flourished, working as the Amirs' viziers, chief secretaries, etc., several of the most outstanding Arabic stylists of the tenth and early eleventh centuries). However, we do not know for sure in which language he wrote his manual on secretaryship, the *Ketāb Zinat al-kottāb* "Book of the adornment of secretaries" (see below), since the Arabic title tells us nothing here. That Beyhaqi did not, in the later part of his life, establish any great reputation as an Arabic stylist can be inferred from the absence of an entry on him in the literary-biographical works just mentioned above.

Of external sources for Beyhaqi's life, we have to fall back on a Khorasanian but non-contemporary source: two notices, one brief but the other more substantial, in the biographical-historical work which Ẓahir al-Din Abu'l-Ḥasan ʿAli b. Zeyd Beyhaqi, called Ebn Fondoq (d. 1169), wrote concerning his home town of Beyhaq (modern Sabzavār), its eminent persons and its role in Khorasanian histori-

[66] See *EI*[2] arts. "al-T͟haʿālibī" (E.K. Rowson), and "al-Bāk͟harzī" (D.S. Margoliouth); *EIr* art. "Bāḵarzī" (Z. Safa).

cal events, the *Tārikh-e Beyhaq* "History of Beyhaq."[67] These notices will be considered below, but even when this external source and the internal information from the *History* itself are combined, the number of hard facts which emerges is small, although, as Marilyn Waldman observed, one can discern significant pointers to Beyhaqi's character and motivations from a careful reading of the *History*.[68]

Ebn Fondoq's two notices comprise first, a mention in a section called "An enumeration of famous histories," each one of which, so he says, "will be the way to companionship, the open space for propinquity, the enclosure for friendship, the touchstone for men's pleasant fancies and inner thoughts ..." He goes on to mention

> ... Khᵛāja Abu'l-Fażl al-Beyhaqi, who was the secretary of Sultan Maḥmud b. Sebüktegin, a master of the [secretarial] art and possessing a mastery of the peripheral aspects and innermost parts of outstandingness. He composed the History of the house of Maḥmud in Persian, comprising over thirty volumes. Some of these were in the library at Sarakhs and some in the library of the madrasa endowed by the Princess Mahd-e ʿErāq, may God have mercy on her,[69] in Nishapur.[70]

Later, Ebn Fondoq devotes a special section to this famous son of his own home town:

> *al-Sheykh Abu'l-Fażl Moḥammad b. al-Ḥoseyn al-Kāteb al-Beyhaqi*
>
> He was Sultan Maḥmud's secretary, acting as deputy for Abu Naṣr b. Moshkān, and as secretary to Sultan Moḥammad b. Maḥmud and for Sultan Masʿud. Then [he became] secretary to Sultan Mowdud and then to Sultan Farrokh-zād. When Sultan Farrokh-zād's period of dominion came to an end, he opted for a secluded retirement and became busy with literary compositions. He was born in the village of Ḥārethābād. His works include the *Ketāb Zinat al-kottāb*, a work

[67] See on him Bosworth, *The Ghaznavids*, 15; Parvaneh Pourshariati, "Local historiography in early medieval Iran and the *Tārīkh-i Bayhaq*," *Ir. St.*, XXXIII/1–2 (Winter-Spring 2000), 140–43, with earlier works on him listed at 140 n. 45; *EI²* art. "al-Bayhaḳī, Ẓahīr al-Dīn" (D.M. Dunlop); *EIr* art. "Bayhaqī, Ẓahīr al-Dīn" (H. Halm).

[68] *Toward a theory of historical narrative*, 39.

[69] I.e. the daughter of the Seljuq Sultan Malek Shāh, who had been married to the Ghaznavid Sultan Masʿud (III) b. Ebrāhim, possibly around 1082–83, and who acquired this title of "the Bride from Iraq." See Bosworth, *The later Ghaznavids*, 83.

[70] *Tārikh-e Beyhaq*, 20.

> incomparable in its genre (*fann*); and the *Tārikh-e Nāṣeri*, extending from the beginning of Sebüktegin's reign to the beginning of that of Sultan Ebrāhim, in which he described and explained their history day-by-day. That work apparently comprised over thirty volumes. I saw some of them in the library at Sarakhs, some of them in the library of the Mahd-e ʿErāq, may God have mercy on her, and some in the hands of various people; but I did not see a complete set. [It is a work][71] of fine expression and eloquence (*bā faṣāḥat va balāghat*), and has transmitted many orally handed-down stories (*aḥādith*).

Ebn Fondoq goes on to mention various incidents in the history of Nishapur, including a record number of snowfalls, sixty-seven in all, during the winter months of 1009–10, and, citing here ʿOtbi's *al-Taʾrikh al-Yamini* "History of Sultan Yamin al-Dowla",[72] the *History* of Abu Saʿd Khargushi,[73] and ʿAbdalakāni Zowzani,[74] the dreadful famine of 1010–11, in which, reputedly (though horror stories like these are something of a topos), recently-buried corpses were exhumed and their bones gnawed or ground up, and in which parents ate their children.

Then follows an extended passage that cites Beyhaqi on the duties and responsibilities of the Sultan's servants and how they should be content with the modest level of their official salaries and not attempt to rival monarchs in accumulating a large personal hoard. For his part, the Sultan, with his retainers and troops (making up the *dār al-molk*) should not be an intolerable burden on those subjects through whose territories they may pass on campaigns or on royal progresses.[75] It is unclear whether these musings come from a lost part of the *Mojalladāt*,

[71] Ebn Fondoq apparently at this point goes back to discussing the *Ketāb Zinat al-kottāb*; possibly some introductory words have fallen out of the text here.

[72] The famed history of Sebüktegin and Maḥmud by Beyhaqi's older contemporary, Abu Naṣr Moḥammad b. ʿAbd al-Jabbār ʿOtbi (d. 1036 or 1039–40). See on him Barthold, *Turkestan*, 19–20; Bosworth, *The Ghaznavids*, 9–10; *idem*, "Early sources for the history of the first four Ghaznavid sultans (977–1041)," *IQ*, VII (1963), 5–7; *EI*² art. "al-ʿUtbī. 3."

[73] Apparently a work by the traditionist and wide-ranging scholar of Nishapur (Khargush = "a great street in Nishapur") Abu Saʿd ʿAbd al-Malek b. Abi ʿOthmān, d. 406/1015–16; see Samʿāni, *Ketāb al-Ansāb*, ed. ʿAbd al-Raḥmān al-Yamāni and M. ʿAbd al-Moʿid Khān, Hyderabad 1382–1402/1962–82, V, 101–02.

[74] I.e. Abu Moḥammad ʿAbdallāh b. Moḥammad, *fl.* in the early eleventh century, poet and anthologist of Khorasan known to Thaʿālebi; see Sezgin, *GAS*, II, 642.

[75] See for a translation of this passage, Bosworth, *The Ghaznavids*, 64–65.

Beyhaqi's complete *History*, or, conceivably, from the *Ketāb Zinat al-kottāb*, since the tone of the passage would accord well with that of the manuals of secretaryship.[76]

After this, Ebn Fondoq ends this entry on Beyhaqi with information on Beyhaqi's latter days in official service:

> On account of a dowry owed to a wife,[77] the Qazi (i.e. Judge) in Ghazni ordered him to be imprisoned, and after that, Ṭoghrïl-e B.rār (?),[78] who was a runaway slave of the Maḥmudi dynasty, seized power in Ghazni, killed Sultan ʿAbd al-Rashid and consigned the monarch's servants to a fortress. Included amongst these last was Abu'l-Fażl-e Beyhaqi, who was sent there from the Qazi's prison. While he was in that fortress, Abu'l-Fażl wrote [in Arabic],
>
> 1. *While you pass a day in happiness, one day of my misery in prison passes.*
>
> 2. *Neither misery nor ease of life has any permanence; no people has lived for ever in ease of life or in misery.*
>
> After a short period, fortune brought about Ṭoghrïl-e B.rār's killing at the hands of Nushtegin-e Zubin-dār.[79] The duration of his power was no more than fifty-seven days, and royal authority [now] reverted to the Maḥmudi dynasty. Nothing good ever comes out of rebellion against the bestower of favour (i.e. the ruler) and no lengthy period [of time] is ever granted; he who unsheathes the sword of rebellion perishes by it (*va-man salla seyf al-baghy qotela behi*). Al-Sheykh Abu'l-Fażl Moḥammad b. al-Ḥoseyn al-Beyhaqi the secretary died in Ṣafar 470 [/August–September 1077].[80]

---

76 *Tārikh-e Beyhaq*, 176–77.

77 Ebn Fondoq's expression *m.h.r z.n.y* must be read, with A. K. Arends in his Russian translation of the *Tārikh-e Masʿudi*, his *Istorya Masʿūda (1030–1041)*, 2nd ed. Moscow 1969, as reported by B. Składenek in his review in *RO*, XXIX (1965), 120, as *mehr-e zani,* and not as read erroneously by W. Barthold, in his *EI*¹ art. "Baihaḳī", as *mohr-zani* "[illegal] engraving of seals."

78 For suggestions regarding this cryptic element in Ṭoghrïl's name, see Bosworth, *The later Ghaznavids*, 42; a possibility is Bozan "the destroyer."

79 I.e. "bearer of the short spear/lance or javelin," presumably an office within the royal household; for the *zhupin* (a characteristic weapon of the Deylamites, though here obviously wielded by a Turk), see below, Year 421 n. 181.

80 *Tārikh-e Beyhaq*, 177–78.

In her book *Toward a theory of historical narrative*,[81] Waldman made a detailed analysis of Ebn Fondoq's information plus that which can be gleaned from Beyhaqi's own *History*, specifically in her section "Bayhaqī's biography and the sources of biographical information."[82] Hence only a résumé of this is necessary here. The first point that arises is the uncertainty over Beyhaqi's birth date, unmentioned by Ebn Fondoq but ascertainable indirectly from two mentions by the historian himself in his *History*, at Gh 209, F 264, and Gh 359, F 458, respectively. At the first place, he states that he was sixteen years old in 1011–12 when he saw a Ghaznavid bride intended for the Ziyarid ruler of Gorgān and Ṭabarestān, Manuchehr b. Qābus, pass through Nishapur en route for the Caspian lands; but in the second place, he describes himself as fifteen years old when he saw the former vizier of the last Samanids, Abu'l-Moẓaffar Moḥammad Barghashi, in retirement at Nishapur in 1009–10. The discrepancy is only slight, and the whole point is hardly worth labouring: Beyhaqi must have been born around 995–96.

His father, whom he refers to as "Khᵛāja," may accordingly have been in official service, so that the roots of Beyhaqi's own secretarial expertise may have lain in the Samanid bureaucracy; we know that many of the prominent officials of the early Ghaznavids began in the service of the Samanids either at the capital Bokhara or in Khorasan.[83] Beyhaqi probably spent much of his early life in Nishapur, the administrative centre for the Samanid and then Ghaznavid province of Khorasan and its long-established cultural focus, and at some point he passed into the state Chancery, the *divān-e resālat/rasāʾel*, as an apprentice, *shāgerd*, under Abu Naṣr Moshkān, whom Beyhaqi was to revere as *ostādam* "my master." The date for this entry is unspecified but must have been in the middle years of Sultan Maḥmud's reign (998–1030), perhaps around 1015 when he was about twenty years old, as suggested by Mujtaba Minovi.[84] Thus his formation as a *dabir* or secretary was under the exacting standards of chancery procedure and the inditing of official documents, *enshāʾ*, of Abu Naṣr Moshkān; much of his

[81] See above, n. 28.
[82] *Op. cit.*, 39–44.
[83] See Bosworth, *The Ghaznavids*, 57–58.
[84] "The Persian historian Bayhaqī," in B. Lewis and P.M. Holt (eds.), *Historians of the Middle East*, London 1962, 138.

training must also have fallen within the notable vizierate for Maḥmud, until his fall from grace in 1024, of Aḥmad b. Ḥasan Meymandi, called *Shams al-Kofāt* "Sun of the Capable Ones," who likewise had an outstanding reputation as an Arabic stylist and *monshi*.[85]

Since Beyhaqi's duties came to include composing the drafts (*savād*) of official documents and correspondence, including letters to outside powers, and then at times making the final, fair copies (*bayāż*) when these were not done by Abu Naṣr Moshkān himself, he had an unequalled opportunity to make personal copies of these documents, written in both Arabic and Persian, and to keep a personal diary of events, all with a view—which must have gradually matured in his mind, certainly by Masʿud's reign (1031–41)—of eventually composing a history of the Ghaznavid sultans from the viewpoint of the central administration and the court (which was, of course, peripatetic and accompanied the monarch on his travels and military expeditions). Beyhaqi's service in the Chancery continued for over thirty years; whether he ever made it to the top as Chief Secretary is uncertain. He states that he was considered for this post when his master Abu Naṣr died, while still in harness, in 1039, but was passed over in favour of the former Head of the Army Department, Abu Sahl Zowzani, allegedly because the Sultan considered him too young.[86] Since Beyhaqi was then around forty-five or forty-six years old, well into what was at that time considered middle age, if not on the verge of old age, this sounds an unconvincing reason. More probably, his rejection was connected with the earlier rivalry of Abu Naṣr Moshkān and Abu Sahl Zowzani. Certainly, he had no love for Abu Sahl, who emerges from Beyhaqi's pages as something like the evil genius for much of Masʿud's reign.

Despite this snub, Beyhaqi continued working in the Chancery, apparently till the reign of Sultan ʿAbd al-Rashid b. Maḥmud (?1049–52), by which time Abu Sahl Zowzani was most likely either retired or even dead,[87] so that it is possible that Beyhaqi at last achieved the plum post of Chief Secretary; the years of Beyhaqi's official career

[85] See on him, *EI*[2] art. "Maymandī" (M. Nazim and C.E. Bosworth).

[86] Gh 600–01, F 800.

[87] A death date for Abu Sahl at some point within the late 1040s or 1050s seems most probable, according to Jamāl Reżā'i, "Bu Sahl-e Zowzani dar Tārikh-e Beyhaqi," in *Yād-nāma-ye Abu'l-Fażl-e Beyhaqi*, Persian section, 222.

under Mowdud b. Masʿud and the two ephemeral rulers Masʿud (II) b. Mowdud and ʿAli b. Masʿud (I), i.e. till ʿAbd al-Rashid's accession,[88] are particularly dark. The cause of Beyhaqi's fall from grace and his imprisonment during ʿAbd al-Rashid's reign must undoubtedly have been more serious, as Waldman pertinently observed,[89] than a dispute over an unpaid dowry and must have been connected with the political rivalries of the time, whose nature is unknown to us. What Beyhaqi mourned, in regard to this period of his life, was not so much the seizure of his personal property (which he probably regained subsequently)[90] as the loss of his personal copies of official documents and his notes on various events (see below); their confiscation implies that the reasons behind his disgrace were political and that his papers contained politically sensitive or even incriminatory material.

At all events, Beyhaqi regained his freedom, apparently with the overthrow of the usurper Ṭoghrïl and the restoration of the legitimate Ghaznavid line under Farrokh-zād b. Masʿud (I) in 1052, but at the price of having been deprived of the copies of diplomatic documents, treaties, etc., which he had carefully made at the time and had kept, these copies having been, so he says, deliberately destroyed.[91] Whether Beyhaqi, now almost a sexagenarian, ever returned to official life is unknown, though mentions in the *History* show that he at least kept in touch with officials at court and in the administration; Ebn Fondoq's assertion that he returned to office under Farrokh-zād and stayed there till that Sultan died in 1059[92] seems dubious, since Beyhaqi was already at work composing his *History* during Farrokh-zād's reign and was to carry on with it during the early years of the suc-

[88] See concerning the confused chronology of the sultans during these years, Bosworth, *The later Ghaznavids*, 37ff., and idem, *The New Islamic dynasties, a chronological and genealogical manual*, Edinburgh 1996, 296, no. 158.

[89] *Toward a theory of historical narrative*, 43.

[90] According to an anecdote in Sadid al-Din Moḥammad b. Moḥammad ʿAwfi's *Javāmeʿ al-ḥekāyāt*, as quoted by Gh.-Ḥ. Yusofi in his *EIr* art. "Bayhaqī, Abu'l-Fażl" (this must be anecdote no. 1728 in Muḥammad Niẓámu'd-Dín's *Introduction to the* Jawámiʿu'l-ḥikáyát wa lawámiʿu'r-riwáyát *of Muḥammad ʿAwfí*, London 1929, 228, cited from Beyhaqi's own *History* ("The *Ta'ríkh-i Náṣirí*"), cf. 62–63), Beyhaqi's property had been sequestered on the Sultan's direct orders by the son of a slave, one Tumān (?).

[91] Gh 294, F 389.

[92] *Tārikh-e Beyhaq*, 175.

ceeding reign of Ebrāhim b. Masʿud (I). Beyhaqi's whole career thus exemplifies what he emphasizes in the *History* (e.g. in his musings on the subsequent fates of various persons who had served the fallen Amir Yusof b. Sebüktegin, see Gh 253ff., F 331ff.), that the service of monarchs is inevitably subject to the vicissitudes of fortune, more specifically, to changes of régime or of state policy which might exalt a person and then reduce him to imprisonment and poverty.[93]

Sir Henry Elliot and John Dowson, in their *The history of India as told by its own historians. The Muhammadan period* (the first European work to contain translated passages from Beyhaqi's *History*, see below, Section 3, pp. 49–50), dubbed Beyhaqi "an oriental Mr Pepys." This is true in that the account of Samuel Pepys' official career in the Naval Office under Charles II during the years 1660 to 1669, as revealed in his celebrated *Diary*, is comparable with the eleven years of Beyhaqi's work in the Chancery as set forth in the *Tārikh-e Masʿudi*. In both we have a detailed calendar of high-level events and many sidelights on the subtle interplay of personal motives, character and emotions with those events; and it is further true that Pepys in his *Diary* was probably writing with eventual publication in mind, since the shorthand system which he used was one known in the mid-seventeenth century. From the *Diary* we have incomparable insights into Pepys' personal character, morals, beliefs, mode of life, likes and dislikes, and foibles, together with information on his marriage and his fumbling infidelities, his medical history, personal finances, etc. Where the two works diverge lies in the fact that Beyhaqi reveals virtually nothing of his private life: what wives he had (except for the snippet of information about the disputed dowry payment, if this is indeed authentic), what children he produced, his life style, what interests he had outside his secretarial work and authorial activity, what illnesses he suffered, how he faced death, etc. Yet this disparity between our knowledge of the two men is just another instance of the frustration of the historian of medieval Islam in attempting to get behind the public façades of the personalities whom he encounters.[94]

---

93 See Julie S. Meisami, *Persian historiography to the end of the twelfth century*, Edinburgh 1999, 106–07.

94 See for these considerations, Bosworth, "An oriental Samuel Pepys? Abu'l-Faḍl Bayhaqi's memoirs of court life in Eastern Iran and Afghanistan, 1030–1041," *JRAS*, 3rd series, XIV (2004), 13–25.

3. Beyhaqi's works

The lost manual for secretaries, the *Ketāb Zinat al-kottāb*, has been mentioned above in section 2, where it is noted that its language, whether Arabic or Persian, is unknown (but if it was originally written in Arabic, and the reflections on the responsibilities of royal servants, etc., cited by Ebn Fondoq in this same section 2, pp. 32–33, are in fact from the *Zinat al-kottāb*, the historian of Beyhaq must have turned them into Persian).

In various places of his *History*, Beyhaqi refers to what he calls the *Maqāmāt-e Abu Naṣr-e Moshkān* "Activities of Abu Naṣr-e Moshkān",[95] giving anecdotes about its subject and episodes from his life, and illuminating his personal character and secretarial skills. If these *Maqāmāt* formed a separate work (see below), like the *Zinat al-kottāb*, they have not survived. They have indeed been regarded as a distinct, separate work by some scholars, e.g. Muḥammad Nāẓim in *The life and works of Sulṭān Maḥmūd of Ghazna*, 1–2; Saʿid Nafisi in his *EI*² art. "Bayhaḳī, Abu'l-Faḍl Muḥammad b. Ḥusayn Kāteb," at Vol. I, 1131a; and Marilyn Waldman, *Toward a theory of historical narrative*, 44. Certainly, numerous extracts from them are contained in the works of later authors like ʿAwfi, Seyf al-Din Ḥājji b. Neẓām ʿAqili, Ḥāfeẓ-e Abru and others; these have been conveniently gathered together by Saʿid Nafisi in his *Dar pirāmun-e Tārikh-e Beyhaqi* "Around the margins of Beyhaqi's History," Tehran 1342/1963, I, 94ff. and II.

However, Gholām Ḥoseyn Yusofi has recently challenged this view, namely, that the *Maqāmāt* were a separate work, in his *EIr* art. "Bayhaqī, Abu'l-Fażl," at Vol. III, 890b–891a. He has equated the *Maqāmāt-e Abu Naṣr-e Moshkān* with the *Maqāmāt-e Maḥmudi* "Activities of Sultan Maḥmud" also mentioned by Beyhaqi, on the grounds that much of the material cited by Beyhaqi on his master pertains to the reign of Sultan Maḥmud, under whom Abu Naṣr had spent a considerable part of his working life. The material on Abu Naṣr's career during this last-mentioned reign would thus most naturally have been included in the lost section of Beyhaqi's *History* devoted to Maḥmud's

---

95 Concerning the apparent meaning, in this context, of the term *maqāma*, see below, Year 421 nn. 435–36.

reign, what Beyhaqi refers to as the *Tārikh-e Yamini* (see below), just as the material on the last decade of Abu Naṣr's life, the years spent as Head of the Chancery for Sultan Masʿud, naturally came within the extant *Tārikh-e Masʿudi*. This seems a feasible view; if the *Maqāmāt-e Abu Naṣr-e Moshkān* had been a separate book, one might have expected Ebn Fondoq to describe it as such, given that material from the *Maqāmāt* was known in the later fifteenth century when Seyf al-Din ʿAqili used it extensively in his biographical work the *Āthār al-vozarā'* "Relics and notable deeds of the viziers".[96]

We thus come to Beyhaqi's *magnum opus*, his *History*, the thirty volumes of which made up, collectively, the *Mojalladāt* "Volumes" or *Tārikh-e āl-e Sebüktegin* "History of the house of Sebüktegin," a complete dynastic history of the Ghaznavids as pictured by a loyal if not uncritical servant of the line. The *Mojalladāt* extended chronologically from the time of the founder Sebüktegin, who had established himself in Ghazna in 977 as the culmination of a line of briefly-governing Turkish gholām commanders of the Samanid general Alptegin (see above, section 1, p. 6) until, presumably, the end of Farrokh-zād's sultanate and the succession of Ebrāhim in 1059. As we have seen, Ebn Fondoq described the whole work as comprising thirty books or volumes. This division, based roughly on length rather than upon units corresponding e.g. to reigns or to extended historical episodes, must have been deliberately decided on by Beyhaqi to make his *History* more manageable, perhaps with the hope, unfulfilled as it happened, that these moderately-sized books/volumes could be more easily copied and disseminated.

Exactly at what point Beyhaqi began his *History* is not quite clear. A general title like *Tārikh-e āl-e Sebüktegin* implies that he began when Sebüktegin took over power in 976 from Böri/Böritegin, and we have mentions by Juzjāni of the *Tārikh-e Nāṣeri* on Sebüktegin and by Beyhaqi himself of the *Tārikh-e Yamini* on Maḥmud,[97] these comprising the first four-and-a-half volumes of the complete *History*,

[96] Saʿid Nafisi opined that ʿAqili may have got his material from the *Maqāmāt* via the Khorasanian author who served the Timurids in Herat, Faṣiḥ al-Din Aḥmad b. Moḥammad, known as Faṣiḥi Khᵛāfi (d. in the mid-fifteenth century), since the *Maqāmāt* are cited in the latter's historical and biographical compendium, the *Mojmal-e Faṣiḥi*. See Nafisi, *Dar pirāmun-e Tārikh-e Beyhaqi*, I, 96 n. 1.

[97] Juzjāni, I, 225, tr. I, 67–68; Gh 26, F 27.

but there are two problems here. The first is that four-and-a-half volumes seems woefully inadequate for a period of over fifty years' combined rule by Sebüktegin and Maḥmud, compared with the intense detail on Masʿud's reign of eleven years only and, very likely, on the ensuing nineteen years (which must have taken up to twenty volumes). Did Beyhaqi only write a sketchy outline of Sebüktegin's period of governorship and the first half or so of Maḥmud's reign, because he knew that his fellow-historian Abu Naṣr ʿOtbi had carried the story of these two potentates up to 1020, albeit in a very different format and style from his own work?[98]

What was possibly only a rapid survey of the dynasty's early years may be connected with the second problem, that of the interpretation of Beyhaqi's words at Gh 261–62, F 342, where he tells how a fellow-historian and contemporary in Ghazna, Maḥmud Varrāq ("the copyist, bookseller") had written a universal history at almost exactly the same time as Beyhaqi was putting together his own *History* of the Ghaznavids, and had taken it up to the year 1018–19, that very year, so Beyhaqi says, in which he started his own work. He goes on to relate that Maḥmud Varrāq's sons had complained to him, after their father's death, "We, his sons, aren't agreeable that you should utilize (lit. "raise up and set down," *bar dāri va feru nehi*) any more than what you've already said," hence Beyhaqi had no alternative but to desist (*nāchār be-istādam*).[99] Does this mean that Beyhaqi had to abjure giving full detail on the period of Sebüktegin's amirate and the first twenty years of Maḥmud's reign, hence confined himself to a mere résumé of the events of these forty-odd years?

What relationship Beyhaqi's work bears to the third extant contemporary source for early Ghaznavid history (i.e. after ʿOtbi and Beyhaqi himself), the *Ketāb Zeyn al-akhbār* "Book of the adornment of historical accounts" of Abu Saʿid Gardizi,[100] is unclear. Gardizi and Beyhaqi were contemporaries, and the former, from his *nesba*, was a native of Zābolestān where lay both Ghazna and Gardiz. Gardizi states specifically states that he himself was close to Sultan Maḥmud and accompanied him during his campaigns in India, Sistan, Khorasan and ʿErāq [-e ʿAjam] (i.e. Western Persia). In the later, historical

[98] See above, n. 72.

[99] Cf. Barthold, *Turkestan*, 21–22.

[100] See above, n. 26.

narrative part of his book, we have a matter-of-fact, unadorned account of the Ghaznavid sultans, their campaigns and conquests which is quite detailed and gives many exact dates, though not approaching Beyhaqi's exhaustiveness. The two extant manuscripts of the *Zeyn al-akhbār* extend to a few months beyond Beyhaqi's abrupt close, covering the events of 1041 during which Sultan Masʿud withdrew to India in the face of what he believed was impending Seljuq pressure, was murdered soon after a rebellion of his army but was avenged by his son Mowdud. With the execution of the assassins, Gardizi's work comes to a close as abrupt as does Beyhaqi's one, but his historical narrative almost certainly originally extended over the following seven or so years, since Gardizi dedicated his work to Sultan ʿAbd al-Rashid.[101]

It is possible that historians coming after Beyhaqi, in particular those working in the later Ghaznavid and Seljuq periods, were able to make use of his *History* while volumes of it were still to be found, although specific information is very sparse. This seems to be the case with the final, historical section of an *adab* work containing material useful for boon companions, storytellers and entertainers, by an author who was connected with the court of the Seljuqs of the East and who apparently wrote at Merv in the opening decades of the twelfth century, Abu'l-ʿAbbās Aḥmad b. ʿAli Qāshāni, called Ebn Bābā. This section of his *Ketāb Ra's māl al-nadim* "Book of the boon-companion's stock-in-trade" is sketchy on the middle years of Masʿud's reign up to the battle of Dandānqān and the Sultan's deposition and death, but has a fuller treatment of the reigns of his successors such as Mowdud and ʿAbd al-Rashid, with much significant information for these dark decades; it seems not unlikely that Ebn Bābā, working as he was at Merv in the eastern Persian lands, was able to draw upon Beyhaqi's *History*.[102]

---

[101] See on Gardizi and his work, Barthold, *op. cit.*, 20–21; Bosworth, *The Ghaznavids*, 10; *idem*, "Early sources for the history of the first four Ghaznavid sultans (977–1041)," 8–10; Meisami, *op. cit.*, 66–79; *EI*[2] art. "Gardīzī" (W. Barthold); *EIr* art. "Gardizi" (C.E. Bosworth).

[102] See for a translation of Ebn Bābā's section on the Ghaznavids, with a commentary, Bosworth, *The later Ghaznavids: splendour and decay. The dynasty in Afghanistan and northern India 1040–1186*, Edinburgh 1977, 132–55, cf. 2.

To return to the *Mojalladāt*. The bundles of volumes making up each individual sultan's reign had individual names, alluding to well-known honorific titles of the ruler in question. Thus volume 1 on the career of Nāṣer al-Din Sebüktegin was the *Tārikh-e Nāṣeri*, and vols. 2–4 on Yamin al-Dowla Maḥmud b. Sebüktegin formed the *Tārikh-e Yamini*. How Beyhaqi himself referred retrospectively to what we at present conventionally term the *Tārikh-e Masʿudi* is not known, but he does in the *History* refer to the *dowla* of Masʿud as *Ḥāfeẓi* (from the Sultan's honorific of Ḥāfeẓ ʿEbād Allāh, cf. Gh 49, F 53) after having characterised the preceding *dowla*s as *Nāṣeri* and *Yamini*.[103] Hence it is quite possible that he called this part of his *History* the *Tārikh-e Ḥāfeẓi*. The names of the subsequent volumes on Mowdud, etc., are also unknown.

In any case, what we possess today of the history of Masʿud's reign is not entirely complete: we have extant part of vol. 5; vols. 6–7; the first part of vol. 8 and then after a lacuna,[104] its last part; vol. 9; and the opening only of vol. 10, followed by the special section that Beyhaqi had promised to devote to Khwarazm under Sultans Maḥmud and Masʿud, but lacking a promised further section on the recent history of Ghaznavid power in Ray and Jebāl, i.e. northern and western Persia. The remainder of vol. 10 must have gone on to recount the story of Masʿud's abandonment of Ghazna and the imperial territories of what is now eastern Afghanistan, his journey to India and his death there (see on these events, above, section 1, p. 23). In its absence, we depend for information on Masʿud's last days, the brief re-appearance of Moḥammad and the triumph of Mowdud, on Gardizi (see above) and Ebn al-Athir.[105]

We are thus left with only a torso of a massive work that might have extended, using the yardstick of Fayyāż's edition, to 6,000 or 7,000 comparable pages of printed text. One inevitably wonders how

---

103 See Gh 99, F 116, and cf. Year 421 n. 397. For the honorifics of the early Ghaznavids in general see Bosworth, "The titulature of the early Ghaznavids," 215–19, 224–27.

104 Concerning this lacuna, possibly covering up to eleven or twelve months, sc. almost the last seven months of AH 424/AD 1033 and the first five ones of AH 425/AD 1033–34, see below, Year 424 n. 211.

105 See Bosworth, "Early sources for the first four Ghaznavid sultans (977–1041)," 11.

so much of the *History* came to be lost, but we do know that the process of loss developed swiftly. Only some ninety years after Beyhaqi's death, Ebn Fondoq was unable to find a complete set of volumes (see above, section 2, pp. 31–32). Some volumes must nevertheless have survived into the thirteenth and fourteenth centuries for a historian like Juzjāni in his *Ṭabaqāt-e nāṣeri* "Nāṣerian tables" (thus named after the author's Delhi Sultan patron), a literary biographer and anecdotist like ʿAwfi in his *Javāmeʿ al-ḥekāyāt* "Collections of anecdotes" and, so it seems, the Kurdish historian of the first half of the fourteenth century Moḥammad b. ʿAli Shabānkāraʾi in his *Majmaʿ al-ansāb* "Collection of genealogies,"[106] probably to utilize Beyhaqi's work, not to mention various Persian and Indo-Muslim authors, up to Abu'l-Fażl ʿAllāmi, Jahāngir and Fereshta, and the Ottoman Turkish bibliographer Ḥājji Khalifa, who at least cited its name and were aware of its former existence.[107]

It is not hard to conjecture the reasons for the *History*'s survival in only an attenuated form. The incentives for copying such a gigantic work, of concern only to scholars on the far eastern fringes of the Iranian world and its Indo-Muslim outlier, cannot have been great.[108] Copies in the libraries of mosques and madrasas of Khorasan may well have perished in the disorders there from the later part of Sultan Sanjar's reign onwards, with the ravages there of the Oghuz and with the subsequent spoliations of the armies of the Anushteginid Khwarazm Shahs in their warfare with the Ghurids over possession of Khorasan, with a culmination in the mass destructions of the Mongols in the early thirteenth century. As for Beyhaqi's original, autograph manuscript—assuming that he copied this out personally—the obvious place for it to be kept would be the capital Ghazna, either in the possession of his putative progeny or in the royal library of the sultans; but we know that public buildings there, including mosques

[106] See on this author, *ibid.*, 18–20; *EI*[2] art. "Shabānkāraʾī" (C.E. Bosworth and P. Jackson).

[107] Sir H.M. Elliot and J. Dowson, *The history of India as told by its own historians. The Muhammadan period,* 8 vols., London 1867–77 (see on this work, below), II, 53–55.

[108] Even with regard to a work on a similar, immense scale, but with a more universal relevance and appeal for the wider Islamic literate classes, sc. Ṭabari's *History*, our knowledge of substantial sections of the text depends on one or two extant manuscripts only.

and madrasas and doubtless their libraries, were devastated in the seven days' pillaging of Ghazna ordered by the Ghurid 'Alā' al-Din Ḥoseyn in 1150 when, for instance, the personal library of the physician and philosopher Ebn Sinā (the Avicenna of medieval Europe) that had been brought from Isfahan over a century before, perished.[109]

The manuscript history of Beyhaqi's work is somewhat curious. According to Yu.E. Bregel'[110] and 'Ali Akbar Fayyāż,[111] a few more manuscripts of the *History* have turned up in addition to the seventeen enumerated by C.A. Storey over sixty years ago,[112] making a total of some twenty-odd. The remarkable thing is that only one surviving manuscript may conceivably be slightly older than the sixteenth or seventeenth centuries (see below), and even out of these early ones, Fayyāż could only date two of them to those latter centuries with any degree of probability (there is a distressing lack of colophons with dates in what seem to be, on palaeographical grounds, the early manuscripts). Hence no basic manuscript (*aṣl*) is known, and we have a chronological gap of four or five centuries during which the manuscript history of Beyhaqi's work is a total blank. One inevitably wonders how some manuscript(s) did manage to survive through these lost centuries for the later, modest florescence of manuscript copying but then seem to have disappeared.[113]

---

[109] See Bosworth, *The later Ghaznavids*, 117.

[110] *Persidskaya literatura, bio-bibliograficheskii obzor*, Moscow 1972, II, 737–41.

[111] *Tārikh-e Beyhaqi*, Mashhad 1350/1971, Introduction, "Noskha-hā-ye khaṭṭi-ye Tārikh-e Beyhaqi", pp. *bist u yak* ff., also printed in *Yād-nāma-ye Abu'l-Fażl-e Beyhaqi*, Persian section, 516–29.

[112] *Persian literature, a bio-bibliographical survey. I. Qur'anic literature; history and biography*, London 1927–53, 253–54, 1271–72.

[113] We do know that one manuscript did survive into the early sixteenth century at least. In the catalogue of the library of the Ottoman Sultan Bāyezid II (1481–1512), preserved in the library of the Hungarian Academy of Sciences in Budapest and copied in 909/1503–04, is listed a copy of Beyhaqi's *Tārikh āl-e Sebüktegin*, interestingly referred to as *ketāb … avvaloho dhekr Abi Manṣur Sebüktegin*, possibly implying that it contained the now lost opening books of the *Mojalladāt* on the founder of the dynasty. (The same catalogue also includes no fewer than nine mss. of 'Otbi's *al-Ta'rikh al-Yamini,* five of them the original Arabic work and four in a Persian (Jorbādhqāni's?) translation, apparently attesting to an interest of the Ottoman Sultans in earlier dynasties headed by fellow-Turks.) See Miklós Maróth, "The library of Sultan Bayazit II," in Éva Jeremiás (ed.), *Irano-Turkic cultural contacts in the 11th–17th centuries*, Piliscsaba [2002] 2003, 121, 124.

As Filippo Bertotti has remarked, it would be good to be able to construct a stemma of the extant manuscripts, but the absence of specific information in the manuscripts about their copying and dating makes this impossible. Nevertheless, it does seem that there are two distinct manuscript traditions, one "Indian" and the other "Persian", with slight differences of approach to the text.[114] Neither is in general superior to the other, but the "Persian" manuscripts seem to display a greater freedom in reconstituting what the copyists thought the text ought to be, and they add explanatory and clarificatory sections such as the introduction to Book 5 of the *History* (Gh 1, F 948–49) and the translation into Persian of an Arabic letter from the new ʿAbbasid Caliph al-Qāʾem and of Masʿud's oath of allegiance to the Caliph (Gh 304–16, F 949–62). Fayyāż thought that one of the "Indian" manuscripts (which he calls the "Gujarāti" one, simply because it was once located in Gujarāt), from the correctness (*eṣālat*) of its language, was the oldest known manuscript and could conceivably go back to the fifteenth century.[115] Many of the manuscripts are in European collections, with a smaller number in Tehran and one in India. Fayyāż surmised again that the comparative surge of interest in copying the *History* and in diffusing manuscripts of it stemmed from a general revival in Persia (one beginning in the eighteenth century under the Zands and continuing under the Qajars in the nineteenth century) of interest in *adab* and the Persian literary heritage.[116] We can only be grateful that this revival of interest belatedly took place; but the downside was that these later copyists were largely at sea when dealing with the names of the many Turkish military men who play large roles on the stage of the *History*, and likewise when dealing with

[114] It is interesting to note that the (in fact, very numerous) mss. of ʿOtbi's *al-Taʾrikh al-yamini* also apparently fall into two groups of texts, one group emanating from the Persian-speaking domain and the other from the Arabic-speaking domain, the second with its stylistic content slightly modified (this latter group including the ms. or mss. used by Sheykh Aḥmad al-Manini for his printed text of Cairo 1286/1869). See R. Rubinacci, "Upon the 'al-Taʾrīkh al-Yamīnī' of Abū Naṣr al-ʿUtbī," in A. Gallotta and U. Marazzi (eds.), *Studia turcologica memoriae Alexii Bombaci dicata*, Naples 1982, 464–67.

[115] Bertotti, *L'opera dello storico persiano Bayhaqī*, Naples 1991, 26–27; Fayyāż, Introduction, "Noskha-hā-ye khaṭṭi-ye Tārikh-e Beyhaqi," pp. *bist u panj-bist u haft, si*.

[116] *Ibid.*, pp. *bist u do-bist u se*.

many place names of what are now Central Asia and Afghanistan and adjacent regions.[117]

Information about the various editions that have been published in modern times is given by Gilbert Lazard in the short section on the *History* in his *La langue des plus anciens monuments de la prose persane*[118] and by Gholām Ḥosayn Yusofi in his *EIr* article "Bayhaqī, Abu'l-Fażl." The *editio princeps* of W. H. Morley, *The Táríkh-i Baihaki containing the life of Masaúd, son of Sultán Mahmúd of Ghaznín* ..., Bibliotheca Indica. A Collection of Works Published by the Asiatic Society of Bengal, Calcutta 1862, was based on three manuscripts from the sixteenth and seventeenth centuries which Morley found in India but which are now deposited in the British Library; it thus represents the "Indian" manuscript tradition. This printed edition was in fact produced at a time when manuscripts of the *History* had hardly ceased being copied. William H. Morley (who was actually dead by the time this text was printed, it being seen through the press by W. Nassau Lees) had a legal and administrative career in British India and in 1859 became Librarian of the Royal Asiatic Society in London, of whose collection of Arabic and Persian manuscripts he had prepared the catalogue (London 1854). His edition, although without any introduction and with only a few variants indicated, mainly for personal and place names, was less correct than subsequent ones but may represent a more authentic copyists' tradition. For its time it was a meritorious one, not deserving the extravagant condemnation of H. G. Raverty,[119] and for many decades to come it was the basic one which historians of the eastern Islamic world and Central Asia, and of the first Muslim penetration of northwestern India, worked, from Sachau through Barthold to Muḥammad Nāẓim in his *Sulṭān Maḥmūd of Ghazna* (see further, below). However, its unattractive Indian Persian typography, its continuous text with no attempt at paragraphing, and the absence of any index or even table of contents, discouraged all but the most dedicated of scholars and probably worked against its wider usage in the West.

---

[117] *Ibid.*, p. *bist u haft*.

[118] Paris 1963, 76–78.

[119] Juzjāni, *Ṭabaqāt-e nāṣeri*, tr. I, 67 n. 2.

The uncritical Tehran lithograph of 1307/1889–90 made by the well-known Indo-Persian scholar Sayyed Aḥmad Adib Pishāvari (d. 1930)[120] and written by a distinguished calligrapher of the time, Moḥammad Ḥasan Golpāyagāni, was based partly on Morley's edition but mainly on a very recent manuscript in the Tehran Majlis Library or on one closely related to it; its text is in general more correct than Morley's edition and tends to represent the "Persian" tradition. A commentary which Pishāvari wrote was incorporated, with corrections, by Saʿid Nafisi in his subsequent edition of Tehran 1319–32/1940–53 (see below).

There is no need to discuss in great detail the modern editions of the twentieth century, listed by Lazard and Yusofi, but some general remarks may be made. It was not until the three-volume edition of Saʿid Nafisi mentioned above that scholars had before them a critical text of the *History*, for Nafisi gave a plethora of variants from several manuscripts and appended extensive historical and biographical notes, using material from both his predecessor Adib Pishāvari and himself, to the text; although what he did manage to put together as a commentary was unfortunately only a small part of what was planned, and what exists is essentially an uncritical compilation, the sheer quantity of material assembled is impressive. The same may be said of Nafisi's two-volume *Dar pirāmun-e Tārikh-e Beyhaqi*, in which all the passages of later Persian works citing or apparently using material from Beyhaqi are given *in extenso* (see above, p. 38). The edition of the *History* by Qāsem Ghani and ʿAli Akbar Fayyāż, Tehran 1324/1946, marked a step forward, since it took into account a Mashhad manuscript, and, not being overloaded with the numerous variants that Nafisi had included in his text, provided smoother reading. But it is Fayyāż's improved text of Mashhad 1350/1971 (with later reprints from Tehran, including in the third one of 1374/1995 a useful glossary of less usual words and phrases, *loghāt va tarkibāt*, occurring in the text, prepared by Moḥammad Jaʿfar Yāḥaqqi) that provides the best critical text so far available: the layout is more attractive, there is more paragraphing and some more provision of headings, and there is European-style punctuation which is usually intelligently done and is helpful in marking off units of text and speech when Beyhaqi is

[120] See on him *EI*² Suppl. art. "Adīb Pī<u>sh</u>āwarī" (L. P. Elwell-Sutton).

being particularly terse and elliptic. This is the text that has provided the essential basis for the present translation. It was unfortunate that Fayyāż's death prevented him from writing a fuller Introduction than the present twelve or so-page survey of the manuscripts of the *History* (see above, p. 44), useful though this is, and his explanatory glosses (*taʿliqāt*) only go up to p. 223 of the edited text (see below). Subsequent prints, e.g. by ʿAli Eḥsāni (Tehran 1358/1980) and Khalil Khaṭib-Rahbar (three vols., Tehran 1374/1995) have not surpassed Fayyāż's achievement. Both these last are based on Fayyāż's text; Rahbar's edition does not have an apparatus criticus but gives instead extensive philological notes on the text, clearly meant for modern Persian readers who find Beyhaqi's archaic usages difficult, plus detailed indices.

Fayyāż meant to tackle some at least of the many difficulties in Beyhaqi's text as it has come down to us in a series of supplementary notes (*taʿliqāt*) appended to his text of the *History*, but, as mentioned above, his death before his text of the *History* went to press meant that he was unfortunately unable to get very far with these.[121] A limited contribution towards filling this gap has been made by Aḥmad Mahdavi Dāmghāni, who in his "Yād-dāsht-hā'i bar Tārikh-e Beyhaqi" "Notes on Beyhaqi's History"[122] deals with certain passages and words of the text, but a full-scale study of the text and its multiple problems is very much a desideratum.

It is relevant to note here that the Beyhaqi memorial volume, appearing at the same time as Fayyāż's edition and also at Mashhad, contains, amongst numerous papers read at a conference on Beyhaqi held in 1349/1970, several articles which help elucidate linguistic, historical and geographical problems within the *History*'s text; these articles will be noted as need arises to cite them.[123] Finally, a recent work by Sayyed Aḥmad Ḥoseyni Kāzaruni provides a study of the author; a detailed vocabulary, with supporting citations, of proper names and

---

121 F 964–83.

122 In *Majmuʿa-i az maqālāt-e ostād doktor Aḥmad Mahdavi Dāmghāni*, ed. Sayyed ʿAli Moḥammad Sajjādi, Tehran 1381/2002, 641–64 (I am grateful to Mr Ashtiany for supplying me with a copy of this).

123 [Mashhad University, Faculty of Letters and Human Sciences.] *Yād-nāma-ye Abu'l-Fażl-e Beyhaqi*, Mashhad 1350/1971, with both English-language and Persian-language sections.

toponyms in the *History*; and some note also of various titles and technical terms occurring in the text.[124]

It was Morley's merit that his pioneering Bibliotheca Indica edition brought Beyhaqi's *History* to the attention of the scholarly community in the West, or rather, to the exiguous handful of European specialists concerned with the medieval Eastern Iranian world, Central Asia and Northwestern India. Hence within a decade of Morley's text's appearance, the German scholar Eduard Sachau (1845–1930), at that time working in Vienna, used Beyhaqi's very detailed information on the relations of Maḥmud of Ghazna with the last Ma'munid Khwarazm Shahs and the province's subsequent history under Ghaznavid occupation in his "Zur Geschichte und Chronologie von Khwârazm," *SBWAW*, phil. hist. Cl., LXXIII–LXXIV (1973). In parallel to this, the Russian scholar Wilhelm Barthold (V. V. Bartol'd) (1869–1930) drew upon Beyhaqi's accounts of Ghaznavid-Qarakhanid diplomatic contacts and military clashes in his doctoral dissertation *Turkestan v epokhu mongol'skogo nashestviya* (St. Petersburg 1900), the basis of the English translation (actually by Sir E. Denison Ross) *Turkestan down to the Mongol invasion* (London 1928). Apart from a lesser amount of material in the works of his two contemporaries ʿOtbi and Gardizi (see above), and material, possibly contemporary but of rather mysterious provenance, contained in the thirteenth-century historian ʿEzz al-Din Ebn al-Athir's general history, *al-Kāmel fi 'l-ta'rikh* "The perfect work on history," Beyhaqi is the main literary source for the history of Khwarazm and Transoxania during the first half of the eleventh century.

Scholars of the calibre of Sachau and Barthold could use Beyhaqi's Persian text directly, but for those non-orientalists interested in the history of northwestern India, some episodes of the *History*'s information on events at Masʿud's court and on the Ghaznavid plunder raids into India and the warfare there with the Indian princes were made accessible in English translation as part of that multi-volume monument to mid-Victorian Anglo-Indian scholarship, *The history of India as told by its own historians. The Muhammadan period*, compiled by Sir Henry M. Elliot and John Dowson (see above, n. 107), with the translated extracts from Beyhaqi at Vol. II, 53–154. These translations

[124] *Pezhuheshi dar aʿlām-e tārikhi va joghrāfiyā'i-i Tārikh-e Beyhaqi, bā dhekr-e ḥavādeth-e zamān-e nevisanda*, Tehran 1374/1995.

introduced Beyhaqi to a wider readership and conveyed something of the flavour of his *History*. Elliot himself made several of the translations, although others seem to have been made for Elliot by native Indian munshees, who at times misunderstood the Persian ludicrously, so that they could not form an accurate basis for the Islamic history of northwestern India in early Ghaznavid times. The Parsee scholar S.H. Hodivala was in fact to devote a substantial section of his *Studies in Indo-Muslim history. A critical commentary on Elliot and Dowson's "History of India as told by its own historians"* (2 vols., Bombay 1939–57), *inter alia* to correcting the mistranslations, thereby providing a searching and valuable exposition of the translated passages and the historical and geographical problems arising from them.

Not exactly a literal translation into French but a very detailed résumé of Beyhaqi's *History*, with several key episodes translated in full, was the survey of Masʿud's reign prefixed by the French scholar and lexicographer Albin de Biberstein Kazimirski to his pioneer edition and translation of the Divān of the early Ghaznavid poet Manuchehri, *Menoutchehri, poète persan du 11ème siècle de notre ère (du 5ième de l'hégire)*, Paris 1886, as its Introduction (pp. 17–131).

Modern translations of the *History* have had to wait until the second half of the twentieth century. An Arabic one, *Taʾrikh al-Beyhaqi*, was made by Yaḥyā al-Khashshāb and Ṣādeq Nashʾat (Cairo 1376/1957 and later reprints) from the Ghani and Fayyāż text. Given the fact that so few modern Arabs have a first-hand knowledge of Persian language, literature, history and culture, the translation performed a service in making available to the Arabophone audience a work with virtually no equivalent, in its scope and insights, within classical Arabic literature. But the translators were not well-equipped for their task in that they clearly had only a very superficial knowledge of background Ghaznavid history and of the administrative and military terminology of the sources on the Eastern Iranian world during the relevant period. When they were defeated by difficult or unusual Persian words or phrases, they simply left them out, and the best they could do with the not inconsiderable amount of Persian poetry quoted by Beyhaqi was to précis it, thus making no attempt to convey the flavour and subtlety of the original verses.

A Russian translation of the *History*, made on the basis of the Ghani and Fayyāż text, was published soon afterwards by the Soviet scholar, working at the Uzbek SSR Academy of Sciences in Tashkent, A. K. Arends, as *Istoriya Masʿūda (1030–1041)* (Tashkent 1962, revised edition, Moscow 1969). The present writer is not qualified to assess the translation, but a favourable review of it was made by the Polish scholar Bogdan Składanek, see above, n. 77. Arends' annotation is minimal and the *Kommentariy* comprises less than forty pages, but the *Prilozheniya* give translations from later works citing Beyhaqi, including the extensive quotations from the *Maqāmāt-e Abu Naṣr-e Moshkān* in ʿAqili's *Āthār al-vozarāʾ*, and there is a *Glossary* of technical terms. A modern Turkish translation by Necati Lugal (1878–1964), to be published by the Turkish Historical Society, is mentioned in the memorial volume devoted to him as being amongst his yet unpublished works at his death,[125] but information seems to be lacking as to whether this was ever subsequently published.

Other scholars have translated certain episodes of the *History* into Western languages as part of e.g. collections of translations from Persian literature (as in Henri Massé's *Anthologie persane (XIe–XIXe siècles)*, Paris 1950), or in general studies on Beyhaqi and his work (as in the twelve Appendices to Marilyn Robinson Waldman's *Toward a theory of historical narrative*, Columbus, Ohio 1980, and the *Scelta di brani in traduzione* in Filippo Bertotti's *L'opera dello storico persiano Bayhaqī*, Naples 1991. A dramatic episode like the arraignment and execution of the vizier Ḥasanak, in which Beyhaqi shows his narrative power and empathy with the victim, has been an especial favourite for translation and literary and historical analysis from the time of Elliot and Dowson's work onwards. See, e.g., Gilbert Lazard, "Un mémorialiste persan du XIe siècle: Bayhaqī," in *Études de civilisation médiévale (IX–XII siècles). Mélanges offerts à Edmond-René Labande à l'occasion de son départ à la retraite et du XXe anniversaire du CESCM*, Poitiers 1974, 471–78; Homa Katouzian, "The execution of Amir Hasanak the Vizier. Some lessons for the historical sociology of Iran," in *Iranian history and politics. The dialectic of state and society*, London and New York 2003, 250–63; and Julie Scott Meisami, "Exemplary lives, exemplary deaths: the execution of Ḥasanak," in *Actas XVI Congreso UEAI*, Salamanca 1995, 358–64.

---

[125] *Necati Lugal armağanı*, Türk Tarih Kurumu, Ankara 1968, p. XVI.

The present translation is thus the first complete one to appear in a Western European language. The difficulties facing the translator—apart from the sheer length of the text, running to 945 pages in Fayyāż's edition—have been considerable. The state of the surviving text, far from satisfactory, has been outlined above, but a great handicap for the translator of any early Persian prose text like Beyhaqi's *History* is the lack of adequate *Hilfsmittel.* Works on the position of Beyhaqi's style within the linguistic and grammatical development of early New Persian prose are surveyed below in section 5, but the absence of an historical dictionary of pre-modern New Persian is a deeply-felt lack. Scholars working in Avestan and Old Persian and in Middle Persian are better off here, as also are Arabists who have the lexicographical works of Dozy, Nöldeke, Blachère and Ullmann, several vocabularies appended to editions of history and poetical *diwāns*, and numerous dialect dictionaries (e.g. for Syrian, Palestinian, Yemeni, Maghribi, etc. Arabic) which often throw light on earlier stages of the language.

The indigenous lexicographical tradition for Persian developed comparatively late. Apart from the succinct *Loghat-e fors* "Language of the Persians" compiled in the mid-eleventh century by the poet Asadi Ṭusi, aimed at explaining some 1,200 archaic and unusual words found in early Persian poetry, Persian lexicography did not take off till the fourteenth century. The first works at this time tended to be concerned with the Persian glosses to the Arabic text of the Qor'ān, but the centre of compilation for dictionaries proper speedily moved to Muslim India, where the court culture of the various Islamic dynasties there was essentially Persian-based up to the nineteenth century; standard, easily accessible works here for scholars, compiled during the seventeenth century, have been Moḥammad Borhān b. Khalaf's *Borhān-e qāṭeʿ* and ʿAbd al-Rashid Tattavi's *Farhang-e rashidi.*[126] Although there are plenty of modern dictionaries of Persian (MacKenzie described them as "legion"), and a work like Dehkhodā's *Loghat-nāma* represents a tremendous achievement, the modern scholar of earlier New Persian still wishes for a convenient dictionary arranged on historical lines and with *shavāhed*, explanatory examples from the literature of the

[126] See on the state of Persian lexicography, *EI*² art. "Ḳāmūs. 2. Persian lexicography" (D.N. MacKenzie); C.A. Storey, *Persian literature, a bio-bibliographical survey. III/1. A. Lexicography. B. Grammar. C. Prosody and poetics*, London 1984, 1ff.

time. J. A. Vullers' *Lexicon persico-latinum etymologicum* has served scholars well for nearly a century and half, but it has the disadvantage for us today of being in a language no longer so universally understood, even amongst scholars, as it was for our forebears. Nor do we have for Persian the lexical studies and vocabularies appended to many modern editions of classical Arabic texts, as has just been mentioned; a work like Fritz Wolff's *Glossar zu Firdosis Schahname* demonstrates for us the breadth and the limits of Ferdowsi's poetic vocabulary but tells us nothing about the words themselves. In several places of Beyhaqi's text this lack of an historical dictionary—which ideally should be for the present purposes one of the language in its Samanid, Ghaznavid and Seljuq stages—has been acutely felt. Beyhaqi uses words which were no doubt transparent to him at the time but which are to modern readers distinctly opaque and even mysterious and have baffled recent editors like Ghani and Fayyāż. Thus for the elucidation of certain architectural terms, frequently used by Beyhaqi hence not rarities in his time, such as *nim-tark* and *khavāza*,[127] context is of limited help, and their precise meaning may never be recovered.

Numerous of the place names mentioned by Beyhaqi when he describes Sultan Masʿud's campaigns, his progresses through his territories or his hunting trips across the countryside of what is now Afghanistan, likewise present problems of identification for us today. In describing such a region, the classical Arabic geographers of the time often lacked much information about what were to them the remote eastern margins of the Islamic world, and even the very useful and informative, almost contemporary, Persian geographical work by an unknown local author, the *Ḥodud al-ʿālam*, with the magisterial commentary composed in our time by Minorsky, does not give every answer. Given the conservatism of much of the toponomastics in this region, the researches of indigenous Afghan scholars like the late ʿAbd al-Ḥayy Ḥabibi, in various of his published works, have been valuable, and if ever the state of present-day Afghanistan becomes more settled, topographical investigations in such little-known and out-of-the-way regions as Ghur in central Afghanistan, which have proved worthwhile in the past for both local toponymy and Islamic archaeology,[128] will hopefully be able to be resumed.

[127] See below, Year 421, nn. 118, 188.

[128] See below, Year 421, n. 446.

4. Characterising the *History*: Beyhaqi as historian

The uniqueness within his age of Beyhaqi as a historian has meant that this topic has been well covered, notably by Kenneth Allin Luther in his article "Bayhaqi and the later Seljuq historians: some comparative remarks;"[129] by Roger M. Savory in his article "Abo'l-Fażl Bayhaqī as an historiographer;"[130] by Marilyn R. Waldman in her chapter "The method of the secretary as historian: an analysis of the structure and contents of *Ta'rīkh-i Bayhaqī*;"[131] by R. Stephen Humphreys in his chapter "Bayhaqī and Ibn Taghrībirdī: the art of narrative in Islamic historical writing during the middle periods";[132] by Filippo Bertotti in his chapters "La tradizione storiografica," "Il fine dell'opera" and "Elementi compositivi e tipologie descrittive della Storia;"[133] and by Julie S. Meisami in her article "Dynastic history and ideals of kingship in Bayhaqi's *Tarikh-i Masʿudi*"[134] and, most recently, in the chapter "Historiography in the Ghaznavid period" in her book on early medieval Persian historical writing.[135] Hence only a few general remarks are required here; for a fuller consideration of this topic, see the above works.

One of the first things that strikes a reader of the *History* is its length and its discursiveness, even in the truncated form which we now possess, and Beyhaqi himself was well aware of this. Anticipating criticism of the work's inordinate length, he asserts the paramount claims of completeness and of doing justice to the actors concerned in the events:

> Other chronicles do not have such length and breadth as this one, since they have dealt with historical events in a comparatively simple and relaxed manner, and they invoke but a whiff of the past. However, now that I have embarked on this task, I want to do this *History* full justice and delve into every nook and cranny so that no aspect of the events remains obscure. And should this book become overlong, and should

129 In *Yād-nāma-ye Abu'l-Fażl-e Beyhaqi*, English section. 14–33.
130 *Ibid.*, 84–128.
131 *Toward a theory of historical narrative*, 51–78.
132 *Islamic history, a framework for enquiry*, revised ed. Princeton 1991, 128–47.
133 *L'opera dello storico persiano Bayhaqī*, 37–87.
134 In *Edebiyat*, III (1989), 57–77.
135 *Persian historiography to the end of the twelfth century*, 79–108.

> the readers become increasingly weary in its perusal, I place my trust in their gracious learning, lest they account me a prolix bore; for there is nothing that is not worth reading, since, after all, there is no tale or episode that does not convey at least one useful point.[136]

The freshness of his ideas on history writing is seen in the contempt which he expresses for what the Oxford philosopher of history R.G Collingwood called "scissors-and-paste history," the juxtaposition of historical facts without any thoughtful analysis of them or the bringing out of any underlying connecting thread and awareness of causation. Hence Beyhaqi denounces the kind of history writing where "so-and-so king sent so-and-so commander to such-and-such battle, and on such-and-such day they made peace, and this one beat that one or that one this, they went on thus."[137] He likewise castigates the popular love of wonders and exaggerated stories:

> [Unfortunately,] the mass of common people are so constituted that they prefer what is absurd and impossible [rather than the truth], such as stories of demons and fairies and evil spirits inhabiting the deserts, mountains and seas, as when some fool kicks up a commotion and a throng of people equally foolish gathers round him, and he goes on to say, "In a certain sea, I saw an island, and five hundred of us landed on that island; we baked bread and set up cooking pots, and when the fire got really hot and the heat penetrated into that ground, it moved, we looked, and [lo,] it was a fish." Or, "On a certain mountain I saw such-and-such things, and an old woman who was sorceress changed a man into an ass, and then another old sorceress smeared his ear with some kind of unguent and changed him back into human form," and other nonsensical tales like these which, when read at night-time to ignorant people, induce sleep. Those people who seek the truth so that they may afford it credence are accounted amongst the people who [really] have knowledge, but their number is exceedingly small: they accept what is honest and true and reject false statements.[138]

As against such a credulous and uncritical approach, Beyhaqi shows an insight into historical method and source criticism:

> Historical reports about the past are said to be of two kinds, and no third kind is recognized: either one must hear them from some person

[136] Gh 11, F 11.

[137] Gh 354, F 451.

[138] Gh 666–67, F 905.

> or else one must read them in a written document or book. The necessary condition for the former is that the informant should be trustworthy and veracious, and, moreover, one's intellect should testify to the soundness of that report and the Word of God must support it, since it has been said, *"Don't give credence to any reports that are not acceptable to your judgement."* The case is exactly the same with a written document or book: whatever historical reports have been read which the intellect finds no reason to reject, the person hearing them should accept as accurate, and wise men should listen to them and accept them.[139]

As a consequence of such principles, he lays down as his own guiding one that, whatever he wrote should be based on reliable documentation, such as official papers which he saw or of which he acquired copies during his professional career, or else on personal observation or the evidence of reliable informants whose credibility was personally known to him. The directness and freshness of his material is frequently emphasized by his interposing phrases such as "I, Abu'l-Fażl, saw such-and-such with my own eyes ..." He was, of course, personally involved in many of the Sultan's campaigns (including Masʿud's last, disastrous expedition to Danadānqān against the Seljuqs) since the divāns or administrative departments accompanied the sovereign and formed part an integral part of the court apparatus. When he had no first-hand knowledge, such as for events before his own career in the bureaucracy began, he sought out the requisite information from some more senior colleague in the administration; thus he got an eyewitness account of Prince Masʿud's youthful bravery in the course of an expeditions into the pagan enclave of Ghur in central Afghanistan from the secretary ʿAbd al-Ghaffār fifty years after the event in question.[140] As noted above, section 2, p. 35, during the course of his official duties Beyhaqi had frequently to make copies of official documents such as contracts of appointment and treaties with outside powers, but lost these when he fell from favour in Sultan ʿAbd al-Rashid's reign so that, in some cases he was unable to quote these documents verbatim. If he had been able to keep his own exact copies, his *History*, so he says, would have had a different complexion.[141] As it was,

139 Gh 666, F 904–05.
140 Gh 109–10, F 130–31.
141 Gh 294, F 389.

he had to spend years in searching for the text of Masʿud's pledge of allegiance, *beyʿat-nāma*, to the new ʿAbbasid caliph al-Qāʾem before he came across it in the possession of the son of his master Abu Naṣr Moshkān.[142]

After the length and discursiveness of the *History*, the other striking feature of it is Beyhaqi's continual use of interpolations and digressions of various kinds—poetry, historical anecdotes, stories with moral and ethical examples, etc.—within the flow of the historical narrative.[143] Beyhaqi himself was aware that these interpolations interrupted the main thread of his narrative, and after giving such passages he often apologises for them and emphasizes that he is now returning to the main thread of his discourse.

The interpolated matter includes a fair amount of poetry, both Arabic and Persian. In his citation of poetry within historical narrative, Beyhaqi was following an old-established, very widespread technique of Arab historians from the compilers of the *Sira* or biography of the Prophet onwards.[144] The Arabic poetical tradition was, of course, so much older and richer than the New Persian one, which had arisen essentially only in the century preceding Beyhaqi's own one, and amidst the whole corpus of poetry cited, on a simple numerical count of poems, fragments and single verses quoted, there is an apparent preponderance of Arabic citations over Persian ones: fifty-two Arabic ones over nineteen Persian ones. These Arabic citations do include three lengthy poems, two of which would be familiar to all literate persons of Beyhaqi's time, namely, part of a *marthiya* or elegy by Abu'l-Ḥasan Moḥammad b. ʿOmar Anbāri on the Buyid vizier Ebn al-Baqiyya and seventeen verses from a *qaṣida* or eulogistic ode of Abu'l-Ṭayyeb Motanabbi addressed to his patron the Ḥamdānid Amir Seyf al-Dowla (the third citation being a composition from Beyhaqi's own

142 Gh 288, F 381.

143 Specifically noted and discussed in detail by e.g. Waldman, *op. cit.*, 53ff., Bertotti, *op. cit.*, 75ff., and Meisami, *op. cit.*, 86ff.

144 See Geert Jan van Gelder, "Poetry in historiography: some observations," in Maróth (ed.), *Problems in Arabic literature*, 1–13. Van Gelder makes the observation (p. 9) that the use of poetry in Persian historical writing does not seem to have been as widespread as in the Arabic one. This may well be true for the earlier period, but closer examination is required: following Beyhaqi, there is a fair amount of poetic citation in a late Seljuq historian like Rāvandi and an early Mongol one like Joveyni, and the usage thereafter becomes an established one.

time, from the reign of Sultan Mowdud b. Masʿud, i.e. a poetic contest, a *monāẓara*, involving an exchange of poems between Abu Sahl Zowzani and a certain Qāżi Manṣur).[145] But most of the remaining Arabic citations tend to be of a single line or of two lines, often of an aphoristic nature and clearly tumbling forth from the recesses of Beyhaqi's memory (not forgetting verses composed by himself, see above, section 2, p. 33) when an historical parallel could be brought forward or a moral pointed by an apposite quotation. In general, Beyhaqi seems to have had a preference for *moḥdath* or "new wave" poetry, that of the high ʿAbbasid period, rather than for that of the preceding Umayyad and pre-Islamic periods; the near-absence of poetry from the latter period (at least, amongst the verses whose authors or origins can be pinpointed; the only named poet would appear to be ʿAdi b. Zeyd[146]) may come from Beyhaqi's clear lack of sympathy with the pre-Islamic past, Arab or Persian, in general.[147]

However, while Arabic citations preponderate over Persian ones in mere number, the Persian ones add up to a considerably greater number of actual lines of poetry than the Arabic ones (325 lines of Persian vs. 148 of Arabic); these tend to be made up of longer quotations and of substantial, complete poems. Samanid poets like Rudaki and Daqiqi were favourites of Beyhaqi. But it is strange that there are no quota-

[145] Rubinacci, in his study of the poetry in ʿOtbi's history, "Le citazioni poetiche nell' al-Taʾrīḫ al-Yamīnī di Abū Naṣr al-ʿUtbī," in *A Francesco Gabrieli. Studi orientalistici offerti nel sessantesimo compleano dai suoi colleghi e discepoli*, Rome 1964, 263–78, made the point (at *ibid.*, 271) that ʿOtbi cites many more verses by Abu Tammām than of Motanabbi; he concluded that, in ʿOtbi's time (sc. the opening decades of the eleventh century), Motanabbi had not yet overtaken Abu Tammām in general popularity, as he was apparently so to do by the time Beyhaqi was writing (in the latter's *History*, Motanabbi is, statistically speaking, the most often-cited of the *moḥdath* poets; see the article of Bosworth cited below in n. 147, at p. 47).

[146] See below, Year 422 n. 346.

[147] See in general on this Arabic poetry, Abu'l-Qāsem "Novid" Ḥabibollāhi, "Maʾākhedh-e ashʿār-e ʿarabi-ye Tārikh-e Beyhaqi va moʿarrefi-ye guyandagān-e ān-hā," in *Yād-nāma-ye Abu'l-Fażl-e Beyhaqi*, Persian section, 744–77; Bosworth, "The poetical citations in Baihaqī's *Taʾrīkh-i Masʿūdī*," in *XX. Deutscher Orientalistentag vom 3. bis 8. Oktober 1977 in Erlangen, Vorträge = ZDMG*, Supplement IV, ed. W. Voigt, Wiesbaden 1980, 41–56. On Beyhaqi's apparent contempt for the pre-Islamic Persian past, see below, p. 61, Year 423 n. 143 and Year 424 n. 91.

tions (always with the qualification that we possess only a small part of the *Mojalladāt*) from Ferdowsi's *Shāh-nāma* "Book of kings"or from other writers in the Iranian epic tradition; this absence seems to be an aspect of Beyhaqi's lack of interest in Iranian legendary history and the pre-Islamic past, to be discussed below. Of his contemporaries, the early Ghaznavid lyric and panegyric poets, Beyhaqi states that he has given several outstanding odes by ʿOnṣori in praise of Sultan Maḥmud, but these must have been inserted in the lost *Tārikh-e Yamini* section of the *Mojalladāt*; in the extant *Tārikh-e Masʿudi* there figure a mere two lines by this poet. Verses by Farrokhi and Manuchehri do not appear at all in the *Tārikh-e Masʿudi*, although both were eulogists of Sultans Moḥammad and Masʿud and their servants; he does, however, mention the court poets ʿOnṣori, ʿAsjadi, Zeynabi and Farrokhi as amongst the masters of poetry of the age.[148] What is, however, notable is that Beyhaqi gives the complete texts of four long, elaborate odes (totalling 261 verses) by one of his contemporaries, the religious lawyer Abu Ḥanifa Eskāfi, who was personally known to Beyhaqi and from whom the historian requested complete texts of the poems.[149] Regarding their themes, notable are the poet's efforts to justify Masʿud's succession and the setting-aside of Moḥammad (still significant and sensitive issues for a poet like Eskāfi writing at the beginning of the reign of Sultan Ebrāhim, Masʿud's son) and, writing towards the end of Masʿud's reign, to hearten and inspirit the Sultan after his disastrous defeat by the Seljuqs.[150] Since little is otherwise known of Eskāfi beyond his name and exiguous citations of his work by later anecdotalists and literary biographers like Neẓāmi ʿArużi Samarqandi, Beyhaqi has performed a signal service for Persian literary history by preserving these texts.[151]

---

148 Gh 280, F 372.

149 Gh 275–80, 381–82, 382–84, 635–38, F 361–71, 487–89, 489–93, 854–62.

150 W.F. Heinrichs, cited in van Gelder, *op. cit.*, 5, would accordingly classify these poems as "commentary" ones, rather than "action" ones, later reflections upon and explanations of events later than what recorded in the historical work in question, but van Gelder (p. 6) rightly questions whether the two categories are so mutually exclusive.

151 On the Persian verses in the *History*, see Żiyāʾ al-Din Sajjādi, "Taḥqiq dar ashʿār u amthāl-e fārsi-ye Tārikh-e Beyhaqi," in *Yād-nāma-ye Abu'l-Fażl-e Beyhaqi*, Persian section, 273–332.

A residue remains of both the Arabic and Persian citations, especially when a single line or two or three lines only are involved, whose authorship is unmentioned by Beyhaqi and whose origins cannot be pinned down. It may well be that some of these had become popular aphorisms whose origins were confused or lost with the lapse of time; only a scholar extremely well versed in the Arabic and Persian literature of the first four centuries of Islam could perhaps pin down more of these verses (as did, for instance, Mirzā Moḥammad Qazvini for many of the citations in ʿAṭā-Malek Joveyni's *Tārikh-e Jahāngoshāy* "History of the world-conqueror" when he was editing the text of this work).

At all events, it seems reasonable to take the inclusion of the poetic citations within Beyhaqi's narrative as being in part for reasons of adornment (*ārastagi, ārāyesh*) and for the adducing of wonders (*ʿajāʾeb*) and of rare and unusual points (*navāder, gharāʾeb*), but also for didactic reasons: Beyhaqi frequently stresses that homilectic and moral benefits (*favāʾed, ʿebar*) are involved, and he uses verses to point morals for specific events (see further on this point, below, p. 65). The implied themes of Abu Ḥanifa Eskāfi's poems have been noted above, and the lengthy set piece of Ḥasanak's fall and execution provides the occasion for adducing both historical anecdotes and verses on such topics as the perils arising from the inexperience of youth or the failure to guard one's tongue. It was nothing unusual for poetic citations to appear in works primarily concerned with history or biography (and he cannot have been unaware of his fellow-historian ʿOtbi's use of poetry in *al-Taʿrikh al-Yamini*); in any case, the taste for poetry as an aesthetic experience was as universal in Beyhaqi's time as it has been at other times and in other regions of the Islamic cultural world.

The didactic element is strong in the interpolated prose passages and stories which, as being both numerous and often lengthy, are such a feature of Beyhaqi's *History*. The range of subject matter from earlier times is fairly limited. There is a single story about the Prophet Moses and his care, while a shepherd in Midian, for a lamb, Moses being, of course, an important figure in the line of prophets leading up to their seal, Moḥammad.[152] Another single story concerns Bozorjmehr, the semi-legendary chief minister of the Sasanid emperor Khosrow

[152] Gh 204–05, F 258–59.

Anushirvān, but this is not really an exception to Beyhaqi's lack of interest in the pre-Islamic past since, as noted below, Year 423 n. 143, Bozorjmehr is treated here as a proto-Muslim martyr.[153] But it must be stressed that Beyhaqi, although himself a Persian, shows virtually no interest in the pre-Islamic past of Persia, and the anecdotes and stories which he inserts in his narrative are, with the partial exception just mentioned, exclusively Islamic; if anything, he shows himself distinctly hostile to what might be called Persian currents and influences surviving into Islamic life and culture.[154] Hence for Beyhaqi, what is really of significance in human history begins with the revelation of Islam with the Prophet Moḥammad, and what is interesting to him personally in Islamic history starts with the ʿAbbasids. Even stories from the time of the Prophet, the Companions, the Patriarchal Caliphs and the Umayyads are very sparse: the Caliph ʿOmar puts in an appearance to elucidate the citation of a line by a poet of the time, Ḥoṭeyʾa, and the fortitude of the mother of the anti-caliph ʿAbdallāh b. Zobeyr, at the time of his death in battle, is adduced as a parallel to the similar *ṣabr* or fortitude of the mother of the executed Ḥasanak when faced with her son's publicly gibbeted corpse.[155]

It is, accordingly, the ʿAbbasid period, merging into the ascendancy of the Buyids over the caliphs, that provides a goodly number of stories for Beyhaqi. One or two historical sources are specifically named, such as the *Ketāb al-Owrāq* "Book of the leaves [of historical writing]" by the ʿAbbasid historian and littérateur Abu Bakr Ṣuli and the *Ketāb al-Tāj* "Book of the crown" by the historian and eulogist of the Buyids Abu Esḥāq Ebrāhim al-Ṣābi.[156] More often, however, Beyhaqi vaguely says that he has drawn his stories from "historical narratives about the caliphs," *akhbār-e kholafāʾ*, or "historical narratives about

[153] Gh 333–36, F 425–28.

[154] Cf. the very unfavourable picture of the Afshin Kheydhar (see below, pp. 63–64), described as *in sag-e nā-khᵛishtan-shenās nim kāfer* "this dog who does not acknowledge his own status, [that] semi-infidel" (Gh 173, F 214, etc.) and stigmatised in other opprobrious terms as a representative of the older Iranian attitudes, and see in general on Beyhaqi's indifference to the pre-Islamic past, Meisami, *Persian historiography to the end of the twelfth century,* 107–08.

[155] Gh 189–93, 238, F 236–42, 308.

[156] See on these two works below, Year 421 n. 141, and (on the latter one specifically) Year 422 n. 199; and for biographical details on Abu Bakr Ṣuli, below, Year 431 n. 31.

the ʿAbbasid caliphs," *akhbār-e kholafāʾ-e ʿAbbāsiyān*. but such stories seem to come from a tradition of historical writing that was more part of *adab* literature than from the sober historical chronicles, in which the stories cannot usually in fact be found.[157] Nor can there be traced, amongst the works of *adab*, the *Laṭāʾef ḥiyal al-kofāt* "[Tales about] the subtleties of the stratagems of capable people," into which Yaḥyā the Barmakid dipped in order to divert and soothe his mind.[158] Perhaps as a result of this, the stories concerning the period before the later Samanids (when Beyhaqi could get first-hand information about this from older contemporaries, see below), are not characterised by historical accuracy. Nevertheless, Waldman suggests that this does not necessarily mean that Beyhaqi was slapdash and careless in handling his materials but may merely reflect the fact that he had to use what material was at hand for him in Ghazna, remote as it was from the Islamic heartlands, material perhaps oral as well as literary; and in any case, what was important for him in retailing these stories was not so much historical reality as the pattern of past events as they paralleled what was happening during Masʿud's reign, i.e. his aim was strongly didactic (see further on Beyhaqi's search for parallels to contemporary events, below).[159] Waldman's conclusions here seem convincing, given the fact that, when dealing with events of his own time, Beyhaqi stresses the care he took to find the best sources, those with authentic and reliable information.

Beyhaqi's stories set in the ʿAbbasid period include one about the arrangements made by Hārun al-Rashid concerning his three sons and the succession to the caliphate after his death (the arrangements set forth in the so-called "Meccan Letters"). Since this interpolation comes within Beyhaqi's narrative of the events of Moḥammad's deposition and Masʿud's assumption of power, the parallel must have been obvious to Beyhaqi's readers, especially as the person who sows dissension between the brothers al-Amin and al-Maʾmun and who controverts Hārun's intended provisions for an amicable division of power is al-Amin's vizier and chief adviser Fażl b. Rabiʿ, whose villainous role here would be applied by contemporaries to that of Abu

[157] See for discussions of Beyhaqi's sources here, Waldman, *Toward a theory of historical narrative*, 69–71, and below, Year 421 n. 141.

[158] Gh 418, F 539.

[159] *Op. cit.*, 71–72.

Sahl Zowzani in the dispute between Moḥammad and Masʿud—another instance of Beyhaqi's apparent belief that bad monarchs become so through the nefarious influence and bad advice of their evil counsellors.[160]

Given the long-lasting interest to medieval Muslims of the story of the Barmakids, their rise to power in the state under Hārun al-Rashid and their sudden fall (a resonance especially strong within the Persian cultural area),[161] it would be strange if Beyhaqi did not allude to them at several places in the course of his narrative. Thus Jaʿfar b. Yaḥyā Barmaki is adduced in connection with the story of Ḥasanak, how the domination of servants within the state will not, in the long run, be brooked by monarchs zealous to regain all the reins of power within their own hands.[162] The justice of Fażl b. Yaḥyā's period of governorship in Khorasan and his care not to bleed dry the tax-payers there—which Hārun at first contrasted unfavourably with the huge sums of money and presents that his successor in Khorasan, the tyrannical governor ʿAli b. ʿIsā b. Māhān, brought in for the Baghdad treasury—is adduced as a parallel to the financial oppression of Masʿud's civil governor in Khorasan, Suri. The parallel is hammered home by the fact that Fażl tells the caliph of the dangers to Khorasan from the Turks in the adjacent steppes, while Beyhaqi emphasizes that the Masʿud's eventual loss of the loyalty and confidence of the people of Khorasan could in large measure be laid at the door of Suri, whose exactions made the subjects there feel that life under the Seljuq Turks could not be worse and might conceivably be better.[163] A brief tale about Jaʿfar's immense administrative efficiency, and his care always to keep abreast of paper work and not let things pile up, is used to illustrate the secretarial competence of the son-in-law of the Vizier Aḥmad b. ʿAbd al-Ṣamad, Khᵛāja Abu'l-Fatḥ Masʿud Rokhudhi, appointed towards the end of Masʿud's reign to the important post of *kadkhodā* or counsellor and adjutant to the Prince Mowdud.[164] Set two or three decades after the Barmakids' time, namely in the caliphate of al-Moʿtaṣem, is the story of how the caliphal general, the Afshin Kheydhar, sought to encom-

[160] Gh 29–35, F 31–37; cf. Waldman, *op. cit.*, 73–74.

[161] See above, Year 422 n. 191.

[162] Gh 179, cf. 193–94, F 222–23, cf. 242–43.

[163] Gh 414–21, F 533–42.

[164] Gh 654–56, F 885–89.

pass the ruin and death of his Arab rival, the lord of Karaj in western Persia, Abu Dolaf Qāsem ʿEjli. This story is used as a parallel to the episode in Beyhaqi's *History* where the newly-released and restored vizier, Aḥmad b. Ḥasan Meymandi, seeks to get vengeance on the courtier Abu Bakr Ḥaṣiri, who had in the past slighted him, but is restrained from exacting the full penalty by Masʿud's discreet intervention, prompted by the Chief Secretary Abu Naṣr Moshkān, just as Moʿtaṣem rescued Abu Dolaf from death at the Afshin's hands.[165]

Whereas these stories revolving round the ʿAbbasids and their servants may be characterised as extra-historical, at least with regard to their absence from the chronicles of the period, those stories relating to the decline of the Samanids in Transoxania and Khorasan and the genesis of the Ghaznavid state are particularly important as first-hand historical evidence, with many unique details absent from the standard historical sources for the age such as those of ʿOtbi, Gardizi and Ebn al-Athir and from the local history of Bokhara and its rulers by Narshakhi. It is true that the tale (taken, so Beyhaqi says, from the otherwise unknown *akhbār-e Sāmāniyān* "Historical accounts concerning the Samanids") of how the Amir Naṣr (II) b. Aḥmad (II) cured his irascibility and fiery temper[166] is probably pure invention, part of the build-up that seems to have occurred in the general eastern Islamic consciousness of the Samanid amirs as being as exemplary, just and pious orthodox Sunni rulers, who always showed proper deference to their distant nominal suzerains the ʿAbbasid caliphs, unlike their rivals the Saffarids and Buyids. The same mythic quality surrounds the tales about Sebüktegin's early years as a recently-captured Turkish military slave within the Samanid lands, the prelude to his eventual service under Alptegin, and about his tenderness and solicitude even for God's animal creation,[167] these latter traits being part of those making up the image of Sebüktegin as "the Just Amir" that seems to have developed very swiftly around this father-founder of the Ghaznavid dynasty.

It is, however, otherwise with the several passages describing the last years of the Samanid amirate and the internecine warfare which characterised them, with ambitious military commanders like Abu

[165] Gh 172–78, F 213–21.
[166] Gh 106–08, F 126–28.
[167] Gh 201–04, F 253–57.

ʿAli Simjur, Begtuzun, Tāsh, Fāʾeq Khāṣṣa, Sebüktegin himself and his son Maḥmud combining with the incoming Qarakhanids Bughrā Khān Hārun or Ḥasan and the Ilig Naṣr b. ʿAli, all of them hastening to dismember the once-mighty but now terminally enfeebled Samanid kingdom.[168] These stories have the stamp of historical authenticity, and have provided much valuable detail on the politicking and military manoeuvring of the various factions, material additional to what we glean from the standard historical sources mentioned above; Barthold was to make good use of them in reconstructing the detailed narrative of the demise of the Samanid state and the complex events in Khorasan and Transoxania at this time in his *Turkestan down to the Mongol invasion*.[169] These events were, of course, taking place around the time when Beyhaqi was born or was a small child, and the campaigning of the various contenders for power affected the neighbourhoods of Beyhaq and Nishapur where he was being brought up; he may well have derived relevant historical information from the oral testimony of older contemporaries who witnessed events.

In a thoughtful discussion about whether one can discern any rationale behind Beyhaqi's use of all these poetic quotations and interpolated stories,[170] Marilyn Waldman suggested that they apparently serve two related purposes: "To reiterate or reinforce the morals of stories in the narrative, but also to expand, contradict, and comment on the narrative stories to which the interpolations are appended or to set up issues to watch for in narrative stories to come,"[171] and that their inclusion requires Beyhaqi's readers to be thinking analogically as they take in the poetic citations or the stories. Such a need is often specifically stated, e.g. when Beyhaqi argues that a wise man (*kheradmand*) would readily understand that two verses on the beloved's treacherousness, cited as being favourite verses of Amir Moḥammad, in fact applied to the latter's own short period of rule, during which his servants were responsible for many ill-conceived decisions and unwise actions (again the motif that the reprehensible actions of monarchs should often in reality be laid at the doors of their maleficent

[168] Gh 199–201, 205–08, 640–42, F 250–52, 259–63, 864–68.
[169] 254ff.
[170] *Toward a theory of historical narrative*, 68–75.
[171] *Ibid.*, 73.

servants).[172] Waldman goes on tentatively to suggest that Beyhaqi, probably without realizing it, was anticipating Ebn Khaldun's idea that history proceeds in cycles and has repeated patterns, and was implying that the problems facing the Ghaznavid monarchs of his time, in particular, their continuing failure to make sensible choices of successors (see above, section 1, pp. 10–11) were universal ones.[173]

In fact, Beyhaqi seems here to have had a significant predecessor in the writer on philosophy and ethics of the Buyid period, Aḥmad b. Moḥammad Meskaveyh (b. *ca.* 932 and died, according to Yāqut, a centenarian).[174] In addition to his important work on philosophical ethics, the *Tahdhib al-akhlāq* "Refining of morals," Meskaveyh composed in Arabic a universal history (one of first-hand value only for his own time, that of the enfeeblement of the ʿAbbasid caliphate and the rise of the "supreme commanders" or *amir al-omarā*'s to dominance in Iraq and western Persia, the most successful and long-lasting of these being his own masters, the Deylamite Buyids). The very title of this history is significant: *Tajāreb al-omam va-taʿāqeb al-hemam* "Experiences of the nations and the successiveness (or perhaps, "alternating patterns") of human endeavours." Mohammed Arkoun has examined Meskaveyh's introduction to his history and has drawn significant conclusions from it. First, he suggests, Meskaveyh held that history was based on a repetition of events, since, if this were not so, there would be no possibility of a wise man (Beyhaqi's *kheradmand*) drawing any conclusions from their pattern, which would be a mere succession of unrelated and unrelatable happenings. Second, great men and, indeed, people in general, are prey to changes of fortune within the pattern of the rise, florescence and decay of societies, unless measures, military or diplomatic, are set in hand to counter the latter process. Third, one must use rationality in considering historical phenomena and not resort to miraculous or far-fetched stories to explain events.[175]

---

172 Gh 76–77, F 87–88.

173 Waldman, *op. cit.*, 72–75.

174 See on him J.L. Kraemer, *Humanism in the renaissance of Islam. The cultural revival during the Buyid age*, Leiden 1986, 222–33; *EI*² art. "Miskawayh" (M. Arkoun); *EAL*, II, 529–30 art. "Miskawayh" (G. Endress).

175 "Éthique et histoire d'après les Tajârib al-umam," in *Atti del Terzo Congresso di Studi Arabici e Islamici, Ravello 1–6 settembre 1966*, Naples 1967, 84–89.

This last point is almost exactly what Beyhaqi says when he denounces the credulousness and irrationality of the un-wise, not *kheradmand,* mass of people (above, pp. 55–56), but Meskaveyh's whole method of history writing, narrative interspersed with anecdotal and moralising reflections and exhortations, is not dissimilar to Beyhaqi's general procedures in the *History*. That Beyhaqi knew the works of the Buyid scholar, his elder by some two generations, can never be incontrovertibly proven, but is nevertheless not improbable: the early Ghaznavid and Buyid dominions were contiguous, they were both parts of the general Arabo-Persian cultural world of the Islamic East and there had been a perceptible, if not extensive, migration of secretaries and other officials from Buyid service into that of Maḥmud of Ghazna.[176] Meisami does in fact assume that Beyhaqi was familiar with the work of his Arabic historian predecessors and, specifically, with Meskaveyh's *Tahdhib al-akhlāq*, whose influence is seen in his musings during the course of the first *khoṭba* or exordium of his *History*[177] on the qualities of the wise and just man contrasted with the vices of the tyrant.[178] Clearly, there is a speculative element present here, but one senses that ideas like these were beginning to form part of the consciousness of thoughtful writers, and especially those with a philosophical bent, so that Ebn Khaldun was by no means a figure without intellectual antecedents.

Beyhaqi certainly found material in the ʿAbbasid and Samanid past histories for explaining the pattern of events in the earlier part of Masʿud's reign, but he does not seem to have been able to come up with an earlier parallel for the all-dominating problems of Masʿud's later years, the incursions of the Turkmens into Khorasan and the pressure from the Qarakhanids on the upper Oxus region. He could, in fact, have found an analogy from later Sasanid history, when the realm's northeastern frontiers were assailed by the Hephthalites from

[176] Bosworth, *The Ghaznavids*, 59.

[177] See on the two *khoṭbas* and on this first one, in particular, below, Year 421 n. 380.

[178] "Dynastic history and ideals of kingship in Bayhaqi's *Tarikh-i Masʿudi*," 62 n. 20 (where Meisami further suggests that Beyhaqi was, in this *khoṭba*, endeavouring to formulate a Persian vocabulary for philosophical terminology, at the side of the familiar Arabic one, his efforts here having parallels in e.g. the work of Ebn Sinā in his *Dāneshnāma-ye ʿalāʾi*); *eadem*, *Persian historiography to the end of the twelfth century*, 82.

the Inner Asian steppes, as retailed for Muslim audiences in Balʿami's translation of Ṭabari's *History* and in the *Shāh-nāma*; but, as noted above, recourse to the pre-Islamic, infidel past was not part of Beyhaqi's chosen equipment as a historian (as already noted, the story of Bozorjmehr and Khosrow Anushirvān was connectible with Islamic salvation history).

Returning to the topic of Beyhaqi's general attitude towards his task as a historian and publicist of the Ghaznavid dynasty's achievement, he was writing during the reigns of Farrokh-zād and then of Ebrāhim, whose calmer and more settled atmospheres he must have found more congenial for writing after the storm and stress of the middle years of the eleventh century. By the time of these two sultans, apart from his enduring, firm loyalty to the Ghaznavid house Beyhaqi can have had little material reason for writing exaggerated eulogies of either his royal masters or his superiors and other colleagues in the administration. Hence in his *History* he states that his aim is to go beyond a mere recital of historical events involving praise of the greatness and the courage of Amir Masʿud, since those are well-known and contemporaries have been able to witness these for themselves. Instead, he says,

> ... my aim is that I should write a foundation for history (*tārikh-pāya*) that will be of permanent value and raise a lofty structure [upon it] in such a way that the memory of it will remain till the end of time.[179]

He seems, accordingly, to have had in his mind the idea of laying down a model for subsequent Persian history writing, although this was not, in practice, to be fulfilled. His position in Ghazna, on the far edge of the Iranian, and indeed Islamic, cultural world, and the speedy loss after his death of so much of the *History*, must have militated against this; a work of some 140 years later like Rāvandi's chronicle of the Seljuqs, the *Rāḥat al-ṣodur* "Comfort for the Soul," would be more in the tradition of ʿOtbi's *al-Taʿrikh al-Yamini* than that of Beyhaqi.

Beyhaqi had the true historian's attitude of impartiality. He records without comment, letting the facts speak for themselves, the episode when Masʿud, influenced by seductive appeals to his cupidity from the Head of the Army Department (*divān-e ʿarż*) Abu Sahl Zowzani but against the advice of his Vizier Aḥmad b. Ḥasan Meymandi and his

179 Gh 96, F 112.

Chief Secretary Abu Naṣr Moshkān, tried to get back the accession money, *māl-e beyʿat*, expended by Moḥammad in an effort to secure the loyalty of the troops and the civilian officials (see above, section 1, p. 15). The attempt was only partially successful, and created a vast amount of ill-feeling, with the Sultan attempting to foist responsibility for the fiasco on to his servants, including the Vizier. Beyhaqi does not mince words when recounting ugly episodes like Masʿud's procuring of the downfall of ministers or of army commanders who had in the past denigrated him or who had aroused his suspicious nature from their association with the previous régime, such as Maḥmud's old vizier, Ḥasanak, the Turkish generals Eryāruq and Asïghtegin Ghāzi, and his own uncle Yusof b. Sebüktegin, noting that during such times the Sultan would often absent himself from court and spend several days in the countryside or on hunting trips, leaving others to do the required hatchet job and thereby avoiding some of the odium.[180]

Yet, in an age of veneration for the institution of kingship as something buttressed by divine support and approval, even letting the facts speak for themselves cannot have been wholly easy for Beyhaqi, let alone the harbouring of strongly critical thoughts about the conduct of monarchs. As with Christians in the Europe of the Middle Ages and the early modern period, say up to the seventeenth century, premodern Muslims were habituated to believe that the king could do no wrong and that, if things went awry, it was the ruler's wicked servants and evil counsellors who were to blame.[181] Nevertheless, Beyhaqi is often explicit in recording the less attractive side of Masʿud's personality: his obstinacy, his self-will and his failure to listen to disinterested advice, all vices subsumed under the single term *estebdād* (lit. "having sole, unfettered power, with no need to listen to anyone else") and his consequent errors of judgement in dealing with the Turkmen incursions into Khorasan. He realized, too, that his account of the Sultan's behaviour at Āmol in Ṭabarestān, when in 1035 he unleashed

---

180 See e.g. Gh 259, F 339.

181 An attitude still prevailing *de facto* in the totalitarian states of the earlier part of the twentieth century, whether Communist or Fascist or simply based on personal despotism; thus many Germans of the Nazi period persuaded themselves, when instances of arbitrary behaviour, tyranny and corruption came to their notice, that these were the work of officials whose excesses were unknown to the benevolent leader ("wenn der Führer nur das wüsste!").

his army on the town's populace so that they could forcibly collect arrears of tribute, with the result that news of the troops' violence and excesses redounded all over the central and eastern Islamic lands, including as far as Baghdad, was very unflattering to the Sultan: "It is very hard for me to let my pen flow with such words, but I have no choice; there is no partiality in history."[182]

With impartiality in setting down the historical record, there should go fairness, and such a sense seems to have been part of Beyhaqi's nature. During the early part of Masʿud's reign he suffered personally at the hands of Abu Sahl Zowzani, and he says of him that "evil and malevolence were engrained in his nature, and along with that evil, he had no compassion in his heart"; but even though Abu Sahl had been dead for several years by the time Beyhaqi was putting together his *History*, he wanted to be fair to his memory and to avoid charges of parti-pris and prejudice (*taʿaṣṣob va tarabbod*) lest readers think him a cantankerous and resentful old man.[183]

5. Characterising the *History*: style and language

The Persian style of the *Tārikh-e Masʿudi* has evoked widely differing, even diametrically opposed, critical comments, as noted by Waldman.[184] At one pole is the *History*'s first critical editor, Saʿid Nafisi, who characterised its style as archaic and sometimes complicated (the charge of archaicness is hardly surprising in a text from the mid-eleventh century, when New Persian prose as we know it was not much more than a century old!),[185] whereas at the other pole is the historian Mojtaba Minovi, who wrote that "In point of style and language also is his book very interesting: it is full of special words, terms, expressions and turns of phrase that make his writing lively and set a model for

[182] Gh 462, F 600–01; cf. Bosworth, *The Ghaznavids*, 90–91.
[183] Gh 178–79, F 221–22, cf. Bosworth, *op. cit.*, 60–61.
[184] *Toward a theory of historical narrative*, 110.
[185] In his *EI*² art. "Bayhaḳī, Abu'l-Faḍl."

composition in an accurate and sparing language,"[186] a judgement essentially held also by Lazard, that it marks the beginning of what may properly be called literature, and is written in a supple and diversified style, suitable both for description and for laying bare the often complicated detail of court intrigue. It thus clearly differs here from the rather unpolished style of Balʿami's rendering of the *Tārikh-e Ṭabari* and the old *tafsir*s or works of Qorʾānic exegesis of the preceding century and betrays the agile pen of the accomplished secretary.[187] Malek al-Shoʿarāʾ Bahār, in the first and most detailed analysis so far attempted of the style and language of the *History*, emphasized its discursiveness (*eṭnāb*) and the elaboration of its sentences and subordination of clauses.[188] Kenneth A. Luther found Beyhaqi's style unadorned and to the point, so much so that, leaving aside the embellishments of the Persian and Arabic verses and the *ʿebar*, stories pointing morals, he thought it fair to say that the *Tārikh-e Masʿudi* was "an extended Ghaznavid intelligence report on the Sultan himself."[189] Going back from modern authors and critics to an authority separated from Beyhaqi by only a century, the historian of Beyhaq, Ebn Fondoq, regarded the style of his fellow-native of Beyhaq as having "lucid expression and eloquence," *bā-faṣāḥat va balāghat*, see above, section 2, p. 32, although he was probably thinking more of the qualities enshrined in Beyhaqi's lost *Zinat al-kottāb*.

Clearly, these very varied judgements indicate that Beyhaqi could change the pace of his narrative according to the subject of the moment, choosing terseness or prolixity as the context seemed to him

[186] "The Persian historian Bayhaqī," in B. Lewis and P.M. Holt (eds.), *Historians of the Middle East*, London 1962, 140.

[187] *La langue des plus anciens monuments de la prose persane*, Paris 1963, 35, 78.

[188] *Sabk-shenāsi, yā taṭavvor-e nathr-e fārsi*, 2nd ed. Tehran 1337/1958, II, 67–68. Under the heading of this use of *eṭnāb*, one should classify Beyhaqi's extensive love of digressions such as the two *khoṭba*s to volumes 6 and 10 of the *History*, and the interpolated pieces of poetry and tales from past, almost invariably Islamic, history used as flashbacks to illuminate contemporary events, discussed above in Section 4. See Meisami, *Persian historiography to the end of the twelfth century*, Edinburgh 1999, 86–87.

[189] "Bayhaqi and the later Seljuq historians: some comparative remarks," in *Yād-nāma-ye Abu'l-Fażl Beyhaqi*, English section, 24; and see the summary of views on Beyhaqi's style in R.M. Savory, "Abo'l-Fażl Bayhaqī as an historiographer," in *ibid.*, 106–10.

to require, and such qualities accord with Marilyn Waldman's observations regarding the labels which scholars and critics have tried to attach to Beyhaqi's work: "... in the current idiom Bayhaqī's style is journalistic rather than scholarly. He reports fully but is not erudite; he is given to popularization and colloquialism; he emphasizes graphic imagery and human interest. His style is not popular nor is it elitist; it appeals to an intelligent, refined, but not scholarly audience."[190]

Historians of classical Persian literature, such as Bahār, Bausani and Lazard, have placed Beyhaqi's *History* in a second period of its development, after a first period running approximately from 950 to 1050, which includes such historical and geographical works as Balʿami's Ṭabari translation, the anonymous *Ḥodud al-ʿālam* "Limits of the world," the anonymous *Tārikh-e Sistān* "History of Sistan," and (although its author was a near-contemporary of Beyhaqi, see above, section 3, pp. 40–41) Gardizi's *Zeyn al-akhbār*, and is characterised by a plain, straightforward style suited to practical rather than artistic ends, a comparative absence of decorative elements like poetic citations, the insertion of digressive tales and a Persian style sparing of Arabic words and of grammatical and syntactic Arabisms in the Persian prose style. The second period includes, in addition to Beyhaqi's *History*, such works of a slightly later date as Key Kāvus b. Eskandar's *Qābus-nāma* "Book of Amir Qābus" (1082–83), Neẓām al-Molk's *Siyāsat-nāma* (1092–93) and the anonymous *Mojmal al-tavārikh* "Collection of histories" (probably written between 1126 and 1131), and is characterised by a more developed, elaborate style, with greater use of rhetorical devices, citations of poetry, metaphors derived from the stock-in-trade of poetry, what in general may appropriately be termed art prose (*nathr-e fanni*).[191]

[190] *Op. cit.*, 118.

[191] See a summary of these phases in Bertotti, *op. cit.*, 87–88, and a detailed consideration of the historiography of both the Samanid and Ghaznavid periods in Meisami, *op. cit.*, 15–140. This second period, in its turn, gives way to a third period of much more ornate prose with an elaborate chancery style in the ascendant, as seen in the later Seljuq historian Rāvandi and, above all, the Mongol-period historian Joveyni, see Bahār, *op. cit.*, II, 357ff., and K.A. Luther, "Chancery writing as a source of constraints on history writing in the sixth and seventh centuries of the Hijrah," in Iraj Afshār and Karim Eṣfahāniyān (eds.), *Pozhuhesh-hā-ye irān-shenāsi nāmvāra-ye Doktor Maḥmud Afshār*, XII, Tehran 1381/2002, English section, 32–44.

As a secretary, Beyhaqi would, of course, be probably bilingual in Persian and Arabic. Whether he knew Turkish is unknown, but that he did is by no means impossible; Tajik officials must often have had need to communicate with monolingual Turkish military men, and Beyhaqi records the Vizier Aḥmad b. ʿAbd al-Ṣamad as addressing a gholām in Turkish.[192] No statistical count seems to have been made of the relative proportions of Persian and Arabic words used by Beyhaqi; Bahār thought that the Arabic words amount to not more than 10% (presumably in what might be termed straightforward historical narrative; one would expect the proportion of Arabisms to increase in the texts of chancery documents and the *khoṭba*s in which Beyhaqi muses on matters of political philosophy and ethics).[193] This is in any case an increase on the proportion in the tenth-century prose texts, the *Tarjoma-ye Tārikh-e Ṭabari* "Translation of Ṭabari's History," the *tafsir*s or Qorʾānic commentaries, etc., but nothing like the proportion in Seljuq and Mongol period historians like Bondāri, Rāvandi and Joveynī. However, it is relevant to consider the types of Arabic words used, and to distinguish within Beyhaqi's Arabic vocabulary words which had established themselves in New Persian in the course of the tenth and early eleventh centuries (e.g. *efrāṭ*, *tamām*, *moqarrar*, and, of course, technical terms of the Islamic religion such as *eʿteqād*, *raḥmat*, *shafāʿat*) and words which Beyhaqi apparently plucks out of his education in Arabic but which were not apparently absorbed into the standard Persian literary vocabulary and do not accordingly appear in the dictionaries of classical Persian (e.g. *tabaṭṭor*, *tarabbod*, *tashammor*, *taṣallof*, *tanaḥnoḥ*, *tanassom*, *moghāyaẓa*, *moghāfaṣa*, *estebṭāʾ*, etc.).

Thus although there is this perceptible Arabic element in Beyhaqi's style, both in regard to vocabulary and to syntax, there is nothing like the thorough intermingling, on both the grammatical and lexical levels, of Arabic and Persian elements with Turkish that we find later in Ottoman Turkish literary usage. On many occasions it seems that Beyhaqi preferred to use indigenous Persian words when one might have expected, from the prevailing Islamic religious background, the established Arabic technical terms of theology, religious practice, etc.

---

192 Gh 655, F 888.

193 *Sabk-shenāsi*, II, 85.

Hence we have *peyghambar* rather than *nabi* or *rasul* "prophet"; *ādina* "Friday" rather than *jom'a*; *namāz* "ritual prayer; worship" rather than *ṣalāt*; *āfaridgār* "The Creator" rather than *khāleq*. God is usually *khodā*, less often *izad* and on one occasion *yazdān*,[194] rather than Allāh. Quotations from the Qor'ān are modest in number and those from Ḥadith quite rare, two of the few examples being the Prophetic ones *al-mo'men mer'āt al-mo'men* "The believer is the mirror of the believer" and *ettaqi sharr man aḥsanta eleyhi* "Fear the evil of a person to whom you have done good."[195] On the secular level, familiar Arabic phrases came easily to Beyhaqi's pen when they seemed apposite in the context. Thus, to cite only four examples, the maxim enjoining mercy for one's fallen foe, *al-'afv 'end al-qodra* "Be forgiving when you are in a position of power," occurs at least three times;[196] in describing the fall of someone from eminence to obscurity, he quotes a saying *ba'd al-'ezz va 'l-raf'a ṣāra ḥāres al-dajla* "after an exalted status and eminence he became a keeper of mangy camels";[197] to make the point that generous offerings by patrons to poets oil the wheels of poetic eulogy, he says *al-lohā taftahu'l-lahā*, lit. "rich gifts open up uvulas," i.e. loosen tongues;[198] and a proverbial saying which must go back to pre-Islamic times, being found in the classical collections of proverbs like the *Amthāl al-'arab* of Meydāni, *yadāka owkatā vafuka nafakha* "your two hands squeezed the skin while your mouth was blowing air [into it]", used when someone does something to his own detriment.[199] Very characteristic is Beyhaqi's very frequent use, within his Persian style, of formulaic Arabic expressions which must have rolled off his tongue as easily as an English speaker might use, in reasonably ordinary speech, such terms as *fait accompli*, *quid pro quo*, etc.: *be-sāḥel al-ḥayāt* "still alive," lit. "on the shore of life"; *maqbul al-qowl* "with pleasing speech"; *elā yowmenā hādhā* "until this present time"; *'alā ayye 'l-ḥāl* "in any event"; *be-morur al-ayyām* "over the course of time;"etc.[200]

[194] Gh 575, F 763.
[195] Gh 105, 467, F 124, 607, and see also Gh 379, F 485.
[196] Gh 132,168, 180, F 158, 206, 223.
[197] Gh 64, F 71.
[198] Gh 280, F 372.
[199] Gh 205, F 259.
[200] Gh 199, 203, 477 and 685, 513, 587, F 250, 256, 620 and 936, 672, 779.

Bahār listed several morphological and lexical features which stem from Arabic equivalents, e.g. the use of Arabic broken plurals (*nokat*, *ṭoraf*, *atbāʿ*, *khoṣamāʾ*) where authors of the Samanid period would have used Persian plural suffixes (*nokta-hā*, *ṭorfa-hā*, *tābeʿān*, *khaṣmān*); use of a Persian construction analogous to the Arabic *mafʿūl moṭlaq*, e.g. *be-farmud tā u-rā zadand zadani sakht*, lit. "he ordered him to be beaten a severe beating," and *amir bār dād bār dādani sakht bā shokuh*, lit. "the Amir held a court session a holding in a very splendid fashion" (noting that such constructions are already to be found in the *Shāh-nāma*); use of Arabic phrases with *tanwīn*, e.g. *moghāfaṣatan*, *ʿazizan mokraman*, *ghāneman ẓāferan*, *ḥaqqan thomma ḥaqqan*; the occasional use of *sajʿ* or rhymed prose (e.g. at Gh 376, F 480, and cf. Year 424 n. 68; this usage was to increase after Beyhaqi's time, see above, n. 191) and use of Arabic *maṣdar*s or verbal nouns, e.g. *bokhl*, *karam*, *lajāja*, where Samanid usage was to make a Persian abstract noun from the Arabic adjective, e.g. *bakhili*, *karimi*, *lajuji*.[201] The use of an Arabic word in parallel to a Persian synonym gave possibilities of what Sir Arthur Quiller-Couch called in English prose style "elegant variation", avoiding the repetition of a word or phrase by substituting a synonym or an equivalent phrase. Hence in regard to verbs, Beyhaqi may use e.g. *āghāz kardan* or *āghāzidan* "to begin" in one phrase or sentence and *ebtedāʾ kardan* in the next, a feature made easy by the frequency in Persian of compound verbs with *kardan*, *namudan*, *shodan*, *gashtan*, etc.;[202] or he may simply employ Persian synonyms to give variety, such as having *izad* for "God" in one phrase and *khodā* in the next one.[203]

Apart from this question of Arabic influences in Beyhaqi's style, one may characterise his Persian style as particularly free in its word order, with a considerable amount of parataxis, i.e. omission of copulas and simple juxtaposing of phrases in order to avoid a clumsy succession of subordinating conjunctions,[204] approaching what one might imagine was contemporary colloquial usage, hence giving

[201] See *Sabk-shenāsi*, II, 70ff., and for a study of some of the linguistic features of the *History*, Khosrow Farshidvard, "Baʿżi az qavāʾed-e dasturi-ye Tārikh-e Beyhaqi," in *Yād-nāma-ye Abu'l-Fażl-e Beyhaqi*, Persian section, 468–515.

[202] See Waldman, *op. cit.*, 116.

[203] Gh 532 ll. 4–5, F 701 ll. 6–7.

[204] Cf. Lazard, *La langue des plus anciens monuments*, 488–91, §§ 848–56.

pace and life to the flow of language. Thus, to cite only three examples, we have *selāḥ-dār bā khᵛishtan dāsht be-afgand* "the Keeper of the Weapons had [a prayer rug] with him and laid it down";[205] *agar methāl-e sālār Begtughdï negāh dāshtand in khalal nayoftādi nadāshtand*... "if they had obeyed the orders of the commander Begtughdï, this disaster would not have befallen; but they did not obey them ...";[206] *ṣad hazār faryād karda budam ke zanān mayārid farmān nakardand* "I had made a hundred thousand appeals for them not to bring any womenfolk, but they paid no heed."[207] Among other syntactical features are variety of ways of forming passive constructions using e.g. verbs like *āmadan, godhāshtan, oftādan, istādan*, though on the whole Beyhaqi's stylistic vigour leads him to prefer active over passive constructions.[208] Where perfect or pluperfect verbs come after the first position in a series, or even when occurring singly, the *ast* or *bud* is often omitted, e.g. *shoda, rafta* "he has gone". Verbs are not always at the end of sentences, but may be followed by adverbs or an adjective qualifying a noun previously mentioned before the verb, e.g. *be-girad-ash ke dozdi-st nā-be-kār* "let him seize him because he's a good-for-nothing thief." The prefix for continuous or habitual action, *mi-* (or, most likely, as Beyhaqi wrote it, *hami-*, see below) was often in his time felt as an independent particle hence separated from its verb e.g. *mi che konad* "what he is doing," *mi ravā dārad setādan* "he holds it licit to accept." In fact, Beyhaqi has various usages of *mi-* that are obsolete or unusual in later Persian usage, e.g. with an imperative verb to give a durative, continuous aspect, e.g. *gush mi-dār* "keep your ears pricked";[209] with a preterite (or, more accurately, aorist) verb to give this same durative, continuous aspect, e.g. *mi-be-shod* "[the situation] was getting out of hand";[210] and *mi-sākhta bud* "he had been reported as plotting," with a pluperfect verb to give a "distanced" or "inferential" sense (i.e. when the speaker has no direct knowledge of

205 Gh 371, F 473.

206 Gh 484–85, F 630.

207 Gh 544, F 719.

208 See in this regard the study of Moḥammad Javād Shariʿat, "Afʿāl-e motaʿaddi va ṭarz-e esteʿmāl-e ānhā dar Tārikh-e Beyhaqi va mafʿul bi-vāseṭa-ye ānhā," in *Yād-nāma-ye Abu'l-Fażl-e Beyhaqi*, Persian section, 364–72.

209 Gh 573, F 760.

210 Gh 612, F 817.

an event from which he is distanced in time).[211] There is much subordination of clauses, usually with *ke* in various senses (result, purpose, introducing direct or indirect speech, or simply temporal succession) or *chun*, and sometimes with a subordinate clause dependent on preceding subordinate clause, hence making the syntax of the whole locution convoluted.

Beyhaqi's narrative is often enlivened by the use of colloquial, familiar expressions. A list of considerable length could be compiled here, but only a few can be given here as examples: *ṭabli bud ke zir-e gelim mizadand* "they were plotting and spreading rumours," lit. there was a drum beaten underneath the covering";[212] *marā dar in kār nāqa va jamali na-buda ast* "[when he will realize that] I had no personal stake in this matter/no axe to grind," lit. "I was neither a she-camel nor a camel stallion";[213] *panba az gush-e u birun konam* "I shall make him come to his senses," lit. "take the cotton out of his ears";[214] *dast u pāy morda* "frightened to death," lit. "with hands and feet dead";[215] ... *par u bāl konand* "... to reinforce and strengthen their position," lit. "... to flap and stretch their feathers and wings ";[216] *tir az kamān be-raft* "the process has been set in motion," lit. "the arrow has left the bow";[217] *khāk u namaki bikhtand* "they made up a tale," lit. "they sifted some earth and sand";[218] *mārā be-khᵛāb karda-and be-shisha-ye tohi* "they have tried to pull the wool over our eyes," lit. "they have put us to sleep with an empty bottle";[219] *zabān dar dahān-e yakdigar karda-id* "you have concerted with each other these words," lit. "you

---

211 Gh 465, F 603. See on this particular usage the study by Lazard, "L'inférentiel ou passé distancié en persan," *St. Ir.*, XIV (1985), 27–42; this particular example falls into Lazard's Category A, "rapport d'autrui." Éva Jeremiás notes (with examples) that the idea of remoteness (*boʿd*) from the speaker's present time was known as significant to early native grammarians of Persian, see her "Kamālpāšāzāda as linguist,"in *eadem* (ed.), *Irano-Turkic cultural contacts in the 11th–17th centuries*, 90.

212 Gh 156, F 192.

213 Gh 325, F 414.

214 Gh 363, F 463.

215 Gh 435, F 562.

216 Gh 472, F 614.

217 Gh 539, F 712.

218 Gh 576, F 763.

219 Gh 607, F 808.

have placed your tongues in each other's mouths";[220] etc. When the general Aḥmad Ināltegin, believed to be possibly in some way related to Sultan Maḥmud, is mentioned, he is described as the Sultan's *ʿaṭsa* "sneeze" (in English, "spitten image", "exact likeness").[221]

From these very sketchy remarks, it is clear that an extended, detailed study of Beyhaqi's language and style by a specialist on the historical development of New Persian is very much a desideratum. A problem in such a study will obviously be the lateness of the surviving manuscripts of the *History*, giving unknown scribes four or more centuries in which to normalise the original text; and the changes introduced may not have been merely orthographical ones but may have involved morphological mutations. Thus Lazard regards it as almost certain that, in place of the verbal prefix expressing continuous or iterative action *mi-* and the preposition *dar* "in", both written mostly thus in the *History*'s text as we have it, Beyhaqi used *hami-* and *andar*, forms still the most usual ones in his time, as older manuscripts of works from this period show.[222] Similarly, the older negative particle *ney* may have been regularised to *na*.[223] Also, dialectical forms were probably ironed out; here Lazard cites *bestākh* and *ostākh* (var. *gostākh*) "bold, confident" as notable examples in Beyhaqi's text.[224] A further problem for the would-be student of Beyhaqi's language style and vocabulary is the lamentable lack of *Hilfsmittel* in the shape of historical dictionaries of New Persian; despite the immense achievement of Dehkhodā in the compilation of his *Loghat-nāma*, Classical Persian lexicography proper has hardly advanced here since J.A. Vullers put together his still useful *Lexicon persico-latinum etymologicum* a century and a half ago (see above, pp. 52–53).

As part of Beyhaqi's preference for Persian rather than Arabic modes of expression, where Arabic uses the noun *ebn* "son of ..." to indicate filiation, Beyhaqi prefers usually to link them by the Persian *eżāfa*, e.g. Aḥmad-e Ḥasan, and this makes it difficult at times to distinguish filiation like this from names which include a descriptive epithet, also

---

[220] Gh 613, F 819.

[221] Gh 401, F 515.

[222] *La langue des plus anciens monuments*, 177–79 §§112–13, and 179–81 §§114–17.

[223] *Ibid.*, 440–41 §727.

[224] *Ibid*,, 77 and n. 10; cf. Bahār, *op. cit.*, II, 79.

linked by *eżāfa*. ʿAli-ye Rāʾeż ("ʿA. the horse trainer") or Bu'l-Fatḥ-e Dāmghāni ("Bu'l-F. from/connected with Dāmghān") or Ḥasan-e Tabbāni ("Ḥ. the member of the Tabbanī family") are all easy. But is Ahmad Ināltegin all one name (an Arabic element + a Turkish one), as seems to be the case with the Turkmen leader Ebrāhim Ināltegin, or should one more probably read Aḥmad-e Inaltegin "A. son of I."? (In texts where the Arabic *ebn* is used, this is sometimes inserted between "Aḥmad" and "Ināltegin" and sometimes not, so there is no conclusive guidance there.)[225]

The dates in the headings for the various years covered by the *History* are written in Arabic (although one cannot be sure whether these stem from Beyhaqi himself or have been inserted by copyists), but Beyhaqi does seem to have been careful to state on which day of the week fell the beginning of the Arabic Hijri year, 1 Moḥarram. Dates are normally given according to the months of the Hijri calendar, although occasionally the Persian and Syrian Christian months are mentioned. The days of the week, however, have their Persian names, and over a month are normally counted from the first to the last day (with *nima* "half, half-way point" marking the middle of the month, i.e. the fourteenth or fifteenth), and not by the Arabic system of counting the first half of the month from its first day and the second half back from the last day, which is only occasionally used by Beyhaqi.[226] As well as such Islamic festivals as the two *ʿid*s, that of the Ending of the Fast and that of the Sacrifice, the Ghaznavid sultans observed the ancient Iranian ones of Nowruz, Mehragān and Sada, and Beyhaqi often at the appropriate points in his narrative describes the celebrations, the latter one, Sada, in its traditional guise as a winter fire festival.[227]

---

225 Cf. below, Year 422 n. 524.

226 See e.g. Gh 25, 533, F 26–27, 702, and cf. Year 428 n. 134.

227 For this last, see Gh 442–43, F 571–72.

Translation of the
Tārikh-e Mas'udi

[The Year 421 (/9 January–28 December 1030)]

[The surviving remainder of the fifth volume]

[Gh 1, F 948] [In the name of God, the Merciful, the Compassionate.

The narrator of this account, Abu'l-Fażl Beyhaqi the secretary, was himself present and relates that when the late Sultan Maḥmud b. Sebüktegin[1] Ghāzi,[2] the Ghaznavid, may God be pleased with him, died[3] in Ghazni[4] and entrusted the repository of the spirit of his precious soul to the Creator of the soul, his eldest son and designated heir, Amir Mas'ud, was in Isfahan. He was intending to proceed towards Hamadan and Baghdad, and was very far from the royal throne (i.e. the imperial capital Ghazna). Accordingly, the trusted counsellors and pillars of the state from Maḥmud's time, including such persons as Amir 'Ali Qarib,[5] the Great Chamberlain[6]; Amir 'Ażod al-Dowla Abu Ya'qub Yusof b. Nāṣer al-Din Sebüktegin, the Sultan's (i.e. Maḥmud's) brother,[7] who was Commander-in-Chief;[8] Amir Ḥasan the vizier, known as Ḥasanak;[9] Bu Naṣr Moshkān, Head of the Chancery;[10] Bu'l-Qāsem b. Kathir, Head of the Army Department;[11] Begtughdï,[12] Commander of the Palace Gholāms[13]; Abu'l-Najm Ayāz;[14] and 'Ali Dāya the Sultan's kinsman[15]—all these, together with others of the outstanding and prominent people, in consultation with each other perceived that the time was opportune for bringing back Amir Abu Aḥmad Moḥammad, the younger son of the deceased sultan, from Guzgānān,[16] which was near the capital, and putting him on the throne in place of his noble father. The Great Chamberlain, Amir 'Ali Qarib, who was the most illustrious of the trusty men of the state, took the lead and assumed direction of the affairs of state.

Amir Masʿud, having reversed his intention of marching on Baghdad, travelled from Isfahan to Ray, [F 949] from there to Nishapur and from there on to Herat. Amir ʿAli, again acting in unison with other prominent leaders and in accord with their advice, imprisoned Amir Moḥammad in the fortress of Kuhtiz[17] at Teginābād.[18] Seeking to exonerate himself with the excuse that what had happened had been for the public good, he composed the following exculpatory petition in collusion with Mengütirek,[19] the Great Chamberlain's brother, and Bu Bakr Ḥaṣiri,[20] the deceased sultan's boon companion, and sent it to the court of the exalted Sultan Masʿud.] [Gh 2]

The text of the exculpatory petition which the pillars of the state of Maḥmud's time sent from Teginābād to Amir Masʿud at Herat

[F 1] *In the name of God, the Merciful, the Compassionate.* May the life of the lord of the world, the most mighty sultan, the designated heir, be prolonged in greatness, auspicious governance, kingship, divinely-aided success, and may he attain his desires and needs in this present world and the next! We servants of the lord have written from Teginābād on this Monday, 3 Shavvāl [421/4 October 1030] concerning the present position of the victorious army which is at this moment encamped here, on the basis that, when the exalted command subsequently arrives, the troops will make their way, detachment by detachment, to the service of the exalted court of the lord of the world, the great sultan, the dispenser of favours (may God prolong the duration of his life and bring forth victory to his battle standard!). For various impediments and hindrances have now been removed and cleared away, and affairs have become straightforward and of one accord, all hearts are united in obedience and all intentions are honest. *Praise be to God, the Lord of both Worlds, and blessings upon His Messenger Moḥammad and upon all his family!*

The decree of the Almighty God will come into effect just as He wills and pronounces and ordains, not as human desires would like in the matter; for by His command—He is praised and raised on high—

the vicissitudes of fate have their operation, and it is His divine decision concerning the carrying out of His beneficence and His trials alike and the implementation of all kinds of successful accomplishments and [F 2] manifestations of power! There is justice in everything which He does and it is by His grace that dominion over the face of the earth passes from this one to that one and from that one to this one, until "*God will inherit the earth and everything upon it, and He is the best of inheritors*".[21]

Amir Abu Aḥmad, may God prolong his health, is a scion from the main trunk of the realm of the deceased Amir, may God illuminate his proof. Each of the branches is strong and sturdy, with fresh blossoms, [Gh 3] and Amir Masʿud himself would never be in accord with or find it acceptable if any of the servants of the royal house or anyone else expressed anything indecorous about him (i.e. concerning Amir Moḥammad), since any such sentiments would reflect back on the main trunk itself.[22]

Since it had been foreordained that Amir Moḥammad should sit for a period of time on the throne of the kingdom of Ghaznin, Khorasan and India, which was the seat of the two Amirs, his father and grandfather, may God's mercy be upon them both, he necessarily assumed his place on that throne and adorned it, and at that time he was fully deserving of it. It was inevitable that he gave commands on every sort of thing, just as kings are wont to do, and the courtiers there of all grades, higher and lower, carried out those commands in an obedient and submissive way, and sedulously observed in this the requisite conditions of obedience.

When the time allotted to him came to an end and the Almighty God bestowed on His servants the greater branch from the trunk of kingly power (i.e. Masʿud)—who was, in fact, the designated heir[23]—and the latter extended his power over the land as the successor of his father (*khalifat*) and as the successor of the successor of God's Chosen One, peace be upon him, at this juncture the humble servants have ineluctably had to hasten towards the true successor and have offered him the obedience which is more incumbent on him [than on Moḥammad]. Also, at this point when the letter from all us servants has been indited for him, we have acted in accordance with the lofty [F 3] command, as set forth by the exalted hand in the succinct, confidential message[24] sent to them, and have kept Amir Moḥammad under guard in the fortress of Kuhtiz.

Then, when all the troops, with their weapons, had lined up from the vicinity of the camp enclosure[25] to far out into the countryside, much discussion and argument went on. 'Ali Qarib said that Amir Moḥammad should either be sent back to Guzgānān with an escort or else that he should be brought, in his own charge, to the exalted court. In the end, it was decided that he should be held in the fortress together with his family, boon companions and the servants of these groups until the lofty command should determine what was to be done with him. The General Begtegin[26] with his cavalry force and 500 of his choicest horsemen are at the foot of the fortress, encamped in the inner town (*shārastān*) of the Zunbil[27] in order to guard the fortress, so that when the humble servants leave this place, [Gh 4] and head for the exalted court, no lapse of security occurs. They selected these two humble servants (i.e. Bu Bakr Ḥaṣiri and Mengütirek) out of the whole group of leading officers to give an exposition of the situation when they should be asked about it.

"It is fitting, having regard to the compassionate feelings of the lord of the world, the great sultan, may God perpetuate his royal power, that he should forgive his servants' previous deeds, since if at that time they acted so as to bring affairs into a peaceful state, and thereby chose to hold fast to the commands of the deceased lord Maḥmud, now that a lord who is more deserving has appeared and his command has become effective, they have carried out completely all the necessary conditions of service and obedience to commands. We await an answer to this petition in the hope that a reply will speedily come back with instructions about what should be done with Amir Abu Aḥmad and all the other matters which need to be arranged so that we may act accordingly. We despatched swift messengers from the body of *kheyltāshs*[28] of the army to Ghaznin, and gave out information concerning what had taken place and how the exalted banner, [F 4] may God grant it victory, had arrived in Herat at a most auspicious time. This was done with the intention that the Queen-Mother Sayyeda and the rest of the majesty's subjects might rejoice and feel thoroughly at ease. We caused this information to be sent to Sind and Hind so that, the Almighty God willing, no unrest should break out in the outlying parts of that domain."

Bu Bakr Ḥaṣiri and Mengütirek set off[29] as described, and in the same manner they also sent three swift-riding *kheyltāshs* to Ghaznin.

On the Friday, they made the formal intercessory prayer (*khoṭba*)[30] here at Teginābād in the name of Sultan Masʿud. The royally-appointed preacher (*khaṭib*),[31] the Great Chamberlain and all the notables[32] were present in the congregational mosque; they distributed large amounts of dirhams and dinars as charitable offerings[33], and it proved a most impressive occasion. A message had gone to Bost that the *khoṭba* should also be made there for Masʿud; they had done this, and everything was done in a worthy manner and with due decorum.

Each day, the Chamberlain ʿAli would mount and ride to the open country outside the town and take up his position there. The notables and court retainers, [Gh 5] the masters of the sword and of the pen, would all come along and take up their places while still mounted, and they would engage in much debate and deliberation until the time of the midday meal. If any fresh item of news arrived from some quarter, they would retail it, and if a crisis arose in some quarter, they would put matters right by despatching letters with riders, as the exigencies of the situation and their own observations saw fit. Then they would return to their tents.[34] They treated Amir Moḥammad very courteously. His personal boon-companions had permission to go to him, as likewise his singers and reciters and musicians, and the cupbearers would bring wine and all kinds of fruits and aromatic herbs.

I heard from ʿAbd al-Raḥmān the singer and reciter,[35] who related: For two or three days, Amir Moḥammad appeared apprehensive and disconsolate,[36] and would send away his entourage at meal times. On the third day, Aḥmad, son of Arslān,[37] said, "May the lord's life be prolonged! One cannot go against the Divine Will. [F 5]. There is nothing to be gained by sinking into gloom. The lord should get down to indulging once more in wine and pleasurable activities, for we are afraid that otherwise he will be overcome by melancholy[38] and, which God forbid, may fall into sickness." The Amir abandoned his self-imposed abstinence and on that day listened to a few songs from myself. Each day, he would gradually indulge a little more, to the point that when the army left for Herat, he was once again drinking wine. However, he was drinking with a heavy heart, and deep sighs served as side dishes to each cup that he imbibed. For peace of mind is a prerequisite for wine-drinking and merry-making, and it is a grave error to suggest wine for alleviating gloom and sorrow. Indeed, it does have an immediate soothing effect and reduces the gloom, but then, when [Gh 6] the wine has had its full effect, the person falls asleep and wakes up later with a dreadful hangover lasting two or three days.

The swift-riding *kheyltāsh*s who had left for Ghaznin returned, and they reported that there was universal rejoicing when the good tidings (i.e. of Masʿud's accession to the throne) reached Ghaznin, and everyone alike, regardless of their social rank and status, celebrated for several days. They slaughtered animals as sacrificial offerings and distributed large amounts in alms, celebrating the re-establishment of order and concord. The senior officer (*sarhang*)[39] Bu ʿAli the castellan[40] had instructed that letters should be written to all the distant corners of the realm with this news, and in his letters he mentioned that when the letter arrived from Teginābād, he gave orders for them to take copies of it and send them to Sind and Hind and likewise to the regions of Ghaznin, Balkh, Tokhārestān and Guzgānān so that the magnitude of this turn of events would become palpable everywhere and induce peace and tranquillity. The swift-riding *kheyltāsh*s who had been despatched reported that "The notables, scholars of religious law[41] and judges, and the state-appointed preacher had remained at the Rebāṭ of Jormoq,[42] because of the recent upheavals, but when we reached there from Teginābād, they were happily reassured and returned to Ghaznin." When we ourselves reached Ghaznin and gave the field officer's letter [F 6] to the castellan, he immediately ordered that barrel-shaped drums[43] should be beaten and trumpets sounded from the citadel and the good news conveyed to all quarters. The Queen-Mother Sayyeda, Sultan Masʿud's mother, together with all the noble, free womenfolk, came down from the citadel and proceeded to the residence of Abu'l-ʿAbbās Esfarāyeni,[44] [Gh 7] Amir Masʿud's steward and agent in the time of Amir Maḥmud. All the religious scholars, the notables and a multitude of common people made their way there to offer their congratulations. The musicians from the town and the trumpet-players from Shādiābād[45] came in procession with all their instruments in order to render service in that place, and they processed to take us on a ceremonial procession.[46] We received more than 50,000 dirhams' worth of gold and silver and fine clothing. It was a splendid day, the like of which no-one could recall. We arrived early in the morning, and at midnight we returned with replies to the letters."

The Great Chamberlain ʿAli Qarib was filled with joy at this news, and wrote a letter to Amir Masʿud.[47] He sent it by the hand of two *kheyltāsh*s and gave an exposition of those happenings, and he sent off all the letters that had arrived from Ghaznin.

On Saturday in mid-Shavvāl [421/14–15 October 1030] Sultan Masʿud's letter arrived by the hand of his cavalry troopers, one a Turk and the other an Arab nomad.[48] They had with them four horses and had made the journey in four and a half days. This was the answer to that letter which the *kheyltāsh*s had conveyed with the news of Amir Moḥammad's imprisonment in the fortress of Kuhtiz. When ʿAli read the letter, he rode out to the open countryside and summoned all the leading men. They came immediately, and Abu Saʿid the secretary read out the letter to the assembly, [F 7] a message filled with much affection and encouragement for all the notables and leading figures[49] and the troops of the army at large. It was written in the hand of the secretary Ṭāher, head of Amir Masʿud's Chancery,[50] and adorned with the exalted royal emblem and motto[51]. There were also some lines in Amir Masʿud's own hand, addressed to the Great Chamberlain ʿAli, with the official form of address "Excellent Commander, Brother" (*Ḥājeb-e Fāżel Berādar*), and words of endearment exceeding all bounds, as if addressed to a person of equal rank.[52]

When Bu Saʿid pronounced the sultan's name, all present dismounted and then remounted, and the letter was then read out. Successively, detachment by detachment, the troops came forward, and the contents of the letter were communicated to them; they kissed the ground[53] and then went back. The royal command to ʿAli was that [Gh 8] he was to send off the retainers, the courtiers and the successive detachments of the army as he saw fit, and then he was to follow on their heels with the army of India, the elephants, the armoury[54] and the treasury, until he reached the court in safety and security. He was to know that all responsibility for the kingdom was to be assigned to him, and that his rank and station excelled all others.

The Great Chamberlain ʿAli announced, "The commanders of groups[55] must be instructed to bring back the troops and make camp. Today I have several important matters to discuss with these leading officers and senior commanders which it is incumbent on me to settle. Then after that, tomorrow, the process of sending the troops off, detachment by detachment, must be put into operation in accordance with the command of the lord sultan." The troop commanders of each army group (*ṭā'efa*) went away, and the whole army went back and encamped. The Great Chamberlain ʿAli returned also. He took with him all the leading commanders of the army, Tāzik[56] and Turk, and they sat down together privately. [F 8] ʿAli gave the letter in Amir Masʿud's own hand, which they had not seen, to the secretary Bu Saʿid to read out.[57]

He had written the following in his own hand: "I am certain now, and I was already certain at the time when our father the late Amir passed away and my noble brother the Amir Abu Aḥmad was summoned to ascend the royal throne, that at the time this was the only way to preserve the interests of the realm. We had ourself conquered a highly-renowned distant territory and were planning to march on Hamadan and Baghdad, for those Deylamites (i.e. the Buyids) were not to be accounted serious opponents.[58] We wrote a letter and sent it with that envoy [ʿAbd al-ʿAziz] ʿAlavi[59] to our brother containing our condolences as well as our congratulations and words of advice. If he had listened, and if he had become our deputy, and if he had immediately sent that which we had sought,[60] we for our part would in no circumstances have made any difficulties for him. We would have summoned such persons from amongst the leading officers and commanders of the army as were required by sound judgement and would have marched on Baghdad, so that the whole realm of the Muslims would have been under the sway of us two brothers. [Gh 9] But our brother was unable to see the right course for his own good, and he may perhaps have perceived of human deliberations as being on a par with God's predestined decree.[61] Now that it has come to this and he is staying in the fortress of Kuhtiz free and unfettered, together with all his household, he cannot be sent, under any circumstances, to Guzgānān. It would be unseemly to bring him with ourself because he has been held a prisoner, and when he reaches Herat we cannot set eyes on him in that condition. The right course is that he should remain unbound, in an honoured and respected state, in the company of all his family and with as many persons there who are useful to him in general, for the command is not that any members of his family or retinue should be detained in captivity. The General Begtegin, [F 9] with that high degree of wisdom that he possesses, is to remain stationed below the fortress with his retainers. Also, we have entrusted to him the governorship of Teginābād and the military security command[62] of Bost, to which latter town he is to send a deputy. He will receive more marks of favour to enjoy in further service to us. We ourself are going to leave Herat and head for Balkh in order to spend the winter season there. Once Nowruz is past, we shall set off towards Ghaznin and will take suitable measures concerning our brother, for there is no-one dearer to us than him. Let all these things to be made known, if the Almighty God wills."

When they heard the contents of this letter, they all said, "The lord displayed perfect justice at the time when he sent the messenger, and now he is acting even more justly; what is the Chamberlain's view regarding this matter?" He replied, "With your consent, this letter should be sent to Amir Moḥammad so that he may know that he is remaining here by the lord's command, [Gh 10] and a custodian for him has been found, and that we have been relieved of the duties related to him." They said, "A message must certainly be sent to him so that he understands the situation and directs his concerns from now onwards to the General Begtegin." The Chamberlain ʿAli said, "Who should convey it to his presence?" They replied, "Whomsoever the Chamberlain nominates." He instructed the religious scholar[63] Nabih and the judge (*ḥākem*) Moẓaffar as follows: "Go to Amir Moḥammad and lay this letter before him, give him a few words of advice, speak gently with him, and explain that the lord sultan's opinion is very favourable regarding him and that, when we humble servants arrive at the exalted court, we shall make it even more cordial." Also, he should be told that in the next two or three days this body of troops will all depart from here and from then on he would be dealing with the General Begtegin. He is a wise and intelligent person and will be duly observant of his exalted rank, and whatever is necessary to be said, he may say to him.

The two departed and informed Begtegin of their mission, since [F 10] without his permission no-one was allowed entry to the fortress. Begtegin designated his personal counsellor and administrator (*kadkhodā*)[64] to accompany them. They went off to the fortress and appeared before Amir Moḥammad and performed all the due forms of obeisance before him. Moḥammad said, "What news of my brother? And when will the army depart and go towards him?" They replied, "The news about the lord Sultan is entirely good. In the next two or three days the whole army will set off, with the Great Chamberlain following after them. We have come for this particular purpose", and they gave the letter to the Amir. He perused it, and a dark shadow flitted across his countenance. Nabih said, "May the Amir's life be prolonged! The Sultan, your brother, will safeguard the Amir's rights and display kindness. The Amir should not have a heavy heart; one should acquiesce in the decree of the Almighty God," and he spoke many fine words on this topic, the gist of that being that what was going to happen had happened, and once again it was time to resume merrymaking and pleasure, for it has been said, '*That which is foreordained* [Gh 11] *will inevitably happen, and worrying about it is superfluous and unnecessary*'."[65] The Amir treated them kindly and said, "Don't forget me!" They returned and told the Great Chamberlain 'Ali what had taken place.

Since the Great Chamberlain had given the order to depart, the whole of the troops dispersed and began to prepare for the journey to Herat. He further ordered that they should make an account of the allowances and expenses for Amir Moḥammad, and gave instructions to the provincial governor and tax-collector at Teginābād to keep a good watch on affairs so that no problems arose. He summoned the General Begtegin and handed over to him an investiture diploma with the sultan's signature and emblem affixed to it[66] for the military security charge of Bost and the governorship of Teginābād. The General stood upright and then set his face toward the direction of the royal court and kissed the ground. The Great Chamberlain gave him permission to depart, lavished praises on him, and said, "Look after your cavalry, and send the rest of your troops who are stationed below the fortress back to the army encampment ground so that they may join up with us. Remain alert and vigilant so that nothing goes amiss." Begtegin thanked him and returned. He sent the troops who were with him back to the army encampment ground, and he summoned the castellan of the fortress and instructed him, "You must keep up an extra high level of vigilance [F 11] now that the army is departing. No person is to have entry into the fortress without my express permission."

Everything now settled down peacefully, and the troops began to depart for the royal presence at Herat.

An account of what Amir Masʿud did after the passing away of his father Amir Maḥmud, may God's approval be upon them both, during the time when his brother was ruling in Ghazna until Moḥammad was arrested at Teginābād, Masʿud's authority was incontestably established and he was able to ascend the royal throne in Herat

Other chronicles do not have such length and breadth as this one, since they adopt a lighter approach to the study of historical events and invoke but a whiff of the past; but here, having undertaken the task, I want to do this history full justice and delve into every nook and cranny so that no aspect of the events remains obscure. And should this book become overlong, and should the readers become increasingly weary in its perusal, I place my trust in their gracious learning, lest they account me a prolix bore; for there is nothing that is not worth reading, since after all, there is no tale or episode that does not convey at least one useful point.[67] [Gh 12]

Regarding what Sultan Masʿud did in Ray and Jebāl, up to the time when he conquered Isfahan, I had related the history of all that in a fitting manner in the story of the remainder of his father Amir Maḥmud's time,[68] and had given it a separate section of its own, as the readers have already seen and read. When the [brief] reign of Masʿud's brother Amir Moḥammad came to an end and they (i.e. the Great Chamberlain ʿAli Qarib and his partisans) placed him within the fortress of Kuhtiz, as I have described, and when the reply came back to the letter which they had written to Amir Masʿud, the latter ordered that they should present themselves at the court in Herat. They made preparations for the journey. [F 12] The exact details of that journey and of their arrival at court I have left for another place, since my prime duty has been to recount the history of Amir Moḥammad's period of power and what Amir Masʿud did during that time, up to the point when he left Ray for Nishapur and then departed from the latter for Herat. For during that period many remarkable things happened which had to be set forth in order to fulfil the requirement of a complete historical narrative. I have now taken upon myself the task of setting down what Amir Masʿud did and what deeds were accomplished through his agency during that period when his father

Maḥmud passed away and his brother Moḥammad came to Ghaznin and ascended the royal throne, until that time when they held him in custody at Teginābād, so that everything is clearly recorded. Once I have finished this, I shall then go back to the story of the army's departure from Teginābād for Herat, with all the details of how they travelled back, with the Great Chamberlain following in their tracks and what happened when they reached Herat. Also, what further happened to Amir Moḥammad when the General Begtegin transported him from the fortress at Teginābād to that of Mandish,[69] entrusted his keeping to the castellan there, and returned.

Amir Masʿud was at Isfahan, and intended to leave the Commander-in-Chief[70] Tāsh Farrāsh[71] there and advance on the region of Hamadan and Jebāl. The household servants had pitched the camp enclosure outside [the town] and he planned to leave that week on Tuesday,[72] 20 Jomādā I 421 [/26 May 1030]. Then the news unexpectedly arrived that Masʿud's father Amir Maḥmud had passed away, that the Great Chamberlain ʿAli Qarib had [Gh 13] taken charge of affairs and that swift horsemen had immediately set out for Guzgānān speedily to bring back Amir Moḥammad and set him on the royal throne. When the Amir became aware of these happenings, he was greatly taken aback by it all, and [F 13] all his forthcoming plans were now set at nought.[73]

Later, after Amir Masʿud had gone from Herat to Balkh and affairs in the state had become settled and harmonious, Khᵛāja Ṭāher the secretary recounted the following to me:

[The beginning of Ṭāher's long narrative:] When this news reached Isfahan, Amir Masʿud sent for me in mid-morning of that very same day and took me aside. He said, "My father has passed away and they have summoned my brother to ascend the royal throne." I said, "May the lord live for ever!" Then he passed over to me the slim, confidential message[74] and said, "Read it." I opened it. It was the handwriting of his paternal aunt Ḥorra Khottali,[75] and she had written, "Our lord Sultan Maḥmud, God's mercy be up on him, passed away at the time of the evening worship on Thursday, 23 Rabiʿ II [/30 April 1030], and our happy time came to an end.[76] I, and all the royal womenfolk (*ḥoram*) are staying in the citadel at Ghaznin, and the day after tomorrow we will make public his death. At the time of the night worship, they buried that monarch in the Piruzi Garden,[77] and we were all grief-stricken at his loss, for it had been a week whose like we had never before experienced. The Chamberlain ʿAli is now in complete charge. After the burial, swift horsemen set off that very night for Guzgānān to enable your brother Moḥammad to arrive here quickly and ascend the royal throne. This aunt of yours[78], by reason of the compassion and kindness which she bears for the Amir her nephew (lit. son), this same night wrote out in her own hand a brief message and ordered that, as soon as possible, two swift couriers (*rekāb-dār*), who had previously come to the Amir on some important items of business, should be designated secretly to convey the message from Ghaznin and with all speed reach the Amir's camp. The Amir knows that his brother is not capable of succeeding in such a great vocation. This house has many enemies, and we womenfolk, and the treasuries, have now become vulnerable and exposed, as if abandoned in the wilderness. The Amir must speedily take over the helm, [F 14] since he is his father's designated heir, and he must not be distracted by that region which he has just conquered; there will be occasions later to conquer other lands, for those works achieved until now were largely the result of his father's great prestige and awesome stature; once the news of his death gets out, things will become very different. Ghaznin is the heart (*aṣl*) [of the empire], then comes Khorasan, and the rest are all subsidiary dependencies (*farʿ*). [Gh 14] Let him consider thoroughly what I have written, and let him prepare with all possible haste to come back lest this royal capital and we ourselves are left in a wasted condition. Let him also speedily send back couriers, for your aunt is anxiously awaiting the arrival of your response; and whatever happens here will be reported to him in writing."[79]

[Ṭāher went on:] When I became aware of all this, I said, "May the lord's life be prolonged! There is no need for consultation; what she has written must be done, because everything she has said is pure and unalloyed good advice. This news should not be revealed to anyone." He replied. "It's exactly as you say. The sensible plan of action is the one she has envisaged. I shall do just that, if the Almighty God wills it, but it is incumbent upon us to go through the process of consultation.[80] Arise, and send for some attendants, and let them summon the Commander-in-Chief Tāsh,[81] the Great Chamberlain Altuntāsh,[82] and the other leading figures and senior commanders so that we might speak with them frankly and hear what they have to say. Then, whatever is decided regarding these affairs, we will put into practice."

I arose and sent servants; the courtiers arrived, and we went into the Amir's presence. When we sat down, the Amir rehearsed to them the situation and gave me the confidential message to read out to them. When I had done this, they all said, "May the lord's life be prolonged! This noble princess (lit. "queen," *maleka*) has given wise counsel and has conveyed the news in a most timely manner. It is a great blessing that this information [F 15] has arrived here, for if the exalted royal presence[83] had left on an auspicious expedition (i.e. to conquer the West) and had turned his attention to an outlying region and an unfinished project, and this news had reached him there, he would inevitably have had to turn back, and this would have been unseemly. What has the lord now decided in this matter?" He replied, "You yourselves, what do *you* say is the right course of action?" They said, "We see no alternative but to hasten back." Masʿud said, "That's just what we think. But tomorrow, we shall order the news of our father's death to be publicly proclaimed. When the mourning ceremonies have been held, we shall send a message to the Son of Kāku[84] and use conciliatory words with him. Without doubt he will already have heard the news before our envoy reaches him, and it suits him well that we should return from this place, and he will therefore agree without a qualm to whatever we stipulate regarding the tribute money.[85] [Gh 15] For in practice, he will not hand over anything of the stipulated amount since he is fully aware of the fact that, when we leave, many critical problems will lie ahead of us, and for a long time to come we shall not be able to concern ourselves with this. However, it will serve us as a face-saving excuse for our going back." All those present exclaimed, "This is extremely sound and well-thought out, and there is no better course of action. The quicker the exalted royal presence can make for Khorasan, the better. The distance is great, and those who have seized power in Ghaznin will harbour more ambitious delusions which will make matters more difficult and protracted for us." The Amir said, "You all go back now, while I look into this more thoroughly, and I shall issue the necessary orders." So those assembled went away.

The next day, the Amir held court, wearing a white tunic, cloak and cloth tied round his head-dress (i.e. as a sign of mourning), and all the leading figures and senior commanders, and all the various components of the army, came to offer their service, likewise clothed in white.[86] Much lamenting went on, and there were three days of royal mourning, with proper decorum , to the approval of everyone.

When the period of mourning came to an end, the Amir detailed an envoy to be sent to ʿAlāʾ al-Dowla Bu Jaʿfar b. Kāku, and he was despatched. He was stationed a short distance away. [F 16] Before this message could arrive, the Commander of the Faithful had written a letter of intercession on behalf of ʿAlāʾ al-Dowla, asking that Isfahan should be given back to him, that he should function as Masʿud's deputy there and that what had been laid down as tribute money, he was to hand over. The bearer of the letter had stayed on, and was being treated in an evasive manner.[87]

But now, Amir Masʿud seized the opportunity of the caliph's letter of intercession, and he sent an envoy to ʿAlāʾ al-Dowla. The letter and message were couched in the following terms: "We have put into effect the Commander of the Faithful's intercession, in complete conformity with his will, for an invitation from the lord to servants is a command and not mere intercession. Since we have now undertaken more momentous matters than those of Isfahan, no more suitable deputy for there can be found than the Amir ʿAlāʾ al-Dowla. If at the outset, when we led an expedition against these lands, sent a messenger and set forth our justification, we had not encountered resistance and obduracy, the present mishap could have been avoided. But there was no way out; we had to accept things as they were. Now, however, the situation has changed. We are giving up the project of conquering that region (i.e. Hamadan and Jebāl), since we have to undertake a more pressing obligation. We are setting out for Khorasan, for the great sultan [Gh 16] has passed away, and the task of administering a vast realm has been neglected there. The task of securing the centre must have priority over attending to the periphery, especially as Khorasan is a great distance away from here and could be lost to us. A military governor[88] will be chosen for Ray, Ṭārom[89] and the conquered lands, with the aim that, in our absence, no breach should take place there in any circumstances. Moreover, should anyone harbour dreams of rebellion and exploit this opportunity to stage an uprising, his dream and opportunity will last only for the little stretch of time that we need to sit down on our father's throne. We shall never again, in any circumstances, allow this region to be neglected, for we have now seen its problems for ourselves and their nature is clear to us.

From the vantage point of our father's throne, the task of administering that region will acquire a new perspective, since there are there, God be praised, large quantities of men, weapons and machines of war. Now the Amir 'Alā' al-Dowla must put these plans into immediate effect, and avoid any bickering and arguing, so that we can leave here with a well-conceived and well thought-out plan in place. [F 17] Then if anyone tries to ensnare him (i.e. 'Alā' al-Dowla, the Son of Kāku), he should not fall for the argument that, 'You should make light of the agreement, given the fact that Mas'ud is about to depart and won't be here much longer'. He should not pay heed to such words, for we are already extremely vexed by this affair, and if we return incensed, the matter will be dealt with in a thoroughly different manner. Farewell!"

The envoy set off and delivered the message. The Son of Kāku listened attentively and thought it a most opportune arrangement, and responded favourably. They spent three days in parleying, until it was decided that, in the absence of the Amir, he should become the Amir's deputy in Isfahan and that each year he should hand over 200,000 Heravi dinars[90] and 10,000 pieces of clothing from the workshops of Isfahan and its vicinity,[91] in addition to Nowruz and Mehragān presents of all kinds, Arabian horses and camels with fine accoutrements and travelling equipment of all sorts. The Amir accepted the Son of Kāku's excuses [Gh 17] and richly rewarded his envoy. He ordered that an investiture patent for Isfahan and the surrounding regions should be written out for Abu Ja'far b. Kāku and a fine robe of honour prepared for him and his envoy sent on his way.[92]

Having sent back the envoy, the Amir departed from Isfahan for Ray, in an elated mood and confident of victory, on 24 Jomādā II [/29 June 1030]. When he reached the city of Ray, the local people had already heard news of his approach, and had made a great effort to decorate and bedeck the city in a manner beyond all measure. The Amir, however, chose to halt on the edge of the city, where they had pitched tents, and declared his intention to depart soon. The populace of Ray, high-born and low-born, came forth and performed profuse acts of service and submission before the Amir. He, for his part, sent his trusty retainers [F 18] into the city to see all the efforts which the people had undertaken and then give him an account of them. He praised the people of Ray for the devoted service which they had shown.

In this same place, reports came to him, by means of letters from trustworthy sources, that Amir Moḥammad had come to Ghaznin and that affairs there were under his control, with the troops all obedient and submissive to him, for it has been said that *"[the people of] this world are slaves of dinars and dirhams"*[93] (i.e. men will inevitably follow their own material interests). The news was a matter of great concern to Amir Masʿud and he immediately decided to send Sayyed ʿAbd al-ʿAziz ʿAlavi, who was noted for his intelligence and shrewdness, on a mission to Ghaznin.[94] At Masʿud's behest, the Divān secretaries composed a letter of greetings and condolences to the Amir's brother, and gave messages on the subject of the inheritance arrangements and the empire. All these happenings were already described in full while narrating the time of Amir Moḥammad's rule, and should suffice.

After he had despatched this ʿAlavi on this mission, the letter of the Commander of the Faithful al-Qāder be'llāh reached Ray conveying condolences and greetings as is customary in such cases. It was a response to Amir Masʿud's letter written from Isfahan concerning Sultan Maḥmud's passing away and his own forthcoming departure for Khorasan, and also his request for a battle standard, a succession diploma and everything which went with that, comprising honorific epithets and titles, since he was Maḥmud's designated heir. The Commander of the Faithful had instructed him in this letter that "All the lands in the regions of Ray, Jebāl and Isfahan that he has conquered are now conferred on him. He is to hasten to Khorasan [Gh 18] lest any threats of disturbance arise in that important frontier region (*thaghr*). The various grants which have been sought, including the standard, the succession diploma and other marks of nobility, are with a messenger who is following closely behind."

At the receipt of this letter, Amir Masʿud was filled with joy and became much heartened, and he ordered it to be read out to the assembled throng to the accompaniment of trumpets and drums. They made copies of the letter [F 19] and sent them to Isfahan, Ṭārom, the regions of Jebāl, Gorgān and Ṭabarestān, Nishapur and Herat, so that people would fully realize that Masʿud was the Commander of the Faithful's deputy and the designated heir of his father.[95]

Also at this time, there arrived swift couriers from Ghaznin bringing letters from Amir Yusof, the Great Chamberlain ʿAli, Abu Sahl Ḥamdavi,[96] the mayor (*raʾis*) Khᵛāja ʿAli Mikāʾil[97] and the *sarhang* Abu

ʿAli the castellan. They all offered their homage and said, "In the interests of peace and stability at the time, Amir Moḥammad was summoned to Ghaznin lest there arose disturbance and unrest in the state. But he is not up to the task, being solely interested in wine-drinking and merry-making. The lord, who is the true designated successor of his father, must hasten, with a firm heart and great zest, so that he reaches the imperial capital as soon as possible, since as soon as they hear of his exalted presence's arrival in Khorasan, they will come forward to offer him service." Amir Masʿud's mother[98] and his paternal aunt Ḥorra Khottali had also written letters and had explained that complete reliance should be placed on what these humble servants said, since what they had said was the truth."

The Amir became much heartened at the receipt of these letters. He held a court session and summoned the leading men from his commanders and retainers, and related these affairs to them. He said, "This is how matters stand; what is your advice?" They replied, "The right course is the one which the lord sees fit to adopt." He said, "If we fix our attention on these [western] lands, we shall face difficulties. We have conquered by the sword so many regions of great repute, but ultimately, these are peripheral regions, and to set one's mind on the periphery [Gh 19] and leave the heartlands as they are would be a grave error. The correct decision for us here is that we should hasten towards Nishapur and Herat and make for the heartland (i.e. Ghaznin). If, as they have written, this matter can be settled without fighting, and if we assume the imperial throne without further strife, [F 20] we can think again about resolving matters in these lands." They replied, "The more correct view is the one which the lord has come up with. The sooner he departs from here, the better." The Amir said, "A military governor must be appointed for here. Whom should we designate, and how large a force of cavalry?" They answered, "Who will the lord choose? For anyone who stays behind here is going to stay behind reluctantly. It is clear that a certain number of men should be left here. If the people of Ray keep to their word and remain obedient, someone in nominal charge would do, but if they do become unruly, even a substantial garrison here will prove inadequate". The Amir said, "Yes, these are my very own thoughts. I want Ḥasan b. Soleymān to remain here with a force of 500 stout-hearted cavalry. Summon the leading citizens of Ray tomorrow so that what needs to be communicated to them about these arrangements can be said, for whatever happens, we are going to depart the day after tomorrow, since we cannot stay here any longer." They expressed their assent and went away. They sent messengers to the notables of Ray with the instruction, "The exalted command requires that, tomorrow, all of you should present yourselves at the door of the royal tented pavilion." They replied, "We will obey the command."

The next day, a large group of the city notables came forth, including ʿAlids,[99] judges, imams, religious lawyers and prominent citizens, and all sorts of their followers, together with large numbers of the common people. The Amir had given orders that a large body of troops should be paraded with a great display of pomp and ceremony. A substantial force of gholāms was stationed at the door of the tent and with many cavalrymen and infantrymen in the grounds outside, laden with weapons. They then held the court session. The senior commanders and great men of the army were seated in front of the Amir and the rest were standing. Then they brought forward the leading citizens of Ray, comprising about fifty to sixty of the more illustrious of them. The Amir gave a sign [Gh 20] that they should all sit down at some distance away and he began to speak. [F 21] Now a speech by this monarch justly deserved universal attention and acclaim, for he would sprinkle his address with mellifluous words and gem-like phrases.[100] His utterances, whether spoken or in written form, must be cited in this History so that that readers will be assured that no hyperbole is implied in [our] account of monarchs. The Almighty God has said, and His word is true, *"and [God] has increased him amply in knowledge and stature; God bestows His kingly power on whomever He wills."*[101]

The Amir then said to the notables, "What is your opinion about our conduct and actions so far? Don't feel inhibited, and speak the truth and don't dissimulate." They answered, "May the lord's life be prolonged! Since we have been delivered from the calamity and tyranny of the Deylamites, and the eminent name of this great house—may it endure for ever!—has come down upon us, we have slept the sleep of security, and night and day we have raised up our hands in prayer that the Almighty God may not remove far from us the shadow of the lord's compassion and justice. For now we can eat well and sleep well and enjoy security of our lives, possessions, womenfolk, lands and property, which was not the case in the time of the Deylamites."

The Amir said, "We are about to depart, for we have an important task ahead of us and it is our main concern. Letters have arrived from the notables and leading figures[102] that our father the sultan has passed away, and they have said that there is a pressing need to hasten back so that the kingdom can be set in order. We are not referring to domains petty in extent, but to Khorasan, India, Sind, Nimruz and Khwarazm, and in no circumstances can they be left alone and neglected, because they are the heartland. When we are done with these tasks, plans for these regions will have to be made; we will either send one of our capable sons, with a full retinue, or else a commander of high repute with a complete panoply of arms and troops. [F 22] For the moment, we are appointing for here a military governor with a small body of troops, as an experiment, so that we can see what effect this will have in regard to your comportment. If we discern obedience and submission, with no hypocrisy or dubious behaviour, we shall act correspondingly with justice and beneficence to such a degree that nothing better can be imagined. But if things turn out the opposite, expect from us a corresponding requital, and in the sight of the Almighty God we would be excused, since you would have brought it upon yourselves. What was done to the region of Isfahan and its people [Gh 21] serves as a thoroughly convincing example to mankind.[103] You must give a firm and decisive answer, and not indulge in sophistry and disputation, so that one can have full confidence in it."

When the Amir had finished his speech, the notables of Ray all looked at each other, and great fear and perturbation were visible on their faces. They made a signal to the state-appointed preacher of the city, who was an aged man, of excellent character, eloquent,[104] and much travelled. He got to his feet and said, "May the life of the monarch of Islam be prolonged! Here in this great court session, with its boundless display of splendour, we are impotent at giving an answer and have shrunk back in fear. If the exalted judgement sees fit and gives the command, let one of the trusty attendants of the court sit down outside, and let we servants make our way to the place [where Ṭāher the secretary is sitting],[105] and we will give an answer." The Amir said, "That's a fitting suggestion."

They conducted the notables of Ray into the great tent where Ṭāher the secretary was sitting. All affairs went through his hands, since he was the most exalted of the secretaries. Ṭāher came in and sat down, and this group of notables came before him, having come to a decision amongst themselves [F 23] what answer they would give. Ṭāher said, "You heard the lord's words; what is your answer?" They replied, "May the life of the most eminent Secretary (Khᵛāja ʿAmid) be prolonged! All of us have agreed upon a single statement. We have spoken with the preacher and what he heard from our lips he will pass on to the Amir." Ṭāher said, "You have done well to ensure that the discussion does not drag too long. What is your answer?"

The preacher said, "These notables and elders of Ray would agree as a group to whatever was said and stipulated for them as tribute, even if it amounted to two million dirhams[106] on the city and its dependent territories, and they would respond obediently. [Gh 22] They say that they were captives in the hands of the Deylamites for nearly thirty years, with the usages of Islam obliterated, since after the time of Fakhr al-Dowla and the Ṣāḥeb Ebn ʿAbbād, the royal power fell into the hands of an incompetent and ineffective woman and boy.[107] Hands were raised in supplication to the Almighty God until He instilled in the mind of the monarch of Islam, Maḥmud, the idea of proceeding here and responding to our cries for help. He freed us from the oppression and corruption of the Carmathians (Qarāmeṭa) and the evildoers, and rooted out those incompetent ones who were unable to maintain us in security, and he expelled them from this land;[108] and when he returned from here in an auspicious manner, he appointed for us a just, benevolent and decisive lord (i.e. Masʿud). Since that lord (i.e. Maḥmud) departed, this lord (Masʿud) has never been at rest and the saddle-felt of his horse has never had time to dry. He was engaged in conquering the world and removing those too tyrannical and incompetent to govern, to such a point that, if this great misfortune of his father's death had not occurred, he would by now have reached Baghdad and have overthrown the other impotent and useless rulers. He would have answered the distress calls of the subjects of those regions and would also have given them a taste of his own sweet justice. Up to the time when his banner was at Isfahan, it is well known that there has been a general officer (*ḥājeb*) as military governor here in our city and its environs, with two hundred cavalrymen, and no-one from the rump of the group of evildoers would have had the temerity to stir. For if someone [F 24] bent on creating mischief had come this way, and even if his military power had amounted to a thousand men, or two thousand, or more or less, right up to ten thousand, the young and the brave from amongst us would certainly have taken up their weapons and joined forces with the lord's military governor to dispose of those mischief-makers, with the victorious help[109] of the Almighty God. If this lord were to advance as far as Egypt,[110] we would undertake this same task, heedless of the difference between the two distances involved. And if, when the lord is relieved of his present tasks—and given his mighty resolve, that should not take long—he decides to return here victorious and in a happy frame of mind, or if he decides to send a commander instead, [Gh 23] it will make no difference, for we shall be even more humble and obedient on that day than we are now. For while we live, we shall not allow the great manifestation of benevolence which we have experienced to slip away from our hands. Indeed, if on this very day, when he has expressed his wish to depart, he should order a whipping-pole to be set up to chastise us all, we should still be obedient. Our reply is these words we have just spoken."

The preacher turned his face towards the assembled crowd and said, "Is this speech that I have just made your words also?" They all answered, "Yes, it is, nay, we go even further than this in our submissiveness."

Ṭāher said, "May God reward you with goodness! You have spoken well, and have shown your deep appreciation of your shepherd and protector." He arose and went into the Amir's presence and reported their response. The Amir rejoiced exceedingly and said, " O Ṭāher, when good fortune comes along, all things fall into shape at once. This is a most wise and sensible reply, and these people deserve all kinds of rewards. Give orders for appropriate robes of honour for the judge, the mayor,[111] the official preacher, the marshal of the 'Alids[112] and the commander of the ghāzis[113] to be made immediately. The mayor, the marshal of the 'Alids and the judge are to have robes decorated with gold and the others are to have gilded ones. Let them don them and then bring [them] forward so that they may hear our words. After that, send them back to the city accompanied by some of the holders of court offices in charge of protocol[114] in the most dignified manner possible.[115] [F 25]

Ṭāher arose and settled himself at some spot, and summoned the keepers of the treasuries. They prepared appropriate robes of honour.

When everything was in good order, Ṭāher went back to the notables of Ray and said, "I conveyed to the lord the answer that you gave. It proved very pleasing and acceptable, and he ordered for those of you notables who hold high offices to be awarded worthy and prestigious robes of honour. Now go ahead with my blessings and proceed to the Royal Wardrobe (*jāma-khāna*) so that you may be clothed in an auspicious manner."[116] The black-clothed attendants[117] conducted all five [Gh 24] to the royal wardrobe and dressed them in their robes of honour. After this, Ṭāher went into the Amir's presence and they brought in the group of the notables of Ray. The Amir made much of them and spoke to them in an encouraging way. They, for their part, offered up fervent prayers and then returned home. The court officials escorted them back to the city in a group and in the most dignified manner possible. The city populace made great rejoicings; they threw down unprecedented amounts of dirhams and dinars, and then sent back court officials in a handsome and joyous manner.

The next day, when the court session had come to its end—the notables of Ray having come en bloc to render service, together with these commanders, and there being more than ten thousand men and women standing watching the spectacle—they caused the notables to be seated within the domed tent (*nim-tark*)[118]. The Amir summoned Ḥasan b. Soleymān, who was one of the great commanders of the mountain regions of Herat, greeted him warmly and said, "We intend to depart tomorrow and are entrusting the military governorship of this province to your care. You heard what the notables said; be prudent and alert so that no untoward incident occurs during our absence. Treat the people of these regions well and be considerate in your conduct. Rest assured that once we have ascended the royal throne and things have worked out to our satisfaction, we shall make provision for these regions and despatch here [F 26] a strong commander with troops, accompanied by a high-ranking and trustworthy secretary (lit. "one of the lords of the pen"),[119] who will all work under his command and for his purposes, so that, if God so wills, the remainder of Western Persia[120] may be seized. The notables and the subjects must be contented with your rule and be thankful for it. Because of our high regard for you, you will enjoy the full panoply of high rank and prestige, with all your needs and desires fulfilled."

Ḥasan b. Soleymān rose to his feet—he being one of those who had the privilege of being seated in this court session—and kissed the ground. Then he stood up and said, "I am your humble and obedient servant, and am not worthy of this high position, but since the lord has conferred it upon me, I shall do my utmost in carrying out your commands." The Amir ordered that he should be taken along to the royal wardrobe and that they should clothe him in a precious robe of honour as the military governor of Ray: [Gh 25] a tunic worthy of his rank made of Rumi brocade, a gold belt weighing five hundred methqāls[121] and other appropriate items. He came before the Amir in his robe of honour and did obeisance, and was graciously received and praised by him. After this, he went on to Ṭāher's tent, and he too showered him with compliments. The notables of Ray were summoned, and Ṭāher explained to them what had just been done. They were filled with joy, and offered up copious prayers and praises. Ṭāher then ordered Ḥasan b. Soleymān to go into the city, dressed in his robe of honour, with a large escort of troops and accompanied by the city notables. They had decorated the city in celebration. They scattered forth large quantities of coins, and installed him with great ceremony in the palace which they had constructed, and all the populace paid him due marks of respect.[122]

The next day, Thursday, 13[123] Rajab 421 [/17 July 1030], [F 27] the Amir Shehāb al-Dowla Masʿud left the city of Ray under an auspicious star and good fortune, with a complete panoply of arms and troops, and all the necessary equipment for the journey. He made camp at two parasangs[124] along his route. Many people had come as far as there (from Ray) to offer service and to watch the proceedings. The following day, he mounted and ordered Ḥasan b. Soleymān and his retinue to return to Ray while he himself rode off at great speed.[125] When he reached Khᵛār in the region of Ray, he entrusted the town to the local leader (*zaʿim*) of the district, gave the requisite orders and went on his way. When he arrived at Dāmghān, Khᵛāja Bu Sahl Zowzani, having fled from Ghaznin, as has been described previously,[126] came forward there to meet him and the Amir made much of him. He had travelled light, carrying little in the way of luxuries. Amir Masʿud's leading retainers furnished him with so many sumptuous items of kit and equipment that he became very richly endowed. The Amir remained closeted privately with him from the afternoon prayer till the middle of the night.

Now in past times, when Amir Shehāb al-Dowla was residing at Herat, the most lavishly-honoured of his servants was this man Bu Sahl Zowzani. But he used to treat people badly, and could be brusque and bilious, given his choleric temperament. Since it is clear what sort of a person he was, I shall say no more, for he has passed away, and death is the final end of all human toil, but good nature and benevolence are preferable [Gh 26] and bring forth benefits both in this world and the next. Now since this eminent person enjoyed a higher status in the sight of Amir Masʿud than his other courtiers, they were filled with envy towards him. They drew up a legally-attested deposition and spread malicious words about the nature of his religious faith. They brought him to Ghaznin during the time of Sultan Maḥmud and jailed him in the citadel there, as I have explained in the *Tārikh-e Yamini.*[127] He has now passed on and those courtiers who drew up the deposition have passed on, and we too must pass on since the days of our life have reached their eventide. [F 28] Concerning this man's religious faith I shall not say anything but good, since I used to see him over a period of something like thirteen or fourteen years, drunk and sober, and at no time did I ever hear anything untoward from him, nor did he ever say anything which could be used as proof of the existence of defects in his religious faith. I am fully cognisant of this that I have written and will bear witness to it on the Day of Resurrection. Those persons who drew up the depositions will, on that Day, find themselves in an awesome assembly, standing there for judgement, and will give their answer. *May God preserve us and all the Muslims from envy, evil nature, faults and lapses through His beneficence and favour!*

Bu Sahl Zowzani's high status, which I have just described, and the extremely warm reception in Dāmghān that he had received from the Amir, and their private colloquy together,[128] induced all the other courtiers to regard him in a different light. They realized the lofty eminence that he had achieved and, with his arrival on the scene, the shattering of their own dreams of high office. As the poet has said, (Poetry)

1. *When Moses came along and threw down his staff, all forms of magic and magicians were set at naught.*[129]

The man assumed a vizier-like status, being at the receiving end of all the Amir's deliberations, and he took the wind out of Ṭāher's sails and those of the other courtiers.[130] Bu Sahl was the one who was now issuing commands on every subject, and this added further to his power and status.[131]

When Amir Shehāb al-Dowla (Masʿud) moved on from Dāmghān, after one parasang he came to a village, which had a very copious subterranean conduit.[132] Here there came into his presence the courier who had been despatched on the orders of Sultan Maḥmud with the letter under the exalted seal and signature conveying praise and thanks for the tribute money sent from Isfahan, [Gh 27] the wardrobe and the treasuries, but also with those [F 29] slim, confidential letters to the army commanders and to the Son of Kāku proclaiming his disapproval of his unruly son (i.e. Masʿud),[133] as I have explained previously.[134]

The courier dismounted, kissed the ground and drew that momentous letter from inside his tunic and held it out. The Amir reined back his horse and one of the senior officers took the letter and gave it to him, and he began to read it. When he had come to the end, he said to the courier, "It's five or six months since this letter was written; where have you tarried all this time and what is the reason for this late arrival?" The courier replied, "May the lord's life be prolonged! When I set out from Baghlān[135] for Balkh, I fell ill and had to stay for a while at Balkh. When I reached Sarakhs,[136] the Commander-in-Chief of Khorasan, the General Ghāzi, was there, and the news arrived of Sultan Maḥmud's decease. He went off to Nishapur, taking me with him and not allowing me to proceed, saying that 'The lord will arrive with auspiciousness; there is no point in proceeding, since the roads have become unsafe, and it is inadvisable for a solitary rider to travel lest some outrage occur.' When the letter reached Ghāzi with the news that the lord had set out from Ray, he gave permission for me to continue my journey. The road to here from Nishapur is very disturbed. I took very keen precautions, so that I was able to arrive here in safety."

The Amir said, "Where are those confidential letters which Bu Naṣr Moshkān gave you, with instructions that you were to keep them well concealed until they could be delivered?" He replied, "I have them safe." He took off his saddle, opened up the layer of saddle felt, took out the letters encased in wax and extracted them from the wax covering them. The Amir said to Bu Sahl Zowzani, "Read them and see what they say." He read through the first one and said, "It deals with the same matter that the lord was talking about." He scrutinised another, and it was identical with the first one. He said, "They are all written in the same way." The Amir took one of them and read it, exclaiming, "It corroborates exactly what they wrote to me from Baghlān when they informed me of the contents of these confidential letters, Praise be to the Almighty God! A monarch in his last days and with all his wishes fulfilled, leaves his son [F 30] with no succour in an alien land [Gh 28] in the midst of many foes.[137] Now if the Almighty God happens to come to the son's aid and lead him to victory and success in several missions, it should have been incumbent upon the father to express his delight and joy, so how can one explain this anger and wrath?"

Bu Sahl and the rest of the courtiers who were with the Amir said, "Maḥmud[138] wanted one thing, and the Almighty God wanted another, and lo, He has bestowed on you, Amir Masʿud, his royal seat, the kingdom, the treasuries and everything that he possessed.[139] These confidential letters ought to be preserved so that people may read them and learn what your father's thoughts were, and what the Almighty God had intended. They should also know about the hearts and minds of the persons who wrote these letters."

The Amir replied, "Do you realize what you are saying? If, at the close of his life, our father thought that a single harsh act was expedient, and he displayed some animus in it, know that one must take into consideration a thousand beneficial acts which he did on our behalf and how he forgave many serious lapses of ours. Those reproofs will now hold a profitable example for me. May the Almighty God have mercy upon him! For no mother can ever give birth to another like Maḥmud. As for those who wrote out the letters, what offence can one lay at their door? They were acting as agents, and agents have perforce to carry out the orders they are given, especially those issued by kings. If we were to command a secretary to write something out, even if the message involved his own destruction, would he have the audacity not to write it?", and he ordered the lot of those secret letters to be torn up and thrown into that subterranean conduit.[140] He spurred on his horse, and ordered the courier to be given 5,000 dirhams.

When wise men come to this story, however noble and praiseworthy the manner of behaviour and habits of this king may have been, they will recognize him as even more laudable, and it will become more firmly fixed in their minds that he was unique in his time.

I, [Gh 29] Bu'l-Fażl, recall to mind two remarkable stories in this connection. One is regarding [F 31] Khᵛāja Bu Sahl and how he was viewed by Amir Masʿud's courtiers. When they saw him, whether they liked it or not, they considered him a great man. For men should strive hard and find an occasion to win a noble reputation for themselves. Once they achieve this, they will be held in respect, both in good times and bad, and their fame and prestige will stay with them till their dying day.

The other story is that concerning those secret letters and their being torn up and thrown into the water. When all those writers of the letters and all those persons to whom the letters had been addressed heard about this incident, they were highly relieved, knowing that Amir Masʿud would not raise the matter again. In such things, kings receive their inspiration from the Almighty God Himself.

As for the story of the courtiers, I have read in the history of the caliphs (*akhbār-e kholafā'*)[141] that when the Commander of the Faithful Hārun al-Rashid left Baghdad, heading for Khorasan (this is a long story, and the reason behind his journey is set forth in the history books), on reaching Ṭus he fell gravely ill and was at death's door. He sent for Fażl b. Rabiʿ,[142] who held the vizierate after the Barmaki family, and when Fażl came he spoke with him privately. He said, "O Fażl, my life is coming to an end and death is near. When I have expired, bury me here, but when you have completed the burial and the mourning ceremonies, send everything which I possess—treasuries, the armoury and other things, gholāms, beasts of burden, in their entirety—to my son Ma'mun at Merv, since Moḥammad (i.e. al-Amin) has no need of them, seeing that he has the position of designated heir in Baghdad, the seat of the caliphate, the army and all sorts of treasuries. With regard to the troops and retainers who are here with me, give them the choice, so that everyone who wishes to join Ma'mun should be allowed to go and not be held back. [Gh 30] When you have done this, go to Baghdad and Moḥammad's court and act as his vizier and counsellor. Hold fast to the arrangements I have made for my three children. Bear in mind that if you and all my other retainers decide to break your vows and choose the path of injustice, it will bring you only misfortune, and the Almighty God [F 32] will not be pleased and you will follow each other into perdition." Fażl b. Rabiʿ answered, "I accept this testament from the Almighty God and from the Commander of the Faithful and will see it through." In that very same night, Hārun passed away, God's mercy be upon him.

Next day, they buried him and performed the appropriate mourning ceremonies. Fażl accordingly addressed the entire assembly of troops and retainers and said, "We must go to Baghdad." They set off, except those individuals who favoured Ma'mun, and either stealthily or openly, without their retinues and possessions,[143] went to Ma'mun in Merv. Fażl set out and went to Baghdad, and the administration of the caliphate devolved on him, while Moḥammad b. Zobeyda was occupied with merry-making and diversions.

After this, Fażl embarked upon a policy of depriving Ma'mun of his title of next designated heir, and told the preachers to make disparaging remarks about Ma'mun from the pulpits and ordered the poets to satirize him—it is a long story and not relevant to my purpose here. Fażl did everything possible to inflict harm and damage to Ma'mun's position, but he could not prevail over the decree ordained by the Almighty God. Ṭāher Dhu'l-Yamineyn set out against ʿAli b. ʿIsā b. Māhān, who was at Ray. They cut off ʿAli's head and brought it to Merv. From there they marched against Baghdad from two directions, Ṭāher from one direction and Harthama b. Aʿyan from the other. The war continued for two-and-a-half years until Moḥammad b. Zobeyda fell into Ṭāher's hands and they killed him, sending his head to Ma'mun's court at Merv. The caliphate was now firmly established under Ma'mun's rule. He remained at Merv for two years and various events took place in this period till the time when he arrived in Baghdad. The affairs of the caliphate were now on a secure basis, and all the causes of disruption, schism and internecine strife were removed, so that all minds were set at rest.

Fażl b. Rabiʿ went into hiding and remained there for over three years until he fell into Ma'mun's hands; that is in itself a long story and is clearly recorded in the histories of the caliphs. Ma'mun was foremost in his era in displaying shrewd judgement, intelligence, learning and chivalry and in all the virtues associated with the great. [Gh 31; F 33] Despite the many acts of disloyalty that Fażl had committed and the evil designs that he had harboured, Ma'mun forgave his offences and pardoned him, and sent him back home on condition that he should not come to the court and render service. After he had spent a considerable length of time idle and unemployed, mediators began to intercede on his behalf, for he was a man of great stature and was owed many favours by everyone. They were biding their time until they managed to soften Ma'mun's heart, and induced him to treat Fażl more favourably, so that Ma'mun commanded him to come and render service at court again.

When this order was announced, Fażl sent one of his people to 'Abdallāh, son of Ṭāher, who was Ma'mun's Great Chamberlain and a close friend of Fażl,[144] with the message that "The Commander of the Faithful has forgiven my offences and has ordered that I should render service at court. I know that I owe all this first to the favour of the Almighty and then to your intervention, and I realize how kindly and graciously you have acted yourself in all this and how strenuously you have exerted yourself on my behalf to bring this about. Since the Commander of the Faithful has ordered that I should re-enter the court service—and you know that I was a man of considerable status and repute in the past, as indeed was my father before me, for our high rank and repute belong to a long-established tradition—you must perform another gracious favour and enquire at what rank or degree I will be placed. This will sound appropriate, coming from you, and you can make the request since you have the post of head chamberlain, and the Commander of the Faithful will not suspect that I had asked for this and that I had initiated this inquiry." 'Abdallāh said, "I am grateful for your words and will do all I can in this matter."

At the time of the afternoon worship, 'Abdallāh went to the court, but since there was no court session, he wrote a letter to the caliphal court in the following terms: "The lord, the Commander of the Faithful, as is fitting for his greatness and his magnanimity, ordered that that sinful one, whom the lord's forgiveness has raised back to life (i.e. Fażl b. Rabi'), should come and render service at the court. All of us have derived lofty hopes from this high favour that he has bestowed. [F 34] Now what is the exalted command, and at what rank should I have him stationed at court when he comes to render service at the caliph's throne?"[145] When Ma'mun's personal attendant (or: eunuch, *khādem*)[146] conveyed this letter to his master—and 'Abdallāh was wont to write many such letters concerning matters of state at times when the court [Gh 32] was not in session, and replies would come back in Ma'mun's own hand—the answer to it came back with the following wording: "O ʿAbdallāh b. Ṭāher, the Commander of the Faithful is cognisant of what you had written and of your request for answers[147] concerning Fażl b. Rabiʿ, the shameless and treacherous rebel. Now that his life has been spared, he is lusting after a rise in his status. He must be kept down in the lowest grade at court, on a par with the lowliest and the most abject of our troopers.[148] Farewell!"

When ʿAbdallāh b. Ṭāher saw the answer couched in these terms, he became very downcast. He sent his original letter with the reply on its reverse by the hand of one of his trusty servants, and in great secrecy, to Fażl and gave him the message, "Now that such a response has come, the best course is that first thing tomorrow, before daybreak, you should come along and sit down in the place that I shall have commanded to be made ready, for there is certainly no point in broaching the subject again now and seeking further guidance from the caliph, for we would not be certain of the outcome and it may well generate more trouble. This lord is of a compassionate and sensitive demeanour, and when he sees you in your present position, it may be that he will not approve of you being humiliated and degraded to such a degree, and in the course of time, this matter may be straightened out."

When this trusty servant reached Fażl and delivered the message, and Fażl had perused the letter and reply, he sent the message, "I will obey whatever is decreed, and I will not deviate from whatever course you, ʿAbdallāh, prescribe and consider to be in my best interests." ʿAbdallāh gave instructions that, in the first of the caliphal palaces, [F 35] they should rig up on the dais a curtain[149] with several *maḥfuri* carpets,[150] and he further laid down that they should install Fażl b. Rabiʿ on that dais before the court session opened. From this dais it was necessary to pass through three other buildings. These residences belonged to whoever enjoyed a high rank or station at court, starting from those who served as commanders of the guard[151] and the troops, until one reached the residences of the Vizier and the Great Chamberlain.[152]

On account of the Commander of the Faithful's decree, ʿAbdallāh had a place made for Fażl in this outer palace, and he now gave him instructions that, very early the next morning, [Gh 33] before daybreak, he was to come along and sit on that dais below the curtain. When the day broke, and people began to arrive, all who came into the first building and saw Fażl b. Rabiʿ, felt compelled to go forward and pay their respects to him, for they had known him at a time when he had enjoyed great power and prestige and they still held him in awe and respect. He, for his part, would ask after each one of them cordially and make his apologies until they left his presence. When the leading figures, pillars of the state, and the chamberlains began to come in, each one of them, according to his own status, would likewise ask after him warmly, and they were paying him the requisite honour and respectfulness. The Great Chamberlain ʿAbdallāh b. Ṭāher adopted an even more reverential attitude towards him, and offered apologies for having installed him in the outer palace, following a direct command that he had to obey. He further filled him with hope, saying that he would leave nothing undone in the way of facilitating care for his interests and favourable speech on his behalf. He passed on and went to his own designated place until it was time for the court session to begin.

When the Commander of the Faithful opened the audience session, all the leading figures, the Vizier, the holders of high offices, the pillars of the state, the chamberlains and the top commanders of the army, the lowly and the noble, went forth according to their status and official rank, and stood or sat down in their allocated places as befitting their rank.[153] ʿAbdallāh b. [F 36] Ṭāher, in his capacity as the Great Chamberlain, went into the Commander of the Faithful Ma'mun's presence and sought instructions, "The servant Fażl b. Rabiʿ has come in compliance with the exalted command. Following your orders, I placed him in the outer palace at a lowly position. What is your command in regard to his presentation?" The Commander of the Faithful thought for a moment and, swayed by his own noble instincts and magnanimous nature, issued an order that Fażl b. Rabiʿ should be brought in. ʿAbdallāh b. of Ṭāher instructed a chamberlain to bring him forward. When the latter entered the exalted caliphal presence, he conducted himself with the utmost humility and performed the obligations of obeisance up to the hilt, pleading ardently for his offences to be forgiven, and he wept, uttered lamentations and supplicated for pardon. The Caliph was moved to compassion and acted kindly towards him; he forgave him his crimes and pardoned him, bestowing on him the rank of those privileged to kiss the caliph's hand.

When the ceremonial session came to an end and all had returned to their places, ʿAbdallāh b. Ṭāher, the Great Chamberlain, enlisted the aid of the Vizier in promoting Fażl b. Rabiʿ's rehabilitation until the Caliph restored him to favour and commanded that he should be allocated a seat in the same palace where the leading notables were placed; and he was given hope of patronage and future service. [Gh 34] ʿAbdallāh b. Ṭāher immediately came out from the Caliph's presence and conveyed to Fażl the Caliph's marks of respect and favour, allocating him a place befitting his stature and raising his hopes for further marks of solicitude. Fażl's spirits were revived by all this, and he remained at the place assigned to him by ʿAbdallāh b. Ṭāher until the latter had finished his duties at the court and it was time for him to leave and head for his own abode. He mounted his horse in order to return to his own residence. Fażl b. Rabiʿ was waiting at the caliphal palace, and when ʿAbdallāh b. Ṭāher turned homewards, Fażl followed him.

ʿAbdallāh reined back his mount and halted, and implored Fażl to turn back. [F 37] Fażl, however, would on no account turn back and rode on instead, with his reins side-by-side with ʿAbdallāh's reins, to the gate of the latter's residence. When ʿAbdallāh arrived at the gate of his residence, he exhibited great embarrassment and concern on account of the excessive civility shown towards him by Fażl b. Rabiʿ and besought him to go back. The latter told him, "For your part, you have shown me such exalted conduct and generosity as befits a person of your lineage, innate nobility and magnanimous nature. As for my part, I consider nothing more appropriate in the world than what I have just done in exchange, and no greater service than that I escorted you, with my rein to your rein, back from the portal of the caliph to yours. For I swear by the Almighty God that, in my entire life, I have never stooped to escorting even caliphs and never ridden rein-by-rein with them, but I do so now in acknowledgement of your magnanimity towards me!"

ʿAbdallāh commented, "It was just as he said, and I for my part accepted wholeheartedly his magnificent gesture towards me, and deem it a great favour from him and an honour which I have earned to ennoble and enrich my own family's heritage."

Fażl b. Rabiʿ turned his horse round and returned to his own house. He found the quarter and his residence thronged with courtiers and men of eminence and stature. He sat down in his place, and offered his apologies and thanks to the guests for their visit before they took their leave, and so it went on until nightfall. ʿAbdallāh b. Ṭāher came along the next afternoon and presented the customary greetings and salutations, and then returned.

This is the end of the story. Wise persons who reflect on this tale will realize of what fibre and mettle these great men of the time were made. [Gh 35]

We now revert to the topic of secret letters, at the time when Maʾmun was at Merv, and Ṭāher and [F 38] Harthama were at the gates of Baghdad and had surrounded and hemmed in Maʾmun's brother Moḥammad b. Zobeyda, and fierce battles were being fought and the struggle was becoming protracted. From Baghdad, various commanders, leading figures and other ranks of people were making approaches to Maʾmun and penning letters in secret. From Merv likewise, a group from Maʾmun's circle were making approaches to Moḥammad and they too were writing letters secretly. Maʾmun had given orders that these secret letters should be placed in some chests[154] and they were being carefully guarded. The same procedure took place on Moḥammad's side (i.e. the letters were stored away and kept).

After Moḥammad was killed, and when Maʾmun arrived in Baghdad, the treasurers brought out before Maʾmun those secret letters which Moḥammad had ordered to be kept under guard, and they described the matter of those letters written secretly from Merv. Maʾmun closeted himself with his vizier Ḥasan b. Sahl.[155] He discussed his own chests and their documents and those of his brother and asked what should be done about them. Ḥasan said, "You should banish the traitors on both sides!" Maʾmun laughed and replied, "O Ḥasan, in that case there'd be no-one left on either side; they would go off and join up with the enemy, and deliver us up to them. We were two brothers, both worthy of the throne. These people could not have known what the outcome of events would be between us. They were merely looking after their own best interests, even though they did a wrongful deed; for servants[156] should maintain their trustworthiness, and honesty always triumphs in the end. Now since the Almighty God has bestowed the caliphate on us, we shall disregard these past actions and will not make them suffer." Ḥasan said, "The lord is right in taking this lofty view, and I was wrong. May the evil eye be far away!" Maʾmun ordered those secret letters to be brought in, and they were thrown on the fire until they were completely consumed.[157]

Wise persons [F 39] will recognize the depth and significance of this story. Both stories are at an end and we can now return to the thread of the history. The aim of recounting these stories has been to add lustre to the history. But they also serve another purpose, so that a talented person who is resolute as well as wise, [Gh 36] and is blessed by good fortune and favoured for promotion by a king, may be able to devise stratagems through which he may advance his position by careful, gradual and measured efforts. [The aim is also] that he should not let himself fall into the habit of thinking that it is difficult to reach a rank which some other person has managed to attain, for that leads to his becoming slothful and lethargic; nor should he be overawed by the amount of knowledge acquired by a person in a certain field and think it impossible that he should attain it, but rather, he should be resolute enough to attain that rank and master that branch of knowledge. For it would be a great defect in a man upon whom the Almighty God has bestowed innate and acute powers of perception and endeavour, thus enabling him to rise to high office or become learned in some topic, not to apply himself fully to that task but to relapse into despondency and despair. One of the great [poets] has very well said on this point, (Poetry)

1. *I have not seen anything [worse] amongst people's defects than failure to carry something through to its completion by those who have the power and ability to do so.*[158]

The value of books, stories and accounts of people's conduct in the past, lies in the fact that people read through them gradually and select what is fitting and applicable. *God is the vouchsafer of fortune and favour!*

When Amir Shehāb al-Dowla set off from Dāmghān, he ordered letters to be written to the Commander-in-Chief of Khorasan, the General Ghāzi, and to the judges, notables, mayor and the tax officials[159] that he was on his way and that it was necessary that the requisite preparations should be made. The Amir continued: "The General Ghāzi, the effects of whose meritorious actions have now become apparent and who has already rendered service with such complete success, will receive an especially prestigious reward. He must come and render service with the troops, [F 40] both those troops who were with him and those who have been freshly recruited, all with their complete panoply of arms. Also, let it be known that those whom he has freshly enrolled will be retained by us in their rank and station according to the way which he has deemed right and seen as fitting, and there are to be bounties and pay increases. We are confident that the supplies of fodder, which the local governors and tax officials and the mayor had to assemble, are prepared and ready, but if anything is amiss, it must be speedily redressed, for our arrival is imminent." [Gh 37]

When the letters arrived by a swift-riding cavalryman (*kheyltāsh*), the General Ghāzi and the others set to work with greater exertion, and completed the unfinished tasks, and all conceivable preparations were carried out by the army.

Amir Masʿud reached the district (*rustā*) of Beyhaq in an assured and triumphant manner.[160] Ghāzi, the Commander-in-Chief of Khorasan, went out to greet and render homage to the Amir,[161] accompanied by a large body of troops with full and splendid trappings. The Amir stood on an eminence, and Ghāzi went forward, kissing the ground in three places. The Amir ordered that great honour and favour should be shown to him, and they took his arm while he advanced and kissed the Amir's stirrup. The Amir said, "You have done your duty. Now we must do ours. Today we appoint you to the office of Commander-in-Chief, and when we reach Nishapur in good state, orders for an appropriate robe of honour will be given." Ghāzi kissed the ground three more times. The black-clothed attendants[162] asked for the Commander-in-Chief's horse to be brought in,[163] and they set him upon it. He stood some distance away from the Amir; and he summoned the troop commanders for the various army groups (*naqibān*) and told them, "You must instruct the troops to come in their proper battle formations and file past the Amir, so that the lord may see them, and the senior commanders (*moqaddamān*) and leaders (*pish-ravān*) are to pay homage smartly." The troop commanders hurried back, informing the troops about this and addressing them, and a deafening clamour arose of trumpets and barrel-shaped drums and the roar of the troops. First of all came large numbers of troops leading their horses (*janibatiyān*),[164] with a complete array of weapons and with horse armour; then fully-armed gholāms bearing banners and streamers;[165] and then a contingent of the Amir's personal guards, comprising a great number of cavalry and infantry. On their heels came individual cavalry detachments, each under a *sarhang* [F 41] clad in fine equipment and a complete array of weapons, and they passed by, detachment after detachment. The *sarhang*s kissed the ground and stood there. It took from breakfast time till the time of the midday worship for them all to file past. Then the Amir [Gh 38] warmly received the Commander-in-Chief Ghāzi and the *sarhang*s and spoke words of encouragement to them, and he rode down from that eminence and went into his tent.

The next day,[166] he mounted and rode off towards the city, a distance of three parasangs. He departed in the afternoon,[167] and reached the city at nightfall.[168] Not many people had remained within the city of Nishapur, since everyone had come out to greet and escort the Amir or else to see the spectacle. They were offering up prayers to God and the Qor'ān readers were reciting the Qor'ān. The Amir addressed some kind words to each of the notables, and especially to the Judge (Qazi) Imam Ṣā'ed, his old teacher and master (*ostād*).[169] The people were anxious to catch a glimpse of this ruler; it was a most memorable day. When the Amir reached the edge of the city, he gave orders to send the people home, and then he set out for the Garden of Shādyākh and encamped there in an auspicious state on 10 Sha'bān of this year [/13 August 1030]. They had decorated the buildings at Shādyākh[170] with a great variety of hangings and carpets which formerly belonged to the vizier Ḥasanak and which the latter had had specially made for these edifices; no-one could ever remember seeing their like, and those who had seen them will confirm the truth of what I have written here.

The following day, he sat down on the throne upon the ceremonial open pavilion[171] in the garden and held court with a great display of magnificence. A large number of gholāms lined up there from the edge of the dais into the far distance, and there were innumerable black-clad court attendants and holders of court offices whose line stretched to the garden gate, while on the plain outside, [F 42] many cavalrymen were positioned. The court retainers and eminent military commanders came in to render service and sat down or stood up (i.e. in accordance with their social rank). The Amir ordered that the Commander-in-Chief Ghāzi should be seated. The judges, legal scholars and ulema came in, praising the Amir and offering addresses of greeting and condolence. The welcome which he gave to the Judge Ṣā'ed, [Gh 39] Bu Moḥammad 'Alavi[172] and Bu Bakr Esḥāq b. Maḥmashād Karrāmi,[173] was such as he extended to no others.

Then he turned to all those present and said, "This is a blessed city and the town and its citizens are dear to me. What you have done in the way of celebrations in my honour, has not been done in any other town of Khorasan. As you know, I have a task before me, which, God Willing, shall be resolved very quickly. When this is over and done with, we shall turn our attention to the people of Khorasan, and this city will be singled out for special consideration. For the present, we are giving orders that the innovations brought in by Ḥasanak[174] are to be declared immediately null and void, and the rules of procedure in Nishapur with regard to the conduct of legal cases (*morāfaʿat*) and other matters should all now revert to the ancient custom. For news of what Ḥasanak and his followers were doing was reaching us at Herat, and we did view it with disapproval; but the time was not right for voicing our opposition. For what they did, they will reap their own rewards. There will now be two sessions held each week in which complaints against injustice and tyranny (*maẓālem*) can be raised.[175] The sessions and the gates of the palace will be thrown open, and anyone with a complaint should come along and speak without any fear or trepidation, so that justice can be meted out. In addition to the said sessions for hearing complaints, the Commander-in-Chief, the General Ghāzi, will be present at[176] the court and other trusty officials will be there too. People with complaints should make their way to them at the court and in the administrative office and should tell them their stories, so that whatever is required to be done, those responsible may do. [F 43] We have further commanded that on this very day the prisons should be inspected and those incarcerated set free, so that the beneficial effects of our coming may reach all hearts. If after this, someone is emboldened to oppress and molest others, he will get a fitting requital." [Gh 40]

When those present heard these royal words, they were filled with joy and offered up profuse prayers and invocations for the Amir. The Judge Ṣāʿed said, "The Sultan has vouchsafed so much justice and benevolence in this session that there is no occasion for any person to add a word; but I have one petition to make, if I may be granted permission to voice it, since this is an auspicious day and a blessed session." The Amir said, "Whatever the Judge says will be judicious and beneficial." The Judge Ṣāʿed said, "The king knows that the house of the Mikāʾilis is an ancient one; its members are notables of some import in this city, and their good works are apparent. I personally, after the benevolence and favour of God, and after the blessings of knowledge and learning, have found prominence and fame through the patronage of the house of the Mikāʾilis; it is incumbent upon me to acknowledge my debt to them. Now the surviving members of the family have suffered great harm on account of Ḥasanak and others. Their lands have remained sequestered; the charitable endowments (*owqāf*) of their ancestors and forefathers are no longer operative; and the pious uses and institutions (*ṭoroq u sobol*) of those endowments have been diverted. If the Amir sees fit, let him make an order in this case, as is befitting his piety and lofty resolution, so that the many members of the Mikāʾili family who have fallen on hard times and into distressed circumstances, may prosper again, and so that those charitable endowments may be reactivated, with their income released for the benefit of those pious uses and institutions."

The Amir replied, "This is most appropriate." He thereupon gave instructions to the Judge Mokhtār b. Bu Saʿd that all those charitable endowments made by members of the Mikāʾili family should be rescued from the hands [F 44] of those who had usurped them and commended to the care of a trustworthy person to oversee, collect the revenues and convey that income to institutions for pious ends. "As for the family's estates," [the Amir continued] "their exact status is not known to us and we do not know what decision regarding these was made by the illustrious late Amir our father. Bu'l-Fażl and Bu Ebrāhim, the two sons of Aḥmad b. Mikāʾil[177] and others of the family, should go to Bu Sahl Zowzani at the Divān and explain to him the circumstances in detail, so that he may then inform us. Whatever needs to be done will be decreed by us. It is incumbent upon the Judge to raise such [Gh 41] items of public policy so that they can be addressed, and he can keep in touch with us by correspondence after we have departed." The Judge Ṣāʿed said, "I will do just as the Amir says," and they offered up profuse praises.

The whole group of the Mikāʾili family and their clients and dependents went along to the Divān and explained their present plight, describing how they would seize and extort a great deal of wealth from all the landowners, stewards, the rich and notable, and whoever they summoned, and thus the most respectable and esteemed ones of the family would be left downtrodden and destitute. Bu Sahl repeated these true accounts to the Amir, and he gave the lands back to the Mikāʾilis, who were thus greatly favoured.[178]

During these days, letters arrived from Ray to the effect that, "When the exalted stirrup moved onwards, a certain member of the Shāhanshāhis,[179] accompanied by a powerful force of resolute warriors, launched an attack on Ray in order to stir up mischief.[180] Their commander, who was one of the surviving members of the Buyid house, sent an envoy to Ḥasan b. Soleymān. Ḥasan asked the notables of Ray, 'What is our answer, and what is to be done?' They replied, 'You should remain silent, and let us give the answer.' [F 45] They brought that envoy into the city, and for three days they were busy at work and they gathered together all the people. Then on the fourth day they brought the envoy out into the open country and set him down on an eminence. Ḥasan b. Soleymān came with his fully-equipped force of cavalrymen and passed by, followed by the people of the city, numbering more than 10,000 men, all heavily armed, the greater part of them infantrymen made up of the city dwellers and the people of nearby regions. When all this throng had marched past, the notables of Ray said to the envoy, 'Did you witness all this?', and they added, 'Our ruler is Sultan Masʿud b. Maḥmud, and we are obedient subjects of his and of his agents; as for your own lord and for those who come here without the authority of our sultan, there await the well-tempered steel of our short spears[181] and swords. Go back, and repeat what you have seen and heard; do not indulge in any trickery, but report that the sultan rescued us from the hands of the Deylamites, and the people of Ray have enjoyed peace and security ever since they were freed from them.' The envoy said, 'I will convey the message accordingly.' He was given the customary reward. He went off and described what he had seen.[182]

A handful of mischievous rabble-rousers who had banded together said to the Buyid prince (lit. 'the deluded one from the Buyid dynasty'), 'The mass of common people present no danger. We should attack, and in a couple of days we will present you with Ray.' They sounded trumpets and prepared to attack Ray.

When Ḥasan b. Soleymān and the notables of Ray got news of their opponents' [Gh 42] approach, they marched out with those troops that they had collected along with others who had arrived in the intervening period when the envoy had come and then gone. When the two opposing groups made contact with each other on the outskirts of the city, Ḥasan b. Soleymān said, 'They are just a bunch of rootless ruffians; it will not take us long to make a graveyard of their corpses. [F 46] We should send an envoy to them and give them a clear ultimatum so that, if they refuse to withdraw, we shall be absolved and forgiven in the sight of the Almighty God for shedding their blood.'

The notables of Ray nominated the official preacher of the city and gave him a message for the deluded Buyid prince, saying, 'Stop! Fear the Almighty God and don't make yourself responsible for the shedding of blood of this band of misfits whom you have collected together. Go back, for you are not our ruler and shepherd. We are showing you some favour on account of your noble birth and straitened circumstances which have driven you to make an importunate demand on us, for we have no fear of this leaderless rabble around you. We are saying all this in order to avoid bloodshed, and you now bear the burden of blame for such an outcome.'

The preacher went off and delivered this message. That deluded Buyid prince and the rabble rose up, made a tumult with one accord, and ignited into a flame, eager to embark upon war. The preacher returned and reported that 'The answer they gave us was, war. Now you know what to do.' Ḥasan b. Soleymān devised a skilful stratagem in deploying his troops, and placed each one of them appropriately. He kept the people who were less well-armed ready as a back-up force. More than fifty to sixty thousand men had come out of the city to the gate. Ḥasan told the mayor and the notables, 'Appoint some men to hold the mass of people back so that they don't stream forth from the city gate, and give orders for them to remain in their place until I and this body of troops who are fully armed and prepared for battle go forth against the enemy.' The mayor and the notables selected some men and took these precautions. *Putting his trust in God, the exalted one*, Ḥasan sallied forth into action in an extremely measured and orderly manner. The infantry, clad for war, stood in front of the cavalry. The enemy also came on the scene, and fierce fighting ensued. On several occasions that God-forsaken lot launched strong attacks, but to no avail, since Ḥasan's battle-line proved [F 47] extremely solid. As the day grew hotter, and thirst and exhaustion overcame the forsaken ones. [Gh 43] Near the time of the midday worship, Ḥasan ordered the great battle standard to be carried forward, and using seasoned and selected cavalrymen, he launched a victorious assault. They hurled themselves at the enemy's centre and captured the battle standard of the deluded Buyid prince, and the enemy was put to flight in total disarray. The Buyid had a choice Arab horse, and he and a few others who also had good mounts managed to make their escape, and the rabble were left on foot in a hopeless position amidst the irrigation channels and gullies. Ḥasan shouted 'Charge now,[183] and strike great terror amongst them by killing as many as you can, so that, after this, they will no longer be able to sharpen their teeth for Ray and come back again!' Ḥasan's troops rode up[184] and began to slaughter the enemy. The people of the city also came out and began to fight, killing large numbers and taking many captives. When the time of the afternoon worship came round, Ḥasan had a herald proclaim an end to the killing and the taking of captives, since evening was approaching. They stopped; night fell, and the defenders went back into the city, while the remnants of fleeing troops, who had concealed themselves in all sorts of places, escaped under the cover of night.

Next day, Ḥasan ordered the captives and the severed heads of those killed to be brought forward. There were 8,800-odd heads and 1,200-odd captives. Ḥasan gave a command that tripods should be erected along the road by which those God-forsaken ones had come, and the heads of the slain were gibbeted on them. They also erected 120 gallows, and they hanged the strongest of those captives and evildoers; it had a most awe-inspiring impact. The rest of the captives were set free and were told, 'Go back, and report what you have seen, and after this anyone [F 48] who wants to end up on the gallows [Gh 44] and meet his doom, let him come forward!' Those captives went off." [The letters from Ray further reported that] "The people of Ray—may the lord's life be long!—kept faith with everything they had promised and left nothing undone in the way of obedience and loyal conduct. Thanks to the splendour and auspiciousness of the exalted empire, a great show of strength was manifested here, with the result that no rebel is likely to attempt an attack on Ray again. If the exalted judgement sees fit, these notables should be extolled for what they did, in order to make them even more desirous of rendering loyal service, if God wills it."

When Amir Masʿud had perused this letter, he was filled with joy, and ordered trumpets to be sounded and drums beaten. They had the bearers of the good news brought forward and heaped great favours and largesse on them. The notables of Nishapur went along to the open prayer-ground[185] in order to give thanks for the Amir's coming to Nishapur and this fresh vouchsafing of victory. They offered up many sacrificial animals and distributed alms, and each day was one of fresh rejoicing for the Amir.

Also during this week, news arrived that the envoy of the caliph al-Qāder be'llāh[186] had reached the vicinity of Beyhaq with such manifestations of bounty as never before bestowed on a monarch in living memory. The Amir was heartened at the receipt of this news, and he ordered a most worthy and ceremonious welcoming reception for the envoy.[187] The people of the city came along to the Judge Ṣāʿed and said that when they had heard that the Amir had reached the neighbourhood of Nishapur, they had wanted to erect festive platforms with arches[188] and make a very joyful occasion. [F 49] But the mayor had said, "That would not be fitting, for a great calamity has befallen the Amir through the death of Sultan Maḥmud, may God illuminate his proof. However desirable such celebrations might seem—and I am telling you this at his express command—it must be left to another occasion." But a sufficient amount of time had passed, and every day things were improving and turning out better; and now the envoy from Baghdad was approaching with all our wishes in tow. "If the Judge sees fit," they said, "let him request the Amir to bring joy to the hearts of the masses of people by the lord's revoking his previous ban and allowing a celebration to be prepared on an unlimited scale." [Gh 45]

The Judge replied, "This is an excellent idea; you have spoken well, and the time is most opportune." The next day he spoke to the Amir and received permission to proceed. The Judge passed this on to the mayor, telling him that a great display should be put on. The mayor returned home and summoned the important persons of the various quarters and markets, telling them, "The Amir has given his permission. Decorate the city and do all that needs to be done, so that the caliph's envoy may know what sort of a city this is and so that the Amir may hold this city even more dear to his heart, seeing that these acts of favour and benevolence emanating from the caliph are being vouchsafed to him in our city." They obeyed the command and went back and strove to produce effects of such splendour as no-one could ever remember, in such a way that, from the gates along the road into the city to the market, there were row upon row of festive platforms and decorative cupolas (*qobba*) as far as the inner city (*shārastān*) and the congregational mosque, where they had made a lodging-place for the envoy.

When these preparations had been finished, and the news came that the envoy was two parasangs away from the city, the officials in charge of protocol went out to meet him, leading with them fifty mounts and with all the troops mounted. They went forward in a great cavalcade, with outfits of unparalleled splendour and led by the Commander-in-Chief. [F 50] Then came a group of the judges, *sayyeds*,[189] ulema and religious lawyers, and a further group of the high officials of the court, the masters of the pen, all with the finest possible array, and they escorted the envoy, Bu Moḥammad Hāshemi, one of the caliph's close relatives, into the city on Monday, 19 Shaʿbān[190] of this year [/22 August 1030].[191] The leading figures and senior commanders of the army detached themselves from the envoy at the city gate and returned to their homes. The officials in charge of court protocol led the envoy into the market and paraded him around, while the people were scattering about dirhams and dinars, pieces of sugar loaf and all sorts of other things, and jugglers were entertaining people; it was a day whose like no-one could remember. The ceremonies lasted until the middle of the afternoon,[192] at which time the envoy's official escort[193] brought the envoy along to the special residence prepared for him. When he arrived there, a most lavish meal was served at the order of the envoy's official escort. In the course of the meal, the envoy extolled Nishapur in Arabic, and offered up profuse prayers and invocations for this ruler, saying that he could not, in his entire life, recall the like of what he had seen that day. When they had finished eating, sweetmeats and dessert of unparalleled quality and quantity were brought in, and 20,000 silver dirhams as a token pourboire and welcoming present,[194] [Gh 46] and the envoy was struck with wonder. The Amir praised the Nishapuris for their efforts.

When two or three days had passed,[195] the Amir ordered that the envoy should be received at court and that the utmost in decorum should be performed. Bu Sahl Zowzani said, "Whatever the lord has to command regarding the army, the court, the government council (*majles-e emārat*), the gholāms, the holders of court offices (F 51) and all functionaries like these, let him give orders to the Commander-in-Chief to put into effect, and let him give me the scope to perform whatever is necessary. I shall ensure that they act correctly by drawing on what I have read and seen on similar occasions at the court of the late sultan." The Amir agreed and ordered them to summon the Commander-in-Chief Ghāzi.

The Amir said to him, "We have given you orders that the caliph's envoy should be presented, with all that he has brought: the investiture patent, robe of honour, marks of favour and honorific titles (*noʿut*). Let the news of what is about to take place here be despatched everywhere. You are to instruct the army that tonight they are to get everything ready, and at dawn they will be present on parade with their complete panoply of arms and full apparel, at the peak of perfection, so that we may then issue our orders." He obeyed the commands and went back. Whatever was necessary to be ordered, he ordered, and whatever command had to be given, he gave. The Amir issued further orders concerning the gholāms and others, and they were put into effect in a regal manner.

The next day, the Commander-in-Chief Ghāzi came to the court and stood there with the whole body of the troops. He gave orders to all the *sarhang*s so that they paraded outwards from the court in two lines with their cavalrymen, the latter accompanied by their battle standards, their fine fabrics stretching in two lines from the gate of the Garden of Shādyākh to a distant point. Within the garden, from before the royal dais as far as the court, there stood the gholāms in two ranks facing each other, with their complete array of weapons and their multi-coloured coats accompanied by the court masters of ceremonies. Mules had been sent to convey the robe of honour from Nishapur, and these had been left at the envoy's disposal. Also, Bu Sahl had discreetly sent someone and had asked for the investiture patent and the caliphal decrees; he had examined them carefully and had prepared the translations of them, had replaced them in their black satin brocade pouches and had sent them back.[196] [Gh 47]

When the official escort for the envoy arrived, the latter, dressed in black, was placed on a steed which was led forth, [F 52] and the flag was given to a cavalry trooper, who brought this along behind the envoy. Directly after the envoy they brought the mules making up the formal procession, loaded with chests containing robes of honour from the caliph, and ten horses, two of them with gold accoutrements and golden horseshoes, and eight with gold-woven[197] horse coverings and head-dresses. They had decorated the envoy's route in a handsome fashion. He passed along while being showered with dirhams and dinars up to the point where he reached the line of the army's cavalry troopers, and the noise of the barrel-shaped drums and trumpets and the enthusiastic shouts of all the people rose up.

The envoy and the leading men were led through the two lines of the army, and from both sides the *sarhangs* were scattering coins to the populace until the envoy reached the throne. The Amir had taken up his seat on the throne and was holding court, and the retainers and courtiers were either seated or standing in attendance. The envoy was brought forward to the appropriate place with the utmost decorum. He came forward and kissed the Amir's hands, and was installed before the throne. When he sat down, he gave greetings from the Commander of the Faithful and conveyed heartfelt prayers and invocations. Amir Masʿud responded in regal terms. Then the envoy got to his feet and placed the investiture patent and the letter from the caliph at the throne. The Amir kissed them, and then he made a sign to Bu Sahl Zowzani to take the documents, and the latter began to read them. When the passage was reached offering greetings to the Amir, the latter rose to his feet, kissed the throne carpet and then sat down. Bu Sahl read out the investiture patent and the letter, together with a succinct Persian translation, in one or two sections.[198]

Then they opened up the chests and brought forth the robes of honour, comprising sewn and unsewn garments. The envoy rose to his feet, and they took out seven one-piece cloaks,[199] one of them black and the rest of fine Dabiqi cloth,[200] made up in Baghdad, of most rare workmanship and of regal quality. The Amir came down from his throne, and a prayer rug (*moṣallā*) was laid down according to the previous practice of Yaʿqub b. Leyth.[201] [F 53] Amir Masʿud put on a robe of honour and performed two *rakʿats* of the ritual prayer.[202] Bu Sahl Zowzani had told the Amir that he should act thus, since his donning the robes of honour was an indication of the caliph's awarding him his father's rule in its entirety. They brought forward the crown, the collar and the riding horse, [Gh 48] together with a sword, sword belts and other presents which it was customary to bring from Baghdad. The retainers and courtiers laid down offerings of money before the throne in vast quantities, surpassing all scales and standards.

They conducted the envoy back again in the most formal and dignified manner. The sultan arose and proceeded to the bath house and changed his clothes, and ordered 200,000 dirhams to be distributed to the poor. Then those attending the feast[203] came in, and a most splendid spread had been prepared. They brought in the envoy and sat him down in the sultan's vicinity. When the food had been consumed, they dressed the envoy in an especially splendid robe of honour, and they conducted him back to his lodging with great pomp. At the time of the afternoon worship on that day, the official escort for the envoy brought presents from the sultan (i.e. for the caliph), comprising 200,000 dirhams, a horse with gold accoutrements, fifty high-quality, seamless garments, and several pouches containing sandalwood, musk and camphor; and he conveyed the sultan's permission for the envoy to leave. The envoy departed at the end of Shaʿbān [/1 September 1030].

The sultan ordered that letters should be written to Herat, Pushang, Ṭus, Sarakhs, Nasā, Bāvard, Bādghis and Ganj Rostā(q)[204] conveying the good news about these honours and status, newly conferred on him by the caliphal court. They made copies of the investiture patent and the letter, and made known publicly the honorific titles (*alqāb*) so that people might address this mighty sultan accordingly and [Gh 49] refer to him correctly in the *khoṭba* (the formal intercessory prayer). The sultan's titles (*noʿut*) were thus as I have written them: Upholder of the Religion of God, Protector of God's Servants, the One who Wreaks Vengeance on God's Enemies and Staunch Defender of God's Caliph, the Commander of the Faithful (*Nāṣer Din Allāh, Ḥāfeẓ ʿEbād Allāh, al-Montaqem men Aʿdā' Allāh, Ẓahir Khalifat Allāh Amir al-Mo'menin*), and the investiture patent enunciated that "the Commander of the Faithful has entrusted to you the lands which your father the Right Hand of the State and Trusted One of the Religious Community, Support of Religion and Refuge of Islam and the Muslims, Friend of the Commander of the Faithful (*Yamin al-Dowla va-Amin al-Mella va-Neẓām al-Din va-Kahf al-Islām va 'l-Moslemin, Vali Amir al-Mo'menin*) had in his possession.[205] Also, [F 54] what you have yourself conquered, including Ray, Jebāl, Isfahan, Ṭārom and other lands, as well as those realms in both east and west which you will conquer in the future, are yours and will be deemed as yours." The envoys bore away these letters with glad tidings, and in those towns and cities which I mentioned above, they made the formal intercessory prayer in the name of Sultan Masʿud, and his fame spread throughout Khorasan. When the caliph's envoy went back home, Sultan Masʿud was strengthened in his resolution, and affairs began to take on a new colour.

Ramażān, the month of fasting, began and they set about observing it. Sultan Masʿud departed from Nishapur in the middle of Ramażān of this year [/16 September 1030]. On this same day, he ordered that the Judge Ṣāʿed and his sons, Sayyed Bu Moḥammad ʿAlavi, Bu Bakr b. Maḥmashād, and the judge and the official preacher of the city, should all be given robes of honour. The Amir reached Herat on 28 Ramażān [/29 September 1030]. He lodged in the blessed Palace (*kushk-e mobārak*)[206] there and celebrated the Festival[207] on such a scale that people averred that no monarch had ever held a Festival like it. They had set up a festive spread for the sultan in the new building which they had constructed in the ʿAdnāni Garden. Other spreads had been set up in the ʿAdnāni Garden itself, and there they installed the senior officers commanding the various divisions of the army (*sarhangān-e tafāriq*) and the swift-riding cavalrymen (*kheyltāshs*). The poets were meanwhile reciting their verses. In the course of the feast, the leading figures of the court, who were sitting at the sultan's own spread, rose to their feet, kissed the ground and said, "Five or six months have elapsed since the lord had a wine-drinking session. If there was good reason for this abstention, it is now past, and affairs are now on the desired course. If the lord's exalted judgement sees fit, let him give orders for some carousing." The sultan gave his assent and summoned wine, and they brought it in. The musicians plucked the strings of their instruments, [Gh 50] the festivities reached a new height and wine was handed round, so that everyone went home merry with wine, with the exception of the Commander-in-Chief, who never drank wine.[208]

Confidential letters were arriving every day from the army in Ghaznin, giving information on what [F 55] they were doing and what steps they were taking, and how, in accordance with what the lord had commanded, they were ordering affairs. In the late morning of Monday, 10 Shavvāl [/11 October 1030], there arrived suddenly at Sultan Masʿud's court Mengütirek, brother of the Great Chamberlain ʿAli Qarib, and the religious scholar Ḥaṣiri the boon-companion. The sultan was informed immediately. He ordered a court session to be held. They came in, kissed the ground and said, "Blessed be the royal lord, for things have become settled! Your brother has been placed in custody." The sultan gave them permission to be seated and made much of them. The letter from the forces at Teginābād was presented, and the sultan ordered that it should be taken and read out. Then he commented, "The Commander has done what we expected of his wisdom and friendship; the rest of those who followed his example recognized our just rights, and the just rights of the subordinates will be observed. You have come in great haste; go back now and rest for a while, and then return at the time of the afternoon worship, so that you may convey messages and explain the situation." They both went back, and they were lodged together in a worthy abode, and copious quantities of food and dessert were sent to them. They had a meal and then went along to the bath-house.

After he had sent the two of them away, the sultan summoned Bu Sahl, Ṭāher the secretary and other notables for a private session, and they talked at length about diverse matters and it was agreed that, at the time of the afternoon worship, the rank of Ḥājeb should be conferred on Mengütirek and that they should dress him in black and award him a fitting robe of honour; Ḥaṣiri was likewise to receive honours. When the time of the afternoon worship came round, they led along two mounts and brought back Mengütirek and Ḥaṣiri, and they came forward. The two of them sat down in private with the sultan, in the same manner as Ṭāher the secretary and Bu Sahl Zowzani had done earlier in the sultan's presence. They handed over their messages and explained the situation. When they departed, the sultan ordered that Mengütirek [F 56] should be taken to the Royal Wardrobe and dressed in a robe of honour appropriate for the rank of *ḥājeb*, that is, a black coat (*qabā-ye siyāh*) and a two-pointed hat (*kolāh-e do shākh*),[209] and then he came back before the sultan. The sultan said, "May this be blessed! Your status now as a commander is to stand immediately below your brother, the Great Chamberlain ʿAli." Mengütirek kissed the ground and went back. [Gh 51]

They clothed the religious scholar Bu Bakr Ḥaṣiri in a very splendid robe of honour, of the quality that is given to the ruler's boon companions. They brought him forward as well, and the sultan also vouchsafed favour to him, saying, "You suffered many hardships in our cause and out of friendship for us during the time of my father;

you have now done us this service, and we are even more beholden to you. This is a preliminary reward, made at the official level; you will see more acts of beneficence after this." Ḥaṣiri offered up prayers and invocations for the sultan and went back. The Amir ordered all the notables and courtiers to go to the lodging of those two men with messages of congratulation, and they fulfilled all the respects due to them in a most substantial manner.[210]

At the time of the evening worship, the sultan ordered that they should compose a reply, with encouragement and promises of favour, in answer to the letter from the army at Teginābād. They also wrote a letter to the Great Chamberlain ʿAli Qarib replete with many a kind word. The sultan affixed his signature and seal and added a section in his own writing. They composed instructions and letters and despatched them. A swift-riding cavalryman and a man from the corps of swift-running, daredevil Arab cavalry troopers[211] were detailed, and at the time of the night worship they set off towards Teginābād. *God is most knowing about the right course of action!*

A reminder of the happenings and events which had taken place previously and an account of the arrival in Herat of the army from Teginābād, and what took place during that time

When, in carrying forward the narrative of this history, I reached the point when these two swift-riding cavalry troopers, the *kheyltāsh* [F 57] and the bedouin Arab (*aʿrābi*), reached Teginābād [Gh 52] with the replies of the Great Chamberlain ʿAli Qarib's concerning the fortress of Kuhtiz and Amir Moḥammad, [and I set forth] what the command concerning all this was[212] which he gave to the General Begtegin, and how ʿAli said to the army, "Tomorrow your troops should be instructed that they are to depart for Herat with such-and-such a force," I left that narrative *in medio*, as is the custom in a history.[213] For it was incumbent upon me to record the history and exploits of Amir Masʿud during the time of his brother Moḥammad's rule at Ghaznin, and I set about this and carried on the narrative from that time again when he set out from Isfahan until he arrived in Herat, in order that readers should have a full and exact exposition. Now I have set about describing the army's departure from Teginābād for Herat, detachment by detachment, with the Great Chamberlain ʿAli on their heels, and every aspect of what subsequently happened, so that it may be known and set on record that I have left nothing out.[214]

When the reply from Herat arrived by hand of the *kheyltāsh* and the Arab rider, it was read out, as I have previously related. Next day, the Great Chamberlain ʿAli Qarib mounted and rode out to the open country and the entire army assembled there. He instructed them, "According to the Sultan's decree which has arrived, you must travel to Herat, so that during the course of today and tomorrow all of you will have departed, except for the army of India which is to go with me. I will form the rearguard and from here will follow in your traces." They acknowledged the order and immediately hurried forth at great speed so that no-one waited for anyone else. The notables and the conspicuous figures of the court circle like the boon companions and others left the greater part of their baggage and impedimenta behind so that these might come on later with the Great Chamberlain, and moved on in haste.

They had taken the vizier Ḥasanak to Herat by night, since an order with the royal seal and signature had come with instructions that he should be sent on ahead of the army. Three cavalry troopers from the retinue of Bu Sahl Zowzani [F 58], who bore a great animosity towards Ḥasanak, had brought this order. The Head of the Chancery, Khᵛāja Bu Naṣr Moshkān, was also in a hurry, but when he was about to set off he went to the Great Chamberlain ʿAli and remained with him till the time of the midday meal and then came back. He then set off in company with Bu'l-Ḥasan ʿAqili, [215] the Judge Moẓaffar, [Gh 53] Bu'l-Ḥasan Karaji[216] and the religious scholar Nabih[217], together with the boon-companions and a host of other people of all sorts. He was very pensive.

I heard Bu Naṣr Moshkān say, "When I said to the Great Chamberlain, 'I am about to leave; is there any matter in Herat that I might be able to arrange until the time when the Great Chamberlain himself arrives in a state of good fortune?' He took me aside and said to me in private, 'Let this be farewell, O my good friend! For a long time we have been at the same place and harbour no grievances against each other.' I replied, 'What does the Great Chamberlain have on his mind that makes him appear so dejected and talk in such a manner?' He said, 'I bear nothing but good will and honest intentions in my heart and I have never been guilty of treachery and duplicitous behaviour. When I said to you "Let this be farewell!" I did not intend to imply that I would not follow after you, but meant farewell in the absolute and ultimate sense of the word, for the reason that, in truth, Sultan Masʿud has for some time now nurtured ill-will against me, and you will not be able to see me for much longer. These finely-phrased letters, with fulsome forms of address, this writing messages to me in his own hand and appointing my brother to the rank of General (*ḥājeb*), are all deceit[218] and cannot be concealed from a man like myself. All this is bait put down so that I may walk into the middle of the trap. ʿAli Dāya is at Herat, together with the General Bilgetegin[219] and other duplicitous and supine (lit. "are neither women nor men") retainers. And now this bunch will also approach the sultan and will convince him that the Great Chamberlain ʿAli [F 59] should be set aside.[220] The General Ghāzi has obtained the post of Commander-in-Chief and he claims to have overall control. How could he bear the sight of me? It is very easy for me, who have charge of this treasury, elephants and a strong force of Indian and all sorts of other troops, and possess a body of gholāms, followers and personal retainers, to take the road for Sistan. With this army I can conquer Kerman and Ahvāz as far as the gates of Baghdad, since I will only be facing a worthless, ill-fated and already depleted rabble, and I shall be safe. But the disturbed state of this house will not subside, and I shall be the efficient cause of it. The kings of neighbouring states [Gh 54] will impute the shame of such an occurrence to my lord, Maḥmud, and will say that a monarch like him enjoyed a long life and subjugated all the rulers on the face of the earth, yet before he died, he did not know how to regulate the affairs of his house, with the result that a situation like this arose. I consider it licit that they should imprison me in some place and incarcerate me so that I might spend the rest of my life seeking God's forgiveness, since my sins are many. But I am aware that these wretched creatures will not allow this prince to keep me alive, for they fear me, and he himself will covet this wealth and other worldly trash of mine and will bring infamy upon himself. At the outset, when my lord passed away, I committed a great mistake; I have now realized this, but it is to no avail. What business of mine was it to bring forth his brother Moḥammad? The two princely-born brothers should have been left to come together and discuss things between themselves, with the courtiers and retainers in their midst as mediators. I myself ought to have been one of them, since I was the one whose advice was most often sought, until the matter was settled. But I did not do this, but acted as an over-zealous nurse more devoted than the real mother herself and put my life on the line. [F 60] Now, at the present time, they have all rushed away from the scene and have distanced themselves from it all. They called me ʿAli the king-maker (*amir-neshān*), and destiny has decreed its own way. Let it be the way that the Almighty God has foreordained. I have submitted myself to my fate, and in no circumstances will I ever opt for infamy.'

I said, 'May the life of the Amir, the Great Chamberlain, be prolonged! May there be nothing but beneficence and goodness! When I reach Herat, if there is talk and discussion, what should I do?' He said, 'There's no good reason to bring up anything about these matters, for the Sultan himself would realize that I have become suspicious and that I have spoken with you about this affair. Thus it will bring down harm on you, and will not do me any good. If some talk or discussion does crop up somewhere or other—though I am convinced that there will not be any before they have me firmly in their clutches—you should observe the rules of companionship and the bonds of gratitude and loyalty[221] until we are able to see what is happening. For you should know that affairs have changed radically; when you reach Herat you will see this for yourself, and you will become apprehensive about your own position. For a gang of people with new-fangled ways and ideas (*qowmi now-āyin*) has taken control of things, in such a way that the men of Sultan Maḥmud's time (*maḥmudiyān*)[222] are made to look like traitors [Gh 55] and outsiders in their midst. In particular, Bu Sahl Zowzani has assumed charge of affairs and established his own rules and conditions and has bought over everybody. Sultan Masʿud is the way he is, and unless perchance he experiences some feelings of remorse and compunction, your days are numbered.' He uttered these phrases, wept, clasped me to his bosom in an embrace and bade me farewell, and I left."

I, Bu'l-Fażl, say this, that there have been few men like ʿAli; and the way in which he had spoken with my master thus was just as if he was actually seeing before his own eyes what was going to befall him and was prescient of it. A long while after they had seized him in Herat, and his career and life had ended, I heard that when he left Teginābād and headed for Sultan Masʿud at Herat, he had written a letter to his counsellor and adjutant and his trusty confidant at Ghaznin by the care of a man called Sh.b.y[223] (his son Moḥsen is still alive today). In this letter, in [F 61] ʿAli's own handwriting, was this passage. "I have set out for Herat, and I suspect that my next encounter with you and my household and family will be at the Day of Resurrection. Because of this, I am not sending you detailed instructions about every topic. If subsequently, through the grace of God, things should turn out otherwise than what I fear, I shall give you the necessary detailed instructions about everything." I heard this passage from his secretary Bu Saʿid after ʿAli's life had come to an end. May God's mercy be upon them all!

When the army reached Herat, Sultan Masʿud rode out into the open country with a great panoply of weapons, equipment and finery. The army came forward detachment by detachment, and offered their service from the depth of their hearts, since they were sincerely attached to the Sultan, and it was exactly as if they had found Paradise and the Garden of Eden here and now. The Amir heaped praises on them all with his express words and to an unparalleled extent. All affairs were now conducted by the General Ghāzi, the Commander-in-Chief. ʿAli Dāya's words also carried weight and he was held in some esteem since he had brought the force of gholāms from Ghaznin and had gone to Nishapur, but his voice was not so influential as Ghāzi's. This vexed him a great deal, but there was not much he could do about it.

The Amir gave a very fulsome welcome to my master Bu Naṣr, but the situation was such that you would have said that the men of the former régime (*maḥmudiyān*) had committed great wrongs and were aliens amongst the men of the current establishment (*masʿudiyān*).[224] Bu Naṣr went each day to do service but kept well away from the Chancery. Ṭāher the secretary presided over the Chancery [Gh 56] in a grand manner and with much pomp.

News arrived that the Great Chamberlain ʿAli had reached Esfezār with the elephants, the treasury, [F 62] the army of India, and the baggage and impedimenta. The Amir rejoiced exceedingly; I heard that he had not thought it at all conceivable that ʿAli would come to Herat, and he was sending out successively trusted envoys to meet him, each bearing fresh marks of benevolence and all kinds of favour and heart-warming cordiality. ʿAli's brother the Ḥājeb Mengütirek wrote saying, "It is necessary for you to come as speedily as possible, for affairs are going according to your wishes."

ʿAli arrived on Wednesday, 3 Dhu'l-Qaʿda of this year [/2 November 1030] before dawn, with twenty gholāms, with his baggage and train of followers and equipment five or six parasangs behind him. It was still very dark. He came by the road to the court and halted in the entrance hall of the old ʿAdnāni Palace. Apart from this palace, there was another palace, very spacious and fine, and beyond that garden, further gardens[225] and buildings constructed by Amir Masʿud. At times the Sultan resided in the ʿAdnāni Palace, holding court there, and at times he stayed in his own buildings. When ʿAli settled himself in the entrance hall, all those who came there displayed towards him the kind of respect reserved for kings, for their hearts and eyes were filled by the imposing figure of this man. He, for his part, was treating everyone with courtesy and was smiling wryly, for he was a stern man and I had never seen him laugh out loud but only smile. He was very downcast, as if he knew what was going to happen.

It became day, and the Sultan held court in those buildings beyond the ʿAdnāni Garden. [F 63] ʿAli and the great men of state came into this garden by this door of the palace, while the Khwarazm Shah and a group of other people came in by that door which is on the side of the inner city.[226] The Sultan was seated on his throne in that open-columned chamber (*revāq*) which is connected with the Spring Hall.[227] He made Altuntāsh sit on the right of the throne and his paternal uncle Amir ʿAżod al-Dowla Yusof [Gh 57] opposite him, while the great men and the dignitaries of state sat or stood according to their status. The Great Chamberlain ʿAli Qarib came forward and kissed the ground in three places. The Sultan raised his hand, summoned him to come before the throne and held out his hand for him to kiss. He laid before the Sultan a most precious bejewelled necklace, and he had with him 1,000 *siyāh-dāri* (?)[228] dinars which were then scattered on his behalf. Then the Sultan made a sign for him to go to his left side. The General (Ḥājeb) Mengütirek took him by the arm. Opposite the Khwarazm Shah Altuntāsh, the Great Chamberlain kissed the ground, took up his seat and then kissed the ground once more.

The Sultan said, "Welcome! You experienced many tribulations in our interest and service!" 'Ali replied, "May the lord's life be prolonged! All this fell short of what I should have done, but because the exalted utterance has expressed itself so, the humble servant feels rejuvenated." The Khwarazm Shah Altuntāsh said, "The lord happened to be far away (i.e. at his father Maḥmud's death) and it would take him long to return and he had many concerns. It would not have been appropriate for him to abandon a land of such fame and won with such valour and return at once. Meanwhile, we his servants were all determined with hearts and minds to seek his service until today when we have found that felicitous state. Your humble servant 'Ali endured much hardship to ensure that no crisis occurred, and although I was far away, I wrote suggesting what I thought was the best course. Now, thanks be to God, the problems have been resolved without any scars being inflicted in the process. The lord is young, he is sitting in his father's place and his wishes have been attained; [F 64] may he be blessed with youth and kingly power for many a long year! Although there are many suitable servants who have recently come into prominence, and others will come along in the future, there are also here a few venerable figures who have grown old in the service of Sultan Maḥmud. If the exalted judgement thinks fit, these should be kept and cherished and not maltreated to please their enemies,[229] for the elders are the ornaments of the kingdom. I say this not out of my own interest, for it is obvious that I have only a small amount of time left in this world; this is merely wise counsel that I am proffering—although the lord is too exalted to have need of advice from humble servants. Nevertheless, as long as I live, I shall perform my duty of proffering such counsel."[230] [Gh 58]

The Sultan said, "The Khwarazm Shah's words are on the same level of esteem for us as my father's. We listen to them willingly and we accept with gratitude his counsel. When was there a time when he did not have regard for our best interests? What he has done at this time is clear for all to see, and everything which he has said and written will remain before our eyes, and indeed will be put into practice."

The Khwarazm Shah rose to his feet, kissed the ground and went out by the same door as he had entered. The Great Chamberlain 'Ali also rose to his feet with the intention of going out, but the Sultan gave a sign that he was to remain seated. The rest of the courtiers departed, and the Sultan held a private discussion with him, with the General Mengütirek, Bu Sahl Zowzani and Ṭāher the secretary likewise seated, while ʿErāqi the secretary was standing there together with Badr, the Palace Chamberlain (*ḥājeb-e sarāy*) also standing in attendance, armed guards (*selāḥ-dārān*) round the throne and a hundred of the gholāms from the palace barracks.[231] The Sultan said to the Great Chamberlain, "Should my brother Moḥammad remain detained there at Kuhtiz, [F 65] or at some other place? In the present heat, there is no point in bringing him to the court just now. Our intention is to set out for Balkh this winter. Then, when the season of spring comes round and we have reached Ghaznin, whatever necessary decision is arrived at regarding him, will be ordained." ʿAli replied, "It is for the lord to issue commands now, and whatever the exalted judgement sees fit, he will ordain. Kuhtiz is a secure fortress, and the General Begtegin is stationed at the foot of the citadel awaiting commands." The Sultan said, "Those few things[232] which he sent off with his adjutant Ḥasan to Guzgānān, what's happened to them?" ʿAli replied, "May the lord's life be prolonged! Ḥasan has had them delivered to the fortress at Shādyākh.[233] He is experienced and far-sighted, and he has not embarked upon something beyond his capabilities. If the exalted judgement sees fit, a trusty envoy can perhaps hasten there and bring back that treasury?" The Sultan said, "Very well! Go back, halt a while and have a rest, for you are much needed for counsel and for various tasks." ʿAli kissed the ground and arose, and the court officials responsible for ceremonial duties made way for him by that same side of the garden [Gh 59] from which he had entered, and he departed.[234]

The Sultan said to ʿAbdus,[235] "Go after the Great Chamberlain and tell him that there is another message, and that he is to wait for a moment in a covered dais[236] close by us." ʿAbdus went off. The Sultan said to Ṭāher the secretary, "Ask the Great Chamberlain, until when have the army been paid their salaries,[237] and which of the troops are most ready prepared for sending off on a campaign? For I am going to send a force to Makrān in order to overthrow that arrogant one, ʿIsā, since he appears rebellious, and his brother Bu'l-ʿAskar, who came as a fugitive from him a while ago and is still here at court, is to be set up in ʿIsā's place."[238] Ṭāher went off, and then came back with the reply, "The Great Chamberlain says that the army's salaries have been fully paid up to the end of the year, and that they are completely ready and prepared, with no-one [F 66] able to bring forward any excuse; every man who may receive his orders is able to go off forthwith." The Sultan said, "Everything has worked out very well. You must ask the Great Chamberlain to come back."

The General Mengütirek kissed the ground and said, "Will the lord give permission for the humble servant ʿAli and those who are with him, to come today to my place, since I have ordered some stew to be prepared?" The Sultan answered cheerfully, "That's most appropriate! Should you need anything else, our own servants will see to it." Mengütirek kissed the ground a second time and went out in a joyful mood. Now for which brother and ʿAli was he acting as host! For they had already fast secured ʿAli, and that message conveyed by Ṭāher about the matter of the army and Makrān had been *a complete charade.*[239] They had already formulated a plan for what was to be done and had ordered the Commander-in-Chief Ghāzi, "When the Great Chamberlain comes into the Sultan's presence, go out immediately, fully armed and with a very large force of cavalrymen, to ʿAli's baggage and possessions, and seize and confiscate the lot." The Commander-in-Chief Ghāzi had gone off to do this. When the General Mengütirek came out, they said to him, "The Great Chamberlain is at present at the covered dais." When Mengütirek reached the dais, thirty gholāms [Gh 60] went into there and seized him, and stripped him of his cloak, cap and boots, just as they had done with his brother. They brought him into a house by the side of that dais. The attendants bore them away on their backs, since they were fastened with heavy fetters; *and that was the last that was ever seen of the two of them!*[240]

This is what happened to ʿAli, his fortune and his retinue, and how it all ended. Only a fool would set his heart on this treacherous and deceitful world and account his ease of life, high rank and governmental authority [F 67] as anything at all. Wise persons will not be deluded by it. ʿAttābi has expressed this very well: (Poetry)

1. *Let my appointed way of death come to me as a person whose mind is at peace, since I have not painfully experienced the terror of those watering-places (i.e. of death).*

2. *For indeed, grave and momentous events are bound up with what are stored up in the interiors (literally, "bellies") of events which are to come.*[241]

He is a great man indeed, who can lay hold of the garment of contentment and who can break down the grip of covetousness! Regarding this meaning, Ebn al-Rumi also hit the mark when he said:[242] (Poetry)

1. *When God clothes you with the garment of good health, and He gives you sustenance which comes and then goes away,* [Gh 61]
2. *Do not envy those who multiply riches, for just as Fate gives to them, it will only take away.*

That master of poetry Rudaki has said, and has well understood the revolutions of fortune and made people aware of them:[243] (Poetry)

1. This present world is purely a dream effect, and the person whose mind[244] is alert recognizes that.
2. Its good things are in fact bad ones, and its happiness in fact grief.
3. How can you see yourself as secure (*hamvār*) in this world, when all its workings are against order (*na-hamvār*)? [F 68]
4. Its actions[245] are not good, although its face is good; it is evil in its deeds and comely in appearance.

In regard to ʿAli, whom they struck down, the lesson clearly to be drawn is[246] that, over the ages, many people were struck down, such as Bu Moslem and others, as is clearly set down in the history books. If people say that ʿAli intended in his heart some mischief, well, the Almighty God alone can know the innermost thoughts of His devotees. I myself have no concern with that sort of thing; my business is to tell in words my story. They have all passed on, but they will come together in a certain place (i.e. at the Day of Resurrection and Gathering Together for Judgement) when secrets will be revealed. The excuse of those wise persons who were able to raise their voices against this powerful man, with his numerous following, was that people said, "What business had he with placing rulers on the throne or arresting them?" Since for this reason, his fortunes were destined to come to ruin, how could he overcome the foreordained decree? *We seek refuge in God from a decree of fate bringing evil!*

When the momentous affair of ʿAli came to its close and the Commander-in-Chief Ghāzi returned from the formal review[247] of ʿAli's property and possessions, whatever gholāms and baggage which he had, had been plundered, and there was some fear that the baggage and equipment of the retainers and troops stationed at the court and troops who had come with 'Ali would likewise be thoroughly plundered. However, the Commander-in-Chief Ghāzi had taken careful precautions so that not a single thread[248] of any of those persons' possessions suffered loss or damage. The leading figures from Maḥmud's reign[249] were stricken with profound fear at this arrest of 'Ali and shrank away into the background. The Sultan sent 'Abdus to the Khwarazm Shah Altuntāsh with a message, saying[250], "In bringing himself to this end, 'Ali did not act worthily and in accordance with his exalted office. Why did he not look to the Khwarazm Shah, and why did he not emulate [Gh 62] his conduct? What business was it of his to raise my brother to the throne? He should have waited until we arrived. He was just one of the retainers and courtiers; what they did, he likewise should have done. If he raised my brother to the throne, why did he then act so faithlessly (i.e. in abandoning Moḥammad's cause)? Why did he sell his soul by swearing such solemn oaths? He was nurturing treason in his heart, and when all this became apparent to us, he was placed under arrest, for that was the most prudent course. No harm will befall his person. [F 69] They have imprisoned him in a certain place and he is being treated well until such time when our views concerning him become favourable. This situation in regard to him has been explained to the Khwarazm Shah so that he may not get a different picture of events."[251]

The Khwarazm Shah Altuntāsh gave the reply, "The wise and safe course for subjects lies in what lords command, and what the exalted judgement sees as appropriate, who else can determine? I had sent this advice to 'Ali from Khwarazm, both in the form of letters and in that of messages, that he should not undertake these extreme courses. But he had become closely involved in a momentous affair; he did not listen in a sensible fashion, and the stroke of fate was such as it was. But he is a man of great renown and much courage, and such men are hard to find. He has those who envy him and are his enemies, but he is also a kinsman; the lord should not discard him because of malicious slanderers, for he has no-one like him." The Amir sent a reply, "I will do this. 'Ali will be of use to me for great enterprises; this was in the manner of a chastisement, and a display of our wrath for his benefit."

I heard from the representative at the court (*vakil-e dar*) of Altuntāsh, Masʿadi, that the Khwarazm Shah was thrown into deep despair and was overwhelmed with fear, but he maintained his poise and equanimity[252] so that they should not realize how perturbed he was. He sent a messenger, in conditions of great secrecy, to Bu Naṣr Moshkān and Bu'l-Ḥasan ʿAqili, saying, "This is how it all will be from now on. What did ʿAli do to have warranted such treatment? I saw from the outset that this gang of parvenus did not intend to permit a single one of the men from the Sultan's father's time to remain. Arrange things, and employ[253] subtle subterfuges and ploys, so that [Gh 63] I may speedily return, for I see no signs of beneficence or gleams of light." Bu'l-Ḥasan, giving an astringent answer as was his wont, said, "O Masʿadi, allow me to proceed on my own, for the Sultan regards me as one of the old guard too; but since he knows for sure that [F 70] I intend nothing but good counsel in what I say, I have set about this matter and shall accomplish it this very day, so that the required result will be achieved and the Khwarazm Shah may return, according to the desires of his well-wishers. However strong may be the position of this newly-jumped up group, in the end, in matters like these, this Amir will consult and speak with the men of his father's reign, for he has tried and tested them over the years."

Bu Naṣr Moshkān added, "I give thanks and feel most indebted to him. The Sultan has shown me handsome marks of favour and has raised great hopes. I heard from trusty informants that no-one has been allowed to say anything adverse regarding me. In spite of all that has been said and done, the Sultan has not yet discussed any subject with me. If the Sultan speaks and enquires about any matter of public policy, first of all I will broach the subject of the Khwarazm Shah, that the latter should, according to his desire, return to his post in Khwarazm. However, it is completely inappropriate for the Khwarazm Shah to set before the Sultan, and to raise with him, the question of his own departing, and if the Sultan should say something to him about this question, it will be better for him to respond by saying that he has become old and is no longer capable of performing any useful tasks, and that his own personal desire is to leave army service and to take up residence by the tomb of the late Amir. One of the lord's sons should go as Khwarazm Shah so that one of his own sons, and all the troops which he has, may be placed under the command of that prince, for this is a charge which must be properly filled. If the case is presented in this manner, he will not be further cross-examined and will be speedily despatched back to Khwarazm; for the Sultan knows that the security of that frontier region cannot be maintained without the Khwarazm Shah's powerful presence and aura."

These two responses, and particularly that of Khᵛāja Bu Naṣr Moshkān, had a most reassuring and uplifting effect upon the Khwarazm Shah Altuntāsh's spirit and he calmed down.[254]

[F 71] The Sultan sent an investiture patent in the name of the Commander-in-Chief Ghāzi for the governorship of Balkh and Samangān,[255] and his retainers speedily conveyed that information to Balkh so that the formal intercessory prayer could be made there in his name.[256] They took matters into their own hands, and Ghāzi had the ultimate say. The private sessions and consultations of the Sultan regarding affairs of the army were held with him, and the old guard from Maḥmud's time were much troubled by this [Gh 64] and grumbled to themselves in rage and frustration. In the end, they brought about Ghāzi's downfall, as I shall later describe.

Saʿid Ṣarrāf ("the money changer"), Ghāzi's counsellor and adjutant, was riding high,[257] but *"for every people there is an appointed day"*.[258] In truth, he managed things well, but he made one single mistake in that they suborned him into becoming a spy (*moshref*) over his master.[259] He was bought over by the award of a robe of honour and the gold-adorned saddle and accoutrements of a horse that he received. He acted as a spy in this way and his master fell into hardship, and he likewise. For a servant's finest embellishment should be his rectitude. After the fall from power of the Commander-in-Chief Ghāzi, Saʿid was pinned to the wheel of fortune and rose and fell, and was in and out of office, *"so that after mighty and elevated status, he became the keeper of mangy, tar-smeared camels"*.[260] At the present moment, in this year [4]50 [/1058], he is at Multan in the service of the Khᵛāja ʿAmid ʿAbd al-Razzāq,[261] having been for many years a boon-companion of his, and having opted for a modest status and a secluded life. I have for you all a detailed account of these events, which is very perspicacious, as will be set forth, if God Most High so wills.

The position of the vizier Ḥasanak now became disturbed. This was because, during his youthful days, he had done various things which ought not to have been done and had not guarded his tongue, and had affronted this great and powerful Sultan for no good reason.[262] The poet has expressed it well, (Poetry)

1. *Keep guard of your tongue; don't say anything which will bring down calamity on your head; indeed, calamity is brought along by speech!*[263]

Also, on the subject of the young, he has expressed it extremely well, [F 72] (Poetry)

1. *Indeed, when youthful ones*[264] *take charge of affairs to the exclusion of the elders, you see defectiveness in some of those affairs.*

I heard from Bu ʿAli b. Esḥāq, who said that Bu Moḥammad b. Mikāʾil used to say, "What's the relevance here of the word *'some'—there's defectiveness in* all *of them!*"

The Vizier[265] Bu Sahl Zowzani had a very great animus against the dismissed vizier Ḥasanak, since the latter, in the time of his vizierate, used to treat Bu Sahl with contempt and scorn, until the Sultan's anger was permanently fixed on him and he wrought on Bu Sahl at Balkh what he wrought. At this juncture, Bu Sahl immediately ordered the Vizier Ḥasanak to be conveyed to the custody of ʿAli Rāyeż,[266] Bu Sahl's retainer, who brought him along to his own house and subjected him to all sorts of humiliations. [Gh 65] People began to talk about Bu Sahl Zowzani's behaviour in this matter and criticized him, for people of high renown owe their good repute to the benevolent way in which they treat a vanquished foe, since that benevolence is more noble than humiliating people, and the maxim "*Be forgiving when you are in a position of power,*" is much praised.[267] There is also the proverbial saying, "*When you have someone in your power, be forbearing*".[268] But Bu Sahl did not consider such conduct incumbent upon himself and took pleasure in exacting retribution. Bu Sahl and Ḥasanak have both passed away, and I have set down these lines hoping that someone might find it useful and instructive.

Bu Sahl Zowzani selected the troop commander Bahrām and provided him with orders under the Sultan's seal and signature and sent him to Janki[269] at the pass leading into Kashmir (*dar-e Kashmir*) with the command to release the Great Khᵛāja Aḥmad b. Ḥasan [Meymandi] immediately, and send him, in an honourable and dignified manner, to Balkh, since he was needed for assisting in important affairs of the kingdom. Janki was to accompany him personally in order to ensure that Khᵛāja Aḥmad's rightful status was observed.[270] This was to be done in such a way that he made this Khᵛāja Aḥmad hopeful of good treatment and showed him respectful service. When the late Sultan had passed away, [F 73] he had protected Bu Sahl from his enemies. This was the underlying reason why Bahrām had been sent to bring Khᵛāja Aḥmad and his family and servants,[271] for in the past, when Bu Sahl had been in straitened circumstances, and had acted as servitor and tutor to the Khᵛāja's children, the latter had been extremely kind to him, and Bu Sahl now sought to make due recompense. When the Khᵛāja's enemies got news of these events, they became highly fearful. I shall give an account of how the Khᵛāja was brought to Balkh, at what date and in what circumstances, and how the vizierate was entrusted to him.

My master Khᵛāja Bu Naṣr Moshkān was filled with trepidation.[272] He did not attend the Chancery; Ṭāher was there in the Divān, and its working was directed by him. When a week had passed, Sultan Masʿud summoned Bu Naṣr, made him sit down and showed him great favour, saying, "Why aren't you attending the Chancery?" He replied, "May the lord's life be prolonged! Ṭāher is there, and he is a highly capable and experienced person, who has come to know very well the lord's various habits and ways. I have grown old, and am past my working days. If the exalted judgement [Gh 66] sees fit, let me come to the court and render service and occupy myself with offering up prayers and invocations." The Sultan said, "What's all this talk about? It is you that I know and am used to. I don't know any Ṭāhers. You must go along to the Divān, for there are many important matters of state at hand, and we should have ten men like you to tackle them, but such men are hard to find and we have only you to depend upon. Your absence from the Divān can in no way be justified. We rely on you ten times more than did our father. You must busy yourself [F 74] with the work and must give the same counsels as you gave to my father, since everything said by you is listened to and the value of your advice and wise counsels has been known to us for a very long time."

Bu Naṣr took his formal leave, and the Sultan sent him along to the Chancery with all honour and respect. He became highly exalted in status, and set about summoning confidential meetings and sessions for advising on state policy. Bu Sahl Zowzani stretched the bowstring on the bow of evil intent and cliquish intrigue, but none of his accusations struck home until that time when he said, "It is possible to exact 300,000 dinars from Bu Naṣr." The Sultan replied, "Bu Naṣr doesn't have such an amount of gold, and where could he raise it from? And if such a sum did exist, his skill and competence are more valuable to me than this sum. You must cut short saying these things about him, for I am not agreeable to your talking about him thus." He spoke with Bu'l-ʿAlāʾ the physician and voiced complaints regarding Bu Sahl, saying, "He said so-and-so concerning Bu Naṣr, but we gave him such-and-such reply," and Bu'l-ʿAlāʾ relayed this to Bu Naṣr.

I heard from Khᵛāja Bu Naṣr, who related: In the course of this week, the Sultan summoned me one day and I had a private audience with him. He said, "These affairs are now going smoothly, *praise and thanks be to God for His benevolence*. I have made up my mind that we shall not proceed so soon to Ghaznin but shall press on from here to Balkh. Also, that we shall shower unprecedented favours on the Khwarazm Shah, who is here at present, whose conduct we have always observed to be correct and whose services are at this time of such great value, and shall send him back to his governorship over Khwarazm with manifestations of favour. Furthermore, we shall enter into an exchange of correspondence with the Khāns[273] and discuss these topics with them until we arrive at the appropriate time for despatching diplomatic envoys and renewing treaties. Then in the spring time we shall proceed towards Ghaznin. What do you have to say about these plans?"

I replied, "Whatever decision the lord has thought out is the very essence of correct decision making, and one should not do other than what he has enunciated." He said, "I need a better answer. [F 75] You must give your counsel openly and without fear, and set forth the defects [Gh 67] of these plans." I replied, "May the lord's life be prolonged! I have some words of advice, but I thought that it would be awkward to express unpalatable words. It may be that what I expound as pieces of advice will be passed on by the lord to his intimate courtiers and prove offensive to them, and they might say, 'It seems that Bū Naṣr's present comfortable existence is not sufficient for him, and he is now aiming for the vizierate and for directing affairs!' The sensible course for me is to devote myself to my profession of secretary, and I beg to be excused from engaging in other discourse." The Sultan said, "Indeed, I am not agreeable to this, and no-one will have the audacity to say anything to me about these matters, since every person has his clearly-designated place."

I replied, "May the lord's life be prolonged! Since the exalted command is in this wise, I will set forth two or three points; in making this exposition of them, the duty of gratitude owed to this great house will be done. The lord should know that the late Amir was a man whose equal, in every respect, the world has never known, and his age resembled a richly-adorned bride in its splendour and magnificence. He enjoyed a long life. He deliberated carefully about things, and fathomed them out thoroughly. He adopted a course of action, established the right path, and left this path behind as his legacy, and departed from this world. It would be preferable in my view if today we followed the late Amir's path and that no-one should be given the liberty to say to the lord, 'the late Amir was faulty in such-and-such matter; it should have been done better than that,' so that the state does not suffer any impairment. Moreover, now that these two mighty armies and opposing views[274] have come together and speak with one voice, the whole surface of the earth can be subdued by means of them and vast kingdoms conquered. It is necessary that [F 76] they should become united and remain so. I have set forth these views at this present moment, and the most important point is this last one. While I remain in his employment, and while there exists an occasion for my words to be heard, I will hold back nothing of what I perceive to be beneficial." The Sultan said, "You have spoken most aptly, and I accept that all these things are to be done in this manner." I offered up prayers and departed, and verily, not two weeks elapsed before the move from Herat got under way, when they managed to reverse those decisions.

One of the great mistakes which had occurred before that time when Amir Mas'ud came from Nishapur to Herat[275], and was noted as such later, was that when the Sultan heard about the state of affairs, and news was arriving from Ghaznin to the effect that "the armies are being gathered together and are preparing for war," and a need arose for more troops [Gh 68] and the Sultan's exalted mind ranged over every possible place, he commissioned an envoy, a most stout-hearted man called Bu'l-Qāsem Raḥḥāl,[276] to go to 'Alitegin,[277] and a letter was written in the following terms: "We are preparing to confront our brother. If the Amir ʿAlitegin will provide us with help in this warfare, including his personal presence on the battlefield, or else by sending one of his sons with a strongly armed and equipped military force, once affairs have come to the desired conclusion, a substantial province that belongs to us[278] will be made over to one of his sons." The Sultans' advisers had not explained[279] to him that the implications and possible repercussions of this affair were momentous, and that ʿAlitegin would not stop at this single province but would make further demands since [F 77] he had not been given a single one of the regions which he sought. Such a man of valour as the Khwarazm Shah Altuntāsh was lost in the débâcle over ʿAlitegin,[280] and the latter plundered Chaghāniyān,[281] as I shall recount in detail in the chronicle of the succeeding years.

The other error was regarding the Turkmens,[282] who had already taken a bite at Khorasan and developed a taste for it but whom the late Sultan had hurled back by the might of his sword to Balkhān Kuh.[283] They were conciliated and were summoned into service as auxiliary forces to swell the army's ranks. They came [into the Ghaznavid lands], with Qïzïl[284], Bogha (Buqa)[285], Köktāsh (Kuktāsh)[286] and other commanders, and did some good service, but in the end they became troublesome, and reverted to their old métier of pillaging and plundering, as we shall set forth, until a commander of the calibre of Tāsh Farrāsh and the regions of Ray and Jebāl were lost because of them. The outcome of these false steps, which they could not admit to or acknowledge, was that Arslān Jādheb[287] and the Commander-in-Chief Ghāzi suffered several setbacks until the time when they expelled those Turkmens from Khorasan; *there is no possibility of turning back the decree of God*,[288] His mention is exalted. These Turkmens had then come into Sultan Masʿud's service, and he had appointed the General Khumārtāsh[289] as Commander-in-Chief over them.[290]

At this moment in Herat, the Sultan deemed it fitting to send an army to Makrān under a strong and powerful commander so that Bu'l-ʿAskar, who had come to Nishapur [Gh 69] some years previously as a fugitive from his brother, might be placed on the throne in Makrān and the deluded and rebellious one ʿIsā be overthrown.[291] Then, on the advice of Altuntāsh and the Commander-in-Chief Ghāzi, Yāruqtughmush[292], Keeper of the Royal Wardrobe (*jāma-dār*),[293] was appointed to command of this expedition, comprising 4,000 cavalry [F 78] from the palace guard (*sovār-e dargāhi*) and 3,000 infantry. The General Khumārtāsh was also instructed to take these Turkmens with him, these last to act under the orders of the Keeper of the Royal Wardrobe, who was their commander. This force set out from Herat for Makrān with full equipment of war, accompanied by Bu'l-ʿAskar.

After their departure, the Sultan said to the Amir ʿAżod al-Dowla Yusof [b. Sebüktegin], "O uncle, you have recently enjoyed a period of quiet and tranquillity. They report that the vassal ruler (*vāli*) of Qoṣdār has become, during this period of weakness in the state, arrogant and unruly. You must proceed to Bost with your personal slave guards and take up your position in Qoṣdār, so that the Qoṣdāri ruler comes back to his senses and forwards two years' instalments of the land-tax, and also so that, through being stationed at Qoṣdār, you provide a substantial support for the army which went to Makrān." The Amir ʿAżod al-Dowla Yusof replied, "A very sound course of action has been adopted, and the lord has only to command whatever he chooses to ordain."

Sultan Masʿud showed him great favour and gave him a precious robe of honour, saying, "Go forth with blessing and auspiciousness. When we move from Balkh towards Ghaznin after Nowruz,[294] we will summon you so that you and I can reach Ghaznin together." ʿAżod al-Dowla Yusof set out from Herat with his personal slave guards and seven or eight senior officers from the Sultan's guard (*sarhang-e solṭāni*), together with 500 cavalry, heading for Bost, Zāvolestān[295] and Qoṣdār. I had reliable reports that Sultan Masʿud had secretly ordered these senior officers to keep watch over Yusof in such a way that he would not be able to go anywhere without their knowing. I also heard that his chamberlain Ṭoghrïl had been secretly appointed as a spy over him so that he might count Yusof's very breaths and report back whatever took place. This wretched fellow pledged to do this, even though Amir Yusof regarded him as his own child, indeed, [Gh 70] as even dearer. They despatched Yusof on that pretext, saying that he had acquired the ambition of becoming supreme Commander-in-Chief and that the army regarded him with a favourable eye, in order that he might be well away from the court for a period of time.[296] [F 79]

An account of the remainder of the events concerning Amir Moḥammad after his arrest, up to the time when he was transferred from the fortress of Kuhtiz to the fortress of Mandish

I have explained previously how, when the Great Chamberlain ʿAli set out from Teginābād for Herat, he took stringent precautions in regard to Amir Moḥammad, according to the exalted command of Sultan Masʿud which had arrived and which provided for the appointment of the General Begtegin and laid on him complete responsibility for that prisoner. Now that I have finished setting forth the story of the armies travelling to Herat and the arrest of the Great Chamberlain ʿAli Qarib, and the carrying out of various other affairs; and having arrived at the point of Sultan Masʿud's departure from Herat towards Balkh, I am interrupting that historical narrative and taking up again the remainder of the story and the circumstances of that prisoner. This is so that there may be set forth in its entirety what happened in that period when the army left Teginābād for Herat and Amir Moḥammad was brought from that fortress of Kuhtiz to the fortress of Mandish and the history becomes complete. When I have finished this, I shall return to the beginning of the narrative of Amir Masʿud's journey from Herat to the vicinity of Balkh, if God wills.

I heard from master ʿAbd al-Raḥmān the singer and reciter[297] that, "when the army departed from Teginābād to Herat, I and those like me who were servants and attendants of Amir Moḥammad were like fish out of water, abandoned on the dry land, and we felt altogether dispossessed and reduced to misery. Yet we could not bear to be any distance away from the foot of the fortress of Kuhtiz, and were hoping [F 80] that Sultan Masʿud might perhaps summon Amir Moḥammad to Herat and that a ray of hope might appear on the horizon. Every day, [Gh 71] and following our old courtly routine, myself and the rest of our company, the musicians, singers and the aged companions, would have an audience with Amir Moḥammad. We would have something to eat there and then go back at the time of the evening worship. The General Begtegin took extremely stringent precautions, but never barred any of us from access to the Amir. He lavished more and more hospitality upon the Amir and seemed only too willing to satisfy the prince's most impossible whims and wishes if asked.[298] Amir Moḥammad now became a little more contented in mind, and began to indulge in wine-drinking, imbibing regularly.

One day, we were drinking wine in that elevated structure (*khażrā*),[299] and we were seated before him, with the musicians playing. In the distance a cloud of dust became visible. The Amir said, "What can this be?" They replied, "We've no idea." He told one of his confidants, "Go down and ride out quickly, and see what this cloud of dust might be." The confidant hastened away and then, after a long while, came back and whispered something in the Amir's ear. The Amir exclaimed, "Praise be to God!", and appeared delighted and rejuvenated, in such a way that all of us thought that it must be a really wonderful piece of good news but did not have the temerity to ask. When it was almost time for the evening worship, we went back home, but he summoned me alone and confided in me with an intimacy such as he had never shown before, and said, "Bu Bakr the secretary[300] has travelled safely to the Garmsir[301] so that he is now proceeding to Iraq and Mecca via the Kerman road. I am much relieved on his account because he did not fall into the hands of this shameless gang, and in particular, Bu Sahl Zowzani, who is thirsting after his blood. That cloud of dust was he; he was travelling on a swift-running camel[302] in a state of complete assurance." I replied, "Thanks be to God, He is exalted and magnified, that the lord's mind is no longer concerned with him." He said, "There is another wish. If that [also] comes about, I will rejoice and be contented regardless of the calamities which have befallen [F 81] me. Go back, and keep this affair hidden." I went home. [Gh 72]

A few days after that, a rider mounted on a swift camel (*mojammez*) arrived from Herat and alighted by the General Begtegin around the time of the evening worship. The Amir was informed of this, and he sent Bu Naṣr the physician, who was one of his boon companions, to Begtegin with a message, stating, "I have heard that a swift courier has arrived from Herat; what news is there?" Begtegin sent back an answer, "Everything is all right. The Sultan has given an order concerning another matter." When it became day, we prepared to go to the fortress to perform our service, but some of the General Begtegin's retainers told us, "Go back today, for an unavoidable matter has arisen for the Amir. An order has arrived containing words of benevolence and good faith, wait so that that affair may be completed. Then you can come again according to your usual routine." This made us extremely worried, and we went back in a very pensive and sorrowful mood.

After two days had gone by, Amir Moḥammad became worried and despairing. He had spoken with the castellan, asking that enquiries should be made of the General, what was the reason no-one had come near him? The castellan sent someone to ask. The General sent his adjutant and counsellor to him and conveyed the message that "A swift courier has arrived from Herat with a letter from the Sultan. He has given an order regarding Amir Moḥammad containing words of benevolence and good faith. A trusty messenger is coming from Herat to the Amir with various vital messages for him, and it may well be that he will arrive today. This is the reason why these words have been said, in order that the Amir's heart may not be cast down, for there is nothing in them but benevolence and kindness." The Amir said, "This is good news," and he became somewhat calmer in his mind, though not altogether. [F 82]

At the time of the midday worship, that messenger arrived, he being called Aḥmad, Keeper of the Royal Washing-Bowls,[303] one of the close retainers and inner circle of Sultan Masʿud. The General Begtegin immediately sent him to the fortress. He remained there until the time of the evening worship and then came back down. After that, it correctly turned out that they were messages containing benevolence on the part of Sultan Masʿud, with the words, "We have now been fully assured about what has happened, and measures for various affairs will now be decreed as is necessary. The Amir, my brother, should have a stout heart and not let himself give free rein to any suspicions, for we intend to spend the winter in Balkh, and when we go to Ghaznin in the spring, plans will be made successively for bringing our brother.[304] [For the present,] it is necessary that an inventory list (*noskhat*) [Gh 73] of what was in the treasury that was sent to Guzgānān with my brother's counsellor and adjutant, should be given to this trusty messenger. Likewise, the gold coinage, clothing and jewels that were taken away from the treasury on his orders and that were either deposited somewhere or are held by him personally or are in the house of his womenfolk—all this is to be handed over to the General Begtegin so that he may bring it back to the treasury. The list of everything handed to the General is to be entrusted to this messenger so that one is kept informed." Amir Moḥammad gave the lists, and what he had personally with him and what the secluded womenfolk of the harem had from the treasury, he handed over to the General. It took two whole days at that time before they had finished with all this; and during these two days, [F 83] they did not allow anybody near Amir Moḥammad.

On the third day, the General rode forth and approached nearer to the fortress. They brought the elephants there with howdahs, and gave the message that the Sultan's command was that Amir Moḥammad was to be conveyed to the fortress of Mandish[305] so that he could be more suitably accommodated there; and the General was to come with the army that was stationed at the foot of the fortress, for the General and those soldiers with him were required to leave for an important purpose. When Amir Jalāl al-Dowla Moḥammad heard this, he wept, realizing what was really happening. They brought him down, willy-nilly, alone from the fortress, and wailing and lamentation arose from his household. When the Amir reached the ground below the fortress, he called out that they were to ask the General, did the royal ordinance stipulate that they were to bear away him alone? The General answered, "No, all his retinue and folk are to go with him, but his children are being got ready in a separate group, since it would be unseemly that they should be borne along with him. I am remaining here until all of them are brought following him, in a proper and respectful manner, in such a way that, at the time of the afternoon prayer, they will arrive and join him safely."

They conveyed the Amir along, with an escort of 300 cavalrymen, accompanied by the castellan of the fortress of Kuhtiz with 300 heavily-armed infantrymen. They placed the womenfolk in litters[306] and the attendants and retainers on mules and asses. Many indignities and improprieties were committed in regard to scrutiny and searches. People voiced their disapproval of the spectacle, and rightly so, since, when all was said and done, Moḥammad was the son of Maḥmud. When Sultan Masʿud heard about this, he reprimanded Begtegin severely, but the matter was left to rest there. That [Gh 74] master of words, the poet Labibi,[307] has expressed himself very eloquently on this situation. (Verses)

1. A caravan was travelling from Ray towards Daskara;[308] a torrent of water came on, and all the people on the bridge perished.[309] (F 84)

2. When a band of robbers saw that[310] from afar, you would have said that each one of them had become a fierce lion [in audacity].

3. Whatever the robbers fancied, they carried away and then went off. There happened to be there another person too, who joined in the pillaging with the robbers.

4. He was a traveller along the road (*rah-ravi*), and found a great deal of money in this way (*dar ān rāh*).[311] When he thus became rich, he became a man of few words, as if his words were a rare commodity.

5. Whatever they asked him,[312] his answer was always just this: "A caravan was pillaged, but another group did well!"[313]

At the time of the afternoon worship, this group caught up with Amir Moḥammad, and when he saw them all reunited with himself, he broke out in thanks to the Almighty God and forgot all thought of profit and loss. The General also arrived and halted some distance away. He ordered that they should put Aḥmad b. Arslān[314] in bonds at that spot and then should take him to Ghaznin so that the *sarhang* Bu ʿAli the castellan might send him on to Multan so that he might be held captive there. They told the rest of Moḥammad's servants and retainers, such as the boon companions and musicians, "You should all go about your own business, since the command is that none of you should go near him." ʿAbd al-Raḥmān the reciter and story-teller related that, the next day, they dispersed, but I and my friend, Nāṣer Baghavi,[315] stealthily went along with him, for the heart's bonds of friendship did not allow us to forsake him. I said, "We will go along to the fortress (i.e. to Mandish) as an act of fidelity, and when they have conveyed him there we will come back."

When they moved on from Jangalābād[316] [Gh 75] and drew near to Gur-e Vāl.sh.t,[317] the fortress of Mandish appeared from afar on the left-hand side of the road. They turned off the road and proceeded in that direction, with myself and that noble-minded[318] man travelling along with them as far as [F 85] the foot of the fortress. We saw a very lofty fortress with a series of staircases with innumerable steps that required a great deal of effort to climb. Amir Moḥammad came down from the howdah, being in fetters and wearing an unadorned hat and shoes and a ruby-coloured satin brocade coat. We saw him, but it was not possible for us to give any respectful greeting or make any sign to him. Tears overwhelmed us, hardly tears, more like the flow of the Tigris and the Euphrates. Nāṣer Baghavi, who was one of the boon companions[319] of this monarch and was good at reciting poetry and singing couplets, wept and then recited a fine extemporisation: (Poetry)

1. O Shah, what was this that befell you! Your enemy came out of your own stock (lit. "out of your own shirt").
2. Your tribulations surpassed all other tribulations; out of your father's estate, your share came out as Mandish.

Two powerfully-built men took his arms and he began to walk with great effort. When he had climbed a few steps, he would sit down for a good while and have a rest. When he had ascended a considerable distance but was still within sight, he sat down. A swift courier came into view from the road. Amir Moḥammad saw him, and did not go on further in order that he might enquire the reason for the courier's arrival, and he sent one of his entourage to the General Begtegin. The courier arrived with a letter. It was a letter in Sultan Masʿud's own hand addressed to his brother. The General Begtegin sent it up at once. The Amir was sitting down on that step along the way up, and we were meanwhile watching. When he read the letter,[320] he fell to the ground in prostration, then arose, proceeded up to the fortress and disappeared from sight. They delivered to that point all the family and entourage of Moḥammad, together with several of his male servants who were included [Gh 76] in the provisions of the Sultan's orders. The General Begtegin and that body of troops of his now returned. I, ʿAbd al-Raḥmān the busybody (*fożuli*), [F 86] as the old men of Nishapur say, "with a dead mother and ten dirhams in debt," came upon those two men who had gripped the Amir's arms and asked, "Why did the Amir perform that prostration?" They replied, "What has it got to do with you? Why don't you sing what the poet says, and that is this verse, (Poetry)

1. *O desert tents, will our time come back again, or is there no way to recover it once it has gone?*[321]

I said, "Indeed, this is an appropriate day for this melody, but I have stood waiting for a while so that I might hear this one further item of what was said and then go away." They said, "It was a letter to him in Sultan Masʿud's own hand with the information that 'We have given orders that the Great Chamberlain ʿAli, who imprisoned the Amir, should himself be consigned to captivity, and his punishment was meted out to him so that no servant should in future venture such boldness against his own lord.' I wished this felicitous news to be passed on to my brother the Amir, since I knew that he would be overjoyed." Amir Moḥammad prostrated himself to the Almighty God and exclaimed, "I am content with everything which has happened to me up to today, since that ungrateful and faithless one has been brought low, and his hopes and ambitions in this present world have come to an end!" I then departed with my friend.

I, Beyhaqi also heard from the same master ʿAbd al-Raḥmān, seven years after I had begun composing this history, on Sunday, 11 Rajab 455 [/10 July 1063], and while I was narrating the story of Amir Moḥammad's reign, that "Out of many outstanding melodies in my repertoire, Amir Moḥammad used very often to ask me for this particular song, to the extent that there were few festive sessions when I did not sing this, the verses being: (Poetry) [F 87]

1. *Your treacherousness is no novelty or cause for wonder, but your being faithful is one of the most novel of novelties.*

2. *It is not a question of your treacherousness but a question of my own eagerness and my accounting as reliable words of falsehood and deception.*[322]

Although these two verses are those of a lover addressing his beloved, a wise person should see them as a moral example, since this was an omen expressed on the tongue of this monarch. There were [Gh 77] during his time many wanton and ill-conceived decisions[323] of which he was unaware, despite the many acts of goodness which he used to perform during the period of his royal power towards both the soldiery and the populace, exactly like the meaning of these two verses. *What has been divinely ordained will happen,*[324] *and what the Almighty God decrees will take place. May God with His favour awaken us from the sleep of the heedless ones!*

After this, I shall set forth what happened concerning this captive Moḥammad in its appropriate place. When the General Begtegin had completed this assignment, he set out for Ghaznin with orders that he was to proceed from there to Balkh, taking with him Sultan Masʿud's mother (*vāleda*) and others of the royal womenfolk and Ḥorra Khottali, in such a manner that they might arrive there with due care.

When all matters had become completely settled at Herat, Sultan Masʿud said to my master Bu Naṣr, "We have issued all the necessary instructions in all matters. During this week we will set off in the direction of Balkh in order to spend this coming winter there, and whatever needs to be negotiated with the Khāns of Turkestan will be negotiated, and we shall turn our attention to the affairs of that region.[325] Khᵛāja Aḥmad b. Ḥasan is also due to arrive and will assume responsibility for the affairs of the vizierate. Then the journey to Ghaznin will be made." Bu Naṣr replied, "The lord's thoughts and decisions contain the very essence of sound judgement and it is incumbent upon us to carry them out in their entirety." [F 88]

The Sultan said, "A letter must be written to the Commander of the Faithful detailing all these recent events, as is the usual practice, so that it may be set forth that all these matters have been settled without any blood being shed." Bu Naṣr replied, "This is one of the things which needs to be done, and it is also necessary to write to Qadïr Khān, so that a courier may carry the message with speed and convey the good news. Then, when the exalted stirrup reaches Balkh in a state of good fortune, plans should be made for despatching a messenger of high status for drawing up the contract and agreement." The Sultan said, "These things must be set in hand speedily, since our departure is near at hand, and these two letters despatched before we set out from Herat."

My master drew up two documents for these two letters in his accustomed manner, one in Arabic to be sent to the Caliph, and one in Persian to be sent to Qadïr Khān; and these [original] documents have been lost, as I have already mentioned in several places elsewhere in this History. A remarkable feature was that Amir Masʿud and his entourage had brought with themselves a group from Western Persia (ʿErāq), [Gh 78] including Bu'l-Qāsem b. Ḥarish[326] and others, and they were seeking to raise them up above my master, on the plea that they were more learned than him. I concede that they composed excellent poetry and were highly competent in the secretarial skills, but the style required for writing from one royal throne to another royal throne is of a different order. A person only becomes aware of that when he embarks on such writing and realizes the full extent of the task. My master, in addition to being the man of wisdom and wide learning that he was, became, through the required refining process of service for Sultan Maḥmud, unique in his age. Out of envy of him, each person of that group prepared a document, and I am ashamed to say what these documents were like. Sultan Masʿud became aware and cognisant of the situation, and subsequently, when the Grand Vizier Aḥmad [b. Ḥasan Meymandi] came into office, he made his favourable attitude towards my master even more clear, so that those envious of him were deflated for good. I [F 89] made a copy of this document as I had done with other ones, and I have thus preserved his fame in this History.[327] The one of them meant for the Commander of the Faithful was also drawn up on these lines, as shall be known, if God, He is magnified and exalted, so wills.

[*The text of the letter to Qadïr Khān*]

In the name of God, the Merciful, the Compassionate. After the opening formulae and invocation: The Khān knows that the great men and monarchs of the age, when they bear friendship towards each other and travel along the way of righteous behaviour, continually strive to bring about mutual harmony and consideration, and then[328] they bring[329] that happy state of affairs to such a high level that they see each other in a personal meeting, one held in a fitting manner. In the course of that meeting, they put in place all the necessary conditions for a bond of strong mutual support,[330] and the compacts and agreements which are envisaged and on which they had expended limitless effort are in fact put in place, so that the houses might become united and all occasions of hostility and suspicion dispelled. They do all this in order that, when the Herald of the Last Days comes for them and they say farewell to the throne of royal power and pass away, their children, who are deserving of that throne and who will sit in their place, can live out their lives in peace and reign undisturbed, with their enemies unable to find and exploit an opportunity to venture against them and succeed in their aims.

The Khān is fully aware what the high status and the affairs of our father the late Amir were like. Of the qualities and virtues associated with great monarchs, [Gh 79] he enjoyed an overabundance. It is not necessary to give an exposition of these since his high status, his magnificence of court and ceremony, and his panoply of arms and military equipment, were evident to all. The Khān further knows that the two deceased masters (i.e. Maḥmud and Qadïr Khān's brother and predecessor, Ṭoghān Khān)[331] strove hard and used the resources of their sincere minds to the full in order to establish on a firm footing such companionship, harmonious agreement and the conjoining of their interests. That encounter with each other at the gate of Samarqand was of such excellence and elegant splendour that news of it reached far and near, and friends and enemies knew about it. It has passed into [F 90] history so that, for many years to come, it will not be effaced from memory. It is certain that they made all these efforts with the aim in mind that their children might rejoice in that companionship and reap the rewards of those seeds that the fathers had sowed. Now, at this present moment, when the throne has passed to ourselves, what should be done is clear to us both: wisdom so ordains, and experience so requires, that great effort should be made to make these lofty edifices of friendship even more strong and sturdy. Friends on both sides will thereby become joyful and content, and the enemies and those envious of us will spend the rest of their days out in the cold, and in dark despair and anxiety. All people on earth will know for certain that both our houses (i.e. of the Ghaznavids and the Qarakhanids), united as they were, have become even more closely bound up with each other. Further, we ask of the Almighty God the most appropriate of heavenly favour for this enterprise, that He may vouchsafe His favour for His servants, *"and that is through His assistance, and likewise all goodness."*[332]

The Khān, may God prolong his might, will have heard that, when our father, may God's mercy be upon him, passed away, we ourself were far away from the seat of royal power by six or seven hundred parasangs, having brought a whole world under our sway. However much we pondered over the alternatives,[333] there were mighty provinces before us, and the people of all those provinces were eager that our great name should be over those regions and they be adorned by our dominion, and the inhabitants raised their hands en bloc to become subjects of ours. The Commander of the Faithful was bestowing honours and esteem and continually urging in correspondence that we should hasten and go to the City of Peace (i.e. Baghdad) and save the exalted status of the caliphate from a group of vile scoundrels who tarnish that exalted status of the caliphate, and remove their weak and abject rule.[334] [Gh 80]

We had come to the decision that, of necessity and unavoidably, the exalted command of the Caliph should be obeyed and that we should attain the felicitation of meeting with the Commander of the Faithful for ourself, when the news arrived that our father [F 91] had passed to the abode of God's mercy. Then after that, we heard that, since we were far away, the retainers and courtiers had immediately summoned our brother Amir Moḥammad from Guzgānān, had set him on the throne and had hailed him as Amir, regarding this as a way of keeping the situation calm, since we were far away. Also, although our father had made us his designated heir during his own lifetime, in his final days his health was failing and some weakness became preponderant over that firmness of judgement which had formed part of his greatness. He did not in reality show vexation and irritability towards us, as is part of human nature, especially on the part of kings for whom it becomes hard to see and acknowledge someone who is worthy of their own place; but he kept us at Ray, knowing that all those lands as far as Byzantium (Rum) and, in another direction, as far as Egypt, would, in their entire extent, become adorned through our conquest of them. He also envisaged that Ghaznin and those parts of India which have so far been conquered,[335] we should leave to our brother so that they would not fall to a stranger, and he would act as our deputy, and we would regard him with the greatest possible esteem and honour.

We despatched an envoy to our brother with words of condolence on Sultan Maḥmud's death and of congratulation on his accession to the throne. We gave messages to the envoy which contained wise counsels for achieving harmony between the two of us and for the pacification of Khorasan and Western Persia and the allaying of worry for thousands and thousands of people. We stated clearly that we had ahead of us, by the order of the Commander of the Faithful, the task of conquering many regions of limitless size and proportion. There had to be mutual support and unity of purpose between the two brothers, and all causes of disagreement and discord had to be dispelled so that the world and all things of value and renown therein might accrue to us. However, the condition for all that was set out as follows:[336] From [F 92] the royal armoury and storehouse,[337] 5,000 camel loads of weapons and 20,000 horses both for riding and as reserve (*markab*);[338] 2,000 gholām cavalrymen, suitably adorned with a complete array of weapons and equipment; and 500 of choice, swift and agile war elephants should speedily be despatched to ourself. A further condition is that our brother should act as our deputy, in such a way that our own name is proclaimed first from the pulpits in the towns, and the formal intercessory prayers at the Friday sermon pronounced in our name at those places and then afterwards in his name. With the minting of dirhams and dinars, and the official embroidery on luxury garments,[339] they are likewise to write our name first and then his. The judges and the postal and intelligence system officials[340] who will spread and communicate these arrangements [Gh 81] are to be chosen at our royal court so that all that needs to be ordained among the Muslims[341] is commanded by ourself.

We personally will become concerned with the region of Iraq[342] and the raiding of Byzantium, and he with Ghaznin and India, so that we may establish in those places the Sunna of our Prophet and keep to the way which our forefathers followed, that the blessed influence of this policy may be perpetuated for our descendants. It was stated in a forthright manner that "if those measures which we have stipulated are not speedily executed, and a policy of procrastination and denial is adopted, we shall inexorably have to return. The conquered lands will have to be abandoned, and we will turn our attention to the task of attending to the realm itself, for that is the essence (*aṣl*) of it all, the rest is subsidiary (*farʿ*). For when one attains the central objective, dealing with peripheral matters will not be hard. If, God forbid, any enmity and hostility[343] between the two of us should arise, it will lead to bloodshed, and suffering, and dire consequences will ensue which will be blamed on our brother; for since we are our father's designated heir and consider this courtesy and fairmindedness as incumbent upon ourself, everybody in the world will know that we have acted with perfect justice."

By the time that the envoy reached Ghaznin, ideas of grasping the throne and the royal power for himself had already swollen our brother's head. He had taken control of the treasuries and had begun to hand out money, and had immersed himself in feasting and pleasure night and day, [F 93] thereby closing the door to his own best interests. Furthermore, a number of persons who had secured an ascendancy over him and gained a dominant role, did not wish the affairs of state to fall into the hands of its rightful claimant who would hold them strictly to the way of duty and obligation, hence they made our brother send back our envoy. They designated their own envoy to accompany him, with a bag full of evasive tricks,[344] and bearing a message that Moḥammad was in fact his father's designated heir, and our father had given Ray to us, Masʿud, so that after he had passed away, each one of us would be content with our allotted portion. If we now abandon our demands in accordance with this agreement, all our demands regarding gholāms, elephants, horses, camels and weapons would be met and despatched, but he would only send them after a treaty pledging that no attempted invasion of Khorasan would take place, and in no circumstances would he act as a deputy ruler for us, nor should any judges or postal and intelligence officials be appointed and sent by us to his domain.

When we received the reply in these terms, it became abundantly clear that Moḥammad would not furnish justice and would not follow the way of righteous conduct [Gh 82]. That same day, we left Isfahan, even though we had intended to march on Hamadan, Ḥolvān and Baghdad. The Commander Ghāzi in Nishapur declared publicly for us and had the formal intercessory prayer (*khoṭba*) made for us, and the ordinary people and the leading figures of those regions all pledged their obedience to us. He had recruited and collected a large number of troops. We, for our part, communicated details of our intentions to the Commander of the Faithful and sought a formal grant of Khorasan and all the other lands of our fathers, together with the lands of Ray, Jebāl and Isfahan which had just been conquered and any lands which we might conquer, by divine favour, in the future—this even though we already had full rights to all these regions—according to his behest, so that everything should be consonant with the divine law (*Shariʿa*).

After our arrival in Nishapur, the Caliph's envoy came in with the grant of investiture, a standard, honorific titles (*noʿut*) and other marks of favour to a number and value such as no ruler had ever received in living memory. By [F 94] a remarkable concatenation of circumstances, the *sarhang* ʿAli b. ʿAbdallāh; Abu'l-Najm Ayāz; and Nushtegin the royal special servant and eunuch (*khāṣṣa khādem*),[345] also arrived from Ghaznin with the greater part of the palace gholāms, and secret letters reached us from Ghaznin that the Great Chamberlain ʿAli [b. Il Arslan], supreme leader of the great commanders (*zaʿim al-ḥojjāb*), and the General Begtughdï, Commander of the Gholāms, had offered their allegiance to us. Bu ʿAli the castellan and the rest of the leading figures of state and high commanders had written and had offered their allegiance and submission, and Bu ʿAli had said that our brother would not be able to direct the affairs of state, and that as soon as our banner appears, they would all come forward offering their submission and service.

We ordered that the group who had come from Ghaznin should be shown marks of favour and that encouraging replies should be written to the notables of Ghaznin. We set out from Nishapur. Twelve days after the Festival [of the Breaking of the Fast], a letter arrived from the Great Chamberlain ʿAli Qarib and the army leaders who were at Teginābād with our brother to the effect that, when news of our advance from Nishapur reached them, they imprisoned our brother in the fortress of Kuhtiz. ʿAli's brother Mengütirek and the religious jurist Bu Bakr Ḥaṣiri, who now arrived in Herat, gave a full account and explanation of all those events. They had sought our instructions so that they might act accordingly.

We ordered a reply, and encouraging and heartwarming response to ʿAli, to all the leading commanders and to the whole army, and in the reply it was specified that our brother should be kept under careful guard in the fortress and that ʿAli and all the army should now come to the court. After that, they began to arrive in successive detachments until all of them reached Herat, and both the armies (i.e. that of Masʿud in Herat and that from Teginābād) were compounded into one force; and both the troops [F 95] and the subjects felt safe and secure in our service and under our rule. Letters were despatched [Gh 83] to the entire realm, including also to Ray, Isfahan and those surrounding regions, giving a full account of these events, so that it would become apparent that matters had been resolved and all the causes of warfare and strife removed. Also, an envoy was sent to the Caliph and letters written detailing these events, and the exalted commands of the Caliph were sought on every topic. We likewise ordered letters to be sent to the Son of Kāku and other local rulers at Ray and in Jebāl and as far as the pass of Ḥolvān intimating how these affairs had been settled easily and smoothly. We explicitly stated that, immediately after this, a commander with a powerful force would be sent in that direction who would firmly secure those territories which we had conquered and conquer others as well. All this was so that they should not indulge in dreams and fall into the delusion that those lands and their affairs would be forgotten and abandoned.

The Excellent Commander, Our Uncle,[346] the Khwarazm Shah Altuntāsh, that wise counsellor, who had, during our absence, given sound pieces of advice to the people in Ghaznin—although they had treated his words with contempt—came to render service here in Herat, and he is being sent back with the most complete favour possible, as befits his position, status and upright conduct. We ourself in the course of this week intend to make a move from here, having achieved all our desires and with the people secure and contented under our rule and command. A letter under our personal seal has gone with instructions for the excellent Khᵛāja Abu'l-Qāsem Aḥmad b. Ḥasan, who had been held a prisoner in Janki's fortress,[347] to come to Balkh and be presented with many a token of favour and encouragement, so that the hand of tribulation may be entirely lifted from him and our reign become adorned by his judgement and good management. [F 96] We have further issued an order for the General Eryāruq,[348] the Commander in India, to come to Balkh also. From Ghaznin we received the letter of the castellan Bu ʿAli informing us that he has handed over to our own treasury officials all the treasuries [left by Moḥammad], comprising dinars, dirhams, clothing, all kinds of fine things and weapons. Thus no causes of dissension have been left, praise be to God, which could disturb one's mind.

Since all these affairs have now reached a satisfactory conclusion, the Khān has been told the good tidings so that he might be fully informed about everything which has taken place, might have his share of this fortunate state, and might spread abroad and disseminate this information in order that it might reach far and near. Thus since the houses are now united—thanks be to God, may His mention be exalted—the happy state which has been renewed for us should be communicated to him also. [Gh 84] Immediately after this, Bu'l-Qāsem Ḥasiri, who is one of my trusty confidants, and the Judge Bu Ṭāher Tabbāni,[349] a judge of the highest calibre, are being designated to come on a mission to those noble lands of the Khān, may God protect them, and to make the agreements afresh. We await a speedy reply to the letter so that we may put on the garment of joyfulness at the renewal of news of the Khān's flourishing state and the progress of affairs on the desired lines. We account that as one of the greatest of divine gifts, *with God's will and permission, He is exalted and magnified.*

This document was despatched by the hand of a swift courier to Qadïr Khān, who was at this time still alive but who passed away two years later. A letter in similar terms was also sent to the Caliph, by the hand of a religious jurist, acting as a semi-official envoy to the Caliph. After these letters had been despatched, the Amir departed from Herat on Monday, in the middle of the month of Dhu'l-Qaʿda of this year [421/14–15 November 1030] for the region of Balkh via the road through Bādghis and Ganj Rustā(q) with the entire army and in full splendour. (F 97)

The Khwarazm Shah Altuntāsh accompanied him on the journey and was pensive and pre-occupied at what might befall him. On several occasions, Bu'l-Ḥasan ʿAqili introduced the topic of the Khwarazm Shah, and the Sultan uttered many words of kindness, expressing his satisfaction with him, saying that he should return to Khwarazm to prevent the outbreak of any potential trouble there. Bu'l-Ḥasan informed Altuntāsh about this, and Bu Naṣr Moshkān likewise spoke to Altuntāsh's secretary about what he had heard, and Altuntāsh became calmer in mind. I heard from Khᵛāja Bu Naṣr, who said that, although Altuntāsh was in such a favourable position, and although the Amir was very pleased with him and valued his many counsels and appreciated the fact that once Altuntāsh had learnt that the matter of the succession had been resolved, he had come speedily to Herat, bearing many gifts and offerings, nevertheless Masʿud's new advisers had prevailed upon him that Altuntāsh ought to be arrested. The Amir, in a private session which he held with his intimate counsellors while on the road, divulged something of this, but we proffered copious advice and said, "He is an obedient servant, and he has numerous offspring, entourage, retainers and followers. He has done no wrong such as to bring down on himself royal rebuke and displeasure. [Gh 85] Khwarazm is a frontier region against the Turks, and Khwarazm in turn depends on him."[350] The Amir replied, "It is exactly as you say. I am content with him, and we have ordained suitable punishment for the person who uttered these deceitful words concerning him. After this, no-one is to have the temerity to say anything except good about him." The Amir then ordered that a robe of honour should be made for him so that he might then depart. He summoned the boon-companion Bu'l-Ḥasan ʿAqili and gave him messages couched in friendly terms for him to convey to Altuntāsh, saying, "I had intended that he should be brought to Balkh and there be given a robe of honour and the command authorising his return to Khwarazm. However, we were afraid [F 98] that he might perhaps stay too long, and perchance some breach or crisis might occur in those lands (i.e. in Khwarazm). Furthermore, the journey between Pāryāb and Andkhudh[351] is a short one; he must get ready to depart from Pāryāb."

When Altuntāsh heard the message, he arose, kissed the ground and said, "It would be better for me, since I have become old, to retire from the army, go to Ghaznin and dwell in the vicinity of the tomb of the late Sultan; but since the lord's command is thus, I shall obey it."

The next day, the Amir arrived in Pāryāb, and ordered that they should garb Altuntāsh in the robe of honour which had been prepared for him. It was a most magnificent robe, and more opulent than what he had been accustomed to receive in the time of Sultan Maḥmud. Altuntāsh stepped forward and performed his obeisance. The Amir clasped him to his bosom and showed him much affection, and he returned home in a most honoured and dignified state. All the leading figures and great men of the court went to visit him and fulfilled the duties of congratulating him in a most handsome fashion. He was given leave to depart the next day.

That night, Altuntāsh sent his secretary Bu Manṣur to me, Bu Naṣr, secretly—this man Bu Manṣur being one of his trusty intimates—and conveyed the message: "I have received permission to depart for Khwarazm, and [Gh 86] tomorrow night they will realize that we have already gone, for I will not seek to request another confirmation before I leave, since I discern some crookedness at work. This monarch is most magnanimous and generous, but, as I read the situation, this motley bunch of people who have gathered round him all act as viziers, and he listens to them and acts upon their words. They will destroy all the well-laid foundations of the realm. [F 99] I am about to leave, and I don't know how you will all fare, for I see no hopeful signs here. You, Bu Naṣr, must safeguard my interests at court just as you have always done, though you yourself are not so secure, since the old order has broken down and things have taken a different turn; but let's see how things develop." I expressed my assent and went back. I now felt more worried and concerned than before, even though I knew more about the state of affairs than he described.

When one watch of the night still remained, Altuntāsh mounted and rode forth with his close retainers, having ordered that no kettle-drums should be beaten lest they realize that he had departed. During the course of the night, they had persuaded the Amir that Altuntāsh must of necessity be incarcerated and that this opportunity should not be wasted. However, by the time they got news of his departure, he had covered ten or twelve parasangs of the journey back to his homeland. They sent 'Abdus after him with the message, "There are several important matters still to be discussed, and several marks of honour which were not conferred. We gave him the authorisation to depart, and he departed, and these matters have been left unsettled and unresolved." They were exercised in their minds whether he would return or not.[352]

When 'Abdus caught up with Altuntāsh, the latter sent back the answer, "I had the order to depart, so, according to the exalted command, I departed, and it would be unseemly now to return. Those matters that have been left outstanding can be dealt with by letter. Moreover, last night a letter arrived from Khᵛāja Aḥmad b. 'Abd al-Ṣamad, my counsellor and adjutant,[353] that the Küjet (*k.jāt*), the Chaghrāq (*ch. q.rāq*) and the Qïpchāq (*kh.f.chāq*) are on the move; some disturbance may well occur in my absence."[354] He then rewarded 'Abdus handsomely for his pains, so that he would plead well on his behalf and set forth his excuses. He mounted his horse and took 'Abdus along with him for one or two parasangs, saying that he had some important matters to discuss with him. He spoke with him privately [F 100] and then sent him back. [Gh 87]

When 'Abdus got back to the army encampment and recounted what had happened, it became abundantly clear that Altuntāsh had become most apprehensive and alarmed at the turn of events. On the same day, many deceitful words had been conveyed to the Amir, and they accused Bu'l-Ḥasan 'Aqili, who had acted as conveyor of messages to Altuntāsh, of treachery and said that he was in league with him. They said that "These men of the former reign (*pedariyān*) will not allow the lord to achieve any of his desires or collect together any wealth. They all put words into each other's mouths and connive together." But the Amir had angrily shouted them down and treated them with cold contempt. Then he summoned me for a private session and said, "It appears that Altuntāsh has gone off in a state of suspicion and fear." I replied, "May the lord's life be prolonged! Why was this? It is not likely that he should have left in a state of suspicion and fear, for he is most loyal and sagacious, and has been the recipient of much favour from the lord. He has expressed his immense gratitude in our presence." The Amir replied, "This was indeed the case, but we hear that suspicions have arisen." I said, "What is the reason for this?" He recounted the story and said, "These people will not allow affairs to run smoothly," and he told me everything that had happened. I said, "I had already pointed this out in Herat, and the lord had then commented that these people did not enjoy such power and scope. But now, from what I hear and see, they have gained an absolute ascendancy. Altuntāsh has raised several points with me while we were riding along together. He did not utter any complaints, but he expressed several words of sincere advice meant for the Amir, for he is wholeheartedly devoted [F 101] to the realm. The thrust of his argument was that 'I do not see affairs proceeding along the right lines. The lord is magnanimous[355] and peerless, generous and forbearing, and noble; but he is too indulgent a listener. All sorts of people have the temerity to talk to him of matters above their rank and station, and they will not leave him alone, while I, Altuntāsh, am only capable of loyalty and plain obedience. Hence I am departing in accordance with the exalted command, but as his servant and devotee, I feel most dejected and shudder with anxiety for this mighty empire. I do not know how this state of affairs will turn out.' This much he said to me, and I can detect no traces of suspicion in these words. [Gh 88] Has the lord heard anything else?" Then the Amir recounted in its entirety what had happened and what they had persuaded him to do. I said that I, Bu Naṣr, would stand guarantee that Altuntāsh will behave obediently and in an upright fashion. The Amir said, "Although such is the case, he must be appeased and won over, and a letter must be written under my own seal and signature, and we shall add a section below it in our own handwriting, for we had sent a verbal message through ʿAbdus to the effect that we had several things to discuss with him, and he sent back an answer in the terms which you heard. If we do not put these words down in writing, he will remain suspicious."

I replied, "The lord can rehearse to me whatever is the best course so that I may be certain and know exactly what should be written." He said, "You must write about the affairs of the realm and our present and future plans: whatever is deemed right and would appeal to him and restore his confidence, so that all his suspicions and fears are allayed." I then set to work and said, "I now know how the letter should be worded. Whom does the exalted command see as suitable for conveying the letter?" He answered, "It should be given to Altuntāsh's personal representative here at court, who can accompany ʿAbdus." [F 102] I obeyed the command and came away, and the letter was indited according to this text that has here been appended:

In the name of God, The Merciful, the Compassionate

After the opening formulae and invocation: We find that the Excellent Commander, our Uncle, the Khwarazm Shah Altuntāsh, occupies the same exalted place in our heart as did our father, the late Amir since from the time of our childhood till the present day he has shown us the kind of concern and affection that fathers have for their own sons. At the time when our father wished to appoint a designated successor to himself, and sought the opinions of Altuntāsh and other leading men about it, he strove hard on our behalf until that momentous affair was resolved in our favour. After that, when envious people and enemies poisoned the late Amir's mind against us and he acted harshly, to the point that he despatched us to Multan and had intended to rescind the decision that he had taken in our favour and bestow the succession on someone else, Altuntāsh proceeded with much tact and employed subtle ploys in order that our position as heir might not be diverted from the rule of succession. He was biding his time and using stratagems, and gathering supporters, until he regained and restored our father's goodwill towards us and our father recalled us from Multan and sent us back to Herat.[356] [Gh 89].

When he set out for Ray, with us accompanying him, and the Ḥājeb came from Gorgānj to Gorgān,[357] and discussions went on about the division of the realm between us brothers Masʿud and Moḥammad, Altuntāsh was most vigilant in acting on our behalf, and sent a message to us secretly with the words, "Clearly, now is not the time for speaking out. You should fall in with whatever the lord sees fit and ordains." We took that fatherly advice, and everything ended up as is evident today.

When our father died and they brought our brother to Ghaznin, the letter which Altuntāsh wrote and the sincere advice which he gave, his personal espousal of our interests and his keeping aloof from our adversaries, were all in that vein which true friends and men of wisdom and goodwill [F 103] say and write. All that was conveyed to me, and its truth has become apparent. When one witnesses a person acting in this manner, one can see how highly he places his faith in friendship and obedience. As for us, having seen in him at all times such devoted allegiance and upright behaviour, it becomes clear how far we would be prepared to go in demonstrating our trust and belief in him: by entrusting an entire province to him, increasing his rank and position, promoting the status of his sons and bestowing titles and honours upon them.

More recently, when we reached Herat, we summoned him so that he might see us and reap the rewards of his beneficial deeds, but before the letter had reached him, he had already set out in order to come and offer his service. We had wished to take him back with us to Balkh, first, to benefit from his sound judgement regarding some important state affairs which we have to tackle and which have been left in abeyance, such as correspondence with the Khāns of Turkestan; making treaties and covenants; cutting down to size our neighbour ʿAlitegin, who has become overweening and rebellious thanks to the recent fallow stretch of weak and indecisive rule; and second, the matter of reinstating and showing and distributing favour amongst retainers and courtiers, according to their worth, status and function, and fulfilling their hopes of favour. We had hoped that all this could have been done in his presence and with his advice and approval. Our other reason for keeping him with us till we reached Balkh was so that he would have an even more worthy and splendid send-off from there.

But because we thought that, since Khwarazm is an important frontier region, and given that he had departed from it already when we had ourself still not reached Ghaznin, it might well happen that enemies would put a different construction on events, and it was imperative that no troubles or crises should arise there in his absence; so we gave [Gh 90] orders that he should return. As ʿAbdus reported, letters had reached him that opportunists and mischief-makers were on the move, and since he had received permission to return, he had left at once with all possible speed. [F 104] On our orders, 'Abdus came after him and met him, and conveyed to him increased honours and largesse from us, and he explained that there were several other outstanding matters that needed to be discussed with him. He received the reply that, since Altuntāsh had set off, it would be unseemly for him to come back and that if there were any other matters and commands, now or in the future, they could be dealt with by correspondence. When 'Abdus returned to the court and recounted this, we found the Commander's decision on this matter an appropriate one. Because of his deep concern for us and our realm, he felt it necessary, having heard through written reports by his trusted advisers that some trouble was brewing in that frontier region, to hasten and deal with the matter headlong; as for these important issues which needed his presence here, they could also be settled through correspondence.

But there is one thing weighing heavily upon us: we are worried in case those envious backbiters of our rule—whose policy it is to do their utmost to achieve their goals, and if not, at least to add to our worries, just like a scorpion bent on biting everything in its path—may have insinuated something. We do not know whether there is any truth in our presentiments and forebodings, but we consider it incumbent upon ourselves to do our utmost to ensure his peace of mind in all matters. Our judgement rendered it imperative that this letter was commissioned and reinforced by our seal and signature, with a section at the end in our own handwriting. Orders have been given to 'Abdus, and Bu Sa'd Mas'adi, his trusty confidant and representative here at court, has been given instructions that they should carry the letter to him swiftly and deliver it, and bring back a reply which may be perused and studied.

There are some other vital matters which, once we arrive at Balkh safely, [F 105] we shall take in hand, such as writing to the Khāns of Turkestan and bringing back the excellent Khᵛāja Abu'l-Qāsem Aḥmad b. al-Ḥasan, may God perpetuate support and assistance to him, in order for the vizierate to be bestowed on him, and the matter of the General Asïghtegin[358] [Gh 91] Ghāzi, who did us such fine service at Nishapur, and who in return for this received the position of Commander-in-Chief. The Khwarazm Shah must also listen to those items that have been conveyed to him in messages, and give full answers that may then be perused and studied. He must know that in all important state decisions we shall confer with him, just as our father, the late Amir used to do, since his judgement is a blessed one. He, for his part, must adopt the same ways and open his heart to us, and offer us his advice in a plain and forthright manner, for he should know that his words occupy an unassailable place in our heart and mind.

The personal hand of Amir Masʿud: "Let the excellent General, the Khwarazm Shah, may God perpetuate his might, place reliance on this letter and have a stout heart, since our own heart is with him. *God is the One who gives aid for the fulfilment of His rights!*"

When ʿAbdus and Bu Saʿd Masʿadi returned, we had reached Balkh. They brought back a reply set out in very respectful and deferential terms and containing much humility and submissiveness together with very well-expressed excuses for the hurried departure. The Amir closeted himself with myself and ʿAbdus and said, "We did well to exert ourselves in regard to Altuntāsh, for we were a hair's breadth away from alienating him, for they had made him deeply afraid and he was going away in haste. With this letter, however, his fears have been allayed and all grounds for apprehensiveness dispelled. He regained his composure and went off a happy man."

Altuntāsh sent a reply to our letter, as follows:

Regarding the matter of the Khāns of Turkestan, [F 106] it is essential to enter into correspondence with them when you have arrived in Balkh, safe and sound, and at the height of good fortune, and subsequently to despatch envoys and seek a treaty and agreement. For it is well-known that the late Amir went to a considerable amount of trouble and expended much money until Qadïr Khān attained the Khanate with Maḥmud's military assistance and he became firmly settled on the throne. At this present time, the former arrangements must be consolidated to augment the friendship; not that the Khāns can be regarded as true friends, but ostensibly amicable relations will remain between us and they will not incite others against us. ʿAlitegin is our veritable enemy, and is writhing with venom like a serpent with a crushed tail since his brother has managed to drive out [his other brother] Ṭoghān[359] Khān from Balāsāghun,[360] thanks to the might and military power of the late Amir.[361] An enemy never becomes a friend.[362] It is nevertheless necessary to seek a treaty [Gh 92] and affect a rapprochement with him, for although no reliance can be placed on that, it has to be done. When this has been achieved, it will be necessary to fill the regions of Balkh, Tokhārestān, Chaghāniyān, Termez, Qobādhiyān and Khottalān with troops, since whenever he finds an undefended spot and an opportunity, he will strike out and plunder.[363]

As for the matter of Khᵛāja Aḥmad, this servant has nothing to contribute in this respect and stands on the sidelines.[364] Whatever the exalted judgement considers the best and most suitable course of action should be done, for it is a matter of public knowledge that between that peerless master and myself there is some ill feeling.

Regarding the matter of the General Asïghtegin, when Arslān Jādheb passed away, the late Amir chose him as worthy of filling Arslān's place out of the many alternatives available to him. The Amir was well acquainted with the other possible candidates, and if Asïghtegin had not been deemed worthy of such an eminent position, he would not have appointed him. He has rendered much good service, and the lord should disregard what people say, and keep the welfare of the realm in view. Since the lord, in the letter which he has commanded to be written to me, [F 107] has ordained that I should set forth sound counsels through correspondence, I have transmitted one point with this trusty confidant—though the lord himself is well aware of all this, and my words, and those of others, are perhaps superfluous—that the late Amir had a long reign and handed over a strong state with firmly-based rules of government to the lord, and then departed this life. If the lofty judgement sees fit, no-one must be allowed to have the audacity and the power to change one single rule or custom of that, for it will subvert the basis of the whole state's affairs. I shall not say any more than this, as this should suffice.

This answer greatly pleased the Amir, and we, Bu Naṣr and Masʿadi, went away. The next day Masʿadi came to me, Bu Naṣr, and brought a message from the Khwarazm Shah, which said, "The enemies had done their work, but the lord Sultan ordained what was worthy of his greatness regarding myself, a servant uniquely sincere and devoid of treacherous intentions, and I know that you are fully aware of the situation. I felt somewhat more at ease in my mind and went off, but you should know for certain [Gh 93] that, after this, should a thousand urgent matters arise at the exalted court and my personal presence be required, I should not be summoned, for I will not come. But on the other hand, I would be prepared to send as many troops as necessary, or if there is a need for service on one of the frontiers of the realm and I am given an order to act as commander and military leader, I shall assume that duty and shall not shrink from expending my soul and body, my wealth and my troops. For I have seen the state of affairs at court and understood them very well. That crowd will never allow any policy to proceed along the correct lines nor will they leave things alone. The lord is not at fault; the fault stems from those who teach and preach evil; I have sent you this so that you can see exactly how things stand."

I, Bu Naṣr, did not keep this secret entrusted to me, and went along and spoke with the Amir. I requested that this message should be kept secret; but it did not remain so. Another scheme was devised for overthrowing the Khwarazm Shah Altuntāsh, an extremely ineffective and flimsy one, and it did not succeed. As a result, the man became even more distrustful; [F 108] this will be recounted subsequently in its proper place.[365]

In the course of this journey, Khᵛāja Ḥasan—may God keep him in good health—who had been Amir Moḥammad's counsellor and adjutant, arrived at the royal camp at Marv al-Rudh.[366] He was coming from Guzgānān and had deposited the treasury (i.e. that formerly in Moḥammad's possession) in the fortress at Shādyākh in accordance with the orders of Amir Masʿud, and had entrusted it to his trusty retainer so that it could be transported to Ghaznin. [367] He had distinguished himself extremely well in carrying out this service, and when he came before the Amir, he distributed money on a large scale and handed over presents of enormous value and other customary marks of service; the Amir showed him favour and spoke to him encouragingly, praising him for his upright conduct and good guardianship. All the pillars of state and leaders lauded him for that uprightness and the manner in which he had served and safeguarded that great treasury. For when he realized what the situation of his lord, Moḥammad, was, he did not set his heart on that wealth and he did allow himself to be waylaid by satanic temptations but followed the path of rightfulness and truth; for he was a man of great wisdom and extensive experience, learned and well-read, and endowed with clear perception and foresight. As a result, he was able to remain in his former high status.

In the course of this journey, Khᵛāja Bu Sahl Ḥamdavi[368] used to sit in the domed tent of the Divān and issue instructions for official business, since he was better informed than the rest and had attained the aura of a vizier, and the Amir regarded him most favourably. [Gh 94] At the same time, Khᵛāja Bu'l-Qāsem b. Kathir was in charge of the Army Department, and the Amir dealt with him regarding army matters. From among the leading civilian officials (*khᵛājagān*) of the court and the accountants,[369] such persons as Ṭāher, Bu'l-Fatḥ Rāzi and others, sat in the Divān close to Bu Sahl Ḥamdavi. [F 109] Bu'l-Kheyr Balkhi, who had been the local governor and tax collector (*ʿāmel*)) in Khottalān during the late Amir's time, ran the day-to-day business of the vizier's department. Ṭāher, ʿErāqi and the other secretaries who had come from Ray worked in the Chancery with Bu Naṣr Moshkān.[370] Ṭāher and ʿErāqi had developed inflated opinions of themselves. Most of the private sessions were with Bu Sahl Zowzani. He personally drew up monetary transactions,[371] put forward pleas to the legal tribunals (*morāfaʿāt*) and enforced confiscations,[372] and people were in awe of him. Messages were conveyed through his intermediacy, together with the greater part of important matters of state.[373]

ʿAbdus was also very close to the Amir, and involved in everything. ʿAbdus's trusty retainer Mo'adhdhen conveyed the Great Chamberlain ʿAli to the fortress of Korok in the mountains of Herat[374] and handed him over to the custody of the castellan there, who was an appointee of ʿAbdus. After this, the Amir dealt with all matters concerning ʿAli through ʿAbdus, and all the letters that came from the castellan of Korok were presented to the Amir through ʿAbdus. The Amir would then send them to my master, and I, Bu'l-Fażl, would write out the replies to the letters according to my master's instructions. I shall subsequently relate what happened in regard to ʿAli until the point when he died. They also bore away Mengütirek and entrusted him to the castellan Bu ʿAli, and they held him prisoner in the citadel of Ghaznin. They arrested the rest of his brothers and his entourage en masse and they confiscated everything they had. They sent ʿAli's son, the field officer (*sarhang*) Moḥsen, to Multan. He was very young at the time, but was wise and capable of self-control; as a result, he found favour and was released from bonds and tribulation and came to Ghaznin. He maintains his old habit of self-control and contentment with his lot, and is occupied with rendering service and displays no appetite for wealth or rank. May he remain in this safe and healthy state!

Sultan Mas'ud reached Shoburqān[375] with auspiciousness and in accordance with the desires of his well-wishers. [Gh 95] He celebrated there the Festival of the Sacrifice[376] and proceeded in the direction of Balkh, arriving there on Tuesday, 15 Dhu'l-Ḥejja of the year 421 [/14 December 1030][377] and lodged at the Palace of the Gate of 'Abd al-A'lā. In that blessed stage of his reign, the whole world, and particularly Balkh at the time, appeared as fresh and resplendent as a beautifully adorned bride. [F 110] The next day, he held court with great splendour, and the leading men of Balkh, who had come to render service with scatterings of coins, returned home with much beneficence and many marks of favour. Everybody was busy with his own work, and the Amir held lively wine-drinking sessions.

I have taken the history of this monarch's activities up to this point. It ought to have been the case that, from that time when the news reached him of his brother's arrest at Teginābād, I should have said he assumed the royal throne. However, I refrained from saying so, since this kingdom was still in the process of rising to its full florescence, and Mas'ud was heading for Balkh. Now, at this moment when he has arrived in Balkh, and the affairs of the realm are running smoothly again, it is necessary to continue this History in a different fashion. First of all, I will compose an exordium (*khoṭba*) and follow it with several sections of general discourse, and then embark on the history of his auspicious time, for this will be a separate book.[378] I seek the best road to success from the Almighty God and assistance to complete this History. "*God, He is praised, is the best of those who give success and the best helper through His grace, the wideness of His mercy and His beneficence. May God grant blessings on Moḥammad and all his house!*" [F 111]

[The beginning of the sixth volume]

The beginning of the history of Amir Shehāb al-Dowla Masʿud son of Maḥmud, God's mercy be upon them both

Abu'l-Fażl Moḥammad b. al-Ḥoseyn al-Beyhaqi, may God's mercy be upon him,[379] continues to relate:[380] Although this section of the History is preceded by what was mentioned previously, nevertheless, in importance (lit. "rank, standing") it takes precedence. At the outset, it must be realized that the late Amir was the blossom of the first shoot of a tree, out of which kingly power became visible; and it came to maturity when the martyred Amir Masʿud sat down on the throne, in his father's place. Those learned scholars who have recounted the history of the just Amir Sebüktegin, from infancy till the time when he found himself in the palace of Alptegin, the Great Chamberlain and Commander-in-Chief of the Samanids, have further described the arduous and momentous tasks which were inflicted on him until [Gh 96] he acquired the office of the emirate at Ghaznin, dying in that high dignity.[381] The task of government then passed to Amir Maḥmud, as has also been recorded and explained by them, and as I myself have recorded up to the end of his life.[382] Those learned scholars did what was incumbent upon them, and I too did what I could, according to my knowledge and capability, until I reached this great monarch, Masʿud. [F 112] I, being bereft of their virtues[383] and not being of their high calibre, have been a mere wayfarer[384] until I arrived here. My aim is not to explain to the people of this present time the exploits of Sultan Masʿud, may God illuminate his proof, because they have themselves seen him and are well aware of his greatness, his courage and his uniqueness in all matters of government and leadership. Rather, my aim is that I should write a foundation (*pāya*) for history[385] and raise a lofty structure upon it, in such a way that the memory of it will remain till the end of time. I seek success in completing that from the Eternal Presence; *God is the vouchsafer of fortune and favour.* Since in writing history I laid down a condition that, at the beginning of each sovereign's reign, I would compose a *khoṭba* and then embark upon narrating the history itself, I now fulfill that condition, *with God's will and His help.*

[*Khoṭba*]

Section

I begin by stating that, amongst the excellent kings of the past are a group who can be regarded as outstanding, and amongst them two have been singled out as particularly memorable. One is Alexander, the Ancient Greek (*yunāni*), and the other is Ardashir, the Persian (*pārsi*). But since our own lords and monarchs have surpassed these two in all things, one should necessarily know that our kings have been the greatest on the face of the earth; for Alexander was a man whose royal flame took light strongly, flared up for only a very short while and was then turned into ashes. His manner of conquering those mighty kingdoms and traversing the inhabited regions of the world was akin to that of a sightseer passing through different places.[386] [F 113] As for those monarchs whom he subdued, when he asked them to submit to him and style themselves his inferiors, it was as if his action was instigated by a solemn oath that he had once vowed to perform and was now going through with it so that he would keep to his word (i.e. all this was triggered by the whim of a moment). But what is the point of just wandering around the world? A monarch must keep a tight rein, for by seizing some realm and region but failing to maintain his grip, and then impetuously moving on to invade yet another land, and repeating the same process and abandoning it, he would have given full scope for all and sundry to call him weak and impotent.

It is generally held that the greatest deeds of Alexander [Gh 97] as recorded in books were that he killed Darius (Dārā), king of the Persians, and Porus (Fur), king of India.[387] Yet he committed a demeaning blunder in relation to each of these two. His great blunder regarding Darius was that he betook himself to Nishapur during the course of his campaign disguised as a messenger to Darius's army; they recognized him and tried to seize him, but he fled, and Darius was killed by his own trusty retainers, bringing about a drastic reversal in the situation.[388] As for the error regarding Porus, this was that when the battle was raging between them and became protracted and Porus sought to engage Alexander in single combat, and they fought each other hand-to-hand. It is not fitting that a monarch should accept such a risk as this, but Alexander was crafty and ingenious. Before he engaged Porus directly, he had prepared a stratagem for killing him. From the direction of Porus's army there arose a mighty shout; Porus was distracted and looked round in that direction, and Alexander seized the opportunity to strike and kill him.[389] Now Alexander was a figure of great stature, a man of din and clamour, of lightning and thunderbolts, as if he were a raincloud in spring and summer which passed over the sovereigns of the earth, shed its burden and disappeared, "*and it is as if he were a summer raincloud which is very soon cleared away.*"[390] And for five hundred years after him, the dominion of the Ancient Greeks that endured and spread over the face of the earth, was governed by a judicious guideline devised by Aristotle (Aresṭāṭālis), Alexander's tutor, when he decreed that "The realm ought to be divided out among [F 114] several kings so that they are continually preoccupied with each other and do not concern themselves with Rum (i.e. Alexander's own heartland of the Greek lands and Ionia in Asia Minor)." These are called "the Party Kings".[391]

As for Ardashir Bābakān, the greatest thing about him which they relate is that he revived the defunct reign of the Persians and established a tradition (*sonnat*) of justice among kings, which was followed after his death by certain rulers, and upon my life, this was a great achievement; but it must be said that it was because the Almighty God had brought the period of the "Party Kings" to a close that matters worked so smoothly for Ardashir.[392] They mention some miracles[393] of these two personages, Alexander and Ardashir, such as prophetic messengers perform; and the members of this great ruling dynasty (i.e. the Ghaznavids) have displayed such lasting deeds and virtuous actions matched by none, such as have already been narrated in this History, and will be narrated later. Hence if a slanderer or backbiter should say that the origin of the great ones (Gh 98) of this mighty family goes back to an obscure slave boy, the answer to him is that, ever since God, His mention is exalted, has created Adam (Ādam), He has decreed that kingly rule should be transferred from one people (*ommat*) to another and from one group to another. The greatest testimony to what I am saying is the Word of the Creator, His majesty is magnified and His names sanctified, who has said, "*Say, O God, possessor of all sovereignty, You give sovereignty to whomsoever You will and take it away from whomsoever You will. You exalt whomsoever*

You will and humble whomsoever You will. All good things come from You; indeed, You have power over all things."[394] Thus one must know that, in the Almighty God's Decree, in removing the robe of royal power from one group and cladding another group in it, there lies a divine wisdom and general concern for the welfare of all creatures on the face of the earth which is beyond human understanding, and no-one [F 115] can fathom this and give a reason for it, let alone being able to express this outwardly and in their discourse. Although this rule is correct and true, and one must inescapably be content with the Almighty God's decree, wise men, if they focus their minds on this veiled procedure, and explore and probe deeply until they acquire illumination by means of this proof, will become firmly assured that the Exalted Creator has knowledge of hidden things and prescience of things still to come. Further, in His knowledge of the Unseen, it would have been envisaged that, in a certain region in some part of the world, a man will appear through whom His servants would become secure and contented and that land prosperous and fecund. God sets up firm rules, such that, when kingly rule arrives from that seed to that man, it will have so come to pass that the people of his age, humble and noble, show themselves submissive to him, and are obedient and docile, and in that obedience they do not give themselves over to any shame. Just as He makes manifest this ruler, He will send with him a group of men as his helpers and servants, suitable for him, one greater, more competent, more worthy, more courageous and more learned than the other, so that that region and its people will become more adorned by that monarch and by those helpers during that period which the Almighty God has decreed. *Blessed be God, the finest of creators!*[395]

The same applies to the divine messengers, God's blessings be upon them all, from the time of Adam to that of the Seal of the Prophets, Moṣṭafā (i.e. Moḥammad, "the Chosen One"). One must observe that, since the latter was the unique one on the face of the earth, God provided him with helpers of such a calibre that, after his decease, they did such exalted deeds and raised Islam to such a high level as is manifest in the histories and biographies of the Prophet (*siyar*); and until the Resurrection, this faith of Islam (lit. "divine law," *shariʿat*) will continue in existence [Gh 99], each day stronger, more apparent and more exalted, "*even though the polytheists may dislike it.*"[396] (F 116)

Further, the matter of the Nāṣeri, Yamini, Ḥāfeẓi and Moʿini dynasty,[397] which is today manifest, and which the Exalted Sultan (*solṭān-e moʿaẓẓam*) Abu Shojāʿ Farrokh-zād b. Nāṣer Din Allāh, may God prolong his existence, holds by inheritance as a lawful inheritance, has likewise come about in this manner. Since the Almighty God was eager that a dynasty with this eminence should become manifest on the face of the earth, He raised the just Amir Sebüktegin from the stage of infidelity to the stage of faith, and bestowed upon him the gift of the Muslim religion. Then He raised him up until, stemming from that blessed tree, there appeared branches many degrees more sturdy than the stem itself. With those branches He adorned Islam, and He entrusted them with upholding the power of the successors[398] of the Prophet of Islam, so that if one ponders over this, Maḥmud and Masʿud were two bright suns concealed by a morning and a sunset glow, and with the passing away of that dawn and dusk, the brilliance of those suns has now become apparent. And now, from those suns, several illustrious stars and countless glittering planets are the offshoot. May this great dynasty endure for ever, each day more powerful, *despite the opponents and the envious ones!*[399]

When I had finished this section, I began another section such as may be closer to the heart and which will be easier to follow and require less mental exertion. Know that God Most High has given one power to the prophets, may God's blessings be upon all of them, and another power to kings. He has made it incumbent upon the creatures on the face of the earth that [F 117] they should follow those two powers and through them recognize that divinely-given straight path. Anyone who considers that as coming from the heavenly firmament, the stars and planets[400] and the zodiacal constellations, is denying the Divine Creator His status, and is a Moʿtazelite, a heretic (*zendiq*), and a materialist and atheist (*dahri*), and his place is in Hell. *We seek refuge in God from the withdrawal of His grace.*[401]

The power specific to the Prophets lies in their evidentiary miracles, that is, things that ordinary people are incapable of doing. The power of monarchs comprises a discriminating intellect, military might, conquests and victory over enemies, together with the justice which they dispense in conformity with the commands of God Most High. For the distinction between divinely-assisted and successful monarchs and a tyrannical rebel is that, since monarchs are characterised by the dispensing of justice, good actions, good behaviour and praiseworthy deeds, they should be obeyed [Gh 100] and acknowledged as chosen by God for their task. Usurpers who practise oppression and evil must be stigmatised as rebels, and holy war (*jehād*) must be waged on them. This is a measure by which those who do good and those who do evil are assessed and show their true nature. One can know by necessity which of those two persons one must obey. In regard to our monarchs (may God be merciful to those who have passed away and give long life to those who are still living!), one must observe how they led their lives in the past and how they live at present—their justice, beneficent behaviour, pious restraint, religious zeal, purity of daily existence, their pacification of persons and lands, and their cutting short the hands of tyrants and oppressors—so that one becomes assured that they have been among the chosen ones of the Creator, His mightiness be exalted and His name sanctified, and that obedience to them has been a divinely-imposed duty and continues to be so. If in the midst of all this some reversal and degradation has befallen some of these monarchs of ours, and they have suffered a disappointment and faced the unexpected—things which tend to happen frequently in this world—wise men should look at these things with the eye of wisdom and not be misled by false deductions. [They should realize that] the Creator's decree, which the Pen has inscribed on the Preserved Tablet,[402] [F 118] never changes; "*There is no deflecting His divine decree, may His mention be exalted.*"[403] Truth must always be recognized as truth, and falsehood as falsehood; as has been said, "*Truth is always truth, even if mankind is ignorant of it, and the light of day is always the light of day, even if a blind person does not see it*".[404] *I ask God Most High to preserve us and all the Muslims from faults and errors by His power, His benevolence and the breadth of His mercy.*

When I finished the *khoṭba*, I saw it as necessary to compose another section that may be of use both to monarchs and to others, so that each class of persons may derive profit from it according to the amount of their knowledge. So I begin by describing those qualities of the wise and just man which entitle him to be called meritorious, and what the defects of the tyrannical person are, such that he may inevitably be called ignorant and uncouth, and it will become apparent that, whoever is stronger in wisdom will attract more praise, and whoever has a smaller intellect will be held in less esteem.

Section

The greatest sages of ancient times have said that, from among the ancient revelations which the Almighty God sent through the prophet of that age was that he told people, "Know yourself, [Gh 101] for when you have come to know yourself, you will understand [other] things." Our Prophet has said, *"He who knows himself* (i.e. his soul) *has come to know his Lord".*[405] This is a succinct expression with many meanings, for how can anyone who is unable to know himself know other things? He is to be accounted among the beasts, indeed, he is even worse than the beasts since they have no faculty of discernment and he has. Then, when [F 119] mulled over, beneath this significant and deftly expressed and pithy saying is to be found much benefit. For whoever knows himself, and realizes that he is alive but will in the end be reduced to nought by death yet will inevitably rise again from the grave through the power of the Almighty Creator, such a person will know his Creator and will realize His difference from His creatures, and will acquire the right religion and the true creed. He therefore knows that he is composed of a mixture of four things,[406] the fundamental basis for his body, and whenever some defectiveness or imbalance occurs in one of these, the correct balance goes awry and deficiency becomes apparent.

Within this body there are three faculties (*qovva*). One is the faculty of intellect and speech, whose seat is in the head in partnership with the heart; the second is that of anger, whose seat is in the heart; and the third is that of desire, whose seat is the liver. Each of these faculties is thought to provide a location for a spirit (*nafs*), even though they all originate in one body. There is much to be said about this matter, but if I indulged myself in explaining that, the thrust of the argument would be lost, so I shall make a few apposite points that may prove generally beneficial. As for the faculty of intellect and speech, it has three seats within the head.[407] One is called the seat of imagination (*takhayyol*), the first level of which can see and hear things. The second level is the one that can discriminate between things and keep them in the mind; after this, it is possible to know truth from falsehood, and the beautiful from the ugly, and what is possible from what is not possible (i.e. *cogitatio*). The third level is that which can understand and retain in the mind whatever it has seen (i.e. *memoria*). From this, one should know that in regard to this analogy, the middle one (i.e. the second seat of the faculty of intellect and speech) is the most important, since it is like a judge (*ḥākem*), to whom resort is made in affairs and who has the responsibility for delivering judgements and issuing ordinances. That first level is like the testimony of a fair and veracious witness who tells the judge whatever he hears and sees (F 120] so that he may take it to the third level to be preserved and where it can be retrieved when asked for.[408] This is the position of the speaking spirit (*nafs-e guyanda*, i.e. the *spiritus loquens*).[409] As for the spirit of anger (*nafs-e kheshm-giranda*), this is the seat of seeking fame and reputation, the repudiating of disgrace, the throwing-off of oppression, and the concern for seeking vengeance when it [Gh 102] suffers tyranny and injustice. As for the spirit of desire (*nafs-e ārzu*, i.e. the *spiritus appetivus*), it is concerned with the love of food and wine and other pleasures.[410]

One must know very clearly that the rationally speaking spirit is the ruler—commanding, masterful and overbearing. He must exercise justice and administer punishment whole-heartedly and firmly but not so as to uproot all, and display kindness but not so as to leave an impression of weakness. Thus anger is the army of this ruler, through which he repairs deficiencies, secures the frontiers, wards off the enemy and protects the subjects. The army must be totally ready, and thus equipped and prepared to carry out his command. Desire is the subject population of this king; it is vital that they should be in complete fear of the king and the army and give them obedience.

Whosoever fits the conditions I have mentioned and deploys these three faculties to the full, in such a way that they interact in a balanced way, deserves to be called virtuous and perfect in intellect and wisdom. Hence if within a man one of these faculties gains an ascendancy over another, there will inescapably arise a deficiency there commensurate with the ascendancy. When the make-up of a man is closely scrutinized, it seems akin to that of the beasts. However, man, to whom the Almighty God has given these two divine favours which are knowledge and works, must necessarily be distinguished from beasts, and is subject to rewards and punishments. Hence one can now, of necessity, know that whoever [F 121] attains this level is obliged to keep his own body under his personal control so that he may traverse whichever way is more praiseworthy and so that he may know the exact point marking the distinction between goodness and evil. He can then incline towards whichever is the more praiseworthy, and be free from what is the more blameworthy and abstain from it.

Given the above considerations, two ways present themselves now, one right and the other crooked, and they bear signs from which the good can be distinguished from the bad. A man of discernment must reflect upon the conduct of other people: whatever appears good to him, he will know that it is good and then compare his own conduct with that; for if he does not find it in accord with that, he will know that it is evil, since a man cannot discern his own shortcomings. A certain wise man has demonstrated that in an allusive fashion, saying that no-one has the eye for discerning faults, (Poetry)

1. *I see that every human being sees the faults of another, but is blind to the fault within himself.*

2. *A man's own faults are in every case hidden from him, whereas the fault within his brother is clear to him.*[411] [Gh 103]

It may happen that a man has a perfect intellect, and the faculties of anger and desire become dominant in him, so that the intellectual faculty is overcome and flees away, and this person inevitably falls into error. It may be that he realizes that he has fallen between two great enemies, both of which are stronger than his intellect, hence he must employ many stratagems with his intellect in order to prevail over these two enemies; as has been said, "*Woe to the strong one caught between two weak ones!*".[412] So when a weak thing falls between two strong things, one can realize what the situation is like, and at that point defects and blameworthy things show themselves while good qualities and merits remain hidden. Men of learning have likened the human body to a house with a man, a pig, and a lion inside it [F122]. By man they meant the intellect, by pig desire, and by lion anger.[413] And they have said that out of these three, whichever is stronger, the house is his. For them, this is a matter of direct observation as well as of understanding through analogy; for whoever is able to keep a firm grip on his body and is able to break the back (lit. "neck") of greed and desire is worthy of being called a wise and self-possessed person; whoever is totally gripped by his passions, to the extent that everything inclines towards desire and the eye of his intellect remains blind, is like a pig; and whoever is dominated by wrath, and in that angry state never inclines towards clemency and compassion, is like a lion.

This topic must necessarily be expounded more clearly. If some captious person should say that, if desire and anger did not have to exist, God, He is magnified and exalted, would not have created them within a man's body, then the answer to that is that in everything which the Creator, may His mightiness be magnified, has created there is some benefit for mankind, general and apparent. If He did not create an appetite, no-one would incline towards food, which is the mainstay of the body, nor towards sexual coupling, which ensures the perpetuation of the race, and no human being would be left and the world would be in ruins. If He did not create anger, no-one would set his face towards exacting revenge, protecting himself from disgrace and oppression, concerning himself with exacting retribution, and shielding his family and possessions from predators, and he would no longer be able to protect his own interests.

But the appropriate and commendable course is that the faculties of desire and anger should obey the faculty of the intellect, and that a man should consider both these faculties as a horse which he mounts and rides how he likes. If it is not docile [Gh 104] and does not provide a good back for the rider, he straightaway instils fear into it by the whip, and thrashes it if necessary, and if required, he hobbles it[414] [F 123] and ties it up securely in its stable so that it cannot be unshackled, for if it were let loose, the horse would destroy both itself and its rider. A man should know that these two enemies within him are enemies of the toughest and strongest breed, so that he should always be on his guard against them lest they deceive and profess friendship as if, like the intellect, they were true friends to him, so that he is led to perform an evil act and harm someone and think that he has acted justly. In whatever he intends to do, he should consult his true friend, the intellect, in order to be secure from the guile of these two foes.

Every servant on whom the Almighty God has bestowed a clear intellect, who lays open to this intellect, which is in truth his friend, circumstances and events, and who by means of that intellect becomes the friend of knowledge, reads the histories of past generations and ponders over[415] them, and also looks at the affairs of his own time—

such a servant can know what good conduct is and what bad conduct is, and whether the consequences of both of them are good or not, and will know what people say and favour, and what constitutes the best memorial a man can leave behind.

There are many sages who direct men to travel along the way of correct behaviour but do not themselves go along that road which they have pointed out. I see a great number of persons who "command people to do what is good and forbid them from what is bad"[416] and tell people that such-and-such a deed must not be done and some other such deed must be done, while considering themselves above all that! In the same way, there are many physicians who assert that one must not eat a certain thing as liable to bring about a certain malady, [F 124] but then go on to eat vast amounts of that same thing. Then there are also philosophers, who are regarded as physicians of morals and who pronounce against many a heinous deed, and yet when they find the coast clear, they indulge in those very acts. Ignorant people, who are incapable of deciphering the consequences of their deeds, can be excused on the grounds of their ignorance; but those perceptive enough to realize the significance of their actions have no excuse.

The wise man possessing firm resolution and determination is he who, because of [Gh 105] his own clear reason, has indeed become single-minded and has subjugated his enthusiasm (*ḥemyat*) for vain desires.[417] So if a man does not find his own resolve sufficient enough, he should select a few persons, the more virtuous and capable of providing sound advice the better, in order to point out his faults to him, and when he is combatting those mighty enemies who are lodged within his heart and soul, and finds them overpowering, he can seek advice from these counsellors and be directed to the right path. The Chosen One (i.e. Moḥammad) has said, "*The believer is the mirror of the believer*" *(al-mo'men mer'āt al-mo'men)*.[418] Galen (Jālinus) was the greatest of the wise men of his age, unequalled in the science of medicine and anatomy (lit. "flesh and blood") and the humours (*ṭabā'eʿ*) of the human body, and unsurpassed in the treatment of moral and ethical aspects, in which context he has some excellent epistles concerning an individual's self-knowledge from which readers may derive much profit.[419] The basic thrust of the argument, according to him, is that "An intelligent person who cannot recognize the error of his ways and finds himself at fault, should make it his duty to select amongst his friends [F 125] the wisest and the one most capable of giving sound advice, and to commission him to enquire into his own circumstances, habits, and manners so that the friend can lay open before him, dispassionately, his virtues and faults. Monarchs are more needful of this than anyone else, for their commands are as incisive as a sword blade, and no-one dares to oppose them and any error of judgement issuing from them is hard to unravel."

I read in the *Akhbār-e moluk-e 'Ajam* "Historical accounts of the Persian Kings", as translated by Ebn Moqaffaʿ,[420] that it was the custom of their greatest and most virtuous monarchs to have the wisest sages of the age present and seated in their company at all times of day and night until they retired to sleep. These men would restrain them and enlighten them about events,[421] and would point out whatever was worthy of praise or blame in the affairs, customs and commands of their proud and powerful monarchs. Then when the king was stirred by a reprehensible passion and wished to give vent to and exercise his wrath, thereby causing much bloodshed [Gh 106] and the destruction of notable families, those wise men would delve into that matter and lay before him the good and bad consequences of his action and would recount to him stories and chronicles of past kings, cautioning and advising him by appealing to the divine law (*sharʿ*). In this way, they enabled him to evaluate the situation through his own intellect and reasoning; that anger and impetuosity of his would subside, and he would do what was incumbent upon him according to the norms of justice and uprightness. For when he is carried away by anger and displays impetuosity, it signifies that a great affliction has overcome [F 126] his intellect and that he has become needful of a physician who can cure that affliction so that the turbulence subsides.

All men, whether they be monarchs or not, have a spirit (*nafs*), which they call the soul (*ruḥ*), most noble and substantial, and have a body (*tan*) which they call the *jesm*, very insignificant and petty. Now while they (i.e. monarchs and people at large) have their appointed physicians and healers for the body so that they can quickly treat any illness which may befall them, and can concoct medicines and dishes in response so that they return to health, it would be even more fitting to select physicians and healers for the soul so that they may cure any affliction there too. For any wise man who does not do this has made a bad choice, since he has neglected the most important aspect and tackled the least important one. Just as those physicians of the body have potions and medicinal plants brought from India and every other place, these physicians of the mind also have medicines; those are the intellect and worthy experiences, whether observed directly or read about in books.

I have read in the historical accounts of the Samanids that Naṣr b. Aḥmad the Samanid was eight years old when he was orphaned by his father's death, since they killed Aḥmad at the hunting ground and the next day raised the child to the royal throne in his father's place.[422] That lion's cub grew up to be a very agreeable prince, and mastered all the arts of kingship and was peerless in his time. But he had in him excessive amounts of devilry, bile, pugnacity and aggressiveness, and he issued drastic commands out of anger so that people kept away from him in fear and revulsion. Despite all this, he would resort to his own reasoning faculty and would realize that this conduct was most reprehensible. [Gh 107]

One day he closeted himself with Balʿami, his senior vizier, and Bu Ṭayyeb [F 127] Moṣʿabi, Head of the Chancery[423]—both of these men being peerless in their time in all branches of learning—and he gave them a full account of his condition. He said, "I know that I am committing a grave error in the way I conduct myself, but I cannot control my anger, and when its flame dies down, I am filled with remorse; but what does this avail, since heads have rolled, households uprooted and the rod applied without limit? What is to be done?" They replied, "It may be that the right course is for the lord to station before himself the wisest of his boon-companions, in whom, together with the complete wisdom which they possess, there may be mercy, compassion and forbearance.[424] Also, he should give them an injunction that, without any holding back, when the lord is carried away by anger, they should make unstinting intercession and dampen down that anger by subtle and gentle methods; and when he ordains something good, they should render it attractive in his sight so that he may ordain more like it. We believe that if the matter is handled thus, matters will return to a normal and beneficial state."

This suggestion was highly pleasing to Naṣr b. Aḥmad, and he approved of their speech and praised what they said. He said, "I'll add another proviso to make this complete: I swear a solemn oath that, whenever I issue an order in a fit of anger, they should not put it into practice for three days in order to allow the fire of my anger to cool down and the pleas of intercessors to sink in. Then at that point I will look into it and make enquiries, so that if it transpires that my anger was justified, they will apply the rod to a moderate extent, say less than a hundred strokes; but if I was carried away unjustifiably, I will annul that punishment and reinstate and promote those persons for whom I had ordered correction, if indeed they merit promotion, and if the punishment is in line with the requirements of the divine law and according to the sentence of the judges, it will be carried out." [F 128] Balʿami and Bu Ṭayyeb replied, "Nothing else remains to be said, and matters have returned to a normal and beneficial state."

Naṣr b. Aḥmad then issued a command, saying, "Go round and seek out within my realm the wisest men, and whatever number may be found, let them be brought to the court so that I may command whatever is necessary." These two eminent men went away feeling very relieved and contented, for hitherto they had to bear the brunt of the calamities.[425] They made a thorough search among the whole body of wise men [Gh 108] in the realm, and out of them brought back seventy odd persons, of high quality, good family and resourcefulness, to Bokhara. They informed Naṣr b. Aḥmad, and he ordered that these seventy odd selected persons should be tested for a year so that, out of these, a handful of the wisest ones might be chosen. This was done, and out of that group three old men emerged, the wisest, most excellent and most experienced. They were brought before Naṣr b. Aḥmad and he tested them for a week. When he found them unique in their high qualities, he told them his secret, wrote out a copy of a very solemn oath in his own handwriting and read it out. He gave the three men permission to make intercession on any matter and to speak entirely freely. This state of affairs went on for a year. Naṣr had become another Aḥnaf b. Qeys in magnanimity and forbearance to the extent that he became proverbial for this quality, and his blameworthy traits were altogether removed from him.[426]

This section has come to an end also, and although I have been somewhat lengthy in my discourse, I know that judicious readers will find it acceptable, for anything penned on paper is worth reading through once; and after this present age, people in later eras will refer to and learn from it. I am convinced that today, as I am composing this History at this exalted court—may it endure for ever—there are men of great stature who would truly have hit the mark if they had embarked on a chronicle of this monarch, Masʿud's, reign, and would demonstrate to everyone that they are accomplished equestrians, and that in their company I am a mere footsoldier [F 129] with a gouty limp,[427] and it would have been more appropriate for them to write and for me to learn, and for them to speak and for me to listen. But since they are taken up by the affairs of state and are pre-occupied by important tasks, and exert their considerable talent and capability to ensure that no crisis ever occurs to gladden the heart of an enemy or an envious party and gratify their wishes,[428] how can they find time for writing history and collecting historical reports and recording them, and how can they put their hearts and minds to it? Hence I myself, functioning as a deputy for them, undertook this task, since it was possible that if I did hang back and wait for them to embark on this task, it would be to no avail for they would never find the time to do it, and when a long period of time elapsed, these historical accounts [Gh 109] would fade from people's memory and the matter would be taken up by someone without my grasp and mastery of the material (lit. "would not have had the horsemanship for this mount"), and the mighty achievements of this illustrious house would be effaced.

I have seen many histories which, before my time, their servants have composed for past monarchs, and in which they have made additions and left things out and have sought to embellish those histories by means of them. Now the position of the monarchs of this house—*may God have mercy on its past monarchs and exalt those who remain alive now!*—is the opposite of that, since, praise be to God Most High, their lofty virtues are resplendent like the shining sun, and the Almighty God has relieved me of the need to put on a false glitter or a cloak of deceit on my account, since I have clear proof for what I have written so far and for what I am going to write in the future.

When I completed these sections from the *khoṭba*, I went back to writing the History, [F 130] and I seek the favour of Almighty God for its completion according to the rules of historical writing.[429]

I have already introduced into the previous historical narrative two episodes in which this great monarch Masʿud, may God illuminate his proof, was involved, so that my readers would become aware of them. One was concerned with those illustrious deeds performed by him after Amir Maḥmud returned from Ray and entrusted that province to him. The other was concerned with the good fortune which came to him after his father's decease, through the favour of the Almighty God, during his brother Moḥammad's governorship in Ghaznin until that time when he reached Herat and his affairs went smoothly and harmoniously and his desires were completely realized, as readers have been informed. There were various remarkable things and wonders that befell him in his father's time; these comprised several events, all of which I have recounted in this History in their appropriate place in the annals of the reign of Amir Maḥmud.

There were also several other points well worth knowing which had taken place in the time of his youth when he grew in stature and his father made him his designated heir. I had heard something about this when I was in Nishapur, not having yet acquired the good fortune of serving this dynasty, may God maintain it, and I was forever seeking to hear an account from a reliable eye-witness, but to no avail, until I embarked on writing this History and became even more eager to succeed in my search. For I have been engaged on this task for many years, and I feared that if those details were not retrieved by the time I reached the blessed era of this monarch Masʿud, their loss would have been deleterious.

However, a felicitous happening occurred in the opening days of the year [Gh 110] 450 [/March 1058] when Khᵛāja Bu Saʿd[430] ʿAbd al-Ghaffār Fākher b. Sharif, Ḥamid Amir al-Moʾmenin,[431] may God perpetuate his exalted status, displayed his magnanimity and sought me out in the corner of my retirement and took the trouble to approach me. He gave me what I was seeking, and [F 131] then wrote it out in his own hand. He is such a reliable authority that anything with the stamp of his intellect and learning upon it requires no other witness. For this Khᵛāja, may God keep him in a blessed state, was in the service of this monarch from the age of fourteen, and experienced many vicissitudes of fortune during that period of service with him, suffered various hardships and performed momentous deeds of great daring and significance in the company of a king like Maḥmud. Hence when the lord attained the royal throne, he inevitably held him in high esteem and with complete trust.

My contact with this Khᵛāja came from the latter part of the year [4]21 [/end of 1030] when the banner of the Martyred Sultan Masʿud reached Balkh. I found him a person of consummate learning. He used to sit in the Chancery with my master, and most of his time would be spent closeted with this monarch in private sessions. It was necessary—indeed, it was a strict duty incumbent on me—that I should have enumerated the full roster of honorific titles (*kheṭāb*) due to him, but in annals and chronicles it is not the custom to include more than I have already done. Everyone endowed with wisdom and discernment would know that *Ḥamid Amir al-Mo'menin* (lit. "The One Regarded as Praiseworthy by the Commander of the Faithful") has the significance of being one of the honorifics awarded by the caliphal court, and can any form of address be more exalted than this?

He acquired this lofty honour in the auspicious time of Amir Mowdud, who sent him as an envoy to Baghdad with a momentous charge. He went off and accomplished this task in such a way as only wise men and persons of wide experience would do, and returned in triumph, as I shall subsequently describe when I reach the reign of Amir Mowdud.[432] Then during Amir ʿAbd al-Rashid's reign, out of all the trusty confidants and servants, reliance was placed on him for missions to the region of Khorasan, with the very important task of concluding a treaty and covenant with a group of eminent persons[433] who at this present time control the province of Khorasan. At that time I had the responsibility for the Chancery, and will give an account of that too in its appropriate place.[434] After that, this Khᵛāja encountered many things, both smooth and rough. [F 132] In this present auspicious reign of the exalted Sultan Abu Shojāʿ Farrokh-zād b. Masʿud, may God prolong his existence and make his battle standard victorious, the governorship (*riyāsat*) of Bost was entrusted to him, and he remained for a good while in that region and did many memorable and beneficent deeds there. Today he is resident [Gh 111] in Ghaznin, in his own house, enjoying respect and honour. I have written down these few points regarding his career, and I will set forth very clearly in this History, in the appropriate place, a detailed account of his circumstances if God Most High so wills. These various points from the notable exploits (*maqāmāt*)[435] of Amir Masʿud which I heard from him (i.e. from ʿAbd al-Ghaffār) I wrote down here so that they might be known. When I finish this, I shall take up the story of this monarch's ascending of the royal throne at Balkh and narrate the history of his auspicious reign.

The episode (maqāma)[436] *concerning Amir Shehāb al-Dowla Mas'ud's designation as successor to the throne* (velāyat al-'ahd) *and what happened to him*

During the months of the year 401 [/1010–11], when Amir Maḥmud marched off to wage holy war against Ghur from Bost by way of the Zamindāvar road, he ordered that his two sons, Amirs Mas'ud and Moḥammad, and his brother Yusof should stay behind in Zamindāvar and also that the heaviest baggage should be left there. These two princes were fourteen years old[437] and Yusof was seventeen years old. He kept them back there because he used to consider Zamindāvar as an auspicious place since it was the province allocated to him for his first governorship by his father, the just Amir Sebüktegin. When that monarch Maḥmud went to Ghur, those [three] Amirs were left at the house of Bāytegin[438] Zamindāvari, who had been appointed governor of that region by [F 133] Amir Maḥmud. The latter ordered my grandfather—the grandfather of myself, 'Abd al-Ghaffār—to take charge of looking after them and to issue to them faithfully their appointed stipends and living allowances as was necessary. I had a grandmother, a woman who was pious and modest, a reciter of the Qor'ān, who knew how to write and who also was well acquainted with Qor'ānic exegesis, the interpretation of dreams, and historical reports about the Prophet. In addition to these achievements, she used to prepare delicious food and most refreshing drinks; she was a marvel at those. Both my grandfather and grandmother were thus engaged in attending to those princes who had been lodged there. They would ask that old woman for sweets and things to eat and make other requests, and she would be meticulous in preparing their requests and presenting them in a most pleasing way, and they used frequently to ask her to regale them with religious sayings and stories, [Gh 112] and they would be enthralled by them. I myself was very advanced for my age and used to attend the school for Qor'ān learning and recitation; and I would render some service, as children are wont to do, and then go back. It happened that Amir Mas'ud said to his tutor, who was called B.sāl.mi (?),[439] "'Abd al-Ghaffār must be taught something of polite learning (*adab*)." He taught me two or three odes from the *Divān* of Motanabbi and *Qefā nabki*,[440] and this made me more self-confident.

At that time, I saw them seated in that manner for which the eunuch (*khādem*) Reyḥān had been appointed by Amir Maḥmud to oversee and regulate. He would bring in Amir Masʿud, and they would set him down first in the place of honour. Then they would bring in Amir Moḥammad and set him down on his right, in such a way that one of his knees would be outside the place of honour and the other on the cushion, and then Amir Yusof would be brought in and set down outside the place of honour on the left-hand side. When they used to mount for outdoor activities and polo,[441] Moḥammad and Yusof [F 134] would be in attendance before Amir Masʿud together with a chamberlain who had been appointed for that purpose. At the time of the afternoon worship, when the tutor would return, first those two, Moḥammad and Yusof, would retire and go away, and then Amir Masʿud an hour after that. The eunuch Reyḥān was supervising all these arrangements, and if he saw anything improper, he would point it out most vociferously.

Twice a week they would mount and go out to the rural areas. Amir Masʿud had the custom that, every time he rode out, he would offer them (i.e. the people of the rural areas) hospitality. Many items of food would be brought out with great ceremony from my grandfather and grandmother, for on many occasions he would ask for things secretly so that no-one in the [royal] kitchen knew about it. There was a young gholām called Qarategin[442] whose job it was to bring messages to my grandfather and grandmother (it is said that this Qarategin was at first a gholām of the Amir; at Herat he was promoted to the rank of troop commander, and from that rank became a general for Amir Masʿud). They used to bring items of food out to the open country at his whim, and the Amir used to invite Ḥasan, the son of Amir Farighun, Amir of Guzgānān,[443] and others of his peers, and bestow presents on them after eating.

Bāytegin Zamindāvari, the governor of the region, was also at first a gholām of Amir Maḥmud, and the latter [Gh 113] held him in esteem. He had a very capable and pious wife, and afterwards, when Amir Masʿud succeeded his father on the royal throne, he used to hold this woman in great esteem out of respect for her past services, as if she were on a level with the lady, the queen mother. On several occasions here in Ghaznin at Amir Masʿud's court sessions—and I was myself present—this woman would talk about old times, and [F 135] would reminisce about those virtuous deeds and ways of the Amir (i.e. of Maḥmud), and this would please Amir Masʿud greatly and he would ask many questions about those places and rural areas and their local fare and produce. At the time when Amir Maḥmud seized Sistan and overthrew Khalaf,[444] this Bāytegin Zamindāvari had brought back with him one hundred and thirty peacocks and peahens. It was said that they were indigenous to Zamindāvar, and there were some of them in our houses. They would mostly hatch their young in the domed roofs. Amir Masʿud used to be fond of them and would come in search of them on the roofs; in our house they had laid eggs in a dome in two or three places and produced chicks.

One day he shouted down from the roof to my grandmother and summoned her. When she came, he said, "I saw in a dream that I was in the land of Ghur, and just like here, there were strongholds there too with many peacocks and cock fowls. I was catching them and putting them under my coat, and underneath my coat they were fluttering and rolling about. You know everything: what is the interpretation of this?" The old woman replied, "If God wills, the Amir will seize the princes of Ghur and the Ghuris will be subjugated." He said, "I haven't taken over my father's authority, so how can I seize them?" The old woman answered, "When you grow up, if the Almighty God so wills it, this will come to pass, for I remember your father, the Sultan, when he was here in his youth and held this province. Now he has seized the greater part of the world and is about to conquer still more; you will be just like your father." The Amir replied, "If God wills." In the end, it turned out just as he had seen in the dream, and the region of Ghur fell under his obedience. He had many fine exploits in Ghur, as will be mentioned in this account of his exploits. During the months of the year 411[445] [/1020–1], [F 136] when it happened that I, ʿAbd al-Ghaffār, came to join the service of this monarch, may God be pleased with him, he commanded me to bring with me several of those peacocks and peahens. Six pairs were brought, and he ordered them to be put in the garden. They laid eggs and produced chicks. There is a breed at Herat derived from them. The princes of Ghur came to render service to the Amir, some willingly, some unwillingly, for he performed such great exploits [Gh 114] [in their land] that they were filled with fear and were reduced to quiescence. For at no time was it indicated, nor was it to be read in any books, that the Ghuris were so obedient and submissive to a monarch as they were to him.

In the year 405 [/1014–15], Amir Maḥmud set out from Bost on a raid against the region of Khᵛābin, which is one of the districts of Ghur bordering on Bost and Zamindāvar.[446] The infidels there were extremely malevolent and powerful, and controlled many defiles and well-fortified strongholds. He had brought Amir Masʿud along with him, and Masʿud performed great deeds in the presence of his father and numerous heroic exploits, including knocking the champion warrior of the Ghuris off the back of his horse.[447] When a group of the Ghuris took refuge in their stronghold, one of their commanders stood on a tower of the fortress and was showing great courage and audacity in the face of the attackers and causing the Muslims much trouble. Masʿud loosed a single arrow at the man's throat, killing him with that shot, and he fell down from the tower. His companions thereupon lost heart and yielded up the stronghold. All this was thanks to one bold, manly shot. When Amir Maḥmud finished the engagement and returned to his tent, he brought in that lion cub for a feast, showered him with favours and ordered an increase in the privileges allotted to him. It was because of these and similar exploits that Maḥmud appointed him, while still in his early youth, as his designated heir, because he perceived and realized that, when he himself should depart from this deceitful abode, no-one apart from Masʿud could preserve this great house, may it always endure! And behold, the clear proof is apparent that it is twenty-nine years since the death of Amir Maḥmud, [F 137] and in spite of the many setbacks (*tanazzolāt*) that occurred, those praiseworthy customs and established practices, the security, justice and the decorum in affairs of government that is in evidence at this great court today, cannot be found elsewhere, and there is no trace of unbelief anywhere in this land of Islam.[448] May this great house always stand firm, may its upholders always be victorious and its enemies crushed, and may the Exalted Sultan Farrokh-zād, the son of this great monarch Masʿud, bask in the enjoyment of power, the fulfilment of his aims and enjoy to the full his royal power and his youth, *through the divine right of Moḥammad and his family!*

In the year 411[/1020–21], the Amir Masʿud went to Herat and marched against Ghur.[449] On Sunday, 10 Jomādā I [/1 September 1020] he set off from Herat with a large force of cavalry and infantry and with five swift and lightly-armoured elephants. The first halting-place [Gh 115] was at Bāshān, the next at Kheysār, and the next at B.r.yān,[450] where he waited for two days for the whole of the army to come up. Then from there he proceeded to Pār and stayed there two days, then from there to Chesht, then from there went forth to Bāgh-e Vazir, that *rebāṭ* [451] being the first point on the frontier with Ghur. When the Ghuris got news of his approach, they took refuge in their securely-built fortresses and prepared for war. Before embarking on this expedition, the Amir had conciliated and won over to his side Bu'l-Ḥasan b. Khalaf, one of the most prominent of the chieftains (*moqaddam*) in Ghur, and brought him into his obedience. The Amir had pre-arranged with him [F 138] to be there with a well-prepared force at this *rebāṭ* when the victorious royal troops arrived. On this day, Bu'l-Ḥasan appeared with a large, well-equipped army which was said to have numbered 3,000 cavalry and infantry. He came forward, rendered service, having brought many offerings[452] and gifts, comprising shields, mailed coats and whatever was special to Ghur. The Amir welcomed him heartily. On his heels there came Shirvān, another chieftain from the frontier region between Ghur and Guzgānān, whom prince Masʿud had conciliated and won over, with numerous cavalry and infantry and bringing boundless presents.[453] Amir Moḥammad, by virtue of the fact that this man's territory adjoined Guzgānān, had used many stratagems and devices to attract this chieftain to his own side and thereby bring him into his own following, although of course he had not responded favourably, since all the world was on Masʿud's side.

When these two chieftains arrived and the Amir was reinforced with their men, he departed from this place on the Friday and set off in the vanguard, unencumbered and ready for battle, with a force of about fifty or sixty gholāms and two hundred infantrymen of the most dashing picked from all ethnic groups.[454] He arrived at a stronghold that had the local name of B.r.t.r, an exceedingly secure fortress and with heavily-armed defending warriors. [Gh 116] The Amir went all round the fortress and looked at places suitable for fighting. That fortress and its defenders did not appear in his sight and to his lofty determination and courage as anything much. He did not wait for the mass of the army to come up, but joined battle with that force of men he had with him, and led the onslaught with his own noble person [F 139], with the gholāms and infantrymen. They shouted the triumphal cry "God is great!" (i.e. the *takbir*). The accursed defenders in the Ghurid stronghold rose up in challenge and with one accord let out a terrifying shout that almost rent the earth asunder. They were under the impression that the entire army consisted of those at the foot of the fortress. The Amir told the gholāms, "Let your hands loose your arrows!" The gholāms began to shoot their arrows, and shot such an intense hail that none of the Ghuris dared to raise his head above [the parapet of] the tower. The infantrymen, exploiting this advantage,[455] began to assault the tower using scaling ropes, and wrought great slaughter, and those accursed ones took to flight. The gholāms and infantrymen cleared out the Ghuris from the fortifications and towers, and killed large numbers of them, took many prisoners and gained great plunder of all kinds. After that stronghold had been taken, the rest of the army arrived, and all of them applauded vociferously the fact that a fortress like that had been taken by such a small number of men.

From there, the Amir marched onwards to the district of R.zān. When the news of the fall of this fortress B.r.t.r had reached the people of R.zān, the greater part of them had fled and only a small number of people remained in those forts (*kushk*). The Amir offered them a guarantee of quarter and of safe conduct with the result that the mass of fugitives returned, agreed to pay tribute, and handed over numerous presents, including gold, silver and weapons. From this vicinity to Jorvas,[456] the seat of Darmish Bat,[457] was ten parasangs. The Amir did not launch an assault and attack on it because this Darmish Bat had sent an envoy and had offered to submit and become a vassal, promising that when the Amir returned to Herat he would come and render service and would hand over the tribute.

The Amir turned away and led the army to the region of V.y.[458] [Gh 117] This last [F 140] is one of the most highly fortified regions in the whole of Ghur, and its men most warlike and valiant. It had been the centre of ruling power for the Ghuris in times past, and every ruler who held that particular place used to control the whole region. Before the Amir began his advance on that place, he sent there a scholar (*dāneshmand*) as an envoy, accompanied by two Ghuris, retainers of Bu'l-Ḥasan b. Khalaf and Shirvān, to act as interpreters,[459] and he conveyed messages couched in strong terms, full of threats and holding out promises of favour, as is the custom (i.e. as a preliminary to military action). The envoys went off, with the Amir following after them. When the envoys reached those deluded ones and handed over the messages, the Ghuris became very haughty and severe, and said, "The Amir is gravely mistaken in thinking that this place and its people are made of the same mettle as those he has just seen and left behind. Let him come, for here there are swords, spears and stones (i.e. for repelling him)!" The envoys went back and conveyed the messages.

The Amir had meanwhile drawn near, and he encamped that night at the foot of the mountain, and weapons were handed out to the troops. The next morning he mounted his steed; kettledrums were beaten and trumpets blown, and they launched an attack on it by scaling the mountain. The Ghuri defenders came into sight like ants and locusts on the summit of that mountain, cavalrymen and infantrymen, all armed to the teeth. They seized the access ways and tracks, sent up a great shouting and clamour, and were hurling down stones from slings. Fortunately, the mountain was only low, and its terrain was partly earth, with tracks going up it from every side. The Amir allotted the various tracks to his troops, and himself went on straight ahead against the mountain, where the fighting was at its most fierce. He placed Bu'l-Ḥasan b. Khalaf on his right hand and Shirvān on his left hand. The accursed Ghuris attacked hard and fought with great strength, especially against the Amir. [F 141] Those deluded ones controlled most of the tracks up the mountain with their arrows, and realizing that the situation was becoming critical, they all concentrated their efforts against the Amir's standard, and the fighting grew intense. Three horsemen from among the Ghuris' champion warriors found themselves directly confronting the Amir. The Amir waded into the fight; he struck one of them on the breast with a blow from a mace of twenty maunds' weight which laid him out flat on his back so that he saw no means of rising.[460] The gholāms pressed forward and unhorsed the other two attackers. That was what made the Ghuris terror-stricken and they took to flight, staggering in their retreat in a desultory manner [Gh 118] until they reached the village at the foot of the mountain in that sector and on that side, and large numbers were killed and taken prisoner.

When the fugitives reached the village, they fortified themselves within it; it was a very strongly-protected place, with many forts on the usual Ghuri pattern. They plunged into the fight furiously, leaving their women and children, and all the baggage and goods which they had sent along to there, in a mighty and well-fortified stronghold which they had in their rear. The fighting went on till the time of the evening worship, with many of those accursed ones killed and many Muslims likewise achieving martyrs' deaths in battle. In the darkness of the night, those accursed ones fled and abandoned the village. All through that night, the victorious army was engaged in plundering and found much booty.

Next morning, the Amir ordered the large kettledrums to be beaten, and he mounted and set out for their stronghold—which was two parasangs away, with many obstacles and narrow places on the way—and they reached there toward the time of the midday worship. They found a very well-defended stronghold; it was said to be the most impregnable one in Ghur, and no-one could remember that it had ever been conquered by force of arms. The Amir encamped there and gave orders for the troops to take up positions around all four sides of it. They spent the whole night making preparations for investing it and set up mangonels[461] in place. When day broke, the Amir rode forth and took charge of operations in his own exalted person. He got the mangonels into action, stones were hurled [F 142] and mines were sunk beneath the two towers facing the Amir. The Ghuris joined battle from the towers and fortifications, in a most fierce manner. Around each tower that they toppled down, large numbers of men would gather and fight hand-to-hand. The fighting went on for four days, becoming more intense each day. On the fifth day, battle was joined by each side with even greater fierceness, and each side made great efforts with a ferocity witnessed never before. The Amir gave orders, and the palace gholāms pushed forward and overwhelmed the Ghuris with arrows, with the stones hurled from the three mangonels supplementing the arrows. The Amir was ordering the soldiers to carry the standard further forward, and he rode closely behind it with a slow and steady gait so that the gholāms, the troops of the army at large (*ḥasham*) and the various ethnic contingents of the forces (*aṣnāf-e lashkar*) took heart and fought even harder. The Ghuris became disheartened and began to flee. At the time of the midday worship, the main wall came down [Gh 119] through the stones hurled by the mangonels, and there arose a cloud of dust, smoke and fire. The stronghold was breached and the Ghuris within it thrown into a panic. The troops converged on the breach from all four sides. Those accursed ones fought fiercely within that breach, parading their martial skills to the full since they were fighting for their lives. In the end, they were routed, and the Amir's troops took the stronghold by the sword. Large numbers of the Ghuris were killed, and many of the Ghuris asked for quarter , which was granted and they became captives. The number of the captives and the amount of plunder exceeded all counts and measures. The Amir gave orders for a herald to go round and proclaim, "I bestow the property, the silver and gold, and the captives on the army, but the weapons that have been acquired are to be brought forward." A large number of weapons of all kinds were brought to the door of the Amir's tent. Those of them which were the most useful or most fine and rare were taken away as the Amir's personal share[462] while the rest were divided up among the troops. He handed over half of the prisoners to Bu'l-Ḥasan b. Khalaf and half to Shirvān for them to transport back to their own principalities. The Amir gave orders for them [F 143] to level that stronghold with the ground so that evildoers should no longer find a refuge there.[463]

When news of the fate of the village and the stronghold and their defenders reached the Ghuris, they all became obedient and submissive; and stricken with fear, they offered to pay tribute. Darmish Bat was likewise filled with fear, realizing that if an attack should be made on his territory, he would be overthrown within a week. He despatched an envoy, displaying a very high degree of obedience and submissiveness, and offering an increased amount of tribute and presents over what he had previously agreed to pay. Bu'l-Ḥasan b. Khalaf and Shirvān, whom he had asked to act as intercessors and to whom he had sent messages, interceded for him, with the result that the Amir accepted his excuses and refrained from attacking him. The Amir gave orders for Darmish Bat's envoy to be sent back with due decorum, on the condition that he give back all the fortresses which he had seized along the frontiers with Gharjestān.[464] Darmish Bat *reluctantly and through necessity*[465] entrusted the fortresses to the Amir's castellans, and sent all that he had pledged to the court while the Amir was still in Ghur; and when the Amir returned to Herat in a state of complete security and good health, he went there to render service, receiving a robe of honour and other marks of favour. Then, together with the other two chieftains (i.e. Bu'l-Ḥasan b. Khalaf and Shirvān), he went back to his own principality.

When the Amir had finished with the affair of this stronghold, he moved on to the district of the stronghold of T.w.r (?).[466] [Gh 120] This also was a very well-fortified and celebrated stronghold. For seven days he was engaged in continuous warfare there, and had to have recourse to help from the heroic warriors of Ghur[467] until the point when the stronghold was conquered by the sword, many Ghuris killed and extensive plunder taken. The Amir installed there his own castellan and returned to Herat. At Mārābād, [F 144] which is ten parasangs from Herat,[468] many presents and weapons from those Ghuris who had agreed to pay tribute in order to avoid attacks on them by the Amir, were forwarded, and all were gathered together with what Darmish Bat had already sent. In the midst of all this, the Amir reminded me, ʿAbd al-Ghaffār, of that dream which he had had in Zamindāvar, saying, "Your grandmother interpreted the dream very accurately, and it has all come true." I made obeisance and replied, "This is a proof of what the lord had dreamt."

This story about Ghur has been mentioned because, in the times of Islam and of unbelief, no monarch had extended such conquering power over Ghur as did the martyred Sultan Masʿud. In the first conquests in Khorasan, God, His mention is exalted, sought to make the Islamic faith more clear and evident through the agency of those great figures from the early years of Islam. They defeated the Persians and drove them out of Madāʾen, and when Yazdagerd fled, he was killed at Merv.[469] But in spite of those mighty and celebrated deeds, they were unable to penetrate into the heart of the land of Ghur. Amir Maḥmud also took that road from Zamindāvar to the borders of Ghur two or three times, but was not able to penetrate the defiles and narrow places of Ghur, though one cannot say that he felt powerless when faced with obstacles, since he had other plans and intentions than those of the youthful ones (i.e. of Masʿud and his troops). In the time of the Samanids, a commander who was called Bu Jaʿfar Ziyādi[470] and who regarded himself as on a par with Bu'l-Ḥasan, son of Simjur, regarding troops, weapons and equipment, attacked Ghur on several occasions at the behest of the Samanids. The governor of Herat provided assistance in the shape of a locally-raised militia (*ḥashar*)[471] and men from his own following. Abu Jaʿfar Ziyādi tried valiantly and showed great courage, but he was not able to penetrate beyond Kheysār and Tulak.[472] [F 145]. No-one penetrated into the Ghur heartlands [Gh 121] to achieve these great deeds in the manner of this august monarch Masʿud; and all have now passed on, God's mercy be upon them all!

An example of the alertness, foresight and circumspection of this munificent monarch was that, in his youth, when he was living in Herat, he used to drink wine without his father's knowledge, and unbeknown to the eunuch Reyḥān, he used to arrange intimate sessions in the cellars of the palace and have musicians and singers, both male and female, brought to him through secret ways.[473] He gave orders for a special summer-house to be built for his midday siesta within the palace of the ʿAdnāni Garden, in which were constructed pipes to control the flow of water in various directions (*mozammal*) and linen hangings (*kheysh*) arranged so that water from a pool would flow and by means of an apparently magical contrivance (*ṭelesm*) run on to the summer house's roof, pass through the pipes controlling the flow of water and moisten the linen hangings.[474] Also, they decorated this summer-house, from ceiling to floor, with pictures from the book called *Alfiyya*, depicting different ways of intercourse between men and women, all of them naked, so that the whole book with its stories and content was illustrated there; and apart from these, they painted other pictures in the same manner.[475] The Amir used to go there at siesta time and would sleep there. It is a mark of young men that they do this and similar things.[476]

Although Amir Maḥmud had a secret intelligence agent (*moshref*) who was always present when his son the Amir was out with the boon-companions, and who used to watch Masʿud's every move (lit. "count every breath") and report back, it was evident that that agent would not be able to penetrate into Masʿud's more private quarters and intimate gatherings. Hence Maḥmud had spies over him drawn from ordinary people, such as a gholām or domestic attendant or old women or musicians and singers [F 146] or others, who would report back whatever information they acquired so that nothing of this son's affairs [Gh 122] would remain hidden from him. Maḥmud would constantly admonish him in his letters and furnish him with advice, for Masʿud was Maḥmud's designated heir and he knew that the royal throne would one day be his. And just as his father secretly had spies (*jāsusān*) over him, so he too secretly had them, from the same ranks, over his father, and they would report whatever was happening. One of these was the eunuch Nushtegin, his special servant (*khāṣṣa*),[477] for no other servant was as close to Amir Maḥmud as him, and Ḥorra Khottali, Masʿud's paternal aunt, was completely besotted by him (i.e. by Masʿud).

It so happened that the information about the summer-house with the erotic paintings was reported to Amir Maḥmud in extreme secrecy, and it was indicated that "When one has passed from the ʿAdnāni Palace there is a large garden. On the right side of this garden is a large pool, and on the left side of this pool is the summer-house in question. There are two locks on it night and day, above and below, and they are opened at the time when Amir Masʿud goes for his siesta there. The keys are held by a eunuch called Beshārat."

When Amir Maḥmud learnt about this state of affairs, he came to the large tent at the time of the midday siesta and told his special servant, the eunuch Nushtegin, about this message, and gave the order, "Tell so-and-so *kheyltāsh*," who was a swift rider unequalled among his class, "that he is to get ready to be sent to a certain place on an important mission, so that he may ride quickly and ascertain the status of this summer-house. No-one must become aware of this matter." Nushtegin replied, "I obey the command." The Amir then went to sleep, and Nushtegin came to his own tent, and detailed a trooper from his own crack cavalrymen (*div-sovārān*), with three of his own choice horses, instructing him to travel to Herat in complete secrecy to Amir Masʿud within six days, six nights and half a day. He wrote in his own hand a brief private message to Amir Masʿud informing him of these developments and saying, "After this cavalry trooper of mine, a *kheyltāsh* of the Sultan's will come, one-and-a-half days after the arrival of this trooper, in order to see that summer-house of yours. This *kheyltāsh* will not be intimidated by anyone [F 147] and will go straightaway to the house and break the locks. The Amir should attend to this matter at once and act as he sees fit." That crack cavalry trooper rode off immediately. Nushtegin then sent someone for the *kheyltāsh* who had been designated for this mission, and he came all ready and prepared. Amir Maḥmud woke from his sleep between the two times of worship,[478] performed the midday worship and having completed it, summoned Nushtegin [Gh 123] and enquired, "Did the *kheyltāsh* come?" He replied, "He came, and is waiting in my tent." The Amir said, "Bring a pen-case and paper. Nushtegin brought these and the Amir wrote out in his own hand an open document setting forth his mandate,[479] in these terms:

In the name of God, the Merciful, the Compassionate

Maḥmud b. Sebüktegin's order to this *kheyltāsh* is that he should go to Herat within eight days. When he reaches there, he is to go straightaway to my son Masʿud's palace. He should fear no-one, should draw his sword and should cut off the head of anyone who impedes his progress. He should go down through the ʿAdnāni Palace, paying no heed to my son, to the garden. On the right side of the garden is a pool, and beside it on the left, a summer-house. He is to go inside that summer-house, take a good look at its walls to ascertain what is on them, and see what there is in that house. Then he is to return immediately, without speaking to anyone, and head back to Ghaznin. It is incumbent upon the Chamberlain Qotloghtegin Beheshti[480] (i.e. Masʿud's door-keeper) to act according to this order, if he values his life, and if he shows any partiality (i.e. for Masʿud's interests), he will lose his life. He must provide the *kheyltāsh* with all necessary assistance so that he maintains his position in our esteem, *with God's will and His assistance. Farewell!*

When this letter had been written, Maḥmud summoned the *kheyltāsh* and he affixed his seal to that official mandate[481] [F 148] and gave it to him, saying, "It is so required that you go to Herat within eight days, do such-and-such and such-and-such, acquire information about all the matters which have been set forth, and keep this affair secret." The *kheyltāsh* kissed the ground and said, "I'll carry out the orders," and went back. The Amir told his special servant Nushtegin, "The *kheyltāsh* must be given a good-running horse from the Royal Stable and 5,000 dirhams." Nushtegin came outside from the palace and spent a considerable time on giving out the horse and the silver and in carefully selecting the best horse, using up the entire day,[482] and when the evening worship had been performed, the *kheyltāsh* was given his needs and he left swiftly.

Meanwhile, that crack cavalry trooper of Nushtegin's, as he had been instructed, arrived at Herat. Amir Mas'ud [Gh 124] ascertained the contents of the brief private message, and gave instructions that the cavalry trooper should be accommodated somewhere. He immediately ordered plasterers to be summoned. They whitewashed the summer house and gave it a smooth, rendered surface as if there had never been any murals on the walls, and put down floor coverings[483] and set everything in order, and no one knew what this was all about.

On the heels of this crack cavalry trooper, and on the eighth day, the *kheyltāsh* arrived near noon. Amir Mas'ud was sitting in the portico in the 'Adnāni Palace with his boon-companions. The Chamberlain Qotloghtegin Beheshti was sitting at the entrance portal together with other door-keepers, retainers and holders of court offices. The *kheyltāsh* came in, dismounted from his horse, drew his sword, tucked his mace under his arm and left his horse. Qotloghtegin immediately sprang to his feet and said, "What's all this?" The *kheyltāsh* did not respond, but handed to him the official mandate and went into the palace. Qotlogh[tegin] read the letter and gave it to Amir Mas'ud, saying, "What's to be done?" The Amir replied, "Every command therein must be carried out." A commotion ran through the palace, while the *kheyltāsh* continued on his way up to the door of that summer-house and took up his mace, [F 149] smashed the two locks, laid open the door and went in. He saw a house with clean, white-rendered walls and with floor coverings and rugs. He came out and kissed the ground in front of Amir Mas'ud, saying, "Servants have no choice but to carry out their orders. This discourtesy was committed by me on Sultan Maḥmud's orders. It is also laid down that, as soon as I have inspected this house, I should return, and I am going now."

Amir Mas'ud said, "You came at your appointed time and carried out the orders of the lord, my father the Sultan. Now stay for one day at our command—for it may be that they gave the wrong directions—so that you may be shown all the palaces and houses." The *kheyltāsh* said, "I will obey your command, even though this is not part of my brief (i.e. Sultan Maḥmud's instructions to him)." The Amir rode forth. Two parasangs away is a garden called Bilāb,[484] a fortified location where he and his retainers had a place to stay. He ordered that all the people in the palaces should gather together there and evacuate the palaces. The womenfolk [Gh 125] and the gholāms accordingly left. Then Qotloghtegin Beheshti, the *moshref* and the postmaster and intelligence officer conducted the *kheyltāsh* round all the palaces and showed each place to him one by one, until he had seen them all and it became apparent that there was no summer-house of the sort which had been reported. Letters were then composed laying out the aspects of the case, the *kheyltāsh* was given 10,000 dirhams and he was sent back home. Amir Mas'ud, may God be pleased with him, returned to the town. When the *kheyltāsh* reached Ghaznin, and had recounted all that had passed and the letters had also been perused, Amir Maḥmud exclaimed, "They are telling many lies about this son of mine," and he cut short any more of those searches and enquiries.

Also in that time of his early manhood and youth, he used to indulge in arduous physical exercises, such as trials of strength, lifting heavy stones, wrestling and suchlike activities. [F 150] He had given orders for the construction of traps[485] for catching pelicans and other birds. I have several times seen him mount and ride forth on days of intense cold and heavy snowfalls, go to the hunting grounds and hunt there on foot, and endure such hardships between the times of the two worships (i.e. in the morning) of an intensity naught but a hard stone could withstand. He used to put his boots on his bare feet with no covering in such conditions of cold and hardship, and would say, "One should get accustomed to such things, so that one would not be helpless when faced with an arduous task or difficult conditions." In the same way, he used to go out hunting lions as far as the meadows of Esfezār[486] and Adraskan, and from those wild lands and thickets to Farāh and Zir.kān and Sh.y.r.n.r (sarbor)[487]. When he had passed by these places, he would come back to Bost and Ghaznin. He used to go after lions alone, and would not allow any of his gholāms or retinue to give any help. He acted in this way because [Gh 126] he possessed such strength and courage that if his weapon failed to deliver the fatal blow, he would himself tackle the lion valiantly and kill it swiftly.

At the time when he was on his way to Multan with the intention of taking up residence there, for his father had become estranged from him on account of allegations fabricated against him[488]—and that is a long story—he encountered a lion in the vicinity of Kikānān[489] at a time when he was suffering from a quartan fever. He had the custom that, when the lion advanced, he would take a short javelin (*khesht*) with a strong handle in his hand, and a short, thick-stemmed spear (*neyza*) so that if he should hurl the javelin and it should prove ineffective, [F 151] he could quickly use his spear to pierce through the lion and hold it fixed on the spot—and he did all this alone, with his own strength and might—so that the lion would twist and turn upon his spear to the point when it became weakened and fell down. It used to happen that the lion would show itself stronger in the struggle, and he would order the gholāms to intervene and hack the lion to pieces with their swords and battleaxes.[490] On this particular day it happened that he hurled his javelin, but the lion dodged aside so that the javelin did not strike home on it and passed over its head. The Amir took up his spear and struck a powerful blow at its breast, but because of his sick condition, he was unable to keep it in one spot as was necessary. The lion was very big, swift-moving and strong, to such an extent that it came on to the spear and showed such strength that the spear broke, and it was about to attack the Amir. Using both his hands, the monarch battered the lion's head and face with all his might so that the lion was overcome and fell down. The Amir pressed down on it and shouted for his gholāms. One of them, called Qomāsh, was the Royal Swordbearer (*shamshir-dār*), which in official terms is called a "bodyguard" (*jān-dār*).[491] He dashed forward and dealt the lion a powerful blow, such that, through the blow, it was all up with it and it fell down dead. All those present remained in a state of amazement, and it was agreed that what had been written in books about the exploits of Bahrām Gur was true.[492]

Later, the Amir grew so sturdy in stature that he did all his hunting from the back of an elephant. I (i.e. ʿAbd al-Ghaffār) once saw him, in the borderlands of India, where he used to hunt from the back of an elephant.[493] They had covered the elephant's face with iron plating, as is the custom. A powerful lion sprang out of the thicket and went for the elephant. The Amir hurled his javelin [Gh 127] and struck the lion's breast, inflicting a serious wound. Mad with pain and anger, the lion sprang up so that it [F 152] reached the nape of the elephant's neck, and the elephant was shaking in fear. The Amir knelt down and struck one blow with his sword, which cut off the lion's two forelegs. The lion fell down on the two stumps and gave up the ghost. All those who were present averred that they could not recall, in the whole of their lives, such a deed on the part of anyone.

Before he had ascended the royal throne, he went forth one day on an outing with Herat as his destination, and he killed eight lions in one day and caught another one with his lasso. When he got back to his tent, he embarked on a feast of merry-making and wine. I, ʿAbd al-Ghaffār, was present. The story of these lions came up, and everyone was saying something in praise. Khᵛāja Bu Sahl Zowzani sent for an ink-holder and paper and composed several verses of exquisite beauty, such as he was wont to utter, since he was the unique one of the age in polite learning, apt diction and poetry. The Amir was highly pleased with these verses, and all present expressed their approval and made copies of them, including myself. I have, alas, lost this copy, but I have written down at this time a few verses that I recalled to mind, even though they are not in proper sequence,[494] so that the story may be made complete.

Verses written by the Sheykh Abu Sahl al-Zowzani in praise of the Most Exalted Sultan Masʿud b. Maḥmud, may God be pleased with them both![495]

(Poetry)

1. *You do not need the sword, the spear, arrows and bowstrings, and Fate itself follows your will.*[496]

2. *You do not embark on any affair that is difficult to obtain except to come back from it with victory in your clutch.* (?) [F153]

3. *All mankind humbles itself in the presence of a man who was hunting down in the chase eight lions.*

4. *When you rise into view, there is no sun or moon, and when you bestow generously, there is no sea or rain* (i.e. more full of bountifulness).

This master had spoken truly, for all these qualities and achievements, and more, were gathered together in this monarch. Poetry of praise fitted him well, and as for the popular saying that "*the finest poetry it that which is most full of lies,*"[497] in his case there was no need to utter a lie. [Gh 128]

His bravery, stoutheartedness and boldness were those that have been mentioned, and his generosity was such that in one night he bestowed 16,000 dinars on a certain merchant called Bu Moṭiʿ Sagzi. There is a story behind this act of munificence. This Bu Moṭiʿ was a man blessed with good fortune of all sorts, and he had a father by the name of Bu Aḥmad b. Khalil. One night, the latter had, by a happy concatenation of circumstances, come to the court on some business that he had with the chamberlain on duty[498] and he remained there till late. By the time he set out to return, the night was far gone. He was afraid lest some untoward incident occur on the road, so he stayed in the entrance hall to the private quarters—he was a well-known person, and [F 154] people used to hold him in great respect. The black-clothed attendants treated him with consideration, and he settled down there. A servant came in looking for a story-teller (*moḥaddeth*),[499] but it happened that there was no story-teller around. Bu Aḥmad, being magnanimous by nature, rose to his feet and went with the servant, and the latter assumed that Bu Aḥmad was indeed a professional story-teller. When Bu Aḥmad arrived at the Amir's large tent, he began to recite a story. The Amir heard the unfamiliar voice of Bu Aḥmad and furtively had a look, and saw him. He said nothing till Bu Aḥmad finished the story, and it was a most marvellous and polished tale. The Amir called out, "Who are you?" He replied, "I am called Bu Aḥmad b. Khalil, father of Bu Moṭiʿ, the lord's companion." The Amir said, "How much money[500] have the financial accountants raised as an account due from your son?" He replied, "Sixteen thousand dinars," The Amir said, "I have bestowed that sum upon him, out of my regard for your age and out of respect felt for him." The old man offered up copious prayers and invocations for the Amir and went back. They had brought a Turkish slave boy belonging to the old man's son to the Amir's palace for him to be purchased. The Amir gave orders that "The slave boy too must be returned, for we do not wish, and it would not be seemly, to exploit them in any way." There cannot be any more complete act of high resolution and magnanimity than this.

He bestowed an even greater amount than this on Mānk b. ʿAli b. Meymun. This Mānk was one of the landowners (*kadkhodāyān*) of Ghaznin and a man of great substance. When he passed away, he left behind immeasurable charitable endowments and other properties, including a residence (*rebāṭ*) where the Khᵛāja Imam Bu Ṣādeq

Tabbāni, may God prolong his state of health and security, [now] lives. The story of this Imam will be recorded in a very exhaustive fashion in its appropriate place, if God, He is exalted and magnified, so wills.

The tale of Mānk b. ʿAli b. Meymun and the Amir happened in this wise. This man used to prepare every year a large quantity of pickles and other appetising tidbits,[501] and [Gh 129] bring them along to Amir Maḥmud [as a present]. When the throne and royal power[502] passed to Amir Masʿud and he came from Balkh to Ghaznin, he presented a large quantity of pickles and fine white linen garments hand-made [F 155] by pious women. The Amir was highly delighted and showed him great favour, and he said, "Mānk b. ʿAli looked after a large flock of sheep from the personal property of my father, God's mercy be upon him. I have now left them to him. Also, the sheep which make up our own personal flock, and which have been brought from Herat, should be given to him so that he might take care of them. When a financial reckoning is made for the care of the sheep, he should be dealt with lightly so that he reaps maximum profit out of this, for he is a pious man and he is of great import to us." The order was speedily carried out. The next year, the Amir went to Balkh, where there were important matters to be tackled, as will be set forth. According to his custom, Mānk b. ʿAli b. Meymun sent a large quantity of pickles, adding to this dried meat (*qadid*) and all sorts of other things. He requested Mikāʾil Bazzāz (i.e. the cloth merchant), who was a friend of his, to present them on his behalf. He also sent a document containing his financial reckoning, which showed him responsible for paying 50,000 dinars and for the 16,000 sheep. He had also written out a petition[503] and had pleaded that the Sultan's sheep, which he was caring for, should be handed over to someone else, since he had become an old man and could no longer keep them, and that there should be a delay and respite for him to pay that sum, for which he was liable, in instalments over three years.

At the time when Mikāʾil Bazzāz arrived and they brought in those pickles, and opened the necks of the large jars and were offering tastings, I, ʿAbd al-Ghaffār, was present. Mikāʾil proffered the document and the petition. The Amir said, "Take them and read them out. He laughed and said, "Our house owes many rights and favours to Mānk. We have bestowed on him this sum owed and the sheep. ʿAbd al-Ghaffār is to go to the Accounting Office[504] and tell the accountants to draw a line across the account and strike out what remains against him." I wrote out the order [F 156] and he affixed the royal emblem and signature, and Mānk secured a respite through this magnanimous act. It requires a great resolution and abundant forbearance to be able to act like that. May God, His mention is exalted, have mercy on that great sovereign!

There is another action showing even more greatness and renown regarding Bu Saʿid b. Sahl. This man was for a long period the counsellor and adjutant [Gh 130] and the Head of the Army Department[505] for Amir Naṣr, the Commander-in-Chief and brother of Sultan Maḥmud, may God envelop them both with His mercy.[506] When Naṣr passed away, Maḥmud, because of Bu Saʿid's suitability and competence, entrusted to him the oversight of all the crown domains at Ghazni. This job is on a level with the headship of the Divān at Ghazni. He exercised this function for a long period. After Sultan Maḥmud's decease, Amir Masʿud gave to him the important office of headship of the Divān at Ghazni, together with the crown domains.[507] He exercised these functions for nearly fifteen years. Then the Amir ordered that an accounting should be made of his Bu Saʿid's activities. The accounting officials looked into his accounts, and there was a sum of 17,000,000 dirhams net for which he was liable. His salary[508] for the crown domains was only one million dirhams. Everybody said, "What's going to become of Bu Saʿid when he is held liable for a huge sum like this?", for they had seen what punishments Amir Maḥmud ordered for Moʿaddel-dār (?), who was the local governor and collector of taxation for Herat; for the special servant Bā Saʿid, who held the crown domains of Ghaznin; and for the collector of taxation for Gardiz, against all of whom accountings were raised, and what punishments he ordered to be inflicted—floggings, amputations of hands and feet, and tortures. But Amir Masʿud was a man with complete modesty and compassion; moreover, Bu Saʿid b. Sahl, had, in past times, done him from the depths of his heart, many acts of laudable service, and also at that period [F 157] when he held the crown domains in Amir Maḥmud's time.

When they showed that monarch, Amir Masʿud, a statement of accounts due from Bu Saʿid of such enormity, he said, "Send for Ṭāher the Chief Accountant and Bu Saʿid,"[509] and he ordered "You must explain fully to me this state of affairs!" Ṭāher was going through the accounts item by item and was demonstrating that, in the end, a million dirhams were due to Bu Saʿid but 16,000,000 dirhams were owed by him and could not be found anywhere. It was incontrovertible that Bu Saʿid would have to pay it out of his personal wealth. The Amir said, "O Bu Saʿid, what do you have to say, and what is the explanation of this sum of money?" He replied, "May the lord's life be prolonged! The tax revenues of Ghazni are a sea whose depth and extent cannot be fathomed. I swear by the Almighty God [Gh 131] and by the lord's soul and head that I am not guilty of any treacherous behaviour. This sum is that still to be collected[510] from many years, and this accounting is rightfully due to the lord from me." The Amir said, "We have bestowed this money on you, since you have a right to it. Rise and return home in good health and preservation." Bu Saʿid burst out weeping with joy in a most heartfelt manner. Ṭāher, the Chief Accountant, said, "It's an occasion for joy and not for grief and weeping!" Bu Saʿid said, "I am weeping because we servants are rendering service to a lord like this who shows us such forbearance, nobility of character and greatness on his part, and if he should take away from us his care, favour and benevolence, what state of affairs would we be in?" The Amir spoke kindly with him, and Bu Saʿid departed. There cannot be a greater nobility than this. All have now passed on, God's mercy be upon them all!

The amount of largesse that he bestowed on the poets was boundless. Thus in one night he bestowed on ʿAlavi Zeynabi,[511] who was a poet, an elephant's load of dirhams, a million dirhams, of such a standard that [a nominal] ten dirhams had in them nine-and-a-half dirhams' weight of silver. He ordered that that weighty gift should be loaded on an elephant and borne to ʿAlavi's house. A thousand dinars or five hundred dinars, or ten thousand dirhams, [F 158] or more or less, were not too great sums for him on several occasions to bestow on poets, and likewise such sums on his boon-companions, secretaries and personal retainers, and he used to seek excuses for bestowing something on them.[512] At the beginning of his reign he bestowed largesse in very great quantities, but in the later part of his reign that benevolent breeze lost much of its force. But the way of time is such that nothing remains the same, and change affects all things.

Amir Masʿud had a very high degree of magnanimity and compassion. Thus one year he came to Ghaznin, and various shortcomings on the part of the household attendants, and offences which could not be passed over, became apparent there. The Amir told the Palace Chamberlain, "These attendants, who number twenty, must receive twenty strokes of the bastinado." The Chamberlain assumed that each one had been ordered twenty strokes of the bastinado. They seized one of them outside the house, and when they had inflicted three strokes, he shouted out in pain. The Amir said, "We had ordered one stroke for each of them, and that we have now forgiven. Stop beating them!" All of them thus escaped the punishment. This is the acme [Gh 132] of magnanimity and nobility of character; how excellent is *forgiveness from a position of power!*[513]

At the time when Amir Maḥmud set out from Gorgān for Ray he laid down a contractual agreement[514] between his sons, the princes Masʿud and Moḥammad, as was required. Accordingly, on that day, a horse was summoned at court for Amir Moḥammad as the Amir of Khorasan, and he returned to Nishapur.[515] The two Amirs Maḥmud and Masʿud, father and son, set out the next day for Ray. When affairs in that region (i.e. Ray) settled down, and Amir Maḥmud prepared to return, he bestowed a robe of honour on his son. A message arrived for Masʿud, delivered by Bu'l-Ḥasan ʿAqili, to the effect that, "As you heard, a horse suitable for the Amir of Khorasan was ordered at our court for my son Moḥammad. [F 159] You are at this present moment our deputy, and you know our commands regarding this limitless governorate. What is your choice: is a horse suitable for an emperor the horse required for you, or a horse suitable for the Amir of Western Persia?" When Amir Masʿud heard this message from his father, he rose to his feet, kissed the ground and then sat down, saying, "Tell the lord, 'How can I express my thanks for so many bounties? For every hour I find a new and unimaginable favour bestowed upon me. There is no greater obligation on lords and fathers than that they should bestow on their dutiful children fine and appropriate names at that moment when they appear in the world. It is incumbent upon the children and becomes a duty for them that, when they grow up, they should show commendable acts of service and thereby enhance their good reputation (*nām*). The lord bestowed on me a very fine name (*nām*), that being Masʿud ("he who is fortunate, happy"), and even greater than that is the fact that it is in the same versificatory or poetic measure as the lord's name (i.e. Maḥmud "he who is praised"), may he live for ever![516] Now that I shall be bereft of close service and attendance on the lord my father, it should be decreed that I maintain this present name of mine until the lord gives additional ones. If the Almighty God wills that I should be called by that title (i.e. Shāhanshāh or Amir of Western Persia), I shall, with the lord's blessing, attain it'." He gave this reply in the presence of myself, ʿAbd al-Ghaffār, and I later heard that, when they told these words to Amir Maḥmud, he was filled with shame and was thoroughly overwhelmed, and had said, "He has spoken most fittingly, for fame comes to man through skilful achievements."

At that time when the two Amirs, father and son, were travelling from Gorgān towards Ray, [Gh 133] a number of Amir Maḥmud's palace gholāms, such as Qāy Oghlan,[517] Arslān and ḥājeb Chabïk,[518] who were subsequently appointed *ḥājeb*s [F 160] by Amir Masʿud, and the head of the gholāms (*amir-e bachcha*), who was in charge of the mass of palace gholāms, and several of the field officers and heads of barrack rooms,[519] were clandestinely making approaches to Masʿud and offering their allegiance, and were sending messages. There was an aged domestic attendant who used to carry their messages to and fro. An inkling of this affair had come to the ears of Sultan Maḥmud, since Amir Moḥammad had some persons who used to ferret out information on the doings of his brother, making Masʿud always appear in an unfavourable light to his father.

One day, at a halting stage [between Gorgān and Ray] which was called Chāsht-khᵛārān,[520] the father had sought to have his son arrested. At the time of the afternoon worship, Amir Masʿud came to render service, stayed for about an hour and left. Bu'l-Ḥasan Karaji[521] came after him and said, "The Sultan says, 'Don't go back, but remain behind in the guard tent (*kheyma-ye nowbati*), for we desire to hold a convivial wine-drinking session, and we wish to hand you wine in our presence so that you may experience this act of favour'." Amir Masʿud sat down in the guard tent, happy at this act of grace. But at that moment, the aged household attendant came in and brought a message from those gholāms, to the effect that, "The lord should be on his guard; it appears that your father is going to move against you." Amir Masʿud rose up at once and straightaway sent someone to his commanders and gholāms, enjoining them to be on their guard, saddle the horses and have their weapons ready at their sides, since things had come to such a pass as this. They began to stir and get busy. These gholāms of Sultan Maḥmud (i.e. those favourable to Masʿud mentioned before) also got wind of this, and the entire army showed signs of agitation. Information about that was at once conveyed to Amir Maḥmud. He was thwarted, and realized that his plan was not going to succeed and that some disturbance might arise which it would be difficult to contain. Towards the time of the evening worship, he sent Bu'l-Ḥasan ʿAqili to his son with a message, saying, "We had the desire today to drink wine and to offer you wine also, but this is an inappropriate time, and we are faced with having to deal with a certain momentous affair. It was not the right time; [F 161]; go back, with good fortune and happiness, for this occasion can take place [at a future date] in Ray; when we reach there in good health and security, you will find this mark of favour." Amir Masʿud kissed the ground and went back [Gh 134] happy and contented.

Immediately, the aged attendant came in and brought the message of the Maḥmudi gholāms, to the effect that, "Things have gone well, and we have resolved in our minds that, if there should be any attempt at harming the Amir, we shall set on foot a revolt since a great number of the gholāms have joined us and have their eyes fixed on us (i.e. are awaiting the signal to move)". The Amir sent back a reply full of thanks, encouraged them profusely and gave them abundant hopes of future favours, and the episode came to an end. After that, Amir Maḥmud drank wine on several occasions, either while travelling or when he was at Ray, but did not pursue the offer of wine to the son, so that Amir Masʿud said privately to his servants and confidants, "Our father had in mind some scheme against us, but God, His mention is exalted, did not want it to happen."

When they reached Ray, Amir Maḥmud encamped at Dowlāb on the Ṭabarestān road near the city, and Amir Masʿud set up his army camp at ʿAli-ābād on the Qazvin road.[522] There was a distance of half a parasang between the two armies. The weather became very hot, and the leaders and great men ordered subterranean chambers to be made for their midday siestas.[523] A very clean and commodious subterranean chamber was constructed for Amir Masʿud, and the period from the time of the mid-morning meal till the afternoon worship he used to spend there, part of the time in sleep and the rest in merry-making and discreetly-veiled wine-drinking sessions and in issuing orders for things to be done. At one time when it was the hottest part of the day, these gholāms and commanders of Amir Maḥmud came to Amir Mas'ud, on foot and disguised in fine cotton, rainproofed garments[524] and sashes wrapped round their faces. The eunuch Piruz Vaziri, who was aware of what was secretly going on, requested entry for them and they went into that subterranean chamber and made the customary obeisance. The Amir welcomed them, treated them kindly and gave them copious hopes of future favours. They said, "May the lord's life be prolonged! Your father the Sultan is very ill-inclined towards you, and he would like to be able to arrest you [F 162] but is afraid to do so. He realizes that he has exasperated everyone, and he believes that a great conspiracy is afoot. If the lord should give the order, all the slaves and gholāms are united in support of you and will seize him, for when we rise up in an émeute, the personnel of the outer court[525] will come and aid us, and you [Gh 135] will be freed from this humiliating situation and find relief from your worries."

The Amir replied, "It goes without saying that I do not approve of you even harbouring in your minds such thoughts, let alone putting these ideas into action, for Amir Maḥmud is my father and I cannot contemplate the smallest harm being done to him. I fondly accept his chastisements, for as a sovereign, he is peerless in the world. If, God forbid, some situation of the kind of which you are speaking should come about (i.e. any harm to the Sultan), the shame of it will not be lifted from our house until the Resurrection. He has become old, weak, and disgruntled, and his life is drawing to its close, but I myself want him to live on until the time when the Almighty God has decreed his fate. I want nothing more from you than that, when the decree of death—from which no person can escape—comes to him, you should give your pledge of allegiance (*bey'at*) to me." He ordered me, 'Abd al-Ghaffār, to make them confirm the above under oath, and then they left.

Between Amir Mas'ud and Manuchehr b. Qābus, the local ruler[526] of Gorgān and Ṭabarestān, there was a continuous correspondence, conducted in deep secrecy, both at the time when he was in Herat and at this present time. Manuchehr had despatched a man called Ḥasan Moḥaddeth ("the story-teller") to Amir Mas'ud, to render service as a story-teller as well as, from time to time, to bring letters and messages to and fro. The letters going to Manuchehr went out in the handwriting of myself, 'Abd al-Ghaffār. Whenever Mas'ud despatched that reciter of stories to Gorgān, he did it under the pretext that the story-teller was bringing back seeds of aromatic basil, oranges, [wooden] platters (? *ṭabaq*) and other things from there. At the time when [F 163] the two Amirs Masʿud and Maḥmud were in Gorgān and were aiming for Ray, this story-teller went to Setārābād,[527] to Manuchehr, and the latter sent him back with a trusty confidant from his own retinue, a man who was nimble-witted and eloquent, in the guise of Bedouin Arabs, with their appearance and their dress. He also sent back secretly to Amir Masʿud, many gifts, together with handwritten messages and letters and with the delicacies and specialities of Gorgān and Dehestān,[528] apart from all that in the generality of presents which was sent to Amir Maḥmud. On one or two occasions, his trusty confidants, this story-teller and his fellow-envoy, came and went on visits and matters ultimately reached a point where Manuchehr sought from Amir Masʿud a treaty made under oath such as is the practice among kings.

Then one night, in that blessed time, after the night worship, [Gh 136], a chamberlain (*parda-dār*), who is at the present time, in the reign of the Exalted Sultan Abu Shojāʿ Farrokh-zād b. Nāṣer Din Allāh, castellan of the fortress of Sakāvand,[529] came and summoned me, ʿAbd al-Ghaffār—and since it was he who came to summon me, I knew for certain that I was being summoned for an important task—I went along, all prepared, with the chamberlain. I found the Amir in his large tent, seated alone on his throne, with an ink-holder and paper in front of him, and with the Treasurer Gowhar-āyin[530]—who was one of the Amir's confidants at that time—standing there. I made the appropriate acts of obeisance and he motioned me to sit down, so I sat down. He said to Gowhar-āyin, "Give the ink-holder and paper to ʿAbd al-Ghaffār." He set these down before me and he himself left the large tent. The Amir tossed over to me the text of the treaty (*noskhat-e ʿahd*) and [F 164] the document containing the oath (*sowgand-nāma*) which he had written out himself in his own hand. He used to write in such a fine way that even those secretaries who were masters of the art of writing were not able to produce its like. (Bu'l-Fażl will cite them in several places in this History, and many of the documents and memoranda of this sovereign came into his hands.)[531] I studied the document intently. There was written "Masʿud b. Maḥmud says thus: By the Almighty God", and that oath which is customary in a formal treaty document, "until the time when the Lofty Amir Falak al-Maʿāli Abu Manṣur Manuchehr b. Qābus will be with us." The requirements and conventions of such documents were set down fully right to the end, in such a manner that nothing could be more eloquently expressed nor could anything be finer.

When I perused it closely, it was as if a bowlful of fire had been poured over my head; I was dumbfounded and terrified of Maḥmud's wrath. Masʿud noticed the signs of perturbation and confusion in me, and asked, "What's the matter? Why are you so downcast and speechless? How do you find this document?" I said, "May the lord's life be prolonged! No master secretary could have written in the manner in which the lord has composed. But there is one aspect which, if I were to mention it, might not come as something pleasant and would not be in place. I can only speak with permission." He said, "Speak out!" I said, "It is not hidden from the lord's mind that Manuchehr is afraid of the lord's father. The lord's father is at the present moment in such a frail state and in such a lamentable condition that it is no longer a secret, [Gh 137] and it is clear that he is nearing the end of his life. News of this has reached all the rulers and the ambitious and overweening princes of adjoining lands. They are fearful, and would like to be able to take their revenge. They are convinced that, when the Sultan has passed away, Amir Moḥammad will not be able to hold on to his father's position and there will be no stability in his rule, and they are apprehensive about the lord Masʿud, [F 165] since his image and his might are firmly fixed in their minds, and they will not be able to achieve their desires. And how can one rely on Manuchehr? For, when this treaty, adorned with and endorsed by the lord's signature, reaches him, he may well ingratiate himself with Sultan Maḥmud by sending it to him, so that he can reap the ensuing havoc and succeed in his aim of acquiring safety and security. Monarchs have in the past used many stratagems, and when a display of enmity and open hostility has failed to achieve results, they have resorted to trickery and deception in order to succeed in their aims. Furthermore, even if Manuchehr does not behave so ignominiously, Amir Maḥmud is shrewd, highly observant, artful and experienced, moreover he has spies and informers watching the lord, and has appointed and stationed watchmen along all the roads. If this man bearing the document is searched, and the text of the treaty is seized and brought to him, how would you be able to extricate yourself from this?

The Amir replied, "It's just as you are saying. Manuchehr has been insistent on the setting up of this treaty because he knows that my father's days are numbered. He wants to bolster up his position in relation to us, for he is a shrewd, ripe-aged and far-sighted person, and I would feel ashamed to deny him this when he has rendered so many acts of service and has shown his desire for close relations." I said, "The best course would be to write something which cannot be used as evidence against the lord and be exploited by Sultan Maḥmud, should the letter fall into his hands." He replied, "How should such a letter be couched?" I said, "Assuredly, the best course would be to write that 'The Amir has continuously sent envoys and letters and sought our favour, and has performed acts of service in a frank and honest fashion, and he has asked that there should be a treaty between us. We have granted his wishes, for we would not think it right if a venerable person pleads to enter into a bond of friendship with us [F 166] and we repulse him and reject his wishes. However, it is an agreed fact that we are the servant and the son of Sultan Maḥmud, and are obedient to his words. Whatever we do in matters like these should be done in accordance with and in the light of his august sovereignty, or else it would not be right, since if it were not so, first the Amir would blame us and then people in general. On the other hand, how could I consent to bringing embarrassment to the Amir (i.e. Manuchehr) by refusing him this? So I have perforce to make this treaty.'" I then wrote out the text of a treaty with this proem[532] and in this manner: [Gh 138]

The treaty document

Mas'ud b. Maḥmud thus states: By God and by God's covenant, and by the Lord who knows the secret thoughts and the public actions of His creatures, that so long as the lofty, victorious Amir Manuchehr b. Qābus remains submissive and obedient to the commands of the lord, the Exalted Sultan Abu'l-Qāsem Maḥmud Nāṣer Din Allāh—may God prolong his existence perpetually[533]—and pays his tribute money, and upholds the terms of that treaty which he has concluded (i.e. with Maḥmud) and has reinforced with solemn oaths and witnesses, and does not alter a single iota of it, I shall be his friend in heart, intent and belief. I will show friendship to his friends and enmity to his foes. I will hold my assistance and military backing ready for him and will put in place all the necessary conditions of concord and unity. I will faithfully act as his representative at the exalted court of the lord my father, and if I discern any rupture in friendship or animosity, I will strive to remedy it. If the exalted judgement of my father should decree that we remain at Ray, I will still remain faithful to Manuchehr regarding these provisions, and in everything which involves the welfare of the realm, of the dynasty and of the people's physical security, I will strive to conform to it. [F 167] As long as he shows his obedience, maintains his present stance and observes the stipulations of the treaty that he has concluded, I will remain faithful to my side of the agreement with him. May I incur the wrath of God, He is exalted and magnified, if I should be false to my oath and break this treaty. From His strength and power and that of the prophets, God's blessings be upon them all, I have placed reliance on my own strength and power. *Written in the year so-and-so.*

He finished this treaty agreement in these terms and sent it to Manuchehr. The latter rendered his service and showed his submission, and his mind was set at rest.[534]

One should take note and appreciate this man ʿAbd al-Ghaffār the secretary's skill and competence in his solicitude for this prince's best interests, his uprightness and steadfastness, and how far these extended. These stories too have come to an end, and I have resumed my main task and the recording of historical events. *Success comes from God!*

In the fifth volume I have related that Amir Masʿud entered Balkh on Sunday [Gh 139] in the middle of Dhu'l-Ḥejja (i.e. the 14th) 421 [/13 December 1030][535] and became busy with directing affairs of state. It was as if the whole world became adorned like a bride, for things became united and harmonious, and retainers, courtiers and subjects had their minds set at rest through their obedience and submission to this lord.

The affairs of the court were all directed by the General Ghāzi, who was Commander-in-Chief and who held the governorships of Balkh and Samangān. His counsellor and adjutant Saʿid Ṣarrāf was secretly an observer and spy over him, and whatever Ghāzi did in private, he would report back. Ghāzi used to come to the court each day [F 168] with a retinue of around thirty Deylamites with gold and silver shields,[536] shield bearers were drawn up before him, several chamberlains with black caps and with sashes before and thirty gholāms behind, in such a way that every person bore some weapon or item of equipment. I never saw the Khwarazm Shah or Arslān Jādheb and the rest of Amir Maḥmud's senior commanders come to court in this fashion. They used to bring his horse into the outer palace at Balkh, as was done in previous times with those of Amir Masʿud, Moḥammad and Yusof. He used to sit in the open portico or loggia (*ṭāram*)[537] of the Chancery until the time when the court was held. ʿAli Dāya, the ruler's relatives and the powerful commanders had a very extensive platform within the palace, and they used to seat themselves there before the court began. The General Ghāzi used to pass by them on his way to the portico. All of them used perforce to rise to their feet and pay their respects to him until he had gone past. It was most offensive for these people to see him in such a lofty position since they had known him in the days when he was of a lowly rank. They would mutter and say things about this, but it was all unjustified and unseemly, for the world revolves round sultans and they raise up to a lofty position whom they like. It is inappropriate for anyone to complain why things are such, for [the Caliph] Ma'mun said in this connection. "*We comprise the whole of this present world; those whom we raise up are brought to a lofty position, and those whom we abase are laid low.*"[538]

In the historical accounts of prominent persons I read that when Ashenās—whom they called Afshin[539]—successfully terminated the war against Bābak Khorram-Din, brought back victory and reached Baghdad, the Commander of the Faithful Moʿtaṣem ordered when Ashenās came to court, the officials of the court were to dismount in his presence and go before [F 169] him on foot until the point when he reached the Caliph. Ḥasan b. Sahl, despite his great eminence in his own time, dismounted on account of Ashenās's presence. His chamberlain saw him walking along, dragging his feet, and he burst out weeping. Ḥasan saw this but said nothing. When he came back to the house, [Gh 140], he said to his chamberlain, "Why were you weeping?" He replied, "I couldn't bear to see you in those circumstances." He said, "My boy, these monarchs have made us great, and they did not become great through us. As long as we are with them, we must necessarily obey them."

The mutterings of that group and their talk would be reported to the General Ghāzi, but he used merely to laugh it off and was not alarmed by it, for that arrogance was planted in Ghāzi's head by

Amir Maḥmud when Maḥmud gave him the office of a man of Arslān Jādheb's calibre, for he could find no-one more worthy of it than him. I have already recounted this episode in the *Tārikh-e Yamini*.[540] In this connection, I recall a remarkable story, which I have set down here so that it may be better known, for it is such stories that add lustre and colour to chronicles.

The story of Fażl b. Sahl Dhu'l-Riyāsateyn and Ḥoseyn b. al-Moṣʿab

They have related that Fażl, the Caliph Ma'mun's vizier at Merv, reproached Ḥoseyn b. Moṣʿab, the father of Ṭāher Dhu'l-Yamineyn, saying, "Your son Ṭāher has changed his demeanour, and has become haughty and proud, and does not know his place." Ḥoseyn said, "O Vizier, I am an aged man, a servant of this dynasty and obedient to it, and I know that you are fully convinced of my wise counsel and sincerity, but my son Ṭāher is even more faithful a servant than I and even more obedient. I can give a very succinct answer regarding him, but it is blunt and unpalatable. If you grant me permission, I will say it." "Granted," he replied. Ḥoseyn said, "May God strengthen the Vizier! The Commander of the Faithful took him into his service from among the lowliest of his retainers and following, split open his breast and took out from there the feeble heart which a person like him has and replaced it with a new heart,[541] [F 170] by means of which he killed Ma'mun's brother, a caliph like Moḥammad b. Zobeyda.[542] Together with that heart which he bestowed, he also gave the means, the strength and the troops. Now at this present time, when his position has reached that high point which is obvious, do you wish him to abase himself before you and be exactly as he was before? Under no circumstance can this ever come about, unless you take him down to the level he was before! I have said what I know; it is for you to command." Fażl b. Sahl fell silent, to the extent that he did not utter a word that day and was highly discomfited. This story was brought to Ma'mun. He found the reply of Ḥoseyn b. Moṣʿab most pleasing and acceptable to him. He said, "These words have impressed me more favourably than his son's conquest of Baghdad," and he bestowed upon Ṭāher the governorship of Pushang, since Ḥoseyn was previously at Pushang. [Gh 141]

And so one story leads to another. I am going to relate a lengthy tale about Dhu'l-Riyāsateyn, who was called Fażl b. Sahl; Dhu'l-Yamineyn, who was called Ṭāher; and Dhu'l-Qalameyn, who was the head of Maʾmun's Chancery,[543] in order that, should anyone not know it, it will now become known to him.

When Moḥammad b. Zobeyda was killed and the caliphate passed to Maʾmun, he remained for over two years at Merv, and that is a long story. The Vizier Fażl b. Sahl sought to divert the caliphate away from the ʿAbbasids and transfer it to the ʿAlids. He said to Maʾmun, "You made a vow in my presence and took an oath that, if God Most High should successfully bring to a close the matter of your brother and you should become caliph, you would appoint a designated successor from among the ʿAlids. Although the succession may not remain within them, you will at least have absolved yourself of responsibility[544] and will have extricated yourself from the vow and the oath." Maʾmun said, "You have spoken very truly; whom shall we make the designated successor?" He replied, "ʿAli b. Musā al-Reżā, who is the Imam of the Age and who lives in the City of the Messenger of God, peace be upon him."[545] He said, "Someone must be secretly sent to Ṭāher, and one should write to him that we intend to do such-and-such, so that he may despatch someone and bring ʿAli back from Medina, clandestinely give the oath of allegiance to him, and send him to Merv in an honourable manner so that the matter of the oath of allegiance and the succession designation [F 171] can be made public here."

Fażl said, "The Commander of the Faithful should write a succinct, secret letter in his own handwriting." He immediately sent for an inkwell, paper and pen, wrote out this letter and gave it to Fażl. Fażl came back home and sat down alone, and wrote out what was necessary to be written. He arranged matters and sent a confidant to Ṭāher with these commands. Ṭāher was filled with joy at this news, for he was favourably inclined towards the ʿAlids. He put that business in hand, as was required, and appointed a trusty person from the close circle of his retainers to accompany Maʾmun's trusty messenger. The two of them went off to Medina and had a private interview with Reżā, showed him the letter of Fażl and conveyed the messages. Reżā was filled with a feeling of intense reluctance, since he knew that this scheme would not go far. However, he gave his assent to it because he was unable to reject Ma'mun's decision, and secretly and in disguise came to Baghdad, and they accommodated him in a handsome lodging.

After a week, when he had become rested and refreshed, Ṭāher came to him at night in a very secret manner, made elaborate obeisance to him and abased himself very deeply. He showed him that letter in Ma'mun's own handwriting and said, "The first person who will make the handclasp of allegiance to you at the behest of my lord the Commander of the Faithful's command is myself. [Gh 142] When I myself have given this allegiance, I have with me 100,000 cavalrymen and infantrymen who will have given their allegiance likewise. Reżā, may God grant him eternal rest, put forth his right hand to make the handclasp of allegiance, as is the usual practice. Ṭāher extended his left hand. Reżā said, "What's this?" He replied, "My right hand is taken up with giving allegiance to my lord Ma'mun, but my left hand is free, hence I have put it forward." Reżā [F 172] was impressed by what he had done and they exchanged the handclasp of allegiance. The next day, he sent off Reżā with many gifts and marks of respect. They brought him to Merv, and after he had rested a while, the caliph Ma'mun came at night to see him, accompanied by Fażl b. Sahl. They greeted each other cordially, and Reżā gave profuse thanks for what Ṭāher had done, and he repeated that incident of the left hand and the oath of allegiance. This pleased Ma'mun very much, and what Ṭāher had done was heartily approved. He said, "O Imam, that was the first hand that clasped your blessed hand; I have now given that left hand the name of the right one. This is the reason why Ṭāher was called *Dhu'l-Yamineyn*.[546]

After that, they made public[547] the matter of Reżā. Ma'mun made him the designated successor, and laid aside the black banners and substituted green ones for them. Reżā's name was placed on dirhams and dinars and on the embroidered *ṭerāz* bands of luxury clothing,[548] and the whole affair became public knowledge. Ma'mun said to Reżā, "You should have a vizier and a secretary to look after your affairs." He replied, "O Commander of the Faithful, Fażl b. Sahl would be a competent person to manage the job of acting as counsellor and adjutant for me, together with 'Ali [b. Abi] Sa'id,[549] the head of the caliph's

Chancery, for writing my letters." Ma'mun approved these words, and he gave orders for these two persons to take full charge of these offices. Because of this, they used to call Fażl *Dhu'l-Riyāsateyn*[550], and 'Ali [b. Abi] Sa'id *Dhu'l-Qalameyn*.[551] I have set forth what I had intended to say regarding these three honorific titles; the rest of the story I have left aside since it is lengthy and clearly displayed in historical accounts.

The Commander Ghāzi became a most unpleasant ogre (lit. "mountain") in the eyes of the men who had served at the court of Maḥmud (*maḥmudiyān*).[552] Every day his position grew more elevated, and his pomp and prestige[553] more splendid, and the favour of Amir Mas'ud himself, may God be pleased with him, towards him surpassed all limits and extent. These marks of favour included presents of food, seating him in the prime place above everyone else, [F 173] summoning him to wine-drinking sessions, awarding him a lofty status and sending him away with splendid robes of honour. Although Ghāzi did not drink wine and had never done so, and although there could not have been a more shrewd and well informed [Gh 143] person than him, each day[554] he became more and more the target of envy and the object of people's gaze. He assembled a force of around a thousand cavalrymen, with suitable fine equipment and arms. But in the end, when things reached their conclusion, the evil eye came down, for the men of Maḥmud's court persisted in using stratagems until they procured the man's downfall and brought him to Ghaznin in bonds.[555] I shall relate the story of what happened to him in its place, since now is not the time.

The Amir used to discuss all the affairs of the army with Ghāzi and he made him his intermediary in matters connected with the army. Everyone came to look up to him in such a way that, each day when he returned home from the portal of the palace, there would be with him a very large following. The men of Maḥmud's former régime were using stratagems, and they used to employ people to broadcast his faults and paint him in a bad light. But it goes without saying that the Amir did not listen to these and such things could not be hidden from him, for no-one had ever seen a better-informed, more noble and more sagacious ruler than he nor had they read of such a man in books. The affair eventually reached such a high point [as follows:] one day, Masʿud was drinking wine and had spent all the night drinking. Early in the morning he held court on the great dais. The chamberlains went forward, according to tradition, and the great men began to come in after them according to a fixed and regular order, and they would either sit down or remain standing. Ghāzi came in through the door. [F 174] It was a long way up to the dais. The Amir gave an order to two chamberlains that they were to go to greet and receive the Commander-in-Chief. No-one could recall such a mark of favour ever being shown before to any Commander-in-Chief. The chamberlains went forward and reached Ghāzi in the middle of the hall. Several people had preceded the chamberlains and had already given him the good news of this favour. When the chamberlains came up to him, he lowered his head and kissed the ground. They took his arms and in a solemn manner set him down in his place. The Amir turned his face towards him and said, "The Commander-in-Chief is like a brother to us, and that service which he performed for us at Nishapur and to such an unbounded extent, is in no way forgotten by us. Part of those obligations of reward due to you has been performed, and yet more remains which will be fulfilled in due course of time. We hear that your position as Commander-in-Chief is resented by a certain group, and that they are resorting to deceit and falsehood. If they try to cause misunderstandings and rifts by making you worried in regard to me, take care not to become worried, for your position in our favour is exactly what you have heard from my own lips."

Ghāzi rose to his feet and kissed the ground, saying, "Since the exalted judgement regarding me [Gh 144] is in this wise, I fear no-one." The Amir gave orders for a special coat to be brought, and they held it on his back; he rose, donned it and kissed the ground. The Amir gave orders for them to bring a hunting belt set with jewels; he summoned him forward and fastened it round Ghāzi's waist with his own exalted hand. Ghāzi kissed the ground and returned home with such gifts and manifestations of favour whose like no-one could remember.[556]

My master Bu Naṣr continued to be in something like a depressed state of mind at Herat, as I have previously described, and the Amir on several occasions made his spirits revive so that he became more assured in mind. Now at this time in Balkh, he became the recipient of much favour. When the courtiers came into the Chancery, they used to speak with my master, [F 175] despite the fact that Ṭāher had assumed the prestige and glory (i.e. as Head of the Chancery). People had seen Ṭāher stand before Bu Naṣr and guard the door of this monarch. The open portico of the outer palace was our Divān. Bu Naṣr sat in that place where he used to sit in times past, on the left-hand side of the portico, where there was more light. The Khᵛāja 'Amid[557] Abu Sahl,[558] may God strengthen him perpetually, who is the Head of the Chancery at this present time of the Great Sultan Abu Shojā' Farrokhzād b. Nāṣer Din Allāh—may this empire endure for ever!—and Bu Sahl Hamadāni,[559] that elegant son of the master, whose father served the great viziers and who is now still alive enjoying an exalted and honoured status, and his brother[560] Bu'l-Qāsem Nishāburi, the highly capable master, and the scholar versed in polite learning (*adibak*) Bu Moḥammad Dughābādi,[561] a man of great learning and with a fine knowledge of polite literature and poetry, but a mediocre (lit. "pedestrian") secretary: all these sat on Ṭāher's left hand. They set down a very large silver inkstand in front of Ṭāher with a black brocade cloth on one side of the rim. Bu'l-Ḥasan 'Erāqi the secretary, although he was considered as part of the Chancery, himself [Gh 145] seldom sat in the Divān and was mostly with the Amir himself, and involved in other activities. He had an assured place in the court circle of this monarch. On this day when the eminent masters of the Divān and the secretaries were seated according to this arrangement, he came into the portico and sat down on the right hand of Khᵛāja Bu Naṣr in the domed tent so that he planted himself between the two masters in the front of the open portico and began to direct affairs. All who came into the Chancery, whether of lofty status or not, when they saw Bu Naṣr would invariably speak with him, and if a letter was required, they would ask him to do it. The boon-companions [F 176] who brought verbal messages from the Amir on some or other important affair of state that would require letters to be written would likewise speak with Bu Naṣr. This meant that, on this side, business was transacted continuously, while on the other, people were just sitting and watching, except that, from time to time, some person from among those who had seen Ṭāher in Western Persia would come in and would seek a letter from Ṭāher concerning complaints of wrongdoing or some favour or grant of permission. He would order it to be written out and they would converse awhile.

When matters had gone on this way for a short while, the Amir one day summoned Bu Naṣr around noon—he had heard what was going on in the Divān—and said, "The names of the secretaries must be written down [in two groups], those who were with you (i.e. in the central Divān based in Ghazna) and those who were with us and were brought back from Ray, so that orders may be given for whatever needs to be done." My master came to the Divān and the names of the two groups were written down. He submitted the document. The Amir said, "The names of ʿObeydallāh, the grandson through his daughter (*nabasa*) of Bu'l-ʿAbbās Esfarāyeni,[562] and Bu'l-Fatḥ Ḥātemi,[563] should not be there, for we will appoint them to some other charges." Bu Naṣr said, "May the lord's life be prolonged! Amir Moḥammad gave orders that I should take ʿObeydallāh into the Divān out of respect for his grandfather. He is a discreet and circumspect youth, with good calligraphic skills, and he will make a very good secretary. The lord gave orders that Bu'l-Fatḥ Ḥātemi should be taken into the Divān in the time of Amir Maḥmud because he is the offspring of one of the lord's retainers." He replied, "It's exactly as you are saying, but these two persons were in the past secret spies and observers for me in your Divān, so it would not be appropriate to have them in the Divān now." Bu Naṣr said, "Alas that I should only learn about this today!" The Amir said, "If you had become aware of this earlier, what would you have done?" He replied, "I would have banished them both from the Divān, for a treacherous secretary is of no use."

The Amir laughed and said, "There's no need to reveal this conversation to them, [F 177] for they would become distressed"—I had never seen anyone more noble-hearted and more compassionate than him—and he went on to say, "We will issue instructions for whatever is necessary. [Gh 146] What was ʿObeydallāh's position?" Bu Naṣr replied, "That of postmaster and intelligence officer at Sarakhs, while Bu'l-Fatḥ held the same function in Tokhārestān." The Amir said, "You may go back." Bu Naṣr went back.

Next day, when the Amir held court and we were all standing in attendance, he called out, and ʿObeydallāh stepped forward from the line of courtiers. The Amir said, "Are you in the Chancery?" He replied, "Yes, I am." He said, "What post did you hold in my father's time?" He replied, "That of postmaster and intelligence officer at Sarakhs." He said, "We have bestowed that same post on you, but you do not meanwhile need to attend the Divān because there are ample staff there already. Your grandfather and father served at the court,[564] and you will be of service to us there. You must come forward with the boon-companions, until an appropriate time, when you will be allotted a seat in the Sultan's circle." 'Obeydallāh kissed the ground and went back to the line. Then he called out for Bu'l-Fatḥ Ḥātemi, and he stepped forward. The Amir said, "An observer and overseer (*moshref*) who is both faithful and competent, is required for Balkh and Tokhārestān, and we have chosen you for the job. 'Abdus, speaking at our behest, will tell you all that is necessary." He likewise kissed the ground and went back to the line. Then the Amir told Bu Naṣr, "Two investiture patents need to be written out for these two and then we can affix our emblem and signature." He replied, "Excellent!" The court broke up. My master went back to the Divān, and the two investiture patents were written out and adorned with the seal and signature. The two of them, 'Obeydallāh and Bu'l-Fatḥ, left the Divān, and no-one was cognisant of the true background to this. I, Bu'l-Fażl, heard this from my master. All those persons have passed on, God's mercy be upon them all.

The official posts and the grants of local administration and tax-collecting were now confirmed for them. The postal and intelligence service of Sistan, an important and prestigious post that in the former reign had been held nominally by Ḥasanak,[565] was now given to the secretary Ṭāher, and the same post for Qohestān given to Bu'l-Ḥasan 'Erāqi. [F 178] At that time, an accounting was made; the monthly salary (*moshāhara*) bill for all those was 70,000 dirhams per month. What greater magnanimity could there be than this? Also, those secretaries who had newly entered the Divān and did not yet have a salary, obtained after this time grants of tax revenues and monthly salaries.

The secretary Ṭāher was becoming disenchanted with the lack of work and began to feel somewhat ashamed, so that he went to the Divān less frequently, and if he did go, he soon came back home and occupied himself with wine-drinking and merry-making, since he enjoyed much wealth (*bazzi*)[566] and luxury, together with many handsome-faced gholāms and had a luxurious life with all its trappings. [Gh 147]

One day, it happened that the Amir had given orders that four men were to be chosen to act as observers and overseers for the whole empire. This was done, and the Amir said to Ṭāher, "Bu Naṣr must be instructed to have the investiture patents for these persons written out." Ṭāher came in and told Bu Naṣr. The latter said, "Very good, we'll have the documents written out." Ṭāher went away in a disgruntled mood and with a long face (i.e. because he had expected that Bu Naṣr would hand over the writing-out of the patents to him), and sent his major-domo to me, Beyhaqi, saying, "I have something that I need to say to you, and there is a message for Bu Naṣr. When you leave the Divān, you must pass by my house." I told this to my master, and he said, "You must go." So, when I left the Divān, I went to him. He had a house in the street of the silversmiths in the inner city of Balkh. I saw a residence, decorated like paradise and with immense luxury, for his noble virtues and lofty resolution were at a level of perfection and he was a highly respected figure. He [F 179] sat me down in the place of honour next to himself, and a spread of highly delicious food, prepared with great refinement, was set before me. His boon companions, musicians and singers, came in. We ate some food, and another place had been sumptuously prepared for a wine-drinking session. We proceeded to there. I saw a display of luxury, boundless and indescribable. We waded in, and the celebrations got under way. After the wine had been passed round a few times, his treasurer came in and five outfits of high-class, costly clothing and a purse containing 5,000 dirhams, were set before me. Then they went out, and following that, much silver and many items of clothing were given to the boon-companions, musicians and singers, and gholāms.

Then in the midst of all that, he said to me privately, "I do not deny the greatness and pre-eminence of the Khᵛāja ʿAmid Bu Naṣr and the position of great prestige which he has acquired since a long time back, but other people are coming on the scene and are finding favour and high positions with the sovereign lord. Although we two are the leading figures in this Divān at this present time, I acknowledge his primacy and am the lesser figure in relation to him. The lord Sultan has the intention of appointing me to an office superior to the one that I hold at present. Until that time when he eventually appoints me, just as I have regard for Bu Naṣr's great position and eminence, I expect that he will likewise recognize my just claims. Today, when the Amir gave orders for these investiture patents for the observers and overseers, he chose me to speak to about it because it is fully apparent to him and others that I am better able to manage the procedures and practices of the Divāns and of grants of financial responsibility and tax-collecting (*a'māl va amvāl*) than him (i.e. Bu Naṣr). But I had regard for his high position and spoke to him about this. I had expected him to suggest that I write out the investiture patents [Gh 148], and when he said nothing, I was offended. I have troubled you to come so that I could tell you this and so that you would be able to explicate and relay this in a way you think fit." In response I said what needed to be said, and made his mind happy. Then larger bumpers of wine were passed around. The day drew to its close, and we all dispersed. [F 180]

The next morning my master summoned me. I went along and he asked me what had happened. I described it all. He laughed and said, "Today I will show you the difference between knowing and not knowing how to deal with Divān transactions."[567] I went back. He took up his place in the Divān, and I went after him. When the court session opened, by a remarkable combination of circumstances, the Amir turned his face towards my master and said, "I had told Ṭāher the story of the investiture patents for the appointments to the Office of Observing and Oversight (*eshrāf*) so that he might speak with you. Have the final copies (*noskhat*) been prepared?" Bu Naṣr replied, "I have done a draft (*savād*), and today they are doing the fair copy (*bayāż*) so that the lord may look through it first and then it can be written out (i.e. in its final form)." He said, "Well done!" Ṭāher was taken aback, and we came back to the Divān. Bu Naṣr took up the pen of the Divān and began to prepare the final copy, and sat me down in front until I had prepared the fair copy. The time passed in doing this until the hour for the midday worship; and then there appeared an investiture patent, concerning which all the great men and leading authorities averred that no-one had ever seen its like for an investiture patent for the office of observing and overseeing nor was ever likely to see one. The patent was written on three quires of paper in my small, closely-written hand.[568] He took it along to the Amir and read it out, and it met with great approval. Various copies of that investiture patent were written out. Ṭāher at once admitted defeat[569] and recognized completely the extent of Bu Naṣr's capability. After that, up to the time when he went out with Tāsh Farrāsh as Vizier of Western Persia he never said any more words about the art of secretaryship and did not bring the matter up again. Although this was the situation, my master gave me a message couched in pleasant terms to Ṭāher. I went off and delivered it, and on receiving this, he became refreshed in spirit and happy. After this time, marks of kindness and correspondence passed continuously between the two of them, and they sat and drank wine together. In such matters (i.e. of conciliating people and smoothing down their ruffled feathers), my master was the unique figure of the age, despite his complete self-control and reserved qualities (*enqebāż*). *May God's mercy and His good favour be upon him!* [F 181]

An Account of the History of the Year 422 (/29 December 1030–18 December 1031)

[Gh 148, F 181] This year the opening day of Moḥarram fell on Tuesday [422/29 December 1030]. On this day, Amir Masʿud went from[1] the Pavilion [Gh 149] of the Gate of ʿAbd al-Aʿlā to the Garden in order to take up residence there. Government offices had been set up there in proper fashion, and additional buildings erected there also. When I went there after a year, the entrance vestibule to the palace complex and the platforms had all been refashioned according to this monarch's orders, for he was so knowledgeable about building and construction work that he used to take scant notice of any (professional) architect and builder. Indeed, the New Palace which can be seen in Ghazni is sufficient witness for my words. In Nishapur, at Shādyākh,[2] there was no portal or courtyard, and it was he who designed them all with his own hand, i.e. that beautiful palace with several smaller mansions (*sarāycha-hā*) and courtyards which still exist today. At Bost, at the polo ground[3] of the army encampment (*lashkargāh*) of his father the Amir (i.e. of Maḥmud), he gave orders for several additional new buildings, some of which are still standing today.[4] This king was a marvel in every art; may the God the Exalted One have mercy on his soul![5]

An official letter with the royal signature and seal had gone from Herat by hand of some of Khᵛāja Bu Sahl Zowzani's retainers summoning Khᵛāja Aḥmad b. Ḥasan [Meymandi] back to the royal court; and Janki, the keeper of the fortress, had released him from his bonds.[6] Khᵛāja Aḥmad had then said to the General Eryāruq, the Commander of the Indian Troops (*sālār-e henduyān*), "You have been placed in a bad light, and it would be therefore advisable for you to accompany me to the court and have an audience with the Amir. [F 182] I will say what needs to be said, so that you may come back here with a robe of honour and tokens of beneficence; for affairs have now become settled, a lord as noble-minded and forbearing as Amir Masʿud now sits on the royal throne." Eryāruq swallowed this enticing lie,[7] fell under the spell of this great man and accompanied him to the court. On the way there, he performed numerous acts of service for the Khᵛāja.

There was no-one among the masters of the pen in that age with greater reputation and prestige than he, Aḥmad b. Ḥasan. At his orders, Sarïgh[8] the Royal Wine Steward[9] released the Khᵛāja ʿAbd al-Razzāq, who was the son of the [former] Grand Vizier Aḥmad b. Ḥasan[10] and who had been imprisoned in the fortress of Nandana, and brought him to his father, and his son thanked Sarïgh profusely in the presence of his father, who said that he was even more grateful to him. The Khᵛāja Aḥmad b. Ḥasan, then told Sarïgh, "Go back to Nandana,[11] for that vital frontier post (*thaghr*) cannot be left unattended. When I reach the court, I shall set forth what you have done [Gh 150] and you will receive favour which will increase your rank. Sarïgh went back, and the Grand Vizier travelled to Balkh in a relaxed and unhurried manner. He came into the Amir's court session and offered the marks of service, exhibiting due obeisance and homage. The Amir greeted him warmly and with the utmost civility and spoke many kind words to him. Aḥmad took his formal leave,[12] went back and took up residence in the house that had been prepared for him. He rested for three days and then came to the court.[13]

Bu'l-Fażl Beyhaqi thus relates, that when this eminent figure had rested sufficiently, the matter of the vizierate was put to him through messages, but he remained adamantly non-committal. Bu Sahl Zowzani was [F 183] embroiled in that and was involved in all transactions; he used to oversee all confiscation orders and public contracts, and control all commercial activities; the Amir's private audiences used to be mainly with him and ʿAbdus. These two had been picked out of all the rest, and were on bad terms with each other. The old guard (*pedariyān va maḥmudiyān*) had put up with that situation in order each to save his own skin.[14] I had never seen my master Bu Naṣr so apprehensive and perturbed in mind as I saw him then.

In response to the series of verbal messages sent to him, Aḥmad b. Ḥasan had said to Bu Sahl [Zowzani], "I have become old, and am quite unfitted for this task. Bu Sahl Ḥamdavi is a capable and experienced person;[15] he should be appointed Head of the Army Department, and you should be the Vizier, while I keep a watchful eye over public affairs from a distance and give any necessary pieces of advice." Bu Sahl protested, "I don't have such high expectations from the lord; how can I be the appropriate person for that high office when I am clearly cut out to be only a subordinate?"[16] The Khᵛāja replied, "Heaven forfend! When you came back from Dāmghān to join the Amir, weren't you at the helm at a time when the affairs of the land were still unsettled? At the present moment, when the lord has assumed royal power and affairs of state are running on an even keel, you will be able to carry out the task in an even more satisfactory way." Bu Sahl said, "That held true when the king had no-one at his disposal, but if a master like you came along, how bold and reckless it would be for me and my likes to aspire to such heights of office! In the presence of the sun, how can an insignificant ant aspire to such heights? We are all useless; a real master has come along, and all other persons [F 184] have become inadequate." Aḥmad said, "It would be well if I thought this over," and he returned homewards. Over two or three days, around fifty or sixty verbal messages on this topic went to him, but he was steadfast in his refusal.

One day when he had come to the court and rendered service and was about to leave, the Amir made him sit down and had a private word with him. He said, "Why doesn't the Khᵛāja consent to accept this job? He knows [Gh 151] that he is like a father to us. We are faced with many momentous problems, and he should not withhold his capabilities from us." The Khᵛāja replied, "I am your obedient servant, and I owe my new lease of life—after and with due reference to the decree of what God Most High has decreed for me—to the lord.[17] But I have become old and unfit for work. Moreover, I am under a vow and momentous oaths that I should never again undertake any official post, since I have suffered much on that score."

The Amir said, "We will make provision for your oaths to be expiated; you mustn't prevent us from going through with this appointment." Aḥmad replied, "If there is no way out from accepting this office, and if the exalted judgement sees fit, let me go and install myself in the portico of the Divān, and I can send a verbal message by means of a trusty confidant to the exalted court, and hear the reply. Then at that point, I will act according to the lofty command." The Amir said, "That's a good idea; which trusty confidant do you desire?" Aḥmad replied, "Bu Sahl Zowzani is already involved in the matter, but perhaps it would be a sound idea if Bu Naṣr Moshkān was also engaged in the proceedings, since he is an upright person, and in former times was fully involved in dealing with my messages and correspondence." The Amir said, "That's a very sound course of action."

The Khᵛāja went back and came into the Chancery, and they cleared the audience hall of the public. I heard from Khᵛāja Bu Naṣr Moshkān, who said: I made a move to leave, but he made me sit down and said, "Don't go, you are needed here, since there's a verbal message for the sultan's court. He will not let me go and retire to some desolate corner, seeing that it is time when I should spend my days seeking pardon from the Almighty God rather than acting as a vizier." I retorted, "May the lord's life be long! The best course for the Amir lies in this view which he has expressed, and it is also very welcome to us servants, but the lord will find it painful and trying. Many difficult problems lie ahead, and these cannot be resolved [F 185] except with the Khᵛāja's far-sighted and clear judgement." He said, "It's just as you say, but I can see here a surfeit of viziers already, a point that I know is not lost upon you."[18] I said, "Things are as you say, but one can only obey orders." Then I added, "What's my particular role in all this? Bu Sahl will suffice for it. I am at the end of my tether because of him and have to use all my ingenuity to keep my head above water." Aḥmad said, "Don't dwell upon and worry about this matter; I have complete trust in you." I took my formal leave.

Bu Sahl came in, bearing a verbal message from the Amir in these terms, "The lord Sultan says, 'In the time of my father, the Khᵛāja suffered many an injury and torment, and incurred much blame. It is a marvel that they left him alive; his remaining alive has been so that he could be the adornment of our age. He must consent to take up office, for it needs someone of his calibre. [Gh 152] There will be assistants (or "apprentices,"*shāgerdān*) and aides (i.e. in the Divān), all of whom will work under your command, so that affairs may settle down and run in an orderly fashion'."

The Khᵛāja replied, "I had made a solemn vow not to accept any courtly office, but since it is the lord who is giving a command and is saying that he will make expiation for breaking the oaths, I will therefore consent. However, there are conditions incumbent upon this office. If I request these conditions in their entirety, and the lord ordains their acceptance,[19] all at once the whole of these office holders and court servants will rise up against me and become hostile, and they will indulge in the same games they used to play in the late Amir's time, and I shall once again find myself in great peril; whereas at the present time, I have no enemies and live a carefree existence. But if I do not insist upon the conditions and do not see them through, I shall have committed an act of betrayal and will be accused of weakness and impotence, and will not be forgiven either by the Almighty God or by the lord. [F 186] If, in the event, I must unavoidably assume this office, I desire acceptance of my conditions for this position in their entirety. If this is acceptable and I find myself invested with these powers, I shall bring to bear whatever is necessary by way of good counsel and sincere advice."[20]

The two of us went off so that these words could be conveyed to the Amir. I said to Bu Sahl, "Since you are acting as intermediary, what's the use of my coming along?" He replied, "The Khᵛāja Aḥmad b. Ḥasan has asked for you; it may be that he has no confidence in me," and he was most annoyed by my involvement in all this. When we came into the royal presence, I held back out of politeness, wishing Bu Sahl to speak. When he started to speak, the Amir turned towards me and asked me to speak instead. Bu Sahl was highly discomfited. I conveyed the verbal message in its entirety. The Amir said, "I shall entrust all affairs to him except for arranging convivial sessions of wine-drinking,[21] polo-playing and contests of equestrian skill.[22] All other spheres of activity fall upon his shoulders, and there will be no criticism or objection raised against his judgement and opinions." I went back and conveyed the answer. Bu Sahl had been very put out, though I did my utmost to defer to him. But what could I do? For neither the Amir nor the Khᵛāja were prepared to do without me. Aḥmad, son of Ḥasan, replied to the Amir, "I will obey the order, and will look into the matter and write out a contractual agreement (*movāżaʿa*)[23] so that it may be submitted tomorrow for the exalted judgement—*may God increase him in loftiness*—and answers made to its stipulations in the lord Sultan's own handwriting, that it may be made firm with the royal seal and signature, and that this arrangement be adhered to just as it was in the time of the late Amir, for you,Bu Naṣr, must well remember how it was done in those days." [Gh 153]

We went off and conveyed the words. The Amir said, "Well done! Tomorrow, these tasks must be completed so that, the day afterwards, he may garb himself in a robe of honour." We replied, "We will inform him," and went away. He called out to me, Bu Naṣr, and said, "When the Khᵛāja comes back here, you should also come, for [F 187] I have something to tell you." I obeyed and then went into the Khᵛāja's presence and recounted [the Amir's words] to him. Bu Sahl went back, and the Khᵛāja and myself remained behind. I said, "May the lord's life be long! I was speaking with Bu Sahl on the way, the first time we brought a message, and I said, "Since you are the intermediary, what is my function?" He replied, "The Khᵛāja has asked for you, since it would appear that he has no faith in me." Aḥmad said, "I asked for you because I sought an upright and God-fearing person for my entourage, one who would not tell lies or pervert words and who would know what to do. This wretched fellow[24] and others imagine that, if I undertake this office, they can still carry on acting as so many viziers by stealth. The first thing I shall do is to squeeze the noose round his neck so that he will squirm in agony and give up playing the vizier for good, and the others will follow suit. I know that he will not be able to last like this and will land in trouble, for this lord has allowed many base hangers-on[25] to secure positions round his throne and has made them emboldened, but I shall do whatever is necessary through good counsel and sound advice, and I'll see what happens."

He went back, and I went into the Amir's presence. He asked, "What will the Khᵛāja set down?" I replied, "The custom has become established that when the vizierate is given to a distinguished person, that vizier writes out a contractual agreement and seeks the conditions for his office, and the lord writes out, in his own hand, the answer to that. Then he affixes his seal and signature to the answer and finally he invokes the name of God Most High that He will hold the vizier to observe the terms. There should then be a written oath of office (*sowgand-nāma*), with all the conditions set out, and the vizier enunciates them orally and pledges in his own handwriting underneath that he will act according to their terms." He said, "You must therefore prepare the document containing those things which we must write down as answer to the contractual agreement, as well as the document containing the oath, so that tomorrow this matter may be completed and, on the day after the Khᵛāja can don the robe of honour, for as things stand, all the affairs of the state are being held up."[26] I replied, "I'll do this." I went back, and these documents were drawn up. [F 188] At the time of the afternoon worship, the Amir perused them in private and informed himself fully about their contents and was pleased with them.

The next day, Khᵛāja Aḥmad b. Ḥasan came to the court and after the public audience ended, he came into the open portico (*ṭāram*) and ordered it to be cleared of the public and sat down. Bu Sahl and Bu Naṣr brought the Khᵛāja's contractual agreement into the Sultan's presence.[27] The Amir sent for an inkstand and paper, and he wrote his answer, in his own hand, to each clause of the agreement one by one. He affixed his seal and signature, and swore an oath to uphold it. [Gh 154] The document was then brought to the Khᵛāja, and when he had read the answers he rose to his feet, kissed the ground, went before the throne, kissed the Amir's hand, went back to his place and sat down. Bu Sahl and Bu Naṣr brought forward the formal oath of office. The Khᵛāja read it out loud and wrote his own signature on it. He called Bu Naṣr and Bu Sahl to bear witness to it. At the completion of that document with the oath, the Amir spoke kind words to the Khᵛāja and gave promises of favour. The Khᵛāja kissed the ground. Then the Amir said, "You should go back home, for tomorrow the robe of honour will be conferred. At the moment, all the affairs of the state are at a standstill and we have many an important matter in hand, and they all need to be dealt with." The Khᵛāja replied, "I'll obey the command," and he kissed the ground and returned to his house.[28] The contractual agreement was borne away with him and the formal oath of office was put in the Archive of the Chancery (*davāt-khāna*).[29] I have set forth the text of the document with the oath and the text of that contractual agreement in the account of the exploits of Sultan Maḥmud (*maqāmāt-e maḥmudi*) which I have put together, the *Ketāb-e Maqāmāt*, and in order to avoid prolixity I have not repeated them here.[30]

It became clear to all that the matter of the vizierate was now settled, and the fact that a person of such eminence was now at the helm reassured them. All those individuals from whom the Khᵛāja had suffered injuries in the past were now thrown into a panic. Meanwhile, Bu Sahl Zowzani became puffed up in a most alarming way and he was pretending to the people that this office of the vizierate had been offered to him but he had turned it down, and [F 189] that it was he who had secured the Khᵛāja's appointment. However, those persons who had any wisdom and sense knew better than to believe him and recognized that Sultan Masʿud was too discerning, of loftier stature and too percipient than to have given the vizierate to someone else while Khᵛāja Aḥmad was alive, for he had a good measure of everyone's stature and capabilities. The clear proof of what I have said is the fact that, when Khᵛāja Aḥmad b. Ḥasan passed away at Herat, the Amir would survey this group, would recall to mind Khᵛāja Aḥmad b. ʿAbd al-Ṣamad and would say that there was no-one more suitable for the office than he. When I reach this relevant point in the History, I shall set forth this matter in full detail.[31] I do not say this because I have suffered much at the hands of Bu Sahl; for Bu Sahl and his ilk have all passed on, and it is evident to me how much time I have left in this world. But I am setting forth the truth, and I well know that wise men and those people who have experience of the world, and who read this today, will not find fault with me for what I have written. For I consider my writing as my direct responsibility which I intend to perform to the full. *May the Exalted God protect me and all the Muslims from errors and lapses, through His bounty and grace and the breadth of His mercy!* [Gh 155]

The next day, this being Sunday, 4 Ṣafar of this year [422/31 January 1031],[32] Khᵛāja Aḥmad b. Ḥasan came to the court and into the royal presence. The leading figures, the civilian notables, the field officers (*sarhang*s), the retainers and courtiers came in after him and performed the requisite rites of service. The Amir turned towards the Vizier and said, "You must don the robe of honour appropriate for the vizierate, for we have many tasks before us. It must [F 190] be recognized that the Vizier is our deputy in everything which appertains to the welfare of the realm, and his commands and instructions are valid in all matters, and no-one is to raise any objections to what he deems advisable." The Vizier kissed the ground and said, "I am obedient to the lord's command." The Amir made a sign to the General Bilgetegin, who was the head of the chamberlains (*moqaddam-e ḥājebān*), to conduct the Vizier to the Royal Wardrobe. He stepped forward and took the Vizier by the arm. The Vizier arose and went to the Royal Wardrobe, and until near the mid-morning, he remained there until the moment when the astrologer[33] deemed the time auspicious for donning the robe of honour. All the retainers and courtiers went back to their places,[34] whether they were seated or on foot, and the Vizier donned the robe of honour—I was there myself, standing and watching the spectacle, and what I am now saying is therefore based on direct observation and from my notes[35] and my diary[36]—there was a coat of fine, gold-threaded silken cloth of Baghdad,[37] the whitest of white in colour, displaying its very delicate and fine pattern; a large turban of fine Egyptian muslin, but extremely delicate and precious and with a very slender and long, laced[38] *ṭerāz* band; and a belt studded with a thousand methqāls of turquoises.[39]

The Ḥājeb Bilgetegin was seated at the door of the Royal Wardrobe. When the Vizier came forth, he rose to his feet and expressed his congratulations, and he placed in the Vizier's hands a sum of dinars and a cloth together with two very large turquoise stones set in a ring. He began to go in front of the Vizier. The Vizier said, "By the Sultan's head, I beseech you to walk along with me as an equal, and tell the other chamberlains to go in front." Bilgetegin said, "The Grand Vizier shouldn't say such things to me, since he knows of my friendship and, moreover, he has donned the lord Sultan's robe of honour, and we servants must observe the dignity and precedence of that," and he went in front of the Vizier accompanied by two other chamberlains and a numerous body of the holders of court offices. They also designated one of the Vizier's gholāms as a chamberlain and he was clad in a coloured coat, since it is not the custom for a chamberlain of viziers to go in front of them dressed in black.

When [F 191] he reached the midst of the palace, other chamberlains came forward to meet him, [Gh 156] conducted him before the Amir and sat him down. The Amir said, "May it be a blessed occasion for the Vizier!" The Vizier rose to his feet, kissed the ground and went up to the throne, and placed a bejewelled collar in the Amir's hands; it was said to be worth 10,000 dinars. Amir Mas'ud placed in the Vizier's hand a turquoise seal ring, with the Amir's name engraved on it, and said, "This is the signet of our realm, and we have bestowed it on you so that it becomes firmly established that the Vizier's decrees come next in validity to our own commands." The Vizier took it, kissed the Amir's hand and the ground, and returned home. He was accompanied by a vast retinue, the like of which no person could recall, so that there was no-one left at the Sultan's court except those on regular duty there (*nowbatiyān*).

He came out by the Gate of ʿAbd al-Aʿlā and went to his house. Visitors of eminence and high-ranking officials began arriving, eager to ingratiate themselves—some out of a genuine, heartfelt desire and others out of fear—and brought with them so many gifts of slave boys, offerings of money and clothing, the like of which had never previously been witnessed for any vizier. They were drawing up a list of what they had brought so that the whole lot could be presented to the Sultan; thus the Vizier did not retain an iota[40] for himself; for they had learnt and been instructed in such things by him, who was the most refined and illustrious figure[41] of the age. He sat there until the time of the midday worship, only getting up to perform his prayers. It was a magnificently memorable day.

The next day, he came to the court (i.e. as Grand Vizier), but not in his robe of honour, for he was wearing, in the manner of former times, a coat and a Nishapuri or Qāyeni turban,[42] clothes which this master had been seen wearing in the past. I heard from his trusted confidants, including Bu Ebrāhim Qāyeni, who was his counsellor and adjutant, and others, that he had twenty or thirty coats, all of one and the same colour, which he used to wear over the year, and people used to conclude from this that there was just one coat and would say, [F 192] "Good gracious! Doesn't this coat ever wear out? Behold, what an awe-inspiring and upright figure!" And indeed, his manly virtues and endeavours were boundless—as I shall set forth subsequently in its proper place—and at the end of the year, a further twenty or thirty coats were made and delivered to his wardrobe.[43]

On this particular day, when he came to render service and the court broke up, Sultan Masʿud went into a private session with the Vizier, a session which went on till the time of the midday worship. Certain people were haunted with fear and were plotting and spreading rumours,[44] which became all too evident later; not that I nor others beside me were privy to [Gh 157] what went on in that session, but when changes began to appear in that some people were rewarded with official posts and given robes of honour, while others were deprived of office, denounced and disgraced, and matters came out into the open, wise people realized that it was all the outcome of that single private session.

When they beat the barrel-shaped drum at court at the time of the midday prayer, the Vizier came out, his horse was summoned[45] and he went back. All this day, till nightfall, those who felt apprehensive about their prospects were coming and making offerings of money. The Vizier summoned the two persons, [first] the secretary Bu Moḥammad Qāyeni, who was one of his personal secretaries and who, during the time of Aḥmad b. Ḥasan's tribulations, served as a secretary to Khᵛāja Abu'l-Qāsem b. Kathir, at Amir Maḥmud's behest, and had later been employed in Ḥasanak's Divān, and [second] the secretary Ebrāhim Beyhaqi, who used to be in our Divān. He said, "Secretaries must necessarily obey orders, and I have the same confidence in you as I had before.[46] You must come to the Divān tomorrow and get busy with secretarial work, and bring along the assistants and copy clerks (*shāgerdān va moḥarrerān*)." They replied, "We obey your command."

The secretary Bu Naṣr Bosti, who is still alive at the present time [F 193] and who is a sound and upright man, with a good knowledge of secretarial skills and a fine calligraphic hand, had been loyal to the Vizier when he was in India and shown concern for him during the latter's time of tribulation and detention, and he accompanied him to Balkh after his release. The Vizier now showed favour to him and ordered him to be given an important post; he went to be a collector of taxation,[47] and amassed a great fortune. (Bu Moḥammad and Ebrāhim are both deceased, may God grant them forgiveness, but Bu Naṣr is still alive, and has remained at Ghazni in the service of the Ghaznavid house; in the time of the vizierate of the Khᵛāja 'Abd al-Razzāq, may he long remain in his official status, he was his Head of the Chancery.) The Vizier also showed favour to Bu 'Abdallāh Pārsi, and the latter used to be busy with all the items of business which came before the Vizier.[48] In the time of the Khᵛāja's vizierate (i.e. his first vizierate, for Maḥmud), this Bu 'Abdallāh was postmaster and intelligence officer at Balkh, and enjoyed an eminent status, but suffered greatly during the period of the Khᵛāja's tribulation. Amirak[49] Beyhaqi, at the time of the Khᵛāja's dismissal, went forth from Ghaznin under a sealed document of committal,[50] as I have related, and they exacted a great deal of money from him. [Gh 158]

The next day, Tuesday, the Khᵛāja came to the court, had an audience with the Amir and then came to the Divān. A prayer-rug of turquoise-coloured satin brocade, had been spread out near his usual prominent place.[51] He performed two *rakʿats* of the worship and then sat down away from the forefront of the Divān. He sent for an ink-stand, which they set down, and also for a quire of paper and a small casket,[52] of the kind that they bring along and set down for viziers. He set to work and wrote there: "*In the name of God, the Merciful, the Compassionate. Praise be to God the lord of the worlds, and blessings upon His Messenger, the Chosen One, Moḥammad, and all his house. God is my sufficiency, and how excellent a guardian is He!*[53] *O God, help me to do what You desire and what is pleasing to You, through Your mercy, O most merciful of those who show mercy! Let there be given out to the poor and destitute, by way of thanks to God, the Lord of the Two Worlds, 10,000 dirhams of silver coinage, 10,000 dirhams' worth of bread, 5,000 dirhams' worth of meat and 10,000 cubits' lengths of fine cotton cloth.*" Those instructions were passed to the Keeper of the Records and Archives,[54] and the Vizier immediately authorised their issue. He then said, "Let those with complaints of acts of oppression and grievances, and those with requests and petitions, be summoned." Several persons were brought forward [F 194], and he listened to their stories and meted out justice, and then sent them back contented, saying, "The sessions of the Divān and the door of the palace are open, there are no barriers or impediments and every person who seeks redress must come forward." People offered up profuse prayers for him and took hope.

The accounting officials and the secretaries had come in and had sat down, following strict rules of decorum, some at one side, some at the other. He turned towards them and said, "Tomorrow you must come prepared in such a way that you will be able to answer whatever I put to you and not try to shift responsibility on to someone else. Up to now, affairs have been conducted in a very unsatisfactory manner. Each person has been occupied with his own personal concerns and the Sultan's affairs have been neglected. I, Aḥmad b. Ḥasan, know you all well and will not put up with the way things have been done up to now. You must change your ways[55] and each person should apply himself to his task." No-one breathed a word, and all of them were filled with fear and remained petrified. The Vizier arose and went home.

That day, until nightfall, they were bringing in more offerings and presents for the Vizier. At the time of the afternoon worship, he sent for the inventory lists and checked them with what the Sultan's treasurers and the court financial inspectors (*moshrefān-e dargāh*) had set down, and these were submitted to the Amir according to their various categories. They comprised limitless wealth, made up of both gold and silver objects; uncut pieces of clothing; valuable Turkish slave boys; horses and camels of high value; [Gh 159] and everything which would be of a splendour and lavishness fit for kings no matter how grand. The Amir was very favourably impressed by all this and said, "The Vizier is not a rich man; why doesn't he take these back?", and he ordered that ʿAbdus should present to him 10,000 dinars, 500,000 dirhams, ten valuable Turkish slave boys, five riding horses from the royal stables, two finely-caparisoned mules and ten camels. When ʿAbdus reached the Vizier's house with those handsome presents, [F 195], the Vizier arose, kissed the ground and offered up profuse prayers for the Sultan. ʿAbdus then went back.

The next day, Wednesday, 7 Ṣafar [422/3 February 1031],[56] the Vizier came to the court. The Amir held a session for hearing grievances and petitions; it was a most august occasion, with much dignity and splendour. When the court session was over, the Vizier came to the Divān, took up his work and set about handling affairs in his own inimitable way. When it was mid-morning, he summoned Bu Naṣr Moshkān, and the latter came to the Divān. He handed over to Bu Naṣr a confidential verbal message for the Amir, to the effect that "The administration of military affairs (*shoghl-e ʿarż*) is in a parlous state, as I have already informed the lord. Bu Sahl Zowzani has the suitable stature and has achieved prominence. If the exalted judgement sees fit, the lord should summon him and order him to be given a robe of honour with the aim of his taking over this office, since this is the most vital of charges. I will bring to bear everything I know by way of guidance and assistance, so that the affairs of the army may run in an orderly fashion." Bu Naṣr went away and delivered the message.

The Amir made a sign to Bu Sahl, who was seated with the Sultan's boon companions in the court chamber, that he was to come forward, and he said a few words to him. Bu Sahl kissed the ground and left the court chamber. Two chamberlains, one from the internal palace household establishment and the other from the outside service,[57] conducted him to the Royal Wardrobe. They dressed him in a very splendid robe of honour and a belt made with 700 methqāls of gold, all of which had been made in the course of the night. Bu Sahl came in and rendered service. The Amir said, "May it be a blessed occasion! You must go along to the Vizier and act according to his instructions; and you should pay close attention to the matter of the army, since it is the most important of all affairs." Bu Sahl replied, "I will carry out these instructions." He kissed the ground and went back, and at once came to the Vizier's Divān. The Vizier made him sit down immediately below himself, and said many encouraging and laudatory words to him. Bu Sahl went homewards. All the great men, courtiers and retainers went along to his house, paid their due respects in an enthusiastic manner and brought along limitless offerings of money. He, too, ordered that the whole of what they had brought should be recorded in a list and he sent it all to the treasury. [F 196]

The next day, a very fine robe of honour was bestowed on Bu Sahl Ḥamdavi, who had been removed from the vizierate,[58] for his new appointment to the Office of the Oversight of the Realm,[59] in such a way that the four persons who had previously been in charge of this office of the Oversight of the Realm [Gh 160] were to become his assistants, together with all the *moshrefs* at court. He came before the Amir and rendered obeisance. The Amir said, "You deserve much for your long service, and have shown great loyalty and done many deeds in our dynasty's cause. You must perform your duties in this office to the full." Bu Sahl Ḥamdavi replied, "I obey your command," and he returned and went along to the Divān. The Vizier set him down on his left hand with great decorum and spoke with him in very cordial terms. Presents were lavished on him too, and he sent along to the treasury what they had brought.

Affairs in the Divāns were now on an even course, and the prestige of the Vizier's Divān was at such a high level that no-one could recall its like in the past, and the Amir bestowed full authority on it. From the outset, the Vizier began settling old scores and quietly uttering fulminations,[60] and he was secretly inveighing against such eminent figures as Bu'l-Qāsem b. Kathir, who had been dismissed from the office of Head of the Army Department, and Bu Bakr Ḥaṣiri and Bu'l-Ḥasan ʿAqili, who belonged to the circle of boon companions at the court. They had in the past stirred up trouble, as I have already related in this History. Regarding Ḥaṣiri, he was something of a bully and, in the time of Amir Maḥmud, he had taken this present monarch Masʿud's side and had bellowed drunkenly in his support in a wine-drinking session and had twice received a beating.[61] As for Bu'l-Qāsem b. Kathir, he had himself been a vizier for a time,[62] and Bu'l-Ḥasan had purchased Aḥmad b. Ḥasan's slave boy.[63] I shall relate later what happened to each of them.

On Sunday, 11 Ṣafar [422/17 February 1031], a very grand and splendid robe of honour had been made ready for the Great Chamberlain Bilgetegin, together with large kettledrums (*kus*),[64] broad standards,[65] a crescent finial for the pole of the standards (*monjuq*),[66] gholāms, [F 197] purses filled with dirhams, strips of uncut cloth for robes and other items similar to those bestowed upon the Great Chamberlain ʿAli Qarib at the gates of Gorgān.[67] When the court dispersed, the Amir ordered them to take the Great Chamberlain Bilgetegin along to the Royal Wardrobe and garb him in the robe of honour, while the large kettledrums, mounted on camels, and the standards, were held at the gate of the palace, and the finial for the pole of the standard, the gholāms, the purses filled with silver and the rolls of cloth were stationed and displayed in the midst of the garden. He came forward with the robe of honour, i.e. a black coat, a two-pointed hat and a golden belt, and proceeded to the elevated structure (*khażrā*) and made the appropriate acts of service. The Amir vouchsafed to him signs of favour. He went back and came into the Vizier's Divān. The Vizier addressed him in very cordial terms. He returned to his house, and the prominent persons and notables lavished presents upon him. The office of Great Chamberlain likewise became firmly established in this eminent figure. He was a man [Gh 161] of a courageous nature, hospitable and chivalrous to an extent rarely seen, but he was also a man ruled by a very short temper and an impetuosity which was generally deemed unbecoming. But no man is without faults; *perfection belongs [only] to the Almighty God.*

A remarkable occurrence befell the religious lawyer Bu Bakr Ḥaṣiri in these days. He committed an offence while he was in a drunken state, thereby giving the Vizier the opportunity to get his hands on him and exact the revenge that he had coveted, and although the Amir brought some relief in his magnanimous, regal way, the man lost all dignity at the time. I have necessarily to relate this so that the whole story may be known; *there is no turning aside of the Almighty God's decree.*[68]

It so happened that Ḥaṣiri, together with his son Bu'l-Qāsem, had gone out into the countryside, to the garden of Khᵛāja ʿAli Mikāli, which was close by. They had drunk vast amounts of wine, had stayed there for the night and then had further drunk morning draughts—this latter practice being a reprehensible one, in which wise men rarely indulge—and had kept on drinking between the two times of worship (i.e. between the dawn and the midday ones). [F 198] Then they had ridden off, still quaffing away, and made their way along the Street of the Devotees (*kuy-e ʿobbād*). When they drew near the Market of the Lovers (*bāzār-e ʿāsheqān*),[69] with the father in a litter on a mule and his son on horseback, accompanied by thirty gholāms, by chance one of the personal retainers of the Khᵛāja came towards them on horseback. The way was narrow and there was great congestion from people passing along. Ḥaṣiri was beset by a wild thought in his drunken state of delirium: why did not this horseman dismount, and why did he not show him proper respect? He swore at him most offensively. The man replied, "O royal boon-companion, what's the meaning of your abusing me? I likewise have a lord, one greater than you and your likes, and that lord is the Grand Vizier." Ḥaṣiri spoke insultingly of the Vizier and said, "Seize this dog, and see if anyone will be bold enough to come to his rescue!", and he insulted the Vizier in even more robust terms. Ḥaṣiri's gholāms fell on the man, gave him several powerful blows on the back of the head and his coat was torn to pieces. His son Bu'l-Qāsem shouted to the gholāms to desist, for he was alert and attentive to the consequences of actions and was a man of great wisdom. (This is borne out by the fact that, at the present time, he has found such an excellent vocation for himself: having made the Pilgrimage, he has left official service [Gh 162] and has chosen to retire to a corner[70] and is immersed in devotional practices and charitable works. May this master and good friend enjoy a long life!) He made profuse apologies to this man and begged him not to tell his master about the affair, since he personally would make up for this the next day, and in compensation for a single coat torn to pieces, he would hand over to him three. Then they departed.

The man stood and pondered for a while but could not keep the matter to himself, since it is the way of mercenary retainers [F 199] and paid lackeys[71] to blow up such incidents regardless of the consequences. This happened on Thursday, 15 Ṣafar [422/11 February 1031].

He hastened along to Khᵛāja Aḥmad's presence and reported the incident, producing a highly inflated account[72] and parading his bruised head and face and torn coat. This was just what the Vizier wanted, since he sought a pretext to chastise and harm Ḥaṣiri, knowing that this was an opportune moment and that, having just the previous day bestowed on him the robe of honour for the vizierate, the Amir was hardly likely to take Ḥaṣiri's side against him today. He was determined to strike while the iron was hot.[73]

The next day, the Amir desired to go on a hunting expedition in the direction of Mikhᵛārān, and they had brought outside the town the camp enclosure and all the cooking utensils, their store of wine and its appurtenances (*sharāb-khāna*) and other items. The next day, the Vizier did not ride forth but wrote a note in his own hand and under his seal and sent it to the [General] Bilgetegin. He conveyed the message that, "If the Amir asks why Aḥmad has not come, you are to place this note in his hand. If he doesn't ask, you are still to give it to him since it's an important matter, and there should be no delay in delivering it." Bilgetegin replied, "I will undertake to do this"; the two were very close to each other.

The Amir did not hold court since he intended to ride forth. The standard and the ceremonial parasol[74] had been brought out, and many gholāms on horses were standing by. There was a call for the she-elephant with her howdah to be brought forth. This was done, the Amir mounted into the howdah and the elephant was driven forward. All the great men of state stood there on foot, ready to render service, and when he appeared, they gave the appropriate obeisance. The Amir reached the gate of the open portico; and when he did not see Khᵛāja Aḥmad, he enquired, "Hasn't the Vizier come?" Bu Naṣr Moshkān replied that it was Friday, and he would have known that the lord intended to go hunting; he had probably not come for that reason. The Ḥājeb Bilgetegin proffered the note, saying that at dawn the Vizier had sent round this note and had told him: [F 200] "Whether the lord asks or doesn't ask why Aḥmad [Gh 163] hasn't come, the note must be conveyed." The Amir took the note, the elephant was held back, and he read it.

He had written, "May the lord's life be long! I did maintain that I was not suited to be a vizier because they wouldn't allow me to perform my task, for they all have inflated illusions of their own and I did not have the strength, in my old age and having just escaped from one calamity, to embark upon further strife with people and turn the world into my enemy. However, since the lord, with his lofty utterances, had high hopes and bestowed regal provisions, and since, after the grace of God Most High, it was to the lord that I owed my life, the exalted command had perforce to be complied with. And yet before ten days have passed, Ḥaṣiri has already nipped this in the bud. Ḥaṣiri was coming back from the garden in a litter, having drunk wine to the lees, and in the Saʿidi market[75] and not in a secluded spot but in the full view of the public, he ordered his gholams to give a trusty retainer of mine a thorough thrashing and they tore his coat to shreds; and when he had declared 'I am Aḥmad's retainer,' Ḥaṣiri had heaped a hundred thousand curses on Aḥmad. In no circumstances will I come to the court after this, and I won't function as vizier, since the contempt and insults of folk like these are more than I can bear. If the exalted judgement could see fit, I could be released from this post so that I could take up residence in a *rebāṭ* or in any fortress which the exalted judgement thinks appropriate. But if he does not grant me release, let him ordain punishment for Ḥaṣiri so that the injurious effects of that affect his wealth and his own person, for he has become too cocksure and arrogant, and the great wealth that he and his son have amassed induces them to act above their station. I can get from father and son 300,000 dinars for the exalted treasury.[76] This note, written in my own hand, is an undertaking binding upon me to do this. Farewell!"

When the Amir read the note, he folded it up and gave it to one of the gholāms of his household who was the keeper of the archives and records, saying, "Keep this safe," and then he urged the elephant onwards. Everyone was saying, "What's going to happen? What will be the outcome of this?" [F 201] While still in the open country, he gave instructions that the Commander-in-Chief Ghāzi, the Commander (*sālār*) in India, Eryāruq, and other notables should go back since they had not been ordered to go out with the hunting party, and he himself was going off with his personal retainers only. Then he summoned the Great Chamberlain Bilgetegin to approach the elephant, and he spoke several sentences to him in Turkish.[77] Bilgetegin then went back.

The Amir summoned Bu Naṣr Moshkān, and a troop commander (*naqib*) hurried off. Bu Naṣr was in the Divān. The envoy said, "The lord is summoning you." Bu Naṣr mounted [Gh 164] and hurried off.

He reached the Amir, and spent a while there. They spoke together for some time and then the Amir sent him back again. He did not return to the Divān but proceeded to the Grand Vizier Aḥmad's house. Bu Naṣr sent back Bu Manṣur the Guard of the Divān[78] with an order that the secretaries were to go home, and we did so.

I followed my master's steps up to the residence of the Grand Vizier, and I witnessed a tumult and a throng of onlookers. I asked someone, "What's happening here?" He answered, "The governor of the town[79] brought along Bu Bakr Ḥaṣiri and his son, without robe and boots,[80] to the Vizier's house and held them fast there. Two posts for punishment[81] were brought; no-one knows what it's all about."

A considerable number of prominent persons had come to render service and were stationed there mounted on their horses, since it was Friday; but no-one was allowed access except for Khᵛāja Bu Naṣr Moshkān, who came and went in. I myself, Bu'l-Fażl, was highly perturbed when I heard the news, for that master Ḥaṣiri and his son had done me many favours. I dismounted and joined the people outside, and remained there[82] till it was almost noon. Then they brought in an inkstand and paper, and I heard this much of what Bu ʿAbdallāh Pārsi spoke publicly, to the effect that "The Grand Vizier [F 202] says, although the lord Sultan ordained that you and your son should each get a thousand strokes, I have had mercy on you and have spared you the rod, but you must pay 500,000 dinars to buy back the imposed corporal punishment; if not, the order is to go ahead with all despatch. Do not tarry lest you suffer both the beatings and paying the money." Father and son both said, "We'll obey whatever he ordains but we request him to be lenient with us, for he knows that we cannot afford one-tenth of this." Bu ʿAbdallāh went back and forth (i.e. with messages) until they settled on the figure of 300,000 dinars, and they gave a written undertaking for this. The order was issued that they were to be taken to the police guardhouse. The town governor took them along to the police guardhouse and had them incarcerated there, and the crowd dispersed. My master Bu Naṣr remained at the Vizier's house drinking wine, and I returned home.

After an hour, the head of the palace household Sengüy[83] came up to me and said, "Khᵛāja Bu Naṣr has sent me and has given the verbal message that you, Bu'l-Fażl, are to go and attend the lord Sultan and convey the message to him that, acting upon your orders, I, Bu Naṣr, went to the Vizier's residence [Gh 165] and, in accordance with the lofty command, poured water on the flame (i.e. assuaged Khᵛāja Aḥmad's wrath), so that Ḥaṣiri and his son did not get a beating; 300,000 dinars were taken on a written bond and they were then brought into custody. The Grand Vizier was greatly cheered and heartened by what the lord had decreed and these fresh favours bestowed on him, and he kept me back to drink some wine. It would have been imprudent of me not to have accepted, and this was the reason for my not coming personally and my sending Bu'l-Fażl—this so that lack of manners and failure to recognize due rights of service should not be imputed to me."

I went off immediately and found the Amir on [F 203] the edge of the town, installed in a garden, busy with merry-making and wine-drinking, with his boon-companions sitting there, while singers and musicians were playing. I said to myself, "This message must be written down and then, if I don't get the chance to speak, he can peruse it himself, and the required aim will be achieved." So I then wrote out a note giving a complete account and went forward. The Amir called out, "What is it?" I replied, "The servant Bu Naṣr has sent a message," and I showed him the note. He told the keeper of the royal inkstand to take it. He took it and gave it to the Amir. When he had read it, I was summoned to the Sultan's travelling throne (*takht-e ravān*).[84] He gave me back the note, saying to me *sotto voce*, "Go back to Bu Naṣr and tell him, 'Things have gone well, and we are full of praises for what you did. When we get back the day after tomorrow, we will give orders for what remains to be done. You did well not to return here but to remain with the Vizier to keep him company while he indulged in wine-drinking.'"

I returned and reached the town at the time of the afternoon worship, and sent for Sengüy. On a piece of paper I wrote, "I went and fulfilled my mission." Sengüy took it and gave it to my master, who perused it. Bu Naṣr remained with the Vizier till the time of the night worship and came back very drunk. Next day, towards dawn, he summoned me. I went along and found him seated by himself. He said, "How did it go?" I recounted to him everything. He said, "Things went well," and then went on, "This Vizier means business; he will wreak his vengeance and destroy[85] his enemies.[86] But this great monarch, like a good shepherd, is cognisant of his subjects' rights and dues. When he read the Vizier's letter, he had to give him succour, for it would have been unfitting to appoint a minister and, in the same week, consent to his humiliation. He acted in a regal manner[87] and instructed the Great Chamberlain to go to the court and [F 204] issue an order to the town governor that he should take Ḥaṣiri and his son along to the Vizier's palace, together with a flogging-master (*jallād*) and the set of two poles for erecting a flogging-frame, and give each of them a thousand blows with the aim that, after this, no-one should have the temerity to mention the Vizier's name [Gh 166] except favourably. But having issued such an awesome command, and although Ḥaṣiri had committed a grave offence, he did not wish his honour and status to be destroyed totally, and someone was sent in haste to summon me. When I came to the Sultan, he said in the presence of the assembled courtiers, 'You didn't wish to come and pay us a visit?'[88] I replied, 'My happiness lies in rendering service to the lord, but the lord commanded me to attend to several important letters for Ray and those surrounding regions, and said, 'You don't need to come, just send the duty secretary'. He laughed, and on all occasions he was a fount of sweetness and wit. He said, 'I do indeed remember that, and I was just jesting.' He went on to say, 'There are some other points that should be written down in those letters. I thought I would put them to you in person rather than through a message,' and he ordered the elephant to be held firm. The elephant keeper (*pilbān*) came down from the elephant's neck, as well as the mahout's assistant and a gholām of the royal guard who was with the Sultan in the howdah. He signalled that he wanted a private talk, and the various people in attendance withdrew to a distance. I stood by the howdah.

"The Sultan first spoke to me about the Vizier's note[89] and said, 'The Great Chamberlain went off to placate the Vizier, and I gave such an order since *raison d'état* necessitated this for that offence which Ḥaṣiri had committed, so that the Vizier would not be disheartened. However, I am indebted to Ḥaṣiri in a way that I am not indebted to any other of my father's boon-companions, and he has suffered much distress in my cause. On no account do I wish to give the Vizier a free hand [F 205] to destroy retainers like these through his vindictiveness. I have given you the task to redress the balance. Keep what I have said to yourself and salvage this situation, if need be by recourse to our direct command or on your own initiative, so that no harm comes to Ḥaṣiri or his son, for we have told the Great Chamberlain in Turkish[90] to keep them both intimidated and apprehensive but to take no further action until you arrive and quell this blaze.' I said, 'I understand, and whatever needs to be done in this matter shall be done,' and I returned in haste. The situation was as you saw, and I told the Great Chamberlain, 'There must be a delay in implementing the exalted command until I am able to see the Grand Vizier.' I told Ḥaṣiri, 'Shame upon you, old man! Every once in a while you have to do something to disgrace yourself [Gh 167] and give your friends a new cause for concern!'" He replied, 'It's no time for reproaches. It was Fate that did it. We must find a way out.'

"Then I was summoned, and straightaway I was given access. On the way, I saw Bu'l-Faraj-e Bosti[91] dressed in threadbare garments and with a water skin on his shoulder. He stopped me and said, 'For nearly twenty days I have been consigned to the stables and to watering the riding beasts; intercede for me, for I know that the Grand Vizier's heart has become hardened,[92] and without your putting in a word for me, things won't come right.' I told him, 'I'm on an important errand just now. When that has been settled, I will do my best for you, and I'm hopeful of success.' When I reached the Vizier, I found him in a state of great rage and irritation. I made the customary acts of service. He received me very kindly and said, 'I heard that you went off with the Amir; what was the reason for coming back?' I replied, 'He sent me back with those important matters concerning Ray, which are well known to the lord. But those letters can be written out tomorrow, since nothing will be thereby lost. I have come to drink a few cups of wine with the lord, on account of that favour which has today been renewed for the lord on the Sultan's part with regard to the affair of Ḥaṣiri.' He said, [F 206] 'You did very well, and I shall hold that to your credit. But on no account do I want you to make any intercession, for in no circumstances will I agree to it, and you will only be left crestfallen. These wretched fellows[93] have forgotten Aḥmad b. Ḥasan, in that for a while they found the field empty (i.e. had the control of affairs to themselves), and could manipulate weak-willed viziers[94] and hold them in contempt. They will be taught a lesson[95] so that they may wake up from their dream!' He turned towards [Bu] 'Abdallāh Pārsi and said, 'Haven't they been stretched out on the whipping-posts yet?' I replied, 'They will be, but the great lord, the Sultan, has issued a command, and I requested the Great Chamberlain that there should be a pause so that I might see the lord.' He replied, 'You've now seen me, and I'm not going to listen to your pleading. They must be thrashed with rods so that they learn their lesson. O Bā ʿAbdallāh, go off and order them both to be stretched out on the posts.' I replied, 'If the decision to beat them is irrevocable, then there must be a delay in inflicting the punishment on them while I have a private word with you and can adequately propound a couple of points. After that, let the lord's command be carried out.' He called out to Bu ʿAbdallāh [Gh 168] to come back. The attendants were dismissed so that the two of us were left alone together.

"I said, 'May the lord's life be long! Going to extremes in affairs is not a laudable thing to do. Great men have said, "*Show forgiveness when you are in a position of power*"[96], and they have opted for and have regarded forgiveness as an unexpected boon (*ghanimat*) when they were strong enough to exact vengeance. The exalted God has vouchsafed to the lord power, but He had also shown his compassion when He released him from such dire tribulations and incarceration (i.e. in India). It is therefore incumbent upon the Vizier to treat kindly those who have harmed him in the past so that the burden of shame and regret for their deeds falls upon them.[97] The lord is very well aware of the story of Ma'mun and [F 207] Ebrāhim.[98] It would be futile for me to expatiate on this episode; I would be carrying dates to Baṣra.[99] Moreover, when the Sultan acted magnanimously and showed his concern for the Vizier's feelings and high status, and sent this old man Ḥaṣiri there and ordered such a punishment, it has to be recognized what pain it brought to his heart, for he holds this man in great affection by virtue of the fact that he suffered numerous afflictions in the Sultan's cause at the hands of his father Sultan Maḥmud. His conviction has been that the Vizier would likewise act as in a noble and magnanimous fashion and refrain from harming this man. In my humble opinion, it would be preferable if he kept the Sultan contented and ordered that this man should be held in custody but not beaten, and that a written bond (*khaṭṭ*) should be taken from him and his son in the name of the exalted treasury, and then the question of that amount of fines and penalty can be left to the Sultan and whatever he commands. My belief is that he will remit the fines and penalty for him. It would therefore be even better if the Vizier himself does the actual interceding regarding that offence so that he will also get the credit for it. The Vizier knows that I myself have no ulterior motive in affairs like this, but only solicitude for the best interests of both sides. What came into my mind I have set forth as far as my capability allows—but it is yours to command—for you know better the consequences of affairs like these.'

"When the Vizier heard those words of mine, he bowed his head and thought for a while. He sensed that these words of mine emanated from elsewhere,[100] since he was not one of those people from whom such things would remain hidden for long. He said, 'For your sake, I revoke the beatings, but their wealth, the father's and the son's, must go to the Sultan.' I paid my respects, and he despatched Bu 'Abdallāh Pārsi and the matter was settled. A written bond for 300,000 dinars was taken from Ḥaṣiri, and both he and his son were brought to the guard-house. After that, the Vizier called for food, wine, and musicians and singers, [Gh 169] and we got down to the feasting. When we had drunk several bumpers of wine, I said, [F 208] 'May the lord's life be long! This is an auspicious day; I have one other request.' He said, 'Say your wish and you will receive a favourable answer.' I said, 'I saw Bu'l-Faraj (text, Bu'l-Fatḥ) carrying a waterskin, and he cuts a very miserable figure as a stable lad. If he deserved to be chastised, he got it, but much also is due to him for his past services to the lord, and the Sultan has acknowledged this and regards him favourably, as did Sultan Maḥmud. If the Vizier sees fit, he should pardon him too.' He replied, 'I have done so; let him be summoned.' He was summoned, and he came forward wearing those ragged clothes of his, kissed the ground and stood there. The Vizier said, 'Have you repented of your foolish prattle?' He replied, 'O lord, the waterskin and the beasts' quarters have brought me to repentance!' The Vizier laughed, and gave orders for him to be taken to the bathhouse and to be garbed in suitable clothes. Afterwards he came forward and kissed the ground. He bade him sit down and ordered food to be brought for him. He ate something, and after that the Vizier ordered several draughts of wine to be brought for him, which Bu'l-Faraj consumed. Then he showed him marks of favour and sent him back home. After this, we all drank a great deal of wine and returned homewards. O Bu'l-Fażl, this Aḥmad is a great master, but he has embarked on a course of settling old scores and exacting vengeance, and I strongly disapprove of the course which he has taken. The Sultan will never see eye-to-eye with him on this score and will not allow him to destroy his own retainers. I don't know what the outcome of all this will be. Keep all this to yourself, go home and get yourself ready to rejoin the Amir."

I got myself ready to go, and went back to Bu Naṣr. He gave me a sealed private note which I took, and set off in the direction of the hunting ground. I reached there towards the time of the evening worship. I found the Sultan had been drinking wine all day and had then gone to the large tent (*khargāh*) and withdrawn from public gaze. I brought the letter to the eunuch (or "the Amir's private servant") Āghāji,[101] gave it to him and settled down in a spot near [F 209] the camp enclosure. Around the time of dawn, an attendant came and summoned me. I went along, and Āghāji escorted me before the Amir, who was seated on the travelling throne in the large tent. I offered up signs of respect, and he said, "Tell Bu Naṣr that what he did in the matter of Ḥaṣiri was very correct and appropriate. We are about to come back to the town, and will issue the necessary orders." He tossed that letter over to me, I took it and went back. The Amir performed the dawn worship and set off for the town. I myself rode back with greater speed. [Gh 170] Near the town I saw my master and the Grand Vizier standing there as part of the ceremonial party for greeting and escorting back the Amir, together with all the senior army commanders and the court dignitaries. Bu Naṣr saw me, but said nothing. I stood there in my place, and the battle standard and the ceremonial parasol of the Sultan came into view. The Amir was on horseback, and this crowd which had come to meet him surged forward towards him.

My master came up with me and made a sign to me. I went forward, and he whispered to me, "What did you do, and what happened?" I explained the situation, and he said, "Just as I thought." They rode on and the Amir appeared. They all dismounted as a token of respect[102] and then re-mounted and rode on. The Vizier was on the Amir's right and Bu Naṣr was in his close proximity, with other courtiers and great men further in front, so that the press was not too great. The Amir was meanwhile speaking with the Vizier until they reached the vicinity of the garden. The Amir said, "What happened concerning this rash and impulsive fellow?" The Vizier replied, "When the lord has in auspicious circumstances reached his destination, I will give a message to be passed on by word of mouth by Bu Naṣr about what happened and what needs to be done." [F 210] He said, "Well done," and they moved on.

The Amir went up to the elevated pavilion, and the Vizier took up his seat in the open portico of the Divān, sitting by himself. He summoned my master and gave him the message, "The lord, as befits his lofty resolution, took into consideration my feelings in the matter of Ḥaṣiri, and as long as I live, I will never be able to give adequate thanks for this particular act of favour. Although Ḥaṣiri is a man given to impudent acts and to vain and boastful talk, he is an aged man, deserving consideration for ancient acts of service, and he was always a unique servant and devotee of the Amir; and because of this very devotion, he has endured many trials and tribulations in the past, just as I myself suffered.[103] His son is wiser and more self-controlled than him, and has the potential for all manner of service. It would be hard to find two persons as capable as these two, and at present, when the lord's service requires many a suitable servant and retainer, how could I regard it as permissible to bring about the ruin of two servants like these?

"My intention was to make it abundantly clear to everyone, high and low, the extent of the exalted judgement's benevolence towards me. My wish was fulfilled, and everyone knows his place. I myself realized this much, that the two should not be beaten, but they were ordered to be incarcerated so that they might become more conscious of their misdeeds. They have given a written bond, obediently and most willingly,[104] that they will offer 300,000 dinars to the exalted treasury, as a token of service. They are capable of handing over this sum, but it would reduce them to penury, and it is unseemly to have impoverished retainers. If the exalted judgement sees fit, my intercession for them should not be refused; this sum should be forgiven them, and both of them should be sent home in a dignified manner." [Gh 171]

Bu Naṣr went away and conveyed this magnanimous message. The Amir was very glad to hear it, [F 211] and gave the answer, "We have commanded that the Vizier's intercession regarding them should be put into effect. What happens to them is for him to say. If he should deem it the correct course of action that they should be sent back to their house, let him send them back and return to them the document containing the stipulated bond (*khaṭṭ-e movāżaʿa*)." Bu Naṣr came back and spoke with the Vizier. The Amir rose and went out from the portico and entered the palace. The Vizier also went back to his house and gave orders for two fine horses[105] from the official stables to be taken to the door of the guard-house. Father and son were set on them and brought to the Vizier in an honoured state. When they arrived, they kissed the ground and then sat down in a courteous fashion. For a while, the Vizier blew hot and cold with Ḥaṣiri[106], and the latter made many an apology—he was a very eloquent old man—and paid his humble respects in manifold ways. The Vizier drew him near and expressed many apologies, exhibited much benevolence and kissed him on the cheeks, saying, "Go back home in your present garb, for I would consider it unseemly to order a change of attire for you myself, and tomorrow the lord Sultan will ordain robes of honour for you." Ḥaṣiri kissed the Vizier's hand and then the ground, and his son did likewise, and they went back to their house in the ʿAlā' Street mounted on the Vizier's horses and with great pomp. The people flocked towards them with their congratulations, and the son was seated with the father [to receive them].

I, Bu'l-Fażl, was a neighbour of theirs, and I went round to them secretly before all the other visitors arrived. Ḥaṣiri said to me, "As long as I live, I shall never be able adequately to recompense Khᵛāja Bu Naṣr, but I am offering thanks and I am addressing invocations to God for him." Of course, I said nothing about what had happened, for it would not have been appropriate. I offered my good wishes and returned. I told my master what had happened. My master mounted his steed in order to offer congratulations, and I came with him. Ḥaṣiri and his son came out a considerable distance to meet us. They sat down, [F 212] and both of them embarked on offering their profuse thanks. Bu Naṣr said, "My own part in all this is obvious (i.e. my part was insignificant); you should offer up thanks to the Sultan and the Vizier," and after these words he left.

One or two weeks later I heard from Bu Naṣr that the Amir, in the course of a private session during a wine-drinking party, related to Ḥaṣiri all that had happened. On that day, Ḥaṣiri was dressed in a yellow, saffron-coloured robe (*jobba*) and his son in a *bondāri* robe,[107] both of great magnificence, and this was the way in which they had been attired for the occasion. The next day they were brought before the Sultan, and the Amir showed them great favour. The Vizier requested that both of them, by the Sultan's command, should be taken along to the Royal Wardrobe and be dressed in robes of honour. Then they came into the royal presence, and from there went to the Vizier. Then both of them were brought back from the Vizier's presence, with a great show of honour, to their own house. The townspeople offered appropriate congratulations. All have now passed on except for Khᵛāja Bu'l-Qāsem, Ḥaṣiri's son, who is still alive with us, may he long survive! God's mercy be upon them all![108]

Whoever reads this episode (*maqāma*) [Gh 172] must look into it with the eye of wisdom and the intention of deriving a moral example, not with that viewpoint of its being just an entertaining tale, so that he may realize what great men these were. I myself have read a story in the historical accounts of the caliphs (*akhbār-e kholafā'*) which took place in the time of Moʿtaṣem and to some degree reminiscent of the episode I have just retailed, but which unfolded in a more momentous manner than that. I have thought it right to include it here since a book, and especially a history, becomes attractive by the insertion of such things, since one story can blossom into another,[109] so that readers' enjoyment may increase and they may become more avid in perusing it, if the Almighty God, so wills. [F 213]

An account of the story of Afshin and Bu Dolaf's escape from him[110]

Esmāʿil b. Shehāb relates,[111] I heard from Aḥmad b. Abi Dovād[112]—and this Aḥmad was a man who, as well as holding both the Supreme Judgeship (*qāżi-ye qożāt*), was also the most outstanding vizier of the age, serving three caliphs[113]—who said: One night, during Moʿtaṣem's reign, I woke up at midnight, and however hard I tried, sleep would not come, and I felt extremely depressed and worried without my knowing the cause of it. I said to myself, "What can it be?" I called out to Salāma,[114] a gholām who used to be at my side at all times, and said, "Tell them to saddle my horse." He replied, "O lord, it's midnight, and it is not your turn tomorrow for service at court, since the caliph has told you that he will be busy with certain business and will not hold open court, and it's no time for riding forth and visiting any other person." I fell silent, for I knew that he was right, but I was restless in mind and felt in my heart that something momentous had happened.

I got up and called out to the servants to light the candles, and I went off to the bath and washed my hands and face. I still found no peace of mind, and I straightaway came back and dressed. They had saddled an ass for me. I mounted and went off without in any way knowing where I was going. In the end [F 214] I said to myself, "The best plan is to go to the court, even though it is not yet dawn. If I am granted an audience, all well and good; if not, I'll return homewards and perhaps this feeling of anxiety will be lifted from my mind."

I rode on as far as the court. When I arrived there, the doorkeeper on duty (*ḥājeb-e nowbati*) was informed. He came up to me at once and said, "What do you mean by coming at this hour? You know full well that, since yesterday, the Commander of the Faithful has been occupied in merry-making, [Gh 173] and your presence would be inappropriate." I replied, "It's just as you say, but let the lord know that I am here; if there is the possibility, he will give orders for me to go in, and if not, I shall return." He said, "Willingly!" and immediately relayed my request. He came out straightaway and said, "Right! Audience has been granted. Enter!" I went in, and saw Moʿtaṣem in a very pensive mood, by himself, not engaged in anything. I gave my greetings and he responded, saying, "O Bā ʿAbdallāh, why have you been so late in coming? I have been waiting for you for a long time." I was astounded when I heard this, and said, "O Commander of the Faithful, I have come before the crack of dawn, and I thought that the lord would be engaged in some diversion, and I was not sure whether I would be received or not." He said, "Then you don't know what has happened?" I replied, "No, I don't." He said, *"Indeed we belong to God and indeed to Him we shall return!*[115] Sit down and listen." I sat down. He went on, "That impudent dog, that semi-infidel Bu'l-Ḥasan Afshin,[116] because he served us well by defeating Bābak Khorram-Din, and waged a long war against him till he finally captured him—we, for this reason, heaped limitless praise on him and raised him to an extremely lofty degree. He was forever asking us to give him a free hand [F 215] over Bu Dolaf—i.e. al-Qāsem b. ʿIsā al-Karaji al-ʿEjli[117]—so that he might seize his personal wealth and his governorship and kill him, for you know to what lengths the enmity and partisan feeling (*ʿaṣabiyya*) between the two of them extends. But I persisted in denying him this because of Bu Dolaf's worthy character and capability and in deference to his long record of service to us, and, furthermore, because of the friendship which exists between the two of you. Last night a serious blunder was committed, for Afshin went on and on about this; I resisted him several times, but he would not give up and I finally consented. Since then I have been filled with compunction, for there is no doubt that, when it becomes daylight, Bu Dolaf will be seized—and the wretched man has no inkling of this—and he will be brought to this thoroughly unprincipled character,[118] who will have him executed as soon as he has him in his claws."

I replied, "O Commander of the Faithful, woe unto me,[119] this is an unjust shedding of innocent blood and God Most High will be displeased," and I began to recite Qor'ānic verses and historical traditions. Then I said, "Bu Dolaf is the lord's servant and the knight[120] of the Arabs. What he achieved in the province of Jebāl and his many feats there, and the way in which he placed his own life at risk in order to bring peace to the province, are all a matter of common accord. Even if this man is put down, his kinsmen and his followers will not remain silent but will rise up in revolt, and a great deal of civil strife will ensue."

He said, "O Bā ʿAbdallāh, it is just as you [Gh 173] say, and I see it clearly. But the matter is now out of my hands, since last night Afshin took my hand and I contracted, with solemn oaths, that I would not rescue Bu Dolaf from Afshin's clutches nor issue any command that he be handed back."

I said, "O Commander of the Faithful, what possible remedy is there for this calamity?" He replied, "I can only suggest that you go this instant to Afshin. If he won't let you in, thrust yourself in, and embark on imploring, beseeching and lamenting in pursuit of this aim; but you are not in any way to convey any message or word from me, long or short. Perhaps in this way he may have regard for your own respected position, since he knows your high prestige and status, and release Bu Dolaf from his grip, and not consign him to destruction but hand him over to you. If he then [F 216] rejects your intercession, Fate will have done its work, and nothing can be done."

Aḥmad related: When I heard this from the caliph, my senses almost failed me. I went back and rode again towards the quarter of the administrative offices (*maḥallat-e vaziri*). I took with me several of my retainers who had arrived, and I sent two or three horsemen off at a gallop to Bu Dolaf's house. I spurred on my horse and rode so fast that I no longer knew whether I was on earth or in heaven; and my gown[121] became detached from me without my noticing it. It was near daybreak. I worried lest I should arrive too late and Bu Dolaf would have been brought in and killed, and the whole affair would be over and done with. When I reached the vestibule of the entrance to Afshin's palace, all his doorkeepers and officials hurried towards me en bloc, as was their custom on previous occasions, and they did not realize that they ought to have turned me away with some excuse, since my coming to Afshin at such a time would be very unpalatable and disturbing for him. They conducted me into the palace and drew the curtain aside. I instructed my retainers to sit down in the vestibule and to keep their ears pricked for any call from me.

When I came into the midst of the palace, I found Afshin seated in the corner of the central dais, with an executioner's leather mat spread open on the platform before him, with Bu Dolaf seated there. He had no clothes on except his trousers and his eyes were blindfolded. The executioner stood there with a naked sword in his hand. Afshin was engaged in verbal wrangling with Bu Dolaf while the executioner was expecting him to give the command "Strike!" in order to cut off his head. When Afshin's eye fell upon me, he was highly perturbed, he went yellow and then crimson with anger, and the veins on his neck stood out. [Gh 175] My customary practice with him was that, when I came to him, he would come forward at the same time and would bow his head so that his head touched my chest. On this occasion he did not move from his place, exhibiting much contempt and disregard. [F 217] For my part, I was not unduly worried or upset at this for I had come on a momentous mission. I kissed his face and sat down. He for his part did not look at me, but I remained patient over that and embarked on some topic with the aim of engaging his attention so that he would not command the executioner to strike with his sword. He nevertheless firmly refused to look at me. I stood my ground and changed tack, eulogizing the Persians (*'Ajam*) because this varlet (*mardak*) was one of them and stemmed from the land of Osrushana. I vaunted the nobility of the Persians over the Arabs, although I knew that this is a great sin—but it was for Bu Dolaf's sake, so that his blood should not be spilt. He wouldn't listen to a single word. I said, "O Amir, may God make me your ransom! I have come on behalf of Qāsem b. 'Isā so that you may display God's greatness and pardon him for my sake; by doing so, you will receive sundry rewards." He replied, with ire and contempt, "I haven't pardoned him and I'm not going to pardon him. The Commander of the Faithful has given him over to me and last night swore an oath that he would say no more about it (i.e. intervene in any way) so that I could do whatever I wished; I have been wanting to do this for a very long time."

I said to myself, "O Aḥmad, your word and your official signature are obeyed in East and West; are you to put up with such contemptuous treatment from a dog like this?" Again I comforted myself with the thought that, whatever degradation might come my way, I had to bear it for Bu Dolaf's sake. I arose and kissed his head and showed my distress, but it was to no avail. I kissed his shoulder yet again, but there was no response. I turned to his hand again and kissed it, and he realized that I was about to kiss his knees. It was then that he said to me angrily, "How long are you going to go on like this? By God, even if you kiss the ground a thousand times it won't do you any good and you won't get what you want." I was so overcome by anger and despair that I began to sweat and I said to myself, "This hunk of filthy carrion and semi-infidel is treating me in such a contemptuous fashion and [F 218] is uttering such abuse! Why should I put up with it? For the sake of this noble-souled man Bu Dolaf, I will take a grave risk, and let Fate take its course! I would rather do this, whatever calamities it may bring me!"

Then I said, "O Amir, I have said and done all that a noble and dignified person should say, [Gh 176], yet you showed me scant regard. You know how the caliph and all the great men of his court, whether those higher in status than you or inferior, respect my honoured status and how my words carry great weight in every part of the realm. Thank the Almighty God that, because of your recalcitrance I am in no way indebted to you in this matter! I have done my bit. Now hear the Commander of the Faithful's message: He orders you not to kill Qāsem ʿEjli or do him harm in any way. You are to send him back to his house at once, for you have been relieved of your duties over him. If you kill him, I shall reciprocate by taking your life in exchange for his."

When Afshin heard these words, his whole body began to shake and he was mortified with fear. He said, "Are you really conveying this message from the lord?" I replied, "Certainly. Have you ever heard me convey the opposite of his commands?", and I called my retainers to come in. Thirty or forty of them entered, all of them pious, trustworthy and credible would-be witnesses (*mozakki va mo'addel*). I said to them, "Bear witness that I am conveying the message of the Commander of the Faithful Mo'taṣem to this Amir Bu'l-Ḥasan Afshin, and it says, 'Don't kill Bu Dolaf Qāsem or harm him in any way. Send him back to his house at once. If you kill him, your life will be taken in requital." Then I said. "O Qāsem!" He replied, "At your service (*labbeyka*)!" I said, "Are you in good physical shape?" He replied, "Yes, I am." I said, "You have no wounds?" [F 219] He replied, "No." I said to my people again, "Bear witness that he is in good physical shape and bodily health!" They replied, "We bear witness."

I went back in a state of vexation and spurred on my horse furiously, as if I were intoxicated or bereft of my reason, and all the way I was saying to myself, "I have made Bu Dolaf's killing all the more certain, for Afshin will presently arrive hot on my heels, and the Commander of the Faithful will say that he never sent this message; and he will return and kill Qāsem." When I reached the servant [on duty at the palace gate], I was in such a state that I was covered in sweat and breathing heavily. The servant sought access for me, and I went in and sat down. When the Commander of the Faithful saw me in that condition, with his usual magnanimity he ordered a servant to wipe off the sweat from my face. Then he said to me in a gentle tone, "O Bā 'Abdallāh. what's happened to you?" I replied, "May the Commander of the Faithful's life be prolonged! I have never had a day like this in my entire life. Pity a Muslim who [Gh 177] has to undergo all this from the defilement of a heathen!" He asked, "Tell me the story." I began to relate in detail what had happened. I had reached that stage in the narrative where I kissed Afshin's head, then his shoulder, then both his hands, and was about to kiss his feet, and Afshin had said, "Even if you kiss the ground a thousand times, it won't do any good; I'm going to kill Qāsem!", when I saw Afshin coming through the door, with his belt and hat on. I froze in my tracks and cut short what I was saying, and I said to myself, "What bad luck that I was not able to tell the Commander of the Faithful the complete story, that, in order to save Qāsem, I delivered a message purporting to come from him that he had never in fact sent. Now Afshin will relate the story of the message and the caliph will reply that he never gave this message; I shall be disgraced, and Qāsem will be executed." This is what was going through my mind, but God Most High willed otherwise, for the caliph had been intensely distressed hearing about my kissing Afshin's shoulder and hands and being about to kiss his feet, and his saying "Even if you kiss the ground a thousand times, it won't do any good!"

When Afshin sat down, he said to the Commander of the Faithful heatedly, "Last night the lord gave me a free hand over Qāsem; is this message of today, which Aḥmad [F 220] brought, that he is not to be killed, authentic?" Moʿtaṣem replied, "It is my message; when did you ever hear that Bu ʿAbdallāh would deliver a message from ourselves or from our forefathers to anyone, and it should not be authentic? Even if, last night, after your continued insistence, we gave in to your requests regarding Qāsem, you should have realized that Qāsem was born into our household.[122] The wise course would have been for you to send for him, to spare his life and to send him back homewards in a seemly manner and with a robe of honour. But to cap it all, to inflict such distress on Bu ʿAbdallāh was the most heinous act of all. But people behave according to their origins and innate nature, and how can the Persians have any love for the Arabs after what they have suffered from their swords and spears? Go back, and be more prudent and more self-controlled in future!"

Afshin arose, his composure shattered, and he limped away. When he had gone, Moʿtaṣem said, "O Bā ʿAbdallāh, how could you bring yourself to deliver a message which had never been given?" I replied, "O Commander of the Faithful, I could not contemplate with equanimity the spilling of a Muslim's blood; [Gh 178] it will be accounted as a heavenly reward for me, and God Most High will not hold me guilty for saying this lie," and I cited several Qorʾānic verses and historical traditions of the Prophet, peace be upon him. He laughed and said, "What you did was the right thing which had to be done, and I swear an oath before the Almighty God that Afshin will not escape from me alive, for he is no Muslim." After this, I offered up profuse prayers and was filled with joy that Qāsem had regained his life, and I wept. Moʿtaṣem said, "Summon one of the doorkeepers'"; he was summoned and entered. The caliph said, "Go to Afshin's house with one of the special royal horses, set Bu Dolaf Qāsem ʿEjli, son of ʿIsā, on it and convey him to Bu ʿAbdallāh's palace in an honoured and exalted fashion." The doorkeeper went off, and I likewise returned homewards. I dawdled somewhat along the way until I knew that Qāsem and the doorkeeper had reached my house, and then I went back to my house. I found Qāsem seated in the entrance vestibule. When he saw me, he threw himself on my feet[123] in gratitude. I clasped him to my bosom, kissed him, conducted him into the palace [F 221] and set him down with fitting solicitude. He was weeping and heaping thanks on me. I said, "Don't thank me, but rather, thank the Almighty God and the Commander of the Faithful for your new lease of life." Mo'taṣem's doorkeeper conducted him to his house with a great show of splendour.

From this story, everyone can recognize what great persons these were. All of them have now passed on, but this good report of them has remained behind as their memorial. My own aim in setting down this tale is so that readers may acquire some benefit from me, and it may be that something of it will be of practical use to someone. Now that I have finished this story, I shall return to continuing the historical narrative. God is the Most Knowing One!

An account of the execution of Amir Ḥasanak the Vizier, God's mercy be upon him.[124]

I will write a section about the advent of the affair leading to this man's execution, and then the story itself will be unravelled in detail. Today, when I am beginning this story, in Dhu'l-Ḥejja of the year 450 [/January-February 1059] in the auspicious age of the Exalted Sultan Abu Shojā' Farrokh-zād b. Nāṣer Din Allāh, may God prolong his existence, out of this group of people of whom I am about to speak, one or two are still alive, living in some secluded corner; and it is several years since Khᵛāja Bu Sahl Zowzani passed away and has the burden of answering for his earthly deeds. That is no concern of ours, even though [Gh 179] through him some harm did come my way; but no matter, since my years have reached five and sixty and I have to follow in his way. In this History which I am putting together, [F 222] I set down nothing that might lead to charges of *parti pris* or hyperbole[125] and make the readers of this account say, "Shame on this old man!" On the contrary, I am saying what should win the readers' assent and spare me from their taunts.

This Bu Sahl stemmed from a line of religious scholars[126] and was distinguished, learned and cultivated. But a streak of wickedness and malevolence was engrained in his nature—*"There is no changing what God has created"*[127]—and along with that wickedness went a certain lack of compassion, and he was forever on the lookout for a mighty and wilful monarch to become angry with a retainer and have that retainer punished and arrested. This man Bu Sahl would then pounce from a corner, exploit the opportunity and stir up things and inflict much suffering on that retainer. He would then boast that "It was I who procured the downfall of so-and-so, and he got what he deserved." But the wise knew that this was not so; they would shake their heads and laugh in private, dismissing him as a mere braggart. But the case of my master Bu Naṣr Moshkān proved an exception, for in spite of all those intrigues against him, he could not procure his downfall. He was unable to achieve his desire regarding him since the divine decree did not favour and assist his plans to make mischief. Moreover, Bu Naṣr was a farsighted man. In the time of Amir Maḥmud, and without betraying his own master, he kept himself in the good graces of this Sultan Masʿud in all matters, since he knew that, after his father, the royal throne would be Masʿud's.

Ḥasanak's case was different. For the sake of Amir Moḥammad and keen on maintaining the affections of Maḥmud and obeying his orders, he offended this prince, Masʿud, and did and said things which even his peers would find intolerable, let alone a monarch, and this is all too similar to the manner in which Jaʿfar the Barmakid and his kin conducted themselves as viziers in the time of [F 223] Hārun al-Rashid when they suffered the same fate as was meted out to this vizier (i.e. Ḥasanak). Retainers and servants need to guard their tongues in regard to lords, since foxes can never contend with lions. Despite his pomp and rank, wealth and number of followers, Bu Sahl was a mere drop of water to an ocean[128] compared to Amir Ḥasanak, leaving aside, of course, in this context, his greater learning.[129] But since Ḥasanak was guilty of overstepping the mark [Gh 180], as I have recounted previously in this History—in one instance he said to ʿAbdus,[130] "Tell your Amir Masʿud that I do what I do at my own master's bidding (i.e. at that of Maḥmud); if the royal throne ever becomes yours, Ḥasanak will have to be executed"—inevitably therefore, when the Sultan Masʿud became monarch, this man had to sit on the wooden mount.[131] And who is Bu Sahl and others like him in all this? For Ḥasanak drew upon himself the consequences of his own audacity and transgressions. In no circumstances can a monarch overlook three things: *corruption*[132] *in the realm* (or, "impugning the monarch"); *the divulging of secrets; and shameful conduct [towards a man's womenfolk]*).[133] *We seek refuge in God from His abandoning us!*

When Ḥasanak was brought back from Bost to Herat, Bu Sahl Zowzani entrusted him to the custody of his retainer ʿAli Rāyeż,[134] and he received all sorts of contemptuous treatment. For since there were no restraints and controls (i.e. from a higher authority), he was subjected to many acts of cruelty and revenge.[135] For that reason, people spoke critically of Bu Sahl, saying that it is easy to kick someone who is already beaten and down. The true, great-hearted man is the one who conforms to the precept, *"Show forgiveness when you are in a position of power." God, His mention is exalted, has said—and His word is indeed true—"... those who suppress their anger and who forgive their fellow-men; God loves those who do good works."*[136] [F 224]

When Amir Masʿud set out from Herat towards Balkh, ʿAli Rāyeż transported Ḥasanak in bonds and treated him with a display of contempt, malice and harsh treatment. I nevertheless heard from ʿAli—he once told me this in confidence—that "although Bu Sahl gave orders for this man to be treated harshly, only one in ten harsh acts was actually inflicted, and much restraint and cautiousness was exercised." At Balkh, Bu Sahl persisted in impressing on the Amir's mind that Ḥasanak was for the scaffold, but the Amir was very magnanimous and noble-minded, and would not respond.[137] One of ʿAbdus's trusty retainers said: One day after Ḥasanak's death, I heard from my master ʿAbdus that the Amir had said to Bu Sahl that "There must be a convincing proof and argument (*ḥojjati va ʿodhri*) for killing this man." Bu Sahl had replied, "Is there any greater justification than that the man is a Carmathian and that he accepted a robe of honour from the Egyptians (i.e. the Fatimids)[138] so that the Commander of the Faithful al-Qāder be'llāh was annoyed, ceased all correspondence with Amir

Maḥmud and still harps on about this. The lord recalls that the Caliph's envoy came to Nishapur bringing a standard, a robe of honour and an investiture patent, and what the terms of the message were concerning this affair.[139] The Caliph's command on this matter ought to be observed."[140] The Amir said, "I'll have to think about this matter." [Gh 181]

This was followed up by another story, recounted to me by my master Bu Naṣr, as related by ʿAbdus—who was on very bad terms with Bu Sahl—to the effect that: Because Bu Sahl spoke at such length about this matter, one day the Amir told the Grand Vizier Khᵛāja Aḥmad b. Ḥasan, when the latter was returning from the court session, that the Vizier should sit alone in the open loggia of the Divān, where there would be a message for him, to be conveyed orally by ʿAbdus. The Vizier went to the loggia, and the Amir summoned me, ʿAbdus, saying, "Tell Khᵛāja Aḥmad: You know all about Ḥasanak's situation, and how in the time of my father he was responsible for inflicting much pain on us, and when [F 225] my father passed away, how many major plots he hatched during my brother Moḥammad's time, although none of them succeeded. But since the Almighty God bestowed the throne and royal power on us with such ease, the wise choice for us is to accept the apology of those who erred and not to delve into the past. However, in regard to this man's religious beliefs, it is said that he accepted the Egyptians' robe of honour, much to the [ʿAbbasid] Caliph's chagrin, and the Commander of the Faithful took offence and broke off correspondence with my father. They are saying that the envoy who came to Nishapur bringing the document conferring the succession, the standard and the robe of honour had been given a message by the Caliph to the effect that 'Ḥasanak is a Carmathian, and should be hanged from the gallows!' We had heard this at Nishapur but do not recall it very well. What is the Vizier's opinion about this matter, and what does he say?"

When I, ʿAbdus, delivered the message, the Vizier remained deep in thought for a long while and then said to me, "What happened between Ḥasanak and Bu Sahl Zowzani that has made him to go to such extreme lengths in seeking Ḥasanak's blood?" I replied, "I don't know for certain, but this much I have heard, that he had gone to Ḥasanak's palace one day, during the period of Ḥasanak's vizierate, on foot and wearing a *dorrāʿa*.[141] A chamberlain (*parda-dār*) had treated him with disdain and had thrown him out." The Vizier exclaimed, "God is above such things as this! Why should one have to nurse such a petty grievance[142] in one's heart?"[143] Then he said, "Tell the lord Sultan that, at the time when I was a captive in the fortress of Kālenjar and they had the intention of killing me, the Almighty God preserved me. I made all sorts of vows and oaths that I would never say anything which might lead to blood being shed, in any circumstances, whether justified or unjustified. At that time when Ḥasanak returned from the Pilgrimage to Balkh and we set out for Transoxania, [F 226] and had face-to-face meetings with Qadïr Khān, after returning to Ghaznin I was imprisoned, without my knowing what had happened regarding Ḥasanak or what the late Amir had said to the caliph. [Gh 182] Bu Naṣr Moshkān has some authentic information about this; you should ask him. The Amir has the final authority; what is required to be ordained, he will ordain. For if Ḥasanak is indeed proved guilty of being a Carmathian, I shall still abstain from saying anything about the shedding of his blood lest he think that I have some personal motive in his punishment. I have spelt this out clearly so that Ḥasanak does not receive false reports of me through others, for I abhor the idea of shedding any creature's blood.[144] But although I have opted for silence in this matter, I shall not withhold my counsel from the Sultan—for that would be acting treacherously—and will advise him not to shed his blood, or anyone else's, for spilling blood is no trifling matter."

['Abdus continued to relate:] When I brought back this reply, the Amir remained sunk in thought for a long time, and then said, "Tell the Vizier [F 227] that whatever is necessary shall be ordained." The Vizier arose and went off to the Divān. On the way, he said to me, 'Abdus, "Try as far as you are able to dissuade the lord from shedding Ḥasanak's blood, for that would bring infamy." I replied, "I obey the command," and returned and spoke with the Sultan. But Fate lay in wait and was doing its work.

After this, the Amir had a session with my master Bu Naṣr. He later gave an account of that private meeting: The Amir questioned me about the story of Ḥasanak, and then after that, about the story of the Caliph, and said, "What do you say about the religious belief and faith of this man and his accepting the robe of honour from the Egyptians?" I embarked on a description of everything regarding Ḥasanak's situation and his going on the Pilgrimage up to that point when he came back from Medina to the Vādi al-Qorā on the road for Syria, received the Egyptian robe of honour, and the reasons why he was obliged to accept it[145] and to take the road back from Mosul (Mowṣel), instead of returning to Baghdad, with the Caliph meanwhile falling under the impression that perhaps Amir Maḥmud had ordered this.[146] All this I explained in full.

The Amir replied, "Then in this case, what was Ḥasanak's crime here? If he had come back by the desert road,[147] wouldn't he have been responsible for the death of all those people (i.e. the pilgrims) with him?" I said, "This was indeed the case, but [Gh 183] they gave such false reports to the Caliph that he took great offence and lost his temper, and called Ḥasanak a Carmathian. There has been correspondence and comings and goings of messengers on this subject. The late Amir, in his usual obdurate and implacable manner, one day exclaimed, 'A letter must be written to this dotard of a Caliph[148] that, in order to show my esteem for the ʿAbbasids, I have exerted my power throughout the whole world, seeking out Carmathians, and if found and proven, I have them stretched out on the gallows. If it had been proven to my satisfaction that Ḥasanak was a Carmathian, a report would have reached the Commander of the Faithful concerning what has been done regarding him. I have raised him up myself, and he is on a level with my own children and brothers; if he is a Carmathian, then I too am a Carmathian.'

Although those were the words [F 228] of a proud monarch, I went along to the Divān and wrote them up in the style in which servants write to lords.[149] In the end, after much coming and going, it was decided that the robe of honour which Ḥasanak had accepted, together with those precious and rare gifts which those Egyptians had sent to Amir Maḥmud, should be sent back to Baghdad with an envoy so that they could be burnt. When the envoy returned, the Amir asked, 'Where did they burn that robe of honour and the gifts?', for the Amir had been considerably chagrined that the Caliph should have called Ḥasanak a Carmathian. Despite all that (i.e. the returning and destruction of the Fatimids' gifts), the Caliph's feelings of alarm and alienation kept on increasing, though in secret and not openly, until the time when Amir Maḥmud received the divine command and died. I, Bu Naṣr, have explained in its entirety what had happened." The Amir commented, "I understand now."[150]

After this private session, Bu Sahl still persevered in his attempts. On Tuesday, 27 Ṣafar [/23 February 1031], when the court dispersed, the Amir told the Vizier, "Take up your place in the open loggia of the Divān, and Ḥasanak will be brought there, together with the judges and professional attesters to legal acts (*mozakkiyān*), so that what was acquired (i.e. by Ḥasanak) may all be written down in a deed of sale (*qabāla*) in our name and legally attested by him personally."[151] The Vizier obeyed the command and went along to the loggia, and the high officials of state,[152] the leading notables, the Head of the Chancery, Khᵛāja Bu'l-Qāsem b. Kathir (despite the fact that he had been relieved of his office), Bu Sahl Zowzani and Bu Sahl Ḥamdavi all came. The Amir sent along thither the religious scholar Nabih and the judge of the army (*ḥākem-e lashkar*)[153] Naṣr b. Khalaf. The judges of Balkh, the Sharifs, the ulema and religious lawyers, the professional witnesses (*moʿaddelān*) and attesters to legal acts—all the persons who were of good reputation and who were held in great honour[154]—were present and seated there. When this throng of eminent persons was properly marshalled, I, [F 229] Bu'l-Fażl, and a crowd of people [Gh 184] were seated outside the loggia by the market booths, awaiting Ḥasanak.

An hour passed before he appeared, unfettered. He wore an ink-colored[155] gown (*jobba*) tinged with black, somewhat frayed, a very clean *dorrāʿa* and cloak (*redā'*), a turban of smooth Nishapuri cloth, new Mikāli boots on his feet, hiding his ruffled (*kālida*) hair beneath his turban with just a little showing. The commander of the police guard accompanied him, together with ʿAli Rāyeż and a large force of infantrymen of all kinds. They took him into the loggia, and he stayed there until the time for the midday worship; then he was brought out and taken back to the guardhouse. The judges and religious lawyers came out after him. I heard this much, that two persons were saying to each other, "What impelled Khᵛāja Bu Sahl to do this? He has brought dishonour upon himself!"

Following them, Khᵛāja Aḥmad came forth with the leading notables and went back to his house. Naṣr b. Khalaf was a friend of mine, and I asked him, "What went on?" He replied: When Ḥasanak came, the Vizier rose to his feet. When he performed this act of courtesy, every person rose to his feet, whether willingly or not. Bu Sahl Zowzani could not control his ire. He half-got to his feet, muttering angrily to himself all the while. Khᵛāja Aḥmad said to him, " You do everything in half-measures." Then he became really piqued. Although the Vizier was insisting that Amir Ḥasanak should sit close to him, he would not accept this and sat on my right hand instead. Khᵛāja Aḥmad placed Khᵛāja Abu'l-Qāsem b. Kathir and Bu Naṣr Moshkān on his right hand (although Bu'l-Qāsem b. Kathir no longer held office, he was still highly regarded), and Bu Sahl on the Vizier's left hand. This, too, made Bu Sahl livid.

The Grand Vizier [F 230] turned towards Ḥasanak and said, "How is the Khᵛāja, and how is he bearing up?" He replied, "One should be thankful." The Vizier said, "You mustn't be downhearted, since such adversities often befall men. One must submit to whatever the Lord ordains, for as long as there is life in the body, there are numerous venues for consolations and release from suffering." [At this stage,] Bu Sahl's self-control ran out, and he said, "Is it worthy of the lord to talk in these terms with a Carmathian dog who will be put to death on the Commander of the Faithful's orders?" This earned him a withering look from the Vizier.

Ḥasanak said, "I don't know who's been a dog; the whole world knows my family and how I have been endowed with prestige and following and all the trappings of wealth. I lived my life and directed the affairs of the realm, and the final outcome of human life is death. If my allotted span of life has reached its end today, no-one can do anything about it, whether it ends on the scaffold or elsewhere. After all, I am no greater than Ḥoseyn, son of ʿAli[156]. This Khᵛāja, Bu Sahl, who calls me these things also happens to have composed poetry in my honour and has stood in waiting at the gate of my palace. But as for his narration of the Carmathian affair, it would be better if he were held on these charges and [Gh 185] not me![157] This is a matter of common knowledge; I know nothing of such things."

Bu Sahl's bile surged within him, he shouted out and was about to utter some abusive words. But the Vizier shouted back at him and said, "Is there no respect for this session of the Sultan's which we are holding here? We have assembled here to do a job. When we are done—and bearing in mind that this man has been in your hands for five or six months—you can do whatever you wish." Bu Sahl became silent and uttered no word until the end of the session.

In the deed of sale[158] all Ḥasanak's goods and properties were recorded as assigned in their entirety to the Sultan's account. They read out the titles of the properties to him one by one and he affirmed that he was selling that property willingly and freely, and he received in return that amount of silver which had been specified. [F 231] The professional witnesses attested it all in writing; the judge [of the army] put his seal upon it in front of the assembled company, and so did the other judges, *according to the practice on such occasions*.[159] When they had finished this, they said to Ḥasanak that it was time to return. He turned to the Vizier and said, "May the Grand Vizier's life be prolonged! In the time of Sultan Maḥmud and at his behest, I used to speak slightingly about the Khᵛāja, which was altogether a mistake; but what could one do but carry out a royal order? They thrust the vizierate upon me when I was not fit for it. I harboured no evil intent regarding the Khᵛāja, and I treated his followers kindly." Then he continued, "I have erred, and am deserving of any punishment which the lord, Amir Masʿud, may ordain for me; but the Beneficent Lord (*khodāvand-e karim*, i.e. God) will not abandon me. I have given up hope of life, but my wives and children deserve consideration, and I beg that the Vizier will forgive me," and he wept. Those present were deeply moved. The Vizier's eyes filled with tears and he said, "On my part, you are completely absolved. You should not be so despondent, for some amelioration is still possible. I have considered the matter and I have pledged to the Almighty God that, if he is condemned, I shall tend to his household."

Then Ḥasanak rose, and the Vizier and the people rose. When they had all gone, the Vizier reproached Bu Sahl harshly, and the latter sought strenuously to apologise to the Vizier, saying, "I was not able to swallow my own anger." The judge of the army and the religious lawyer Nabih reported the proceedings of the session to the Amir. The Amir summoned Bu Sahl and took him severely to task, saying, "Granted that you have been desperately striving after this man's blood, still you ought to have shown some respect for our Vizier's dignity and status." [Gh 186] Bu Sahl replied, "I remembered that lack of respect and due recognition which he showed towards the lord at Herat in the time of Amir Maḥmud, and I was unable to control myself; such lapses won't occur in the future." I heard from the Khᵛāja ʿAmid ʿAbd al-Razzāq [b. Aḥmad b. Ḥasan], [F 232] who said, "On the eve of Ḥasanak's execution, Bu Sahl came to my father at the time of the night worship. My father asked, 'What brings you here?' He replied, 'I shall not go away until the lord falls asleep lest he write a note to the Sultan interceding on Ḥasanak's behalf.' My father retorted, 'I would have written, but you have now wrecked everything. This is a grievous matter,' and he went off to his bed."

All that day and night the plans for Ḥasanak's execution were taking shape. They arranged for two men to be dressed up in the garb of messengers who had ostensibly come from Baghdad and had brought a letter from the Caliph that Ḥasanak the Carmathian had to be put on the scaffold and stoned to death so that never again should a person go against the Caliph and don a robe of honour given by the Egyptians, or convey pilgrims through their lands.[160] When these preparations were all made, on the next day, which was Wednesday, 27 Ṣafar [/23 February 1031],[161] Amir Masʿud mounted his steed and headed for the hunting ground and three days' merry-making, together with his boon-companions, his special intimates, and his musicians and singers.[162] In the town, he ordered the town governor to erect the gallows on the edge of the prayer ground[163] of Balkh below the inner town. The crowds were already making their way there.

Bu Sahl mounted his steed and rode up to the gallows and halted near there on an eminence. Cavalrymen and infantrymen had gone to bring Ḥasanak. When they brought him round from the edge of the Lovers' Market and he reached the middle of the inner town, Mikāʾil, who had halted his horse there, came up to him, called him a vile hireling[164] and hurled obscene insults at him. Ḥasanak did not look at him and made no reply. The mass of the people heaped curses on Mikāʾil for this despicable conduct and for the loathsome things he had uttered. And it does not bear repeating what the more refined and cultured had to say about this Mikāʾil.[165] (After Ḥasanak's demise, this Mikāʾil, who had married the sister of Ayāz, suffered several misfortunes and endured many tribulations; he is still alive today, [F 233] and has devoted himself to prayers and recital of the Qorʾān. When a friend behaves badly, how can one avoid setting it down?)

Ḥasanak was brought to the foot of the gallows—*We seek refuge in God from an evil fate!*—The two messengers were stationed there, supposedly having just arrived from Baghdad, and the Qorʾān reciters were intoning the Qor'ān. They ordered Ḥasanak to take his clothes off. He put his hand inside his clothes and secured the strings of his *ezār*[166] and tied its ankle-strings, and drew off his gown and his shirt and threw them away together with his head covering. He stood there naked except for his *ezār*, with his hands held together, with a body as [Gh 187] white as silver and a face finer than many a painted picture. All the people were weeping from grief. They brought along an iron helmet with a visor, intentionally narrow so that his face and head would not be covered. An order was shouted out, "Cover his head and face lest they be marred by the stones, for we shall be sending his head to Baghdad for the Caliph." They kept Ḥasanak in this state; his lips were moving and reciting something, until a larger-sized helmet was brought. In the midst of all this, Aḥmad, the Keeper of the Royal Wardrobe, came along mounted, turned to Ḥasanak and delivered this message, "The lord Sultan says, 'This is your own wish, which you had sought, saying, "When you become monarch, hang me from the gallows!" We wanted to spare you, but the Commander of the Faithful has written that you have become a Carmathian and you are being put to death in accordance with his command.'" Ḥasanak of course made no reply. [F 234]

After that, they covered his head and face with the larger-sized helmet that they had brought. They bellowed out to him, "Run!", but he did not breathe a word and took no notice of them. Everyone said, "Have you no sense of shame, making the man you are about to kill run to the gallows?" There was nearly a great riot; the cavalrymen charged towards the crowd and quelled that commotion. Ḥasanak was taken towards the gallows and delivered to the dais where he was placed on a mount he had never tried before (i.e. the gallows). His executioner bound him firmly and brought down the halter. The order was shouted out for people to stone him, but no-one touched a stone and everyone was weeping uncontrollably, particularly the Nishapuris. Then they distributed silver coins to a handful of rabble so that they might hurl stones, but the man himself had died because the executioner had thrown the noose round his throat and strangled him.

This was Ḥasanak and his fate. He was fond of saying, God's mercy be upon him, that "the supplications of the Nishapuris will save me," but they did not avail. If he usurped the lands and water of the Muslims, neither the lands nor the water remained for him;

and such great numbers of gholāms, estates, goods, gold, silver and wealth proved profitless in the end. He passed on, and this band who had concocted this plot passed on too. This is a tale rich in moral lessons. All these objects of contention and strife for the sake of the paltry vanities of this present world, they left behind. How foolish is the man who binds his heart to this world, which furnishes comforts and ease of life only to take them back with a vengeance![167]
(Poetry)

1. *By your life, this present world is no place of permanent abode when once its covering is removed from the eye of the beholder.*

2. *How can people remain in it permanently, when its continuance is only attained by the ways of annihilation?* [Gh 188]

Rudaki says, [F 235]

1. To this transient world, it is not right for the guest to bestow his heart forever.

2. Beneath the ground you must sleep, though you may sleep now on satin brocade.

3. What is the use of a large retinue, if one has to enter the grave alone?

4. Beneath the earth, the ant and the fly will keep you company, supplanting the one who tends to your locks now

5. As for the one who tends to your tresses, though rewarded in dinars or dirhams for his service

6. He will lose heart and leave, seeing your cheeks so pallid and sallow—after all, he is not blind ![168]

When all this was over, Bu Sahl and the people left the foot of the gallows, and Ḥasanak remained there alone, alone as he had come forth from his mother's womb.

Later I heard from Bu'l-Ḥasan Ḥ.r.b.li,[169] who was a friend of mine and one of Bu Sahl's close intimates, to the effect that: One day, Bu Sahl was drinking wine and I was with him. It was a well organised occasion, with numerous gholāms standing around to wait upon us, and musicians and singers all making music and singing mellifluously.

Meanwhile, he had ordered that Ḥasanak's head should be brought in, unknown to us, and kept in a large dish with a domed lid. Then he said, "The first fruits of the new season have been brought in, let's have some!" Everyone said, "Let's eat!," so he said, "Bring it in!", and they brought in that dish and removed the lid. When we saw Ḥasanak's head, we were all badly shaken, and I was taken aback in horror. Bu Sahl laughed. He happened to have a cup of wine in his hand, and he poured it out on to the garden, and they took the head back. Next day, and in private, I reproached him at length, but he said, "O Bu'l-Ḥasan, you're a chicken-hearted fellow. This is the way to deal with an enemy's head!" This story circulated, and [F 236] everyone blamed him extensively for this episode and cursed him. On the day they executed Ḥasanak, my master Bu Naṣr did not touch his food and appeared extremely downcast and pensive, to an extent that I had never before seen, and he was saying, "What hope is there now?" Khᵛāja Aḥmad b. Ḥasan was in a similar mood and did not go the Divān. [Gh 189]

Ḥasanak was left hanging on the gallows for almost seven years, with his feet shrivelled and withered so that no trace was left of them when the order eventually came and he was taken down and buried, and no-one could tell the head from the torso. Ḥasanak's mother was a woman of great fortitude. I heard that for two or three months they kept the news from her. When she did hear, she did not wail and lament as women are wont to do but, rather, wept with such pain that all those present wept tears of blood at her distress. Then she said, "What a great man this son of mine was, that a monarch like Maḥmud gave him this present world and a ruler like Mas'ud the next one!"[170] She carried out the mourning rites for her son very appropriately. Every wise man who heard this approved, and it was fitting that he should.

One of the poets of Nishapur uttered this elegy concerning his death, and it is noted down here:

1. They cut off his head, he who was the head of the élite, the adornment of the age and the crown of the realm.

2. Whether he was a Carmathian, a Jew or an infidel, to ascend the scaffold from the seat of power was a dreadful thing.[171]

There have been similar cases to this in the world. When 'Abdallāh b. Zobeyr occupied the caliphate in Mecca, and he secured control of the

Ḥejāz and Iraq, and his brother Moṣʿab took over Baṣra, Kufa and the Savād as his deputy, ʿAbd al-Malek b. Marvān [F 237] marched from Syria against Moṣʿab with a large army which comprised his troops, military equipment and stores.[172] A great battle took place between them and Moṣʿab was killed. ʿAbd al-Malek returned to Syria, and sent Ḥajjāj b. Yusof to Mecca with a numerous and well-equipped army—and the accounts of these episodes appear in all their detail in the chronicles. Ḥajjāj came with his army and joined battle with ʿAbdallāh. Mecca was besieged, and ʿAbdallāh blockaded himself in the mosque of Mecca. The fighting intensified, mangonels were brought into action against the Holy House, and stones were hurled until one corner was brought down. When ʿAbdallāh's situation became too desperate, he stopped fighting. Ḥajjāj sent a message to him, saying, "You have only one or two more days left until you are taken captive, and I know that you won't come forth under any guarantee of safe conduct that I personally may offer, therefore come forth on the authority of ʿAbd al-Malek, so that I may send you to Syria unfettered and in an honoured and respected state. Then ʿAbd al-Malek will know what has to be done, and no more devastation will occur within the sacred area (Ḥaram) and no more blood will be shed."

ʿAbdallāh replied, "I'll think about this." That night [Gh 190] he took counsel with those of his remaining retainers. The majority of them advised that he should surrender in order to avoid civil strife (*fetna*) and to save himself. He went to his mother, Asmāʾ, who was the daughter of Bu Bakr al-Ṣeddiq, and explained the whole situation to her. Asmāʾ pondered for a while and then said, "O son, was this rebellion of yours against the Umayyads motivated by religious or by worldly considerations?" He replied, "I swear by God that it was all in the cause of religion, attested by the fact that I have not taken a single dirham for the sake of this present world, as you well know." She said, "In that case, resign yourself to death, slaughter and mutilation just as your brother Moṣʿab did, for your father was Zobeyr b. ʿAvvām, and your grandfather on my side was Bu Bakr Ṣeddiq.[173] Bear in mind [F 238] the conduct of Ḥoseyn, ʿAli's son. He was noble-minded and refused to submit to ʿObeydallāh b. Ziyād." He replied, "O mother, I too am inclined towards what you are saying, but I wanted to know what you felt and thought about this matter. Now that I know, I look forward to martyrdom and death; but I am apprehensive lest when I am killed they should mutilate me." His mother said, "Once a sheep is slaughtered, it feels no pain when it is carved up and skinned."

All night, ʿAbdallāh prayed and recited the Qorʾān. Just before dawn, he made the major ablution (*ghosl*) and performed his dawn prayers communally with the rest of the worshippers and recited the suras *Nun va 'l-qalam* (LXVIII) and *Hal atā ʿalā 'l-ensān?* (LXXVI) in the course of two *rakʿats*.[174] He donned his mailed coat and girded on his weapons—among the Arabs no-one ever made war on foot as he did—and went and clasped his mother to his bosom and bade her farewell. His mother straightened up the mailed coat on him and stitched up round the armpit, and said, "Fight on against[175] these evildoers so that you may attain Paradise!"[176] just as if she might be sending him on a pleasant errand.[177] And of course, she did not give way to lamentations as womenfolk usually do. ʿAbdallāh came forth. He found his forces scattered and in disarray, having abandoned him, except for a group from his own family and close retainers who wished to show solidarity with him and who were well-equipped with breastplates, mailed coats, helmets and weapons. He called out, "Turn towards me!", and they all turned towards him. ʿAbdallāh then recited these verses: (Poetry)

1. *Indeed, when I recognize my appointed day I show endurance, when some of them recognize it but then deny it.*[178]

When they arrived at the battlefield, they halted. (It was Tuesday, 17 Jomādā I of the year of the Hejra 73[/4 October 692].[179]) Ḥajjāj b. Yusof came out from one side with a numerous army, and arranged them in battle order. He placed the men from Homs opposite the entrance to the Kaʿba, the men from Damascus opposite the gates of the Banu Sheyba, the men from Jordan [F 239] opposite the gate leading to Ṣafā and Marva, the men from Palestine opposite the gates of the Banu Jomaḥ, and the men from Qennasrin opposite the gates of the Banu Sahm.[180] Ḥajjāj and Ṭāreq b. ʿAmr were stationed with the mass of the army at Marva, and they held there a great battle standard.

When ʿAbdallāh b. Zobeyr saw a boundless army placed so as to face him from every side, he turned to his own followers and said, "*O house of al-Zobeyr, if you give yourselves up willingly for me, we shall be people of a distinguished house among the Arabs. We shall have been extirpated [in God's cause]*[181] *to the last man but shall not be tainted by any dishonour. So now, O house of al-Zobeyr, let sword blows not affright you, for indeed, I have never been present at any encounter without being borne out wounded from amongst the slain, and what I have experienced of the treatment of wounds is worse than the pain I have experienced from the actual receipt of the wound.*[182] *Gird your swords as you guard your faces. I don't know any man of you who has broken his sword and has lived to tell the tale.*[183] *If a man loses his weapons, he is as defenceless as a woman. Avert your eyes from the gleaming sword blades, and let every man busy himself engaging his opponent. Don't be distracted by asking about me, and let no-one* [F 240] *say, Where is ʿAbdallāh b. al-Zobeyr? Indeed, if anyone asks about me, I shall be in the front rank of warriors." Then he recited,* (Poetry)

1. *What keeps back Ebn Salmā [from baseness] is that he cannot live for ever, and one day he must meet his appointed destiny* (al-manāyā) *whichever way he turns.*

2. *Hence I am not one to purchase life at the expense of disgrace, nor one to seek a ladder to climb for fear of death.*[184]

Then he said, "In the name of God, O freeborn men, attack!" He lashed out on every side, like a charging lion. There was no direction where he sallied forth with less than ten men confronting him, nine of whom fled before him in terror like foxes fleeing before lions. They were fighting to the finish, the battle raged fiercely [Gh 192] and the enemy was numerous. ʿAbdallāh fought so strongly that all the men in front of the doors were thrown back towards Ḥajjāj and they were almost routed. Ḥajjāj ordered the battle standard to be borne forward. Fresh troops and famed champions came forth from the centre of the battle line, and men of both sides engaged closely with each other. In this confused mêlée, a stone hit ʿAbdallāh b. Zobeyr on the face violently, and blood streamed down his face. He cried out, saying,

1. *Our wounds do not flow with blood on to our heels, but rather, the blood drips down on our feet.*[185]

Another stone came along, and hit him harder on his breast, such that his arms trembled from its impact. One of ʿAbdallāh's clients (*mavāli*)[186] saw the blood and shouted, "They've killed the Commander of the Faithful!" He had not been spotted by the enemy because he had kept his face covered, but when they heard the client's words and realized that he was ʿAbdallāh, many troops rushed at him and killed him. They carried off his head and brought it before Ḥajjāj. The latter performed a ritual prostration (*sajda*), and a cry arose that ʿAbdallāh b. Zobeyr, had been killed. The Zobeyrids stood firm [F 241] until they were all killed, and the revolt came to an end.

Ḥajjāj entered Mecca and ordered that the corner of the Kaʿba which had been devastated by stones from the mangonel should be repaired and other buildings restored. He sent the head of ʿAbdallāh b. Zobeyr to ʿAbd al-Malek b. Marvān and ordered that his body should be gibbeted. They brought the news of his killing to his mother. She did not lament at all but exclaimed, "*Indeed we belong to God, and to Him we shall return!* If my son had not acted as he did, he would not have been the son of Zobeyr or the maternal grandson of Bu Bakr Ṣeddiq."[187] Time passed. Ḥajjāj asked, "What's this old woman doing?" They related her words and described her fortitude, and he exclaimed, "God, the Mighty One, is above all this! If ʿĀʾesha the Mother of the Faithful and this sister of hers Asmāʾ had been two men, the caliphate would never have passed to the Umayyads! This is true courage and fortitude! We must devise a stratagem to get her to pass by her son to hear what she has to say." A group of women were given this task, and they persevered and inveigled Asmāʾ into being led in that direction. When she saw the gibbet she realized that it was her own son. She turned to one of the women, one of the noblest of the women, and said, "Isn't it time that this rider was brought down from this horse?" She said no more and left. Ḥajjāj was told of this. He was dumbfounded and gave orders for the corpse of ʿAbdallāh to be taken down and buried.[188] [Gh 193]

Although this story is long, it contains many beneficial examples, and I described two situations in order to make plain that one should not express excessive wonder at Ḥasanak's fate, for he was not alone in this and greater figures than him had faced similar afflictions. Moreover, if his mother did not lament openly but spoke such words of defiance, let no-one make the accusation [F 242] that this could not be so, on the premise that there is a great difference between men and women, for "*Your Lord creates what He wills and whatever He chooses.*"[189]

When Hārun al-Rashid had ordered that Jaʿfar b. Yaḥyā the Barmakid should be killed, he ordered that he should be cut into four pieces and the pieces gibbeted on four gallows. (That tale is very well known and I have not included it, for it would have taken too long and would have added to the readers' weariness and made them forget the main narrative and hurl abuse at the author, Bu'l-Fażl.) Hārun had secretly placed agents so that should anyone pass beneath Jaʿfar's gibbet and exhibit signs of sorrow and compassion, they could seize him and bring him before the caliph for punishment. When some time had elapsed, Hārun came to regret his overthrowing of the Barmakids. A man from Baṣra passed by one day. His eye fell on one of the gibbets on which the quarters of Jaʿfar had been placed and he recited to himself,

1. *Were it not, by God, for fear of the denunciation of a slanderer, and an eye* (or: spy) *of the caliph which* (or: who) *never sleeps,*
2. *We would circumambulate the trunk on which you are gibbeted and would kiss it* (estalamnā) *just as pilgrims kiss the [Black] Stone*[190]

This episode and the man's verses were reported to the caliph at once, and the man was brought as a captive before him. Hārun said, "You had heard our proclamation; why did you commit this fault?" He replied, "I had heard it right enough, but I have obligations to the Barmakids [Gh 194] in return for favours on an unheard-of scale. I wanted to fulfil discreetly my debt of obligation to them, and I did so. I was admittedly at fault, in that I did not observe the lord's command. If the Barmakids deserve that state, then I too shall be content [F 243] with whatever is meted out to me." Hārun asked him to narrate the story (i.e. of his dealings with the Barmakids), and the man told it. Hārun wept, and forgave the man.[191] These lengthy tales are not devoid of marvels, subtle remarks and moral examples.

I have read in the historical accounts of the caliphs[192] that a certain secretary related that "Bu'l-Vazir entrusted to me the department responsible for collecting the poor-tax and for issuing salaries and living expenses (*divān-e ṣadaqāt va nafaqāt*) in the time of Hārun al-Rashid.[193] One day after the fall of the Barmakids, I looked into a very old register and I saw written on one leaf, 'At the Commander of the Faithful's command, there was conveyed to the Amir Abu'l-Fażl Jaʿfar b. Yaḥyā al-Barmaki, *may God prolong his brightness*, such-and-such an amount of gold, such-and-such an amount of silver,[194] such-and-such an amount of textiles and carpets, such-and-such amount of clothing, perfumes and various luxury items and such-and-such an amount of jewels, in total, thirty million dirhams' worth.' Then afterwards I came to another leaf on which was written that, on that day, expenditure was authorised for purchase in the market of four dirhams and four-and-a-half *dāngs*'[195] worth of reed matting and naphthalene for burning Jaʿfar b. Yaḥyā the Barmakid's corpse". *The immortal God*[196] *is above all this!* I, Bu'l-Fażl, have studied many books, especially historical accounts, and have culled pieces from them, and I am inserting them in the midst of this History so that those entranced or seduced [by the attractions of this present world] may wake up from their dream and act in such a manner that brings them benefits both now and hereafter. *God is the One who, through His graciousness and the breadth of His mercy, renders possible whatever He pleases!*

They likewise gibbeted on the gallows the Vizier Ebn Baqiyya[197] at the time when ʿAżod al-Dowla Fanā-Khosrow, captured Baghdad and the son of his paternal uncle, Bakhtiyār—who [F 244] was called ʿEzz al-Dowla—was killed in a battle which took place between the two of them.[198] This is a long story, and comes in the historical accounts of the Buyid dynasty, in the *Ketāb-e Tāji*, which the secretary Bu Esḥāq composed.[199] This Ebn Baqiyya, the Vizier, was a most haughty and overbearing person—a man of great learning, great wealth and high eminence, but impetuous.[200] He used to serve as vizier both to the caliph al-Ṭā'eʿ le'llāh [Gh 195] and also to Bakhtiyār. In the course of the struggle which took place between Bakhtiyār and ʿAżod al-Dowla, Ebn Baqiyya was guilty of several acts of incivility, and was foolhardy and domineering. He did not consider the consequences, since, in dealing with a man like ʿAżod al-Dowla, and given his own master Bakhtiyār's feebleness, he did those things which he should not have done; but one cannot prevail against the decree of Fate. Inevitably, when ʿAżod al-Dowla captured Baghdad, he ordered him to be placed on a scaffold, and he was killed by being made the target for arrows and stoning.[201] The following verses were recited as an elegy upon him: (Poetry)[202]

1. *Loftiness* (i.e. from his being gibbeted) *during life and death, you are indeed one of the miracles!*

2. *It is as if the people, when they stood around you, were visitors seeking your bountifulness in the time of your munificent gifts.*

3. *It is as if you were standing among them like a preacher, and all of them were standing up at the opening of the ritual prayers.*

4. *You extended your arms towards them, showing solicitude*[203] *for them, as you were wont to extend them when bestowing gifts.*

5. *Since the bosom of the earth was too narrow, after your death, to encompass your loftiness,*

6. *They made the sky your tomb and the robe of the dust-raising winds the substitute for your shrouds.* [F 245]

7. *Because of your greatness in the minds [of people], even now you continue to pass your nights in the care of faithful guardians and watchmen.*

8. *Torches are lit around you at night, just as they were with you when you were alive.*

9. *You mounted a steed on which previously Zeyd*[204] *rode high in bygone years,*

10. *And that is an excellence in which there is consolation and which removes from your eyes the reviling of enemies.*

11. *Before I saw your one, I never saw a trunk* (i.e. Ebn Baqiyya's gibbet), *which was able to embrace generous acts.*

12. *You did harm to the onslaughts of Fate* (i.e. by warding them off through your generosity), *so they rose up, and as a result, you are the one slain by their vengeance.*

13. *You used to provide protection from the turns of fate brought about by the passing of the Nights, so that they turned on you, seeking their revenge,*

14. *And your fate* (*dahr*, lit. "time") *made the beneficence towards us launched in that time into great acts of evildoing.*[205]

15. *You were a cause of happiness and fortune* (or, lucky star," *saʿd*) *for one group of people, but when you departed, they were scattered by strokes of ill fortune* (or, "evil stars," *monḥesāt*). [Gh 196]

16. *There is a violent thirst for you embedded within my heart which can only be assuaged by flowing tears.*

17. *If only I were able to perform the obligations owed to you and the necessary duties,*

18. *I would fill the earth with poems strung together [in your praise] and express through them my lamentations, alternating with the mourning women.*

19. *But I am compelled to restrain my feelings in regard to your loss, out of fear lest I be numbered among those guilty of crimes.*

20. *You have no tomb over which I can implore the gentle rain to fall, since you have become the target for impetuous rain showers.*

21. *May the greetings of the Merciful One be continuously upon you! May they bring acts of mercy, in the morning and the evening alike!*

These fine verses are by Ebn al-Anbāri, and the verse which he recited, "You mounted a steed on which previously Zeyd ..." has the intended reference to Zeyd b. ʿAli b. al-Ḥoseyn b. ʿAli b. Abi Ṭāleb. This Zeyd's patience ran out on account of the tyranny of the Umayyads, and he led a rebellion during the caliphate of Heshām b. ʿAbd al-Malek at a time when Naṣr b. Sayyār was amir of Khorasan. The story of this rebellion is a long one and is set down in the chronicles. At the end of it all they killed him, may God's mercy be upon him, placed him on the gallows and [F 246] left him there for three or four years.[206] *May God give judgement between him and the whole of the Messenger's house, and the Umayyads!* The poet of the house of ʿAbbās is inciting Bu'l-ʿAbbās Saffāḥ to slaughter the Bani Omeyya in an ode which he recited, the name of the poet being Sodeyf. I shall cite this verse from that ode: (Verse)

1. *Recall to mind the places where al-Ḥoseyn and Zeyd were felled, and also one slain in the vicinity of al-Mehrās.*[207]

I have brought to a close this narrative of Ḥasanak's execution, and in the course of this composition I have added several stories and intriguing points which are very long and wearisome. I hope that readers may perhaps forgive this and accept my excuses, and not regard it as too great a great burden. I now return to the main business of the History, and there are many marvels hidden behind the veil (i.e. are still to be revealed) which, if life remains for me, will be set forth, if God Most High wills. [Gh 197]

The story of the despatch at this time of envoys to Qadïr Khān for the renewing of the agreement and compact between the two sides

When Amir Maḥmud held his meeting with Qadïr Khān and their friendship became firmly cemented with a marriage alliance and an agreement, as I have already explained previously in great detail, the contractual agreement stated that, on our side, the lady (*ḥorra*) Zeynab (i.e. Maḥmud's daughter),[208] may God's mercy be upon her, was betrothed to Yaghāntegin[209], Qadïr Khān's son, who was at that time referred to as Bughrātegin[210] and who was alive till last year, i.e. 449 [/1057–8]. Qadïr Khān displayed such overweening ambition [F 247] that he overthrew Arslān Khān and slew such a noble and eminent brother.[211] But no sooner had his affairs become settled when he died and became one with the earth.[212] The poet expresses this succinctly:

1. *When something is completed and made perfect, its defectiveness is close at hand; expect decline and decay when someone says "It is completed!"*[213]

It is most strange to behold the way in which certain of the children of Adam lead their lives, killing each other for no good reason and destroying one another on account of the transient, tinselly trappings of this world, and then they themselves leave it all and go alone beneath the earth with much agony and affliction in their wake. Where is the benefit in all this, and what wise man would choose this way? But what else can they do when such things do not go well, since no-one can get the better of Fate! One of Qadïr Khān's daughters was betrothed to Amir Moḥammad, since Amir Maḥmud was at that time doing his best to buttress Moḥammad's position in every way he could.[214] For how could he know what destiny had in store?

When, subsequently, Amir Moḥammad was thrown into captivity and it became impossible to bring that daughter of Qadïr Khān, and there was a need to renew the marriage alliance in the name of Amir Masʿud, the latter held a private meeting on Monday, 3 Rabiʿ I of this year [/28 February 1031][215] with the Vizier Khᵛāja Aḥmad and my master Bu Naṣr. They discussed various aspects of this matter, until the decision was reached that two envoys should be sent with a letter, [F 248] one envoy to be selected from the group of boon-companions and the other from the judges, in order to conclude the compact and agreement. They agreed upon Khᵛāja Bu'l-Qāsem Ḥaṣiri (who is still alive today, and long may he remain so!) [from the first group], and [Gh 198] upon Bu Ṭāher Tabbāni [from the second group], who was one of the leading figures of the Tabbāni family, and a unique figure in learning, knowledge, piety and discretion [from the second group]. In addition to all these, he had a very fine stature and a handsome appearance, and his handwriting and penmanship matched his mien; I have seen few calligraphic hands in Khorasan as excellent as his. That noble-hearted man remained for three years in the land of the Turks and then returned fully contented; but when he reached Parvān[216] he passed away. I shall relate this story in its appropriate place. My master wrote down the letter and the text of two sets of instructions for oral delivery (*moshāfaha*)[217] by the envoys on this matter in a most exquisite manner. That copy (i.e. the one by Bu Naṣr) has been lost and therefore I have made another copy of it so that it can be read and its intricate and subtle manner appreciated.[218] I am first of all going to relate a story concerning those Tabbānis since it has a connection with several points regarding monarchs. Then after that, the texts will be written out, since from every section of such documents remarkable points and wonderful things may be gained. I am fulfilling my task, and if at times I try people's patience, I seek their indulgence, [F 249]

The story of the Tabbānis

The fame and notable deeds of the Tabbānis stem from the Imam Abu'l-ʿAbbās Tabbāni. He is the forbear of the Khᵛāja Imam Bu Ṣādeq Tabbāni, may God preserve him in good health, who has at the present time found a fitting way of life and is in the Rebāṭ of Mānk b. ʿAli b.

Meymun.[219] In the course of one day, he gives over a hundred *responsa* on legal problems[220] and is regarded as the Imam of the Age in all sciences. I am going to recount in this section of the History how he first became attached to this royal house. Then, with God's will and permission, I am going to set forth the positions of religious leadership, the judgeships and the offices to which he was appointed in the time of the monarchs of this dynasty. The forbear of this Bu'l-ʿAbbās was the disciple of Yaʿqub Abu Yusof, son of Ayyub, at Baghdad, Bu Yusof Yaʿqub Anṣāri being the Chief Judge for Hārun al-Rashid and pupil of the Imam Abu Ḥanifa; he was one of the indisputably authoritative Imams and one of the partisans of free choice and free will,[221] without any rival.[222] Abu'l-ʿAbbās was likewise accounted one of the followers of Abu Ḥanifa, as I saw written in the *Mokhtaṣar-e Ṣāʿedi* composed by the Judge, the Imam Abu'l-ʿAlā' Ṣāʿed (who was the tutor (*mollā*) to both Sultan Masʿud and Moḥammad, the two sons of Sultan Yamin al-Dowla), in the section called basic principles for resolving legal questions,[223] "This is the word of Bu Ḥanifa and that of Bu Yusof, Moḥammad, Zofar,[224] Bu'l-ʿAbbās Tabbāni and the Judge Abu'l-Heytham."

There was a religious lawyer from among the Tabbānis called Bu Ṣāleḥ, the maternal uncle of the mother of this Bu Ṣādeq Tabbāni. [Gh 199] Sultan Maḥmud gave him an official appointment during that time when he was at Nishapur as Commander-in-Chief for the Samanids, and despatched him to Ghaznin to be an Imam there [F 250] for the adherents of Bu Ḥanifa. He was sent by him in the year 385 [/995].[225] He used to teach in that college (*madrasa*) situated at the Gate of the Men of Bost. The Chief Judge Abu Soleymān Dāvud b. Yunos, who is still living as the foremost and greatest scholar in this town—although he has gone well into the vale of years[226] and is almost bedridden—and also his brother, the upright Judge Maḥmud,[227] were both pupils of Bu Ṣāleḥ and learnt the religious sciences from him. Bu Ṣāleḥ was so highly regarded by Amir Maḥmud that when he passed away in the year 400 [/1009–10], Maḥmud said to the Vizier, Khᵛāja Abu'l-ʿAbbās Esfarāyeni, "Go along to this Imam's college and conduct the funeral ceremonies there, since he has no son to take charge of his obsequies. I would have thought it right and proper as far as my own faith and conviction are concerned to have carried out this duty personally, but people may cavil at this and find it unseemly (i.e. for a king). We have no servant with greater prestige and authority than yourself, and you are our Vizier and our deputy." Bu Beshr Tabbāni, may God have mercy on him, was likewise a great Imam of the time of the Samanids, and his horse had accoutrements of gold, regarded as a very great mark of honour at that time when strict rules of decorum were observed.[228]

If a reader of this book should say, "Why does Bu'l-Fażl have to go on at such length in his discourse?", I would reply that I am writing a history covering fifty years, taking up several thousand pages, and containing many a name of prominent and significant figures from every rank and profession, and if in all this I can also pay some tribute to my fellow-citizens[229] and shed more light on the history of such an illustrious family as that one, my readers should understand the reason and make allowances for me.

I shall now return to the beginning of the story of Sultan Maḥmud's role as Commander-in-Chief for the Samanids and in this context retail several worthwhile[230] snippets of various kinds, since [F 251] there is evident profit in this, and shall include the despatching (i.e. of his embassy to the Qarakhanids) of this Imam Bu Ṣāleḥ Tabbāni as an envoy.

The coming of Bughrā Khān,[231] father of Qadïr Khān, to Bokhara and the onset of the decline of the Samanid dynasty took place in the month of Rabiʿ I 382 [/May-June 992],[232] and is a long story. He carried off immeasurable quantities of wealth and valuable hoards from the treasuries of the Samanids. Then he became indisposed with haemorrhoids. When he decided to return to Kāshghar, he brought forth ʿAbd al-ʿAziz b. Nuḥ b. Naṣr al-Sāmāni, awarded him a robe of honour and said, "I heard that they have usurped your dominion from you. [Gh 200] I have now given it back to you, since you are courageous, just and of good conduct. Be stout-hearted, and if ever you need help, I shall be there with it."[233] The Khān went back to Samarqand, and his illness grew worse and he died, may God have mercy on him;[234] *but for every human being in the world there is a fixed number of breaths decreed and an allotted term of life.*[235]

The Well-Pleasing Amir[236] [i.e. Nuḥ (II) b. Manṣur (I)] re-entered Bokhara on Wednesday, 14–15 Jomādā II 382 (/17 August 992),[237] seized this paternal uncle of his, ʿAbd al-ʿAziz, held him captive and blinded both his eyes with camphor, and Abu'l-Ḥasan ʿAli b. Aḥmad b. Abi Ṭāher, the confidant of the Well-Pleasing Amir, recalled: "I was there when they were blinding this wretched soul. He lamented greatly and wept, and then he said, 'The great consolation is that there will be a day for punishment and recompense in the next world and a Just Arbiter, who will act on behalf of the oppressed against their oppressors.' Indeed, if this were not so, the spectacle would have been too painful for most people to bear."[238] [F 252]

When the Well-Pleasing Amir was established in his capital, and Bu ʿAli Simjur became excessively impertinent and contemptuous, the Amir wrote a letter to the Amir Sebüktegin and sent an envoy, and asked if Sebüktegin would graciously take the trouble to come and meet him on the plains near Nakhshab,[239] so that they could resolve this problem together. The Just Amir Sebüktegin went with a numerous, well-equipped army, including many elephants. He also brought with him Amir Maḥmud, since the Well-Pleasing Amir had ordered Sebüktegin to bring him along so that the office of Commander-in-Chief of Khorasan could be entrusted to him. They proceeded, had a meeting together and the supreme command was given to Amir Maḥmud. Sebüktegin and Maḥmud returned together to Balkh, and Maḥmud was given the honorific title of *Seyf al-Dowla* ("Sword of the Realm"). The Well-Pleasing Amir also led an expedition from Bokhara with a powerful army. They all joined forces and headed for Herat. Bu ʿAli Simjur was there with his brothers and with Fāʾeq and a mighty army.[240] For two or three days, envoys went back and forth to see if a peace agreement could be reached, but to no avail since Bu ʿAli's army would not agree to it. Outside the gates of Herat a fierce battle took place on Tuesday, 14–15 Ramażān 384 [/23 October 994].[241] Bu ʿAli was defeated and retreated to Nishapur, and the Amir of Khorasan Nuḥ returned to Bokhara. The Amir of Guzgānān, Abu'l-Ḥāreth Farighun, Sultan Maḥmud's father-in-law,[242] and the just Amir Sebüktegin, marched towards Nishapur at the end of Shavvāl of this year [/6 December 994]. Bu ʿAli Simjur [Gh 201] fell back to Gorgān.[243] I have left this story at this juncture so that it may be related at a subsequent time, because I had noted another story which I shall now relate, with many a rare feature and well worth knowing, and which concerns the Amir Sebüktegin. *God is most knowing about what is best!* [F 253]

The experiences of the Just Amir Sebüktegin concerning what occurred between him and his master who brought him from Turkestan, and Amir Sebüktegin's dream[244]

The Sharif Abu'l-Moẓaffar b. Aḥmad b. Abi'l-Qāsem al-Hāshemi, called al-ʿAlavi,[245] related to me a story in Shavvāl of the year 450 [/ November-December 1058]—and this is a great, noble-minded and most honourable man, and of a fine lineage. He is, furthermore, cultured and a good poet, having composed around 100,000 verses of poetry concerning this present and former monarchs, may God be pleased with them all and may He grant long life to the exalted Sultan Abu Shojāʿ Farrokh-zād Nāṣer Din Allāh![246]

He narrated thus: At that time when the Just Amir (i.e. Sebüktegin) went to Bokhara for a meeting with the Well-Pleasing Amir (i.e. Nuḥ b. Manṣur), he sent my grandfather Aḥmad b. Abi'l-Qāsem b. Jaʿfar al-Hāshemi to the Amir of Bokhara, and sent with him also the Amir of Guzgānān by virtue of the fact that he was the Commander-in-Chief of the Army, so that they might arrange matters. The Well-Pleasing Amir heaped favours on him and gave him a document conveying a formal grant of investiture remitting the land tax on gardens which he held.[247] When my grandfather died, Amir Maḥmud made this remitted sum over to my father and ordered a formal grant of investiture (i.e. for the property), since he had become the ruler of Khorasan, the Samanids had been overthrown and he had become the monarch.

My grandfather continued to relate: When we finished with the battle at Herat and were proceeding towards Nishapur, the custom was that, each day, the Amir of Guzgānān and all the important commanders, those of the Samanids and those of Khorasan, would come to the door of the just Amir [F 254] Sebüktegin's tent after the [afternoon] worship and would remain waiting there in their saddles. When he came out to mount, all these notables would dismount until he mounted and then they would ride to the next staging-post along the road. When he reached [Gh 202] a staging-post called Khākestar,[248] he encamped there for a day and gave many charitable offerings to the poor. After the afternoon worship, he mounted and rode around in those plains,[249] accompanied by all the leading figures. At various places in those steppelands there were mounds and hillocks. We saw a mound. Amir Sebüktegin exclaimed, "I've found it!," and he reined in his horse and made five or six gholāms get down on foot, and said, "Dig in such-and-such a place!" They began digging and went down a little way. A thick, iron pin came into view, such as is found in stables (i.e. for tethering horses to it); its ring had become separated from it. They pulled it out. Amir Sebüktegin examined it. He dismounted from his horse and offered up thanks to the Almighty God, prostrated himself, wept copiously, called for a prayer rug and performed two *rakʿat*s of the ritual prayer. He ordered this pin to be brought away. He mounted and stood there. The accompanying notables asked, "What's been happening just now?" He replied. "It's an unusual story; listen!"

"Before I found myself in Alptegin's palace, my master the slave dealer transported me and thirteen of my comrades across the Oxus to Shoburqān and thence to Guzgānān. The father of the present Amir was at that time the ruler of Guzgānān.[250] They brought us into his presence. He purchased seven slaves other than myself, but did not choose me and five others.[251] My master travelled onwards from there in the direction of Nishapur. At Marv al-Rudh and Sarakhs [F 255] he sold four more gholāms. I and two of my comrades were left. They used to call me 'Sebüktegin the lofty,' and by chance, three of my master's horses had become saddle-sore under me. When we reached this place Khākestar, another horse had become sore under me, and my master beat me severely and placed a saddle on my own neck. I was very depressed on account of my situation and fortune and my ill luck that no-one would purchase me. My master had sworn an oath that he would take me to Nishapur on foot, and he did so. That night I went to sleep in a highly depressed state. In a dream I saw Kheżr[252] come to me, question me and say, 'Why are you feeling so depressed?' I replied, 'Because of my ill-fortune.' He said, 'Don't be depressed, I bring you the good news that you will become a great and celebrated man, such that one day you will pass through these steppelands with numerous important persons, and you will be at their head. Be of good heart, and when you attain this station, act benevolently towards God's subjects and mete out justice, so that your life may be prolonged and the ruling authority [Gh 203] may remain in your offspring's hands.' I answered, 'I offer up thanks.' He said, 'Give me your hand and make a pledge.' I gave him my hand and made the pledge. He squeezed my hand firmly, and I then awoke from my dream. I still felt that squeeze on my hand. I rose in the middle of the night, performed the major ablution, began performing the ritual worship until fifty *rakʿats* had been done, prayed for a long time and wept. I was feeling much stronger. Then I took away this pin, went out into the plain and thrust it down into the ground as a marker. When day broke, my master loaded up and searched for the pin and could not find it. He gave me a good beating with a whip and swore solemnly that he would sell me for whatever price offered. I walked the two stages to Nishapur. Alptegin was at Nishapur with a great retinue, as Commander-in-Chief for the Samanids, and my master sold me and my two comrades to him. What happened subsequently is a long story, until I reached this rank which you now see." *God is most knowing about what is best!* [F 256]

The story of the Just Amir Sebüktegin with the female deer and her young, his tender behaviour towards them and his dream[253]

I heard at Bost, also in the year 450 [/1058], from ʿAbd al-Malek the accounting official—a noble-spirited man, a capable secretary, a marvel at accountancy and a good raconteur—who related:

At that time when Amir Sebüktegin seized Bost and the power of Bāytuz and his partisans was overthrown,[254] there was a chieftain (*zaʿim*) in the region of Jālaqān called Aḥmad b. Bu ʿOmar,[255] a wealthy and upright old man. Amir Sebuktigin chose him from among all the men of the region, treated him with favour and took him into his own entourage. He became so close a confidant that he would be summoned every night and would remain with the Amir till a late hour, and the Amir used to hold private sessions with him, telling him of his joys, sorrows and secrets. This old man was a friend of my father, Aḥmad b. Bu Nāṣer the accounting official. One day while I was there, he related this story to my father, saying, "Amir Sebüktegin was conversing with me one evening, and was laying open to me the circumstances and secrets of his past adventures and experiences. Then he said, 'Some time before I ended up at Ghaznin, I mounted my steed one day around the time of the afternoon prayers and went out into the open country at Balkh. I had only one horse, [Gh 204] and it was very fleet-footed, so that any hunting prey which came before me was unable to escape. I spotted a female deer with her young. [F 257] I urged on my horse and made a strenuous effort. The fawn became separated from its mother and was distressed. I captured it, placed it over my saddle and turned homewards, the day having by now reached the time of the evening worship. When I had ridden onwards for a while, a sound reached my ear. I looked back, and it was the fawn's mother following in my tracks and making sounds of lamentation and imploring. I turned my horse round, hoping to capture her as well, and I gave chase, but she sped away before me like the wind. I turned back. The same thing happened two or three times, and the poor thing kept coming back and moaning plaintively until I was in the vicinity of the town. She was still following me and making piteous sounds. I felt sorry for her and said to myself, "What good is this young deer to me? I should be kind to this loving mother," and I threw the fawn back on to the open plain. It ran towards its mother, and they gave cries and both went off towards the steppeland. I returned homewards. The night had grown dark and my horse had not had its barley feed. I felt most depressed and went to sleep in my quarters in a sorrowful state. In a dream I saw an old man, most radiant with intelligence, who came close to me and addressed me, "O Sebüktegin, because of that compassion which you showed for that mother gazelle and gave this young one back to her, and left your horse without its barley feed, we have bestowed on you and your offspring the town called Ghaznin, and Zābolestān; I myself am the messenger of the Creator, *may His glory be extolled and His names be hallowed, and there is no god but He!*" I awoke, and felt assured and strong-hearted, and I always had this dream in mind until I reached my present status. I know for certain that royal power will remain in my house and among my descendants until that time which God, His mention is exalted, has decreed!' " [F 258]

The story of Moses the divine messenger and the lamb, and his compassion for it[256]

When the old man of Jālaqān finished his story (i.e. about Sebüktegin and the young gazelle), my father said: "That was a fine and marvellous dream. Compassion and pity are indeed admirable qualities, especially when bestowed upon these dumb, harmless creatures, [Gh 205] such as cats and the like. For I have read in the historical accounts of Moses that, when he was a shepherd, he was driving the sheep one night towards their enclosure; it was the time for the ritual worship, and a dark night with heavy rain pouring down. Near the enclosure, a lamb ran away. Moses became flustered and chased after it, meaning to beat it with a stick when he caught up with it. But when he did collar it, his heart went out to it, he clasped it to himself and patted its head, saying, 'You poor thing! You have nothing to fear behind you and nothing to hope for ahead of you, so why did you run away and abandon your mother?' And although it had been pre-ordained that he would be a divine messenger (*peyghambar*), this act of compassion made his prophethood (*nobuvvat*) all the more secure and strengthened."[257] [F 259]

I have set forth these two remarkable dreams and this tale so that it will be known and confirmed that this royal authority will remain in this great house for a long time. I now return to the thread of the story which I had begun (i.e. about the Tabbānis) in order to complete it.

The remainder of the story of the Tabbānis

The Amir Sebüktegin remained for a while at Nishapur until the matter of Amir Maḥmud was settled, and then he set off back to Herat. Bu ʿAli Simjur sought to proceed from Gorgān to Pārs (Fārs) and Kerman and seize those provinces, since the climate of Gorgān was unhealthy and he feared that he might share Tāsh's ill-fate, who had died there. But he could not relinquish the thought of Khorasan and Nishapur; there is no remedy for a self-inflicted wound, and it has been proverbially said, "*Your two hands have fastened up [the skin] and your mouth has blown it up.*"[258] When he heard that Amir Sebüktegin had gone to Herat and that Amir Maḥmud had only a small force of men, he was tempted to recapture Nishapur. On the first day of Rabiʿ I of the year 385 [/5 April 995] he set out from Gorgān, accompanied by his brothers and Fāʾeq al-Khāṣṣa and with a strong, well-equipped army. When news of his action reached Amir Maḥmud, he withdrew from the town and encamped in the Garden of ʿAmr b. Leyth, a parasang away from the town. The Commander Bu Naṣr b. Maḥmud, the grandfather on his mother's side of Khᵛāja Bu Naṣr N.v.ki/Nuki—who is at present the mayor of Ghaznin—joined up with him.[259] The mass of the common people of the town flocked to the side of Bu ʿAli Simjur, and made a great show of joy at his coming, took up their arms [Gh 206] and set out to give battle. It was a battle aimed at opening up a breach. Amir Maḥmud fought valiantly, and since there was no adequate defence to stop them, they broke through into that garden, [F 260] and he left for Herat. His father, Sebüktegin, sent forward a force of cavalrymen and began gathering together an army. A large number of men, including Indians, Khalaj[260] and men of every kind, was assembled. Bu ʿAli Simjur took up his position at Nishapur and ordered the *khoṭba* to be made there in his name: "*No victor was ever seen more like a defeated one than he*".[261]

The Amirs Sebüktegin and Maḥmud marched out from Herat, leaving the ruler of Sistan at Pushang but brought along with them the latter's son with a fully-equipped army.[262] When Bu ʿAli heard reports of their approach, he left Nishapur for Ṭus in order to give battle there, and the enemy came up after him. Amir Sebüktegin sent an envoy to Bu ʿAli with the verbal message, "Your house is an ancient one and I do not wish to be the one who destroys it. Accept my sincere advice and opt for peace, so that we may return to Merv and you can be the deputy of my son Maḥmud at Nishapur. I can then step forth and intercede, so that the Amir of Khorasan (i.e. the Samanid ruler) may regard you favourably. In this way, everything will turn out well, and sources of fear and suspicion will be removed. I know that all this will not please[263] you, but look at it wisely and take stock of the situation, and you will realize that I am speaking the truth and offering fatherly advice. Rest assured that I have nothing to worry about and that I do not say these words from a position of weakness. With the great army which I have, everything is possible, with the strength of the

Almighty God, but I am seeking the path of peace and righteousness and not pursuing the way of tyranny and injustice."

These words fell not unfavourably on Bu ʿAli's ears, since he perceived the possibility of a reverse. He related these words to his commanders. They all replied, 'What sort of talk is this? We must give battle!" Bu'l-Ḥoseyn b. Kathir, father of Khᵛāja Abu'l-Qāsem, [F 261] was very eager to accept this peace offer and gave much good counsel, but to no avail in the face of what Fate had ordained would come to pass. We seek refuge in God! When luck runs out, all plans go wrong! The poet has said, [Poetry]

1. *When God decrees the departure of all prosperity from a people's house, they undertake wrong courses of action.*[264]

During the night of Sunday, 19–20 Jomādā II 385 [/21–2 July 995],[265] [Gh 207] they engaged in battle and fought each other furiously. The forces of Bu ʿAli and Fāʾeq severely hammered the greater part of Sebüktegin's army, and the latter was almost put to flight. But Amir Maḥmud and Khalaf's son, with a highly select, battle-experienced and fresh cavalry force suddenly appeared from an ambush and inflicted a mighty blow on Fāʾeq and Il-mengü,[266] so that they were routed. When Bu ʿAli saw this, he was put to flight, and he fled precipitately to the pass leading to the river[267] so that he might from there follow his own way. They captured a group of his leading men and commanders, including the General Bu ʿAli, Begtegin Morghābi, Yināltegin,[268] Moḥammad, son of the General Ṭoghān, Moḥammad Shārtegin,[269] Lashkar-setān[270] of Deylam, Aḥmad b. Arslān the treasurer, Bu ʿAli b. Nushtegin and Arslān of Samarqand,[271] and together with these captives, they took back those of their own men, and their elephants, who had been captured in the battle of the breach. Bu'l-Fatḥ Bosti[272] says concerning the battle, [Poetry]

1. *Have you not seen what Abu ʿAli encountered, when I previously saw him as a man of judgement and shrewdness?*

2. *He rebelled against the ruling power, hence there hastened against him men who could uproot Abu Qobeys.*

3. *He made Ṭus his strong refuge, but Ṭus became more ill-fated for him than Ṭoweys.*[273] [F 262]

The dominion of the Simjuris came to an end, in such a way that one did not succeed another (i.e. the line was cut off) and they did not secure a permanent foundation on the earth.[274]

Bu ʿAli made his way to Khwarazm, where he was arrested, but his gholām Il-mengü stirred up trouble against the Khwarazmians until they released Bu ʿAli. After that, he was hoodwinked by the plausible lies of the Amir of Khorasan and, notwithstanding his arrogant behaviour in the past, arrived in Bokhara. Then after going back and forth at the Well-Pleasing Amir's court for some days, they seized him and several of his senior commanders[275] and plundered everything they had, including the beasts of burden, weapons, valuables and equipment. At the time of the evening worship they bore away Bu ʿAli and fifteen other men to the citadel and imprisoned them there, this being in the month of Jomādā II of the year 386[276] [/June-July 996].[277] Amir Sebüktegin was at Balkh, and kept sending envoys and messages to Bokhara, saying, "Khorasan will never be at peace while Bu ʿAli is in Bokhara. You should send him to us so that he may be incarcerated in the fortress of Ghaznin." The Well-Pleasing Amir's trusty advisers said that it would be unseemly to despatch him there. The procrastination on their side was met by persistence and intimidation on Sebüktegin's side. But the power of the Samanids had reached its end, and whether they liked it or not, [Gh 208] they had to send Bu ʿAli and Il-mengü to Balkh in Shaʿbān of this year [/August-September 996]. One of the religious lawyers of Balkh told the story, "I saw these two figures on the day they were brought to Balkh. Bu ʿAli was mounted on a mule, with knee-high boots[278] and wearing a robe [F 263] of green *ʿattābi* cloth[279] and a silken turban. When he reached K.jājiyān,[280] he asked, "What do they call this place?" They said, "So-and-so." He replied, "The astrologers made the prognostication for us that we should come to these parts, but we did not know that it would be in this wise."

The Well-Pleasing Amir repented of his sending Bu ʿAli, and said, "Our neighbouring rulers are chiding us."[281] He wrote a letter and sought for Bu ʿAli to be sent back. Sebüktegin's representative at the Samanid court wrote to him that an envoy was coming requesting this act of service. Before the envoy and the letter could arrive, Sebüktegin despatched Bu ʿAli and Il-mengü with one of his own commanders to Ghazni and they were imprisoned in the fortress of Gardiz. When the envoy arrived, Sebüktegin sent a reply, "Khorasan is in turmoil and I am occupied with restoring order there. When I have accomplished this, I will go to Ghaznin and will have Bu 'Ali sent back."[282]

Bu 'Ali's son Bu'l-Ḥasan ended up at Ray at the court of Fakhr al-Dowla. They treated him with great honour and assigned him a monthly allowance of 5,000 dirhams. But on account of his affection for a woman or a boy, he returned to Nishapur and went into hiding. Amir Maḥmud ordered strenuous efforts to be made in ferreting him out; he was seized, and carried off to Ghaznin and imprisoned in the fortress of Gardiz. *We seek refuge in God from the reversal of fortune!*[283] The Simjuris were overthrown, and Amir Maḥmud became firmly established as Commander-in-Chief of Khorasan and became a powerful figure. His heart was, however, fixed upon Ghaznin. Whenever he came across a man or woman who was an outstanding exponent of his or her craft or profession, he would despatch that person to there.[284] Bu Ṣāleḥ Tabbāni, whose fame and lofty status I have set forth, was one of these. This tale has now come to its close; it is not devoid of many remarkable aspects and wonders. [F 264]

This Imam Bu Ṣādeq Tabbāni, may God preserve him[285] and prolong his lifespan, who is now in Ghazni (his maternal uncle was Bu Ṣāleḥ, whose circumstances I have explained), was at Nishapur occupied with scholarship. When Amir Maḥmud made a firm compact and agreement with Manuchehr the governor of Gorgān and chose a noble lady to be conveyed there, and when Khᵛāja 'Ali b. Mikā'il, was intending to set off, in the year 402 [/1011–12],[286] Amir Maḥmud said to him, [Gh 209], "The Tabbānis and their disciples adhere to the correct line of the legal school (*madhhab-e rāst*) of the followers of the Imam Abu Ḥanifa, may God have mercy on him, so that no possible criticism can be levelled at them. Bu Ṣāleḥ has passed away; when you arrive in Nishapur, enquire whether there are any members of the Tabbāni family left, and which of them would be suitable for Ghaznin and our court. Cultivate them all, and on our behalf give them hopes of favour, and promise of places in our service and beneficence." He replied, "I'll do as you command."[287]

When the noble lady was brought to Nishapur, I, Bu'l-Fażl, was sixteen years old at the time[288] and saw the Khᵛāja's arrival and the great effort which had been made at Nishapur, including the erection of festive platforms with arches[289] and their decoration, whose like I never saw again at Nishapur. ʿAli b. Mikāʾil made much of the Tabbānis, and gave Bu Ṣādeq, Bu Ṭāher and other members of the family hopes of handsome treatment from the Sultan's court. Then he continued onwards to Gorgān, conveying the noble lady to there. Amirak Beyhaqi accompanied them, with the charge of reporting everything which went on (at that time he was functioning as a secretary in the Chancery as apprentice under ʿAbdallāh the secretary). I saw him as a debonair young man, finely dressed and turned out. Khᵛāja ʿAli returned from Gorgān. The people of Gorgān had made great efforts at ceremony and show. He reached Nishapur and from there travelled on to Ghaznin. [F 265]

In that year when the Sultan gave Ḥasanak permission to go on the Pilgrimage, that is, the year 414 [/1023–4], Amir Maḥmud also instructed him, "When you reach Nishapur, convey our favour to Bu Ṣādeq Tabbāni and others." When he arrived there, he made much of the Imam Bu Ṣādeq and others, and gave hopes of handsome favours. He went on, performed the Pilgrimage and set off back for Balkh. Amir Maḥmud was there, making preparations to travel at Nowruz for the meeting with Qadïr Khān. Ḥasanak took the Imam Bu Ṣādeq with him, together with several other religious scholars from Nishapur. (Bu Ṣādeq was an outstanding figure in the religious sciences[290] and had acquired a great deal of learning (*fażl*) apart from the religious sciences.) He arrived in Balkh. The Amir asked Ḥasanak what the present situation of the Tabbānis was. He replied, "Bu Ṭāher holds the judgeship of Ṭus and Nasā, and it was not possible to bring him along without the exalted command, but I have brought along Bu Ṣādeq." The Amir said, "Well done!" They were involved in many important affairs, and Bu Ṣādeq was sent back, another factor here being that Ḥasanak did not want to send him on to the Sultan's court since he had set his heart on a plan and had talked about it with Bu Ṣādeq at Nishapur, that he would build a very finely-appointed college at the head of the Alley of the Basket-Weavers in order to install Bu Ṣādeq to teach there. But one must know that outstanding merit (*fażl*), although it may be kept hidden, will in the end become publicly known, just like the scent of musk.[291]

Bu Ṣādeq attended a disputation session[292] [Gh 210] with Abu'l-ʿAbbās the Judge of Balkh, the Judge ʿAli Ṭāyaqāni[293] and other scholars, and very complex questions of differing interpretations[294] were discussed. Bu Ṣādeq joined in and surpassed them all,[295] to such an extent that these leading, senior scholars averred that they had never seen a religious scholar like him. Bu Bakr Ḥaṣiri and Bu'l-Ḥasan Karaji conveyed this report to Amir Maḥmud. [F 266] He was very appreciative of all this and summoned Bu Ṣādeq into his presence and saw him, and intellectual topics were aired during his audience session. The Amir regarded him with approval and said, "Plans must be made for the journey to Transoxania, and from there back to Ghaznin," and Bu Ṣādeq went back home from that court session. Amir Maḥmud formed the intention of crossing the Oxus. He bestowed on Ḥasanak a robe of honour and commanded him to return to Nishapur. Ḥasanak said to Bu Ṣādeq, "This monarch has his sights fixed on a great enterprise and is going to an unknown land. Enemies abound and one cannot know what might befall. You are a learned scholar, unaccustomed to travelling, and you should not risk a calamity. Go back to Nishapur with me, in an honoured and exalted state. Once the Sultan becomes freed from this important affair, I myself will head for Ghaznin and take you with me so that you may take up residence there." Bu Ṣādeq returned with him to Nishapur.

The Amir had held his meeting with Qadïr Khān, and he came back to Ghaznin in the summer and decided on the expedition to Somnāth. He ordered a letter to be written to Ḥasanak, to the effect that "You should stay at Nishapur, since we are undertaking a raiding expedition to far-away regions, and when we return safe and sound to Ghaznin, you must come and render service." The Amir set out and raided Somnāth[296] and returned in a healthy and contended state. On the way home he ordered a letter to be written to Ḥasanak, saying, "You must hasten to render service, and bring Bu Ṣādeq Tabbāni with you, for he is of use to our court." Ḥasanak set out from Nishapur, accompanied by an extensive retinue of judges, religious lawyers, prominent men and notables in order that they might greet the Amir. They received marks of favour and robes of honour according to their status and rank, and returned to Nishapur. The Amir gave orders that this Imam Bu Ṣādeq should be retained at the court; he bestowed marks of favour and ordained for him a monthly allowance. A short time after that, he appointed him Chief Judge of Khottalān, since there were twenty-odd colleges there with charitable endowments attached for their support (*owqāf*).[297] During the whole of his time there, his words were obeyed and he enjoyed power and prestige in a regal fashion. He is here now at this great royal presence [F 267] (i.e. the court of Sultan Ebrāhim in Ghaznin)—may it endure for ever and may he also [Gh 211] enjoy long life!—since great benefit is to be derived from him, and he has taken up permanent residence in the Rebāṭ of Mānk b. ʿAli b. Meymun.[298] Monarchs entrusted to him confidential matters, and he conducted important embassies. When I reach the time of the monarchs (i.e. of those coming after Masʿud), I shall set forth what they commanded him,[299] *if God Most High so wills and if He holds back the appointed term* (i.e. grants the author continued life).

The Judge Bu Ṭāher Tabbāni was in Nishapur at the time when Amir Masʿud had headed for Nishapur from Ray. He had gone forth a distance of several stages to meet and escort the Amir, accompanied by the Judge Bu'l-Ḥasan, son of the Judge, the Imam Abu'l-ʿAlā', and he had sought the office of Chief Judge of Ray and those regions and had received a favourable answer. But when they reached Nishapur and the Judge Bu Ṭāher came there, the Amir said to him, "We intended to send you to Ray to be Chief Judge there, but now we have given that office to Bu'l-Ḥasan. You yourself are to come with us, so that, when state affairs become more regularised, you can exercise the office of Chief Judge of Nasā and Ṭus, and your deputies are there already. We shall add to it the charge of Judge of Nishapur, but we are now sending you on a great and important mission to Turkestan to conclude a marriage contract and agreement. When you complete that, and come back to the court, you are to make your way to Nishapur, with favour and a robe of honour, and take up your residence there and exercise the office of Judge of Nishapur, with deputies for yourself in Ṭus and Nasā, for our opinion of you is of the highest." He offered obeisance, and came with the Amir to Herat. Affairs now assumed a settled state. The Amir went on to Balkh and these circumstances which I have previously set forth attained a completed form. This Judge Bu Ṭāher, may God have mercy on him, was appointed to go on a diplomatic mission with Khᵛāja Bu'l-Qāsem Ḥaṣiri, may God keep him safe, to Kāshghar and the court of Qadïr Khān in Turkestan.[300]

Since the story of the Tabbāni family has been given, I am now going to set down here the texts of these letters and sets of verbal instructions (*moshāfaha-hā*)[301] [F 268] so that they may be known, if God Most High so wills.

An account of the text of the letter and the two sets of verbal instructions sent with the two above-mentioned envoys who set out for Turkestan[302]

In the name of God, the Merciful, the Compassionate

When we reached Balkh in a state of well-being and victoriousness —may the life of the exalted Khān be prolonged!—and all affairs of the realm became orderly, we composed a letter, despatched by a swift courier, so that all that which God Most High had empowered us to do, from the time when we marched to Isfahan until this present time when [Gh 212] we arrived here, including unimaginable victories, may become well known and that, given the bond and the unity between the two houses which is so firmly established, a portion of the resulting fortune and credit may be gleaned here by you. Through our envoys, we have sent a memorandum concerning the marriage alliance and agreement so that the firm foundations of friendship between us, over which we expended so much toil and trouble to establish, will become even firmer and more solid.

Now we have sent our brother and trusted confidant Abu'l-Qāsem Ebrāhim b. ʿAbdallāh al-Ḥaṣiri, [F 269] may God prolong his glorious state, who is one of the trusted members of our court, in the rank of the especially close boon companions. The late Amir, our father, may God illuminate his proof, held him in great affection and esteem, and consulted him on matters concerning the welfare of the kingdom; today he is the most valuable and useful legacy and relic of that era, and his competence and ability in offering sound advice are only too apparent. He has been sent as an envoy so that he may convey our most pleasant and purest benedictions and greetings to the Khān. He will embark upon what he has been instructed to do until the matter is brought to its fruition[303] in a thoroughgoing fashion and according to the correct procedures, and will then return home.

The Judge Abu Ṭāher ʿAbdallāh b. Aḥmad al-Tabbāni, may God prolong His favour for him, has been attached to him, so that when it is approved that the marriage contract and agreement should be concluded according to the terms brought by the envoy, the Judge may perform all the relevant legal conditions, in accordance with the requirements of the *Sharīʿa*. This Judge is one of the leading religious scholars of the court. He has conducted many an important mission and embassy, and in each one of these his sound counsel and piety have been apparent.

The envoy Abu'l-Qāsem has verbal instructions, since in those instructions words can be spoken more openly, in such a way that when he receives the appropriate permission, he may reveal their contents. He has another set of verbal instructions with him concerning an important matter, but if this matter is not raised in discussion he will not present them; if however it is subsequently discussed, he will necessarily show them so that the intended aims may be achieved. Our trust in him extends to such a point that, if the discussion gets bogged down with questions and answers and becomes protracted, whatever he says is exactly the same as if it comes from our own mouth, since what needs to be said he has already rehearsed with us in several of our court sessions and he has heard unequivocal answers, so that he would not have to refer back to us for instructions for any matter to be settled, and can return home with everything agreed upon and completed. He also has with him a list (*tadhkera*) (i.e. of presents to be offered), as has been the customary practice, and there has always been such exchanging of presents and winning over with precious gifts on the part of both sides, [F 270] so that when these are looked at favourably, any faults in them may remain hidden.

It befits the Khān's exalted magnanimity that the envoys are not kept too long but sent back swiftly with their wishes granted, [Gh 213] for the people of our two great lands look forward to the establishment of friendship between us. When the envoys are sent back homewards, with their mission achieved, envoys from that well-guarded land (i.e. the eastern Qarakhanid kingdom) should be attached to them,[304] with the aim that, when they reach our royal presence, we likewise may bring about all the conditions of friendship and concord, as have been sought, *with the permission of the Almighty God.*

The first set of verbal instructions

"O brother and trusted confidant Abu'l-Qāsem Ebrāhim b. ʿAbdallāh al-Ḥaṣiri, may God prolong your remaining span of life, when you present yourself at the Khān's court, you must convey to him our greetings with an affirmation of his greatness and awesome presence. Also, you are to set forth the insignificance of the list of presents which have been sent with you as tokens of friendship and solicitude, in the most attractive way possible, and to say that these trifling things are sent by way of adhering to the customary practice. Then after this, excuses should be sought, and presents and tokens of friendship on a scale worthy of both sides be offered. Then say [F 271] that the Khān will be aware that, at the present moment, the people of the two great regions who are under the rule of us two powerful monarchs, and those outside, in the neighbouring lands, near and far, are closely watching to see what form the friendship between the two of us will take, so that when the relations between the ruling houses which, God be praised, are now one, become more firmly linked together in unity and concord, our friends and well-wishers may become joyful by it, for they will be able to live their lives in security and peace of mind. Enemies and evil-doers will become sorrowful and downhearted, since they will know that they will have to put up the shutters and go out of business.[305] Therefore, it would be better if there were a proper contract between us two friends, with a mutual bond of marriage attached to it, for when marriage and personal links are established, all contentious talk is cut short, and slanderers and mischiefmakers will find themselves out of a job. And when the foes of both sides realize that we speak and act with one voice, they will be deprived of all their strength[306] and will know that opportunities for mischief will no longer come their way and that they will never get their wishes. The blessings of co-operation and mutual help would soon become apparent to both sides ...[307] including conquering new provinces and embarking on noteworthy and far-flung raiding expeditions against the infidels, thereby bringing joy to the souls of departed monarchs. For when we revive and make fresh their custom (*sonnat*) of launching raids against the infidels, they will be pleased with us and [Gh 214] the blessings emanating from that will accrue to us and our descendants.

"When this section of the proceedings is confirmed and settled, and the Khān decides to conclude the agreement, ask for an appointed day deemed as appropriate for solemnising the agreement.[308] Then request that the notables, the trusty courtiers of that noble house, the paternal uncles, the brothers [F 272] and the sons [of the Khān], may God long keep them in their exalted states, together with the leading judges and ulema, present themselves at the Khān's court. You yourself, bringing with you the Judge Bu Ṭāher, are to go there and present the document setting forth the agreement which was given to you, so that its conditions may be confirmed, and you are to say that, when this agreement has been made and the envoys from that well-protected kingdom, who have been given leave to depart in your company, reach our court and see us, we likewise will ratify the agreement on the basis of that same document which we have sought and which is in your possession, in such a fashion that no addition or deletion be admitted. It is certainly necessary that nothing of the conditions set out in the agreement document should be changed or altered, since the aim is complete correctness and mutual benefit. At no time has it ever been considered reprehensible that one should insist on exactitude in such great and notable matters, for the more correctly couched a treaty, the better and more beneficial it would prove.

"If any trusted retainer from their side should suggest some improvement concerning one of the clauses of the agreement, you should heed his words and answer fairly and act freely in the ensuing debate, for you will be able to judge for yourself on the spot, and we will give our consent to whatever you decide and will put our name to whatever passes muster with you. However, it is incumbent upon you that whatever you agree to should not reflect any diminution in the status of our realm. If you find yourself baffled by a thorny problem for which you have received no instructions from us, refer back to us for a decision and send letters by swift couriers so that the problem in question may be resolved. For this is a momentous and protracted mission and it may not come right in a session or two or even more, and there is scope for doubts and indecisions, and therefore it will acceptable if you arrive at the court later than planned. What is important is that you return with a well-executed and accomplished mission, with no further need for any other mission or review.

"When the matter of the agreement is settled, the Judge, may God prolong his state of health and preservation, is to ask the Khān to read out aloud, in their entirety, those conditions and solemn oaths which are written in the text of the agreement [F 273], in the presence of those assembled. Extreme care should be taken that the agreement is correctly drawn up in conformity with the requirements of the religious law. Then after that, the leading figures are to write on it their attestations of witnessing and their signatures, as is the usual practice.

"After the agreement is settled, speak with the Khān to the effect that, 'Since an affair of such excellence has gone through, and its blessed effect will extend to future generations, we have reached the opinion that there ought to be, from the side of the Khān, [Gh 215] two marriage links, one for ourself and one for our son Abu'l-Fatḥ Mowdud, may his firm position be prolonged, who is our eldest son and who will succeed to the kingly power after us as our covenanted successor. That bride (*vadiʿat*) who is to be nominated for ourself should be from the noble virgins of the Khān's own family, and the other bride should be from the children of the Amir the Khān's son, Bughrātegin, the covenanted heir to the throne. But it is necessary that these two noble ladies should be princesses of noble lineage on both sides.[309] If the Khān sees fit to agree to these requests and gives us an affirmative answer, as befits his lofty spirit, high resolution and bountiful traits of character (and in no possible way would it be admissible, and on account of his chivalrous nature it would be unfitting, that we should receive a refusal in this matter), it is confirmed that, when he gives us this answer, whatever he may ask, we shall agree to it in its entirety, so that this friendship may be so firmly established that time[310] will not have the power to tear it asunder. When he signifies his agreement—and I know that he will, since in all aspects he is peerless in his magnanimity—you are to take the solemn engagement the next day, so that on that same day, these two marriage contracts may be concluded most auspiciously. Take the Judge Bu Ṭāher with you so that both contracts may be concluded and so that he can perform all the required legal conditions and formulae. Set the dowry for those two brides—the one who is to be mine [F 274] at 50,000 Haravi dinars, and that for the other bride, that of our son, at 30,000 Haravi dinars. When you come back from the session where the marriage contracts have been concluded, give orders for the treasurers who are with you to bring out and hand over the offerings of money and the presents, which have been sent with you, to the Khān, the heir to the throne, and the queens and mothers of the two brides, and to the paternal uncles, relatives and court retainers, may God prolong their firm position and the security and safety of them all, according to what that document, which you have with you, expressly stipulates.

"You should also make the necessary apology, explaining the fact that what has at this present moment been hurriedly despatched is a mere formal offering,[311] and when the litters for conveying the brides (*mahd-hā*) are sent for the brides to be brought back in a blessed and auspicious fashion, appropriate and customary presents, as befits both sides, will accompany the litters. For the time being, this array of presents should be looked upon with a compliant eye.

"After these proceedings have been carried out and everything is settled, request permission to return, and bring with you the envoys of the Khān who have been nominated, so that when everyone arrives at our court in a state of health and preservation, we may likewise follow the example of the Khān and [Gh 216] put in place what is necessary in these matters for conducing to an increase of friendship and concord, if God Most High so wills."

The second set of verbal instructions

"O brother and trusted confidant Abu'l-Qāsem al-Ḥaṣiri, may God prolong your remaining life, I am thinking that it may happen that they will ask you about the affair of our brother, the Amir Abu Aḥmad Moḥammad, may God prolong [F 275] his health and safe condition, and will say, 'When Sultan Maḥmud and Qadïr Khān had their meeting together at the gate of Samarqand, and concluded the marriage contracts and agreements, there was a promised liaison in the name of our brother, the conditions of this being well known. What should be done now regarding this? For that arrangement can in no way now be put into effect, yet the *Shariʿa* does not allow it to be left in a state of perpetual abeyance.'[312] If more or less nothing is said about this topic, and if they show regard for our feelings in this respect and leave that matter to us, do not yourself add anything on that subject until that time when the envoys from that noble quarter reach our court in your company. Then if at that time they *do* say something on that score, we will answer them as we see fit. But if they do bring it up now, then we have hereby ordered that your answers should be laid out for you in these instructions so that you will know how to pick your words and there will be no need for you to refer back for briefing.

"[So, if necessary,] tell them that it is well known how dearly and preciously the late Amir, may God illuminate his proof, held us when we were a child, and how he singled us out above all his offspring. When subsequently we emerged from school and a period of time elapsed, in the year 406 [/1015–16] he made us his covenanted heir, and first of all, oaths were required of his brothers, Naṣr and Yusof, followed by his relatives, close retainers and courtiers, and they gave a solemn undertaking that, if the decree of death were to come upon him, the royal throne should go to us. He put in place every binding document and precaution necessary for this matter, and he gave us the governorship of Herat and that of Guzgānān to our brother, after he had been made to swear an oath that he would place himself under our command and in our obedience when we ascended the imperial throne. All those things which are customarily given to designated heirs, comprising gholāms, precious objects, arms and equipment, a counsellor and adjutant to act as a vizier, chamberlains and attendants, he ordained for us in the fullest possible measure.

"In the year 408 [/1017–18], he ordered us to proceed to Herat since it is the central point [F 276] for Khorasan, and he gave orders for the leading court figures, judges, local governors and tax-collectors, notables and subjects to come and offer us service, and all of them gave ear to what we said. In addition to this, he sought that the news should spread far and near that we were his deputy and his covenanted successor. We remained for a considerable period of time in Herat, and [Gh 217] everyone in Khorasan acted in accordance with the commands we gave. This continued until troublemakers and envious ones filled the mind of that lord with animosity against us and painted a picture of mischievous and wrong actions, no part of which God Most High had brought into being and which He had never permitted to enter our heart. They devised stratagems to alter the good opinion which he had of us, and he was, moreover, taken in by what they wrought. Furthermore, that aspect of human nature which could not contemplate anyone who was worthy of his own, Maḥmud's, place, led him to treat us in a harsh fashion. He recalled us from Herat and sent us to Multan, and we were in effect held captive there for a period of time, even though it was not called by the name of 'captivity.' He elevated the status of our brother, ordered various acts of favour in respect of him and bestowed all sorts of beneficence in order to make us feel discomfited. Yet despite all this, he did not deprive us of the title of covenanted successor and did not make any alteration or change in that arrangement, and when our enemies and those who envied us did suggest change and alteration through their devious words and sly allusions, he would shout at them to desist.

"Meanwhile, we were patiently enduring and had entrusted our affair to God Most High until, in accordance with His grace, it would be appropriate to make the mind of that lord show kindness towards us, since we were guiltless. It became clear to him what they had wrought—since in the time of our grandfather the Just Amir (i.e. Sebüktegin), [F 277] exactly the same troubles had been stirred up—to the point that Maḥmud comprehended the situation and spoke words to the effect that 'We inflicted wrongs on Masʿud, just as we suffered from our own father,' and he summoned us back from Multan, extending his favour to us in the same measure as in times past, and sent us back to Herat.

"Nevertheless, although these circumstances were set straight in this wise, the calumniators still did not allow that monarch's mind to become completely favourable to us. At times they would say that we were exacting a pledge of obedience (*beyʿat*) from the army, and at other times they would say that we were intending to attack Kerman and Western Persia. They caused troubles and misrepresentations of this sort so that his mind never became completely free of doubts regarding us. Letters containing reproaches were continuously arriving and he kept throwing in our teeth the praiseworthy activities of our brother. We, meanwhile, were showing patient endurance, since God Most High will never abandon His servants who are upright, who depend entirely upon Him and who maintain an attitude of patient endurance.

"Because of the numerous misrepresentations and troubles which they wrought, affairs reached such a point that, each year when he would summon us to Ghaznin, at the court and in government policy sessions (*majles-e emārat*) he would order the protocol for going there, for being seated and for going back, to be exactly the same for us two persons, Masʿud and Moḥammad. Then after that he gave an order, for that period of time when we would be at court, [Gh 218] that for one day the figure enjoying primacy should be ourself and the next day our brother.[313] Every day there would be messages sent to us containing, in varying degrees, reproaches and harsh words, while those to our brother would contain expressions of affection and bestowal of praise. Furthermore, when he, Maḥmud, sought from the Caliph a grant of more honorific titles for himself, and at the same time sought further titles for ourself and for his brother Yusof,[314] he had given a command that, on the letter to the caliphal court the name of our brother should be written first. We did not exhibit any dismay, and declared, 'This is as it should be,' so as not to give them any further pretext.

"When Sultan Maḥmud led an expedition against Ray and came to Gorgān, and the excellent Commander, our Uncle, the Khwarazm Shah, arrived there—and he had already made up his own mind that he would leave us at Ray, and that Moḥammad should be appointed to Khorasan [F 278] and the seat of imperial power (i.e. Ghaznin)—he consulted with the Khwarazm Shah and the leading figures of the army on this matter. They did not have the temerity to give a direct answer but requested that they might give their replies through messages. This was agreed to, and many words and messages passed to and fro until a decision was reached in that they effected an agreement between ourself and our brother that, when our father should pass away, we should not attack each other—since Moḥammad did not in any case have the permission to take away from me the designation of covenanted successor—and that our brother should subsequently hand over our share *in toto*. He sent our brother to Khorasan, and took us with him and conquered those regions. He entrusted them to us and turned back on account of illness and his impending death.

"He left us at Ray with such a lack of matériel and troops that we were regarded as easy prey by everyone, and with the further motive, that our name should be tarnished, and that we should come back in a sorry state, with our tail between our legs.[315] But the Almighty God, through His grace, held us within His care[316] in such a way that in the course of one winter many of our aims were achieved, including the battle at Sar-e Jahān[317] and the capture of the Sālār of Ṭārom, and after that, the onslaught against the Son of Kāku and the capture of Isfahan, those episodes being known to the Khān in full detail; if he does not know them fully, Abu'l-Qāsem Ḥaṣiri can give an exposition of them, for he knows them well. From there, we intended to attack Hamadan, Ḥolvān, Kermānshāhān and Baghdad, but the news of the decease of that mighty sovereign and strong pillar, our father, reached us at Isfahan, and the foundations of the realm became enfeebled. We had the intention of observing the terms of his testament so that no conflict should ensue, but [F 279] Moḥammad's supporters did not let this happen and, willy-nilly, an expedition to Khorasan and the homeland [Gh 219] had to be made, as has been previously set forth in its entirety by hand of a courier and the Khān made cognisant of it.[318]

"At the present time, since the direction of the state has necessarily become firmly established in our hands, and our brother passed into our power—his position during our father's lifetime was the one which has been set forth in this set of verbal instructions, and after our father's death things happened as they did, until the idea of becoming ruler came into my brother's mind, together with the desire for giving orders, for sitting on the royal throne, and for issuing incalculable wealth from the treasuries and lavishing it in gifts—how can it be right that he should be released? For in no circumstances can two swords exist in one scabbard or be placed there, for they would not fit. The wisest course for him, for the army and for the subjects is that he should be held in some place on our authority, in the most comfortable conditions possible. Releasing him would generate extensive security threats. When a certain amount of time has elapsed and when affairs have become completely harmonious and peacefully ordered, then, at that time, according to what God Most High has decreed, and according to what the prevalent conditions require, decisions will be made concerning my brother Moḥammad, *with the Almighty God's permission.*

"When this set of verbal instructions is studied in the light of the complete wisdom which God Most High has given to the Khān and in the light of the other elements of greatness and masterfulness given to him, we know that [F 280] he will consider us as excused in regard to what has been said and he will not consider it appropriate to bring up mention of the marriage contract which was made in our brother's name. For he, may God make perpetual His goodness towards him, has so written[319] that he is, up to the present moment, taking as much care for our welfare and interest as for his own. We ask for success from God, His mention is exalted, so that this friendship which we have embarked upon may be fully achieved; *indeed, He is the best of those who give success and provide succour.*

"If occasion does not arise for setting forth [the subject matter of this] set of verbal instructions which contain the account of our brother and the marriage contract, and the Khān and his advisers pay no attention to it, then these instructions should be laid aside. If subsequently any words should pass regarding this topic, herein are trenchant answers in this set of instructions; present them and clarify the situation. Say whatever needs to be said—for you were a witness to all these matters and saw them all—so that there would be absolutely no further room for debate and doubts, *if the Almighty God so wills.*"

Behold, the texts of the letter and of each of the two sets of verbal instructions were on this wise, and much profit may be gained by pondering over them, [Gh 220] *if God Most High so wills.*

Amir Masʿud had a private session with the Vizier Khᵛāja Aḥmad b. Ḥasan and the Head of the Chancery, Bu Naṣr Moshkān. These two envoys were summoned, and that meeting dragged on till the time of the afternoon worship. What needed to be discussed with the envoys was covered, and [F 281] instructions were given, and the document with the list of presents was made out: the presents for the first audience with the Khān, and presents for the occasion of the concluding of the marriage contract, all very lavish and appropriate. There were two gold goblets set with jewels, together with strings of pearls; gold-embroidered garments and other garments of all kinds, Rumi, Baghdadi, Isfahani and Nishapuri, suits of multi-coloured fine linen and cloths for turbans; musk, aloes wood and amber; two jewelled collars, regarded as unique; all these were designated for the Khān, his son Bughrātegin, the queens, the brides, the paternal uncles, the chamberlains and the courtiers. Everything that had been set down in the list was fetched out of the treasuries, paraded in front of the Amir, and entrusted to the envoys. A treasurer was appointed, with assistants and with porters from the treasury, who would accompany the envoys. The envoys went away. Bu ʿAli, the official in charge of organising diplomatic missions and hospitality, was summoned, and two impressive robes of honour were given for taking along to the envoys. All preparations were made, and on Monday,[320] 10 [–11] Rabiʿ I 422 [8 March 1031] they departed from Balkh.

After this, I shall set forth in its appropriate place, if God Most High wills, the story of these envoys and what happened when they reached Qadïr Khān's court at Kāshghar in regard to the agreement and the marriage contracts and the matter of the marriage contract originally made for Moḥammad, the lengthy stay there of the envoys, the discussions which went on, and the swift couriers and envoys who came and went with letters and replies, until that point when the affair was settled. [F 282]

An account of the arrest of the General Eryāruq, Commander of the Indian army, and how that affair unfolded, until he was killed in Ghur, God's mercy be upon him[321]

I have already given an account of Eryāruq, the Commander in India at the time of Amir Maḥmud, [Gh 221] and how he became puffed up and overweening so that he was generally regarded as being quasi-rebellious, and how during the reign of Moḥammad, he did not go over to their side (i.e. that of Moḥammad's partisans), and then, at this time of Amir Masʿud, how the Grand Vizier Aḥmad b. Ḥasan, enticed him back from India by a certain stratagem.[322] When Aḥmad met with Amir Masʿud he had said, "If India is to be of any use to us, Eryāruq should not be allowed to go back there again." [I have also set forth how] Eryāruq came each day to the palace with an escort of court officials and ceremonial shield-bearers,[323] making an entrance together with the Commander-in-Chief Ghāzi, and how the swagger and air of superiority[324] of these two individuals were hard to bear for [F 283] the men from the time of Maḥmud's régime. For this being the case, these two eminent figures, Eryāruq and Ghāzi, did not have anyone to furnish them with sound advice, and neither of these two Commanders-in-Chief had a worthy counsellor and administrator, seasoned and well-versed in secretarial practice; for it is only too evident what can be expected from Sa'id Ṣarrāf and minions like him of obscure background and little worth. It would be true to say that the Turks seek out such men and pay no heed to the consequences, so that they inevitably face pitfalls ahead; for in spite of the fact that they are energetic and innately generous, and regardless of their resources and material trappings, they have little experience or notion of administrative matters and are lacking in prescience,[325] so how can they possibly avoid falling into adverse situations? When the Maḥmudiyān became apprised of this situation, and discovered an opening by means of which they could trip up these two persons, they conspired together in devising stratagems to bring the two commanders low.

Fate assisted these circumstances. First, the Amir instructed 'Abdus to suborn the counsellors and adjutants of Eryāruq and Ghāzi and secretly to usher them into an audience with him. The Amir showed them much kindness, gave them hopes of future advancement and induced them to watch over their masters' every move[326] and relay everything which went on to 'Abdus, who would then report to the Amir. Those two worthless nonentities were taken in by the blandishments they received, which were beyond their wildest dreams, and could not comprehend that, once their masters fell, they themselves would be *"meaner than a discarded horseshoe and lower than the dust"*.[327] How could they have known, for they had neither gone through any [F 284] professional training (*shāgerdi*) [Gh 222] nor read any books.[328]

These two men got busy, and whatever went on they would convey, true or false, and divulge to 'Abdus. These reports hardened the Amir's attitude towards Eryāruq, and Ghāzi also fell somewhat lower in his estimation. The Maḥmudiyān became more outspoken, and when they expatiated on these matters in the Amir's presence and found him receptive, they schemed together and plotted that first, they would devise a stratagem for Eryāruq to be brought low, and then with him out of the way and Ghāzi isolated, it would become feasible for them to overthrow him too. The Maḥmudiyān also got wind of the news about the position of the two counsellors and administrators (i.e. those of the two generals) and realized that both had been duped and suborned, for in their cups the two counsellors and administrators had boasted that they were the Sultan's servants. The

Maḥmudiyān therefore began to make much of them, plying them with gifts and convincing them that "If their present masters were removed, the Sultan would bestow important offices on them."

The second misfortune arose in this way. The Commander-in-Chief Ghāzi was a wily person whom even the accursed Satan (Eblis) was never able to trip up. He had always been abstemious, but when he achieved all his desires and his pitcher[329] became filled to the brim, he turned to wine and started drinking. When the Amir heard of this, he plied both of the commanders with wine. Drinking is a great evil when carried to excess, and those who over-indulge in wine can easily be manipulated. In his capacity as Commander-in-Chief, Ghāzi began wooing and conciliating the army, and each day would bring back a detachment of troops to his house and would hand out wine and presents, and Eryāruq would be present there, [F 285] and Ghāzi likewise would be Eryāruq's guest at times. In the wine-drinking sessions of both commanders, once the wine took effect, the Turks[330] would praise these two commanders in Turkish, and would scoff at the Great Chamberlain (i.e. the General) Bilgetegin as effeminate (*mokhanneth*), ʿAli Dāya as an old woman, and the Commander of the Palace Gholāms Begtughdï as blind and lame. They would speak of others, too, in similar terms, finding faults and reviling each in turn.

After these two Commanders-in-Chief had been overthrown, [Bu] ʿAbdallāh, Begtughdï's counsellor and administrator, told me: One day, the Amir had not held court and was drinking wine. Ghāzi and Eryāruq went back together, taking along with them many men, and they drank wine. The Commander Begtughdï sent me secretly to Bilgetegin and ʿAli, and he gave the verbal message that these two impertinent fellows, Ghāzi and Eryāruq, were overreaching themselves. If Bilgetegin and ʿAli deemed it a good course of action, they should ride out with about twenty gholāms on pretext of a hunting expedition so that Begtughdï, with Abu ʿAbdallāh and a number of gholāms, could join them, and [Gh 223] together they would come up with a plan of action. Bilgetegin and ʿAli Dāya said,[331] "That's a very good idea; we will go off in the direction of Mikhᵛārān until the Commander Begtughdï arrives." They mounted and rode off. Begtughdï likewise mounted, taking me with him, and they brought along with them goshawks (*bāz*), hunting cheetahs (*yuz*) and other hunting birds and beasts (*javāreḥ*). When they had travelled about two parasangs,[332] these three, Begtughdï, Bilgetegin and 'Ali Dāya, halted on some high ground with their three counsellors and adjutants: myself; Bu Aḥmad T.k.l.y,[333] the Great Chamberlain's counsellor and adjutant; and Amirak, 'Ali's trusted confidant.[334] They sent away the gholāms, together with the falconers,[335] for the hunt, and the six of us, Begtughdï, Bu 'Abdallāh, Bilgetegin, Bu Aḥmad T.k.l.y, 'Ali Dāya and Amirak, remained behind.

Our masters embarked on their discussion, and for a while aired their worries about the Amir and the hold that [F 286] these two Commanders-in-Chief had established on him. Begtughdï said, "The remarkable thing is that, within the palaces of Maḥmud (i.e. in the gholām households of these palaces), there was no-one of lowlier status than these two, and they have kissed the ground before me a thousand times; but both of them began to display an air of valour and boldness, Ghāzi through being exceptionally shrewd and sly, and Eryāruq by virtue of being a supreme ass, until Amir Maḥmud promoted them and bestowed on them a high rank so that they achieved eminence. Ghāzi performed very creditable services for this Sultan, Mas'ud, at Nishapur[336] and attained this high rank. Although the Sultan's attitude is unfavourable towards Eryāruq but well-disposed towards Ghāzi, it will be possible to turn the Sultan's mind against Ghāzi too, since Ghāzi and Eryāruq have fallen into the habit of drinking wine together and making fools of themselves. But until the downfall of Eryāruq is achieved, no plans can be made regarding Ghāzi; then, once one prop goes the whole edifice will fall down and both of them will fall into disgrace and we shall be freed from our present degrading plight." The Great Chamberlain and 'Ali suggested devising a plan to poison Eryāruq, or else despatching directly someone to dispose of him. The Commander Begtughdï said, "These two schemes are futile and won't get us anywhere. We ourselves will be disgraced, and they will be strengthened in their position. The best course is for us to lay aside such plans and put on a show of friendship, and at the same time employ people to stir up trouble by blowing up and broadcasting whatever the Turkish troops and these two commanders say, and we'll see what happens then." They settled upon this plan, and the gholāms and falconers returned, bringing back a great amount of game. The day had grown late, and the game hampers were thrown open for a repast, and the attendants, gholāms and retainers all ate. Then they returned, and put in hand what they had concocted for these two persons.[337]

Several days passed regarding this affair. [Gh 224] The Sultan's attitude towards Eryāruq hardened, and he held a private session to discuss his possible arrest. He raised complaints about Eryāruq to the Vizier, saying, "The situation is reaching a point critical enough to enmesh and destroy Ghāzi as well. The realm[338] cannot endure such things [F 287]. It is not right for the army commanders to be so insubordinate and act in away that even the royal princes would not have the temerity to emulate. It has become incumbent on us to seize Eryāruq, for once he is arrested, Ghāzi will mend his ways. What does the Vizier have to say about this?" The Grand Vizier remained deep in thought for a while, and then said, "May the life of the lord of the world be prolonged! I am on oath never to betray the good interests of the realm in any way. The matter of the commander and of the army is a most delicate one, and it is the responsibility of the monarch. If the exalted judgement sees fit, he will excuse me in this one matter, and whatever he himself considers to be the right course, he will act upon and issue commands. If I should say something regarding such topics, it may happen to be at variance with the lord's judgement and will cause him to regard me unfavourably." The Amir replied, "The Vizier is our deputy and the most trusted of all our servants, and one must necessarily discuss such matters with him, so that he may express whatever he knows on the subject and we shall be listening. Then we shall turn it over in our own mind, and that which judgement renders necessary, we shall command."

The Vizier said, "Now I am able to speak. May the lord's life be prolonged! What was said regarding Eryāruq the other day when I came to the court for an audience,[339] was a word of advice in the context of India, for when this man was there, he displayed some boldness and insolence, as well as winning fame and prestige, which he subsequently squandered away; for when the late Amir summoned him, he exhibited some reluctance and hesitation in going, and this was noticed and widely commented upon. When Amir Moḥammad summoned him, he did not go and retorted "The father's designated heir is Amir Mas'ud; if Mas'ud assents to the succession of his brother and does not leave Western Persia for Ghaznin, then I shall come and render service." But when he heard the lord's name (i.e. that Mas'ud had succeeded to royal power) and I gave him the necessary briefing, he came along with me (i.e. to the Sultan's court). Until now, I have not heard of any rash action and acts of disobedience on his part [F 288] so as to cause alarm. As for this intemperate behaviour, brash display of possessions and pomp, and unauthorised wine-drinking with Ghāzi and the Turks, all that is very easy to attend to, and I myself can rectify it all in one session and nothing further needs to be said about it. The lord's dominions have increased in extent, and competent persons are needed; men like Eryāruq are hard to find. I have set forth what I had in mind, and it is now for the lord to command." The Amir answered, "I see it now and it's all just as you have said. This matter must be kept secret until I've given it more thought." The Khᵛāja said, "I obey," and went back. [Gh 225]

The Maḥmudiyān did not cease from stirring up trouble, to the point that they insinuated to the Amir that "Eryāruq has become suspicious and mistrustful, and is in league with Ghāzi to foment some mischief; if they can't pull this off, they'll decamp;[340] and one must bear in mind that the greater part of this army owes allegiance to Eryāruq." One day, the Amir held court and all the people were assembled. When the court session was over, the Amir commanded, "Don't go away, since we're going to drink wine." The Grand Vizier, the Head of the Army Department and the Head of the Chancery also sat down with the Amir. Small trays of delicacies began to arrive; one was placed before the Amir seated on his throne, one before Ghāzi and Eryāruq, one before the Head of the Army Department Bu Sahl Zowzani and Bu Naṣr Moshkān, and one in front of every two boon-companions (Bu'l-Qāsem Kathir was sitting in the ranks of the boon-companions). Accompanying dishes of *lāgoshta* and *reshta*[341] had been ordered, and large quantities were brought. Then when these prominent figures had eaten, they got up and came back to the loggia of the Divān, sat down and washed their hands.

The Grand Vizier heaped praises on both of the two commanders and spoke of them in handsome terms. They replied, "We receive nothing but encouragement and favour from the lord, and we are ready to sacrifice our lives in his service; but other persons are preying on our minds, and we don't know what should be done." The Vizier said, "This is mere fancy[342] and sheer delusion; the Amir will resolve the misunderstanding at once. Wait a while until I am finished [F 289] and he summons you both." He went forward alone and sought a private audience and repeated these words, and he besought the Amir to restore their spirits with a fresh display of favour. After that, he said, "It is for the lord to judge according to what he deems fit and commands." The Amir replied, "I understand."

All those in attendance were recalled, and the musicians and singers came in and started performing, and there was much merriment and lively talk. When the day's course reached the time of the midday prayer, the Amir signalled to the musicians and singers to stop. Then he turned towards the Vizier and said, "Hitherto we have ordained consideration for these two army commanders as was befitting. With regard to Ghāzi, he came from Ghaznin at the time when we were still at Isfahan, and rendered us memorable and matchless service at Nishapur. In regard to Eryāruq, when he heard that we had reached Balkh, he hastened, in company with the Vizier, to render service. But we keep hearing that certain persons, envious of their state, [Gh 226] are engaging in idle talk[343] and are making them feel ill at ease. They should banish those thoughts from their minds and should place their confidence in what we have said, for we shall not pay heed to what others say about them." The Vizier said, "There is nothing left to be said here; what greater solicitude can there be than this which the exalted utterance has spoken?" Both of the commanders kissed the ground and also kissed the throne, and returned to their places and sat down in an exultant mood. The Amir ordered that two coats of special quality and woven with gold thread should be brought, together with two swords with their belts encrusted with jewels, said to be valued at 50,000 dinars each. He summoned them both into his presence a second time and ordered that the coats should be placed on their backs and that they should fasten them up with their own hands, and with his own hands the Amir threw the sword belts over their necks. They kissed his hand, the throne and the ground, [F 290] went back, mounted and rode off, accompanied by all the court office holders, until they got back to their residences. I, Bu'l-Fażl, was on duty in the Divān this day; I witnessed all this and noted it down in the journal of events for this year.[344]

After their departure, the Amir ordered two gold sets of wares and utensils for festive sessions (*majles-khāna-ye zarrin*)[345] to be prepared for the two commanders, with goblets brimming with wine, dishes for dessert and pots of narcissus. He told the boon-companion Bu'l-Ḥasan Karaji, "Go to the Commander-in-Chief Ghāzi, and these will be brought on after you, and three of the court musicians and singers will come with you. Also, give him this message, 'You did not get your full measure before you came away from our feast; so now drink wine with the boon-companions accompanied by the music and singing.'" The three singers and performers went with him, and personal attendants carried away these royal presents. He ordered the boon-companion Moẓaffar to go to Eryāruq with the three singers and those gifts. The Vizier delivered a topical discourse (i.e. on the Amir's magnanimity to his faithful commanders) in his own inimitable way, and returned home around the time of the afternoon worship. The others also began to go back home. The Amir remained there till around the time of the evening worship, then arose and entered the palace briskly. The Maḥmudiyān were most grieved by the new turn of events. Neither they nor anyone else could divine what was in store. Fate was making itself heard with eloquent tones, but no-one was listening (Poetry)

1. *O you who spend the night sleeping in a happy state at its outset, indeed, turns of Fate often strike at dawn.*

2. *Do not rejoice in a night whose early part is agreeable, for often the latter part of a night kindles a fire* (i.e. one of strife or violence).[346]

These two boon-companions Bu'l-Ḥasan Karaji and Moẓaffar made their way to these two commanders with these gifts and along with the performers and singers. They rendered due service, and when they heard the Sultan's message they quaffed wine in a convivial manner and rejoiced greatly. When they were on the verge of falling into a drunken state, [F 291] they gave horses, gold accoutrements, clothing, silver and Turkish gholāms as presents to the two boon-companions, [Gh 227] and sent them back in a handsome manner. The performers and singers, too, were given robes and silver, and they went back and Ghāzi went to sleep. It was Eryāruq's habit that, once he embarked on a wine-drinking spree, he would drink for three or four days and nights, and this night he drank till daybreak on account of those glad tidings and royal favour that he had received.

The next day the Amir held court. The Commander-in-Chief Ghāzi, freshly puffed up with self-esteem, proceeded to the court with a great display of pomp and ceremony. When he took his seat, the Amir asked why Eryāruq had not come. Ghāzi replied that he had the custom of drinking wine for three or four days and nights continuously, especially now on account of the joyfulness and favour of the previous day. The Amir laughed and said, "We must also drink wine today, and we will send Eryāruq a round." Ghāzi kissed the ground with the intention of going back but the Amir told him to stay, and they set to drinking. The Amir ordered that Amirak Siyāhdār Khomārchi[347] be summoned; he was a seasoned wine drinker, and Eryāruq was much attached to him. (Amir Maḥmud had also sent him to Eryāruq when the latter was in India to instruct him to pay a visit to the court and return, in that very same month that Maḥmud himself passed away, as I have previously set forth.) Amirak came into Amir Mas'ud's presence. The Amir said, "Fifty flagons of wine will be brought with you to the Commander Eryāruq's house; go and keep him company, since he is very fond of you, until he becomes drunk and goes off to sleep. Tell him also 'We [F 292] have granted you leave not to attend court and to drink wine in your customary fashion.'"

Amirak departed. He found Eryāruq bent double (or: "rolling about"),[348] wandering round the garden and quaffing wine, while the musicians and singers were performing. He conveyed the message. Eryāruq kissed the ground in gratitude and wept profusely, and he bestowed substantial rewards on Amirak and the attendants. The latter went back, and Amirak remained behind. The Commander-in-Chief Ghāzi stayed with the Amir until noon and then he went back, taking with him several senior officers and his chamberlain, and sat down to drink wine. He distributed on that day a considerable sum of dinars and dirhams, horses, gholāms and clothing. Meanwhile, Eryāruq, as was his custom, kept falling asleep and getting up and sipping some soup (*reshta*)[349] and drinking wine again so that he became utterly oblivious of what he was doing,[350] and he went on in this manner for that day and night and the next day, without resting.

The next day the Amir did not hold court, and he had made arrangements for Eryāruq to be arrested. He came and sat in the open, upper gallery opposite the loggia of the Chancery, we ourselves being within the Divān, and men were sent secretly to bring back news of Eryāruq.

In the midst of this, at the time of the midday worship, 'Abdus arrived and whispered something into the ear of Bu Naṣr Moshkān. The latter arose and told the secretaries to go back since they were going to clear the garden. [Gh 228] Apart from myself, Bu'l-Fażl, all arose and went away. Bu Naṣr said to me *sotto voce*, "Send your horse back, and sit at the entrance hall of the Divān, for something important is about to happen. Stay there to the end and be vigilant, take in everything that happens, and then come back to me." I said, "I'll do that." He went off, and the Vizier, the Head of the Army Department and all the rest went back.

The General Begtegin, son-in-law of 'Ali Dāya, came into the entrance hall and went up to the Amir, stayed there for an hour and then returned to the entrance hall. The General then summoned Moḥtāj, the Commander of the Police Guard (*amir-e ḥaras*) [F 293] and spoke confidentially with him. The latter went away and brought back 500 footsoldiers of all colours and races[351] and fully armed, and sent them back to the garden, where they were to remain in concealment. The troop commanders of the Indians came along bringing a force of 300 Indians, and they also took up positions within the garden.[352] A chamberlain and a black-uniformed court official (*siyāh-dār*)[353] went to Eryāruq and said, "The Sultan wishes to hold a wine-drinking feast, the Commander-in-Chief Ghāzi has already been sent for, and he is summoning you to attend as well." But Eryāruq was in such a drunken state that he could hardly move. He said, "How can I come in this condition? What kind of service can I render?" The black-uniformed court official[354] Amirak, whom the Sultan had deputed to stay close to Eryāruq, said, "May the Commander-in Chief's life be prolonged! The lord's command must be observed and you must go to the palace, for when he sees you in this state, he will excuse you and send you back home. Not to go would appear most unseemly, and unfavourable interpretations would be put on it." Amirak managed to win over to his side Eryāruq's chamberlain Altuntegin, so that at last Eryāruq agreed that he had no choice but to go. He called for his clothes, boots and cap and put them on, and summoned a massive retinue of gholāms and 200 footsoldiers. Amirak said to Eryāruq's chamberlain, "This is unseemly—he's merely going to a wine-drinking party—ten shield-bearing gholāms and 100 footsoldiers would be sufficient."[355] The chamberlain had that throng of troops sent back, while Eryāruq himself had not the faintest idea what was going on in the world around him.

When he reached the court, the General Begtegin and the Commander of the Guard Moḥtāj met him and helped him dismount, went before him to the loggia and seated him there. Eryāruq stayed there for a moment and then arose, saying, "I'm drunk and cannot stay here; I'm going back home." Begtegin said, "It would be unseemly to go back without the royal permission; remain here until we inform the Amir." He sat down in the entrance hall, and I, Bu'l-Fażl, was observing him closely. He summoned Ḥājji the watercarrier, who came and held a pitcher of water before him. He was putting his hand inside the pitcher and bringing out pieces of ice and consuming them. Begtegin said, [F 294] "O brother, this is unseemly behaviour for an army commander, crunching chunks of ice in the entrance hall! Go inside the loggia and do what you like there!" He came back into the loggia. (If he had not been drunk, the intended arrest of him would have been a much more drawn-out affair.)

When he sat down in the loggia, fifty palace senior officers (*sarhangs*) [Gh 229] from the élite front-line troops of the army (*mobārezān-e sarghowghā'*) suddenly burst in, and Begtegin came in, took Eryāruq to one side, and the field officers came in from left and right and seized him so that he was unable to move at all. He cried out to Begtegin, "O unchivalrous brother, have you brought this down on me?" More gholāms came in and pulled off his boots—he had two daggers[356] in each boot—and Moḥtāj entered. Very strong fetters were brought and placed on his legs. They took off his coat, and they found poison and amulets in the front part of the coat, all of which they removed from him and took outside. Fifty footsoldiers surrounded him. Other footsoldiers ran and seized his horses, trappings and gholāms. Eryāruq's chamberlain and three gholāms sprang up and escaped in full view. His gholāms took up their weapons and went up on to the roof, and a mighty commotion ensued.

The Amir was with Begtegin during the arrest of Eryāruq, and minions had been hastily sent to Begtughdï, to Bilgetegin and to the leaders of the army, with the information that such a task was at hand so that they could mount, and they had all mounted, fully armed. When they bound Eryāruq, and his gholāms and retainers raised an outbreak, this group of armed men went off to Eryāruq's residence. Many other cavalrymen from every ethnic group joined up with them, and a fierce fight broke out. The Amir sent ʿAbdus to Eryāruq's supporters with a message, "Eryāruq was a reckless man who did not know his own place, [F 295] and you were yourselves in peril through your association with him. The public weal lay in his being arrested today. We are your lord;[357] don't act like children, and cease fighting. Your weakness in numbers is only too apparent; you will be killed within an hour, and it will not do Eryāruq any good. If you behave and control yourselves, we will treat you well and reward you." He also took with him a verbal message and a substantial heart warming reward for Eryārug's chamberlain. When ʿAbdus delivered this message, it dampened things down at once, and the chamberlain and Eryāruq's gholāms kissed the ground in obeisance. The revolt collapsed immediately; Eryāruq's residence was seized and seals affixed to its doors. By sundown, it looked as if it had never been inhabited by a soul. I myself went back and told my master Bu Naṣr everything that I had seen.

When the time of the night prayer had passed, Eryāruq was transported from the loggia of the Divān to the town citadel, and ten days later he was despatched to Ghaznin and entrusted to the castellan Bu ʿAli. He, in accordance with the royal command, held him in the fortress for a while in such a way that no-one realized that he was a prisoner there. Then he was sent to Ghur in the custody of Bu'l-Ḥasan Khalaf,[358] to be incarcerated in some place. This is the end of the account of him, and I [Gh 230] shall describe in its appropriate place how he came to his end and how he was killed. His arrest took place at Balkh on Wednesday, 19 Rabiʿ I 422 [/6 March 1031].[359]

The day after the arrest, the Amir sent to Eryāruq's residence Piruz Vaziri the eunuch,[360] Bu Saʿid the overseer (*moshref*) (who is still alive today and living in the Rebāṭ of Kandi;[361] he had not yet been given the title of "overseer" because the office of the Overseer of the Court and Palace [F 296] was in the name of the Judge Khosrow), Bu'l-Ḥasan b. ʿAbd al-Jalil and Bu Naṣr the accounting official.[362] Eryāruq's accounting official and his adjutant, who had both been arrested, were brought there, the doors opened and a large number of luxurious objects were brought forth. They handed over a list stating that there was very great wealth in India. It took three days to make a complete inventory of Eryāruq's property and possessions and to present it to the royal court. Those gholāms of his who were of high calibre were placed in the barrack rooms (i.e. of the royal palace), and those of only moderate quality the Amir bestowed on the Commander-in-Chief Ghāzi and the leading army commanders.[363] The Amir appointed Bu'l-Ḥasan b. ʿAbd al-Jalil and Bu Saʿid the overseer to go to India and bring back Eryāruq's property and possessions, and they both departed speedily. Even before Eryāruq's actual arrest, swift-riding cavalrymen[364] had gone armed with letters ordering Eryāruq's retainers (i.e. those in India) to be detained as a precaution.[365]

The next day, following Eryāruq's arrest, Ghāzi came to the court, appearing intensely troubled and apprehensive. When the court broke up, the Amir held a private session with the Vizier and Ghāzi, and said, "The position of this man is one thing, and the position of the other servants is another. He had become haughty and had risen high in the time of our father to the point that he perpetrated many an unlawful execution, while the provincial tax-collectors and the postal and intelligence service officials never dared to expose him fully, fearful for their own safety, since the roads had been blocked and no-one could travel without his express authorisation. He had not come back from India at our father's demand and would not come, and if they had launched an expedition against him, he would have stirred up a great deal of mischief. The Vizier [F 297] had to adopt many a crafty wile in order to bring him back.[366] Such a servant is of no use. I have related all this so that the Commander-in-Chief should not fill his mind with worries on account of what has taken place. His own position is quite different, as was that service which he rendered for us when we were at Isfahan and from there marched on Khorasan."

Ghāzi kissed the ground and replied, "I am merely a servant; if the Amir orders me to leave my present post and become a muleteer, I would still deem it a source of pride. Issuing commands is the lord's prerogative, for he knows his servants best." The Vizier then spoke some fine words, delivered in his own inimitable way, both in the context of Eryāruq and as a way of [Gh 231] restoring Ghāzi's morale. They both then departed. The Vizier sat down with Ghāzi in the loggia of the Divān and summoned my master Bu Naṣr, so that he could describe and enumerate in their entirety the acts of impetuousness and the manifold transgressions which Eryāruq had committed, as if he had been prompted by those hostile to the realm, in such a way that Ghāzi was struck with amazement and said, "In no way could these actions be overlooked." Bu Naṣr went away and spoke with the Amir, and brought back soothing responses, and these two masters both spoke reassuring words so that Ghāzi's mind was set at rest and he returned home.

I heard from Khᵛāja Bu Naṣr that Khᵛāja Aḥmad had told him: "This Turk (Ghāzi) has become suspicious, since he is intelligent and shrewd, and things like this do not pass over his head. Alas for a man like Eryāruq, who would have been able to conquer another vast region apart from India, and I would have been his guarantor. But this lord appears to believe every word he hears (i.e. of the slanders and insinuations), and those who are scheming won't let him alone until they have undermined everything. Mark my words; Ghāzi too is as good as finished." (Bu Naṣr continued:) The Vizier rose and went to the Divān, and appeared fraught with care. This [F 298] wily old man[367] had said to me, "They have made gangs out of the Maḥmudiyān and Masʿudiyān, each busy with their own particular agenda. May God, His mention is exalted, grant us a favourable outcome!"

An account of the arrest of the Commander-in-Chief Asïghtegin Ghāzi and how events unfolded until he was sent to the fortress of Gardiz, where his allotted span of life came to an end, God's mercy be upon him

It would be injudicious of me to write something which appears untrue, for these men whose story I am recording have passed away long years ago and their feuds and animosities have been relegated to the Day of Resurrection. The truth is that Sultan Masʿud had no desire whatsoever to arrest Ghāzi and would never have sanctioned any violence done to him, and he would have given him that command of the army of Western Persia which was given Tāsh. But two rare sets of circumstances conjoined here, and the preponderant power of Fate gave a helping hand so that the commander was thus brought down; *there is no turning back God's decree.*

One element was that the Maḥmudiyān fastened on this man, and persevered with their stratagems, slanders and incitements, and the Amir's mind became full of all that he had heard, until they achieved their aim. The other more serious underlying factor was that the Commander Ghāzi was still young and with scant regard for his elders, and because of his immaturity, he did something rash and unwise that led to his downfall, without his lord wanting this to happen. [Gh 232, F 299]

It happened that, after the downfall of Eryāruq, Ghāzi grew suspicious, kept himself to himself, gave up wine-drinking, and was coming and going like a lost soul. In private, he used to express his despair to anyone with whom he was talking, and would weep.[368] The Maḥmudiyān were meanwhile exaggerating things out of all proportion, were spinning lies and were purveying these to the Sultan, till matters reached boiling point and the Amir's mind became clouded with doubt; despite all this, he was bearing all these things patiently in a truly regal manner.

In their machinations, the Maḥmudiyān went as far as this: There was a woman in Nishapur, the wife of Ḥasan b. Mehrān, and she was very wise and experienced in the ways of the world. She was the daughter of Bu'l-Fażl Bosti and had been left a widow after Ḥasan's death, but although many notable suitors for her hand had come forward, she had refused to marry again. This widow was the foster-mother of a servant maid (*kanizak*) who was in charge of all the womenfolk in Ghāzi's residence, and she used to be a frequent visitor there. The widow had a good calligraphic hand and wrote excellent Persian. The group of plotters managed to find agents, without anyone finding out, who under the guise of purported well-wishers were able to deceive her and feed her with the news that "The Amir intends to arrest the wretched Ghāzi, and the time has drawn near; it's going to take place on so-and-so night." This woman went along and told the servant maid, and the latter came and told Ghāzi, filling him with intense fear, and saying, "Find a way to save yourself while you are still free, lest they seize you unawares, as with Eryāruq." Ghāzi became very distressed, and said to the maid, "Ask this noble lady if she can come here and enlighten us further on this, and I'll see that she is rewarded well if this danger passes." The maid asked her to come, but she answered, "I'm too scared to come, but I will let you know what is happening through brief notes. You know how to read and can inform the Commander."[369] The maid said, "That's a very sound idea." The widow began to send off messages setting forth what she had heard.

But [F 300] the Maḥmudiyān were showing themselves past masters in this game of subterfuge, and this woman had no way of knowing that she was being manipulated, until Fate's workings had their effect. At the time of the afternoon worship on Monday, 9 Rabi' II 422[/5 April 1031],[370] they told this woman, "Tomorrow, when Ghāzi comes to the court, they intend to arrest him." They worked up this ploy and offered proofs for it. The woman immediately penned a note reporting the situation to him, and the maid told Ghāzi. Ghāzi was stung by the news, since others too had instilled fear into him. At once and in secret, in such a way that his counsellor and administrator Sa'id Ṣarrāf and others of the outside staff (*biruniyān*) were left unawares, he gave orders for the horses to be shod—it was the time of the evening worship—and he gave out that the Sultan was sending him off that very night to a certain place on a mission, so that the news of this would not be made public. [Gh 233] His treasury was opened up, and whatever was comparatively light in weight, jewels, gold, silver and clothing, he gave to the gholāms to carry away. After the time of the night prayer, he mounted. This servant maid and four other maids were given mounts, and he waited until all the gholāms were mounted. Mules were loaded up with light loads, and likewise swift-running camels. (He was staying in the palace of Arslān Jādheb, in a distant part of Balkh, very far from the Sultan's palace.)

He rode on and came to a parting of the ways, with one road leading towards Khorasan and the other towards Transoxania. Since he was undecided, he halted and said, "Which way shall we go? For I have fled to save my life." The gholāms and retainers said, "Whichever direction your judgement decides; if they come in pursuit of us, we'll fight to the death." [F 301] He pronounced, "The best course is to make for the Oxus, we shall cross over it and find safety, whereas Khorasan is far away." They replied, "It's for you to command." So he aimed towards Siyāh-gerd[371] and sped onwards. Before the night was through, he reached the Oxus. He rode along the bank of the river from the Rebāṭ of Dhu'l-Qarneyn until he was opposite Termez (Termedh).[372] He found a boat with ample room in it. There was no wind, and he found the Oxus calm. He crossed the river safely and stood on the farther bank. But then he said, "It was wrong of me to enter enemy territory. I shall forfeit my good name, since there is here such an enemy of Maḥmud's domains as ʿAlitegin. It would be better to make for Khorasan." He returned to the original bank (i.e. the Afghan shore). It had become daylight. He performed the dawn worship, and was about to turn around in the direction of Kālef and take the road to Āmuy[373] and seek refuge at the Khwarazm Shah's court in order to secure his intercession with the Sultan and to restore his position. But he looked up, and a band of the Sultan's troops came into view, composed of lightly-armed, swift cavalry and hand-picked warriors. In the middle of the night word had been brought to Amir Masʿud that Ghāzi had left in the direction of Siyāh-gerd, and the Amir had come forth and had sent troops in all four directions. Ghāzi now became very distraught.

The next day, when we went to the court, there was a great tumult, and armed men were rushing on each other's heels. The Sultan, appearing preoccupied and distressed in mind, summoned ʿAbdus, and gave him his seal ring and wrote out a guarantee of safe conduct in his own hand, with the message "Your envious foes have at last done their work, but you can still salvage the situation. Come back and deprive them of their victory, for we regard you in exactly the same esteem as we did in the past," and he pronounced solemn oaths. ʿAbdus went off with all haste until he reached Ghāzi. The Maḥmudiyān had sent forward a force of picked troops and had secretly given an order to crush Ghāzi and, if possible, to kill him.[374] The two forces were in close proximity of each other. Ghāzi [Gh 234] had intended to cross the river once more in order to escape this [F 302] pursuing army, but this was not to be, for the wind had picked up and the Oxus was turbulent so that his boat was of little use. When the pursuing army charged, intent on taking his life, he was compelled to stand his ground and fight, for he was a doughty warrior. His gholāms set about fighting furiously and a fierce battle ensued. Contingents of the Sultan's army were arriving on the scene one after the other. Ghāzi felt dispirited but was fighting on, so that many an arrow became embedded in his shield. An arrow struck hard at his knee, bringing him down; and it seemed as if he was about to be killed.

'Abdus arrived on the scene and stopped the fighting, and heaped blame on the army, telling them that they had no orders to engage in battle: "Why did you attack? You should have halted face-to-face with Ghāzi and awaited further orders." They replied, "We were forced to engage them in battle, for he tried to cross the river, and when this proved impossible, he attempted to flee in the direction of Āmuy. We had to stop him, for we feared the Sultan's chastisement. Now that you have arrived, we have ceased fighting and have awaited further orders." 'Abdus went up to Ghāzi, who had halted on an eminence, in a sorry state. 'Abdus said, "O Commander-in-Chief, what devil enticed you from the way of obedience and made you fulfill your enemies' wishes?" He broke down and wept, saying, "Fate decreed thus, and they filled me with fear." 'Abdus replied, "Don't be downhearted, for the situation can be retrieved," and he conveyed to him the letter of safe conduct and the seal ring, and passed on the verbal message and mentioned the Amir's oaths. Ghāzi dismounted from his horse and kissed the ground, while the Sultan's army and his own gholāms stood on the two sides. 'Abdus consoled him. Ghāzi took off his weapons. An elephant with a howdah had arrived and Ghāzi was placed in the howdah, and his gholāms and retainers were given encouraging promises. 'Abdus sent on Ghāzi's shield, just as it was [F 303] with the arrows still stuck in it, by hand of swift riders, with a message recounting everything that had happened. Halfway through the night, the shield reached the court and when the Amir saw it, and heard 'Abdus's message, he was relieved. Khᵛāja Aḥmad and all the notables had come to the court and remained in attendance, until the Amir told them to return home and they left. He speedily went inside the palace, and at that same time, food was served.

By daybreak 'Abdus had arrived with the army, and Ghāzi with his gholāms and retainers were all brought in. The Amir was informed, and he came out of the palace and spoke with 'Abdus in private for a while. Then 'Abdus came away and brought to Ghāzi a message couched in encouraging terms, saying, "the royal command is that you should be lodged in the Moḥammadi Palace[375] situated opposite the Private Royal Garden (*bāgh-e khāṣṣa*) and rest there until tomorrow, when commands will be given for what needs to be ordained. They bore Ghāzi there and set him down. Abu'l-Qāsem [Gh 235] the oculist (*kaḥḥāl*) was immediately brought there to extract the arrow (i.e. from his knee) and to apply medicaments. He rested there, and food was brought from the royal kitchen. A string of royal messages kept arriving with heart-warming promises of favour. He ate a little and then slept. The gholāms had their horses taken away from them, and they were themselves lodged in the barrack rooms; food was brought to them and they took their rest. A force of about a thousand footsoldiers was stationed to the left and the right of the palace without Ghāzi being aware of it. ʿAbdus went back after seeing to it that Ghāzi had settled down and was reposing with his maidservants.[376]

It became day. The Amir held court, and the notables were present. He said, "Ghāzi is a man of integrity and experience. In this instance he committed no fault, for he had been intimidated. This matter will be looked into and the person responsible duly punished." The Grand Vizier and the notables there said, "This must be done." Through one of his personal servants, ʿAbdus relayed this piece of news [F 304] to Ghāzi, who was overjoyed. After the court session, the Amir sent Bu'l-Ḥasan ʿAqili with Yaʿqub b. Dāniyāl[377] and Bu'l-ʿAlāʾ, who were his personal physicians, to Ghāzi, with the message, "You should not be downcast; they contrived this against you, and we are going to investigate this affair, and whatever needs to be ordained, we shall ordain, so don't be downhearted that you have been brought here and lodged in this garden of our brother, for our wish is that you should be near us and that the physicians should look after you and this affliction remedied. Whatever is required for you will then be commanded."[378]

When Ghāzi heard this, from his seated position he kissed the ground, since it was not possible for him to stand up, wept and offered up many prayers, saying, "They plotted against me until such an error was committed. It is for the servants to err and for their masters to forgive. Your servant does not know how to supplicate eloquently, but the lord will act as his magnanimous nature decrees." Bu'l-Ḥasan returned and reported what Ghāzi had said. When the Maḥmudiyān heard these accounts, they became extremely disconsolate and embarked upon a stratagem to ensure that the fallen Ghāzi should never rise to his feet again. When Ghāzi's adjutant and retainers saw this turn of events, they emerged two or three days later from various nooks and crannies and went to him.

I shall not prolong this story any further. The Maḥmudiyān persisted in maligning Ghāzi to such an extent that every day he fell lower in the Amir's esteem. Since they were constantly supplying the Amir with adverse reports, and since Ghāzi had also been forced to commit an error of judgement, with Fate lending a helping hand here, the Amir became more ill-disposed towards him and gave the matter further thought and realized that it was beyond repair.[379] [Gh 236]. He summoned ʿAbdus, had a private session with him and said, "This unruly rogue [F 305] is of no use to us, for he forfeited his reputation through what he did. Also, we are losing the loyalty of the Pedariyān in the process. It is wrong to stir up a whole world for the sake of an individual who has committed such an act of betrayal. Go to Ghāzi there and say, 'Since a serious error was committed, it is in your own interest for you to be away from us for a while and reside in Ghazni, so that gradually and in the course of time this blot on your honour is removed and the damage repaired.' When you have said these words, take away from him all his retainers and attendants, with the exception of those two women in his household who are to be left with him. Despatch to the Divān all those retainers whose possessions are substantial enough to be confiscated. Saʿid Ṣarrāf should be brought in and should be told to come along to the court, for he is of some use. Send all Ghāzi's gholāms to our palace so that a thorough investigation may be made of the wealth which is in their hands and that they may be brought to the treasury, and there, those who are suitable for the palace can be retained, and whatever decision seems appropriate to make regarding those who are not suitable can be ordained. Make certain that no item of this man's wealth, immoveables and moveables alike,[380] remains concealed. When you have done all this, appoint a body of footsoldiers to guard Ghāzi in such a way that no-one is able to see him without your knowledge. Then after this, whatever our judgement deems necessary will be ordained."

ʿAbdus went away and delivered the Amir's message. When Ghāzi heard it, he kissed the ground and wept, saying, "The welfare of servants lies in whatever their lords ordain. An obligation of service is incumbent on me. If the lord's judgement sees fit, I should be kept in a place that will guarantee my personal safety, for enemies are after my blood. Then when the time appears appropriate and the lord's heart becomes better disposed, and a new muleteer is required, I shall be there ready.[381] Also, I would request that the Amir should allow me to have these women of my household and some clothing and food which of necessity one needs. O ʿAbdus, give me your hand and undertake for me from God [F 306] that you will always remember me," and he was weeping as he uttered these words. ʿAbdus replied, "Things are not as dire as you imagine; you must not be despondent." Ghāzi said, "I'm not a child, and I realize that after today I shall not see you any more." ʿAbdus gave him his hand and pledged his fidelity, and drew him to himself and embraced him. He then turned away and went out, [Gh 237] sat down on that large dais, and whatever the Amir had commanded, he carried out in its entirety, so that by the time of the afternoon worship, all was done.

He went back to the Amir's presence, having appointed footsoldiers to guard Ghāzi, and he told the Amir all that had taken place and laid before him the lists (i.e. of the confiscated property). A great quantity of wealth, comprising both immoveables and moveable property, came to light. The gholāms were brought to the barracks, and they were questioned about what they had[382] and were told that whatever the Commander had given them was liable to be returned.[383] The Amir summoned them before him, and he sent the cream of the bunch to the palace barracks and the remaining ones he bestowed on the leading commanders (or: "chamberlains") and palace staff.[384]

When this affair was satisfactorily settled, the Amir said to ʿAbdus, "Ghāzi must be despatched to Ghaznin." He replied, "How does the lord command this to be done?", and what Ghāzi had said to him, how he had wept and had clutched his hand, he related in its entirety. The Amir was much grieved by this and exclaimed to ʿAbdus, "This man is innocent. The Almighty God watches over His servants, and he must be shielded from any harm. We have entrusted him to you; take careful charge of his affair." ʿAbdus said, "What exactly does the lord ordain?" He answered, "Arrange for ten camels to be got ready, with litters and covered carriers, and three mules, and a large quantity of clothes for Ghāzi and also for the servant maids to wear, three cooks, [F 307], and 1,000 dinars and 20,000 dirhams for living expenses. Tell them also to write a letter under the royal seal to the castellan Bu ʿAli that comfortable quarters are to be made ready in the citadel of Ghaznin for him and his retinue, and Ghāzi is to be held there with them, but in fetters, for this precaution is a necessary condition of imprisonment.[385] Three Indian slaves should be purchased for serving him and attending to his needs. When all this has been made ready, secretly and so that no-one realizes, they must be sent off in the middle of the night, with an escort of three hundred Indian cavalrymen and two hundred footsoldiers, also Indian, and an advance guard.[386] You yourself are to nominate a trustworthy person to accompany Ghāzi on your behalf and to ensure that no harm is done to him and no demand made on him until he is conveyed safely to the citadel of Ghaznin, and you are to bring back a reply (i.e. a letter confirming his safe arrival) from the castellan Bu 'Ali in his own hand." 'Abdus came along, all this was set in hand, and Ghāzi was transported away, "*and this was the last time anything was heard or seen of him*," since he was never seen again.[387] I shall relate the story of his decease and that year in which he died in another place.[388] [Gh 238]

The account of these two mighty commanders has now reached its end, and it has proved a lengthy one. But this could not be avoided, since from the outset it was set forth as a precept that all aspects of an episode should be described in their entirety, and since both of these two were men of great eminence, I have kept to my rule, for even if the matter is drawn-out, it is not devoid of interesting points and awe-inspiring aspects.[389] Behold, what was the final destiny of the two army commanders? Everything came to naught, as if they had never been. By God Most High's command, the hand of time and the passage of the heavenly firmament have wrought many such things in the past [F 308] and will wreak many things in the future. The truly wise are those who are not duped by the deceitful favours that fortune offers, being aware that she might well take them all back in a most despicable manner and without recompense. One must emulate in this regard the way of noble-minded persons and scatter the seeds of benevolence in both this present world and the next, so that one's good reputation remains behind. One should not devour and appropriate everything for oneself, for no man has ever achieved fame in this way.

In ancient times there was a man called Zebreqān b. Badr, who enjoyed great wealth. He was only concerned with his own belly and his own attire, and displayed little compassion for anyone else, so that, as a result, the poet Ḥoṭey'a said about him, (Poetry)

1. *Leave aside noble deeds, and do not even try to seek them out; be what you are, a guzzler of food and one obsessed with clothes.*[390]

I have read that, when this ode of Ḥoṭey'a was recited to Zebreqān, his boon-companions said, "This is a nasty satire which Ḥoṭey'a has recited about you." Zebreqān went to the Commander of the Faithful ʿOmar b. Khaṭṭāb, complaining and seeking redress, pleading, "Give me justice!" ʿOmar ordered Ḥoṭey'a to be brought in, and the latter said, "I don't perceive any nastiness and vituperation in this; and in any case, reciting poetry, with all its fine nuances and intricacies, is not the Commander of the Faithful's métier. Let him summon Ḥassān b. Thābet,[391] and ask him to say truthfully and on oath what he can tell us about this verse." ʿOmar sent someone, and Ḥassān was brought in, he being by then blind. He sat down and this verse was read out to him. Ḥassān said to ʿOmar, *"O Commander of the Faithful, he didn't just satirize Zebreqān, he shat on him!"*[392] ʿOmar smiled and motioned them to depart. This verse has remained immortalized, and it is four hundred odd years since it has been written down and recited, and lo! I have quoted it afresh[393] so that someone might read it and find it profitable, for a good reputation remains a permanent memorial. [F 309]

This verse of Motanabbi is very finely composed, (Poetry) [Gh 239]

1. *The memory which survives of a noble youth is his second life: what he needs basically provides his daily nourishment, and the superfluities of sustenance are mere diversion.*[394]

If I were to start writing on this theme, it would become very long, and this admonition is sufficient for those blessed with intelligence and knowledge. I recall three lines of verse written by Abu'l-ʿAtāhiya apposite for the predicament and times of these two commanders. I have noted them here because they are rich in moral observations: (Poetry)

1. *You have wasted your life in going to-and-fro; you desire sons, and you desire family and wealth.*
2. *Did you not see the monarch of former times when he passed onwards; has any group of people in this present world attained what he attained?*

3. *When a people get a tight hold on kingly power, they will encounter a time when their tight hold on that kingly power is loosened.*[395]

Rudaki has also well expressed [this]: (Poetry)

1. The grandees of the world have all passed away; faced with death, all have bowed down their heads.
2. They all lie deep in the earth, those who erected such tall palaces. [F 310]
3. After a life of ease, and from among myriads of luxuries,
When it came to the end, they took with them nothing but a shroud.
4. Gone are all their rich blessings: what they wore, what they bestowed and what they devoured.[396]

This tale has reached its end, even though it was rather lengthy, for *what is fresh and singular* (al-badiʿ) *is never wearisome.*

After Sultan Masʿud had unburdened himself of these two matters, and Eryāruq and Ghāzi had been borne away to Ghaznin, as I have set forth, he embarked upon feasting and hunting in the vicinity of Termez, as was the custom of his father Amir Maḥmud, and he left Balkh on Thursday, 19 Rabiʿ II 422 [/15 April 1031],[397] accompanied by most of his courtiers and retainers. My master Bu Naṣr went along too, for out of prudence he would not stay behind on such occasions, so that he could be present on the scene and ensure that no plots were hatched against him. I accompanied him on the journey, and when we reached the bank of the Oxus, the Amir dismounted, and embarked on merry-making and wine-drinking. (Gh 240) He imbibed continuously for three days. On the fourth day, he mounted his steed and went off to hunt lions and other game. He killed four lions with his own hand (he was a marvel for bravery and courage, as has been recorded in several places in the History) and a great deal of other game of all kinds was also hunted. He called for food, and the game hampers were brought in; they devoured food and set about drinking. He ate and drank on the way until he reached his tent and stayed up carousing most of the night.

The next day, he mounted and came to the side of the Oxus.[398] Boats were brought to this shore, and the citadel [of Termez] had been adorned with all kinds of weaponry.[399] Many infantrymen had come [F 311] with their senior officers (*sarhangs*) to render service and were stood on that opposite side of the Oxus bank. The Amir got into a boat, and the boon-companions, the musicians and singers, and the gholāms had climbed into other boats. They sailed until they reached the foot of the citadel. The castellan of the citadel at this time was Qotlogh, Sebüktegin's gholām,[400] who was a man endowed with much dignity and gravitas. The castellan and the group of senior officers kissed the ground and scattered coins as alms, and the footsoldiers likewise fell to the ground in obeisance. Trumpets were blown from the citadel and drums beaten, and great shouts were raised. Platters of food were brought out, according to the custom at Ghaznin, comprising lamb,[401] game, fish, pickles and thin cakes of bread.[402] The Amir was delighted with all this. They kept on eating, and wine flowed, and the sounds of the musicians and singers floated up from the boats. On the river bank, the musicians and singers of Termez, the women dancers and drummers, amounting to more than three hundred, struck up and were dancing and playing. Rarely have I seen elsewhere festivities of the kind I saw in Termez. They went on in such a fashion that no-one had ever seen their like.

In the midst of all this, five cavalrymen arrived, two sent from the Amir Yusof b. Nāṣer al-Din from Qoṣdār, where he resided at that time, as I have mentioned, and three sent from the Commander, the Keeper of the Royal Wardrobe, Yāruq-tughmush,[403] and they brought the news of the conquest of Makrān, the killing of ʿIsā b. Maʿdān, the entrusting of the reins of power[404] to his brother Bu'l-ʿAskar and the restoration of order [Gh 241] in this province. (I shall give the full story of this subsequently.) They spoke with the Amir, and a skiff[405] was sent, and the bearers of good news were conveyed alongside the Amir's boat. When they came aboard the Amir's boat, they rendered service and [F 312] handed over the letter. Bu Naṣr Moshkān took the letter—he being in the boat conveying the boon-companions—and rose to his feet and read out the letter in a loud voice. The Amir was highly delighted, and he turned towards the castellan and the senior officers and said, "This town of yours has always proved auspicious for our dynasty, and today we hold it as even more blessed because such excellent news has arrived and such an extensive province has been conquered." Everyone, men and women alike, kissed the ground, as did likewise the garrison of the citadel up on its roof, and with one voice they bellowed out a mighty cry of jubilation. Then the Amir turned towards the local governor and tax collector and the mayor of Termez, saying, "We remit for the subjects 100,000 dirhams of the land-tax due this year. An accounting should be drawn up for this sum owed by them, and quittances (*barāts*) should be issued in such a way that the sum remitted is equitably spread out. Fifty thousand dirhams should be given out from the state treasury as gifts for the foot soldiers of the citadel garrison, and 50,000 dirhams for these musicians and singers and dancers." They replied, "We obey," and a shout arose that the lord Sultan had commanded such tokens of regard as these three grants; and everyone, from the eminent to the lowly, offered up profuse prayers.

Then the Amir said to the castellan, "Follow after us to the army encampment, together with all the senior officers of the citadel so that robes of honour and gifts are also presented to you in the traditional way, for tomorrow we intend to leave here for Balkh." They sailed across in boats, and towards the time of the midday worship arrived at the army encampment. The Amir embarked on drinking wine. The castellan of Termez and the senior officers came in, and the Great Chamberlain Bilgetegin seated them beside himself in the domed tent (*nim-tark*). Bilgetegin then gave a verbal message to his representative at court Ṭāher b. K.n.d.h[406] to tell the Head of the Army Department Bu Sahl Zowzani, who was drinking wine with the Sultan, to let the Amir know that the castellan and the senior officers had arrived. Bu Sahl passed on the message. The Amir said, "Go to the smaller tent and tell the treasurers and the overseers to give them all robes of honour, in accordance with what has already been decreed, and to bring them for an audience with us." Bu Sahl Zowzani came out, and [F 313] the matter was arranged. The castellan and the senior officers donned the robes of honour and came into the royal presence. The Amir ordered that the castellan Qotlogh and Bu'l-Ḥasan b. Bā Naṣr,[407] who had been granted robes of honour and gold trappings for their mounts,[408] should be given places to sit, while the rest were to stand there. All were given goblets of wine and they drank and rendered service. The Amir said, "Go back, be on the alert and stay watchful, and you will enjoy our beneficence permanently." They replied, "We obey!" They kissed the ground, departed and took their places in the boats and returned to the citadel. The Amir drank wine until midnight, and arose early at dawn the next day. The large kettledrums were beaten, and they rode off and made camp at Siyāh-gerd. [Gh 242]

The next day, on Friday, 27 Rabiʿ II [422/22 April 1031], he entered Balkh, and observed the auspicious sight of the new moon of Jomādā I. He left the garden and lodged in the palace of the Gate of ʿAbd al-Aʿlā. He gave instructions that all impending business should be dealt with, since it was time to leave for Ghaznin and they were to depart in a week or two. They obeyed the command and busied themselves with matters at hand. *God is most knowing about the right course!*

An account of events in the province of Makrān and what went on there during the time of Amir Maḥmud[409]

When Maʿdān, the governor of Makrān, passed away, a dispute arose between his two sons ʿIsā and Bu'l-ʿAskar, and soon a quarrel in words gave way to a clash of swords, with the army and the populace inclined towards ʿIsā. Bu'l-ʿAskar fled and arrived in Sistan, [F 314] at a time when we (i.e. the Sultan and his entourage, including Beyhaqi himself) had gone to Somnāth.[410] That truly noble-hearted man Khᵛāja Bu Naṣr Khᵛāfi lodged him in a handsome fashion, and fed and entertained him lavishly with wondrous hospitality.[411] Khᵛāja Bu'l-Faraj ʿĀli (*sic*) b. al-Moẓaffar, may God perpetuate his exalted status—who at this present time, in the fortunate (*farrokh*) reign of the exalted Sultan Abu Shojāʿ Farrokh-zād b. Nāṣer al-Din, *may God prolong his life and grant victory to his servants*, holds, together with his deputies, the office of the Overseer of the Realm and who is a man unique for learning, intellect and knowledge of the religious sciences and of polite learning—had come this year to Sistan, and he had there struck up a great friendship with the Khᵛāja, my father, and has many stories about their friendship and their time together, and at present he is my friend. In this same year, his late brother Khᵛāja Bu Naṣr also came to Qāyen.[412] Both these two later came to Ghaznin and rendered much service, rising to such high office that Bu Naṣr attained the headship of the Army Department and died while in that office. He was a most learned and handsome man, cultured and wise. He is survived by his eldest son, who has had assigned to him the office of the overseer of Ghaznin and its vicinity.

Bu Naṣr Khᵛāfi explained Bu'l-ʿAskar's situation, and after our return from the Somnāth expedition, Amir Maḥmud sent a letter to Bu Naṣr instructing him to send Bu'l-ʿAskar to the court with due decorum, and he did so. Amir Maḥmud showed him favour and kept him at the court. News of this reached his brother, the governor of Makrān, who became extremely worried[413] and fearful. He sent the Judge of Makrān, together with the headman of the region and several of the pious men and notables from amongst his subjects, to the court bearing letters and depositions (*maḥżar-hā*) stating that "I am my father's designated successor, and if only my brother had not acted in a hostile manner but had exhibited a conciliatory attitude and followed our father's injunctions, [Gh 243] no favour or benevolence would have been denied to him. Now, if it pleases the lord, he could retain me in this province and stipulate whatever is incumbent upon me, just as that great and just Amir (i.e. Sebüktegin) had stipulated for my father,[414] and on the appropriate occasions I will send what is due together with tokens of service for Nowruz and Mehragān. [F 315] Whatever my brother needs and whatever the lord commands, will be regularly sent without any niggardly reservations. My trusty agent will hand over a document with whatever terms of the contractual agreement (*movāżaʿat*) may be fixed, so that I can put it into practice in accordance with my obedience and submission. Let an envoy from the exalted court be designated, and let him bring with him an investiture patent for the province—and, if the exalted judgement so bestows, a robe of honour, since I have made the formal intercessory prayer in the lord's name. In this way my resolve will be further strengthened, and this region, in which I have made the intercessory prayer for the lord, may become completely settled and at rest."[415]

Amir Maḥmud responded favourably, the necessary arrangements were made, and the Makrānis were sent home. Ḥasan Sepāhāni (i.e. Eṣfahāni) Sārbān[416] was despatched as an envoy to bring back the land-tax of Makrān and Qoṣdār, and a very splendid robe of honour and an investiture patent was sent with him. The matter of Makrān became properly settled, and Ḥasan Sepāhāni returned with the tribute of Makrān and Qoṣdār, accompanied by an envoy from Makrān and with much wealth and valuable items brought as presents for the Amir and the great men of the court, comprising gold, pearls, amber and other specialities of those lands, and also with a contractual agreement pledging that, annually with the land-tax, there should be 10,000 Haravi dinars for the brother Bu'l-ʿAskar, apart from clothing and luxury products; and they had brought with them the specified amount for one year. This proved satisfactory, and the envoys from Makrān were sent back.

Bu'l-ʿAskar remained at the court and was occupied with rendering service. Amir Maḥmud ordered him to be assigned a monthly allowance of 5,000 dirhams, and he used to receive two robes of honour per year. I never at any time saw him drink wine in the Amir's sessions nor play polo nor engage in other such things that I had seen Abu Ṭāher Simjuri,[417] and men of their status do, [F 316] for Bu'l-ʿAskar was a person of some gravitas and with a powerful build. From time to time, on the odd occasion when there was a grand reception, he would be invited to the feast but would be given leave to depart once the trays had been cleared (i.e. before the start of the heavy wine-drinking bout). He used to come with us on journeys, including that year when we went to Khorasan and we were diverted towards Ray,[418] and the journey grew even more protracted. It was the time when the rulers of the surrounding regions had had brief, wishful dreams from which they later woke up to find themselves fatherless[419] and without a province (for Amir Maḥmud was suffering from the frailty of old age and his end had drawn nigh). ʿIsā of Makrān was one of those dreamers. Amir Maḥmud had encouraged Bu'l-ʿAskar's hopes by promising that, upon his return to Ghaznin, he would provide Bu'l-ʿAskar with an army and that a mighty commander would accompany him [Gh 244] to drive out his brother from the province, and that Bu'l-ʿAskar would be entrusted with the province instead. But he never found the time for this on his return to Ghaznin, and failed to carry out his promise; nor was it possible for Amir Moḥammad to carry out his father's dying wishes during the period of his own rule, for he faced a far more momentous challenge. He too made much of Bu'l-ʿAskar and conferred robes of honour on him, and gave him hopes of this; but this never came about because of the subsequent turn of events (i.e. Moḥammad's deposition).

When matters became settled and on an even course for Amir Masʿud at Herat, as has been recorded in the fifth volume of the History, he appointed the Keeper of the Royal Wardrobe, the General Yāruq-tughmush, together with a powerful force of palace troops along with the Turkmens of Qïzïl, Buqa and Köktāsh, who had become clients of the Sultan[420] and had entered his service,[421] and sent them to Sistan, and from there they proceeded to Makrān. He sent Amir Yusof with a strong military force to Qoṣdār, saying to Yāruq-tughmush, "Yusof is a reinforcement for you, so that if help is needed, he can send troops, and if needs be, come himself." He had secretly given the commander of this army [F 317] instructions to keep an eye on Yusof. The underlying motive behind sending Yusof to Qoṣdār was so that for a while he would be far away and out of sight of the bulk of the army, for he was their Commander-in-Chief. In the end, he was arrested during this year in Balq[422] at the bridge of Khumārtegin when we were coming to Ghaznin. The story of that will come later, in the seventh volume.

When ʿIsā of Makrān heard reports of these armies and of his brother, he prepared for war and assembled a force of 20,000 infantry from Kich, Rig,[423] Makrān and every district and ethnic group, together with 6,000 cavalry. The General Yāruq-tughmush, the Keeper of the Royal Wardrobe, reached Makrān (he was a very alert and sharp-eyed commander and a renowned warrior). He had with him senior commanders and a well-equipped army, eager to fight. A force of 2,000 cavalry of the royal guard (*sovār-e solṭāni*) and the Turkmens were ordered to hide in ambush within local date-palm groves. Large kettledrums were beaten, and the Makrāni marched out. He was seated on an elephant and brought forward his army, comprising cavalry and infantry and ten choice elephants. They joined battle and there was much bloodshed. Both armies fought fiercely and acquitted themselves well. The Keeper of the Royal Wardrobe nearly faced a breach in his lines, but he advanced, a great shout rose up from the army, the champions and outstanding warriors provided help, the troops were unleashed from the ambush and the Makrāni turned in flight. They came upon him in a defile whither he was fleeing, killed him and bore off his head. [Gh 245]. Large numbers of his troops were killed, and for three days the town and its environs were plundered, with a great deal of wealth and beasts falling into the army's hands. Bu'l-ʿAskar was then placed on the throne as Amir. When he was firmly in control and the people of those regions became quiescent under him, the Keeper of the Royal Wardrobe went back with the army, as will be mentioned subsequently. The governorship of Makrān was firmly established in Bu'l-ʿAskar's hands until the time when he died, as will be recorded in this [F 318] history of the life and times of kings.[424]

May God, He is exalted and magnified, have mercy on them and may He bring about happiness and prosperity for the great Sultan Farrokh-zād in his life, youth, good fortune and kingly power!

[The end of the sixth volume]

[F 319] [The beginning of the seventh volume]

An account of the departure of Amir Masʿud from Balkh to Ghaznin

At the end of the sixth volume I said that—at the beginning of the month of Jomādā I 422 [/26 April 1031]—the Amir went back from the garden to the Palace of [the Gate of] ʿAbd al-Aʿlā and gave orders that all outstanding matters should be dealt with since he intended to proceed towards Ghaznin in that very week, and everything was accordingly settled. When he was about to go, he said to Khᵛāja Aḥmad b. Ḥasan, "You must remain in Balkh for another week, for all sorts of people are being left behind in Balkh—local governors and tax collectors, judges, the military governors of various towns and individuals seeking redress for their grievances—so that you may hear what they have to say and send them all back. Then come and join up with us at Baghlān, for on the way to Samangān we intend to stop at various spots and hunt and carouse awhile." He answered, "I obey, but I shall need with me one of the Chancery secretaries to write down any commands that the lord may issue, and a treasurer to issue a robe of honour in case this has to be given out to someone." The Amir said, "That's a good idea. Tell Bu Naṣr Moshkān to nominate a secretary, and the Vizier should have one of the treasurers standing by, with dirhams, dinars and clothing so that the Vizier may give orders for whatever he deems the best course of action. He should arrange matters so that within ten days he can tie up everything and join us at Baghlān."

My master Bu Naṣr chose me, Abu'l-Fażl, and a treasurer was nominated [F 320] in the person of Bu'l-Ḥasan b. Qoreysh, the treasury secretary. This Bu'l-Ḥasan was a most competent secretary who had served the Samanids and had been in their treasuries at Bokhara, and the Vizier Khᵛāja Bu'l-'Abbās Esfarāyeni had brought him with him. Amir Maḥmud had complete confidence in him. He had two assistants (*shāgerds*), one of the two being 'Ali b. 'Abd al-Jalil, the cousin on his father's side of Bu'l-Ḥasan b. 'Abd al-Jalil; all have passed on, may God have mercy on them. [Gh 246] I mention their names for two reasons: one is that I knew them well and had spent some time in their company, and so I wanted to say something about each of them; and the second is to describe the workings of the different offices as they were in previous times so that the readers of this History might gain some experience and deduce some moral precepts from my account.

On Sunday, 13 Jomādā I [422/8 May 1031] Amir Mas'ud set out from Balkh and encamped in the garden of Khᵛāja 'Ali Mikā'ili, since affairs had not yet been settled and the garden was near the town. Khᵛāja Abu'l-Moẓaffar 'Ali, son of Mikā'il, offered lavish hospitality there on a regal scale[425] to such an extent that it became a talking point. The prominent persons of the court were given food and hospitality, and sumptuous presents, gold and silver were offered to the Amir. The Amir went away from there in a state of contentment and well-being. He rode on joyfully, wine-drinking and hunting, from one host to another: at Kholm,[426] and at Piruz-e Nakhchir,[427] and in Badakhshān it was the turn of Aḥmad b. 'Ali b. Nushtegin, the Master of the Royal Stables,[428] who was the governor of those regions, and at Baghlān and in Tokhārestān [F 321] the Great Chamberlain Bilgetegin had the honour.

The Grand Vizier Aḥmad b. Ḥasan used every day to hold a formal session in his residence at the Gate of 'Abd al-A'lā, and would preside over it till the time of the midday prayer and would deal with administrative matters. I used to be with his secretaries, and I would write down whatever he commanded and would carry on my work. He would give orders for robes of honour and largesse to be given out on the Sultan's behalf. When we had performed the midday worship, those visitors from outside the Divān would go back home, and the Grand Vizier would have the secretaries and his own entourage and myself join him at his spread, and we would eat and then return. This went on for a whole week until all the tasks were completed, and I myself received numerous bounties. Then the Grand Vizier departed from Balkh and, despite the fact that an elephant with a howdah and a mule with a litter were available to him throughout the journey, he would sit down in the midst of a travelling litter (*takht*) with its window screens[429] drawn, and five men would carry it. He came also from India to Balkh conveyed in this fashion, since it provided a softer and more comfortable ride.

We came up with the Amir at Baghlān, [Gh 247] where he had been engaged in carousing and hunting, and was awaiting the Vizier. When the latter came in, he narrated in full all that he had achieved. The Amir was very pleased. He remained there one more day and then the army travelled onwards via the road through the valley of Zirqān and Ghurvand.[430] They emerged and encamped for three days of merry-making with wine and hunting on the enchanted, paradaisal plain.[431] No-one could remember a time like this, and the world appeared resplendent as a bride, and the mighty monarch rode along in a leisurely way, secure and carefree, until the party reached Parvān. [F 322] From there they travelled on in the same ebullient and joyful mood to the next staging-post of Balq.[432] Each day yet another group of the people of Ghaznin would arrive to meet the party on its way and offer their obeisance; for instance, Moẓaffar, the mayor of Ghaznin, the deputy for his father Khᵛāja ʿAli, came forward at Parvān with numerous presents of rare sweets and delicacies, and others came fast on his heels till we reached Balq. Those who came along would find favour according to their status and rank. *God is most knowing about what is best!*

An account of the arrest of the Amir Abu Yaʿqub Yusof b. Nāṣer al-Din Abu Manṣur Sebüktegin the Just[433]

The arrest of this Amir happened here at Balq. This incident had a lengthy dénouement which has to be set down so that the whole episode becomes comprehensible. Amir Yusof was a man completely devoid of any rebellious traits who would never seek out any mischief or invite trouble.[434] In the time of his brother Sultan Maḥmud he used to be so occupied with attending the royal audience twice a day that he had no time for anything else. Also, during his own leisure time, when he was free of these courtly duties, he sought his own pleasure, with merry-making and bouts of wine-drinking. Given such circumstances, and given his youthfulness,[435] together with his having been born into luxury, wealth and power for which he had never had to exert himself, it is clear how much experience he had acquired. When Amir Maḥmud passed away, and there was no longer anyone holding on to the end of the leash,[436] Amir Moḥammad came to Ghaznin and assumed the throne, and he gave the post of Commander-in-Chief to his paternal uncle Amir Yusof, and events took the course that they did and which I have set forth previously. [F 323] That period of kingly rule, and his time as Commander-in-Chief, was but a brief phase, too short for him to have been able to acquire much discernment and awareness. Then such an event took place as the confinement of Amir Moḥammad in the fortress of Kuhtiz at Teginābād (i.e. with the connivance of his own courtiers). Although those responsible did so out of their support for a great monarch (i.e. Masʿud) and expressed their firm allegiance to him, [Gh 248] kings may accept such protestations of deep attachment at the time but they do not put their trust in such persons.

[In this context,] I have read in the historical accounts about Yaʿqub b. Leyth that he led an expedition to Nishapur with the aim of seizing the Amir of Khorasan, Moḥammad b. Ṭāher (II) b. ʿAbdallāh b. Ṭāher (I). The notables at Moḥammad's court tried to make approaches to Yaʿqub and sent speedy couriers with letters, saying, "You must hasten very quickly, so that the frontier region of Khorasan, extensive as it is, does not perish; for our present ruler is not capable of anything except indulgence in pleasurable pastimes." However, three of the oldest and the most learned of the elders made no attempt to turn to Yaʿqub and attach themselves to him, but remained steadfast at their posts at Moḥammad b. Ṭāher's palace until Yaʿqub b. Leyth arrived. They arrested Moḥammad b. Ṭāher and seized these three men and brought them before Yaʿqub. Yaʿqub said, "Why didn't you try to ingratiate yourselves with me, as your friends did?" They replied, "You are a great monarch and will become an even greater one. We shall give you our truthful response, so long as it does not kindle your wrath." He said, "I won't get angry; speak your mind!" They said, "Has the Amir ever seen us before today?" He replied, "No, I haven't." They continued, "Have we ever sent him any letters, or has he ever corresponded with us?" He replied, "No, never." They went on, "We are thus an old and aged group of persons who have all served the Tahirids for many years, and during their rule have enjoyed many acts of favour and have become well established in office. Would it be right for us to follow the path of ingratitude (*kofrān-e neʿmat*) and ingratiate ourselves with their opponents, even though [otherwise] our heads may be chopped off?" They added, "So this is our situation, and today we are in the Amir's hands and our master has been overthrown. Let him do with us what is pleasing to the Exalted God [F 324] and what befits his own chivalrous nature[437] and magnanimity." Yaʿqub answered, "Go back to your homes and rest assured that such nobility should be preserved and will prove of value for us; you must remain permanently at my court." They returned home, secure and offering up thanks. After this, Yaʿqub ordered that those who had tried to ingratiate themselves with him should be arrested, their possessions confiscated, and they themselves banished.[438] He promoted the three men to high office and relied upon them in affairs of the realm. I include stories like this so that slanderers do not rush into producing false charges critical of this great monarch Masʿud but, rather, speak justly, for the nature of monarchs, and their manners and customs, are not like those of the rest and they see through things that others cannot.

Another contributory factor was that, in order to retain Sultan Maḥmud's favour, Amir Yusof was drawn to Amir Moḥammad's side, thereby alienating the other party (i.e. Masʿud's). Amir Yusof had two daughters, one of them already grown up [Gh 249] and nubile, and the other still very young and not yet at a marriageable age. Amir Maḥmud gave the former, nubile one to Amir Moḥammad, and the marriage contract was concluded; the other one, who had not yet reached puberty, he betrothed to Amir Masʿud so that he should not be offended, but no marriage contract was concluded. Amir Maḥmud ordered a lavish marriage ceremony, whose like no-one could recall, in Amir Moḥammad's palace which was opposite the Lesser Square (*meydān-e khord*). When the palace was decorated and preparations were completed, Amir Maḥmud mounted and came there, showed great favour to Amir Moḥammad, conferred on him a robe of honour fit for a king and bestowed many gifts. They went back and left the palace for the bridegroom[439] and the noble womenfolk. By a stroke of Fate, a fever gripped the bride. At the time of the night worship a litter was brought, the river of Ghaznin became filled with women of high status, and many candles and torches were lit so that the bride could be transported to the Royal Palace. But the hapless bride, still innocent of the ways of this world, [F 325] and bedecked in gold, precious ornaments and jewels, breathed her last while still seated there, and everything came to naught. This became known immediately and was conveyed to Amir Maḥmud. He was much saddened by the news, but could do nothing against the strokes of Fate, for God, His mention is exalted, inflicts things like that on His servants so that they may perceive their own helplessness.

The next day, he ordered that the marriage contract for the other daughter, who had been betrothed to Amir Masʿud, should be concluded for Amir Moḥammad.[440] This came as a great disappointment to Amir Masʿud, but he could not say anything. The girl was still very young, and they postponed bringing her to her future house (i.e. that of her future husband). Time passed and circumstances changed, Amir Maḥmud died, and the end of the affair was that this girl arrived in the women's quarters of Amir Moḥammad at that moment when he came to Ghaznin and assumed the throne, she being reportedly fourteen years old. That night when she was brought from our quarter by the mill from her father's palace to the government headquarters,[441] I witnessed much pomp and ceremony, beyond measure. After the imprisonment of Amir Moḥammad, the girl was sent to be with him in the fortress. She was there for a while, but then felt homesick and returned, and she is at the present time here in Ghazni. Amir Masʿud felt much aggrieved by this unjust behaviour on the part of his paternal uncle, and the preponderant power of Fate also lent a hand so that Yusof fell from his throne-like position into a pit.[442] *We seek refuge in God from the adversities of fortune!*

When affairs for Sultan Masʿud at Herat became settled and assumed an even course, as I have set forth previously, he sent the Keeper of the Royal Wardrobe, the General Yāruq-tughmush, to Makrān with a massive army in order to restore order there and to place Bu'l-ʿAskar on the throne.[443] He sent Amir Yusof to Qoṣdār with ten *sarhangs* and an army contingent as a supporting force for the Keeper of the Royal Wardrobe and to hasten the settlement of affairs in Makrān. [Gh 250]

But this was a mere pretext, for his intention was to get Yusof away from the court and away from the eyes of the army, and to have him interned, as it were, in Qoṣdār with those *sarhangs* acting as his keepers. Meanwhile, on the orders of the Sultan, Yusof's personal chamberlain Ṭoghrïl, whom he held dearer than his own offspring, was secretly suborned on the orders of the Sultan, and arrangements were made [F 326] for him to act as a spy over Yusof and report back whatever went on; as a reward for this, he was offered the prospects of high promotion.[444] This gullible Turk swallowed this poisoned bait and did not realize that ingratitude can be an ill-omened thing. He used swift messengers to convey secretly from Qoṣdār to Balkh a medley of truth and falsehood[445] to ʿAbdus, and this would then be relayed to the Sultan. How could Yusof know that his very life and soul and beloved one was spying on him? At times, and especially while under the influence of wine, he would mutter and grumble and indulge in loose talk and say, "What prompted us to bring all this upon ourselves, for we are sure to be dealt with one after the other? This is only to be expected, since we all acted disloyally and broke our pledge; we shall see where the affair will end."[446] All this was written down, and a lot more embellishments added, further hardening the Sultan's attitude towards Yusof.

Ṭoghrïl went so far in the revelations which he sent back as to write, "Yusof is getting ready to defect to Turkestan, and has been engaged in correspondence with the Khāns and their followers." The Sultan secretly ordered letters to the leading commanders who had been asked to keep an eye on Yusof, saying, "Great care must be taken in watching over Yusof until he comes back to Ghaznin. When we leave Balkh for Ghazni, we will summon him. If he opts for going off in another direction (i.e. absconds to Turkestan), he must be stopped and seized and brought before us in fetters. But if he does proceed directly to Bost and Ghaznin, what we have just commanded should of course be kept from him." Those leading commanders followed their orders, and all the requisite safeguards were put into effect. We were at Balkh, and on several occasions—three or four [F 327] or five times—swift camels arrived from Qoṣdār bringing fine citrons,[447] pomegranates and sugar cane, and delivering letters from Yusof filled with expressions of subservience and reporting on the situation in Makrān and Qoṣdār. The Amir was ordering replies couched in handsome terms, addressing him as "Exalted Amir, Our Uncle, Abu Yaʿqub Yusof b. Nāṣer al-Din," and he wrote that "On such-and-such a day we intend to leave Balkh. The affairs of Makrān have become settled, and accordingly, you too should leave Qoṣdār soon so as to reach Ghaznin at the same time as ourself and so that your just rights may be properly recognized."

Amir Yusof left Qoṣdār and reached Ghaznin before Sultan Masʿud. When he heard that the Sultan's army train and entourage was heading from Parvān towards Ghaznin, he set out with his son Soleymān, the ungrateful Ṭoghrïl [Gh 251] and fifty gholāms, travelling very light, for the ceremonial welcoming. When one watch remained of the night, the Amir had departed from Setāj[448] heading for Balq, where they had set up the enclosure for the army camp (i.e. for the next stop). He was in a howdah on a female elephant, with torches lit, and they rode on talking and exchanging stories as they went along. Near the town of Balq, a torch became visible from afar on the plain from the direction of Ghazni. The Amir said, "It could be Yusof my uncle, whom we have summoned, and who has come to greet us," and he ordered two troop commanders to go and meet him. They galloped towards the torch, arrived there and hurried back, reporting, "May the lord's life be long! It is indeed Amir Yusof!" After an hour he arrived. The Amir reined in his elephant, and Amir Yusof dismounted and kissed the ground, while the Great Chamberlain Bilgetegin and all the notables and great men accompanying the Amir also dismounted. Yusof's horse was summoned and he was helped to mount in a most decorously respectful manner. The Amir asked after his welfare in an exceptionally warm and cordial manner. [F 328] They rode along, and the Amir was conversing solely with him until it became day and they dismounted for the dawn worship. The Amir exchanged that elephant for a horse and they rode along, with Yusof at his left side, and they were conversing till they came to the army encampment. The Amir turned to ʿAbdus and said, "My uncle has come lightly equipped; tell them to set up here, right in front of the camp enclosure, an awning,[449] platforms and tents, and my uncle can be installed here and be near us." He answered, "I'll do so."

The Amir went into the tent enclosure (*kheyma*) and installed himself in the large tent (*khargāh*), and Amir Yusof was placed in the domed tent (*nim-tark*) while they set up the platform and the canvas shelter.[450] So he went there and other tents were erected, and his gholāms came and were settled down. They brought in trays of food and set them down—I myself was observing all this from the Divān—but he did not touch anything and was sunk in his own thoughts to an inordinate extent, for he had a foreboding of the approaching calamity. When the trays were removed and the leading personages of the court began to disperse, the Amir ordered the area to be cleared for a private audience and summoned ʿAbdus, and kept him for a long time. Then he came out and went to Amir Yusof, and they were alone and talked for a long time. ʿAbdus was coming and going, and there was much talk and Yusof's treacheries[451] were being enumerated. The final outcome was that by the time of the midday worship, three senior officers (*moqaddam*) from the Indian troops were placed in position there with 500 fully-armed Indian cavalrymen and three Indian troop commanders accompanied by 300 picked infantrymen, and a saddled mule was brought in and held ready. I saw Amir Yusof [Gh 252], rising to his feet, still with his cap, boots and belt on. He clutched his son to his bosom and wept, took off his belt and threw it down, and said to ʿAbdus, "I entrust this child to the Almighty God, and [F 329] after Him, to you." He said to Ṭoghrïl, "Be of good cheer! O ungrateful wretch! Was it for this that I brought you up and held you dearer than my own children, so that you could be duped into wreaking such a deed against me? You will get your just deserts in the course of time!" He mounted his mule and they conveyed him to the fortress of Sakāvand. After that, I never saw him again, and the next year, 423 [/1032], when we came back from Balkh a letter arrived when we were on the road that he had died in the fortress of Daruna,[452] may God's mercy be upon him.

The story of this Ṭoghrïl is rather a short tale but it has remarkable features, and I ought to tell it; I shall then return to the main narrative of the History.

An account of the story of this gholām Ṭoghrïl al-ʿAżodi[453]

In his looks, pleasing stature, fine complexion, elegance and sharp wit, this gholām was one in a thousand. The Khātun of Arslān had sent him from Turkestan for Amir Maḥmud. This Khātun had the custom of sending to Amir Maḥmud each year an exceptional gholām and a choice, virgin slave girl by way of a gift, and the Amir used to send her in return fine linen turban cloths, delicate muslins for shawls, pearls and Rumi brocade. The Amir found this Ṭoghrïl pleasing, and had him as one of a group of seven or eight gholāms acting as cupbearers subsequent to Ayāz.[454] Two years passed. It happened one day that the Amir was drinking wine in the Firuzi Garden over the roses,[455] with countless hundred-leaved roses strewn about.[456] [F 330] These radiantly handsome cupbearers[457] entered in a pre-arranged order, two-by-two. This Ṭoghrïl entered, clad in a ruby-coloured coat, with his companion wearing a turquoise-coloured one, and both of the two moon-faced ones began to hand round the wine. As Ṭoghrïl stood there with dark-coloured wine in his hand, Amir Yusof, already befuddled by the wine, became transfixed by him, and however much he struggled to restrain himself, he could not take his eyes off him.

Amir Maḥmud was surreptitiously watching and observing his brother's infatuation and bewitchment, but he behaved as if nothing was amiss and let an hour pass by. [Gh 253] Then he said, "O brother, our father Sebüktegin died when you were still a child, and on his deathbed he had said to the secretary ʿAbdallāh, 'It is decreed that the domain of Ghaznin should be in Maḥmud's keeping, for it is beyond Esmāʿil's ability. Tell Maḥmud from me that I am concerned about Yusof and have entrusted him to you. You must bring him up as you see fit and cherish him like your own offspring.' You know that, to this end, we have accorded you several acts of benevolence. We considered that you had grown up suitably behaved (*bā adab*), but you're not as we imagined. Why are you fixing your gaze on our gholāms during our wine-drinking session? Would you like anyone to stare at your own gholāms during a drinking bout? And yet your eyes have remained fixed on this Ṭoghrïl for a long while. If it were not out of respect for my father's soul, you would receive a proper chastisement. I have forgiven you this one time, and I have presented this gholām to you, since we have many like him. Be on the alert that such a lapse does not occur a second time, for you cannot play such games with Maḥmud." Yusof was reduced to confusion, rose to his feet, kissed the ground and said, "I repent, and an error like this won't occur again." The Amir said, "Sit down!" [F 331] He sat down, and that was the end of the matter, and the carousing got more lively. The wine had its effect on Yusof, and he went homewards. Amir Maḥmud called out to one of his personal eunuchs[458] called Ṣāfi—he had charge of the gholāms like him—and said, "Send Ṭoghrïl to my brother." He was sent to him, and Yusof rejoiced heartily. He lavished gifts on the eunuchs and gave out much money as alms. He raised up this gholām to a high status, with Ṭoghrïl becoming his personal chamberlain, and he held him dearer than his own children. And when the soft, clear down of youth began to yield to darker and longer shadows and the onset of manhood,[459] Yusof sought a wife for him from a prominent family, and was so excessively prodigal over Ṭoghrïl's betrothal and the wedding celebrations that it drew forth the disapproval of many a wise observer; and for his pains, his master, Yusof, was chastised and punished in the way that I have already set forth.

After his master's death, although Ṭoghrïl found some sort of advancement and favour with Sultan Masʿud, he was soon shunned as a pariah both by the Sultan and by others; he experienced adversity and died young with his ambitions unfulfilled. The consequence of ingratitude is always thus! May God, whose mention is exalted, keep us and all the Muslims in His protection and may He grant the best divine guidance so that it will lead to thankfulness for His blessings and the thanks of His servants who are the recipients of bounty, *through His beneficence and the abundance of His mercy!* [Gh 254]

After the demise of Amir Yusof, his retainers became scattered. Various squabbles and upheavals befell Bu Sahl, grandson of Lakshan, his counsellor and administrator,[460] and he was forcibly compelled to disgorge his wealth. He was a most learned, wise and circumspect person. In the end he was given the governorship and tax-collecting responsibilities of Bost, since he was a native of the town, and died while in that office. Khᵛāja Esmāʿil suffered many hardships and experienced numerous vicissitudes. [F 332] He looked after the interests of Yusof's household, took charge of the affairs of this Amir's children, held himself responsible regarding their concerns, and underwent a chequered period until he gained further recognition and became engaged in more private and personal tasks for this monarch. He proved his capability and trustworthiness on several occasions and thereby achieved prominence, with the result that at present, in the auspicious time of the Exalted Sultan Abu Shojāʿ Farrokh-zād b. Nāṣer Din Allāh, the office of stewardship of the palace and oversight of the crown domains, and many other tasks, are entrusted to him.

He pursued these tasks for a long time in such a way that no blame or reproach rebounded upon him.

Regarding Āmuy,[461] when he experienced this débâcle in the state of affairs, he focussed his attention on his own spiritual salvation and, having served Yusof, he gave up serving earthly masters and chose the *meḥrāb* (i.e. attendance in the mosque), prayer, the Qorʾān and asceticism, and has remained steadfast in this to date. On several occasions, the monarchs of this house sought to appoint him to an office. For a while he held the command of the ghāzis of Ghaznin,[462] and carried out the task admirably; but in the end he found people to intercede for him so that he was able to extricate himself from that. Several times they wanted him to undertake missions, but he so contrived that he got out of it. In the year 449 [/1057–8] they were pressing him into accepting the post of the overseer of the charitable endowments of Ghaznin, hoping that in this way the task would be carried out to perfection, but he again managed to find ways to stop them. It is a mark of true manliness to act thus and to trample upon greed and concupiscence; the Almighty God will not abandon and leave in deprivation any of His devoted servants. [F 333].

Regarding Bu'l-Qāsem Ḥakimak,[463] who was one of Amir Yusof's boon-companions and a capable and cultured man, he also refused to serve anyone else, and kept to his old loyalties in his own noble way. Today, these two are alive here in Ghaznin, and are friends of mine.[464] What else could I do but to take note and acknowledge all the friends I knew, and this is not too removed from the conventions of history. Now that I have set down this story, [Gh 255], I shall return to the main thread of the history of Sultan Masʿud after the arrest of Amir Yusof and his consignment to the fortress of Sakāvand.

The next day, he moved off from Balq and travelled onwards. At Shajkāv,[465] the senior officer (*sarhang*) Bu ʿAli the castellan and Bu'l-Qāsem b. ʿAli Nuki (Navaki?),[466] the postal service and intelligence officer, came to meet him, for it was customary for them to come as far as here to welcome the royal party. The Amir was most gracious to them in a manner appropriate for each one of them. The castellan presented piles of delicious delicacies, in his own inimitable way, and the Amir was most pleased and complimented them both before sending them back to Ghaznin. He instructed the castellan to plan ahead with foresight and to station a full force of infantrymen from

Khalqāni (?)[467] onwards to the palace, since the road would be lined with a series of festive platforms and arches, so that no untoward incidents should occur. The next day, Thursday, 8 Jomādā II 422[468] [/2 June 1031], the Amir rode towards the capital and seat of government with a very splendid array and with the townspeople of Ghaznin, men, women and children, streaming out excitedly to see him. At Khalqāni (?), so many ceremonial cupolas had been carefully set up[469] that even the old men were saying that they could not remember anything like it in the past; and showers of coins were scattered as alms on an unparalleled scale. There was such a press of people [F 334] that it was most difficult and troublesome to get past those festive platforms; and a great crowd of people went out to the dry river bed and the Shābahār plain.[470] Towards the time of the midday prayer the Amir arrived at his splendid palace (*kushk-e maʿmur*) and installed himself there in resplendent glory. His paternal aunt, Ḥorra Khottali, following her practice of previous years with Amir Maḥmud, sent the Amir large quantities of finely-prepared delicacies that pleased him enormously.

That day, at the time of the afternoon worship, he did not hold court, and when night fell, the royal party withdrew privately, and all the harem concubines[471] and the noble, free women came to see him. All this day and night, [Gh 256] throughout the town there was so much jollity, with music-making and wine-drinking and people sauntering about and playing hosts to each other, that no-one could recall its like. The next day the Amir held court, sitting upon the dais of state on the throne of his father and grandfather. The townspeople began to come in successive groups, and the retainers, the troops stationed at the court, the army at large and the townspeople distributed showers of coins on a lavish scale, for truly on this day a mighty sultan had installed himself on the throne of the state. The poets recited many a poem, as is evident from the collections of their poetry (*divāns*); I have not offered any examples of these here in order to avoid prolixity. A great multitude of people stayed until the time of the midday worship. Afterwards, the Amir arose and entered his palace and imbibed wine without the boon-companions.

At the time of the afternoon worship he did not hold a court session nor on the next day either, but he mounted and rode off [F 335] by way of the clover fields to the Firuzi Garden, where he visited and shed tears at the tomb of his father, and he ordered 20,000 dirhams to be given to those persons tending the tomb. He said to the religious scholar Nabih and the judge of the army Naṣr b. Khalaf, "A large workforce must be assembled and set to work so that this charitable hospice (*rebāṭ*) that the late Amir decreed, may be built promptly, and the income (*ṭoroq va sobol*) accrued from the pious endowments for this hospice used with great care for its upkeep. My father had a great affection for this garden, and because of this, he gave orders that he should be buried here. Out of our great respect for him, we regard this worthy site[472] as hallowed ground so that we shall only visit it to pay our respects. All kinds of festive greenery more suited to pleasant pastures (*nazeh*)[473] should be rooted out, and people with outdoor pleasures in mind[474] should be discouraged from coming here." They replied, "We'll do this," and those present offered up profuse prayers. He came out of the garden and took the road across the open plain, accompanied by the retainers and courtiers and other prominent men, and came to Afghān-shāl.[475] He halted at the tomb of the Just Amir Sebüktegin and visited it and prayed there.[476] He ordered 10,000 dirhams to be given to those living nearby and tending the tomb, and from there returned to the Royal Palace and administrative headquarters. The leading figures of the administration installed themselves in the Divāns on the next day and set to work.[477]

On Tuesday, 20 Jomādā II [/14 June 1031] he went to the Maḥmudi Garden and held a wine-drinking party. He found the place very much to his liking and gave orders that the Divāns and the necessary furnishings and equipment should be brought to there. All the palace residents came there, with the gholāms and the womenfolk. The Divāns of the Vizier, of the Head of the Army Department, the Chancery and the Office for Palace Administration and Crown Domains, the notables and prominent figures, all were installed there and things settled down into the usual routine. The men of the army, the ordinary populace, as well as those [Gh 257] of high rank and eminence, were contented and devoted to this awe-inspiring lord. [F 336] The Amir, too, conducted himself in a pleasing and appropriate manner, and had he persevered that course of conduct, no mishaps would have occurred. However, apart from the Grand Vizier Aḥmad b. Ḥasan, there were also those playing at being ministers behind the scenes[478] and oblivious to the common weal. In order to further their own selfish aims, they tailored their plans to make them seductive to a monarch, especially if the monarch happened to be young and wilfully bent on his own pleasure.

The process of discontentment and the way they alienated all hearts from this monarch began thus: Bu Sahl Zowzani and others insinuated to the Amir in private that "The accession payments[479] and presents which your brother Amir Moḥammad gave out must be recovered, since it is a serious loss and a gross piece of injustice to leave a sum of more than seventy or eighty million dirhams in the hands of the Turks and Tāziks and other ethnic groups of the army (*aṣnāf-e lashkar*) for an enterprise that was abortive (i.e. Moḥammad's brief sultanate)." They embellished and made this matter more pleasing to the monarch's mind, saying, "These men of the old guard of your father's time, in their insolence and hypocrisy, do not want the lord to reclaim this money, because they themselves are implicated in it and have taken some money; they realize that it ought to be given back and they don't like it. The right course is that the treasurers should make out a list of all the monies which they have paid out and have it sent to the Army Department. I, Bu Sahl, will make out assessments of money to be collected (*tasbib*) for each of the soldiers, and documents authorising the collection of money due (*barāt-hā*) will be written out so that the entire amount may be recovered.[480] Meanwhile, the troops' pay allotments (*bistagāni*) should not be given out for one year until the money arrives back in the treasury from the army and the Tāziks (i.e. the non-Turkish, Persian civilian officials). For they have been amassing money for forty years, and all of them have become enriched; what have they done to deserve being allowed to hold on to such enormous wealth?"

The Amir said, "That's a good idea," and he went into a private session with the Grand Vizier and spoke about this plan. The Vizier replied, "It is the lord's prerogative to command whatever he wishes, but has he given this proposal sufficient thought?" The Amir said, "I have thought about it, and it is the right course; there is a great deal of money involved." Aḥmad said, "Allow me to think about it too, and then, [F 337] whatever I arrive at as being judicious, I'll set forth, for a quick answer won't do. Then whatever the exalted judgement deems fit, he can ordain." The Amir said, "Very good." Aḥmad went back, and devoted all the day and night to thinking about this matter, and the whole enterprise appeared to him as most sinister and murky, for he was one of those eminent, gifted and experienced men to whose perspicacious minds [Gh 258] these underhand schemes do not remain a mystery for long.[481]

The next day, when the Amir held court and the courtiers had gone back, the Amir said to the Vizier, "What view have you come to regarding that matter discussed yesterday?" He replied, "I will go to the open loggia of the Divān and then deliver my response in a verbal message." He said, "Good!" The Vizier came into the loggia and summoned Khᵛāja Bu Naṣr and had a private talk with him, saying, "You've heard the news of what they've been up to?" He replied, "No, I haven't." The Vizier said, "They've made the lord Sultan eager to take back what his brother gave out in payments for the army, the notables of good birth, poets, even down to trumpeters and players of the ordinary-sized kettledrums[482] and jesters. The lord has spoken to me about this and I have found the entire scheme thoroughly unacceptable. I didn't say anything about it at the time, since I observed that the Amir was hungering for the recovery of this wealth, so I told him that I would think about it. I pondered over it all yesterday and last night, but however much I looked into it, I could not see any merit in going through with this scheme, since it will only lead to much infamy and ill-repute. Moreover, a great deal of this money will have been lost and will prove to be irretrievable. What's your opinion about this matter?"

Bu Naṣr said, "The Grand Vizier is the leader and master of us all, and what he perceived is the only right way, and I myself am saying exactly what he has said: that no-one in any time or age has ever done this or heard of such a thing being done. Nothing has come down to us about this from the era of the ancient kings of [F 338] Persia, and as for after the advent of Islam, one has not read anywhere of the caliphs or the rulers of Khorasan and Western Persia demanding the return of money given as accession payments; but today, such arguments will be utterly ineffective. Anyway, I, Bu Naṣr, already have everything that Amir Moḥammad bestowed on me—gold, silver, uncut garments, coats, turban cloths and whatever else—intact and ready, for I had, with good reason, feared such an eventuality. I will send these gifts back to the royal treasury this very day before they make out assignments for the money to be collected and thus bring shame upon me, for it will prove futile to argue about such things. In my case, it is easy to give back the money, since I have it to hand, and if I did not, I would be able to hand over the appropriate mulct; but it is much more difficult for the one-horse troopers and lesser people, and there will be much wrangling and discussion and many headaches. I don't know where it will all end, for they will not, as we have seen, leave this tender-hearted and compassionate ruler to himself; and all the norms and established traditions will be turned upside down; let's see what Fate has in store!"

The Grand Vizier said, "You must go off and deliver a robust and uncompromising message from me. I do this out of compunction[483] so that tomorrow, when this ill-favoured measure goes through—and he may well [Gh 259] come to regret it—I shall have absolved myself of all responsibility and he will not be able to say that there had been no-one there to point out the disreputable nature of this enterprise." Bu Naṣr went away and delivered a robust and uncompromising message, but it was to no avail, for the shadowy, mischief-making ministers (*vozarā' al-su'*) had tied up the whole affair securely. The Amir's answer was that "The Vizier speaks eloquently; we will think it over and whatever we deem necessary, we will ordain." Bu Naṣr came back to the loggia of the Divān and gave a full account of what had been said, and added, [F 339] "It won't do any good!"

The Vizier went to the Divān. When my master Bu Naṣr went back to his house, he secretly sent a trusty envoy to the treasurers and requested them to draw up a list of everything—gold, silver, clothing, coats and various luxury goods—which had been bestowed on him during Amir Moḥammad's period of rule and royal power, and send it to him. They did this and sent him the list. He gave back everything, and it was immediately sent to the treasury, and he got back a written document from the treasurers as a receipt for that list. This news was brought to the Amir, and it pleased him, since Bu Sahl Zowzani and others had said that all the repossessions would be like this (i.e. the money would be collected easily). For those two or three days, Bu Manṣur the accounting official, the treasurers, the overseers and the treasury secretaries were installed there, and they drew up lists of the presents and robes of honour which had been given out to the leading figures, the pillars of the state, the courtiers and all sorts of people during the period of his brother Amir Moḥammad's exercise of royal power. It was an immense and measureless sum of money. The Amir saw those lists and gave them to Bu Sahl Zowzani, saying, "We intend to go on an hunting expedition involving the rounding-up of game,[484] and this will take about twenty days.[485] After our departure, tell them to make out the assignments of money[486] intended for this group of persons and to be collected from that group, and those assigned to that one from this one, so that the monies become adjustments of payments[487] and what has to be brought to the treasury is brought." He replied, "I'll do that." This day, Friday, 1 Rajab of this year [/24 June 1031], after performing the ritual worship, he proceeded towards the hunting enclosure, with a complete array of weaponry and provisions, while the Grand Vizier, the Head of the Army Department and the Head of the Chancery remained in Ghaznin.

After he left, the assignments were put into operation, and a babble of voices and protests, of an unprecedented volume, arose, and such a sense of notoriety was generated as would be difficult to describe. To everyone who came to the Grand Vizier and complained, the answer was, "This is the Sultan's and the Head of the Army Department's doing; I have no share in this affair;" and everyone of the boon-companions, courtiers and others [Gh 260, F 340] who spoke with the Amir, would receive the reply that "This is the Vizier's and the Head of the Army Department's doing," and he gave out the distinct impression that he personally did not know what was going on. There ensued heavy-handedness and harshness, and in the end, many fortunes were lost; at a stroke public sympathy was destroyed and those feelings of goodwill and support, which had been so apparent of late, withered away. Bu Sahl's name was on everybody's lips, and they saw everything as his doing. Although he possessed accomplices, their names never came up in this matter, and he acquired a bad name for himself. He regretted his action but it was of no use. There is a proverb, "*Measure a thing and then cut:*"[488] he cut the cloth first without taking the correct measurement and then he tried to sew it all up, with the result that, from the boots to the coat, it all came out tight and ill-fitting.[489]

An account of the torrent[490]

On Saturday, 9 Rajab [2 July 1031], between the dawn and the midday ritual worship, a gentle drizzle started to come down, in such a fashion that it just made the ground slightly damp. A group of herdsmen and their flocks had encamped in the dry bed of the river of Ghaznin and had penned their cattle there. Although people told them, "Get away from there, for it's unwise to settle in the path of a torrent,"[491] they took no heed until it began to rain harder, and then they arose in a slothful manner and ensconced themselves at the foot of those walls adjoining the quarter of the blacksmiths, seeking shelter—this being another mistake. They rested there, having tethered a large number of mules belonging to the Sultan on that side of the river which extends towards Afghān-shāl among the trees as far as the walls of the mill, and had set up stables and pitched tents, and had planted themselves down, feeling safe and secure. That, too, was an error, since they were right in the path of the torrent. Our Prophet, Moḥammad the Chosen One, has said, "*We seek refuge in God from the two dumb and deaf things!*"[492] and by these two dumb and deaf things he meant water [F 341] and fire. At that time, the bridge of Bāmiyān[493] was not as now; it was a sturdy bridge erected upon sturdy columns and on it were two rows of shops facing each other, as at present. When it was destroyed by the flood, the merchant ʿAbaveyh,[494] that pious and generous man, may God's mercy be upon him, constructed a bridge with a single arch, displaying great elegance and beauty. Such munificent works remain behind and serve as memorials to their founders.[495] [Gh 261]

At the time of the afternoon worship, such an amount of rain fell on the bridge that no-one could remember its like, and the rain persisted until some time after the evening worship. Then early in the night itself, a torrent came down such that even the very old averred that they could never recall its equal. It swept down suddenly out of the blue and uprooted many trees. The herdsmen fled and saved each his own skin as did also the muleteers. The torrent carried off cattle and mules, and reached the bridge, which created a bottleneck, for how could so much mud,[496] tree trunks and drowning beasts all get through all at once? [F 342] The channels under the arches of the bridge became blocked so that the water could not get past, and it flowed over the top of the bridge. Fresh tides of torrential water kept arriving to reinforce the flood, like waves of wrathful and unruly troops. The waters mounted and overflowed from its banks, and swept into the markets, reaching the quarter where the moneychangers lodged, inflicting much damage. The greatest calamity of all was that the torrent uprooted the entire bridge, together with the shops, from its foundations and water found its way everywhere. It also destroyed many caravanserais that were ranged along, and the markets were entirely obliterated. The waters reached the lower foundations of the citadel,[497] which already existed before the time of Yaʿqub b. Leyth; for it was ʿAmr, Yaʿqub's brother, who restored the inner city and the citadel of Ghaznin.[498] Master Maḥmud Varrāq has given an excellent exposition of these events in the history which he composed in 450 [/1058–9] spanning several thousand years and going up to the year 409 [/1018–19]. [Gh 262] He put down his pen [at this juncture] and that [accounts] for the fact that I myself began from this year [40]9 [/1018–19] onwards. This Maḥmud is a reliable and veracious authority. I had much to say in his praise, and I have seen as many as ten to fifteen scarce works of his on different topics. When the news of my proposed eulogy and exposition of his work reached his children, they called out to me and declared that, "We, as his children, do not wish you to delve into our father's words any further than you've already done."[499] I was compelled, therefore, to desist.

This great torrent brought people incalculable loss. The next day, people stood and watched the spectacle from both sides of the river. [F 343] Towards the time of the midday worship, the force of the torrent began to slacken. For several days there was no bridge, and only with difficulty could people cross from one bank to the other until the they were able to repair the bridge. I heard from several reliable local Zāvolis[500] that, after the torrent subsided, people were finding gold, silver and damaged articles of clothing that the torrent had thrown up. The Almighty God knows how much bounty the wretched and the hungry found in all this![501]

The Amir returned from his hunting trip involving the rounding-up of game to the Garden of a Hundred Nightingales[502] on Saturday, 16 Rajab [422/9 July 1031] and stayed there for seven days engaged in merry-making and wine-drinking, till he had his rest from chasing beasts and wild animals,[503] having had good hunting, and then he came from there to the Maḥmudi Garden.

Letters had arrived from Ray a few days earlier saying that all was going well and that the Son of Kāku and the neighbouring princes were peaceful and were honouring their agreements, since the show of might had driven all thoughts of rebellion from their mind. However, the letters went on to say that "It is necessary to have here a powerful and experienced commander, since the province of Ray is very extensive, as the lord has seen, and although at present there is no crisis, the potential for one is there."

The Amir had a private session with the Grand Vizier Aḥmad b. Ḥasan, and the prominent personalities and pillars of the state, the masters of the sword and pen, and they discussed these matters. The Amir said, "The tax yield for that broad and extensive province is substantial, and in no circumstances can the region be relinquished after having been taken by the sword. There are no credible opponents remaining there worthy of our concern, for had that been the case, I would have tarried there longer until I had taken Baghdad; for one can say that in the whole of Western Persia there is no capable military commander worth his salt, [Gh 263, F 344] but just a group of indolent[504] Kiyā'is.[505] We need a most vigilant, alert and capable commander at Ray and an able counsellor and administrator (*kadkhodā*). Who are worthy of these two posts?" All remained silent, waiting to see what Khᵛāja Aḥmad would say. The latter turned to those assembled there and said, "Give the lord your answers!" They replied, "It is more fitting if the Grand Vizier takes the lead and says what needs to be said, so that we can then offer our contribution according to our knowledge and understanding."

The Vizier said, "May the lord's life be prolonged! Ray and Jebāl form an extensive province with a considerable tax revenue. In the time of the Buyid dynasty there were powerful imperial monarchs (*shāhanshāhān*) there, with counsellors and administrators like Ṣāḥeb Esmā'il Ebn 'Abbād[506] and others. The books relate how the Samanids exhausted their treasuries over the control of Ray, for Abu 'Ali Chaghāni and his father would go there over a long period and conquer Ray and Jebāl, but then the Buyids would return with a well-equipped army and drive them out, until both Chaghāni and his son forfeited their position and power, thanks to this venture, and were toppled, and the command in Khorasan passed to Bu'l-Ḥasan Simjur. He was shrewd and astute rather than bold and valiant, and held his ground until he negotiated a contractual agreement between the Samanids and the Buyids and Fanā-Khosrow[507] so that, every year, four million dirhams should be brought from Ray to Nishapur to be given to the army there. A lasting peace was maintained and the swords remained in their scabbards. That contractual agreement remained in force for thirty years until Bu'l-Ḥasan died and both the Samanid and Buyid states fell apart, and Amir Maḥmud took over Khorasan.[508] Subsequently, the late Amir would often discuss the affairs of Ray with me in private sessions, saying that an attack on it ought to be made. I would reply, 'It is of course for the lord to decide, but at the moment that province is of little significance and [F 345] its ruler is a woman.' He used to laugh and say, 'If that woman were a man, we would have had to keep a numerous army at Nishapur.' And while that woman remained in power, he made no move against Ray.[509] When he did make a move, and it fell easily into his hands, he set up the lord Masʿud there. That province is a very long way away from us; it was under the power (lit. "shadow," *sāya*) of one lord, and now it is ruled by another.[510] I would prefer those regions to be entrusted to the Son of Kāku, for although he can be regarded as something of an enemy, he is a man with whom an equitable arrangement can be made and there will be no need for a powerful army and a commander to be stationed there. A contractual agreement must be arranged with him on the basis of tribute which he is to pay annually, and the judges and the postal service and intelligence officers of the exalted court [Gh 264] should be attached to him and his deputies in those regions."

The Amir said, "I have thought about this, and it's a good idea. But it has one major flaw, and it's this: while previously the Son of Kāku controlled only Isfahan, he still managed to give Majd al-Dowla and the people of Ray a great deal of trouble and vexation. Now today, if he secures his rule over Ray, Qom, Qāshān (Kāshān) and the whole of those regions, he will behave correctly for a couple of years, but subsequently will have delusions of grandeur and will act in the manner of the Buyids[511] and gather together people round him; inevitably, the need would arise for sending a powerful commander with a strong army to overthrow him. The region of Isfahan should be sufficient for him as our deputy, and the commander and the adjutant and administrator whom we are now sending will be watching him closely. Ray and Jebāl will remain in our hands and the Son of Kāku will be forced to grit his teeth and bear it."[512]

The Vizier said, "In this judgement, the lord has right on his side. Concerning the people of Gorgān and Bā Kālijār, what does he say and deem the right course?" The Amir said, "Bā Kālijār is not a bad person, but the general state of Gorgān and Ṭabarestān is fraught with difficulties because that child, [F 346] the son of Manuchehr, has not yet become sufficiently mature, as is required, and is not driven by the desire and the will to act as a king.[513] If Bā Kālijār stays away from that region, that territory and its surrounding mountains will fall into disorder, and we will necessarily have to despatch a military commander there." The Vizier said, "It thus becomes imperative to nominate a commander of great reputation. All are there for the lord's scrutiny, whether in office and engaged in service, or whether [at present] held in custody and hoping for release through the lord's compassion and pity." The Amir said, "In no circumstances should one trust those who are interned, for each of them is there for a great offence, and it would be inappropriate to place reliance on them again. As for those leading figures at court who are in office, such as the Great Chamberlain, the Commander of the Palace Gholāms and others, they cannot be removed from their present posts for that would cause trouble. We will have to find others."

The Vizier said, "What does the lord think about ʿAli Dāya? He is a prominent and capable figure, and during the lord's absence (i.e. in western Persia and then Khorasan), he rendered such valuable service as is well known. Or Ayāz, who is a good commander and who was close to the late Amir in all matters?" The Amir replied, "ʿAli is eminently well-fitted and experienced; we intend to appoint him to a great charge, as will be discussed with the Khᵛāja. Ayāz has been raised in the lap of luxury and has achieved a place dear to one's heart; but although he was very much formed and fashioned by our father,[514] he has never been far from the palace and has not experienced the rough and tumble of life and he is still very green.[515] [Gh 265] He should stay with us for a while, but outside the palace, and try his hand at different tasks in order to gain experience, and then we shall take another look at him and give the necessary orders."

The Vizier answered, "I have set forth all I know, and clearly the lord has already deliberated and come to a conclusion about this, and his exalted judgement is superior to all others." The Amir said, "My mind has settled upon Tāsh Farrāsh, since he is one of our father's old retainers and was with us at Ray.[516] We established him there in an honoured position in which he has remained ever since. He must now proceed to Nishapur at once [F 347] and reside there for two or three months—since there is an important matter,[517] as will be discussed with the Vizier—so that he may completely dispose of the matter and then go back to Ray. When we go to Balkh this winter, we will appoint a counsellor and administrator for the region, a postal service and intelligence officer, and other persons who need to be nominated, so that they can embark on their duties." The Vizier said, "The lord has thought it out very thoroughly and has made a wise choice, but a strong supporting force of fully-armed and equipped troops, must be sent along." The Amir said, "This must be done. Whatever needs to be ordered, will be ordained," and the assembly dispersed.

The Amir ordered that a particularly fine and splendid array of outfits should be got together for Tāsh: a golden belt, a two-pointed hat, saddle ornaments containing 1,000 methqāls of gold, twenty gholāms, 100,000 dirhams, six male elephants and three female ones, ten measured pieces of fine quality cloth for robes, large kettledrums, a standard and other accoutrements, and all this was done to perfection.

When there were two days remaining of this month (i.e. on 28 Rajab 422/21 July 1031), the Amir held court. When this was over, the Amir ordered Tāsh Farrāsh to be conducted to the Royal Wardrobe, and invested with the robe of honour and brought back. The Amir said, "May this robe of honour for the supreme command of Western Persia be auspicious for us and for you! We have, as you know, many servants, but we have conferred this title and favour upon you because you served us well at Ray and were our commander there. Since you are doing your utmost to render us service, so we in turn do our best to endow you with bounties, higher rank and prestige." Tāsh kissed the ground and said, "Being one of the lord's lowliest slaves, I have not attained this status and rank on my own; it was the lord who ordained all this as befits his magnanimous nature. I shall strive hard, and will pray for success and favour from the Almighty God [F 348] so that I may perhaps be able to render some worthy service," and he kissed the ground and went homewards. The great men of the court [Gh 266] came up to him and paid due respect to him in a most appropriate fashion.

A week later, the Amir had a private session with Tāsh, which also included the Grand Vizier Aḥmad b. Ḥasan, Khᵛāja Bu Naṣr Moshkān and Bu Sahl Zowzani. The Amir gave Tāsh orders regarding Ray and Jebāl, and said, "You must stay in Nishapur for three months, giving the troops who have been assigned sufficient time to reach there. Suri, as head of the Divān [of Khorasan],[518] will pay their salaries, and then you can proceed fully prepared and equipped. We have given orders to Yaghmur,[519] Buqa, Köktāsh and Qïzïl, together with the whole band of Turkmens at Nishapur, that they should join you and that the General Khumārtāsh should be their commander. You must strive to have these chiefs[520] arrested, since it has become evident to us that they are harbouring malicious intentions in their heads. But you must also keep the Turkmens contented and entrust them to the leadership of Khumārtāsh, and then head for Ray." He answered, "I'll obey the command," and went back.

The Vizier said, "May the lord's life be prolonged! It was a mistake at the outset to bring in these Turkmens and to set them down in the heart of our own territories.[521] On that day, we—Altuntāsh, Arslan Jādheb and others—spoke at length, but it was to no avail, for the late Amir was guided by his own autocratic judgement, and he committed that error. So many knotty problems[522] appeared as a result that the Turkmens were driven out ignominiously from Khorasan with their tails between their legs. And then the lord brought them back. At the present time when these people have been pacified and attached to our service, it is appropriate to place them under the leadership of one of our generals, but it is bad policy to remove their chiefs, for it will alienate the Turkmens and they will no longer act in a trustworthy manner."

The Amir replied, "Some of their chiefs have actually sought this, and it should be done, and they will settle down." The Vizier said, "I have been out of touch with such affairs for several years, and clearly the lord is more knowledgeable. [F 349] That which the exalted judgement sees, servants cannot see, and the right course lies in that." He arose, and on the way to the Divān he said to Bu Naṣr Moshkān and Bu Sahl Zowzani, "This is a most ill-conceived decision, but I did manage to absolve myself from all responsibility for it and you two are my witnesses," and he left.[523]

A few days after this, the Amir said to the Vizier, "India cannot properly function without a military commander there; whom do you think should be sent?" He answered, "The lord knows his servants, and he will have thought about a servant suitable for this post. It is a very great and prestigious responsibility. Since there was a man of

Eryāruq's calibre there, leaving an aura of awesomeness and grandeur, [Gh 267] a person of his stature is needed as a replacement. Although the affairs of state depend for their success first and foremost on the lord's own majestic presence, nevertheless an experienced commander is essential, a man who has had adequate training in the past (i.e. in warfare and administration)." The Amir said, "I have set my mind on Aḥmad b. Ināltegin,[524] even though he has not served an apprenticeship under military commanders. He has been our father's treasurer, rendering him service in all his journeying, and he observed and knew the circumstances and the ways of the late Amir."[525]

The Vizier thought for a while, for he had been on bad terms with this Aḥmad because the latter had made much mischief at the time when the Vizier was on trial and his possessions put up for auction,[526] and he exploited the situation and was buying up the Vizier's goods and effects at very low prices. Then the Vizier had been imprisoned, and had not been able to secure any requital and compensation until now when he ordered that an audit (*shomār*) should be made of Aḥmad b. Ināltegin; he pressed him hard and relentlessly, until a sum of money was extracted from him.[527] But at this moment, since the Amir had preferred and chosen him, the Vizier sought to mollify him and pour balm on his wounds. The other point was that the Vizier was on very bad terms with the Judge from Shiraz, Bu'l-Ḥasan b. ʿAli, by reason of the fact that on several occasions Amir Maḥmud had said, as was his wont, "How long do we have to put up with these airs and graces of Aḥmad? It's not as if there's a dearth of potential viziers for us! Here's one for a start, the Judge from Shiraz!" [F 350] (This Judge was in no way comparable to this great and eminent figure [i.e. to Khᵛāja Aḥmad b. Ḥasan], but kings can say whatever they like, and it is never any good arguing with them and offering proofs and reasons.)[528]

In this court session, the Vizier went along with the idea of pitting such a formidable figure as Aḥmad b. Ināltegin against the Judge from Shiraz and seeing the latter discredited. He said, "May the lord's life be prolonged! This has been very well thought out, and there's no-one suitable except Aḥmad. But in his case we need safeguards through a formal oath and through the requirement of his leaving a son here as a hostage." The Amir replied. "Exactly so. Let the Vizier summon him, and let him give orders and carry out whatever is required in this respect."

The Vizier came to his Divān, and Aḥmad was summoned. He came, but was very apprehensive in case this was another possible unpleasant surprise (i.e. another episode like the financial accounting he had had to undergo at the Vizier's hands). The Vizier made him sit down and said, "You know that there has been a settling of accounts with you going back several years, but you must also know that I have made a solemn oath to do my utmost in the Sultan's concerns. You should not [Gh 268] therefore be under the misapprehension that I harbour a grievance against you and bear you evil intentions, and accordingly adopt a wary and discontented stance. For where it is a question of the Sultan's interests and welfare, as a servant of the realm I can only offer wise counsel and solicitude."[529]

Aḥmad kissed the[530] ground and said, "Such baseless ideas would never cross my mind. It is not as if I am seeing the lord for the first time today, for I have known him for several years.[531] The wisest course for this humble servant lies in what the lord Sultan commands, and in what the lord, the Grand Vizier, advises." The Vizier said, "The Sultan today held a private audience, [F 351] and discussions took place on all sorts of topics, the most important being the matter of India, concerning which he said, 'There is a man there who is from the learned and secretarial classes,[532] namely the Judge from Shiraz, but he is hardly the man to lead an army. What we need is a commander of great fame to proceed there, lead expeditions against the infidels and collect the tribute (*kharāj*), just as the Judge is in charge of collecting the regular taxation and money due (*'amal-hā u māl-hā*). That commander should venture out on wars against the infidels when he thinks fit, extract the tribute and appropriate elephants and smite the heads of any rebellious Indians.' When I asked, 'The lord is familiar with all his servants, whom has he in mind to be the Commander-in-Chief?', he replied, 'My mind is fixed on Aḥmad b. Inaltegin.' I saw that the lord thought very highly of you, and I also recounted what I knew of your bravery and your capabilities. He ordered me to summon you and to convey to you encouraging words from the exalted court session and to take charge of all the preparations for your departure. What is your response to all this?" Aḥmad kissed the ground, rose to his feet and said, "I, as a servant, cannot find words to express my gratitude for this act of favour, and I do not consider myself worthy of this high status. I remain a servant pledged to obedience and will obey whatever has been ordained and will do my utmost, so that it will become evident that nothing in the way of solicitude and wise counsel will remain undone." The Vizier gave him encouragement and spoke to him kindly, and sent him away

He summoned the boon-companion Moẓaffar the judge, and recounted to him what had happened, saying, "Tell the Amir that he should give orders for Aḥmad b. Ināltegin's robe of honour to be made ready, of finer quality than the one which was made for Eryāruq when he was appointed Commander-in-Chief of India, and Bu Naṣr Moshkān is to write out the investiture patent for him, to be adorned with the royal seal and signature, so that when he dons the robe of honour, the necessary procedures and orders for confirming the appointment may be put in place; thus he will be able to leave soon, get down to work and lead expeditions against the infidels at the appropriate time." Moẓaffar went off and delivered the message. The Amir ordered Aḥmad's robe of honour to be prepared, as well as drums (*ṭabl*), a standard, large kettledrums (*kus*) and all the other trappings issued for commanders-in-chief.

On Sunday, 2 Shaʿbān of this [Gh 269] year [422/25 July 1031], the Amir ordered that Aḥmad b. Ināltegin should be conducted to the Royal Wardrobe and be dressed in a very splendid robe of honour. He came into the royal presence girded with a gold *hazārgāni* belt and a two-pointed hat, [F 352] and with his equipment and accoutrements likewise *hazārgāni*, and made the customary offerings of service.[533] The Amir showed him much favour, and he went back to his house in a fine display of splendour, and people came to offer fitting recognition of his position. The next day, he came to the court. The Amir had a private session with the Grand Vizier and Khᵛāja Bu Naṣr, Head of the Chancery, and Aḥmad b. Ināltegin was summoned and received verbal orders directly from Amir himself. From there the three of them, the Grand Vizier, Bu Naṣr and Aḥmad b. Inaltegin, went into the loggia of the Divān and sat down together in private. The investiture patent and the contractual agreement, together with its written-out responses,[534] each document confirmed by the royal seal and signature, were brought in with Aḥmad. They brought forward the document containing the oath and he took the oath, as is the usual custom, putting his own signature to it. It was shown to the Amir and entrusted to the Keeper of the Archives.

The Vizier said to him, "That wretched, bone-headed fellow from Shiraz[535] wishes to have the military commanders under his own orders, for he had had some dealings with an ineffective nonentity like ʿAbdallāh b. Qarategin.[536] But when he heard the name of Eryāruq and he realized that a stout-hearted man[537] had entered the scene, he sought to send his own tax-collector and an overseer.[538] He sent Bu'l-Fatḥ Dāmghāni and Bu'l-Faraj Kermāni, but they never managed to get the better of Eryāruq. The process of Eryāruq's subsequent downfall had its roots elsewhere: he was too headstrong and autocratic. You, as the Commander-in-Chief, must operate in accordance with the contractual agreement and the responses to it. Certainly, don't meddle in the fields of collecting the regular taxation and extracting wealth, so that tongues cannot wag against you, but fulfil your duties as Commander to the full, in such a way that the little wretch does not get the better of you and consider you an easy prey. Bu'l-Qāsem b. Bu'l-Ḥakam, who is the postmaster and intelligence agent [F 353] and a trustworthy person, will transmit news of what is happening when he thinks fit, and will see to it that the ordinances of the Sultan and of the Divān are delivered. Neither of you needs to bother his exalted majesty directly; anything which needs a written answer should be sent to me in full, and you will be furnished with firm answers. The exalted judgement has laid down the requirement that several persons from the leading figures of the Deylamites, such as Bu Naṣr b. Ṭeyfur and others, should be despatched with you so that they may live far away from the court, since they are a group of aliens (i.e. with no ties to the court);[539] also, several persons who have been involved in factional and partisan behaviour (*taʿaṣṣob*) in their own regions, like Bu Naṣr Bāmiyāni, the brother of the leader of the notables (*zaʿim*) of Balkh, and the paternal cousin of the headman of the town (*ra'is*). Also, a bunch of unruly and factious palace gholāms, who had carried out and been convicted of acts of treachery, will be set free, awarded presents and given the impression that they have been accepted back into the fold. You must [Gh 270] take these men along with you and treat them with great care and kindness, but not one of them is to cross the Chandrāha river[540] without the Sultan's command and your own knowledge and permission. When you go out on raiding expeditions, you are to take this bunch with you, and take great care that there is no fraternisation with the army of Lahore (Lāhur) nor any wine-drinking or polo-playing. Keep spies and watchmen over them, for this is one of those important priorities which must be attended to at once. Bu'l-Qāsem, son of Bu'l-Ḥakam, is a dab hand at this. He will receive instructions to join forces with and carry out whatever is necessary in this matter. The exalted commands on other matters, and the investiture patent and the responses to the contractual agreement, have been prepared. Regard all that you have just heard in confidence as royal commands,[541] and keep it to yourself. When you have all arrived there at your posts, you will report new developments as they occur, [F 354] with each person having regard for matters directly relevant to him, so that necessary orders are given and each person can act upon the instructions received." Aḥmad b. Inaltegin replied, "Everything is clear to me, and I shall do my utmost to ensure that things run smoothly," and he returned home.

The Vizier sent a message after him through his personal chamberlain Ḥasan, to tell him in person that "The exalted command is that your son should remain here, although of course you will be able to take with you your family and daughters. Make arrangements for your son to remain at your residence with a tutor and overseer and guardian, since he will have more space and freedom there, for the lord, solicitous of your feelings, did not wish your son to be placed in the barracks of the palace gholāms. I felt too embarrassed to tell you this myself, and one should not require a hostage from you; and although the Sultan has not given any specific order regarding this,[542] one cannot dispense with customs and traditions, and I have no choice but to safeguard the interests of the state, in matters small and great, and likewise the good interests of you and your likes."

Aḥmad answered, "I will obey the command, and my personal interest, today and in the future, lies in whatever the Grand Vizier deems correct and commands." He rewarded the chamberlain handsomely and sent him back on his way, and he made the necessary arrangements for the son. All the other affairs connected with the position of Commander-in-Chief, including equipment, weapons, gholāms, etc., he arranged in the way he had seen done in the past,[543] for he was a marvel at organising such things. When he had completed all the preparations, he sought, and received, permission to depart.

On Saturday, 24 Shaʿbān [422/16 August 1031],[544] the Amir mounted and, with a great retinue of people, came to the plain of Shābahār seated on the travelling throne (*mahd*) on an elephant, halting on the dais.[545] Aḥmad b. Inaltegin came into his presence, [Gh 271] dressed in a ruby-coloured coat and offered up obeisance. A very splendid procession, with numerous troops bearing their complete panoply of arms, went past, comprising the senior officers, Deylamites[546] and [F 355] other ethnic groups who had been designated to accompany him. After them came 130 royal gholāms, most of them youths whose beards and body hair had begun to grow (i.e. they were just past puberty), whom the Amir had liberated from their slave status and who were now entrusted to Aḥmad. Accompanying them were three palace senior officers with three banners bearing a lion device and short spears, in the tradition of the palace gholāms. Then there followed suit large kettledrums, Aḥmad's own banner—of red brocade with a crescent-shaped finial on top (*monjuq*)—seventy-five gholāms, and number of pack and riding camels.

The Amir said to Aḥmad, "Go forth with pride and joy, be on your guard, acknowledge the worth of all this magnificence, keep our own person before your eyes and show praiseworthy service so that you'll find yourself worthy of even greater favour." He replied that, whatever was incumbent by way of service, he would do. He made obeisance, the horse for the Commander-in-Chief of India was summoned,[547] and he mounted and rode off. *It was the last encounter with him,* for he was led astray by malicious and corrupting influences and forsook the path of rectitude, as will be subsequently related in its place.[548]

The Amir came back to the Maḥmudi Palace at Afghān-shāl, for he had done full justice to the joyous month of Shaʿbān,[549] and, as prescribed by Boḥtori in the verse that follows, had indulged in many bouts of merry-making and wine-drinking, (Poetry)

1. *Give me to drink, [O my two companions,] since the month of Shaʿbān has come round, the first vintage of the pure and choicest wine!*[550]

They returned the furnishings and household equipment to the Palace and got ready for the holy month of Ramażān. On Monday, the first day of Ramażān [422/22 August 1031], they began the fast. On Tuesday, the Amir took his place on the great dais, and broke his fast with the leading figures—it was a magnificent display that had been made—and then the two Princes [F 356] Saʿid and Mowdud[551] sat down in their turn, accompanied by the chamberlains and boon-companions, at the trays of food, while the swift-riding cavalrymen and troop commanders sat at other rows.[552] The Sultan [usually] used to break his fast alone in the palace.

The Amir ordered that a review should be made of the prisons and the fortresses of Ghaznin and its surrounding regions, and that lists with the names of those imprisoned should be written out[553] so that the Amir[554] might peruse them and give the necessary instructions regarding each individual case. He gave orders for a million dirhams to be issued from the treasury for the poor and deserving of Ghaznin and adjacent areas. Letters went out to the whole of the kingdom for the anointing of mosques with the aromatic substance *khaluq* and for a review of the jails.[555] However, he issued no instructions concerning the money to be expended on religious and charitable purposes (*zakāt*) which his father used to give each year, but no-one thought it opportune to say anything on this topic since [Gh 272] great kings give orders for whatever they deem most pleasing to themselves, and it is not for their servants to make any criticism; for those who want to stay in office, silence is the better option in such cases.[556]

During the course of this summer, Bu'l-Qāsem b. 'Ali Nuki, the postmaster and intelligence agent of Ghaznin, asked Khvāja Bu Naṣr Moshkān to take his sons into the Chancery. (I had observed such friendship between them which surpassed that of brothers.) Bu Naṣr responded favourably to him. His eldest son Moẓaffar possessed wisdom and held official posts,[557] both in the time of Amir Maḥmud [F 357] and in this present reign. In the time of Sultan Maḥmud, together with the secretarial post and the monthly salary which he had,[558] he was also appointed as secret overseer over the palace gholāms, in such a way that the purveyors of food to the barracks used to come to him and tell him whatever secrets they had gleaned from the gholāms, and he would write down clearly the gist of those pieces of information and submit them in his own hand and without any intermediary. In these secret affairs, Amir Maḥmud had complete trust in him,[559] and I observed that Moẓaffar several times received substantial gifts of money. He was a very dear friend of mine, a capable young man with a good calligraphic hand, but in secretarial skills rather pedestrian and mediocre.[560] He died young, *God's mercy be upon the son and the father.*

My master discussed Bu'l-Qāsem's sons with the Amir, and received his consent for their appointments. He brought Bu Manṣur, Bu Bakr and Bu Naṣr into the Chancery and sent them before the Amir, and they offered service and money offerings. Bu Manṣur was learned and cultured, with a fine calligraphic hand, and at the Amir's behest, he was sent to Lahore with Amir Majdud, as I will set forth.[561] Irascibility and devilry were engrained in this Bu Manṣur; he died while still in his youth, God's mercy be upon him.

Bu Bakr was likewise learned and well formed in polite learning, with a good calligraphic hand, and he remained in the Divān for a period of time, but he had in him a streak of deviousness, which led to his undoing—*there is no way of avoiding Almighty God's decree*—as I shall set forth in its appropriate place. He was dismissed from the Chancery, but in deference to his father's service in the past, the monarchs treated him compassionately, and he was made overseer of the district of Giri.[562] He has been there a very long time, and is still there today in the year 451 [/1059].

Khᵛāja Bu Naṣr was the youngest [of the three brothers], but was of noble pedigree on both sides—*"an inherent quality of birth comes out in later progeny"*[563] [F 358]—with a father like Bu'l-Qāsem and, on his mother's side, a lineage from the chamberlain Bā Maḥmud, who was the chief [Gh 273] of the chamberlains of Bu'l-Ḥasan Simjur.[564] Thus it was to be expected that he should turn out as he did, and he remained in the Chancery through the sagacity and the discretion that he possessed. He became a secretary, with a good calligraphic hand, and he acquired the office of postmaster and intelligence agent of Ghaznin, and meanwhile was appointed to various other posts, all of them prestigious, such as that of the postmaster and intelligence officer of the army and further offices, whose enumeration would take too long. Finally, it happened that in the fortunate time of the just Sultan Abu Shojāʿ Farrokh-zād b. Nāṣer Din Allāh, he became employed in the Chancery. When need arose for an experienced headman (*raʾis*), with a distinguished and ancient ancestry for this exalted capital and town, the choice fell on him. He was awarded a suitable robe of honour, and at this present moment when I am writing this book he occupies this post, as well as that of the postal and intelligence service. He is one of my old-established friends. The readers of this History must endure necessary tedium and frustration with grace and nobility of mind if

I spin out the story too long, since unavoidably, the claims of friendship must be satisfied, especially as this friendship is a very old one. *God is the One who grants success for the completion of my intention, through His grace!*

On 3 Ramażān [422/24 August 1031], the Amir said to the Great Chamberlain Bilgetegin, "You should send some men to organise a corvée in the district of Khār-margh, since we intend to go hunting."[565] The Great Chamberlain came to our Divān and summoned the sons of Niyāzi the Qowdkash,[566] to whom the duty was customarily entrusted, and he asked for the register which was usually kept in our Divān for such occasions. Orders were written out, and swift-riding cavalrymen set off and got together a force of foot labourers (or: "local militiamen").[567] On Saturday, the thirteenth of this month [Ramażān 422/3 September 1031], the Amir went off in the direction of Kharvār and Khār-margh, [F 359] and enjoyed some excellent hunting, returning to Ghaznin on Sunday, 23 or 24 Ramażān [/13 or 14 September].

On Monday, 28 or 29 Ramażān [/18 or 19 September],[568] he sat in state for the festival of Mehragān, and several showerings of coins, presents and luxury goods and beasts, of unlimited numbers and extent, were brought forward as offerings.[569] Suri, the head of the Divān [of Khorasan] had sent an endless array of things through his personal representative at court[570] as presents. In the same way, the representatives of the great men in charge of outlying provinces, like the Khwarazm Shah Altuntāsh, the Amir of Chaghāniyān, the Amir of Gorgān, the governors of Qoṣdār and Makrān, and others, brought many things. It was a memorable day.

On Wednesday, the Festival [of the Ending of the Fast] was celebrated. The Amir had ordered an army review (*taʿbiya*) on a scale such as [Gh 274] I had seen in the time of the late Sultan his father, on those occasions when it happened that the envoys or notable and eminent men from Western Persia and Turkestan presented themselves at the royal court. When the appropriate hour for the start of the Festival had arrived,[571] the Amir went from the main square to the great dais. A magnificent spread of food had been laid out, and the Amir sat down there. The courtiers and retainers, and the great men, were seated there; poets came forward and recited verses, followed by musicians and singers who began to play and sing. Wine was handed round, both where the Amir sat and at another spread where the *sarhang*s, the swift-riding cavalrymen and the various ethnic groups of the army sat. There were great vessels filled with wine, so that people staggered back from the table drunk. Having drunk several goblets at the feast, the Amir left the table and mounted the main great throne (*takht-e bozorg-e aṣl*) on the dais of the court. A reception had been prepared the like of which no-one could remember. The Vizier, the Head of the Army Department, the Head of the Chancery and the boon-companions came forward for it. The court musicians and singers, and those from outside, struck up, and such merry-making got under way that all possible traces of gloom and melancholy were banished from the very edifice. The Amir ordered that the less well-known poets[572] should receive 20,000 dirhams; 50,000 dirhams [F 360] were conveyed to the house of ʿAlavi Zeynabi[573] on an elephant; ʿOnṣori was given 1,000 dinars; and the musicians and singers and the clowns received 30,000 dirhams.

Those poems that were recited have all been set down in poetical *divāns*; if I were to record them here too, it would take up too much space, since the masters of poetry had recited a great deal of verse therein describing the court session and the wine, welcoming in the Festival and in praise of monarchs. However, I have written down here an especially fine ode which is in my possession and in which are described the passing away of Sultan Maḥmud, the accession of Moḥammad, the coming of Amir Masʿud from Isfahan and all other events. For it so happened that, when I had reached this very point in writing this History, I fell into the company of Master Bu Ḥanifa Eskāfi. I had already heard how cultivated he was and widely read in all branches of knowledge, but when I met him, I understood better the meaning of this verse of Motanabbi.[574] (Poetry)

1. *I used to deem the reports [about him] exaggerated before I met him, but when we met, actual experience made the reports seem inadequate.*[575]

In the course of discussions with him, I said, "Had you lived in former times and had the monarchs of the age seen your verses, your reward would not have been less than the lavish favours that they used to bestow on other poets. But now you must compose an ode and revivify that past with your poetry, so that history may become adorned by it."[576] He composed this ode [Gh 275] and sent it to me. If someone can eulogize a past ruler with such fine verses, who knows to what heights his poetry would soar if a monarch now should look favourably at him and commission an ode! Today, *thanks be to God and thanks for His benevolence*, no town anywhere can vie with Ghaznin in its prosperity, populousness, security and peace of mind and its being blessed by such a just, benevolent Sultan—may this monarch and the people of the town endure for ever! But the market for learning, *adab* and poetry is now rather flat, and [F 361] those skilled in these crafts are deprived of support.

Since I introduced a long section at the beginning of this History in praise of Ghaznin, this exalted capital—may it ever remain standing!—I consider it necessary, and regard as an obligation, to mention persons who are from this town and have learning and merit, and especially a man like Bu Ḥanifa, of whom the least part of his excellence lies in poetry, and who teaches belles-lettres and the religious and legal sciences without any stipend or allowance, and who freely shares his knowledge with the public. From this point onwards, I intend to rely on his learning and generosity, to the extent that I shall seek out from him whatever verses I find necessary and suitable for inclusion in the History. Here follows this ode that I had asked from him, so that it may be perused closely: (Ode)

1. When a man has mastery over his craft and if fortune smiles, he can convert the dark earth into pure gold, for all to see.

2. The heavens regard the person as noble and magnanimous who does not quibble about the triviality of the task.

3. A rider who is bereft of a horse that knows the way, is bound to take a tumble and fall captive to overriding Fate.

4. God bears up to the span of the heavens that person who makes light of the terror of the cave.[577] [F 362]

5. Be magnanimous, and do not despair if given a paltry task, since from time to time, a flower sprouts out of a thorn by chance.[578] [Gh 276]

6. Consider good fortune (*dowlat*) as a lofty fortress, with its gate secure, but through his own exertions, a man is able to find his way in.

7. Proficiency and ability manifest themselves at once in a person, just as one's picture does, reflected in a mirror.

8. To rise up early at dawn becomes the mark of the man, for [in the pale light of] a cloudy day, the hawk can better attain its prey.[579]

9. Wine, sleeping, the rebbeck, roasted meat, with herbs and bread, have levelled more than a thousand palaces with the ground!

10. When you have seen for yourself the king's feasting and that military prowess of his, its palpable joyfulness and victoriousness are more than it is possible to count. [F 363]

11. That very thing (i.e. Fate) which led your brother to corruption, that same thing also tied your brother to a hundred nails.

12. When the day darkens (i.e. when ill fortune overwhelms one) and a man's fortune is reversed, he himself will see the evil coming his way rather than the good.

13. No-one ever drew any benefit from deceitfulness and trickery; have you not read your *Kalila va Demna* ten times?[580]

14. When the exalted judgement (i.e. the Amir) discerned that the best course was to return from Balkh and roundly secure his kingdom,

15. There was not a single couple in the town of Ghaznin who were not intoxicated with anticipation of his imminent arrival, not even for a brief while.

16. The people of Ghaznin were all agog, waiting to set eyes on that face, so like a rose in spring.

17. They were all transfixed in anticipation when the sun of [all] kings arose with its effulgent rays from the heavens and emerged from the travelling throne.

18. He entered the state capital, in the manner of his grandfather and father before him, having attained his perfect fulfilment and having made praise of God his rule of life.

19. From that time when the entire world came under his domination, no-one came to any harm, not even through a trifling nosebleed.

20. He returned to his homeland where he was born and raised, for in order to turn into a pearl, the rain drop comes back to the sea (i.e. to its original home).[581] [F 364]

21. He went around the world, revolving like the firmament itself; and not like other kings, for the sake of silver offerings.

22. The monarch is like the firmament, and no one has said of the firmament that it has more than one focal point.[582] [Gh 277]

23. O you who are successful in kingship, may you live long out of thanks for the great bounties, which we receive increasingly from serving you.

24. It is because God created you from earth,[583] that the revolving heaven itself is one of the servants of the earth.

25. Driven by the hope that it might kiss the dust under your feet; year in and month out, the wind bears a cloud of dust up into the heavens.

26. The blade of your sword showers dirhams unto the foe's head, so that you can throw him into prison and pay the keeper with the dirhams from his head. (?)[584]

27. If you have not seen a mountain in motion, give one or two glances at that mount of yours!

28. He rushes forth, like an old man in pursuit of piety, and stands his ground, like a young man bent on sin.

29. Your army is not just human kind, but is it perchance the host of Fate, since it is not possible to restrain them with defensive gates and walls.

30. God forbid that anyone of the army should find mutilation and death, but if so, it would be from his eagerness to attack, just like Jaʿfar Ṭayyār.[585] [F 365]

31. At that time when, like eyelashes close together in search of sleep, the two powerful armies engage in fighting with their spears;[586]

32. there is such a clash of swords, and bowing and prostrating by their blades, that the air itself seems to have donned a headband of steel.

33. The vultures of the heavens have driven away the vultures of the earth, because they have such a wide choice from the many bodies which fall from the horses' saddles.[587]

34. The air is filled with thin, silk threads of the foaming horses,[588] and the clamour of the warriors echoes throughout the regions of the earth.

35. [On your side,] your men have brazen hearts seeking valour, [while on their side,], the foes are all pleading tongues, craving quarter.

36. Your prudence and your audacity complement each other, in the same way as festive bouts and wine lovers go together!

37. When the firmament saw the peacefulness of the creatures of the world resting upon you, it made a pact and the world as a whole declared its allegiance to you.

38. Because of your glorious generosity, gold and silver have lost their value in the world; does not everything become valueless when there is a surfeit?

39. O lordly one, the proof of divine truth is firmly held in your hands, even though falsehood should prevail a while, it will not last forever. [F 366]

40. The guardianship of the world is not a task for everyone, even though a man may be experienced and dexterous and have abundant wisdom.

41. The same benefit does not come from the moon as from the sun, even though the beneficial effect of the moon is not[589] negligible.

42. Of ideal rule over the army and the populace, your royal lineage is the exemplar, sent by the Almighty God.

43. For you will not be able to find from the heavens a better master than your father [Maḥmud]; what your father did, you too should emulate by night and by day.

44. Strive for meting out justice, and at night enjoy the sleep of the just (lit. go to sleep secure from all evil), for it is only the unjust who lay awake, apprehensive of the consequences of their misdeeds.

45. From one father, it is not surprising that there should be two sons, one good and one bad, since both the pulpit and the gallows can be made from the very same tree.

46. That person whom you raise up to a mighty status is not truly exalted, because the person whom you render exalted may speedily be abased.

47. The truly exalted person is that person whom the Supreme Artificer of the World (i.e. God) renders exalted, without the influence of the heavenly bodies.[590]

48. Things do not always happen as you would wish and would like, but it is the outcome of what the Just God has decreed. [F 367]

49. A little Jewish boy[591] whom his mother consigned to the river out of fear of Pharaoh, that evil-natured one with a heart black as pitch,

50. Did not Pharaoh pick him up from the water, and out of compassion not for a moment let go of him?[592]

51. He whom God creates for kingship will be raised out of a pit and placed upon the throne, in the way Joseph (Yusof) was.[593]

52. There is a proverb: "The loftier the head, the greater the headache," it is a true adage, a hangover (*khomār*) comes from wine and wine comes from that same hangover.[594]

53. If you do not believe me, it is easy to convince you: read an account of this king's remarkable deeds and then see if you can find anyone like him.

54. The master of the world, the monarch of the age, Masʿud, through whom the religion of Aḥmad (i.e. Moḥammad, the Prophet), the Chosen One, has become exalted!

55. He speaks of glory in the same way as the religious devotee speaks of pious restraint; he recoils from injustice and oppression as the lover shrinks (lit. flees from, *ferār*) from the pain of separation.

56. When someone comes to him with a grievance, he does not fix his gaze on him, lest he is rendered speechless on account of the Shah's awesomeness.

57. No-one ever touches his coat of mail (i.e. is able to get near him in battle)[595] since one must cast away the skin of a serpent just like the serpent's head. [Gh 279]

58. He resembles intelligence, because he has made knowledge (*ʿelm*) his treasure and troops, and he resembles justice because he has made forbearance (*ḥelm*) his palace and fortress. [F 368]

59. If his father awarded him (i.e. Masʿud) the governorship of Ray, it was out of affection and compassion and not with the aim of making mischief.

60. When a lioness wishes to make her cub able to fend for itself (i.e. be weaned), she sends it forth from the thick grassy cover (*morghzār*, lit. "meadow"), not out of hostility or casting it forth [but so that it can stand on its own feet].

61. When that Shah (i.e. Maḥmud) sought to separate you from himself (i.e. by appointing Prince Masʿud to the distant governorship), he did not give you silver or gold or horse accoutrements (*zin*) or finery (*zeyn*) in excessive amounts (i.e. as compensation, or, as it were, a bribe).[596]

62. [Is it not the case that] a mother and father give a greater share to that son, out of all their sons, who is weak and distressed?[597]

63. In order to give Masʿud scope to prove his innate talents to other monarchs, Maḥmud did not treat him as well as he should.[598]

64. When the mother takes away the child from her milk, making black the breast (i.e. making it unattractive, and thereby weaning the child), this does not arise out of hostility.[599]

65. As a result of the gentle chastisement of fathers, sons have a comfortable station in life; through the wick of a candle being trimmed, the flame blazes up more brightly.

66. When the world was set in good order under that prince of religion Maḥmud, stretching from Somnāth to the frontiers of Bolghār,

67. He seized the whole world, just like Faridun, and divided it up, since the Shah was, like Faridun, successful in his deeds.[600] [F 369]

68. Since the rulership of this present world appeared contemptible in his sight, his lofty resolution became conformable to the joyfulness of the Abode of Rest (i.e. he abandoned earthly existence for the eternal joy of the next world).

69. Another day of resurrection (or "upheaval," *qiyāmat*) became apparent in the world (i.e. when Maḥmud died); the eschatological Day of Resurrection will come when the moon grows feebler in its transit (i.e. when the world comes to an end).

70. [This day of resurrection or revival of royal power became apparent] from the fact that Masʿud held kingly power like his grandfather and father, through numerous swords and spears in those regions and lands.

71. Reasons of state thus decreed for a while that the small star Sohā[601] became in the moon's place, for a certain time respected.

72. When conditions at that focal point of the world (*kaʿba-ye molk-e jahān*, i.e. Ghaznin) reached such a stage that the wind of neglectfulness snatched the coverings[602] away,[603]

73. The lord of the world (i.e. Masʿud) laid aside unnecessary distractions[604] and girded up his loins for strictly necessary work (*fariża* "obligatory acts of worship").[605]

74. He sent a messenger to his brother; he gave a message containing a thousand acts of kindness and favour,

75. Saying, "That it is only fitting for you to enjoy the seat of power in our name, which should be emblazoned on embroidered cloth worldwide and engraved on coins."

76. The message was of no avail, since the mirror of good fortune had become rusty for Moḥammad through the speech of envious ones.

77. They were no idle words,those that Alexander wrote as a memento: [that when fortune smiles] three (coveted treasures), a horse, a sword, and a maiden, come through the royal gates all at once.[606] [Gh 280]

78. When the banner of the victorious Shah from Isfahan set out early for the well-ordered royal court , in a stately manner, suitably adorned, [F 370]

79. From the midst of the dust surrounding the advancing concourse of troops, the shining face of the emperor of the age appeared, just as in the dark night, the moon of the fourteenth day appears.[607]

80. Before the town of Nishapur could rejoice at the sight of Masʿud, a great crowd of people, like the waves of the sea, came out to greet him.[608]

81. Do not consider any attribute more noble than that of prophethood, for there have remained from the Prophet many great memorials (or traditions, *āthār*) in the world.[609]

82. Did you hear that the Prophet, when he wished, was magnanimous; coming to him was not a difficult task for Ṣoheyb and Salmān.[610]

83. They coin a proverbial saying that the physician comes uninvited (i.e. unnecessarily) when a healthy person is tending a sick one.

84. When the Shah arrived in Herat, you could see men from his father's army coming from every direction in successive columns, like ants.

85. Look carefully, for my ode has turned out like the Discriminating Scripture (*Forqān*),[611] since it bestows equal knowledge to the heart and the eyes.

86. Even though, there was time when I feared that I would not be able to unfold the scroll (i.e. be unable to complete the poem).

87. For the words themselves saw so many original meanings embedded in them, that they appeared wearied and unable to act as a guide (the signifiant and signifié dichotomy). [F 371]

88. Because I stem from Ghazni and am still youthful, I see no market for my knowledge (i.e. no opportunity for fully exercising my poetic talents).[612]

89. O lord, a fine poem is like a garment, whose weft never becomes separated from its warp.

90. From the record of your great achievements, I bring forward these wonderful things; indeed, from out of the sea they bring forth royal pearls.

91. Do not compose poetry, but if you have no choice,
compose the kind that encourages good deeds and removes the bad.

92. Admit that the words of the poem are like lustrous pearls,
Admit that the meanings convey a magical beauty.

93. As long as hardship and suffering remain part of the transient world,
You should live and enjoy a hundred worlds in bliss.

94. As long as the heavens are bringing along the months and years (i.e. as long as time continues to elapse), you [O Masʿud,] remain for ever thus, Shah and chief!

95. As long as the anemone blooms upon the mountain, and as long as the rain continues to fall from the sky,

96. Remain firm like a mountain, and laugh like the anemone (comparison of red lips and red petals opening); and gallop furiously fast as the revolving firmaments and like a rain bearing cloud, pour down your bounty on earth.

So there comes to an end this elegant satin brocade of a panegyric ode, in which honeyed words and their significant meanings [F 372] are clasped in an embrace. If this learned and excellent person should find just treatment from the tyrant Fate, and if some king should bolster his poetic talent by royal benevolence, in the same manner as the masters of preceding ages like ʿOnṣori, ʿAsjadi,[613] Zeynabi and Farrokhi found patronage in their time, he will be able to parade his (hair-splitting) ingenuity and discrimination in the choice of words and make his rivals appear lowly by contrast, *"For indeed, gifts unlock the tongue,"*[614] and he may perhaps find it, since he is still a young man *and that is not difficult for God*.[615] This story has come to its end.

On Sunday, 5 Shavvāl [/25 September 1031], Amir Masʿud mounted and was on a travelling throne on an elephant.[616] [Gh 281] He came to the plain of Shābahār with a most impressive display of pomp and ceremony, including elephants and files of led horses and camels, in such a fashion that thirty horses had accoutrements set with jewels, turquoise, jade and other rare things; 300 gholāms decked with gold and silver, and all with coats of *saqlāṭuni* cloth and Rumi brocade; and fifty other led horses and camels with gold accoutrements. The palace gholāms all went on foot at the head of the procession, carrying arrows, bows and gold and silver maces. There were also shield bearers from Merv[617] and 3,000 infantrymen, comprising those of Sistan, Ghaznin,[618] Herat, Balkh and Sarakhs; numerous troops, prominent persons, retainers and pillars of the state—I, Abu'l-Fażl, had gone to watch this and was there on my horse.[619]

The Amir, seated on the travelling throne, ordered that the elephant should be reined in on the raised platform (*dokkān*).[620] [The Grand Vizier] Khᵛāja Aḥmad b. Ḥasan, the Head of the Army Department and Khᵛāja Bu Naṣr Moshkān, were positioned close by the elephant. [F 373] He held a session for listening to complaints of wrongdoing, petitions for redress were asked for, those persons complaining of injustice were heard, and they were then sent back. The Amir summoned the boon companions, and called for wine and for musicians and singers, and the notables were asked to join the wine-drinking session. Platters of little dishes of delicacies (*navāla*) and pies and pasties (*sonbusa*) were served round for those desirous of them.[621] Wine circulated, and the musicians and singers were playing their instruments and singing. It was a gloriously resplendent day, when gaiety and mirth were given full rein.

In the mid-morning, there arose the noise of large kettledrums, drums and trumpets, for on this day Tāsh Farrāsh was setting off for Khorasan and Western Persia by way of Bost. First of all, the Commander, the Keeper of the Royal Wardrobe Yāruq-tughmush, entered, in full panoply of arms and with his well-groomed retinue, who filed past while he stood there and rendered service. After him came Maḥmudi *sarhangs*, three with golden belts and seven with silver belts, all fully arrayed. After them Gowhar-āyin, Treasurer to this monarch, whom the latter had raised up and promoted to high office, came in, and also several generals and *sarhangs* of this monarch with troops of cavalrymen. The cavalrymen were filing past, while the senior officers (*moqaddamān*) were standing there in attendance.

Then the Commander-in-Chief [for Khorasan and Western Persia] Tāsh entered, with large kettledrums, a standard, and a complete panoply of arms and equipment, accompanied by 150 of his own gholāms and 100 royal gholāms [Gh 282] who had been set free and handed over to him. Tāsh dismounted and made his obeisance. The Amir ordered that they should all be seated, and the horse for the Commander-in-Chief of Western Persia was sent for.[622] Wine was handed out to Tāsh and likewise to the senior officers who had been designated to accompany him. Three or four rounds of wine were given out. The Amir instructed Tāsh, "Be vigilant, for we have entrusted you with an important task, and pay heed to the instructions of the regional counsellor and administrator who is to follow you regarding all matters related to the welfare of the state. Keep sending us letters, and you will receive in return replies giving you directions on how to proceed. A postmaster and intelligence officer will be appointed from among our trusted officials so that he can have full scope and authority [F 374] to report back to us in a very detailed manner. You must treat these prominent men and senior commanders, who comprise both former retainers of my father (*pedariyān*) and persons in our own service, according to their status and rank, so that, as we have already ordered, they may be obedient to you and carry out your commands and things go smoothly in an orderly fashion. I am hopeful that God, the Exalted one, will facilitate the conquest of the whole of Western Persia at your hands."

Tāsh and the others said, "We will obey the commands." They dismounted and kissed the ground. The Amir said, "Go forth in God's name with fortune's blessing, joyfully and with decorum!" They mounted and went off in the direction of Bost. It will be necessary to have afterwards in this History a highly detailed section regarding the supreme command of Tāsh and the function as regional counsellors and administrators of the two high civilian officials (*ʿamid*) Bu Sahl Ḥamdavi and Ṭāher Karaji,[623] for it contains much significant matter worth understanding.[624]

The Amir returned and came back to the Royal- Palace. He engaged in a drinking session lasting two days. On the third day he held court, and said, "Unfinished business must be settled, because we intend to go to Kabul in order to lead an expedition from there against whichever region seems to need attention." He said to the Great Chamberlain Bilgetegin, "We ordered the elephants to be driven and brought to Kabul for a review to be held; when will they arrive?" Bilgetegin answered, "The riders have been gone now for some days, and during the course of this week they should be bringing back all the elephants to Kabul." He said, "Excellent!"

The court session broke up, but he kept the Grand Vizier back, together with the Head of the Army Department, Bu Naṣr b. Moshkān, and the Great Chamberlain Bilgetegin and the General Begtughdï, and they had a private session together. The Amir said, "In which direction should we march?" The Vizier replied, "What is the lord's own view, and what has he been thinking about?" He said, "My own inclination is to offer our thanks to God for these numerous blessings and acts of favour, recently restored to us without experiencing any hardship or civil strife, by leading an expedition against the infidels into the distant regions of India. We shall thus have revived the tradition (*sonnat*) of our forefathers, carry out acts of valour and manifest our thanks. [F 375] A great impression of fear and awe will be instilled in India, and they (i.e. the pagan Indians) will know that even if our father has passed away, we will not allow them [Gh 283] to have vain illusions and become bloated and relish their state of false security."

The Vizier answered, "The lord has thought this out very well, no other way is suitable, and the wise course of action will be whatever the exalted judgement deems appropriate. But there is room for a question, and since this matter has been introduced with consultation and discussion in mind, I shall say what I think so that the lord can hear it clearly and we servants who are present can likewise hear it to see whether it is a sound course of action or not; then, whatever is most agreeable should be acted upon. The lord sent a senior commander with a great reputation, accompanied by a powerful force, to India, hence there is a fully-prepared army there. The men of Transoxania have again begun to come forward. The Bā Saʿidān[625] should assemble also, an effective expedition against the Indians can be mounted this year, and the heavenly reward for this will be credited to the lord's account. Another general has gone to Khorasan and Ray. It will take some time for this commander to settle matters there, and it will reinforce and strengthen this general's hold on that region if the lord takes up his position in Khorasan. ʿAlitegin is still licking his wounds and harbouring feelings of rancour in his heart,[626] with his brother overthrown and he himself left without succour.[627] Talks about marriage contracts and a diplomatic agreement have been undertaken with Qadïr Khān, envoys have gone forth and are at present involved in discussions, but according to the letters that we have received from them no final decision has yet been reached. If the exalted banner launches an attack on India, all these affairs will be left unresolved and may well become more complicated and intractable. ʿAlitegin is near Balkh and has large numbers of men at his disposal, since the Seljuqs have joined up with him. If he does not attack Balkh and Tokhārestān, it may well be that he will march against Khottalān, Chaghāniyān and Termez and stir up trouble, and besmirch our good name. In my opinion, the soundest course will be that the lord should go to Balkh this winter so that, thanks to the aura of his presence, the envoys will be sent back with their mission fulfilled, and with the marriage contracts and [F 376] diplomatic agreement firmly concluded. A regional counsellor and administrator should be appointed to follow after Tāsh from Balkh, for until such an official is sent, all affairs will be held up. The problem of ʿAlitegin can be brought to a successful conclusion either by war or peace, for delusions of grandeur were induced into his mind at that time when the lord marched on Khorasan while his brother Amir Moḥammad was on the throne, and the Amir sent him a message promising him Khottalān.[628] That ambition (i.e. to acquire Khottalān) has remained with him ever since. Furthermore, news has arrived from Baghdad that the Caliph al-Qāder be'llāh is ill and has despaired of life, and has entrusted affairs to his son al-Qāʾem. If news of his decease should arrive, it will be best for the lord to be in Khorasan. Also, envoys should be designated for Gorgān and a contractual agreement should be made with them. Apart from this, other matters [Gh 284] may arise, and all are things that would require immediate attention. When all these considerations have been met and the affairs of state placed on an even keel, then an expedition against the infidels in far-flung regions can be contemplated for next year, and with complete peace of mind." [He turned to the other advisers and said,] "What does the present company think about what I have just said?" They all replied, "What the Grand Vizier perceives and is privy to is well beyond our knowledge and capacity, and his good counsel and solicitude are well known to the lord." The Amir said, "The correct decision is what the Vizier has just expressed, and nothing else will do. He is like a father for us. The decision has been made on these lines; go back home and get ready, for we shall set out this week." All those present at that private meeting returned homewards, having offering up praises to the Vizier and wished him well; for he was matchless in his time.

The Amir set off from Ghazni on Thursday,[629] mid-Shavvāl [422/15 October 1031] and arrived in Kabul. He stayed there for three days, and a review was held of the elephants, amounting to 1,670 [beasts], male and female. He was pleased, for they appeared very stout and healthy. The head of the elephant keepers (*moqaddam-e pilbānān*) was a man of such stature as [F 377] the General Bu'l-Nażr,[630] and the sons of Qara Khan[631] and all the elephant keepers were under his orders. The Amir showed favour to Bu'l-Nażr and praised him lavishly, saying, "This noble-minded man has experienced many trials and tribulations in our cause and has suffered great injuries from the late Amir, to such an extent that, on a single occasion, he was beaten with a thousand strokes, but he remained loyal to us throughout that interrogation, and in truth he sacrificed his body and soul for us. Now is the time to pay him his due, for it is a shame that such a man, given his competence, his good counsel, his eloquence, and the training which he has had at court in correct etiquette and ceremonial procedures, should be head keeper of the elephants."

Khᵛāja Aḥmad replied, "Bu'l-Nażr does indeed deserve this, and a man like him should be allotted a place by the lord's throne and put in charge of the royal messages." The Amir ordered him to be taken along to the Royal Wardrobe and to be garbed in the robe of honour suitable for a chamberlain, a robe that he had worn in the past.[632] He came forward with a black coat, two-pointed cap and belt adorned with gold; he performed the customary acts of obeisance and then returned to his own tent. All the prominent men of the court paid the necessary respects and acknowledgements due to him. After this, he rose each day to greater prominence until that time when he was appointed to the office of head of the chamberlains (*zeʿāmat-e ḥojjāb*), as I shall mention in the appropriate place and record its date. At the present time, in the year 451 [/1059], he is still alive, praise be to God—and long live the Exalted Sultan Abu Shojāʿ Farrokh-zād b. Nāṣer Din Allāh, who showed him much kindness and who acknowledged his past service to the realm. Today he leads armies and performs deeds of valour, as I shall set forth. When he is in Ghaznin, he proffers advice on the governance of the kingdom. If an envoy arrives, he arranges the customary ceremonies. Officials of various backgrounds, former servants of Maḥmud, [Gh 285] of Masʿud and of Mowdud, all bring their problems to him; he holds the prestigious post of custodianship of the citadel of Ghaznin, and has one of his personal chamberlains [F 378] called Qotloghtegin running it for him (i.e. as his deputy).

After reviewing the elephants, the Amir indulged in wine-drinking festivities. He gave robes of honour to the elephant keepers through the Great Chamberlain Bilgetegin. A hundred male elephants were chosen to accompany the exalted banner to Balkh, and the remaining elephants were driven back to their quarters. The Amir left Kabul and reached Parvān, and stayed there for five days, hunting and carousing, until the baggage, impedimenta and elephants crossed the pass (*bazh*) of Ghuzak.[633] Then he crossed the pass and drank wine at Chowgāni (?),[634] and from there came to Valvālej,[635] staying there for two days then setting off thence for Balkh and entering the town on Tuesday,[636] 13 Dhu'l-Qaʿda 422 [/1 November 1031]. He stayed for a week at the Gate of ʿAbd al-Aʿlā Palace and then proceeded to the Great Garden. All the baggage and equipment were brought there and the Divāns were set up there, and according to those instructions which the Amir had given and the layout which he had sketched out, the entrance portico, the open spaces, the Divāns, etc. and the barrack quarters for the gholāms, had all been set up, and that great water channel which runs through the Garden had been utilized for fountains.

When they were in Ghaznin, Bu Sahl Zowzani had schemed against the Khwarazm Shah Altuntāsh, had stirred up troubles and had aroused covetous desires at the Amir's court. This led to Altuntāsh's fall from favour, and Bu Sahl too suffered much adversity as a result while he was in Balkh and remained in that plight for a while, but this is not the appropriate place to recount it. I shall first record the arrival of this monarch at Balkh, and give an account of several urgent tasks that he already had to deal with and some which turned up later, and how they were dealt with, and only then will I embark upon a full discourse (*maqāma*) (i.e. on Bu Sahl and Altuntāsh) for it contains many remarkable aspects and rare observations well worth knowing.[637] [Gh 286]

On Tuesday, the twentieth of this month (i.e. of Dhu'l-Ḥejja/8 December 1031), news arrived that the Commander [F 379] of the Faithful al-Qāder be'llāh, *may God illumine his proof*, had passed away, and that the Commander of the Faithful Abu Jaʿfar the Imam al-Qāʾem be-amr Allāh, *may God perpetuate his ruling power*, who is still alive in this present year 451 [/1059] (and may he long remain alive!)[638] and who was the covenanted heir, had been raised to the throne of the caliphate.[639] The pledge of allegiance had been made, and the leading figures of both of the two branches of the Hashemites, the ʿAlids and the ʿAbbasids, together with the whole of the people of Baghdad, were content to give obedience and follow him. To all the regions from one end of the world to the other,[640] letters were written, and envoys went forth in order to extract the pledge of allegiance from the prominent figures amongst the governors.[641] The religious lawyer Abu Bakr Moḥammad b. Moḥammad al-Soleymāni al-Ṭusi, the envoy appointed to the Sultan's court,[642] had come to Khorasan for this important mission.

Amir Masʿud was plunged into deep thought by this news. He had a private session with Khᵛāja Aḥmad and my master Bu Naṣr and said, "What should be done regarding this matter?" The Vizier replied, "May the lord's life be prolonged in good fortune and magnanimity so that all lifetime benefits and rewards are accrued upon him![643] Although this report is authentic, the wise course might nevertheless be for this news to be kept concealed and for continuing to make the formal intercessory prayer in the name of al-Qāder.[644] The envoy, as it has been written in the letter, is following after the report of these events and may soon arrive. When he does arrive and has had a period of rest, he can be brought into the lord's presence in a fitting manner so that a letter of commiseration and of greeting can be given to him and he can return homewards. The next day the lord can sit and hold the customary three days of mourning. After that, he can go to the Friday mosque on the Friday for the customary practice of greeting the new caliph to be carried out by making the formal intercessory prayer for Qāʾem and with the scattering of coins as alms." The Amir said, "That's exactly the right course." They accordingly kept this news secret and did not make it public. On Sunday,[645] 10 Dhu'l-Ḥejja [/28 November 1031], the customary celebration of the Festival of the Sacrifice was carried out with great pomp and ceremony, and there were all sorts of decorations and spectacles.

On Friday,[646] mid-Dhu'l-Ḥejja of this year [/2–3 December 1031], a letter arrived, saying that the envoy Soleymāni had reached Shoburqān. From Ray to there, the provincial governors, the local governors and tax-collectors, and the sultan's officials had shown great solicitude for him and had followed the customary practices of going out and greeting him and escorting him. The Amir summoned Khᵛāja ʿAli b. [F 380] Mikāʾil and said, "An envoy is coming. Get ready and go out ahead with a great body of Sharifs of the ʿAlids[647], judges, ulema and religious lawyers, as a welcoming escort, and with the great men of the palace and the holders of court offices following on your heels, and bring the envoy into the town in a fitting manner." ʿAli made a great effort, surpassing all measure, since he was the leader and spokesman of the town notables (*raʾis al-roʾasāʾ*) and arranging such activities had been his responsibility and the responsibility of his auspicious family [Gh 287]—may this house remain for ever with the descendants of the Khᵛāja ʿAmid Abu ʿAbdallāh al-Ḥoseyn b. Mikāʾil, may God prolong his firmly-established position; *how excellent is the progeny of this great religious leader* (ṣadr)*!*[648]

He went off to welcome and to escort back the envoy, followed by Bu ʿAli, the official responsible for entertaining envoys, and with the court office holders and with numerous beasts of burden led along. When the envoy drew near to the town, three generals, Bu'l-Ḥasan Karaji and the boon-companion Moẓaffar the judge, who both spoke Arabic well, and ten *sarhang*s with about a thousand cavalrymen, went out to greet him, and brought the envoy back into the town with great ceremony on Friday,[649] 22 Dhu'l-Ḥejja [/10 December 1031]. He was lodged in the Alley of the Basket Weavers in a fine, handsomely-decorated palace, and straightaway, much delicately-prepared food was brought in. *God is most knowing about what is best!*

An account of the arrival from Baghdad of the envoy and the public announcement of the death of the Caliph al-Qāder be'llāh, may God be pleased with him, and the making of the khoṭba *according to custom for the Imam al-Qā'em be-amr Allāh, may God perpetuate his existence and prolong his exalted role and elevated position*

When the envoy had enjoyed a period of rest and refreshment—they entertained him very lavishly for three days[650]—the Amir said to the Vizier, "The envoy has had his rest; he must be brought into our presence now." The Vizier said, "It is indeed time; how should it be done?" The Amir replied, "I have decided that the best procedure would be that we should go back to the [Gate of] ʿAbd al-Aʿlā Palace for a few days, since it is more compact and better-furnished for such affairs, and there are two palaces there. The gholāms and holders of court offices can be stationed there according to the usual practice, [F 381] and, moreover, the customary practices of greeting the new caliph and of mourning for the old one can be carried out there more appropriately. Then when we have completed these duties, we will come back to the Garden." The Vizier said, "The lord has thought this out very well, and it should be done thus."

They held a private session, and the Great Chamberlain, the Commander of the [Palace][651] Gholāms, the Head of the Army Department and the Head of the Chancery were summoned and they all came. The Amir gave them all the necessary orders concerning the envoy, the letter required for him to take back to the caliph, the troops, the holders of court offices and the palace gholāms; and they went back. The Amir mounted at the time of the afternoon worship and returned to the Gate of ʿAbd al-Aʿlā Palace. All the baggage and impedimenta were brought there, and similarly, all was settled and in order in the Divāns. [Gh 288] The decision was made that, on the first day of Moḥarram [/19 December 1031], which would be the beginning of the year, the envoy should be brought in, and my master Bu Naṣr b. Moshkān, gave Bu ʿAli, the official responsible for looking after envoys, an order such as was customary. The letter (i.e. that to be sent back to the new caliph) was brought and was perused; it had been written setting forth accession greetings and condolences. At the end of this whole document (*qeṣṣa*) was written this letter and the pledge of allegiance so that they could be studied. Several times I sought for this letter till I found it at this present time, when I had carried the History up to this point, in the possession of the son of my master Kh^{v}āja Bu Naṣr, *may God prolong his state of health and preservation and have mercy on his father.* If my papers and documents had not all been deliberately destroyed, this History would have had a different complexion. *May God judge between me and the person who did that!* The Great Chamberlain and the generals arranged to the last detail the matter of the troops, the palace gholāms and the holders of court offices.[652]

The History of the Year 423 (/19 December 1031–6 December 1032)

[Gh 288, F 381] The first day of this month of Moḥarram was a Thursday. Everything was prepared before daybreak. [F 382] When the dawn broke, 4,000 palace gholāms stood on both sides of the Government Headquarters several rows deep. Two thousand of them had two-pointed (or: "winged") hats and costly belts studded with ten hooks as their accoutrement,[1] and each gholām had a silver mace. The other 2,000 had four-winged hats and were girded with a *kish*, a belt, a sword, a quiver (*shoghā*) and a bow case (*nim-lang*),[2] and each gholām had a bow with three arrows in his hand. All of them had on coats of Shushtari satin brocade. Three hundred gholāms from the Sultan's personal guard stood in the rows on the dais in the vicinity of the Amir, with even more splendid uniforms, two-pointed hats, gold belts and golden maces, and there were several of them who had belts set with jewels. There were also fifty or sixty Deylamite shield-bearers[3] guarding the door within the palace. All the great figures at court, the provincial governors and the chamberlains, had on two-pointed hats and golden belts, and outside the palace the holders of court offices were stationed. A large number of elephants were held there. The troops of the army, bearing their weapons and armour for the horses, wearing many-coloured uniforms of satin brocade, and having with them litters and weapons, stood in two lines facing each other with their standards, so that the envoy might be led through them. The official charged with the reception and entertainment of envoys[4] went off with mounts that were led along and a numerous retinue, and they set the envoy on his mount and brought him along. A great noise of trumpets and [Gh 289] of large, barrel-shaped drums, of the type borne on elephants' backs,[5] arose; one would have said that it was the Day of Resurrection. They conducted along the envoy with these elaborate, impressive ceremonies. He witnessed things that he had never seen in his life, and was bedazzled and dumbfounded by it all, and entered the palace.[6] The Amir was seated on his throne in front of the dais.

The caliph's envoy, who was robed in black, made his greetings. The Grand Vizier Aḥmad b. Ḥasan responded. He alone was seated in the Amir's presence; the rest were standing. The General Bu'l-Nażr took the envoy's arm and led him to a seat. The Amir [F 383] called out, "How did you leave the lord, the Commander of the Faithful?" The envoy replied, "May God, His mention is exalted, reward the exalted Sultan! The Imam al-Qāder be'llāh, the Commander of the Faithful, may God illuminate his proof, has passed away! '*Indeed we belong to God, and to Him we shall return*'. It is a great calamity, but the divine blessing of our new caliph's continued existence is of greater import. May God Most High grant the late caliph a place in Paradise, and may He perpetuate the life of the new lord of religion and of this present world, the Commander of the Faithful."

The Grand Vizier spoke very eloquently in Arabic in this same vein, and gave an indication to the envoy in the course of his address that he should proffer the letter. The envoy rose to his feet and brought up to the throne the letter, which was contained in a black satin pouch[7] and presented it to the Amir, and returned to his designated place and sat down. The Amir called out to Khᵛāja Bu Naṣr. He came up to the throne, took the letter and stepped back, and stood facing the throne. He opened the pouch and read out the letter. When he came to its end, the Amir said, "Read out its translation so that everyone will be aware of its contents." He read it out in Persian, in such a fashion that the entire audience averred that he was matchless in this.[8] They conducted the envoy back and escorted him to his house with great ceremony.

The Amir prepared to hold mourning ceremonies, and the next day, when he held court, he wore a white cloth tied round his head-dress and a white cloak, and all the retainers, courtiers and chamberlains came in wearing white also.[9] The envoy was brought in as a witness to these things. The markets closed, and the populace and people of all ranks came forward in successive groups. This went on for three days, and the envoy was brought along, and at noon, when the Amir arose and the audience ended, he would be escorted back. When the three days were over, the people returned to the markets and the administrative offices re-opened their doors, and barrel-shaped drums and ordinary-sized kettledrums (*dohl va dabdaba*) were beaten to mark the occasion.

The Amir summoned Khᵛāja ʿAli [b. Mikāʾil] and said, "Give orders for decorative platforms and arches to be erected from the court to the entrance of the Friday mosque, and for a full display of pomp and ceremony, for Friday is approaching and we intend to come in person to the Friday mosque so that the investiture proclamation (*khoṭba*) can be read out concerning the [new] Commander of the Faithful." He replied, "I'll do that." He went back and [Gh 290] summoned the notables of Balkh, giving them the necessary instructions. They got busy on this work on the [F 384] Monday, Tuesday, Wednesday and Thursday, and they decorated Balkh from the Gate of ʿAbd al-Aʿlā to the congregational mosque in such a fashion that no-one could ever remember seeing Balkh like it. They set up a large number of festive platforms and arches from the markets to the head of the street of ʿAbd al-Aʿlā, and from there to the court complex and the streets where the notables resided. They carried on setting up decorations throughout the night till daybreak on Friday. By then, the town appeared so well prepared that nothing additional was required.

The Amir held court on Friday, and when it broke up, Khᵛāja ʿAli b. Mikāʾil said, "May the lord's life be long! Everything that the exalted command ordained regarding the decorative platforms and arches and decorations has been completed; is there any additional command? The Amir said, "Instructions must be given for the subjects to come in and settle down quietly, and for every group to be in its place. They are to take care regarding the platforms and the goods and things which they have brought with them. They should not indulge in any displays of jollity and merry-making until we ourself pass, so that not a single sound is heard. Then when we have gone past, they are free to do just as they like, for when we have performed the worship we shall return along the other side of the inner city to the Garden." He said, "I obey." He went back and passed on this order. The black-coated court attendants appeared, and they secured complete compliance from people.

At the fullness of noon, the Amir mounted his steed. Four thousand gholāms, with all that splendour which I have previously mentioned, that is, on the day of the envoy's ceremonial entry, went forward on foot, with the Commander of the Palace Gholāms Begtughdï at the rear of them. Next came the gholāms of the Sultan's personal guard, with the Sultan's standard, the holders of court offices and the chamberlains at their head and the Great Chamberlain Bilgetegin at their rear. After the Sultan came the Grand Vizier with the other senior officials (*khᵛājas*) and the court notables, and after the Grand Vizier, Khᵛāja ʿAli b. Mikāʾil, along with the judges, the learned and religious figures, and the mayor (*zaʿim*) and notables of Balkh. The caliph's envoy was with them in this procession at the right hand of ʿAli b. Mikāʾil. The Amir [F 385] came with this concourse to the congregational mosque, going most sedately, in such a manner that, apart from the sound of the drums[10] and the cries of "Keep back!"[11] from the holders of court offices, no other sound was to be heard.

When the Sultan halted at the mosque, he installed himself below the minbar (pulpit). They had draped the minbar from top to bottom in brocade woven with gold threads. The Grand Vizier and leading figures of the court sat down. ʿAli b. Mikāʾil and the caliphal envoy sat down a further distance away. The official preacher and orator performed the due sequences of the *khoṭba* [Gh 291] and the worship. When he had finished this and the people reposed themselves, the Sultan's treasurers came in and placed at the foot of the minbar five silken purses containing 10,000 dirhams as an offering to the caliph. Following that, other offerings were presented on behalf of the royal princes, the Amir's sons; the Grand Vizier and the Great Chamberlain; and then the rest. The attendants were shouting out, "So-and-so's offering," and then "So-and-so's offering," and they were setting them down until a vast amount of gold and silver was deposited. When it was all done, the Amir arose, mounted his steed and went round by the foot of the inner city, with the gholāms, retainers and courtiers, towards the Great Garden. The Grand Vizier accompanied him. The treasurers, the treasury secretaries and the accounting officials conveyed the offerings to the treasury by the road through the market. Khᵛāja ʿAli b. Mikāʾil mounted, taking with him the envoy, and they came out through the groups of stalls in the market.[12] The people of Balkh celebrated enthusiastically and they scattered as alms many dinars, dirhams, precious items and all sorts of things. This took all day, and it was nearly time for the evening worship when they reached the Gate of ʿAbd al-Aʿlā. ʿAli then went back by another route, and he conducted the envoy, with the accompanying retinue, to his own residence. An elaborate reception had been prepared. They dined, and ʿAli gave the envoy a fitting offering of money[13]; this munificent gesture pleased the Amir very much.

Next day, the Amir gave instructions to Bu Naṣr Moshkān for him to go to the Grand Vizier and proceed with the concluding of an agreement (*ʿahd*) with the caliph and the arrangements for sending back the envoy. Bu Naṣr went to the Divān of the Vizier. They talked privately and summoned the envoy there, [F 386] and had a lengthy discussion until they agreed upon what had to be settled, to the effect that the Amir would conclude an agreement, in accordance with the document which had been brought by the envoy, on the condition that when the envoy returned to Baghdad, the Commander of the Faithful should send a fresh investiture patent which should include in it Khorasan, Khwarazm, Nimruz, Zābolestān, the whole of Hind and Sind, Chaghāniyān, Khottalān, Qobādhiyān, Termez, Qoṣdār, Makrān, Vāleshtān,[14] Kikānān,[15] Ray, Jebāl, Isfahan and all the territory up to the pass of Ḥolvān, Gorgān and Ṭabarestān. Also, that the caliph should not enter into correspondence with the Khāns of Turkestan, and should bestow no honorific titles nor send robes of honour without this house (i.e. the Ghaznavids) being the intermediary,[16] as it was in past times, when the late caliph al-Qāder be'llāh had so arranged with the late Sultan Maḥmud, *may God envelop him with His mercy.* Also, this envoy Soleymāni should return to resume this arrangement, bringing with him a matchless robe of honour as an expression of the Commander of the Faithful's fond approval. Also, the caliph is to give permission for an attack to be made on Kerman from Sistan, and one on Oman (ʿOmān) from Makrān, [Gh 292] and the Carmathians are to be overthrown. A vast army has been assembled, and we need more territory. The army must be put to work. Were it not for our respect for the sanctity of the caliph's court, an attack on Baghdad would have been unavoidable so that the Pilgrimage route might be kept open, for our father had left us at Ray for this very purpose, and when he died, had we not been compelled to return urgently to Khorasan, at this present moment we would have been in Egypt or Syria. We have capable sons mature enough for undertaking such activities,[17] and others are on the way to this; they must be given tasks to perform. We are on friendly terms with the Buyids, and are not going out of our way to harm them in any way; but they have to be more vigilant and restore the caliphate to its former dignified state and keep open the Pilgrimage route. [F 387] Our subjects have been instructed to prepare themselves for undertaking the Pilgrimage and have been assured that they will be accompanied by one of our commanders. We have given our pledge regarding this, and if the Buyids do not exert themselves in this matter, we will act strongly (i.e. against the Buyids whose lands lay across along the Pilgrimage route), for we are answerable for this to God Most High, since there has been bestowed upon us not only great power and prestige but also countless troops all fully equipped and ready for action.[18]

The envoy said, "Everything said here is true and just. An official memorandum should be written out which I can show as a proof of this." They replied, "Very good," and sent him back. Bu Naṣr told the Amir everything that had happened, and he approved this warmly. On Thursday, 15 Moḥarram [423/2 January 1032], the judges, notables and sayyeds of Balkh were summoned, and when the court session broke up they were brought in. 'Ali, son of Mikā'il, also came in. The official charged with the reception and entertainment of ambassadors brought in the envoy, and the Grand Vizier, the Head of the Army Department, Bu Naṣr Moshkān, the Great Chamberlain Bilgetegin and the Commander of the Palace Gholāms Begtughdï were likewise present. My master had translated the document affirming allegiance and its formal oath into Persian, in a translation as fine and delicate as Rumi brocade and containing all the conditions. He presented the translation, along with the Arabic original, to the envoy who perused them and read them out aloud so that all those present heard him. The envoy said, '*May the Almighty always watch over you!*'[19] This is a precise rendition of the Arabic original and nothing is amiss, and I shall tell the Commander of the Faithful, *may God perpetuate his existence*, accordingly" Bu Naṣr read out the original Arabic document in its entirety, and the Amir said, "I have listened to it all and noted it down in my mind; give me the Persian version." [F 388]

Bu Naṣr handed it over to him, and Amir Mas'ud began to read it out aloud—and amongst all the monarchs of this house I never knew anyone who could read and write Persian the way he did. He read out the agreement to its very end, [Gh 293] without any pause or hesitation, and then they fetched the royal inkstand and he wrote his signature below both the Arabic and Persian copies of the agreement, that which had been brought from Baghdad (i.e. the Arabic) and the

[Persian] translation which my master had made. They had brought in another inkstand from the Chancery, which they set down, and the Grand Vizier and those present wrote out their signatures as witnesses to the documents. The Commander of the Palace Gholāms Begtughdï did not know how to write, so Bu Naṣr signed on his behalf. The envoy and the local representatives from Balkh were sent back, and the chamberlains likewise went home.

The Amir stayed behind with these afore-mentioned three, the Grand Vizier, Bu Naṣr and the Commander of the Palace Gholāms Begtughdï, and said to the Vizier, "We must send back the envoy." The Vizier replied, "Yes, certainly. Bu Naṣr should compose a letter, an official memorandum and list of verbal messages, and these should be submitted for the approval of the exalted judgement. The Amir should bestow an appropriate robe of honour and presents for the envoy, and entrust to him the customary offerings for the exalted caliphal presence so that he can take his leave." The Amir said, "What should be sent for the caliph?" Aḥmad said, "Twenty thousand *man*s of indigo has been the traditional amount in the past for the caliph personally and 5,000 *man*s for the court entourage,[20] as well as the entire sum presented to the caliph on that day when the investiture was formally proclaimed from the pulpit and which is now kept in the treasury. What does the lord ordain, of clothing, jewels and perfume, to be sent further? It is well-known and established what should be given to the envoy. I have read in the historical accounts about ʿAmr b. Leyth that, when his brother Yaʿqub died in Ahvāz, the Caliph Moʿtamed, who had harboured so much grievance against Yaʿqub and had fought and vanquished him, despatched Aḥmad b. Abi'l-Aṣbagh on a diplomatic mission to ʿAmr, Yaʿqub's brother. An undertaking had been made to ʿAmr that he should turn back (i.e. from southwestern Persia, the provinces which Yaʿqub had conquered) and should remain at Nishapur until the investiture patent, succession agreement and standard should reach him there. ʿAmr promptly gave the envoy 100,000 dirhams and sent him back homewards. But when the envoy came to Nishapur with two servants (*khādem*s) and two robes of honour, and splendid presents, bringing with them a standard and a document confirming ʿAmr's succession, 700,000 dirhams were expended on them and their mission.[21] [F 389] This envoy Soleymāni has come with a momentous mission and charge; he should be given an appropriate robe of honour and 100,000 dirhams. Then if he returns and brings back what we have asked (i.e. Masʿud's demands as detailed above), the Amir should give him whatever the exalted judgement deems fitting."

The Amir said, "This is very sound sense," and he embarked on enumerating the list of the additional presents for the caliph to the Vizier, who wrote them down: 100 pieces of clothing, all of high value and of every kind, ten of them woven with gold; 50 vesicles of musk; 100 pastilles of camphor; 200 bales (*mils*)[22] of linen, of the highest quality; 50 valuable Indian swords; a golden goblet of 1,000 methqāls' weight filled with pearls; ten jacinths; twenty superlatively fine Badakhshāni rubies; [Gh 294] ten Khorasani horses, specifically, from Khottal,[23] with satin brocade caparisons and head covers; and five valuable Turkish slaves.[24] When this was written out, the Amir said, "All this must be made ready." The Vizier replied, "Very good," and he went back and sat down in the loggia of the Chancery. The treasurers were summoned and were given orders, and the Vizier and his officials went back. The treasurers prepared all this, and the Amir saw it and was pleased. My master Khᵛāja Bu Naṣr drew up the copy of the letter in his inimitable way, for he was the very paragon of the age in penmanship. I myself, Bu'l-Fażl, wrote out the fair copy of this, since letters to the caliph's court, to the Khāns of Turkestan and to neighbouring monarchs used all to be written out by myself. I kept copies of all of them, but they were deliberately destroyed. A thousand pities that those paradisal gardens (i.e. eloquently-composed documents) are no longer extant, for this History would have become truly exceptional because of them. But I do not despair of the Divine Beneficence that they may be one day returned to me, so that everything may be set down and that the status of this outstanding master (*ṣadr*, i.e. Bu Naṣr Moshkān) may be more widely known to people; "*That is easy for God.*"[25] The memorandum was written out, and Khᵛāja Bu Naṣr showed it to the Vizier. Then at that point he wrote out each of the two in fair copies, [F 390] in Persian and in Arabic.[26] He read both of them out in the Sultan's court, and they were received with great approval.

On [Tuesday,] 20 Moḥarram [423/7 January 1032], the envoy was brought in, and he was given a very lavish array of presents,[27] of the kind given to men of religious learning, including gold equestrian trappings weighing 500 methqāls, a mule and two horses. He was then sent back. All the presents earmarked for the caliph were brought to him anon, and the envoy himself was given personally 100,000 dirhams and twenty precious robes. As his own personal gift, the Grand Vizier sent the envoy a mule with a caparison and head covering, together with 500 dinars and ten sets of clothing. My master Bu Naṣr sent the reply letter to him by hand of the official charged with the reception and entertainment of envoys. The envoy set out from Balkh on Thursday, 22 Moḥarram [423/9 January 1033], and five swift couriers (*qāṣeds*) were sent with him, so that he might send them back, one at a time, with news of current events, and might send two of them back from Baghdad with an account of what was happening and what had been done. A spy was secretly inserted amongst the whole troupe of attendants travelling on foot[28] and those leading the horses,[29] [Gh 295] and he was instructed to send back, by hand of these couriers, an account of all events, great and small. (Amir Masʿud was a wonder in doing this sort of thing;[30] I shall set down in several places what he ordained on such occasions.) Letters went by couriers of the postal and intelligence service[31] to all the provinces which lay along the envoy's route, with instructions for them (i.e. the people of those provinces) to go out and meet and escort him with due ceremony and to entertain him lavishly so that he might travel along in comfort.[32]

When I have finished this story, it will be necessary to fulfil what I had promised concerning writing out the letter from the caliph and the letter with the text of the accession document. [F 391]

The text of the letter [from the Caliph][33]

In the name of God, the Merciful, the Compassionate

From the servant of God and His helper (vali), *ʿAbdallāh Abu Jaʿfar al-Emām al-Qāʾem be-amr Allāh, Commander of the Faithful, to Nāṣer din Allāh al-Ḥāfeẓ le-ʿebād Allāh al-Montaqem men aʿdāʾ Allāh Ẓahir khalifat Allāh Abu Saʿid, client* (mowlā) *of the Commander of the Faithful, son of Neẓām al-Din va Kahf al-Eslām va ʾl-Moslemin Yamin al-Dowla va-Amin al-Mella Abuʾl-Qāsem Vali Amir al-Moʾmemin—the exalted official motto, "My source of assistance is in God"—greetings upon you!*

The Commander of the Faithful expresses to you praise [Gh 296] *for God, apart from Whom there is no god but Himself, and asks that He pray over Moḥammad His prophet, may God bless him and his house and grant him peace. As for what follows:*[34] *May God ensure your good preservation and protection, and allow the Commander of the Faithful to make use of your services, and with extensive favour, noble gifts and precious manifestations of beneficence for you and with you, and may He never deprive you of Him!*

Praise be to God, the Conquering One through His mightiness, the All-powerful One through His eminence, the Permanently-existing One, the Pre-existent One, the Exalted One, the Compassionate One, the One exercising supreme sovereignty, the All-dominating One, the Vigilant One, the Haughty One, the One possessing favours, overwhelming power (jabarut), *splendour and the invisible world* (malakut), *the Living One who never dies, the One who cleaves the heavens for the dawn and the One who seizes souls. No difficulty is impossible for Him and there is no escape from His decree. No human sight can apprehend Him. No night or day come over Him successively. He establishes for every term of life a written decree, for every human activity a way of entry, for every project embarked upon a way out and for every living thing a fixed, determined term: "God brings the term to an end for those souls at the time of their death, and those who have not died, in their sleep; those souls for whom He has decreed death, He retains, and* [F 392] *the others He sends back until a designated term. Indeed, in that there are signs for a people who reflect."*[35] *He is the One unique in lordship, the One who ordains for everyone whom He has created a span of continued life for a determined spell, as a decree of His for all created beings and as an act of justice in what is foreordained. No angel brought near [the heavenly throne]*[36] *goes forth from Him, nor any prophet is sent, nor any pure one* (ṣafi) *because of his acting sincerely towards Him, nor any sincere friend* (khalil) *because of his sincere friendship for Him, nor anyone who speaks* (kalim) *because of his speaking intimately with Him.*[37] *The Almighty God says: "Every community has a term fixed for it, and when its term comes, they will not linger behind for a single hour nor will they go in advance."*[38] *He also says, His name is exalted, "Indeed, it is We who inherit the earth and whoever is upon it, and to Us they shall be made to return."*[39]

Praise be to God, who chose Mohammad, may God bless him and his house and grant him peace, from the best of houses, who selected him from the most noble of origins and who singled him out for Himself from the most excellent of Qoreysh in acquired nobility (ḥasab) *and the most noble of them in inherited lineage* (nasab)[40], *the most excellent of them as to root* (aṣl) *and the purest of them as to branches* (farʿ). *He sent him as a light shining forth, bringing good news, conveying warnings, providing guidance and as a divinely-directed one, and as a well-pleasing messenger, summoning men to Him and giving them guidance towards Him, and as a proof coming from Him so that he might warn those who wrought evil and as good news for those who do good deeds. He then conveyed the divine message, brought about a state of security, gave wise counsel to the community* (omma), *fought strenuously in the way of God and acted as His servant until death*[41] *came to him. May God bless him and his house and grant him peace, and raise him in nobility, dignity and power!*

Praise be to God, who chose the Commander of the Faithful from amongst the people of that religious community (mella), *whose green shoot was lofty, whose foundations were solid,* [Gh 297] *whose root was firmly compacted and whose origin strongly implanted, and whose roots were adorned and whose branches were kept inviolate! He selected him from amongst the community whose fire-steel blazed forth strongly, and He picked him out from the core of the caliphate, whose meteoric gleam gives illumination. He provided him uniquely with a handsome disposition, singled him out with pure qualities and endowed him specially with praiseworthy ways, amongst which were the most vital, most fitting, truest and most worthy of which were submission to God Most High's command* [F 393] *and decree, and contented acceptance of its adversities and harmful effects, and he fulfilled all of that sort of thing. The caliph followed, continued in the way and pursued his path along the road of his pious forbears, and kept to their illuminating, clear track. In his position of fortunate circumstances, he keeps his tongue moistened in expressing thanks. He faces up to the calamities which have come upon him with the patient endurance with which God Most High has endowed him, and he meets adverse strokes of fortune with his acceptance of their being inflicted in accordance with what the One whose supreme position is exalted has endowed him. He fulfils the necessary duty of giving thanks in both situations* (i.e. the good and the bad) *to his Creator and Master, and he binds up the good circumstances of life with what makes them firm and beneficial, and the adverse circumstances with taking thought for what will dispel them. He sees that what is given to him regarding both sets of circumstances is an enveloping benefit and that the proof for him in believing that there is something beneficial in both of them together is decisive. He is not excused punishment from his Lord, He is praised, but he acknowledges his awareness of His vouchsafing goodness, content in times of distress with his being afflicted and tested so that he might be worthy of receiving a greater share of God's beneficence, and gain an enhanced share of heavenly reward. The profit from all aspects is of no use to him, nor does the advantage concern him however circumstances have turned out, because of his knowledge that God, He is glorified, brings favours and beneficence into existence through His grace, makes decisions concerning them in accordance with His justice, ordains the course of things by His wisdom, controls their varying aspects with His will and puts them into effect through His will. He is alone in his heavenly power and in His creation, and He directs their affairs according to His express decree, and He makes incumbent upon all of them submission to His commands and contentment and conformableness to His decrees. So glory be to Him, than whom no other is to be praised for agreeable things and harmful ones [alike], and blessings be upon Him, the One for whom there can be no suspicion regarding His decisions for matters of hardship and of ease alike. He, mighty is His name, says, "We afflict you with evil and good as a test, and to Us you are made to return."*[42] [Gh 298]

When God Most High acted with his entire freedom of will in transferring the God-fearing, pure and righteous Imam al-Qāder be'llāh—may God's prayers be upon him living and dead, and may He sanctify his spirit in the future continued existence and in the dwindling away into absorption in God[43]*—to the place of His exaltation and the abode of His vouchsafing benevolence at the point of his arrival at the completion of his appointed term of life and his attaining the final part of his allotted span, and [when God] joined him up with his forefathers the Rightly-Guided Caliphs, may God's prayers be upon them* [F 394] *all, as an example of what God Most High has ordained for all living creatures existing apart from Himself and for every created being which His two hands have formed. The passing* *of the Commander of the Faithful into the abode of rest was easy for him because of his knowledge of God's giving for him in compensation entry into the fellowship of the pure prophets and His granting him what God the Lavisher of Beneficence had prepared for him of rest, lavishing of favours and residence in the abode of permanency. But the stinging of the scorching and the inflicting of the pain of separation entailed for him humiliation and silent grief and caused him sorrowfulness and anxiety, and he remained poised between the state of giving orders and prohibitions, uttering the formula of belonging to God and returning to Him*[44] *and yielded himself up to the One who has the power of creation and giving commands, the One who brings things into existence and the One who takes things back. He is never controverted in issuing his ordinances and His acts of breaking down and building up are never opposed: "Those who are in the heavens and the earth make request of Him; every day He is engaged in some business."*[45] *The Commander of the Faithful sought refuge, as a consequence of this approaching event that drew close and destructive stroke that came near, in what God desires for him and has made incumbent for him. He made himself submissive, he uttered the formula of belonging and returning to God after being filled by fright and affliction, and he said, "Indeed we belong to God and to Him we shall be made to return." He sought a heavenly reward, and he endured patiently, he was contented and gave thanks after exercising his skill over every hard and distressful episode and after repulsing every painful stroke of misfortune, since the judgement of the Imam al-Qāder be'llāh, may God be pleased with him and sanctify his spirit, was a shining star and his judicious character a firmly-fixed mountain. He was fiercely unyielding in religion and firm in his resolution in giving obedience to God, the Lord of the Worlds. May God pray over him and through this prayer set him down in the Paradise Gardens of easeful living and guide him on a straight road. He, may God sanctify his spirit, was fine in his actions and noble in his character; no-one exceeds his degree amongst the righteous Imams, and he makes manifest his proof amongst the worlds.*[46] *"Indeed, He does not cause the reward of those who do good to become wasted."*[47] *The Commander of the Faithful has pictured in his mind, through his keen understanding and his clear thought, the deflecting of his mind from the grief of these misfortunes towards the desire for the reward of the grief and the recompense, and he has placed his eager desire for* [F 395] *God Most High in entrusting back to his Master his security and his setting on foot that which he requests. He asks that He will favour the pure Imam al-Qāder be'llāh, God's prayers be upon him and His good will and forgiveness, with the good actions which he has offered and which will draw him close to His side, and bring near to him what He previously granted from His side, until the angels meet him announcing the good tidings of forgiveness and communicating to him noble gifts and divine approval. God, He is blessed and raised up above all men, says, "Their lord announces to them glad tidings of mercy and goodwill from Him, and Gardens of Paradise prepared for them in which is enduring delight, where they will abide for ever; indeed, there is with God a mighty reward."*[48]

The Commander of the Faithful invites you to respond favourably to what God has entrusted to him and has made incumbent by express designation (naṣṣ) *to him from the pure Imam al-Qāder be'llāh, may God make noble his resting-place and illuminate his tomb, in order that he may repair the splits, uphold the divine prescriptions* (sonan), *bind together the state of security which was scattered, heal the state of weakness and the breaches, mend the deviations and restore the deficiencies, uphold God's right regarding his subjects, and preserve what He asked him to preserve concerning His creatures. He then held a general court session in the presence of the supporters and leading men of the ʿAbbasid cause, the great men and prominent figures*[49] *of the family, the leading figures from amongst the judges, religious lawyers, professional witnesses, ulema, exemplary figures* (? amāthel) *and righteous men. They invited the Commander of the Faithful to become eager in upholding God's right amongst them, they bound themselves to what God had made incumbent upon them of obedience, they struck their hands together in making oaths of allegiance with approval, submissiveness, seeking blessings and favourable hopes for the future. God had illumined their sight, made pure their hearts, led them aright towards guidance and had showed them the way to grasping "the firmest handgrip".*[50] *The affair became one of great importance and its loss something which is injurious. Every adverse stroke of fortune fell away, every disaster became bright, everything dispersed and scattered became joined together again and every advantageous thing manifest and revealed.*

The Commander of the Faithful has issued this letter of his when all affairs have become straightforward for him and the matter of government has become submissive to him. He has risen to the lofty position of his ancestors the Rightly-Guided Caliphs and he has taken his place in the place of the divinely-guided Imams who were his predecessors, [F 396] *the blessings of God be upon them all, putting on the garment of the victorious power of God Most High in regard to what he keeps secret and proclaims publicly, manifests openly and conceals, choosing to gain His approval in whatever he looses and binds, comes up to and seeks out, holding fast to God's command in what He decrees, coming close to Him in what he draws near to and approves, seeking for the reward which is with Him and fearing an adverse Last Accounting. He does not choose someone as an intimate because he is a close relative, nor does he keep back a distant person* (i.e. one not connected through kinship links) *from what he merits. He does not use his faculties of thought and reflection for anything except in protection of his own private area and pasturing flocks until he is able to facilitate the implementation of rights* [Gh 300] *and to repair breaches. He keeps secure the flocks of beasts and renders the water sweet. He puts down causes of internecine strife, extinguishes their fire, pulls down their beacons, destroys their traces, tears apart their followers and scatters their partisans. He asks God for assistance in what He has set him to govern and His right guidance in what He has entrusted to him for watching over, [that He should grant him strength]*[51] *in all his affairs and intentions, and that He should help him towards the right course in his intended plans and judgements.*

So stretch forth your hand—may God render you useful for me through God's blessing and His good favour—for giving allegiance[52] *to the Commander of the Faithful, and may all those who are in your circle and those others whom your capital city shelters, stretch forth their hands for it. For you are the shining meteor of his state*[53] *which is not extinguished, its advance scout*[54] *who never becomes tired, and its sword which is never still. Continue to follow on the most praiseworthy of your ways, the most rightly-guided of your character traits, the most attractive of your qualities and the most generous of your attainments, in taking good care of what we have entrusted*[55] *to you, keeping guard of it and watching over it. Be a compassionate father and a tender mother for the subjects, for indeed the Commander of the Faithful has appointed you as their shepherd to govern them, and he has summoned you to rule over them. Take unto yourself an efficacious oath in accepting this letter, and exact it from all those at your court with the attestation of the Commander of the Faithful's trusted servant Moḥammad b, Moḥammad* [F 397] *al-Soleymāni, so that it may be an enduring witness before God and before the Commander of the Faithful laid upon you and upon them; compliance with it is incumbent and binding.*

Know that the place you have in the Commander of the Faithful's eyes is the place of a trusted, reliable person, one not suspect or to whom doubtful views can be imputed, since he has delegated the power of command to you, he seeks strength for himself through you and he has not sought help from anyone else against you, knowing that you follow in it the ways of those with pure hearts and are one of those enjoying happiness. For indeed, happiness is linked with that and blessing from God is bound up with it. All manifestations of goodness will become profuse for you through it and will be for you complete and permanent. Affirm to high and low in society that the Commander of the Faithful will not neglect their welfare nor will he be remiss in looking after them, taking, in this, firm hold of the command of God, the Lord of the Worlds, where He says—and He is the most veracious of those who utter words—"Those who, if We establish them in the land, will perform the worship, hand over the poor-tax, urge to what is good and restrain people from what is disapproved; to God belongs the consequence of affairs."[56]

This is the confidential message of the Commander of the Faithful to you, may God make attractive your enjoyment of life and may He always grant requests from you! Receive it with consideration for it and by lauding its high status, comprehend fully the whole of what it contains in order that mention of it may be spread to the whole community, that joyfulness and rejoicing may be completed by it, and that they may place their trust in what God has revealed to them of the Commander of the Faithful's tender care for them [Gh 301] *and his regard towards them with the eye of compassion. Arrange for invoking the name of the Commander of the Faithful from the minbars of your kingdom, making it heard, communicating it, introducing it and repeating it. Hasten to send to the Commander of the Faithful a reply to this letter, with your choice of what came from him in it, for indeed, he shows an earnest desire for it and requires it to be sent. Inform him of your beneficial measures in the lands over which you rule*[57] *and the soundness of what you desire and are putting into execution. [Give information also in your reply] about your remaining in the straight way with the most praiseworthy of fixed intentions in offering obedience to him* (i.e. the Commander of the Faithful) *and the most attractive ways of conduct in following him. Indeed, he is awaiting that* (i.e. Masʿud's reply) *and requiring it and watching out for it and expecting it, if God wills.*

Greetings to you, and God's mercy and blessings, and may He bless His servant[58] *the Commander of the Faithful through you, together with outstanding favours, substantial largesse and precious gifts for you and in your house, and may He never remove these from you! May God grant blessings on Moḥammad and all his house! Our sufficiency is in God alone!* [F 398]

The text of the agreement giving allegiance (ʿahd)[59]

In the name of God, the Merciful, the Compassionate

I have given allegiance to our lord and master ʿAbdallāh Abu Jaʿfar, the Imam al-Qāʾem be-amr Allāh, Commander of the Faithful, an engagement of obedience, following him, content with him, out of free choice, with full faith in him, with an open proclamation and an inner affirmation, with the sincerity of my intention and the purity of my conscience, the soundness of my faith and the firmness of my resolve. I give my obedience without constraint and from free choice, without any compulsion; on the contrary, affirming his excellence, acknowledging his right, recognising his charisma, confident of the excellence of his regard [for me], cognisant of his knowledge of the good interests of those, from the high and low levels of society, who hold firmly to the agreement with him, of the restoring of what is in disarray, of making future consequence secure, of calming unrest, of honouring the saints, of subduing the deviationists (molḥedin) *and humiliating the refractory ones. All this is based on the fact that our lord and master, the Imam al-Qāʾem be-amr Allāh, the Commander of the Faithful, ʿAbdallāh, and His successor on earth, imposes on me the obligations of obedience to him and sincere advice, since his imamate and his governing power are incumbent on his community, and observing his rights and fidelity to their covenant with him is obligatory for them. I have no doubts about this and I have no hesitations regarding him; I do not disregard his orders and do not incline towards anyone but him. Moreover, I am the friend of his friends and the enemy of his enemies, whether they be high or low in estate, near or far, present or absent. I am firmly attached to my allegiance to him, fulfilling the agreement and renouncing, in a contrary situation, the protection in the covenant.*[60] *In that I am in private exactly as in public, and my interior feelings regarding it are the same as my external ones, and I acknowledge that my obeying this promise of allegiance which has infused my spirit and my firm attachment to that which is incumbent upon me, for our lord and master al-Qā'em be-amr Allāh, the Commander of the Faithful, is one with integrity of my intention, uprightness in my resolution and steady persistence in my views and judgement,* [Gh 302] *[I further declare] that I will not work towards anything which will in any way destroy the promise of allegiance; I will not place upon it any interpretation opposed in sense to it; I will not pursue any course harmful to the caliph, whether in prosperity* [F 399] *or adversity; I will not leave aside any sincere advice to him in any circumstances whatsoever, whether close ones or distant ones. I will not clear my mind of the intention of giving support to him in all circumstances, nor will I change anything of what I have contracted to do in this offering of allegiance. I will not go back on the agreement nor will I repent of it. I will not sully my intentions and my conscience by acting contrary to it, nor will I oppose him at any time or in any circumstances with what might injure him. Furthermore, I am in the same position concerning this oath of allegiance, in keeping to its conditions and faithfully observing its stipulations, in regard to his secretaries, servants, chamberlains, and all his retainers and connections.*

Together with that, I have sworn, of my own free will and without constraint, in complete security of mind and free from fear, an oath for which God will hold me responsible on the day when I am made to appear before Him and will require of me the recognition of His rights on the day when I shall stand in His presence.[61] *I say: By God, there is no god but He, the One who knows the unseen and what is visible, the Merciful, the Compassionate, the Exalted,*[62] *the Sublime, the Conquering, the One who attains His goal, the Victorious, the Destroyer, the One whose knowledge penetrates the lands and the heavens. His knowledge of what has gone before is like His knowledge of what is to come. Also, I swear by the Most Beautiful Names of God,*[63] *by His sublime miraculous signs, by all His definitive words, by all the agreements and compacts*[64] *which God made with His creatures; by the Mighty Qor'ān, by the One who sent it down and the one who came with it (i.e. the inspiring angel Gabriel); by the Torah, the Gospels, the Psalms of David, the Discriminating Scripture*[65]*; by Moḥammad the Prophet, the Chosen One, may God bless him and all his house and grant them peace; by the members of his family, the pure ones, by his Companions, the chosen ones, and by his wives, the pure ones, the mothers of the faithful, peace be upon them all; and by the angels brought near [the Heavenly Throne] and the prophets sent down. Indeed, this oath of allegiance of mine, to which my tongue and my hand have contracted, is an oath of allegiance offering obedience. God, His splendour is exalted, is aware from me that I have laid it upon myself, that I will fulfil totally what is contained in it and that I have a sincere desire to uphold it and to give support to those adhering to it. I offer that with a wholesome mind, with no dissembling*[66] *or scheming or defectiveness or trickery, until the time when I shall meet God, fulfilling my engagement concerning the oath of allegiance, keeping in a safe place what I was engaged to do regarding it, without raising any suspicion of evil* [F 400], *breaking its provisos, interpreting it in a wayward fashion or breaking my oath,*[67] *since those who swear allegiance to those possessing the power of command, "The hand of God is above their hands; whoever breaks faith is only breaking it to his own hurt. To the one who fulfils what he has pledged to God, He will give a mighty reward."*[68]

This oath of allegiance to which I have obligated myself, to which I have stretched out my hand and over which I have clasped hands, with what has been laid upon me in it involving fidelity, friendship, sincere advice, help, obedience, harmonious relations, effort and zeal, [Gh 303] *is God's agreement; indeed, His agreement is a thing whose fulfilment is required.*[69] *It is an agreement which He has made binding upon His prophets and messengers, peace be upon them, and on each one of His servants, it being one of the most firmly-concluded of His covenants. I take upon myself the obligation of holding fast to what of the agreement he has laid upon me and not changing it, of being obedient and not being rebellious, and of having a pure heart and not being afflicted by doubt. I follow the straight path and do not deviate from it, and I hold fast to that for which I have given an undertaking to God with the firmness of obedient persons holding to their obedience and of those persons with obligations and faithfulness holding to their obligations and faithfulness.*

If I break this oath of allegiance, or any part of it, or change any of its stipulations or negative any of its features or alter any of its aspects, whether secretly or openly, or by using some trickery or by some wayward interpretation or by asserting the possibility of an exception from it[70] *or by making an act of reparation after breaking it or by circumventing it, or by abandoning what I have given my soul to and the agreements and covenants of God which I have bound myself to observe, or by turning aside, moreover, from the ways of persons who do not treat lightly what has been entrusted to their safe keeping and who do not consider licit fraud and trickery, and whom nothing keeps back from fulfilling the undertakings made under contract, hold to firmly—[if I do any of these things,] then I have abjured and denied the Mighty Qor'ān, the One who sent it down and the one* (i.e. the angel Gabriel) *who came down with it and the one to whom it was revealed* (i.e. Moḥammad), *and I have thrown off all connection with God and His Messenger, and God and His Messenger are likewise freed of all connection with me, and I have renounced belief in God's angels, His books, His messengers and the Last Day.*

Also, everything which I possess at the moment when I pronounce this oath, or will possess during the remaining part of my life—wealth in the form of money or silver coinage, jewels, buildings, clothing, carpets and furnishings, moveables, landed property, estates, pasturing herds, arable land, [F 401], *milch beasts or other types of property that one usually possesses, whether great in value or small in significance—is to be given as alms to the destitute in various aspects of the way of God, the Lord of the Worlds* (i.e. in various charitable ways), *and may it be forbidden for me that all that given as charity, or any part of it, should revert to my wealth and property by any legal subterfuge* (ḥila) *or by any means or methods, or by any equivocation in faith. Also, may every slave whom I own, male or female, at the mo-*

ment when I utter this oath, or whom I may own at any future time in my life, become freed for God's purposes, and may nothing revert to me from their clientage to me (valā'). *May every animal which I possess, comprising horses, mules, asses and camels, or which I may own during the rest of my life, be freed in the way of God; and may every wife whom I have married, or may marry during the rest of my life, be subject to a triple divorce,*[71] *one which is irrevocable and cannot be nullified.*

In what I have said there is to be no introducing of confusions or obscurities derived from any of the legal schools (madhāheb), *in which a way out or attenuation*[72] *of things like these* (i.e. the promises detailed above) *may be used. If I break any of the conditions of this allegiance of mine, or if I go against any one of it basic principles, or if I make exceptions to my oath, or if I make expiation for infringements of it, or if I introduce a wayward interpretation of it, or express with my tongue the opposite of my real belief, or if the external sense of my words does not match the inner meaning of my acts, then I shall be obliged to make* [Gh 304] *the Pilgrimage to God's Holy and Ancient House in the hollow of Mecca thirty times, to be done on foot and not riding. If I do not fulfil this oath, may God not accept from me anything in exchange or its equivalent, except after my adherence to its stipulations;*[73] *may He abandon me on the Day when I shall have need of His aid and support; may God consign me to dependence on my own resources and strength and keep me away from access to His resources and strength; and may He deprive me of prosperity and fortune in this present life and forgiveness in the next one!*[74]

This oath is my oath and engagement of allegiance, and the engagement of allegiance written down in it is my own one to which I have sworn from its beginning to its end, an oath which I fully intend to fill. It is obligatory upon me, laid upon my neck and with all its parts interlocking with the others. The intention in the whole of it is the intention of my lord 'Abdallāh Ja'far the Imam al-Qā'em be-amr Allāh, the Commander of the Faithful, may God prolong his existence for a period which will fulfil the welfare of this present world and religion, and for a life conducive to all good interests, which will raise high his banners, make noble his pronouncements, [F 402] *exalt his words, strike to the ground his enemies and make glorious his friends. I take God Most High as my witness to all this; He is sufficient as a witness for this.*

[The translation into Persian of Qāʾem be-amr Allāh's letter to Sultan Masʿud]

[Gh 312]

[The translation into Persian of the oath of allegiance of Sultan Masʿud, may God be pleased with him][75]

[Gh 316, F 402]

An account of the circumstances involving Khᵛāja Abu Sahl Moḥammad b. Ḥoseyn (Ḥasan)[76] Zowzani the Head of the Army Department and his arrest

I have already mentioned in this volume that before[77] we had left Ghaznin at the time when Sultan Masʿud had already decided to leave Ghaznin for Balkh, Bu Sahl Zowzani had instigated some mischief regarding the Khwarazm Shah Altuntāsh and had given full vent to his powers of intrigue and the ability to arouse rapacious instincts (i.e. within the Amir's mind).[78] For this reason, he later suffered a great calamity. I shall rehearse the story of these machinations in full and explain the reason for his arrest.

I heard from Khᵛāja Bu Naṣr that Bu Sahl had planted in the Sultan's mind that "The Khwarazm Shah Altuntāsh has become devious, and he ought to have been seized at Shoburqān, whence he left in a wrathful state. Powerful commanders like ʿAli Qarib, Eryāruq and Ghāzi have all been overthrown, but the Khwarazm Shah Altuntāsh remains at liberty enjoying great might, weapons, equipment and an army. Were he to be overthrown likewise, and replaced in Khwarazm by a trusted servant chosen by the lord, a substantial domain, a treasury and a large army would accrue to the realm." The Amir said, "But how can this be achieved? An army there, led by a mighty commander, is required for such a task." Bu Sahl replied, "It's very easy, so long as this [Gh 317] matter remains secret. The lord should write in his own hand a brief note to the commander Monjuq,[79] leader of the Küjet troops, a loyal courtier who is in Khwarazm[80] and who is thirsty for Altuntāsh's blood, so that he can arrange to seize and kill him. There are in the Khwarazmian capital around 3,000 [F 403] cavalrymen of the royal army (*ḥasham*), and it is clear how many the Khwarazm Shah and his personal retainers amount to (i.e. they are inferior in number); he can easily be overthrown. Since the confidential note will be in the lord's own hand, it will not be doubted, and none of the secretaries and others will hear about it."[81]

The Amir said, "That's a very sound plan. You are the Head of the Army Department; make a list of all the names (i.e. of the commanders to be suborned)." He did just that, and the Sultan wrote out the secret letter in his own hand and inserted the name of each of the important officers according to their rank and status. Bu Sahl did not realize that this plan could not remain a secret and that the Khwarazm Shah would slip out of his hands; the latter was unrivalled in his alertness and intelligence. He was not to be overthrown this easily, and a whole world would be stirred up. Notwithstanding Almighty God's decree, one must know that Khorasan was lost as a result of the affair of Khwarazm and that Khᵛāja Aḥmad b. ʿAbd al-Ṣamad, the Khwarazm Shah's counsellor and administrator (*kadkhodā*), was uniquely adept and seasoned in managing affairs. All this will be narrated in its appropriate place.

My master Khᵛāja Bu Naṣr related:[82] When this secret letter in the Sultan's hand was despatched, the Amir divulged that secret to ʿAbdus. ʿAbdus told it in a drinking session to Bu'l-Fatḥ Ḥātemi, who was his close confidant, and told him that he thought Bu Sahl would bring about the downfall of this mighty house; ʿAbdus and Bu Sahl were sworn enemies. Bu'l-Fatḥ Ḥātemi told this next day to Bu Moḥammad Masʿadi,[83] the Khwarazm Shah's representative at court (*vakil-e dar*), out of friendship and was handsomely rewarded. Masʿadi immediately sent off a message in a cipher arranged with Khᵛāja Aḥmad b. ʿAbd al-Ṣamad and divulged full details of the plot. Bu Sahl had planted agents along the road to Khwarazm, and these agents were intercepting letters and were on their guard. Masʿadi's coded letter was brought back. The Sultan sent a verbal message to the Grand Vizier, saying, "Why should the Khwarazm Shah's agent at our court devise a code and write letters in it? Be on your guard and find out!" Masʿadi was summoned to the Divān—I, Bu Naṣr, was there at the time [F 404]—and he was asked about the code. He replied, "I represent an eminent personage here at court, and I draw substantial allowances and a stipend and other financial benefits, and in exchange I have given a rigorously-binding pledge that I should speedily report back whatever concerns my master's interests. The lord (i.e. the Grand Vizier[84]) knows that I would not do anything harmful, and Khᵛāja Bu Naṣr knows me well. [Gh 318] Since this was a matter of some import, I wrote this message in code. They said, "What's this important matter?" He answered, "It's not possible for me to say." They said, "You must necessarily speak. This question is being phrased in these terms out of deference to the respected status of your master Altuntāsh, otherwise, the question would have been put in another manner."[85] He replied, "Since there's no other way, I must seek from the lord Sultan a guarantee of protection from punishment." They referred back, and a guarantee from the Sultan was put in place. He then retailed those circumstances which he had heard from Abu'l-Fatḥ Ḥātemi, and the latter from ʿAbdus. When the Vizier had taken in all that, he became pensive and plunged into deep thought, and he turned to me, saying, "You see what they're doing?" Then he said to Masʿadi, "Had you written something previously?" He replied, "Yes, I had, and this was sent to confirm it." The Vizier said, "Since he represents an eminent personage here at this court, and draws allowances, a stipend and other financial benefits, and in exchange has given a firm pledge,[86] he had no choice. But Bu'l-Fatḥ Ḥātemi must be punished since he told a lie."

Then the Grand Vizier secretly said to me, Bu Naṣr, "Tell the Sultan that this secret should not be revealed to ʿAbdus and Bu Sahl Zowzani till we see what happens. Masʿadi is to be told[87] to write a letter in code at once, to be sent by one of his own swift couriers, and another letter by the agent of the state postal and intelligence service (*askodār*), with the message, "The previous letter was without substance and should be disregarded."[88] [F 405] This is the only wise course of action just now until tomorrow, when we can see[89] whether that letter has reached there, what is happening, what they are doing and what course of action we can consider. The Sultan must stop this affair and should make Ḥātemi the scapegoat for this episode, even though this matter cannot remain hidden and there will be a very grave crisis." I myself went and delivered the Vizier's message. When the Sultan heard it, he was dumbfounded and lost for words. I sat waiting. He turned towards me and said, "Whatever words can be used to salvage the situation must be used, to the effect that Bu'l-Fatḥ Ḥātemi has uttered this lie, that there is enmity between Bu Sahl and ʿAbdus, and that this scoundrel Ḥātemi has muddied the waters to such an extent and conjured up such lies." I went back and reported to the Vizier what had happened. The Vizier spoke reassuring words to Masʿadi, and on the basis of the draft that I, Bu Naṣr, had drawn up on this subject, he wrote out two letters in code, one to be sent by hand of a swift courier and the other by the Sultan's cavalryman, to the effect that "What was written previously was a product of mischief-making by Bu'l-Fatḥ between the two men of note (i.e. Bu Sahl and ʿAbdus), since they were on bad terms with each other, and for this reason Ḥātemi was punished for what he did." Masʿadi was sent back homewards. Bu'l-Fatḥ received 500 strokes of the stick and was deprived of the office of the oversight of Balkh which had been given to him. [Gh 319]

When Masʿadi went away, the Vizier had a private talk with me and said, "You see what they have done? They have stirred up a whole world. We are dealing with Altuntāsh and not with a man of straw,[90] and he has, moreover, at his side a man like Aḥmad b. ʿAbd al-Ṣamad; how could this plot ever work with them? Altuntāsh [F 406] has been lost to us. He is a wise old Turk and mindful of his own reputation; if this were not the case, he could wreak havoc on us. To cap it all, I myself have been kept well away from all such activities as these (i.e. the intrigues of Bu Sahl and his partisans), as you can see for yourself, nevertheless Altuntāsh will lay the responsibility for all this at my door! Go to the Amir and tell him, 'All things considered, something has been going on without my knowledge. If the lord sees fit, he should put me in the picture so that the required remedies may be applied.'" I went off and conveyed the message. The Amir became very heated and said, "There is nothing to worry about on this score. All that Bu Sahl had managed to say to us before I bellowed at him was that Altuntāsh had slipped away with impunity at Shoburqān. Then ʿAbdus had gone and poured out his heart to Ḥātemi and had told him that Bu Sahl would never stop mischief-making, and Ḥātemi had made a proper meal out of all this,[91] until he received his just deserts and got his punishment." I said, "This is all quite innocuous, may the lord's life be prolonged! This affair can be salvaged, provided that nothing else has been going on." I came along and repeated it all to the Vizier. He said, "O Bu Naṣr, the deed has been done and it was done in secret; they kept us in the dark, and you'll see what will come out of it all!" I then went home.

After that, at the time of the noon worship, I was seated in the Amir's presence. The official despatch bag (or box *askodār*) from Khwarazm had been brought to the Divān, secured with a ring and sealed.[92] The janitor of the Divān knew that every despatch bag that arrived like that [Gh 320] must be very important. He brought it in. I took it and opened it. It was a letter from the postmaster and intelligence agent, the brother of Bu'l-Fatḥ Ḥātemi. I gave it to the Amir. He took it and read it, and became highly perturbed. I knew that something grave had happened. I did not say anything, [F 407] and made a formal gesture requesting leave to depart. He said, "Don't go!" I sat down, and he gave a sign for the boon-companions and door-keepers to leave. The court session ended and no-one remained. He tossed the letter over to me and said, "Read it!" It was written that "Today, Friday, the Khwarazm Shah held court, and the courtiers and retainers came in. The commander[93] Monjuq, the general commanding the Küjet auxiliary troops (*sālār-e Kūjātān*), was drunk. He did not take his usual seat, but came on further. The Khwarazm Shah laughed and said to him, 'Last night the general must have put away rather more drink than usual, and must have had a late night.' The commander snapped back, 'It is your overwhelming bountifulness that drives me to revelry and wine-drinking. Your misguided bounty will be the death of me. One must first afford bread before one can get to wine; and he who is blessed with bounty can provide the wine himself.' The Khwarazm Shah laughed and said, 'Don't talk like a drunkard in my presence.' He replied, 'Yes, indeed, a man who has a full belly thinks that the famished are drunken and mad; it is our fault that we put up with this.' The Khwarazm Shah's Commander-in-Chief, Tāsh Māhruy,[94] shouted at him, saying, 'Do you know what you're saying? A most exalted person is talking to you in a jovial way and laughing, but you seem oblivious of your rank and station. If it were not for the respect due to this exalted court, the response to this would have been the sword!' The commander shouted back at him and laid his hand on his sword.[95] The commanders and gholāms waded into him and a mêlée ensued. He was hurling abuse and grappling with them, while the Khwarazm Shah was shouting out that they should leave him alone. In the course of that fracas, Monjuq received several kicks in the groins and on his chest. He was carried back to his house, and at the time of the midday worship he died and yielded up his soul to the exalted court (i.e. of God). May the lord of the world enjoy long life! The Khwarazm Shah summoned me and said, 'You who are the royal postal and intelligence agent, have witnessed the incident; now report what really happened so that a report of a different complexion isn't sent to the exalted court.' I have given a full report, so that the exalted judgement [F 408]—may God increase it in sublimeness—can be apprised of the affair, if God Most High wills." There was a note wrapped inside the folded letter with the information that "When this happened to the commander Monjuq, the Khwarazm Shah ordered precautions to be taken regarding his household and property so that nothing should go wrong. His secretary, along with the commander's son, were brought to the Divān and held there until a decision should be made, *with God's permission*." [Gh 321]

When I finished reading the letter, the Amir said to me, "What do you say? What's behind it all?" I replied, "May the lord's life be prolonged! I am not a clairvoyant, but this much I know, that the Khwarazm Shah is a very intelligent, powerful and self-possessed person, and no-one would dare to instigate such a brawl in his presence to such an extent that a commander of the calibre of Monjuq is killed unintentionally. At all events, there must be something at the bottom of this. The postal and intelligence officer is unable to write anything openly except according to their wishes and at their direct dictation. He has been bound by an oath (i.e. from us, the Amir) to send us secret reports of anything going on there by whatever means at his disposal. We cannot get to the bottom of this affair until his undercover letter[96] arrives." The Amir said, "O Bu Naṣr, why should I any longer keep this secret from you? Bu Sahl prevailed upon us to do such-and-such, and there is a secret letter in our own handwriting saying such-and-such. Once the letter of the Khwarazm Shah's representative at court arrived, they must have killed the commander Monjuq and concocted something like this story as a pretext. We are not at the moment concerned about the commander's being killed but with the fact that the secret letter in our own handwriting should not fall into their hands and lend itself to lengthy repercussions. The detention of the commander's son and his secretary must have a deep-lying reason, and that secret letter may be in the possession of that wretched secretary.

What's to be done here?" I said, "The Grand Vizier will know how to handle this; without his actual presence, the matter cannot be resolved." He said, "This affair must be kept secret for tonight, until the Khᵛāja comes tomorrow." I went back very downhearted and perplexed, for I knew that the Khwarazm Shah was now completely outside the Sultan's control, and all night I was prey to apprehension. [F 409]

Next day, at the end of the court session, the Amir had a private audience with the Vizier and asked for those letters. I presented them and he gave them to the Vizier. When he had finished perusing them he said, "The poor commander came to a wretched end; we can deal with this." The Amir said, "There is another related matter here that the Vizier has not yet heard about and which I told to Bu Naṣr last night. Bu Sahl prevailed upon us to do things that led to the despatch of a secret letter, in our own handwriting, to the commander Monjuq. Our immediate concern is that the secret letter should not fall into Altuntāsh's hands." The Vizier replied, "The secret letter may well be in the hands of that secretary and we can no longer depend on the Khwarazm Shah.[97] Let us only hope that this does not breed[98] any further mischief! However, I personally reckon that it won't in fact do so, since this Turk is old and wise, and he will know[99] that the lord [Gh 322] has been put up to do this by others. Altuntāsh and I have never been on the best of terms, and at all events he will lay the blame for what has happened at my door. It must be said that, by coming up with such a misguided scheme, Bu Sahl acted mischievously and showed little gratitude for all the favours bestowed upon him by the lord. I do not understand why all this has been kept secret from me, for I would have pointed out the right and the wrong ways of proceeding in this venture."

The Amir said, "What had to happen, happened; what can be done now?" He replied, "An answer should be written back immediately to the postal and intelligence officer, and this case of the commander should not be blown up out of all proportion. Certainly, nothing should be written to Altuntāsh until we see what happens next, but this much should be mentioned, that 'The commander acted foolishly and did not observe the responsibilities of his status, and the divine decree gave a helping hand to this and he died. However, his rights should be respected in regard to his offspring, and his cavalrymen should be allocated to his son.' Whether they will or not is a different matter. At all events, the postal and intelligence officer's letter will arrive secretly [F 410] one of these days, provided he is able to send one and the roads have not been blocked, and he will explain fully what has happened. Then we can put together another scheme in the light of what we have read. The brother of this Bu'l-Fatḥ Ḥātemi is the deputy postal and intelligence officer there; Bu'l-Fatḥ must have ventured upon this in order to ingratiate his brother at court." The Amir said, "That's correct, since at that time when Bu'l-Fatḥ was in Bu Naṣr's Divān, he used to write to us and inform us about our father Maḥmud's activities, and he did this for the sake of his own father who was in the Divān of the Amir's deputy (*khalifat*, i.e. Masʿud) at Herat."[100] I, Bu Naṣr, said, "Alas that I should be hearing these words only today!" The Amir answered, "What would you have done if you had heard about it then?" I said, "I would have had his clothes ripped off his back in disgrace and thrown him out of the Divān, for a treacherous secretary is of no use at all." We arose and went home.

The Amir had summoned the Head of the Army Department Bu Sahl, had lashed him with his tongue and had poured scorn on him, saying, "When will you cease furnishing erroneous advice? If, after this, you ever say a word in my presence about any matter except in regard to military affairs, I aver, I'll have your head cut off!" ʿAbdus was likewise summoned, and he spoke to him severely and at length, "You have revealed the secret with which we had entrusted you![101] You are nonentities beneath contempt[102] and will get your just deserts!" [Gh 323] After this the Amir used to appear pensive and preoccupied, and he would only discuss matters of interest on different issues with the Grand Vizier and myself, Bu Naṣr. The pretensions of this clique (i.e. of Bu Sahl and his cronies) were deflated, since it had become apparent that whatever they said and thought was based on error.[103]

One day, I was in my house, and I was told, "A traveller[104] is at the door and is saying that he has an important piece of news." I had a premonition that he had come from Khwarazm. I told them to bring him in. He came in and asked to see me alone. He split open the staff which he held, and he extracted and handed over to me a slim piece of paper [F 411] addressed to me from Bu ʿAbdallāh Ḥātemi, the deputy postal and intelligence officer. He had written, "I have had to use many a subterfuge and to offer this traveller money and assurances of further rewards at the royal court, before he would agree to embark on this dangerous mission. He has been an eye-witness to events here, and if he reaches the exalted court in safety he will deliver my verbal messages, for he is an alert and resourceful man. His words should be heard and given credence, if God wills."

I said, "What's the message?" He replied that Bu ʿAbdallāh says as follows:

What I had written previously, to the effect that the commander Monjuq, in a brawl which occurred at the Khwarazm Shah's palace, had received several kicks in the groins and on the chest and had died, was in accordance with that text drawn up by the Khwarazm Shah's counsellor and administrator, Aḥmad b. ʿAbd al-Ṣamad. They rewarded me with silver and clothing, and had I written anything different, it could well have been fatal for me. The truth is that on the day before he was killed, the commander had given a great feast and had invited a bunch of rabble-rousers from the Küjet and Chaghrat troops,[105] and he had uttered complaints about the Khwarazm Shah in public and had spoken some unseemly words, going as far as to say, "The world does not stand still. Altuntāsh and Aḥmad are only concerned with their own interests and those of their sons and gholāms; but this situation cannot last for ever, for it is clear how long I and these other free men can endure these wretched conditions." The Khwarazm Shah was informed of this. Next day, during the court session, he said to the commander Monjuq, "Yesterday and last night you gave a feast?" He replied, "Yes." The Khwarazm Shah said, "Couldn't you find any meat or delicacies, that you had to make a meal of me and my counsellor and administrator (i.e. slander us behind our backs)?"[106] The commander hurled back at him an even harsher reply. The Khwarazm Shah smiled and looked at Aḥmad, and when the commander had left, he said to Aḥmad, "You saw how the wind from the royal court has swollen up the commander's head?"[107] Aḥmad replied, "It will be blown away from there (i.e. we'll soon put a stop to it)," and went back to his house.

It was the custom that, each Friday, Aḥmad would go back home (i.e. from the court or from his Divān) earlier during the course of the morning,[108] [Gh 324] and everybody would go to convey their greetings and pay him their respects. I myself was present there. The commander came in and began a diatribe against Aḥmad, and [F 412] in the course of this he said, "What was the Khwarazm Shah trying to tell me today?" Aḥmad replied, "My lord is forbearing and generous; if he were not, he would have answered you with his club and sword. What business have you and your likes to talk above your station just because you've had some rough wine?"[109] The commander replied with more verbal abuse as if he was slapping Aḥmad in the face. Aḥmad said, "This wind (i.e. this truculence) blows from the royal court, but you ought to have kept it quiet for a while until that moment when the office of the Khwarazm Shah had come to you." The commander said, "With you at the helm, the Khwarazm Shahs won't last long,"[110] and he got up with the intention of going away. Aḥmad said, "Seize this dog!" The commander said, "You won't get me!" Aḥmad snapped his hands and said, "Let him have it! (*dehid*)." Two hundred men burst in, as had been pre-arranged. The commander had reached the middle of the hall when they laid into him with sword, battle-axe (*nāchakh*)[111] and ordinary axe (*tabar*), and killed him. They tied a rope round his feet and paraded him round the town. They broke into his house and arrested his son and his secretary. They compelled me to write a letter according to a draft of their own, as you have already seen. Next day, they sought from his secretary the secret letter that they said had come from the royal court. He denied that the commander had ever given him anything. They searched through the commander's house and his papers but could not find any secret letter. They put the secretary through severe torture; he confessed and yielded up the letter to them. They took it but they did not show it in public or divulge anything about it so that no one learnt about its existence. For three days the Khwarazm Shah did not hold court, and remained closeted in private meetings with Aḥmad. On the fourth day, Friday, the court session was held just as it was normally held each day, but with even greater pomp and ceremony. At the time for the Friday worship, the intercessory prayer was pronounced according to the usual practice.[112] There is no hint of anything resembling a rebellion, but I am kept well away from everything except routine official business, and they are acquiring additional gholāms and horses far above the normal level. Whatever I am able to write from now onwards will be at their dictation and no reliance should be placed on it. [F 413] I now have to deal with travellers and secret messengers, and I am in fear for my life. *God is the One who provides sufficiency!*

I wrote out a copy of the verbal message and brought it to the palace. The Amir read it, and was highly perturbed, saying, "This must be kept sealed up until tomorrow when the Vizier comes," and I did that. The next day, when the court [Gh 325] broke up, he had a private session with the Grand Vizier and myself. When the Vizier had read the deputy postal and intelligence officer's letter and the copy of the verbal message, he said, "May the lord's life be long! Such is the result of unconsidered actions. We must renounce all hope of the Khwarazm Shah, for we shall get nothing further from him. Let us hope to God that he does not initiate further trouble by joining forces with 'Alitegin, since they are close to each other, and create great havoc." I, Bu Naṣr, replied that he would certainly not do this, and he would have regard for the rights of the deceased lord (i.e. Sultan Maḥmud), and he would realize that some evil-motivated person had misled the lord in this affair. The Amir said, "What can I do about the letter in my own hand, which they have acquired as evidence against me? And if they do use it as evidence of my complicity in the plot, how can I deny it?"

The Vizier replied, "This deed is done, but there is one possibility remaining, and so long as we act at once, it may perhaps assuage matters for a while. The deed is retractable, even though it may cause the lord some anguish, but the affair of Altuntāsh and that important frontier region cannot be gainsaid." The Amir said, "How's that? I am even ready to give away one of my beloved sons in order to bring this affair to a close and prevent further aggravation." The Vizier replied, "The lord's best interests must always be uppermost for me, and my words should not be misinterpreted as implying that I am speaking out of personal bias and cannot abide one of the servants of your exalted court." The Amir said to the Vizier, "I have never suspected this and never will!" He replied, "The person behind this débâcle has been Bu Sahl, and Altuntāsh [F 414] bears serious grudges against him. Although the secret letter went out in the lord's handwriting, it should be clear to Altuntāsh that Bu Sahl must have used many a trick to wrench this letter from the lord's hands. Bu Sahl himself must be made the sacrifice for salvaging this position: the lord should order his arrest, since he was the proponent of two misguided plans and policies, and it will take a long time to recover from their deleterious effects, and the lord himself now has regrets about both of them. One is the episode when the accession payments of the lord's brother the Amir Moḥammad were clawed back, and the other is that he made Altuntāsh suspicious and resentful. For when he is placed in captivity, this evil can be laid solely at his door. A letter can be written by the lord on this matter so that Altuntāsh's suspicions and resentments may be dispelled; although he will not come to the court, at least he will not ally with an enemy and will not stir up trouble. I myself can likewise write a letter and give him a clear, objective account. When he realizes that[113] I have had no part whatever in this affair,[114] he will listen to my words and our task will be accomplished." The Amir said, "That's an excellent plan; tomorrow I shall order Bu Sahl's detention. [Gh 326] The Vizier must take precautions regarding him and his partisans, both here and in the provinces, lest he slip through our hands and the whole plan be aborted." He replied, "I'll do exactly this," and we went back homewards. On the way, the Vizier said to me, "This lord has now realized that, in this case, the chickens have come home to roost, but in a way this may prove beneficial and prevent similar incidents in future."

The next day, when the court rose, the Vizier went to his Divān and Bu Sahl to the Army Department. I was left in sole charge of the Chancery, and letters speedily went out with instructions that Bu Sahl's partisans and properties in Merv, Zowzan, Nishapur, Ghur, Herat, Bādghis and Ghaznin were to be seized. When these letters went out, the Amir's command reached the Vizier, conveyed orally by the boon-companion Abu'l-Ḥasan Kudyāni,[115] with the message, "Letters in connection with that matter which yesterday [F 415] was discussed face-to-face with the Vizier were despatched to the provinces, and swift-riding couriers went forth; the Vizier will now bring to completion the matter regarding that man." The Grand Vizier summoned Bu Sahl, together with the subordinate officials of the Army Department, and he demanded the accounts relating to the army. He then sat privately with his assistants and they were busy with going through the accounts. He gave secret orders, and the duty commander (*ḥājeb-e nowbati*) rode off and went to Bu Sahl's house with a body of inquisitorial agents and trusty retainers of the Vizier, and they sequestered Bu Sahl's residence, arrested all those of his retainers and hangers-on who were at Balkh,[116] and reported back to the Vizier what they had done. The Vizier came back from the Divān and gave orders that Bu Sahl should be taken to the citadel. The duty commander set him on a mule, and with a numerous escort of cavalrymen and footsoldiers, conveyed him to the citadel. En route, two household servants (*khādems*) and sixty gholāms were brought to the duty commander; they came before him, and were taken to the palace.[117] Bu Sahl was conveyed to the citadel and was placed in fetters. He fell a victim to his own machinations.[118] The Amir was informed of what had happened.

The next day, after the court had dispersed, the Amir had a private session with the Vizier, and I was summoned. The Amir said, "The affair of Bu Sahl is now finished with, and good riddance,[119] since the man stood in the way of good government!", and he went on to say, "What should be done now?" The Vizier answered, "The best course would be for Masʿadi to be instructed to write a letter at once to the Khwarazm Shah, as is the normal practice for an agent at court to write, and to explain that 'The exalted court has ascertained that [Gh 327] Bu Sahl had been responsible for treacherous acts in the state, and was still indulging in them, to the point that he stirred up such trouble with regard to a great and prestigious old dignitary [F 416] like the Khwarazm Shah on the first occasion when the latter came to court, until he was compelled to go back irate and bitter.[120] Even then, Bu Sahl did not desist, but persisted in plotting against the Khwarazm Shah and others. The exalted judgement has therefore deemed it advisable to relieve him of responsibility for the Department of the Army and to have him interned, so that the kingdom and those who serve it are freed from his mischief-making and machinations.' Then at that point I, the Vizier, will confide in secret to him (i.e. to Masʿadi, the Khwarazm Shah's agent) so that he can write a letter in code to the effect that 'All this was done by the lord Sultan because Bu Sahl had been biding his time and had already written out a draft until he found an occasion when the Sultan was befuddled from wine-drinking. A confidential note was then written out in the Amir's hand and in line with that draft and sent off at once to Khwarazm. The following day, when the lord had reconsidered that matter and had demanded the return of that note, Bu Sahl had asserted and sworn an oath upon the lord's life and head, that he too had had second thoughts about that letter and, having realized that it was all a mistake, had torn it into pieces. When it became evident that he had lied, the Sultan ordered for him to be punished appropriately.'

This letter will go off today, and then one week later Bu Naṣr will write a letter and will explain fully the situation, and the Khwarazm Shah's mind will be reassured. I myself will also write, and a trusted envoy will be sent from the exalted court, a man of solid judgement, able to speak forcefully and eloquently, so that he may go to Khwarazm, convey the letters, deliver the verbal messages, find out for himself how things are and then return. Although all this is mere subterfuge, and although it won't convince those wily and experienced persons and they will realize that it is a mere palliative,[121] it will have introduced some element of conciliation which may appease the Turk. This [F 417] son of his called Satï (S.t.y)[122] should also be made much of tomorrow, given the rank of a chamberlain and a gift of 5,000 dinars allotted for him so that that old man's mind may be soothed."

The Amir replied, "All this is sound advice, and must be carried out in its entirety. The Vizier should know that, henceforth, everything which is done in the kingdom, whatever financial measures are envisaged and whatever measures are planned, will all be put into effect under his direction, and he is the one who is to be consulted." The Vizier kissed the ground and wept, and he said, "The lord [Gh 328] should know that these three or four old men who have been left here are better than a thousand young men. The Almighty God has preserved them on earth to bolster up and strengthen the lord's empire, and they should not be hastily spent and thrown to the wind."[123] The Amir summoned him forward to himself, clasped him to his bosom and praised him lavishly, and he showed the same favour to myself. We went back. The Vizier summoned Masʿadi and had a private session with him. I, Bu Naṣr, made a draft document, and he wrote out that which was to be written out both explicitly (*be-ẓāher*) and in code (*moʿammā*), and they were despatched. A week later, the Vizier designated Bu'l-Qāsem Dāmghāni to go to Khwarazm; this Bu'l-Qāsem was an old man, wise and eloquent.[124] The Vizier composed a very finely-phrased letter from himself personally to the Khwarazm Shah, and I wrote out a letter from the exalted court session on the basis of this draft, as follows:

An account of the royal ordinance (*methāl*) issued from the court of Shehāb al-Dowla Abu Sa'id Mas'ud to the Khwarazm Shah Altuntāsh

In the name of God, the Merciful, the Compassionate

The Excellent Commander, Uncle, the Khwarazm Shah, may God preserve his strength, [F 418] is today like a father to us, and he is the mainstay of the empire. In all circumstances he has shown himself an upright, sincere and God-fearing person, and has demonstrated his true beliefs and opinions without any dissembling. We shall never forget[125] what he did after our father, the late Amir, had passed away, when he offered his sympathy and sincere advice to those persons who had newly emerged on top (*now-khāstagān*) at Ghaznin.[126] And then one must bear in mind his subsequent visit to the court, coming as he did with the purest of intentions and free from malice, and his offering of sincere counsel on matters of government and how to consolidate it,[127] in a manner that merits an entire chronicle on its own. That person whose faith and belief are such as this, who feels such loyalty towards the state with which he identifies wholeheartedly and who does his utmost to show his appreciation of the bounties bestowed upon him by the late lord and the present one, and who also strives to do the same regarding the rest of the royal household, can know that, both in this present world and in the next, he will achieve perfect happiness in accordance with the saying, *"He lived in a state of good fortune and left behind a praiseworthy name"*.[128] May his excellence always remain, and may no ear ever hear of his demise! It is true to say that on his part there have always been uprightness and genuine faith, singleheartedness and devotion for us, while on our part and in response to that, [Gh 329] fitting reward and consideration have not been forthcoming. Indeed, on the contrary, many misdeeds have been perpetrated by opportunists[129] and mischief-makers, as well as by those of our officials young and inexperienced enough to be heedless of the consequences of their actions. As a result, we are now filled with shame, and given our genuine faith[130] and perennial concern for his welfare and best interests, blame ourselves for our failings.[131] However, we have complete faith in his valour and sound judgement [F 419] and are confident that he will focus on our essential affection and trust and will dismiss these minor aberrations from his mind,[132] and will always remain for us the same unique, sincere and singlehearted Altuntāsh. If those envious mischief-makers have tried, or are trying, to catch his ear or to show him things to trouble his mind, he should envisage in his mind's eye the very person of the late Amir, Sultan Maḥmud, may God illuminate his proof, and meditate upon his many blessings and favours and the bonds between them, and not on what those driven by envy and opportunists place in front of him. For Altuntāsh possesses sufficient wisdom, power of discernment, forethought and careful consideration to remain steady as a rock against such vicious currents. We seek from the Almighty God success in seeing that his rightful dues are recognized, and if anything has arisen that has been injurious to his lofty stature or is unpleasant in his eyes, that it should be remedied. *He, praise be to Him, is the One in charge of that, and the One who grants favours and success through His munificence and the breadth of His mercy!*

When we set out from Ray to secure the seat of royal power left by our father and reached Dāmghān, Bu Sahl Zowzani joined up with us. In times past he had done us service and had endured great tribulations in our cause. He had remained in the citadel at Ghaznin,[133] and it seemed to us at the time that he was the best person for giving sincere advice and he appeared as the most solicitous of the servants. We had no-one in our entourage from amongst the elder statesmen of the realm to administer and carry through the correct course of action, and we were about to embark upon a momentous task. Inevitably, since he was the foremost person in evidence, he would make pronouncements on every topic and his words would then be buttressed by our approval. [F 420] He began to loom larger and larger in the public eye and people began to look up to him, as is the usual way. There were a few others, such as Ṭāher, ʿAbdus and other persons who joined his coterie. His kept his status until we reached Herat. Our brother was kept under arrest somewhere, and the retainers, courtiers and the whole of the army came to offer their service at our court. The old guard from Maḥmud's time (*pedariyān*) were disregarded and elbowed aside, and this man was directing affairs till matters reached a stage when he thought he held a higher office than that of the vizierate itself. [Gh 330]

When we had delved into matters more deeply and in perspective, and had the occasion to know this man better and to test his abilities, we saw the wisest course of action as being to order the most worthy Khᵛāja, Abu'l-Qāsem Aḥmad b. al-Ḥasan, may God perpetuate his firm position, to be summoned back from India, thus ending his long period of adversity, and we entrusted the vizierate to his capable hands. At the same time, we gave this Bu Sahl responsibility for the Army Department so that he would be concerned with one job only and our court would be relieved of his arrogant and presumptuous ways. But he could not see what was in his own best interests, and those inflated delusions of grandeur never left his head, and he could not desist from being conceited and overbearing, to the extent that all the notable figures at our court became irate and discontented on account of him. Persons who had been entrusted with official posts, posts beyond the capabilities of others and for which they were uniquely suitable, sought to be relieved of their duties, and they lost their sympathy for our cause and thus endangered the very fabric of the state. Despite all this, he still kept on uttering slanders about the leading army commanders and fabricating lies about them, just as he has done now about the Commander (i.e. Altuntāsh) and has caused him distress; he has manipulated the commander Monjuq and created a fracas through him, and he has urged us to change the good opinion concerning the Commander, who is like a father and an uncle to us.

When the activities of this man surpassed all bounds, and his highly treacherous acts [F 421] became apparent to us, we ordered his dismissal from the Army Department, and he was imprisoned and had his wealth and property confiscated so that other rash persons might be chastened by his example and consider this a warning. Doubtless the Commander's trusty agents will have informed him about this matter and the details of how it was carried out. Now at this present time, we have bestowed much largesse and favour upon the Commander's son Satï, a son and a trusted confidant of ours; he has received the rank of a chamberlain and is as dear to us as our own offspring, for who can be more worthy of this position than he, by virtue of being the son of such a father[134] and of having nobility in status and worthiness? These favours are insubstantial in comparison with what is due to the Commander. If fitting and well-deserved favours have not so far reached the Commander from our court, they will from now on be sent regularly so that all the feelings of enmity and suspicion which this malevolent soul (i.e. Bu Sahl) has aroused may be dispelled. The excellent Khᵛāja, the Vizier Aḥmad b. Ḥasan, has, on our instructions, sent a trusty envoy and has dealt with matters at greater length and more openly, and has conveyed messages following our very own verbal instructions. [Gh 331] The Commander should place full reliance on that and purge his mind of former misgivings. That very same trusty messenger should be sent back speedily, and the Commander should request in full whatever he requires and whatever would contribute further to his peace of mind so that, *with God's permission*, they can be met and carried out.

This letter was written out, and the trusted envoy from the Vizier's Divān went off and returned. For the moment everything appeared quiet and tranquil, and no great calamity arose.[135] [F 422]

The final period of the Khwarazm Shah's life turned out to be riddled with fears and anxieties until a powerful army was appointed from the Sultan's court, and he, Altuntāsh, was given the order to come with the army of Khwarazm to the Oxus. The two armies joined together under his command and he marched off to fight ʿAlitegin. They engaged in battle at Dabusi,[136] and ʿAlitegin was given a drubbing, with many of his troops killed. The Khwarazm Shah was hit by an arrow and put out of action, and the following night he died. Khᵛāja [Aḥmad b.] ʿAbd al-Ṣamad, that capable, knowledgeable and experienced man, concluded during the course of the night, before the Khwarazm Shah's death became publicly known, a peace agreement with ʿAlitegin, the latter being grateful for that peace. The next day, Aḥmad withdrew that army, the treasuries and the palace gholāms, and employed many subtle stratagems until he got them safely back to Khwarazm, as I shall set forth in its appropriate place.[137]

I, Bu'l-Fażl, heard a more detailed and accurate account of the killing of the commander Monjuq from Khᵛāja Aḥmad b. ʿAbd al-Ṣamad, in that year when Amir Mowdud reached Donpur,[138] avenged the Martyred Sultan (i.e. Masʿud), went to Ghaznin and assumed the throne and appointed Khᵛāja Aḥmad as his Vizier. After acting as Vizier, Khᵛāja Aḥmad b. ʿAbd al-Ṣamad only survived for a short time and then passed away, God's mercy be upon him.[139] One day, I was sitting down with this Khᵛāja, having gone to deliver a verbal message, and Bu Sahl Zowzani had not yet come back from Bost. He said to me, "When is Khᵛāja Bu Sahl arriving?" I replied, "There has been no news from Bost as yet, but he should be [Gh 332] arriving in about ten days' time." He said, "Will the Amir entrust him with the Chancery?" I replied, "Who is there more qualified than he? He held it in the time of the Martyred Amir." Then after that, the conversation turned to the topic of Khwarazm and the commander Monjuq, and I was retailing the story of these events, since I had been in the midst of all that. He said, "It's just as you said and events happened just like that. But there is one point which you're unaware of [F 423] and which is worth knowing about." I replied, "If the lord sees fit, let him set it forth, since it may be of use for me"—I was intending to compose this History, and wherever I found an item of interest, I would seek it out. I asked him for information about the precise manner of the commander Monjuq's death, and he responded as follows:

"On the first day when the Khwarazm Shah appointed me as his counsellor and administrator, he established the custom that, each day, I would go into his presence alone, I would sit down and would stay there for one or two hours. If he called out that there was to be a court session, others would come in. Whether there was some important matter or not, he would have a private session with me and would say, 'What did you do last night, what did you eat and how did you sleep? I myself did so-and-so.' I would say to myself, 'What kind of a whim is this, that he holds a private session every day?' Till one day we were at Herat, and a very important matter came up overnight, and a letter arrived from the late Amir (i.e. Sultan Maḥmud). The matter was dealt with during the aforesaid private session and no-one got wind of it. He told me, 'I set aside a period for private talk every day on account of a day such as that.' I said to myself, 'How grossly mistaken I was! The Khwarazm Shah was perfectly right!'

"It was the same in Khwarazm. When Masʿadi's letter in code arrived, the next day, he had a private audience with me. This session became protracted, and he appeared despondent and wept, saying, 'May this gang of evil and vicious advisers be accursed, since they brought about the destruction of an incomparable man like ʿAli Qarib, as well as men like Ghāzi and Eryāruq! They nearly got me too at Shoburqān,[140] but the Most High and Blessed God preserved me. Now they have set their hands to the same sort of tricks and plots; but they don't realize that a man like the commander Monjuq will not be able to procure my downfall; and suppose I were to be overthrown, how could such an extensive province of the Sultan be preserved from enemies? Yet if they perpetrate a thousand such deeds, I will not tarnish my own good name and reputation,[141] for I have become old, and death may arrive at my door at any time.'

"I replied, 'It's exactly like you say, but we must show our teeth so as to make manifest our power and also to show the court [F 424] that the Khwarazm Shah is not asleep and that they cannot so easily and frequently encroach upon his power.' He said, 'When the commander Monjuq brings his rebellious pretensions [Gh 333] into the open, he must be arrested.' I replied, 'We must do something more drastic; a head into which a monarch like Masʿud has drummed delusions of becoming Khwarazm Shah must be chopped off, or else a very great deal of harm will ensue.' He said, 'But this would be a most infamous and degrading deed!' I replied, 'Let the lord leave this one to me!' He said, 'I have done so.'

"This private audience took place on a Thursday. The confidential letter in the Sultan's handwriting had reached the commander Monjuq and had made him feel extremely cocksure. He held that great feast on this same Thursday, and he engaged in a splendid celebration. On the Friday, the commander attended the formal audience of the Khwarazm Shah. He was drunk, and uttered much abuse and threatening words. The Khwarazm Shah endured this, although Tāsh Māhruy, the Khwarazm Shah's Commander-in-Chief, hurled insults back at him. I went to my house and prepared to deal with him. When he came up to me, as was the usual practice, since everyone used to come to me each Friday, I perceived him as puffed up and swollen-headed to an immeasurable degree. I began to confront him volubly and to chastise him, asking him why he failed to observe the bounds of polite behaviour towards the Khwarazm Shah and why he had hurled abuse. He flew into a rage—and he was a fellow by nature vain, foul-mouthed and highly conceited—and began raising his voice and hurling abuse. I clapped my hands, which was the pre-arranged signal for action, and a multitude of men from the Küjet came in and hacked him to pieces. The Khwarazm Shah only became aware of the news when the sound of the turmoil rose up from the town; for they had tied a rope around his feet and were dragging him along. I summoned the postal and intelligence officer's deputy, and gave him silver and clothing to send off that report which you have read. The Khwarazm Shah summoned me and said, 'O Aḥmad, what's happened?' I replied, 'We've taken the appropriate course of action.' He said, 'What will you tell the court?' I replied, 'I've seen to that,' and I told him what I had written. He said, 'You're a brave fellow!'[142] I replied, 'One cannot conduct oneself as a Khwarazm Shah in any other way! The event had a most awesome impact on everyone.' " [F 425]

Since the matter of this captive Bu Sahl Zowzani has come to its end, I considered it incumbent on myself to give the story of another captive.

Story

I have read that when the sage Bozorjmehr abandoned the religion of the Zoroastrians (*din-e gabragān*), since it was a faith full of defects, and embraced the religion of the Prophet Jesus, the blessings of God be upon him, he composed a testament (*vaṣiyyat*) for his co-religionists in the following terms:[143]

"I have read in the books that, at the end of time, a prophet will appear whose name is Moḥammad the Chosen One. [Gh 334] If I live long enough, I shall be the first person to join his faith; and if I do not live long enough, I am hopeful that at our gathering together for the Last Judgement we will be made part of his community (*ommat*). You likewise make the same testament to your children, so that you may attain Paradise." This news was brought to Kesrā Nushirvān. Kesrā wrote a letter to his governor, "Immediately you read this letter, send Bozorjmehr to the palace in heavy bonds and chains." The governor arrested him[144] according to the royal command. The news spread within Fārs that the prisoner would be taken away the following day. Men of learning were coming to Bozorjmehr and saying, "You replenished us from the fount of your knowledge and did not hold anything back until we became filled with learning; you were our shining star which showed us the way of right guidance; you were for us the pure water which quenched our thirst; and you were the fruit-laden orchard from which we plucked all kinds of fruit. The king is angry with you and they are taking you away. You are not one of those sages who would turn away from the way of right guidance, so give us a memento of your knowledge." [F 426]

He said, "I give you my testament, that you should recognize the unicity of the Almighty God and give Him obedience. Know that He sees your actions, good and evil alike, and He knows what you hold in your hearts. Your lives are according to His decree. When you reach your final destination, your return is to Him, and there will be a gathering-together for judgement and a resurrection, with questioning and responding (i.e. concerning men's actions on earth), rewards and punishment. Speak only good things and do good deeds, for the Almighty God, who created you, did so in order that you should do good. Take care not to do any evil and stay far away from the wicked, since those who wreak evil have but a short life. Be pure at heart, and keep your eyes and ears and hands and private parts from illicit pursuits and other people's chattels. Know that death is the final abode of life, and that although you may live long, you have to make your way there in the end. Put on the garment of modesty, which is the garment of the pious. Make it your custom to be veracious, for it preserves one's honour; men love those who speak the truth and such persons do not suffer perdition. Avoid telling lies, because a liar, even though he may give true testimony, is turned away. Envy diminishes a person, and the envious will never be at peace since he will be perpetually at war with the decree of God, mighty is His name, and envy will carry off people before their appointed time. The avaricious person is never at rest, for he may be seeking after things that have not been allotted to him. Keep your distance from women, for they consume wealth and destroy households. Whoever seeks purity in his own wife should not hanker after [Gh 335] other men's wives. Do not find fault with people; since no-one is faultless, the person who is oblivious to his own faults is the most ignorant of men. A good temper is the greatest of the gifts of the Almighty God; keep far away from an evil temper, for that places heavy shackles on heart and foot: a man with a foul temper is forever in great agony, while others, too, are in distress because of him. A good disposition is of value in this present world and the next one, and is worthy of praise in each of the two worlds. Whoever is greater than you in age, hold him in greater honour and take care to pay him due respect, and do not be disobedient towards him. Do not place your trust for everything in hope alone, to the extent that you neglect your work.

Those who constructed towns, villages, buildings and subterranean irrigation channels, and were anxious about the material concerns of this [F 427] world, have left it all behind and have passed on, and those works have become old and effaced. I have said enough, and I know that our next encounter will be on the Day of Resurrection."

When Bozorjmehr was brought into Kesrā's open courtyard, the latter gave orders, "Bring him before me just as he is, in bonds and fetters." When he was brought forward, Kesrā said, "O Bozorjmehr, what marks of honour and official ranks are left that you did not obtain as a result of our favourable opinion towards you? You reached the status of a vizier, and the government of our kingdom rested on you. Why did you abandon the faith of your fathers? As the great sage of the present age, why did you give out to the people that this monarch, the army and the subjects are not on the right path? Was it your intention to stir up the kingdom against me and to bring out both nobles and commoners alike in rebellion against me? I shall kill you in a manner that no sinner has ever been killed before, for your sin is a heinous one—unless, of course you repent and return to the faith of your ancestors and fathers so that you receive a pardon, for it will be a pity to kill a sage like you when there is none like you!"

Bozorjmehr replied, "May the king's life be prolonged! People call me the sage, the one possessing knowledge and the wise man of the age, but since I came out of the darkness into the light, I am not going back to the darkness and thereby become a man without knowledge and wisdom." Kesrā said, "I will order your head to be chopped off." Bozorjmehr replied, "The Judge before whom I shall go is just; He does not require testimony, but He inflicts retribution and will deprive you of His mercy." Kesrā became more angered than ever. He said, "Take him back (i.e. to the prison) until we give orders about what is to be done." He was taken back. When Kesrā's anger subsided, he said, "It would be a pity to bring about this man's destruction." He ordered him to be incarcerated in a chamber, very dark, like a tomb, [Gh 336] to be chained up with heavy iron fetters, to be clothed in a coarse woollen garment and to be allotted as his ration each day two pieces of barley bread, one pinch of salt and a pitcher of water. He appointed watchmen who were counting his very breaths and reporting them back to him.

He remained in these conditions for two years. One day, they heard no words from him. They informed Kesrā, who became worried, and ordered Bozorjmehr's dungeon to be opened up. They brought his friends and his family to him so that they might speak with him in the hope that [F 428] he might give an answer. They brought him forth into the light, and found him strong in body and unchanged in looks and bearing. They said, "O sage, we see you in thick, coarse wool, heavy fetters and in a confined, dark place. How is it that you retain your natural mien and a sturdier physique than before? What's the reason?" He answered, "I have made for myself a digestive composed of six things; each day I eat a little of it to stay like this." They said, "O sage, if you see fit, teach us about that electuary (*maʿjun*) so that, if something should happen to one of us or to one of our friends and such a situation comes up, it would be at hand." He replied, "First, I had firm trust that whatever God Most High may have decreed, will be. Second, I was content with His decree. Third, I have put on the shirt of fortitude, because there is nothing like fortitude for tribulation. Fourth, if I cannot endure patiently, I do not at any time let melancholy and impatience get a hold on me. Fifth, whenever I reflect that some created being is in a worse position than I, I give thanks. Sixth, I do not thus despair of the Almighty Lord, who from hour to hour gives hope of deliverance." They conveyed back to Kesrā what had occurred and what he had said. He said to himself, "How can one kill such a sage?" But in the end he ordered him to be killed and mutilated. Bozorjmehr went to Paradise and Kesrā to Hell.

I know that whoever reads this will not find fault with my bringing in this story, since it is not without value and the History becomes adorned by such tales. I now return to the thread of the narrative, *with God's will and help; success comes from God!*

[An account of the Khwarazm Shah's going, by way of the Bokhara road, to attack ʿAlitegin in Transoxania, and the Khwarazm Shah's death][145]

Having had Bu Sahl Zowzani placed in prison, Amir Masʿud had a private session with the Vizier Aḥmad b. Ḥasan on the topic of the Army Department, and who [F 429] should be appointed to assume responsibility for this charge. The Vizier replied, "Amongst the secretarial cadre, Bu Sahl Ḥamdavi is the most fitting." The Amir said, "We have appointed him to the office of Overseer of the Realm.[146] It is a most important charge, and we don't have anyone else like him. Another person must be found." [Gh 337] The Vizier replied, "The lord is well acquainted with other possible alternatives; whom does he designate?" The Amir said, "I like Bu'l-Fatḥ Rāzi, for he has worked for several years under you." The Vizier replied, "He is most presentable,[147] of good character and capable, but he has one fault: he is somewhat ponderous and over cautious, whereas this post requires wide vision and a vigorous approach."[148] The Amir said, "Assistants may be over-cautious and of limited vision, but when they become masters and gain recognition, they act quite differently. He must be summoned and must be made hopeful of receiving the post." The Vizier answered that he would do so.

When he went back he summoned Bu'l-Fatḥ Rāzi and talked privately with him and said, "Today, there has been discussion regarding you, and you were the Sultan's choice for heading the Army Department. I have known you and tried and tested you over a long period. You must have sought after this post without my own permission and prompting, and must have promised to make economies;[149] such things cannot be hidden from me, Aḥmad. In any case, I would have sought this post for you; but it would have been better if you had kept me informed; but all is well and I shall overlook this. One must act confidently and perform one's task correctly. In no circumstances will I accept cuts (i.e. in manpower and salaries) being made by reducing the size of the army, because it would lead to a breach in the realm's security and the harmful consequences of that would be great; but if you can track down the thefts and breaches of trust that have been perpetrated by Bu'l-Qāsem b. Kathir and his subordinates,[150] and can recover them for the treasury, you will have done a praiseworthy act of service." [F 430] He replied, "I have acted as the lord's (i.e. Aḥmad's) accounting officer for twenty years now, and he has put me to the test and found me upright. I used to observe breaches of trust taking place, and I wanted a good legacy and reputation to survive from during the time of the lord's vizierate. I therefore drew up a list of these economies and explained them in the royal presence. If your lofty judgement sees fit to overlook the fact that I did not bring them to your attention, no more errors like this will occur." Aḥmad said, "I have overlooked them; go back home; this office has been confirmed for you."

The next day, Saturday, Bu'l-Fatḥ was brought to the Royal Wardrobe, and he put on a robe of honour appropriate for the office of Head of the Department of the Army. As part of that outfit he girded on a belt of 700 [methqāls' weight of gold] and came forth, offered up service and went back to his house. The court notables and the army leaders paid the requisite gifts and presents to him in a praiseworthy manner. The next day, he came to the court and got a firm grip on the job. He was [Gh 338] a quick-witted and capable man, and while Khᵛāja Aḥmad b. Ḥasan was alive, he did not have an open field to himself; but when the Vizier passed away, he did have the field all to himself and set about making economies in the army, and because of that, many troubles ensued. I shall detail these one by one in their appropriate place.

At this time, confidential letters arrived from secret agents in Bokhara, with the information that ʿAlitegin is certainly not acting in a peaceable manner, but uttering threatening words and is preparing an army. He has two great grievances on his mind. The first is that the late Amir, Maḥmud, had the meeting with Qadïr Khān envisaging that the Khanate of Turkestan, with all its splendour, should pass from their house (i.e. of ʿAlitegin).[151] The second is that the present lord, Masʿud, had led him to hope, at a time when the Amir had not yet achieved full control over his realm, that if ʿAlitegin were to send a supporting army led by one of his sons, the lord would cede to him a province. But since things became settled and unity was achieved without any fighting or upheaval, and the throne passed to the lord without a rival contender, ʿAlitegin is bent on finding [F 431] an occasion to wreak mischief, although so long as the lord remains at Balkh he does not need to worry.[152]

When the Amir became apprised of this situation, he summoned the Grand Vizier Aḥmad b. Ḥasan and Bu Naṣr Moshkān to a private meeting to ask their opinion on this matter, and there was an exchange of views on all aspects. The Amir said, "ʿAlitegin is an implacable enemy with misguided ambitions. The best plan would be that he should be uprooted from Transoxania. If Qadïr Khān's son Bughrātegin, who is connected with us through matrimonial ties,[153] is able to intervene, he can be our deputy,[154] and we will send him our sister who is betrothed to him so that he will become an in-law of ours, and deputy, and thus we shall be rid of this opportunist ʿAlitegin. If Bughrātegin does not come, then we will give orders that the Khwarazm Shah Altuntāsh should head towards Transoxania with a powerful army, for Khwarazm is in a settled state (i.e. it can safely be left). A son of his with a contingent of troops can remain behind and will be sufficient[155] (i.e. for keeping control of Khwarazm)."

The Vizier replied, "Transoxania is a vast province. The Samanids, who were rulers of Khorasan, made their capital there.[156] If it comes into our possession, that will be a momentous achievement. But ʿAlitegin is a shrewd and wily person, and has been ruling there for the last thirty years. If the Amir has Altuntāsh in mind, it would be best for a very distinguished envoy to be sent to the Khwarazm Shah in order to convey a verbal message[157] about this proposal for an attack on ʿAlitegin. If he offers an excuse (i.e. for not leading this expedition to Transoxania), [Gh 339] and still harbours in his mind that episode of the commander Monjuq, this matter will have to be shelved, for without his military strength, ʿAlitegin cannot be overthrown. In that case, another course of action will have to be devised. On the other hand, if he seems eager to move (i.e. against Transoxania), [F 432] it would imply that that resentment no longer festers."

The Amir said, "This is the sensible course; who shall go as envoy?" Khᵛāja Bu Naṣr said, "We should send Amirak Beyhaqi, the postal and intelligence officer of Balkh, and if we wish the Khwarazm Shah to march forth, ʿAbdus should be sent as counsellor and administrator of the army."[158] The Amir said, "No-one else but him will do." ʿAbdus was summoned immediately, and my master wrote out the text of the letters in a most remarkable and distinctive style. A worthy robe of honour was ordered for the Khwarazm Shah, to be accompanied by five elephants, male and female, and other robes of honour for Khᵛāja Aḥmad b. ʿAbd al-Ṣamad and the Khwarazm Shah's immediate entourage[159] and for the royal courtiers and retainers. ʿAbdus left Balkh to go to the Khwarazm Shah. The Khwarazm Shah attacked ʿAlitegin and was killed. In that period, Sultan Masʿud dealt with several matters, all of high importance. Those will have to be set down, since this is the necessary task and way of procedure for history writing.

On Tuesday, 2 Rabiʿ I [/17 February 1032], the Amir went off towards Monjuqiyān[160] on a hunting expedition, and since the landscape was covered by a riot of colours, green, yellow and red (i.e. grass, wild flowers, etc.) it provided a fitting venue for a lavish festal display and he ordered the palace gholāms to set up awnings afar where he enjoyed a drinking session. He came back to the Garden in the last days of Rabiʿ I.

On 1 Rabiʿ II [/17 March 1032] some swift couriers sent by ʿAbdus arrived with the news that "Things are going according to plan. Altuntāsh put on the robe of honour and made preparations for going out to war."

The Amir had appointed the secretary Ṭāher to go off to Ray as counsellor and administrator of the army that was with the Commander-in-Chief Tāsh-Farrāsh. The postal and intelligence officer and the treasurer were also appointed. Ṭāher's robe of honour was got ready. The Amir gave the post of treasurer to the boon-companion Bu'l-Ḥasan Karaji [F 433] and that of postal and intelligence officer to Bu'l-Moẓaffar Ḥabashi,[161] and the appointment as Commander (*sālār*) there to the Keeper of the Treasury (*khazina-dār*) Gowhar-āyin. He gave appointments to the General and former Keeper of the Royal Wardrobe for Maḥmud, Yāruq-tughmush, and to several other men from amongst the generals and field officers from Qom, Kāshān, Jebāl and its surroundings. On Tuesday, 6 Rabiʿ II [/22 March 1032] [Gh 340], robes of honour were made ready, they donned them and came forward, and the Amir showed them marks of favour. On Thursday, the eighth of this month [/24 March 1032] they were sent off.

On this same day,[162] news arrived that Nushirvān, son of Manuchehr, had died in Gorgān, and it was said that Bā Kālijār, his maternal uncle, had plotted with the Great Chamberlain of Manuchehr and they had poisoned him—this child not having yet achieved puberty—so that Bā Kālijār might seize the royal power.[163] Letters had arrived in Ghaznin to the effect that "No male member of the house of Mardāviz and Voshmgir[164] has been left, on whom the royal power can be bestowed. It would be a fitting appointment if the lord Sultan were to retain as governor in this land Bā Kālijār, who was directing all affairs during Manuchehr's time." The answer went forth that "That was a sound course of action. At Mehragān, the exalted banner will set out for Balkh. Envoys should be sent so that what needs to be stipulated with them may be laid down."[165] When the Amir reached Balkh, Bu'l-Maḥāsen the leading personage[166] of Gorgān and Ṭabarestān arrived there, together with the Judge of Gorgān, Bu Moḥammad Besṭāmi, the Sharif Bu'l-Barakāt, a high-ranking Deylamite and Shiraj Leyli (?), and they were brought into the court. Then the Grand Vizier embarked on arranging the issues at hand: the amirate was to be assumed by Bā Kālijār and he was to send his daughter from Gorgān.[167] My master wrote out the fair copy of the investiture patent for Bā Kālijār, and a very splendid robe of honour [F 434] was made up and entrusted to the envoys, who themselves were given robes of honour. An order was given to Ṭāher that he was to seek out the arrears of stipulated tribute and what had just now been stipulated, and send it all to Nishapur to Suri, the head of the Divān, so that it might be conveyed to the capital with the taxation yield of Nishapur.[168]

On the eighteenth of this month (Rabi' II [/3 April 1032]), a letter arrived with the news that the mother of Bu Naṣr Moshkān had passed away. She was a wise woman. My master once told me that "At the time when Sultan Maḥmud, having made Ḥasanak his vizier, had fallen out with him, despite the affection he had held for him, my mother said to me, 'Look, my son, when the Sultan bestows the vizierate on someone, in spite of his affection for him, within a week he will regard him as a foe; for the Vizier will become his co-partner in the realm, and kingship cannot be shared'." Bu Naṣr remained at home to receive condolences, and the due ceremonies of mourning were carried out with due decorum. The Grand Vizier arrived to offer his sympathies, and his eye caught sight of the ornamental garden there,[169] which resembled Paradise with its profusion of blossoming jasmine and other sweet-smelling plants, myrtle, narcissus and cypress trees. He said to Bu Naṣr, "Had we not come here on such a sad occasion (i.e. the death of Bu Naṣr's mother), we would have done justice to this garden with our merry-making, [Gh 341] just as in the same way, in Sultan Maḥmud's time, we enjoyed the ornamental garden at Ghaznin." They brought his horse to the side of the portico where the mourning ceremonies were being held, and he mounted. Bu Naṣr kissed his stirrup and said, "May the lord live long! Your gracious visit here is a source of lasting pride for me, and it will not be surprising if this garden acquires that same auspiciousness that the garden at Ghaznin had." Although the Amir had sent a message of sympathy through Bu'l-Ḥasan ʿAqili, he himself graciously reiterated his condolences when, on the Wednesday, Bu Naṣr went to render service at the court.

[The story of the garden at Ghaznin and the Vizier's coming to it][170]

I am relating the story of the garden at Ghaznin and the Vizier's coming to it, for one thing because it illustrates the high status [F 435] of my master, to whom a vizier[171] of such eminence as Aḥmad b. Ḥasan came in order to give condolences and offer up prayers. I heard from my master that the late Amir, Maḥmud, one day held a wine-drinking banquet at Ghaznin, and large numbers of roses had been brought. At dawn, I sent to the Amir all the hundred-petalled roses which had just bloomed in my garden, and went on myself afterwards to render service. The Grand Vizier, the courtiers and retainers then arrived. The Amir was engaged in wine-drinking. He kept back the Vizier and myself, and great jollifications went on. Towards noon, the Vizier said, "May the lord's life be prolonged! It is a custom, on occasions like this when the season for the roses to blossom comes round, to drink a special bumper of wine,[172] since they are our guests for only forty days, especially when the roses are like these, matchless in colour and fragrance." The Amir replied, "Bu Naṣr has sent them from his own garden." The Vizier said, "One should see this garden!" The Amir said, "Are you fishing for an invitation?" He said, "Of course." The Amir turned towards me and said, "What do you have to say about this?" I replied, "May the lord's life be prolonged! Foxes do not have the temerity to go out hunting with cheetahs for fear of enraging the lion. My hands are tied." The Amir said, "What if the lion gives his permission?" I answered, "In that case, yes, it can be done." He said, "I have given permission; you must do it." Both of the two eminent officials expressed their obedience. They brought in bumpers of wine, and a lively celebration got under way, and the wine-drinking session came to its end. A week later, my master spoke to the Sultan and received permission, and Khᵛāja Aḥmad came to the garden. A splendid and extensive reception had been prepared. At the time of the afternoon worship, the Amir sent Bu'l-Ḥasan ʿAqili there with a verbal message, saying, "You must keep Bu'l-Ḥasan there, and we have ordered that tomorrow, [F 436] at first light, there should be wine-drinking, for at dawn the garden is at its best." Both of the masters were made joyful by this act of favour, and the next day, great festivities took place, and then at the time of the afternoon worship, they all dispersed. [Gh 342]

On Tuesday, the twentieth of this month (Rabiʿ II [/5 April 1032]), a letter from ʿAbdus arrived by swift riders with the message that "The Khwarazm Shah has marched from Khwarazm to the vicinity of Āmuy and has sent me back to the court, according to the plan." The next day, the Sultan mounted and came out to the open plain, and began to inspect the commander and the army that had been appointed to join up with Altuntāsh. Up to the time for the afternoon worship, the cavalrymen, with their complete equipment and weapons, went past in review, together with a numerous force of infantry, said to number 15,000. When the army had gone past in its formations, the Amir called out to these two commanders, Begtegin Chowgāni, one of Maḥmud's former commanders (*pedari*),[173] and Masʿud's own commander (*masʿudi*) the Master of the Royal Stables Böri,[174] and to the senior officers, "Be alert and vigilant, and prevent the troops from imposing on the populace, whether on home ground or within enemy territory, so that they do not commit acts of injustice (i.e. restrain them from plundering). When you reach the Commander-in-Chief Altuntāsh, serve him well and obey his commands and never oppose him in any way." They all replied, "We obey!", dismounted, kissed the ground before the Sultan and rode off. The postal and intelligence officer Amirak Beyhaqi was seconded to act as postal and intelligence officer for that army.[175] The Amir summoned him into his presence, and held a private session with the Vizier and Bu Naṣr Moshkān, and issued instructions on all sorts of topics. Amirak too took his formal leave and went off.

On Monday, 1 Jomādā of this year [/15 April 1032], ʿAli Dāya was brought to the Royal Wardrobe and dressed in a robe of honour appropriate for the office of Commander-in-Chief, since the Grand Vizier had said that there was no person of senior status more outstanding than he and that he had weapons, equipment, troops and gholāms. He was garbed in a robe of honour of the quality which, according to ancient custom, was bestowed on Commanders-in-Chief. He went back homewards, and people came to pay their respects to him in a handsome fashion. The next day, he set off towards Khorasan with 4,000 cavalrymen from the royal army, who were all instructed to obey the commands of Tāsh Farrāsh and those of the secretary Ṭāher, and to take up their positions at Ṭus and act as a supporting force for those troops.[176] [F 437] ʿAli Dāya was to maintain the morale of the troops and ensure that no crisis arose in Khorasan.

A letter in code arrived from Amirak to the effect that "When the Khwarazm Shah saw the army despatched by the Sultan, he was at first stricken with fear that ʿAlitegin had his forces deployed for action. He drew back, and had brought back the boats from the middle of the Oxus,[177] until his counsellor and administrator Aḥmad b. ʿAbd al-Ṣamad put fresh heart into him. Nevertheless, the Khwarazm Shah still appears [Gh 343] like someone beset by anxieties, and I made a point of visiting him frequently until he appeared somewhat calmer. Let us hope that it will all end well, for at the outset at least, things look gloomy." The Vizier said, "The Khwarazm Shah did not turn back, but carried on; this task will be accomplished and will not give rise to any calamities."

Couriers of the postal and intelligence service had been stationed on the road to Balkh with the aim of intercepting news. Every day, a courier was arriving. Then towards noon a despatch bag arrived fastened with a ring and sealed,[178] with a message to the effect that "When the Khwarazm Shah crossed the Oxus, ʿAlitegin got news of it. He entrusted the city of Bokhara to the ghāzis of Transoxania, and took with him to Dabusi his treasury and the lighter equipment, with the intention of making a stand there. He ordered 150 of his élite gholāms to garrison and guard the citadel there. When the Khwarazm Shah heard this, he sent ten senior officers with a cavalry force to attack Bokhara, while he himself went with the [main] army formation and seized control of the roads to the left and the right so that no attacks from ambushes could take place. When he reached Bokhara, ʿAlitegin's military governor there fled to Dabusi, and the ghāzis of Transoxania and the townspeople came forward offering their obedience, showed submission to the exalted empire of the Ghaznavids and stated that they had long wished to become subjects of the Most Mighty Sultan, the Monarch of Islam, Shehāb al-Dowla. The Khwarazm Shah showed them favour, and gave orders [F 438] that the citadel was to be invested and taken by force of arms. Seventy choice Turkish gholāms fell into his hands; they were kept in one group so that they could be sent to the exalted court. The citadel and fortress[179] were plundered, and a vast amount of booty and beasts of burden fell into the troops' hands. The next day, the Khwarazm Shah set out for Dabusi. Spies arrived with the news that "ʿAlitegin has brought a large army, comprising his own troops as well as the Turkmens and Seljuqs[180] and a locally-raised militia,[181] and is intending to give battle at Dabusi, which is adjacent to Ṣaghāniyān[182] and is a terrain suitable for ambushes, with many trees and streams. Victory and divinely-aided success will result for the exalted empire!"

The Amir had ordered a dais to be erected on the other side of the Garden facing the elevated pavilion (*khażrā*). It was a very lofty and broad dais, with appropriate height, and it overlooked the Garden. Before it was a large pool, and there was an extensive open space such that the troops could draw up there in two ranks facing each other. It had taken a considerable amount of time for it to be erected, but now it was completed. The Khᵛāja [Abu] ʿAbdallāh al-Ḥoseyn b. ʿAli b. Mikāʾil[183] had been ordered [Gh 344] to ensure that the work of construction was well done, since the Amir intended to hold court on this new dais on Tuesday, 18 Jomādā I [/2 May 1032]. On this day, he held a public audience there, and so many offerings of money were presented that they appeared limitless. After holding court, the Amir mounted and rode to the review ground nearby, and they played polo and practiced archery. Meanwhile, a magnificent feast was prepared and brought on to the dais. The Amir went from the review ground to the bathhouse and from there to the feast. The notables and other dignitaries were summoned to the spread, [F 439] and began to eat. Wine was handed round, and they came away from the feast well intoxicated. The Amir took a siesta. Masses of flowers were brought in. Royal orders had been given that those present were not to return home because a session of wine-drinking was to follow.

My master came from the flower garden to the Divān. The despatch bag from Amirak Beyhaqi arrived fastened by a ring and sealed.

My master opened it and the colour drained away from his face. It was the practice that, when letters used to arrive, he would write a note and would give it to Bu Naṣr, the Guard of the Divān,[184] for transmission to the household servant. If it was important, he would entrust it to me. He took up this confidential letter himself and bore it to the Amir's private servant, Āghāji.[185] Āghāji relayed the information. They were summoned and he entered. The musicians and singers were dismissed and the Grand Vizier summoned. The Amir came forth from the palace and had a private session with them until the time of the afternoon worship. The Vizier went back and my master resumed his place in the Divān. He sent for me and I began to make a copy of the letter. It was from Amirak Beyhaqi, and ran as follows:[186]

When Altuntāsh reached Dabusi, ʿAlitegin's vanguard came into view. He ordered the large kettledrums to be beaten and trumpets to be sounded. He moved forward with his forces in full formation, and they encamped facing the enemy with a wide river between them.[187] A short, sharp engagement[188] took place, and both the sections of the army which were in advance positions received reinforcements. The army of Altuntāsh halted and encamped during the interval between the two worships (i.e. the noon and afternoon ones), and the vanguards fell back. The Khwarazm Shah stood on an eminence, summoned all the commanders and leaders and addressed them [Gh 345] thus, "Come what may, there will be a battle tomorrow. Return to your positions, and be vigilant tonight. If any noise of military activity is heard, don't become fearful and don't leave your positions, for I have taken due precautions in devising a subterfuge and in maintaining a vanguard, and I have prepared for war so that, when the enemy appears, we will be in full control of the situation." [F 440]

He took with him Amirak Beyhaqi[189] for a meal, and the counsellor and administrator (i.e. Aḥmad b. ʿAbd al-Ṣamad) and his close retainers were summoned. When he had finished eating, he had a private session with Aḥmad, the Commander-in-Chief Tāsh [Māhruy] and several of the *sarhangs* who had been in Sultan Maḥmud's service, saying, "This ʿAlitegin is a serious foe. He remained quiescent on account of his fear of the late Sultan. Subsequently, and when order had been restored, he was given hopes of gains; had those hopes been fulfilled, this man would not have embarked on a policy of wreaking havoc and would not have displayed his opposition. When the secret agents wrote that he was making trouble, the lord Sultan sent 'Abdus to me and issued orders on this matter. What alternative had I but to carry out the orders, since those mischief-makers had already blackened my reputation with the Amir? Now, the matter has come to the sword. Tomorrow's battle will be a fierce one, and I am not one to take to my heels. If events take a wrong turn, I shall not take myself back to Khwarazm, and if I am killed, it will be no matter, as I shall find martyrdom in the lord's service. But the rights of my ancient service should be observed in regard to my sons." They all answered, "If God Most High so wills, things will go well and there will be a victory."

Then he gave orders that advance guards should go out to all four quarters and that all the precautions given out by the chief commander, and relayed, should be carried out. The commanders and leaders went back. The enemy launched attacks on several occasions, there was a great clamour, and the enemy retreated with their tails between their legs.

When dawn gleamed, the Khwarazm Shah stood on an eminence with his generals and senior commanders around him and with the army formations drawn up in their places. He said, "O noble comrades! When day [F 441] breaks, a very insolent and crafty enemy will come forward, and he has a united and single-minded army; they will fight with their very lives. We have come to take their lives [Gh 346] and possessions and to uproot them for good. Be sharp-witted and vigilant, and keep your eyes fixed on my battle standard in the centre, for I shall be there personally. If, God forbid, you drag your feet, disaster will ensue. The mighty Oxus lies before you, and Khwarazm as a bolt-hole is very far away. In truth, I myself shall never take to flight, and if you desert me, you will have subsequently to face the lord [Sultan]. What I know, I have said." They replied. "The Khwarazm Shah has done us justice, and we will lay down our lives."

The Khwarazm Shah stood in the centre, and he designated the most doughty of the army's troops who were on the flanks to take up their places adjacent to the centre so that, if need should arise for troops on the right flank or the left flank, he could direct them there. He told Begtegin Chowgāni and the Master of the Royal Stables Böri to take up their positions on the right wing with a very strong force.

He held his Commander-in-Chief Tāsh on the left flank together with some troops from the army sent by the Sultan (i.e. the army sent from Balkh to join Altuntāsh). He stationed a strong rearguard behind each flank. He ordered five valiant *sarhang*s with their crack troops to hack in two any man deserting from the army, and he set about despatching the choicest of the cavalry to face the vanguard.[190]

At daybreak, the large kettledrums were beaten and the trumpets sounded, and a clamour rose up. The Khwarazm Shah went forward with his army formation. When they had proceeded a parasang along the river bank, the water became fordable,[191] and therefore presented a strategically dangerous spot. A group of cavalrymen from the vanguard galloped back to bring the news that ʿAlitegin had crossed the water and had taken up his position on a very extensive plain, with the river and a thick grove of trees on one side and, on the other side, his army stretching into the distance, and it was here that the battle was going to take place. They were relating that ʿAlitegin had made three places for ambushes in the direction of his baggage and impedimenta and his rearguard, with the intention of advancing from the river bank and creating a diversion from behind. Although the Khwarazm Shah [F 442] had stationed his counsellor and administrator with the baggage and impedimenta and with a strong rearguard, he now sent back one thousand each of cavalrymen and infantrymen in order that they should be ready to withstand that group of ʿAlitegin's troops. He hurriedly despatched some troop commanders (*naqib*s) to Aḥmad and the rearguard, and he gave a verbal message to the senior commanders who were drawn up on the bank of the river to put them in the picture as well. Then Altuntāsh moved forward, and the troops engaged with each other. He took with him Amirak to act as an observer and bear witness to his conduct, and he stationed Amirak, with himself, on an eminence. From his red banner and ceremonial parasol they spotted ʿAlitegin also standing on raised ground.

The two armies became locked in battle, [Gh 347] and there was a furious engagement, the like of which, so the Khwarazm Shah said, he could not recall during the whole of his lifetime. ʿAlitegin's right wing launched an attack on the Khwarazm Shah's left wing around the time of the midday worship, they pressed hard and the Khwarazm Shah's troops took to flight. The Khwarazm Shah raised a shout and despatched reinforcements from the centre. They were unable to stand fast, and the army's left wing fell back in retreat. Only his Commander-in-Chief Tāsh Māhruy was left; 200 of his cavalrymen were driven into the river and all of them perished.[192] The Khwarazm Shah sent his right wing against the enemy's left wing, and they stood firm in a commendable manner. The enemy fought very bravely, and as a result, large numbers were killed and wounded on both sides, and the army's right wing fell back. The General Begtegin Chowgāni and the Master of the Royal Stables Böri with their force of 500 cavalry were wading into the fray. The numerically superior enemy attacked them, and there was a danger that they might all be killed. The Khwarazm Shah and the centre advanced from their position and launched an assault on ʿAlitegin's centre, joined by Begtegin and Böri with the cavalry force which had been driven back. ʿAlitegin likewise moved forward to attack with his centre and left wing. The Khwarazm Shah seized a lance and dashed forward. When the troops saw his standard, they rushed forward like a mountain of iron, and so many from each side were killed that the cavalry found it difficult to manoeuvre. Both armies fought on unrelentingly until nightfall, when [F 443] they disengaged from each other, so that the outcome of the battle remained unresolved. If the Khwarazm Shah had not taken to battle himself, that mighty army would have been wiped out.

An arrow had struck the Khwarazm Shah and had penetrated the very spot where a stone from amongst those hurled from a fortress in India had hit his left leg.[193] But behold his courage! He felt the pain, but did not show any sign of it on the battlefield. He ordered one of his gholāms to extract the arrow, and he bound up the wound. When he reached the army encampment, he found the troops and retainers (i.e. those of the rearguard and those detailed to guard the baggage and impedimenta) stood fast in their place, no disaster having occurred. He put fresh heart into those who had been pushed back and kept them stationed in their positions.[194] Although the enemy had several times tried to draw them into ambushes, his counsellor and administrator Khᵛāja Aḥmad and those troops and retainers who had been deployed there had taken care and had averted any possible disaster. The Khwarazm Shah praised them warmly, and although he was wounded, no-one got to know about it. He summoned the senior commanders and dismounted from his steed. He rebuked some of them [Gh 348] and they offered their apologies, which he accepted and said, "Go back, and return at dawn well prepared, so that we can polish off the enemy decisively, for they have been battered, and had it not been for the onset of night, we would have clinched the victory." They replied, "We'll do so."

He kept back Aḥmad and myself, Amirak Beyhaqi, and said, "This army would have been wiped out today had I not dug in my heels and stood fast, and had I not hazarded my life.[195] But an arrow hit me in the very same place that a stone once struck. Nevertheless, I shall take the field tomorrow regardless." Aḥmad said, "It is inadvisable to go into battle in a wounded state. It may well be that for some reason [F 444] a lull will occur in the middle of the fighting, depending on what the enemy is up to: for I have sent out spies who will return before dawn." Altuntāsh sent out scouts, men who had had a period of rest, and I myself went back.

At daybreak, a man came and summoned me urgently. I hurried to Altuntāsh. He said, "All night I was unable to sleep on account of this wound. Just an hour ago, the spies came in and reported that ʿAlitegin was in a very parlous and troubled state because he had lost so many men, and is resolved to send envoys and discuss peace terms. Nevertheless, although this is the case, we have no choice but to use subterfuge, mount our horses and go forward."[196] Aḥmad said, "What does the Khᵛāja (i.e. the narrator Amirak) say?" I replied, "The leading commanders of the army should be summoned and it should be given out that we will go forth to battle, so that the army should mount. Then we should quickly send someone forward who will return from the direction of the enemy's lines to where our own vanguard is stationed, with the information that the enemy will not come forward to fight since an envoy is to be sent. Thus the Khwarazm Shah can have a respite, and then we shall see what the position is." The Khwarazm Shah answered, "That's a good plan." The prominent leaders and senior commanders were summoned; they saw the Khwarazm Shah and then went back, and they stood ready on their mounts.

The large kettledrums giving the signal for battle were beaten. The Khwarazm Shah called for his horse, and mounted it with some effort. The horse made a sharp movement, and by an ill chance he fell off right on the side of his wound and broke his hand. They bore him secretly into the camp enclosure, to his private tent, and laid him on his bed. His senses ebbed away. He summoned Aḥmad and Amirak and said, "This has come upon me, and I am only able to see to myself. Do what you think is best, so that the enemy doesn't get his wish and this army of ours is not wiped out." Aḥmad wept and said, "Things will turn out better than the lord thinks, these matters will be taken care of." He brought Amirak to the army, [Gh 349] and told them that "There will be no fighting today; it is being said that 'Alitegin has been hurt and will send an envoy. Despatch a succession of scouting parties to the opponents' camp. [F 445]. If the enemy offers battle, we should mount our steeds and wade into the fray; but if they send an envoy, then a decision should be made on the basis of an appraisal of the situation at that time." They replied, "That's a very good plan." They set out, large kettledrums were beaten and they were keeping a keen lookout.

This old wolf, Aḥmad, had observed the fighting of the previous day and the weakened condition of his master, and during the night had sent someone to 'Alitegin's counsellor and administrator, Maḥmud Bik. He had conveyed a verbal message with a proposition and had said, "This audacious conduct and transgression started with you, as a result of which the Sultan sent the Khwarazm Shah here. When we crossed the Oxus river, it would have been advisable and the wiser course if your master had sent an envoy and had sought pardon for those impertinent words and high-handed conduct that had offended the Sultan, so that the Khwarazm Shah could have intervened, interceded on his behalf and set things right, and so much blood would not have been spilt. But Fate took a hand. I am not saying all this from a position of weakness, for you have already had a taste of our might, and the lord Sultan is at Balkh and our troops and reinforcements are lined up one after the other. We counsellors and administrators are agents acting for the great men; we have an obligation to keep an eye on the public weal. Although the Khwarazm Shah is unaware of what I have said, and if he knew, I should be in deep trouble, yet I do not wish any more blood to be shed. I have discharged my obligations as a Muslim and what is due from our presence in this land; you should do whatever you know to be the best course for yourselves."

'Alitegin's counsellor and administrator and 'Alitegin himself regarded the message as offering a favourable opportunity, and that same night designated an envoy, a distinguished 'Alid from the important families of Samarqand and they gave him messages. Towards noon of this day, the army had mounted in its formations. The envoy arrived, and Aḥmad told the Khwarazm Shah what he had done without his knowledge. Although his injuries were all-consuming, [F 446] and he was to leave this world that very night, he responded, "O Aḥmad, I am gone! My sons must not suffer any harm from this, should the Sultan say that I was in league with ʿAlitegin." Aḥmad replied, "We have passed beyond this stage. The best course is to follow what I have arranged so that we can make peace and leave here in safety towards Āmuy and cross to the other side of the Oxus. Then I shall set the record straight. A trusted confidant of the Sultan's like Amirak is here, and what has happened is as clear as daylight. [Gh 350] If action like this had not been taken, we would have been in deep trouble. The Khwarazm Shah must now endure for an hour the discomfort of sitting formally and receiving the envoy." The Khwarazm Shah put on his boots and cap and came to the great tent, and the gholāms, a great throng of retainers, troops and prominent persons stood by. The envoy came into his presence, kissed the ground, and was given a seat close to the Khwarazm Shah. They talked of making peace. The envoy said, "ʿAlitegin says, 'The late lord Sultan used to address me as his son, and when this present Sultan, Masʿud, marched against his brother and against Ghaznin, I offered him the services of my troops and my son; is this my reward now! Since the Khwarazm Shah is now the most senior and venerated figure of the realm, I shall forget what has passed in order to appease the Sultan. He should proceed to the Oxus, encamp there with his army and act as intercessor, so that the lord Sultan may accept my excuse and a state of goodwill obtain, as existed in the time of the late lord Sultan, and no more blood be shed.' "

The Khwarazm Shah replied, "He has spoken with great fairness. I shall see that these things are done and will perform this act of good will. The war has ended. We will head for the Oxus and encamp there." The ʿAlid offered up invocations for Altuntāsh, and they brought him back to the tent and seated him there. The Khwarazm Shah said to Begtegin, the Master of the Royal Stables Böri and the other commanders, "What do you have to say, and what are your views?" They answered, "The lord Sultan's command is that we should follow the Khwarazm Shah and follow his orders. Our one-horse troopers (*yak-sovāragān*) were badly mauled [F 447] and were driven away with such ignominy; had not the Khwarazm Shah stood firm like that and been prepared to fight to his last breath, an irretrievable disaster would have occurred. The Khwarazm Shah has been wounded and many men have been killed." He cut them short, "Don't get involved in talk and discussion at this moment, but whether riding or on foot, maintain your formations, use maximum caution and post advance look-outs on all four sides, for one should never feel safe and secure from the enemy's wiles." They replied, "We'll do so."

The Khwarazm Shah got up, but his weakness grew worse, and he had three spasms of diarrhoea. He summoned Aḥmad and said, "I am near my end. Settle the matter of the envoy more quickly." Aḥmad wept and came out of the camp enclosure and sat down in the great tent. He bestowed on the envoy a fine robe of honour and fitting largesse, and sent him on his way. He also sent with the envoy a quick-witted, eloquent man from amongst his trusted retainers, and they agreed that, when the 'Alid reached 'Alitegin, he should send back our own envoy. 'Alitegin should have retreated one stage back [Gh 351] before our envoy's return. We will likewise travel a stage's journey towards Āmuy in the course of tonight.

The army halted to encamp, and look-outs were designated for all four directions. The Khwarazm Shah's dysentery and weakness grew worse. He summoned the household servant (*khādem*) Shakar,[197] the major-domo of the palace, and said, "Send for Aḥmad." When he saw Aḥmad he said, "I am gone. It's not the time for grief and there should be no weeping. Death comes as the end for all men. You people should stand shoulder-to-shoulder and so contrive that my death remains a secret tonight and tomorrow. If, when you have travelled one stage, it becomes known publicly, you can act according to the situation. For if, God forbid, news of my death should reach 'Alitegin before you cross over the Oxus, [F 448] you and this army will experience what you have never before experienced in your lives. When Amirak goes with the army to the court and enters the sultan's presence, he should relate fully all that has happened to me, explaining that, although there is nothing dearer than one's life, I sacrificed mine in furtherance of the Sultan's interests, and I hope that, in recognition of my services, he will look after my sons. I have no strength left for any more words, and am occupied now in yielding up my life and uttering my last words as a devout believer."[198]

Aḥmad and Shakar wept. They came out, and began making the necessary arrangements. At the time of the afternoon worship, the Khwarazm Shah was in such a state that no more hope was left. Aḥmad went to his own large tent, summoned the troop commanders and gave the message for the army that "Peace has been firmly established. 'Alitegin has covered a stage in the direction of Samarqand, and by the time of the night worship the envoy reached our advanced post, and the advance guard has been sent back, since the Khwarazm Shah intends to make a move.[199] Wait for the signal of the large kettledrums. The right wing,[200] the vanguard and the rearguard should go along with their arms ready and in battle formation, since, despite the peace agreement, we are in enemy territory and we cannot afford to feel secure from the foe." The senior commanders were in agreement with this.

This is the final goal of all mankind, as the poet has said,

1. *Indeed, a man who has travelled along for seventy years to a watering place is near to drinking his last.*[201]

The truly wise man is that person who seeks out contentment with his lot and temperance, for naked came he into this world and naked will he depart from it.[202] There appears in the historical traditions the following: "*He who sets out with faith in his heart is preserved in sound bodily health and has with him his daily sustenance; it is as if he acquired for himself the goods of the entire present world*".[203] May God Most High grant the favour of acts of beneficence, and may He procure for us the fortune of happiness in this world and the next![204] [F 449]

When the Khwarazm Shah died, it was not possible to make a coffin and its appurtenances, for fear of the news of his death becoming public. [Gh 352] They got ready the elephant litter and, before dawn, laid him in the litter, and posted there an attendant to hold him, and they gave out publicly that "He can't ride on a saddle because of his wound, and is travelling in the litter for comfort and ease." But the news of his death had spread amongst his own gholāms. The household servant Shakar ordered the large kettledrums to be beaten, and the whole of the army, with its weapons, in its battle formation and with numerous lit torches, set off, so that by the time of the dawn worship, seven parasangs had been covered, and the personal tent (*kheyma*), the large tent (*khargāh*) and the large camp enclosure (*sarāy-parda-ye bozorg*) had been erected. He was brought down from the elephant, and the news of his death spread about generally. Aḥmad and the household servant Shakar summoned a few people, including close retainers, the physician and the judge of the army, and instructed them to set about washing the corpse and preparing the coffin.

Aḥmad sent away the troop commanders and summoned the leading personages of the army, telling them that there was a message from the Khwarazm Shah: each commander was to bring a contingent of the army with him. They all came, fully armed, and the troops halted there. Aḥmad bade the commanders dismount, and he talked to them in private and related to them what he had arranged before the Khwarazm Shah's death, that is, his writing to ʿAlitegin's counsellor, his sending an envoy and the peace agreement, up to the stage they had reached at present. The commanders bitterly lamented the Khwarazm Shah's death and lavished high praise on Aḥmad, and they said, "We must now get ourselves to Āmuy as speedily as possible." The Khᵛāja replied, "ʿAlitegin appears in a bruised and crestfallen condition. Today he is twenty parasangs away from us, and by the time news of the Khwarazm Shah's death reaches him we shall have reached Āmuy. Some of the more bold and brazen of the Khwarazm Shah's gholāms have got wind of his death. I have put you to this trouble and brought you here so that you might exercise complete control and restraint over them.[205] We should mount at the time of the afternoon worship and ride all night so that we can reach the river by daylight and strive to cross the Oxus very speedily." They replied that it was a well thought-out plan and that they would all obey his command and whatever he decreed. He sent for the household servant Shakar and told him [F 450] to summon the Khwarazm Shah's senior officers. When these commanders arrived, he asked them to be seated, but they were too respectful and mindful of Aḥmad's status, hence reluctant to sit down in his presence, and he had to insist vigorously until they agreed to sit down.

He said, "You know how hard the Khwarazm Shah strove so that you could attain to your present rank and status. He passed away last night—for death comes to all men—but the lord [Gh 353] Sultan, may he live long, is alive and well. The Khwarazm Shah has worthy and able sons, and he himself did much valuable service. When these leading commanders of the Sultan's army and Amirak, who are the Sultan's trusted confidants, arrive at the court and set forth what has happened, the Sultan will install one of the Khwarazm Shah's capable sons in his father's place and send him to Khwarazm. It was on this assumption that I have made the peace agreement with ʿAlitegin, who is now far away from us. We shall depart at the time of the afternoon worship in order to reach Āmuy very quickly. The chief commanders of the Sultan's army will make for Balkh and we for Khwarazm. If you pledge your word to me and persuade the palace gholāms to act sensibly, when we reach Āmuy, largesse will be distributed from the Khwarazm Shah's treasury. You will thus preserve your good reputation and will not be dishonoured. But if—God forbid!—you act in an unruly fashion and stir up a tumult, you know how you fare in numbers;[206] within the space of an hour these 6,000 cavalrymen and personal retainers would despatch you to the next world. Even if a handful of you nevertheless manages to join up with ʿAlitegin, you will have no prestige left in his sight nor any assurance of a safe haven. I am not mincing my words[207] so that there can be no illusions about this. All the leading commanders who are sitting here are of one accord with me on this," and he turned to the assembly, saying, "You're all of the same accord?" They replied, "We all follow your orders obediently."[208]

Aḥmad made them swear binding oaths, and they went away and spoke with the gholāms. The whole body of gholāms raised a riot, made a din and ran for their horses and arms. These senior officers mounted their steeds, and Aḥmad ordered[209] the troops to mount en masse. When the gholāms saw this, they debated with their own commanders for a while, and the commanders came to Aḥmad and said that an agreement had been arrived at: they were seeking an undertaking from the exalted Khᵛāja Aḥmad [F 451] and a sworn oath that he would not harm them but treat them with exactly the same consideration as in the Khwarazm Shah's time. The Khᵛāja Aḥmad replied that this was just and proper that they would be treated with even greater consideration than in the Khwarazm Shah's time. They went to-and-fro, and Aḥmad swore the required oath, but told them that they would be deprived of their horses for this one night only and should ride on camels, then the next day, their horses would be given back to them; and this arrangement would only be done for this first stage. They thought about it for a while, and finally they agreed in the following manner, saying that they would be obedient to the Khᵛāja's orders on condition that out of every tent of ten gholāms, one gholām should ride a horse and travel with the field officers so that they would feel secure.

Aḥmad assented and expressed his approval. On this basis, they went back, had something to eat, got prepared and ready, rode all night and halted the next morning; but the horses were not given back to the gholāms, and they were proceeding in this way till they crossed the Oxus [Gh 354] and reached Āmuy, where Amirak Beyhaqi remained.[210] Aḥmad said, "Since this mighty army has arrived back safely, I had the intention of coming to the exalted court at Balkh; but the news of recent events will reach Khwarazm, and it will be a formidable task to maintain order there. Relate to the Sultan what you know, and the monarch will ordain favourable consideration, out of recognition of this ancient house's due." They all showered praise on Khᵛāja Aḥmad and bade him farewell. Khᵛāja Aḥmad ordered the gholāms to be given back their horses. I myself had prepared a résumé of this confidential letter; I prepared this detailed version for the exalted judgement to study, if God Most High so wills.[211]

These stories may appear out of place in a typical chronicle. For most historians record how a certain king sent a certain commander to a certain battle, and on such-and-such day they made peace, and this one beat that one, or that one beat this one, and they leave it at that;[212] but I intend to perform my duty to the full.[213] [F 452]

[When Amirak's despatch reached Balkh,] the Grand Vizier and my master were in a private conclave. They sent for the two Bu'l-Ḥasans, Bu'l-Ḥasan b. ʿAbdallāh and Bu'l-Ḥasan b. ʿAbd al-Jalil, and I was also present. Letters were composed. [First,] to Amirak Beyhaqi, with the instruction that he was to come on ahead of the army. [Second,] Begtegin and Böri were ordered to stay at Kālef and Zam[214] and to ensure that our army did not harass the populace, and they were informed that Moḥammad Aʿrābi[215] was coming to take up his position at Āmuy with the army of Kurds and Arabs. [Third,] a letter went to the Amir of Chaghāniyān with a full exposition of these events, so that he might be on the alert that ʿAlitegin was going to send an envoy and that he should accept his approach in order to avoid any mischief being generated.[216] [Fourth,] a letter went to the Khᵛāja Aḥmad b. ʿAbd al-Ṣamad—previously, he had the official form of address of "Our Sheykh" (*Sheykhonā*), but now he was addressed as "My Sheykh and My Trusty Confidant (*Sheykhi va-Moʿtamadi*)"—containing much favour and encouragement. There was written, "Since the Khwarazm Shah lavished and yielded up his precious life in this act of service, we must of necessity recognize the rights of that kind and venerable old man in regard to his sons, who are here at our court and have been trained and educated in our service. One of them, as the exalted judgement decrees necessary, will be sent very shortly to take charge of those affairs (i.e. in Khwarazm) in the required manner". [Fifth,] a letter was written to the army of Khwarazm to commend them for their recent service and performance (i.e. in campaigning against ʿAl-itegin). These letters had the Sultan's official signature and emblem affixed to them and were signed by him personally.

The next day the Sultan held a court session [Gh 355] and summoned Hārun,[217] son of the Khwarazm Shah, who was descended from the Rāfeʿi family on his mother's side. (Rāfeʿ b. Sayyār was ruler in Khorasan before Yaʿqub, son of Leyth, with his seat at Pushang;[218] the Khwarazm Shah had married Hārun's mother when he was at Herat during the time of Yamin al-Dowla, before he acquired the office of Khwarazm Shah.) Hārun remained in the court audience hall for an hour, and it was evident [F 453] that he was the one who would succeed to his father's place. Those present went back home between the noon and afternoon worships.

Hārun's investiture patent for the governorship of Khwarazm was written out for him as deputy for the prince, Amir Saʿid b. Masʿud.[219] In the investiture patent this royal prince was set down as the Khwarazm Shah and given appropriate honorific titles, and Hārun was styled "deputy (*khalifat al-dār*)[220] of the Khwarazm Shah." The royal emblem and motto were affixed, and letters were written to Aḥmad b. ʿAbd al-Ṣamad and the army saying that Aḥmad was to act as counsellor and administrator (i.e. for Saʿid). Hārun had the official form of address of "My Son and My Trusted Confidant." The robe of honour for Hārun was got ready on Thursday, 8 Jomādā I 423 [/22 April 1032],[221] but at half the value of what his father's robe had been. He was dressed in it, and from there he went home and received people's cordial congratulations. Satï, another son of the Khwarazm Shah Altuntāsh, cut a more dashing and impressive figure than Hārun and had hoped that he would be sent, and now felt depressed and disappointed. The Amir showed him favour and said, "You are needed for more important services than this." He kissed the ground and said, "The welfare of servants lies in what the lord deems fit, and I would not barter one day of service and being able to look upon the lord for all the benefits and blessings of ruling in this present world."

On the Friday, Hārun came to the covered loggia of the Divān. Bu Naṣr had written out the text of the oath of allegiance to the Sultan and presented it to him. Hārun read it out loud, and the notables and prominent persons attested it as witnesses. Afterwards, he came before the Amir and sought permission to depart. The Amir said, "Be vigilant, and hold our own person before your eyes so that your position may become more elevated. Aḥmad is in the place of a father to you; obey his instructions; treat the retainers and servants of your father well, and recognize the service which each one of them has given; and do not forget our great favour in taking you into our service." But later he [F 454] forgot his obligations and after a few years, when Khorasan was in turmoil on account of the Turkmens, this inexperienced youth [Gh 356] became a prey to diabolical temptations until he lost his life. I shall set forth, in its appropriate place, what various events took place, until Khᵛāja Aḥmad b. ʿAbd al-Ṣamad was summoned and invested with the vizierate, and his own son took his place (i.e. as counsellor and administrator) at Hārun's side. The conduct of affairs passed into the hands of a pair of youths, and they became entangled in their feuds and forfeited their lives, and that land and its surrounding regions was thrown into chaos. Such is the fate of him who renounces allegiance to the lord of the throne, Amir Masʿud![222] Then I shall continue this section, and then come back again (i.e. to the main thread of the History) and relate many remarkable deeds, if God Most High so wills.

Amirak Beyhaqi arrived, and gave a detailed account of the events. The Amir's mind had been made hostile towards him, since the Grand Vizier had a grudge against him on account of his own retainer (*chāker*) Bu ʿAbdallāh Pārsi. This was because Amirak had gone off to Balkh in order to arrest Bu ʿAbdallāh and to take over the office of postal and intelligence officer at the time of the Vizier's period of tribulation.[223] The Vizier was forever seeking an opportunity, and exploited the opportunity of this journey to Bokhara to conjure up distorted accounts of him, and deployed such master-strokes of cunning until the office of postal and intelligence officer of Balkh was taken away from Amirak and given to Bu'l-Qāsem b. Ḥātemak. However, the Sultan put fresh heart into Amirak, saying, "We shall ordain for you a more important post, for we have never discerned on your part any disloyal act." There can be no more generous and scrupulous person than the Sultan![224] I shall set forth what happened to Amirak subsequently.

When this basis for affairs was thus established, and the weather in Balkh became hot, the Amir set out from Balkh on 22 Jomādā I 423 [/16 May 1032] [F 455] on the road to the Vale of Gaz,[225] bent on carousing and hunting. On 11 Jomādā II [/25 May] he took up residence in the Maḥmudi Palace, which is the government headquarters at Ghaznin, and then in the middle of this month [/29 May] proceeded to the Maḥmudi Garden. The horses were sent out to the meadows and the royal camels were sent off, according to past custom, to the pasture grounds at Rebāṭ-e Karvān.[226] *God is most knowing about what is best!*

An account of the story and the adventures of the envoys who went from the court of Ghazna to the court of the caliph and what happened to them, and how they returned

When Soleymāni, the Commander of the Faithful al-Qā'em be-amr Allāh's envoy, was being dispatched homewards from Balkh, [Gh 357] the Amir had expressed his concerns regarding the Ḥajj pilgrimage and the blockage of its route (i.e. through brigandage), and had asked that strenuous efforts should be made to open up the road.[227] An answer arrived, to the effect that "The caliph, issued an order from the seat of the caliphate Baghdad to the Buyid house, and they restored and set right the Pilgrimage road, repaired the cisterns and no impediment has remained. An eminent commander should now be appointed from Amir Mas'ud's court, and the pilgrims of Khorasan and Transoxania should come." Orders were sent to Khorasan to get preparations under way speedily, and people were eager to visit the

House of the Almighty God. Amir Masʿud nominated Khᵛāja ʿAli b. Mikāʾil as leader of the pilgrims, and he exerted himself to the utmost in carrying out the customs and ceremonies far beyond the call of duty, for he was endowed not only with wealth and means but also imbued with a spirit of chivalry. The Sultan appointed the religious scholar Ḥasan Barmaki[228] for the embassy, since this latter person had gone on embassies on two or three previous occasions and had been to Baghdad. My master composed letters to the caliph and the caliph's vizier,[229] and letters were also written to Tāsh Farrāsh, the commander in Western Persia, and to the secretary Ṭāher and others.

On Sunday, 21 of this month [Jomādā II /4 June 1032], Khᵛāja ʿAli b. Mikāʾil donned a splendid robe of honour, such that [F 456] he was a vision of splendour,[230] and was given accoutrements of gold for his horse, a ceremonial cloth (*ghāshiya*) and the official form of address of "Khᵛāja." At that time, "Khᵛāja" used to be a very lofty title, but nowadays the rank of *khᵛāja* has been cast away and this form of address abandoned. I shall now give a story that happened at Nishapur as a kind of ceremonial covering to this episode.[231]

Story

There was a certain eminent person (*khᵛāja*) called Bu'l-Moẓaffar Barghashi who was vizier to the Samanids.[232] When he finally realized that Samanid rule had reached its end, he devised a way out for himself. He gave a handsome payment, 5,000 dinars, to one of the Samanids' physicians, and made an agreement and undertaking with him.[233] One day when there had been a great freeze-up, he rode his horse on the ice, deliberately fell off it, let out a wail and feigned unconsciousness. [Gh 358] He was brought back to his house in a litter, and alms were bestowed and sacrificial beasts were offered up in limitless quantities at that time. Verbal messages were brought to him, and the Amir came to ask after him. He offered up obeisance by gestures, and the physician brought in a wooden splint and a cloth impregnated with pitch, and diagnosed a broken leg. The Amir would make enquiries of the physician each day, and the latter would say, "He suffered a serious accident," and [F 457] every day he would be inventing a different excuse. The Amir fell into despair, and state affairs became neglected, until Bu'l-Moẓaffar appointed a young man, who was a trusted confidant, as assistant to the Amir, acting as the Vizier's deputy. That young man got the idea into his head of becoming Vizier, and the Amir was attracted by him. Meanwhile, each day the physician would give the Amir disappointing news regarding him.

When the Amir gave up hope of him, he meanwhile was sending the lighter and more portable items of his possessions to Guzgānān whenever he had an opportunity, and he purchased a fine estate there. After that, he wrote out a document listing what he possessed—gold and silver, moveable property, beasts of burden and slaves. He summoned religious lawyers and notables, and in their presence he swore verbal oaths that he owned nothing of immoveable and moveable property, apart from the estate in Guzgānān and what was listed in this document, in his direct possession (*melk*), nor had he deposited anything in trust (*amānat*) with someone else. He sent this to the Amir, and requested leave to go and reside on that estate, on the grounds that "This climate (i.e. in the Samanid capital Bokhara) doesn't suit me, and there I shall offer up prayers for the state." The Amir believed him and was agreeable; he gave permission for him to depart and relieved him of his post. He granted to him estates in Guzgānān and wrote an instruction to the Amir of Guzgānān to cherish and esteem him, and he gave him leave to depart.[234]

He possessed a number of camels and a number of people who used to be in his service and look after his interests.[235] He resided there until the Samanids were overthrown. He sold the estates in Guzgānān and went to Nishapur with a sound body, a happy heart and a cured leg, and settled there. I, Bu'l-Fażl, saw this Bu'l-Moẓaffar at Nishapur in the year 400 [/1009–10] as an old man, full of dignity, tall in stature, with a ruddy complexion and hair as snowy white as camphor; he used to wear a white *dorrāʿa* over several *molḥam* silk garments of Marghozi manufacture.[236] He used to ride a lofty steed, with ornamental coverings and trappings, accoutrements of iron inlaid with silver [Gh 359] and very chaste, a white leather saddle pommel and [F 458] a covering which his stirrup attendant used to carry under his arm. He never went to pay greetings and attend upon anyone, he never allowed anyone to come near him and he never mixed with any persons. There were three old men, of the same age as himself, who were his boon-companions; they used to sit with him and he never used to bring anyone else to that place. He was the owner of a garden at Moḥammadābād on the edge of the town, and he spent most of his time there. If some important person died, he would come to the mourning ceremony. I saw him, at a time when I was fifteen years old, when he had come for the mourning ceremony of Esmāʿil Divāni.[237] The Khᵛāja Imam Sahl Ṣoʿluki; the Judge Imam Abu'l-Heytham; the Judge Ṣāʿed; the Head of the Divān at Nishapur; the mayor or headman of Pushang; the military governor Begtegin; and the Amir's Chamberlain, the Commander-in-Chief,[238] were all present at the ceremony.[239] They gave the place of honour to him, and they showed him great respect. When he turned to go home, the Grand Vizier's horse was summoned for him. He died still maintaining this self-restraint and lofty status. Amir Maḥmud used to call him "Khᵛāja," and they used to address him thus in written documents. On several occasions he sought to offer him the vizierate, but he refused.

There was a man in Nishapur called Abu'l-Qāsem Rāzi, and this man, Bu'l-Qāsem, used to bring up and train slave girls. He would bring them to Amir Naṣr and go back with handsome payments. On one occasion, he had brought several slave girls. Amir Naṣr gave Bu'l-Qāsem a fine muslin head-cloth and wrote out for him a letter of commendation (*ʿenāyat-nāma*). The people of Nishapur greeted him appropriately; he brought along the letter, and it was read out in the sessions for hearing complaints and receiving petitions.[240] I heard from my father that the Judge Bu'l-Heytham said *sotto voce*—he was a man with a fund of jokes and pleasantries—"O Bu'l-Qāsem, take note: acting as a pimp is better than functioning as a judge!" At that moment, Bu'l-Moẓaffar Barghashi was coming out of his garden at Moḥammadābād. He saw Bu'l-Qāsem Rāzi mounted on a valuable horse, with precious gold-encrusted girths and accoutrements on it, and an ample ceremonial cloth, adorned all over with designs and pictures. When he saw Bu'l-Moẓaffar Barghashi, he dismounted and kissed the ground. Bu'l-Moẓaffar said, "May the robe of honour (i.e. the turban cloth) bestowed by the Commander-in-Chief be blessed!", and Bu'l-Qāsem performed the act of service a second time. [F 459] Bu'l-Moẓaffar rode off. When he was some distance away, he said to the stirrup attendant, "Throw that ceremonial cloth beneath that wall!" [Gh 360] He threw it down there, not daring to ask why. A week went by. Bu'l-Moẓaffar expressed his intention of going out riding. The stirrup attendant said to one of the boon-companions, "What does he ordain in regard to the ceremonial cloth?" The boon-companion came back and answered, "He says, 'A length of Dāmghāni cloth should be kept inside the coat, and when I get down from the horse, it should be placed over the raised part of the saddle.'" This was done until the end of his days. The old-established boon companions bandied this story about in the convivial session. Bu'l-Moẓaffar said, "Since Bu'l-Qāsem Rāzi became a person with a ceremonial cloth, it's not possible for us to have a cloth borne before ourself." This episode became public knowledge in Nishapur and the report reached Sultan Maḥmud. He became angry and heaped reproaches on his brother, and an order emanated from the court to the Amirs Moḥammad and Masʿud regarding ceremonial cloths and saddle-coverings, and harsh words and threats went forth. But nowadays, anyone who has fifty dirhams and can purchase a ceremonial cloth has one borne before him. Monarchs may not be aware of these things, but it is the task of informers and spies to deal with these affairs so that such delicate matters do not go unnoticed. For whatever is written down on a piece of paper is better than the blank paper itself, even though that too can disappear.

Now we return to the thread of the History.

After the award of the robe of honour to ʿAli b. Mikāʾil, Amir Masʿud went to the Garden of a Hundred Nightingales[241] and then came out to the open country. ʿAli b. Mikāʾil passed before him, with the most comprehensive outfit and equipment possible. He dismounted and offered up service. My master appointed a secret informer and spy to accompany him, with the arrangement that swift envoys conveying reports could keep arriving back at intervals, and he used to give them payments, so that the work should not be neglected and anything remain hidden, since he used to keep a register in which he would set down important matters. Amir Masʿud had a great gift for setting up this sort of surveillance (i.e. over his servants), and there are many subtly intriguing stories about him in regard to this matter. Khᵛāja ʿAli and the pilgrims set out towards Balkh in order to travel to the caliph's capital at Baghdad. [F 460]

The Sultan stayed for a week in the Garden of a Hundred Nightingales. He gave orders for the old Palace of Maḥmud Zāvoli[242] to be decorated, since they were going to perform the circumcision ceremony for several of the royal princes.[243] They adorned it with several kinds of fabrics set with gold and with many jewels, and with the utensils and accoutrements for convivial session[244] decorated with gilding and vessels filled with amber and camphor. Large amounts of musk and aloes wood were placed in there. They took such pains to achieve their effect that no-one could remember its like. At the beginning of the month of Rajab [/13 June 1032] there was a feast and celebration for all the courtiers and retainers. On the Thursday (3 Rajab/15 June) the Sultan mounted and went to the White Palace with seven of the royal princes, senior commanders, chamberlains and kinsmen from the royal family. They stayed there for a week until these circumcision celebrations came to an end. Then he returned and came back to the government headquarters. [Gh 361]

On the fifteenth of this month [/27 June 1032], swift envoys arrived from Turkestan, sent by Khᵛāja Bu'l-Qāsem Ḥaṣiri and Bu Ṭāher Tabbāni, and they had mentioned that "We were obliged to remain in Kāshghar for a long time, and they held us back there." He gave commands for the envoys to be given lodging and ordered largesse for them, until they had taken their rest. He himself desired to go to Herat, and they rode that way and a camp enclosure was erected on the outskirts of Herat. On the first of the month of Dhu'l-Ḥejja [/8 November 1032] he hunted lions at the Rebāṭ of Shir o boz[245] and killed several lions with his own hands, and he engaged in wine-drinking. In the middle of the month (i.e. 14–15 Dhu'l-Ḥejja [/21–2 November 1032]) he came to Herat with a great display of splendour and a complete array of equipment, arms and impressive might. He held this town in particular affection for he had had a very pleasant time there in the past.[246]